Owned, An Ethological Jurisprudence of Property

This book draws upon domestication science to undertake a radical reappraisal of the jurisprudence of property and intellectual property.

Bringing together animal studies and legal philosophy, it articulates a critique of dominant property models and relationships from the perspective of cognitive ethology, domestication science and animal behaviour. In doing so, a radical new picture of property emerges. Focusing on the emergence of property models through prevailing ideas of human domestication and settlement, the book challenges the anthropocentrism that informs standard approaches to ownership and to authorship. Utilising a wide range of examples from ethology and animal studies, the book thus rethinks the very nature of property as uniquely human.

This highly original contribution to the fields of property and intellectual property will appeal not only to legal scholars in these areas, as well as in animal law, but also to legal theorists and others working in the social sciences with interests in posthumanism and animal studies.

Johanna Gibson is Herchel Smith Professor of Intellectual Property at Queen Mary, University of London, where she teaches and researches in intellectual property, creative industries, and animal law and welfare. Gibson is the author of several other Routledge monographs, including *Intellectual Property, Medicine and Health* (2017), *The Logic of Innovation* (2014), *Creating Selves* (2006), and *Community Resource* (2005). Along with the humans, she shares her home with four rescue dogs and four rescue cats, all arriving with wildly disjunctive stories.

Owned, An Ethological Jurisprudence of Property

From the Cave to the Commons

Johanna Gibson

LONDON AND NEW YORK

First published 2020
by Routledge
2 Park Square, Milton Park, Abingdon, Oxon OX14 4RN

and by Routledge
52 Vanderbilt Avenue, New York, NY 10017

Routledge is an imprint of the Taylor & Francis Group, an informa business

First issued in paperback 2021

© 2020 Johanna Gibson

The right of Johanna Gibson to be identified as author of this work has been asserted by her in accordance with sections 77 and 78 of the Copyright, Designs and Patents Act 1988.

All rights reserved. No part of this book may be reprinted or reproduced or utilised in any form or by any electronic, mechanical, or other means, now known or hereafter invented, including photocopying and recording, or in any information storage or retrieval system, without permission in writing from the publishers.

Trademark notice: Product or corporate names may be trademarks or registered trademarks, and are used only for identification and explanation without intent to infringe.

British Library Cataloguing-in-Publication Data
A catalogue record for this book is available from the British Library

Library of Congress Cataloging-in-Publication Data
A catalog record for this book has been requested

ISBN: 978-0-367-35657-6 (hbk)
ISBN: 978-1-03-208338-4 (pbk)
ISBN: 978-0-429-34213-4 (ebk)

Typeset in Galliard
by Apex CoVantage, LLC

To that dog

Contents

Acknowledgements ix
Preface: the hunter and the farmer and that dog xii

Introduction: Owned, a dogged tale of property 1

PART 1
Domestication, the stone age 29

1 *Canis familiaris* – the invention of domestication 31
2 The imitation of domestication 55
3 Socialisation 81

PART 2
Territory, the space age 103

4 Marking territory 105
5 Resource guarding 132
6 Separation anxiety 153

PART 3
Dominion, the machine age 175

7 Predatory drift 177
8 Pack fiction 200
9 Wild abandon 220

PART 4
Altruism, the social age 249

10 Shared interests 251
11 Resocialisation 280
12 *Res familiaris* 302

    Not the end of it 325

    Bibliography 327
    Index 359

Acknowledgements

This began as one book, and then two, and at times I worried that this would spawn yet another before making it to press. There is something extremely productive about the sociability of an ethological jurisprudence. Once you start looking, there are connections everywhere.

The first person I mentioned this idea to was a very brilliant, very kind jurist, Sir Henry Carr. It really started out as a conversation about our dogs and sharing various photographs and anecdotes, while everyone around us seemed to be talking very seriously about the law. And then I said I would love to understand what dogs could teach us about law. Henry wasn't just polite; he was genuinely enthusiastic. The last time I saw him he asked me how the project was coming along, and I mentioned it was going well but much more to do. The last thing he said to me was, "I look forward to reading it!" as he gave me a hug. The loss of Henry this summer was a denial of one of the most accomplished legal minds on the bench. But it was also a devastating loss of one of the most generous.

I have a few people I would like to thank, some of whom may not be expecting it. First, I am grateful to Emily Hudson for setting an animals question on the Oxford Intellectual Property Moot in March 2018. This really started the ball rolling, especially as Barbara Lauriat invited me to speak at the Conversazione giving me a chance to put some early ideas together. And to David Vaver, thank you for your question. If my answer was too short, that is the topic of the next book, so I will be sure to send you a copy.

I am also extremely appreciative of my own ethology professors and their enthusiasm when I studied animal behaviour. I am so grateful to Andrew Tribe for his guidance when I was his student and almost his PhD student (until I opted for a PhD in law instead). And to Clive Phillips for being incredibly supportive and generous with his time and guidance; it has been a privilege to have his insight and encouragement. I would also really like to acknowledge Judith Blackshaw, with whom, as an undergraduate in my first year of university, I took my first animal behaviour class. I am not sure if she ever knew how inspirational she was to me, but she was talking about the mutual benefits of accommodation that welcomed people with their pets (in fact, the triadic benefits, with properties better kept when everyone is happy) long before now, when people are just getting around to arguing about it.

There are indeed some very wonderful people working in human-animal studies, and fortunately for me I had the chance to test some of my research at the International Society for Anthrozoology in the summer of 2018 and at the same time meet some of the best of them. I would like to thank Tania Signal for her immediate friendship, her brilliance and scholarship, and her fabulous sense of humour. She turned a conference into park life! And to Emily Plec, who fascinated us with a life completely unmonitored by social media, leaving us all bewildered as to what to do with photos in the absence of a tag. I am looking forward to the next project and to keeping in touch the old-fashioned way . . . by email!

And a huge thank you to Alan McElligott for his indefatigable friendship, his great humour, his endless understanding, and his contagious enthusiasm . . . and for the goats, the great trips to visit the goats! Here's to many dog walks with you and Jack the Lab! And Malcolm Langley, our super archive librarian who kept me furnished with things I had or had not noticed and let me keep things so long the shelves look empty without them. Many thanks to Malcolm for the coffee, the curiosity, and the conversation.

And from a long list of brilliant colleagues to a possibly unfairly shorter one. First, I want to make a very special thank you to Mayes Al-Jassas and Shirley Abranches for being the best unofficial (or official!) research assistants with whom I have ever worked. They tracked down rare books, missing books, and centenarian pamphlets wrapped in rice paper. Nothing was too much trouble, and I will always be grateful to them for their support and especially their interest as well. And, of course, to Gbemisola Adedoyin-Adeniyi, the problem solver, technology magician, stationery fancier, and keeper of the good pens, I owe a special gratitude. Bemi keeps the whole place (and me) together.

And thank you to Ian Walden, the Director of the Centre for Commercial Law Studies, Queen Mary, University of London, for his support and enthusiasm in the development of animal law as a new teaching area in the School of Law. It has been wonderful to be able to build this new area and to see the great range of students recognising the importance of the "animal turn" in law. Indeed, to all my colleagues at the Centre for Commercial Law Studies, Queen Mary, University of London, thank you for your community. And, of course, I am enormously grateful to Colin Perrin and Nicola Sharpe at Routledge for their dedication to the project and their incredible professionalism and proficiency in their care for the final realities of the book.

I have some friends and family to thank, some of whom are human. My very special thanks go to Great Uncle Bulgaria, also known as Peter, who, despite being an awful backseat driver, is a very treasured friend. And to Kathy and Kristie who will always put up with a rant when needed and somehow always seem able to fix everything. And, of course, to Phillip, who lived through the process, all I can say is I'm sorry, I am about to start another one. And to Kitty Pryde, Poly Styrene, and Lora Logic, who may or may not be cats, thanks for the friendship (and the stares). And to Bulldog Drummond, prolific purrer and avid keyboard *worrier*, a big fan of the sprawl, cut, and waste, many seemingly inspired moments were victims. He also added a lot of text, but that is more ambiguous, and I apologise for all the random Hs and Js that the copyeditors must have found (his favourite keys). And to my wonderful mother, Dawn, my amazing and clever mother, and to my brother, John, my generous and put-upon brother, my greatest thanks of all. . . . Well, along with the dogs, that is: Aubrey Beardsley, the Sheepdog; Huw Le Lytle, the Bedlington Terrier; Howard Spring, the Parson Russell Terrier; and Jefferson Airplane (Jeff), the Border Terrier cross. And to all the dogs I have ever shared my life with, and there are many. It really is their story.

And if there's anything missing (and there is), it's because there is so much more to say. It is truly a book of "passionate interests."

Preface
The hunter and the farmer and that dog

(*Loosely based upon the friendship of Niko Tinbergen and Konrad Lorenz . . . and That Dog.*)

Once upon a time there were two ethologists, and they were great friends.

One ethologist liked to devise ways to stalk his subject, to hide and conceal, all the while pretending at indifference. His endeavour was one of the hunter and the hunted.

The other ethologist liked to share with his subject, to come out into the open and become friends, collaborators. He chose to share his space, to contribute to the flourishing of his friends, to make kin. His endeavour was that of the farmer.

The first ethologist watched and saw and learned about many things. And the animals gave him every reason to credit their ingenuity and knowledge, and their world grew before his eyes. But his own world did not grow larger.

The second ethologist bumped into, joined in, touched, and inhabited new worlds. His own world embraced a whole new social life. He spoke of love, and his social world grew and grew. But were the animals given all the credit they were due?

Where the first ethologist saw the amazing independent creativity of the animals at home in their vital worlds, he did not get to enjoy the enormous potential of participation.

And where the second saw the enormous potential of collaboration, of attachment, of kinship, he never really saw the creative individuals for who they were.

The first ethologist said to his friend, "Do you really think it is all about basic drives? Do you really think it is all about competition?" The second ethologist said to his friend, "But do you really think it is all about keeping our distance when really there are so many wonderful little stories to tell?"

Despite their differences, the two ethologists remained firm friends. Each brought something remarkable to the friendship. And together they made the most astonishing and invaluable contributions to the study of ethology and to animal lives everywhere. Together. Two worlds.

This is also the story of (at least) two systems of property. The first is rivalrous and competitive. It pretends it is objective when in fact there is so much more at play.

The second is cooperative, generous, a field of shared interests, a proliferation of imaginative imitations.

How we might bring these worlds into contact is the adventure ahead. And our guide, our teacher, is that dog. How might we make friends of hunters and farmers?

This will be the story of how to reconcile these insights by revealing them through a third. A dog. That first dog.

This is the story of experimentation and emotion, of imagination and innovation, of socialisation and sympathy. The smellable, sniffable, chewable. This story is the smell of success. That dog's success.

This is the story of that dog.

Introduction
Owned, a dogged tale of property

> [I]f you like to play with your dog, and enjoy seeing him catch a ball or dash into the sea to retrieve a stick, don't you think you are better off than others who do not care about dogs at all?
>
> Tinbergen N (1954) *Bird Life*, OUP, London, 5

This is the dogged tale of property, from the cave to the commons. It is a story of losing track, looking back, and making tracks once again. This is a story of passionate interests. After all, "law is to be found in life."[1]

You do not have to love dogs to read this story, but it always helps.

The road ahead

> Jurisprudence today stands in great need of more hypotheses.[2]

This book started with some possibly surprising hypotheses. What can animals other than humans teach us about law?

What insight into the disputed terrain of property might they be able to offer? How might taking the perspectives of other animals enlarge and expand the legal world? How might a genuine ethological jurisprudence be developed?

For that I have chosen that dog as our guide. First, because of the startling role dogs have played in our own domestication. Second, because that dog has an uneasy relationship with property to which many people have strong and impassioned responses. Often the welfare of dogs is somewhat subjugated to the interests of owners (particularly in training discourse and the often promoted "quick fix" for unwanted behaviours). Indeed, the pet dog seems at times one of the more vulnerable domestic species,[3] not least because so much of dog welfare is obscured by cultural mythologies. It really is time for that dog to get a hearing, so to speak. And third (but doubtfully finally), that dog and other animals have extraordinary ways not only of negotiating territory but also of marking place, sharing space, and managing resources. As will be seen, an ethological jurisprudence is ultimately about the "one problem of property," as it were – empathy.

On this journey, as well as that dog, there are many other animals. However, the often-favoured term, nonhuman, has not been used in the present work.

Indeed, it seems to be as inadequate as that of animal, particularly with the advent of artificial intelligence in these same discussions, also referred to as nonhuman. As flawed as it might be, the term animal is used mainly because, quite other than nonhuman, its identity does not depend upon the human. Nonhuman seems to reaffirm an anxiety about defining these individuals against the boundary of human exceptionalism; that is, that there is something distinctive, immutable, and impassable about the exceptional boundary of humanness. This belief is quite contrary to the underlying rationale of an ethological jurisprudence, with the relations and the potential of an ethological approach of continuity and communication. Indeed, in this text, except where in direct comparison to another animal species, humans will be referred to as human animals instead.

Why is property the obvious place to start to build an ethological jurisprudence? Ethology has a particularly important relationship with property. First, it is to question the presentation of property as natural (and as a natural right) through a consideration of the social and relational development of property through domestication and other multispecies assemblages to present an alternative history, as it were. At the same time, the animal introduces a particularly critical perspective on property, given the way in which animals are characterised through property relations and identified and commodified as property. Indeed, the confrontation between ethological substantiality and authenticity on the one hand, and, on the other hand, the popular constructions of animals through property relations as predators, strays, wild, and so on, is striking.

Further, somewhat in defiance of the developments in affective science and embodied cognition, popular animal training and learning discourse remains wedded to a narrative of radical behaviourism and inescapable instinct. While the animal is enslaved by instinct, the human animal is free to accumulate. The relationship between human exceptionalism and property, and the development of the theory of predatory drift in human property relations in this work, emphasise a presumed species uniqueness about property. This commitment to exceptionalism and distinction for humans, and the biological biographies accorded to taxa, species, and breeds, readily complies with the construction of animals as mechanistic objects of property. In addition to this, the enfolding of dogs within (economic) society is extensive, with certain sectors of dog training notably adhering to a commodity culture of owners and problems, producing results quickly rather than transforming the culture of dog ownership and the relationships between dogs and humans. At the same time, however, despite the research evidence, the rhetoric of exceptionalism, the relationship between economics and property, particularly in the context of intellectual property policy and debate, belies a belief in the drive narrative and constructs its own radical behaviourism of incentives.

What is property?

What is property? The etymology of the word itself is intriguing in the context of the present discussion, with its attachment to the "proper" and indeed notions of manners and courtesy that are thus implied. Notably, the term is contested even within legal discourse, with considerable disagreement over what it encompasses in terms of rights and ownership. But perhaps of most particular note of all, property suffers from the ambiguity arising from its application to things: "Property in its true and original sense means solely a right, title, interest, or ownership; and consequently, to call material things like land, houses, money, cattle, etc., property is as great an absurdity as to call them right, title, interest or ownership."[4] In this journey towards a greater empathy within the law, this slippage to the discourse of things is hugely disruptive to the true relational quality of property: "For property is a term commonly applied to both *objects* that are said to be owned as well as the *rights* exercised over such objects."[5] And this confusion between rights and things is at the heart of the confusion in the general population as well.

This obsession with "thingness" is something that an ethological jurisprudence sets out to challenge, not only from the perspective of the "objects" of property themselves, namely, the animals in this story, but also in terms of the reification of the relations within property, the affiliation and indeed kinship that is at the heart of greater empathy within the law. In other words, how might the owner, the trespasser, the nuisance, the user, the consumer, the animal, that dog contribute to the co-constitution of a property relationship? And what kinds of fascinating transformations might this suggest in contemporary connections, sympathies, understanding, and materialisation of the property relation?

This journey is from the cave to the commons, from the fence to incorporeal property, that is, intellectual property. But what is really fascinating is that in many respects all property is incorporeal. All property is digital. All property is always already about relations that, while possibly articulated through objects, cannot be reduced to objects that are merely indexical of the co-constituted legal and social space. What if that third, that "object", is that dog? Importantly, what emerges is the multiple and simultaneous interests that inhere in property. The bundle of sticks to be thrown and to be fetched. That dog is a not a chair. An item in which property rights might exist, yes indeed, but an interest that is served by competing and often primary interests. Simply calling upon rights, however, does not necessarily account for the sociable nature of these relations. Indeed, in many respects, rights discourse charges an adversarial and arguably property-like approach, embedding the original discourse sought to be overturned. In framing the discussion of sentientism as a demand for rights, are we asking the wrong question? Is this asking an unwilling audience simply to view all animals as human animals? And is this merely to reaffirm an already compromised approach? What is needed is a reconsideration of the nature of the very fundamentals of rights discourse. In other words, how might a repositioning of our viewpoint maximise the relations that exist through various rights, duties, and interests? Indeed, how does a shift in this space recast the property system in its relational potential? Arguably, what is needed is a genuine ethological jurisprudence in order to emphatically transform the interpretation of those relations within the law. And the point at which this begins is property.

First of all, property is, quite simply, *not* the law of things. Although property may sometimes cover relations that are transacted in respect of things, property covers so much more: "Property organizes the world for us, assigning resources to owners, apportioning rights and duties, constituting markets, organizing concepts of citizenship and political identity, and grounding dissent and protest. . . . Property provides both a rationale for dispossession and a ground for its opposition."[6] An ethological approach reviews the relations as distinct from the fixed ideals. As Paracelsus says in Borges's short story of the philosopher's stone, the Platonic ideal writ large, "The path is the stone. . . . The stone is the point of departure."[7] That is, the object is merely a point for relations, and these are the fundamental values of a functioning property system. These are the paths, crisscrossing and overlapping. The problem that is confronting this sociability is that the object has been taken for the relation. And this must be addressed.

Thus, property is not the law of things. But property does seem to be the law of everything. From liberty to publicity, everything seems to be driven by a rhetoric of rivalry and property and, above all, "a woefully inadequate conception of what property is," that is, the perceived dominion of ownership: "Paradoxically, scholars who focus on developing the implications of substantive norms such as liberty, autonomy, equality and social justice tend to use the ownership model. They do so because the absolutist conception of property expresses strong and widely shared claims about the power of individuals to shape their own lives."[8]

Assistance towards an ethological jurisprudence will come from the early twentieth century and the work of Wesley Newcomb Hohfeld.[9] In his exacting attention to the fundamental legal concepts of property, he created a scheme of connections, of relationships, neither ranked nor relegated. Hohfeld's scheme emerges as a truly sociable connective of property relations.

The things about humanity

> Many animals have possessions – beavers have dams, spiders webs and magpies shiny objects, for instance – but only humans have a sophisticated material culture that we depend upon for survival.[10]

Ownership is certainly implicated in the rhetoric of individual intentionality and freedom. And the "woefully inadequate conception" is one almost invariably articulated as a one-sided relationship to a thing. This language of ownership in respect of place, of things, and, above all, of identity, characterises the dominant model of property and its attending discourse.

The extrinsicality of ownership is particular to this relationship of absolute dominion as distinct from affiliative relation. Ownership is the language of "thingness," and the implication is that this materialism somehow makes us uniquely human[11] while at the same time rendering animals "things," incapable of "being" through property. And by the same perspective, the emphasis on "things" simply complies with the logic of human exceptionalism.

However, another late nineteenth- and early twentieth-century thinker challenged this predatory march of property language that coupled the rise of industrialisation. Gabriel Tarde[12] maintained that society could not be defined through this assumed objectivity and indifference. If there is a "thing" for Tarde, it is society itself, and thus it is never static but always experienced through connections, always dynamic and sociable. Tarde's thinking admonishes the Cartesian dualism that sustains the narrative of human exceptionalism – human and animal, machine and culture, there is no outside to these relations. *Every thing is a society*.[13] "What is society? It could be defined, from our point of view, as each individual's reciprocal possession, in many highly varied forms, of every other."[14] Thus, rather than the fixed identities of the one-sided *being*, an ethological jurisprudence, as will be seen, is concerned with the dynamic socialities of *having*, always already in connection and in relation.[15]

Just making observations

> And sociology also, including the sociology of law, must be a science of observation.[16]

> He was, let us not forget, almost incapable of general, platonic ideas. It was not only difficult for him to understand that the generic term *dog* embraced so many unlike specimens of differing sizes and different forms; he was disturbed by the fact that a dog at three-fourteen (seen in profile) should have the same name as the dog at three-fifteen (seen from the front).[17]

Ethology is grounded, as it were, in observation. The law too is about making observations and rendering a judgment. The early days of ethology were arguably dominated by an anxiety over affecting a convincing scientific objectivity, a distance and an extrinsicality, a dispassion and indifference, it was nevertheless not unprejudiced: "When ethologists discuss animal communication, we almost never find any suggestion that subjective experiences may occur in the animals under study. The reductionist, behaviorist tradition still dominates our thinking."[18] Indeed, this very affectation of impartiality may be in and of itself a manipulation of the observation and the representation: "In the behavioral sciences, as in the physical sciences, our databases are derived from *relations* that exist between observers and their subjects. . . . Any given form of investigation can do no more than provide a single window of perception. . . . To put the matter metaphorically, multiple windows can provide a more complete picture of the landscape. Single-dimensional perspectives need to become multidimensional (as are animals)."[19]

An ethological jurisprudence takes an affective scientific approach, following the traditions of a cognitive ethology and taking the perspective of critical anthropomorphism,[20] a term introduced by Gordon Burghardt, accepting anthropomorphism as an interpretive strategy, "to take on real targets – critiquing the science done and the explanations offered."[21] Through this perspective, Burghardt is responding to the earlier work of Donald Griffin, one of the founding figures of modern cognitive ethology, who called for a greater attention to animal experiences, awareness, and consciousness in research. Indeed, the affected indifference of anthropocentrism, the pomposity of anthropodenial[22] and human exceptionalism, is what Griffin argues is the true offence of anthropomorphism: "the prevailing view implies that only our species can have any sort of conscious awareness or that, should animals have mental experiences, they must be identical with ours, since there can be no other kind. It is this conceit which is truly anthropomorphic, because it assumes a species monopoly of an important quality. The attitude resembles, in many ways, the pre-Copernican certainty that the earth must lie at the center of the universe."[23] It is imperative to look back and consider: "The alternative is to postulate some special form of human uniqueness, not demonstrable objectively – an unparsimonious procedure, to say the least."[24] Indeed, taking a lead from Donald Griffin, just because the phenomena observed in the following chapters might seem startling to traditional approaches to property analysis does not mean they are able to be disregarded: "It is very easy for scientists to slip into the passive assumption that phenomena with which their customary methods cannot deal effectively are unimportant or even nonexistent."[25] Indeed, lawyers have been exposed to similar conditioning.[26] What is advocated is more blue-sky thinking in law, as it were: "It thus does not make sense to play off improving the living conditions of people against studying the behavior of animals (or doing any other kind of basic research). If we confess ourselves to the principles of liberty, equality and basic human rights, we need to be able to do both!"[27]

Thus, an ethological jurisprudence is indeed a process of observation, but observation with an open eye, intruding upon pretensions of objectivity and participating in the world of its subjects, seeing that dog at three-fourteen and that dog at three-fifteen.[28] It is a process of emotions and passionate natures[29] and a jurisprudence of passionate interests.[30] That dog will interrupt, intrude, and become a complete and invaluable nuisance. In this way, worlds will collide, and it is in these productive collisions that innovation upon traditional perspectives is possible. Through this process, it is necessary to take perspectives and exercise a critical anthropomorphism in order to realise the potential of these relations. As the anthropologist, Edward Adamson Hoebel, observed, without this kind of interaction with the observed, without the abandonment of the affectation of objectivity, it is not possible *to take on real targets*. "Specifically, if he has no idea as to what constitutes law, he will be unable to see law."[31]

To see the law, it is necessary to engage with the law, to enter the environment and move about, to take on the relations within the law, and to accept the act of culpable observation. The process is informed by Jakob von Uexküll's theory of the *Umwelt*, variously translated as surroundings or environment. *Umwelt* is the animal's "perceptual life-world,"[32] but it is argued that human animals suffer from an "excentricality" when it comes to their own life-worlds: "No, humans do not have an Umwelt. On the contrary, what characterizes us is the absence of a stabilizing, species-specific enclosure bubble."[33] The drift towards the combative away from the relations of an ethical life, of familiar production, must be resisted. And for that, a resocialisation of property through an ethological jurisprudence is needed. This interaction between observation, communication, and *Umwelt* is of immediate significance to Donna Haraway's approach to *respecere*, looking back and taking account in an interspecies exchange of mutual respect and sociability.[34] As Vinciane Despret advocates through her philosophical ethology, we need to build "an ethos for which the 'natural conditions' are, in an undetermined manner, of the nature of the animal and of the nature of the one who questions him, an ethos where 'natural condition' never means neutral condition." Critical anthropomorphism is a functional and deliberate way in which to substantiate the relations of property and indeed of law: "this anthropomorphism is something more than a simple attribution: as long as his body is producing and being produced by a new identity, this experience is a new way of being human, which adds new identity. Therefore, being anthropomorphic means here to add new definitions to what it is to be a human being."[35] And that is genuinely relational.

That dog is key to the story of property's resocialisation. That dog looks back.[36]

Animal modelling

Animal modelling occurs throughout science right through to studies of social competence. There is considerable evidence of a human-like social competence in dogs,[37] and in some respects the proximity between dogs and humans is even closer than that between chimpanzees and humans.[38] This means that dogs have become a subject of particular interest in a range of cognitive studies,[39] including aging[40] and dementia.[41] This research in turn often feeds back into the availability of improved veterinary treatments and regimes for dogs through a kind of comparative approach to one health and one welfare.

The present work is a kind of animal modelling in the law, except that the dog is not a model. This is about that dog. That dog is not a metaphor. This approach is not allegorical. That dog is not a proxy human, an analogical tracing, and it is certainly not to use that dog to erect a nonhuman foil to the human. This is much more than animal modelling. Through these sociable relations, this is jurisprudence *being-with* the animal, or indeed, *becoming-with*: "To be one is always to *become with* many."[42]

One of Aesop's fables is about a hunter searching for the tracks of a lion. He comes across a woodman and asks if he has seen any tracks, to which the woodman offers to show him the lion himself. But the hunter does not want to see the lion, "it is his track only I am in search of, not the lion himself."[43] Although this is a fable about courage (in deed as well as in words), it is perhaps also a telling tale about being and having. Throughout, property will emerge as relations, through the tracks and connections of sociable territories, as distinct from the static externalities of objects. It is the tracks we are in search of. The path is the stone.

This puts in mind the rhizomatic connections explored by Deleuze and Guattari, of overlapping tracks and intersecting communications: "Is it not of the essence of the rhizome to intersect roots and sometimes merge with them?"[44]

They describe animals as rhizomes, "in their pack form,"⁴⁵ and "Burrows are too, in all of their functions of shelter, supply, movement, evasion, and breakout."⁴⁶ The burrow is thus a kind of creative assemblage of making home: "Perhaps one of the most important characteristics of the rhizome is that it always has multiple entryways; in this sense, the burrow is an animal rhizome."⁴⁷ Indeed, the Iguana performs this very collective work, at the same time seemingly confounding the ordinary principles of ownership: "Here, 'owner' means the female temporarily in possession of the burrow. However, since a female cannot build a burrow in a single shift but must take numerous rests, the 'interloper' may be the female who has done most of the digging on the burrow, and hence in a different sense may be the owner."⁴⁸

The sociability of property relations is always "at work," as it were: "But the land exists also for society. . . . Society has an interest in bringing the treasures of the ground to the surface. If the owner neglects to do this, the law gives the right to anyone else who is ready to do so to 'burrow' and to 'search.'"⁴⁹

Indeed, that dog likes to dig.

Why an ethology of property?

There is often a rather unfair, and, if taken at face value, scientifically implausible stereotype imposed upon dogs; namely, that they "live in the moment." It suggests a certain enthusiasm for life while at the same time diminishes that dog as an intentional, historical being, rendering them a nomad of history, wandering and feckless: "The beast lives *unhistorically*, for it 'goes into' the present, like a number, without leaving any curious remainder. It cannot dissimulate, it conceals nothing; at every moment it seems what it actually is, and thus can be nothing that is not honest."⁵⁰ Animals are configured as outside history, ahistorical, and thus without the necessary "prestige" in order to intend and engage historical impact. However, as this story follows that dog through the first domestication event, through the erection of monuments and landmarks, through social play and aesthetic performance, the relationship between "the moment" and property becomes clearer. This same imposition of ahistoricity has been perpetrated against so-called primitive or traditional cultures, both through the denial of property systems as well as the ossification of cultures and identities. As Deleuze and Guattari explain: "nomads have no history; they only have a geography . . . the defeat of the nomads was such, so complete, that history is one with the triumph of States. We have witnessed, as a result, a generalized critique dismissing the nomads as incapable of any innovation. . . . History has always dismissed the nomads."⁵¹ Indeed, the theories of domestication, such as that dog as itinerant scavenger, through to that dog's rendering by ownership as stray, feral, homeless, "History has always dismissed the nomads."⁵²

Animals other than humans have been crafted through the history of ownership. And indeed, as this story will tell, the history of property is inextricably bound up with domestication, evolution, and the scientific revolution of the late nineteenth and early twentieth centuries. Animals are thus central to this history, key historical figures, not merely because they have been rendered objects and artefacts within it, but rather, and much more significantly, they are collaborators in that history, architects of the same space. Indeed, that dog is the inventor of domestication.

But within popular discourse, including the language of trainers themselves, the traditional domestication myth that the dog is a tamed wolf, with all the human intentionality that goes with that, is surprisingly persistent and accepted. Indeed, this continues to embed within dog training discourse the tenets of radical behaviourism and unconditional conditioning theories, as it were, in a wholly Cartesian paradigm of human exceptionalism and the instinctual beast. This not only provides ongoing support for very basic approaches to training through physiological stimuli and responses, often denying the cognitive elements and admitting aversive techniques, but also fuels an almost visceral kneejerk reaction to notions of emotion and consciousness as naïve anthropomorphism, despite the evidence emerging through canine cognitive science. In three years of reviewing training threads in social media, the reactionary language around anthropomorphism is almost ubiquitous, tenacious in its exceptionalism and extremely damaging to modernising the understanding of training paradigms and human-dog bonds.[53]

At the same time, shifting the perspective on property helps to explore and confound the dominant narratives of human exceptionalism and the recalcitrance with respect to any exploration of anthropomorphism, peeling back the thin veneer of anthropodenial.[54] In doing so, it makes for good science and good law to exercise the precautionary principle with respect to the existence of emotions, consciousness, and culture in animals, rather than rely upon presumptions against emotional life for want of exacting proof.[55] The latter is precisely the wrong way to apply the precautionary principle and the right way to lead to perverse conclusions and destitute relations. Propertyless, as it were.

The predatory turn

What emerges through this exploration of the story of property is the truculence and combative shift in property relations. Property drifts from its social origins in that first domestication through what is called here "predatory drift." This term is taken quite unselfconsciously from the same (fraught) term in dog training discourse for reasons to be made clear in later discussion. This predatory turn can be recognised in politics, anthropology, sociology, science, law, and language, and indeed throughout social life.

It appears in stark relief in the history of the modern dog. From the story of domestication and the interspecies family to the demonisation of the wolf as an aggressive, warring pack animal, rather than the reality of the family social organisation, through to the translation of these misconceptions in modern dog training discourse, the travel of predatory drift is clear. Fictions can indeed travel very far on the momentum of belief, notwithstanding the biological (or other) realities undermining them.[56] It is a drift which has cast the user, the consumer, the trespasser as the trespasser as stray, homeless and the owner as indomitable, defensive, and territorial. Predatory drift is property's homesickness.

How will this story make home and find the abode of ethics in property? The concept of familiar production was introduced in *The Logic of Innovation*, proposed as a transformation of the way in which relations within intellectual property are conceived.[57] In other words, familiar production presents a shift away from notions of "the public, "the population," the anonymous user," towards the smaller, individual sociality of the family. From *in rem* to *in personam*; that is, property is always reducible to a fundamental relation between two beings.[58] On the other hand, the crowding and the restriction of resources, as it were, will always be a welfare issue. And the loss of space through the crowding of consumers in the artificial scarcity of intellectual property, generalising their interests and restricting their access, will always present a potential welfare issue that must be addressed through an analysis of those relations. Property is not a thing; it is a bundle of sticky things.

Indeed, the neglect of Gabriel Tarde's writings for almost a century is an example of this predatory drift, a turning away from the sociology of the individual, the interspecies dyad, towards the grand gestures of the population, the species, of human exceptionalism. However, in familiar production, in the social age of property, we look back. As Deleuze and Guattari note, Tarde responded to Durkheim's "great collective representations, which are generally binary, resonant, and overcoded," by explaining "that collective representations presuppose exactly what needs explaining, namely, 'the similarity of millions of people.' That is why Tarde was interested instead in the world of detail, or of the infinitesimal."[59]

And for this, the discussion looks back to Gabriel Tarde.

Imitate this

> In nature no animal is solitary throughout its life history.[60]

> It is now proper to bring to light a general observation, a special side of which I have just been indicating in pointing out the passing of unilateral into reciprocal imitation. The mere play of imitation has resulted, then, not only in extending it, but in making it two-sided as well. Now, this effect which imitation produces upon itself, it also produces upon many other connections between people. Ultimately it transforms all unilateral into mutual relations.

> We ceased long ago to believe in Rousseau's 'social contract.'[61]

To refer to property simply as the law of things is thus at best reductive and at worst entirely misleading to the point of injustice, especially in the context of debates over animals as property.[62] This is where Gabriel Tarde's universal sociology offers an opportunity to reorient the perspective on the extrinsicality and fixation of representations of society offered by traditional property narratives and indeed in sociology – the "thingness" of society, as it were: "Tarde's sociology of imitation proposed a conceptual apparatus for engaging with the paradox itself."[63] As Bruno Latour explains, "Instead of saying, like Durkheim, that we 'should treat social facts as a thing', Tarde says that 'all things are society', and any phenomenon is a social fact."[64] That is, *every thing is a society*. Things themselves are conduits for interrelational action: "the little *imitations, oppositions*, and *inventions* constituting an entire realm of subrepresentative matter."[65]

Although recognised primarily as a sociologist, Gabriel Tarde began his career in law. Born in 1843 he became a magistrate in 1867 and continued in that role for 27 years, during which time he studied widely across a range of disciplines and their interactions, including biology, philosophy, and sociology.[66] As a magistrate, he is said to have developed an international reputation in criminology[67] and a keen interest in the question of "the large part that imitation plays in criminal conduct."[68] He was subsequently appointed as Head of the Bureau of Statistics of the Ministry of Justice in 1894 and did not commence his academic career until 1900 when he was appointed Professor of Modern Philosophy at the Collège de France, a post he held until his death in 1904.[69]

Putting harmony and cooperation at the centre of this narrative as the fundamental encounter in evolution, as distinct from the warring narrative of predator and prey, and declaring this contact ("the first tie") a necessary precondition of society itself, Tarde's sociology dismantles the traditional social contract as fiction, not a cause.[70] At the same time, Tarde's critique of Darwinism arrests the Cartesianism that continues to characterise property debates today, particularly in relation to animals:

> Instead of explaining everything by the supposed supremacy of a *law of evolution*, which compels collective phenomena to reproduce and repeat themselves indefinitely in a certain order, – instead of thus explaining lesser facts by greater, and the part by the whole, – I explain collective resemblances of the whole by the massing together of minute elementary acts – the greater by the lesser and the whole by the part. This way of regarding phenomena is destined to work a transformation in sociology similar to that brought about in mathematics by the introduction of the infinitesimal calculus.[71]

Tarde's microsociology[72] resonates with the concept of familiar production[73] that is developed in more detail in the context of the concept of *res familiaris* later in this work. Indeed, "Tarde, an attentive reader of Darwin and Marx – among countless others – makes no attempt, at any point in his sociology to distinguish human from natural *societies*."[74]

Living, as we are, through our own *fin de siècle*, as it were, Tarde is part of a "fresh" pre-history of *fin de siècle* thinkers that are enticingly resonant today: the jurist, Wesley Newcomb Hohfeld, and his work of fundamental sociability in legal relations; the psychologist, Margaret Floy Washburn, the first woman to receive a PhD in psychology[75] and the real personality behind the development of animal behaviour beyond automata towards emotional, sentient beings; anthropologists, including Bronislaw Malinowski for his challenge to the disregard of property and law in so-called primitive peoples; the philosopher, Henri Bergson, and his "instinct" for sympathy; the sociologist Georg Simmel, and his advocacy for the interactions of sociability; and generations of ethologists and animal scientists who have informed and reformed our multispecies society beyond the reduction of life to mechanism.[76] As Tarde might say, this is some small effort at restoring the biography of the names,[77] not unlike his own, which is almost invariably omitted from every standard treatise on sociology.[78]

The contemporaneity of *fin de siècle* thinking in law, sociology, and science offers particular insight into the progression of property. Tarde was writing during a period of rapid professionalisation and the exponential growth of industrialisation and technologisation during which many disciplines began self-consciously defining themselves against these new technological benchmarks. Rediscovering Tarde has provided an opportunity to examine shared themes through the science and jurisprudence of the late nineteenth and early twentieth centuries towards understanding the impact of scientific developments on property and law. Indeed, ethology had its own anxieties about fashioning itself as a discipline against a background of distinguishing itself from psychology and embarking upon refining a disciplinary identity[79] – something which has been curiously, yet possibly, invaluably unsuccessful.

Further, with the organisation of professions came the possibility of an economy of skills through the recognition and scarcity of expertise. It is notable that in the volatile pre-World War II period in Europe, this professionalisation and acknowledgement of expertise was an important defence against the populist State. In 1933, English biologist and sociologist, Alexander Morris Carr-Saunders,[80] and his collaborator, Paul Alexander Wilson, published *The Professions*, examining the role and organisation of professional associations in society. In the present climate of rising populism and anti-expert rhetoric, their insights continue to be relevant:[81]

> Professional associations are stabilizing elements in society. They engender modes of life, habits of thought, and standards of judgement which render them centres of resistance to crude forces which threaten steady and peaceful evolution. But the service which they render in so doing is not sufficiently appreciated. It is largely due to them and to other similar centres of resistance that the older civilizations stand firm. The new civilization of America is threatened by forces which bend the social structure this way and that; they may put its delicate mechanism out of gear or even shake it to the ground. In no other country can public opinion be so easily exploited by experts in that art; movements are set on foot, demanding support in the cause of uplift, whose ambitions know no bounds and whose successes bewilder Americans and astonish the rest of the world. . . . The family, the church, the universities, certain associations of intellectuals, and above all the great professions, stand like rocks against which the waves raised by these forces beat in vain. In America the community requires protection not against the State but against itself.[82]

But at the same time, this means that the populist rhetoric of anti-intellectualism and anti-expert is easily mounted as a generalised counter to these collective identities. And indeed, these kinds of organised and professional structures are potential mechanisms for dominance and control, presenting a possible cartel-like administration of a particular profession. The weakness of the traditional professional structure is that it too is constructed within a narrative of predatory drift, and so it too is easily dismissed within that same narrative. The liability in all these systems is that the individual has been erased in society's predatory drift towards the generalised crowd: "[I]t is a serious mistake to think, in the midst of social interests which preponderate even in modern societies and which embrace the so-called natural interests that there are no individuals or individual interests."[83] The feral wanderer, outside the law, demands to be recuperated: "Canine tales demand a hearing."[84]

An ethological jurisprudence seeks to reinvigorate a relational, multispecies, interactional property of "the little *imitations, oppositions,* and *inventions*"[85] and disturb the predatory drift towards "the view that the individual is not an independent center of force, but only a fleeting datum of experience, that he is a product of heredity modified by environment, and that he does not exist for himself, but is a passing phenomenon in a complex of other phenomena. Here, it would seem, there is no need or scope either for the evaluation or for the weighing of interests. So far as human will has any function, it can be thought of only as serving a universal process."[86]

An ethological jurisprudence is necessarily setting about weighing those interests in a personal process, always already *in personam.*

Fin de siècle interdisciplinarity

Evolutionary theory (and particularly the narrative of natural selection and the combative notion of "survival of the fittest") continues to influence property discourse and interpretation today. The considerable influence of evolutionary theory in the area of social and cultural development (including property and other social institutions)[87] led many early anthropologists to consider so-called primitive peoples to have no concept of property.[88]

One particularly influential example is the early treatise, *Ancient People*, from the anthropologist and social theorist, Lewis Henry Morgan.[89] Although evolutionary social theory does suggest an absence of property in early civilisations, Morgan does not entirely discount the concept of property in "savage society," and indeed he explicitly documents examples of personal property. Nevertheless, he questions the capacity for real property in nomadic societies based upon what appears to be a notion of unanchored wandering as distinct from territory: "Its dominance as a passion over all other passions marks the commencement of civilization. It not only led mankind to overcome the obstacles which delayed civilization, but to establish political society on the basis of territory and of property. A critical knowledge of the evolution of the idea of property would embody, in some respects, the most remarkable portion of the mental history of mankind."[90] This "civilisation" filter, as it were, through which property is defined, arguably continues in force in contemporary debates over traditional knowledge. In this significant work, Morgan sets down the perceived relationship between rivalrous property and a developed society: "The growth of property is thus closely connected with the increase of inventions and discoveries, and with the improvement of social institutions which mark the several ethnical periods of human progress."[91] This perceived relationship between property and progress is now mainstream, and the defence and combat over property territories are profoundly conditioned.

Morgan was also a great influence on Karl Marx and Friedrich Engels, for whom the narrative of a distinctly human mastery over the natural environment was driven by an evolutionary theory of production. Tim Ingold notes that, following Marx and Engels, most histories of human development in relation to the environment can be characterised by the terms collection and production: "The distinction between them was first coined by Friedrich Engels. In a note penned in 1875, Engels pointed to production as the most fundamental criterion of what he saw as a kind of 'mastery' of the environment that was distinctly human."[92] It is notable that this distinction has much in common with the evolutionary theory of social development of the nineteenth century and, as such, with related theories of human domestication. Domestication emerges as a critical event in the history of human society.

However, as the body of anthropological knowledge grew, the appreciation of a kind of "work" in hunting territories began to challenge the dismissal of notions of property in hunter-gatherer societies:[93]

> Until very recently it has been maintained generally that the hunting peoples of the world lacked completely any concept of individual ownership in land. This attitude has been current since the time of Lewis H. Morgan, who categorically assumed that such a characteristic was to be found only among peoples endowed with civilization, as he defined the term. In the last few years, however, detailed investigations have not only disproved this contention, but have demonstrated that among many of the hunting peoples individual ownership of land is not only a recognized principle, but in fact often a most outstanding culture characteristic.[94]

And as will be seen in later discussion, in this kind of property system there is an interesting communication between the land and environment and the owner or territory-holder, inviting a relationship interpretation rather than object-led.[95] Through a discussion of animal territories, the importance of this kind of approach to overlapping spaces will be explored.[96]

Properly speaking, modern conceptions of property in land did not emerge until agriculturalism.[97] Tarde describes what is perhaps better clarified as modern property as "a prime agent in civilisation" arising "from a group of agricultural inventions."[98] In other words, property as a social institution is considered to have been facilitated primarily by the settlement and territory-building of agricultural societies.[99] This relationship of co-evolution, as it were, has been made more explicit in recent research. For example, Samuel Bowles and Jung-Kyoo Choi maintain, "The advent of farming around 12 millennia ago was a cultural as well as technological revolution, requiring a new system of property rights,"[100] proposing a relationship of co-evolution between farming and agriculture as a social and cultural institution and the emergence of property rights as part of the social organisation of that cultural life.[101]

Tarde also notes that a form of common property preceded new private property rights[102] and throughout *Laws of Imitation* attributes this to the imitative revolution arising from the fundamental invention of domestication. As such, it is the sociable property in imitation that is perhaps being lost through the construction of the desire for private property as a perceived dominion rather than a relation. Indeed, the concept of "owner" did not come about in use until much later than the emergence of agriculturalism;[103] however, individual property relations are nevertheless in evidence in ancient and non-agricultural societies.[104] Thus, a distinction between "ownership" and "private property" has important ancient roots. This distinction between ownership and property is arguably in play in Tarde's own account:

> [W]e must recognise the facts that this desire, one which arose from a group of agricultural inventions and which is a prime agent in civilisation, was preceded by a desire for common property (the North American pueblos, the Hindoo village-community, the Russian mir, etc.); that, as a matter of fact, it has not ceased to grow up to the present day at the expense of the latter desire, as is proved by the gradual division of undivided property, of our common lands, for example; that it is no longer growing, however, and that when it once enters into competition with desire for superior subsistence and for more general well-being, it will withdraw before the rival to which it itself gave birth.[105]

The ages of property

The story of property thus narrated settles into four "ages," from the cave to the commons.

The first age is the Stone Age, the age of the first domestication and that dog. As Tarde declares, "What do all our modern inventions amount to in comparison with this capital invention of domestication?"[106] That is, in comparison with the invention that made possible all further innovation and social development? But who invented domestication? For that we must go to the source – that dog. And from that first domestication, the imitation of domestication thus sets human animals forward on a path to modern society, a process through which they are socialised and "humanised." But if "this capital invention" of domestication made all else possible, is that future of humanity distinctly canine? "If, as may be reasonably presumed, human social groups developed out of some form of animal family, they had their origin in a type of association differing profoundly from that which is called to mind when the dictum is cited that the family is the foundation of society."[107]

The second is the age of territory, the Space Age. This is an age of socialisation through mobile territories and overlapping spaces. Boundary-making is less about exclusion than it is about connection, sociability, and at times even welcome interference. This is an age of animals erecting landmarks, building monuments, and creating works. And yet the recognition of these achievements is largely hampered by a creeping attachment to fixation and the visual as human animals modernise the creative landscape.

The predatory turn in property emerges in the age of dominion, the Machine Age, an adversarial, warring shift in property relations, as it were. This predatory turn reaches its peak in the intellectual and political endeavours of the late nineteenth and early twentieth centuries in particular, a period of intense self-consciousness about charting an impassable canyon between the exceptionalism of humans and a machinic behaviourism of animals, abridged to a simple mechanism of incentives. It is in this age that the theory of "predatory drift" is posited, a term unashamedly and strategically taken from dog training discourse. The taking is strategic because the term is without basis in actual ethology and science. The term is a construct, a mythic imposition upon the ongoing reduction of the animal subject to drives and instinct. Similarly, developments in property are preoccupied with establishing property rights as natural, almost pre-existing, always already before the social, as such. In this age of dominance, property shifts from its social origins, from its territories of relations to the boundary-making of things and the rivalry of place. The so-called acquisitive instinct for accumulation thus obscures the genuinely social origins of property as well as the highly constructed and ultimately illogical assumptions underpinning this approach. And yet, the supremacy of the perspective on property as absolutist dominion is persistent and resilient. We need to look at things differently.

We are experiencing the second wave of the predatory turn, our own *fin de siècle*, as it were, with recognisable pessimism. The link between the late nineteenth- and early twentieth-century *fin de siècle* and the rise of fascism in Europe, where territories are reterritorialised as boundaries, as distinct from the genuine territories of relations, is important in this history of property. This was also a period of expansive colonisation and complete reconfiguration of resources through industrialisation,[108] including the development of *Lebensraum* (living space) into an imperialist and ultimately Nazi ideology.[109] As communication technologies and globalisation did not so much shrink the world as transform it into a seemingly single system and thus ultimately consumable ideas, the subscription to the crowd, to the "pack," to the increasing momentum of predatory drift seems secured. Presented as instinct, this second wave of predatory forces harnesses the "conservatism of crowds . . . reborn in fascism."[110] This predatory drift creates strays, ferals, and itinerant wanderers.

But an ethological jurisprudence seeks to challenge the biological determinism of such predatory drift in property systems, returning the conscientious attention to the relations and a convergence upon shared interests. Indeed, this is to return the social as the primary relation, as distinct from conflict as the primary interaction. As Tarde explains: "In the midst of a nature where the essence of every force seems to be to struggle, where every being kills its fellows in order to live, where fratricide is the law, this conception of essentially harmonious faculties, in absolute contrast with this spectacle, is a singularity which does credit to the soul of man."[111]

Tarde rejects the simple "survival of the fittest" provided by evolutionary theory and puts cooperation at the heart of human development. Indeed, cooperation is the passion that animates the Social Age, the age in which principles of altruism and sociability are the sympathetic affinities through which familiar production is propelled. This is the age of shared interests and genuine mutualism, of familiar production. Through a resocialisation of property, assisted by Hohfeld's relations, a genuine *res familiaris* is possible. Although Tarde writes, "I do not see how the doctrine of evolution can continue and can, without maintaining any shocks, account for this phenomenon,"[112] several decades later it did indeed account for this reciprocity through the theories of cooperation[113] and reciprocal altruism.[114] Tarde was, once again, seemingly ahead of his time.[115] He was not alone, however, in this thinking that cooperation and indeed sociability might be far more important than combat. The Russian zoologist, Karl Federovich Kessler, proposed the law of mutual help in 1881, just a few months before he died, in which he declared sociability to be the fundamental quality of development,[116] paving the way for Peter Kropotkin's theories of mutual aid.[117] And this altruism could no longer be considered uniquely human: "Darwin's whole thesis that man is descended from other animals requires that man's altruistic drives have precursors among his animal ancestors."[118] Through the central character of cooperation, evolution becomes a dialogue between two beings: "Far from being smothered by competition, cooperation was possible precisely because the individual was important. It was through his seeking out of others that all the goodness in the world was born."[119]

Once again, the prejudice of the observer changes the observed, and the history of the study of altruism is an important illustration of this: "Deeply held commitments to individuals, atomism and egoism have moved psychology to underestimate the frequency of altruism and to seek explanations of examples of altruism that are based in the self-interested motives of the altruists."[120] Indeed, it is "to take the altruism out of altruism."[121] The economics-based models of competitive acquisition and accumulation, despite the biological rhetoric attached to them, are simply not supported by the science. As Warder Clyde Allee notes: "a ruthless struggle for existence is not the whole, or even the major contribution of current biology to social philosophy and social ethics."[122] Further, Allee wholly rejects the purported scientific basis for a warring, combative social structure of pitiless and unaccountable competition and geopolitics:

"Those who assert that the whole trend of science is to lend support to the present war system in settling international disagreements are relying on a mistaken, outmoded phase of biological thought to bolster up a much older and unreasoned drive toward conflict. The philosophy that condones war is not based on all the biological evidence or on recent interpretations made in the light of that evidence."[123] The co-option of science by the discourse of predatory drift is simply not correct; or as Oskar Morgenstern says somewhat more emphatically: "Economists simply don't know what science means. I am quite disgusted with all of this rubbish."[124]

It is indeed all about property but not because property is all about things. It is because everything is about property. Everything is about relations. And property is about everyone.

How to restore this sociability? We need to take a walk.

That dog is a nuisance!

> Everything which belongs to a thought without image – nomadism, the war-machine, becomings, nuptials against nature, capture and thefts, interregnums, minor languages or stammering of language, etc. – is crushed and denounced as a nuisance.[125]

Movement is a nuisance to property. Nomadism is an annoyance. Smell exasperates intellectual property. An ethological jurisprudence is a similar intrusion, bringing in scents, and strays, and scratches on the floor. In a way, an ethological jurisprudence is outside the accepted or desired behaviours and organised life of an orderly property discourse. But that is the nature of the sociable territory into which this story is entering.

The idea that some dog behaviours might be deemed "nuisance" behaviours is important. The focus is on the human animal as owner, not on the property as relation. The relationship is thus one-sided, concerned with inconvenience rather than the positive welfare of that dog and the explanation of the behaviour: "Problem behavior is a personal rather than a physical construct, as it describes any behavior that is problematic for the individual reporting it. The problem is not the animal's behavior per se, but rather the problem it poses to the reporter."[126] This is a curious inconsistency in dog welfare, compared with other species, in that positive welfare is not gaining traction in a large area of training practice. The emphasis is entirely upon the owner. But what is happening in the relation? What is that dog trying to communicate? From frustration, to boredom, to separation anxiety, the behaviour is often treated as an object, a thing – observable, mechanical, and resolvable through a "quick fix." However, such methods that focus upon the thing ignore the relation at their peril, and certainly to the detriment of that dog, as later discussions will explore. Further, such behaviours may be part of the normal repertoire of communication resources for that dog, so the implications of silencing them are significant.

An ethological jurisprudence focuses upon the relation; that is, instead of all attention on effects and enforcement, with the other party (the visitor, the consumer, and so on) always already after the event, the concern and indeed respect is for the relations prior to "enforcement," whatever that might be, towards a resocialisation of property. Joseph Agassi writes, "the major cause of the nuisance value of philosophers to scientists is intellectual."[127] An ethological jurisprudence welcomes the nuisance of both. Indeed, ethology is used to the trouble: "with respect to facts described, questions asked, methods employed, and theories ventured, ethologists looked toward a number of different disciplines, at different times, with an eye to impressing or influencing practitioners in those areas."[128] There is, after all, a distinct nuisance factor in interdisciplinarity. And that should be encouraged.

That dog is thus a crucial protagonist in shifting those intractable positions. So, let's walk with that dog. And I hope this book will prove an utter nuisance.

Notes

1 Radin M (1938) A Restatement of Hohfeld, *Harvard Law Review*, 51(7), 1141–1164: p. 1141.
2 Cairns H (1941) *The Theory of Legal Science*, U of North Carolina P, Chapel Hill, 73.
3 Indeed, there is little regulation on training, other than the provisions against unnecessary suffering and the restriction on some procedures (e.g., tail docking) as provided in the Animal Welfare Act 2006. New legislation is attempting to regulate puppy mill operations as well. However, farm animal welfare is more closely regulated at the EU level by a range of instruments, particularly with respect to handling. Dogs seem to, in many ways, slip between the cracks.
4 Hallowell AI (1942) The Nature and Function of Property as a Social Institution, *Journal of Legal and Political Sociology*, 1, 115–138: p. 120.
5 Hallowell AI (1942) The Nature and Function of Property as a Social Institution, *Journal of Legal and Political Sociology*, 1, 115–138: p. 120.
6 Blomley N (2016) The Territory of Property, *Progress in Human Geography*, 593–609: pp. 594–594.
7 Borges JL (1983/[1992]) Paracelsus and the Rose, *The Antioch Review*, NT Di Giovanni (trans.) 50(1/2), 395–398: p. 396.
8 Singer JW (2000) *Entitlement*, Yale UP, New Haven, 12–13. As Singer explains: "however . . . the ownership model hinders our ability to address these normative goals adequately. It does so because ownership is a woefully inadequate conception of what property is. It hides from our view consideration of the systemic consequences of alternative property regimes, and it takes our attention away from considering which relationships can be characterized as just and which ones should be seen as oppressive" (13).
9 Hohfeld WN (1913) Some Fundamental Legal Conceptions as Applied in Judicial Reasoning. *Yale Law Journal*, 23(1), 16–59; Hohfeld WN (1917) Fundamental Legal Conceptions as Applied in Judicial Reasoning, *Yale Law Journal*, 26(8), 710–770.
10 Lawton G (2014) The First Things Humans Owned, *New Scientist*, 25 March.
11 Lawton G (2014) The First Things Humans Owned, *New Scientist*, 25 March.
12 Also known as Gabriel de Tarde. Tarde dropped the aristocratic "de" during his lifetime, but it was resumed by his various publishers and commentators (and son) after his death. He will be referred to as Gabriel Tarde in the present work.

13 Tarde G (1893/[2012]) *Monadology and Sociology*, T Lorenc (trans.), Re-Press, Melbourne, 28.
14 Tarde G (1893/[2012]) *Monadology and Sociology*, T Lorenc (trans.), Re-Press, Melbourne, 51.
15 Tarde G (1893/[2012]) *Monadology and Sociology*, T Lorenc (trans.), Re-Press, Melbourne, 52–53.
16 Ehrlich E (1936) *Fundamental Principles of the Sociology of Law*, Harvard UP, Cambridge, MA, 473.
17 Borges JL (1942/[1962]) Funes, the Memorious, in *Ficciones*, A Kerrigan (trans.), Grove Press, New York, 107–115: p. 114.
18 Griffin DR (1976) *The Question of Animal Awareness: Evolutionary Continuity of Mental Experience*, The Rockefeller UP, New York, 54. Donald Griffin was one of the leading figures in the development of a cognitive approach to ethology, shepherding in an affective science of comparative psychology: "I suggest that behavioral scientists now have the opportunity, and perhaps an obligation, to explore and discuss the implications for this traditional, behavioristic viewpoint of recent discoveries about communication behavior in animals" (55–56). This is discussed further in Chapter 10, "Shared interests."
19 Fentress JC (1992) The Covalent Animal: On Bonds and Their Boundaries in Behavioural Research, in Davis H & Balfour D (eds.) *The Inevitable Bond: Examining Scientist-Animal Interactions*, Cambridge UP, Cambridge, 44–71: p. 45.
20 Burghardt GM (1985) Animal Awareness: Current Perceptions and Historical Perspective, *American Psychologist*, 40(8), 905–919. See further the earlier article co-authored with Harold Herzog which notes that in addition to a presumed exceptionalism of the human species, a failure to address the situated nature of the observer can also lead to species-specific presumptions based upon cultural prejudices: "Our culturally based anthropocentric notions of decent behavior frequently color our judgments, often erroneously, as with pigs, rats, vultures, hyenas, and certain predators. Positive attitudes may be similarly misplaced." See Burghardt GM & Herzog HA, Jr (1980) Beyond Conspecifics: Is Brer Rabbit Our Brother?, *BioScience*, 30(11), 763–768: p. 766. See further the discussion of Konrad Lorenz's wolf studies and Nazism in Chapter 8, "Pack fiction."
21 Burghardt GM (2007) Critical Anthropomorphism, Uncritical Anthropocentrism, and Naïve Nominalism, *Comparative Cognition and Behavior Reviews*, 2, 136–138.
22 Waal F de (1999) Anthropomorphism and Anthropodenial: Consistency in Our Thinking about Humans and Other Animals, *Philosophical Topics*, 27, 255–280.
23 Griffin DR (1976) *The Question of Animal Awareness: Evolutionary Continuity of Mental Experience*, The Rockefeller UP, New York, 69.
24 Griffin DR (1976) *The Question of Animal Awareness: Evolutionary Continuity of Mental Experience*, The Rockefeller UP, New York, 71.
25 Griffin DR (1976) *The Question of Animal Awareness: Evolutionary Continuity of Mental Experience*, The Rockefeller UP, New York, 56.
26 Griffin DR (1977) Anthropomorphism, *BioScience*, 27(7), 445–446: "In the analysis of animal behaviour we have been strongly conditioned to avoid anthropomorphism as a cardinal sin against scientific standards" (445).
27 Goymann W (2019) On the Importance of Studying Animal Behaviour: Or Any Other Kind of "Blue Sky" Research, *Ethology*, 125, 501–502: p. 502.
28 Borges JL (1942/[1962]) Funes, the Memorious, in *Ficciones*, A Kerrigan (trans.), Grove Press, New York, 107–115: p. 114.

29 Bekoff M (2000) Animal Emotions: Exploring Passionate Natures, *BioScience*, 50(10), 861–870.
30 Tarde G (1902/[2007]) Economic Psychology, A Toscano (trans.), *Economy and Society*, 36(4), 614–643.
31 Hoebel EA (1946) Law and Anthropology, *Virginia Law Review*, 32(4), 835–854: p. 840.
32 Sagan D (2010) Umwelt after Uexküll, in Uexküll J von (ed.)(1934/[2010]) *A Foray into the Worlds of Animals and Humans*, JD O'Neil (trans) U of Minnesota P, Minneapolis, 1–34: p. 2.
33 Winthrop-Young G (2010) Bubbles and Webs: A Backdoor Stroll through the Readings of Uexküll, Afterword to Uexküll J von (1934/[2010]) *A Foray into the Worlds of Animals and Humans*, J D O'Neil (trans), U of Minnesota P, Minneapolis, 209–243: p. 220.
34 Haraway D (2008) *When Species Meet*, U of Minnesota P, Minneapolis, 19. The concept is discussed in more detail in later chapters, see in particular Chapter 9, "Wild abandon".
35 Despret V (2004) The Body We Care For: Figures of Anthropo-zoo-genesis, *Body & Society*, 10(2–3), 111–134: p. 130.
36 The refrain of looking back is taken from the title of a scientific paper looking at the interspecific communicative abilities of dogs in a comparative study with socialised wolves. The authors found that a key difference in the behaviour of dogs is that they look at the human's face, thus demonstrating not only a communicative competence but also, and importantly, an accounting for the other in that communicative interaction. See Miklósi Á (2003) A Simple Reason for a Big Difference: Dogs Do Not Look Back at Humans, But Dogs Do, *Current Biology*, 13, 763–766.
37 Buttner AP (2016) Neurobiological Underpinnings of Dogs' Human-Like Social Competence: How Interactions between Stress Response Systems and Oxytocin Mediate Dogs' Social Skills, *Neuroscience and Biobehavioral Reviews*, 71, 198–214; Hare B & Tomasello M (2005) Human-Like Social Skills in Dogs?, *TRENDS in Cognitive Sciences*, 9(9), 439–444; Miklósi Á et al. (2004) Comparative Social Cognition: What Can Dogs Teach Us?, *Animal Behaviour*, 67, 995–1004; Cooper JJ et al. (2003) Clever Hounds: Social Cognition in the Domestic Dog (*Canis Familiaris*), *Applied Animal Behaviour Science*, 81, 229–244.
38 MacLean EL et al. (2017) Individual Differences in Cooperative Communication Skills Are More Similar between Dogs and Humans Than Chimpanzees, *Animal Behaviour*, 126, 41–51.
39 Bunford N et al. (2017) *Canis Familiaris* As a Model for Non-Invasive Comparative Neuroscience, *Trends in Neurosciences*, 40(7), 438–452.
40 Mazzatenta A et al. (2017) The Companion Dog as a Unique Translational Model for Aging, *Seminars in Cell & Developmental Biology*, 70, 141–153; Gilmore KM & Greer KA (2015) Why Is the Dog an Ideal Model for Aging Research?, *Experimental Gerontology*, 71, 14–20.
41 Studzinski CM et al. (2006) Visuospatial Function in the Beagle Dog: An Early Marker of Cognitive Decline in a Model of Human Aging and Dementia, *Neurobiology of Learning and Memory*, 86, 197–204; Studzinski CM et al. (2005) The Canine Model of Human Cognitive Aging and Dementia: Pharmacological Validity of the Model for Assessment of Human Cognitive-Enhancing Drugs, *Progress in Neuro-Psychopharmacology & Biological Psychiatry*, 29, 489–498.
42 Haraway D (2008) *When Species Meet*, U of Minnesota P, Minneapolis, 4.

43 Aesop (1998) The Hunter and Woodman, in *The Fables of Aesop*, The Folio Society, London, 67.
44 Deleuze G & Guattari F (1980/[1987]) *A Thousand Plateaus: Capitalism and Schizophrenia*, B Massumi (trans.), U of Minnesota P, Minneapolis, 13.
45 The complex legacy and interpretation of the term, "pack," is considered in detail in Chapter 8, "Pack fiction."
46 Deleuze G & Guattari F (1980/[1987]) *A Thousand Plateaus: Capitalism and Schizophrenia*, B Massumi (trans.), U of Minnesota P, Minneapolis, 6–7.
47 Deleuze G & Guattari F (1980/[1987]) *A Thousand Plateaus: Capitalism and Schizophrenia*, B Massumi (trans.), U of Minnesota P, Minneapolis, 12.
48 Maynard Smith J (1979) Game Theory and the Evolution of Behaviour, *Proceedings of the Royal Society of London*, 205(1161), 475–488: p. 481.
49 von Jhering R (1913) *Law as a Means to an End*, The Boston Book Co, Boston, 386–387.
50 Nietzsche F (1874/[2015]) *The Use and Abuse of History*, A Collins (trans.), Martino Press, Mansfield, 5.
51 Deleuze G & Guattari F (1980/[1987]) *A Thousand Plateaus: Capitalism and Schizophrenia*, B Massumi (trans.), U of Minnesota P, Minneapolis, 393–394.
52 Deleuze G & Guattari F (1980/[1987]) *A Thousand Plateaus: Capitalism and Schizophrenia*, B Massumi (trans.), U of Minnesota P, Minneapolis, 394.
53 In a brief project review, József Topál describes it thus: "One of the popular interpretations among laypeople of the emergence of the dog is that domestication led to an 'artificial' animal that was created by man 'in his own image." He notes further the results of surveys of pet owners which suggest that "as the result of living closely with their dog many of pet owners are disposed to form the subjective impression that the dog is an animal possessing human-like skills. Until recently, behavior experts put down this approach as one of the striking examples of human anthropomorphism leading to nonscientific (nonparsimonious) explanations regarding dog behavior," or a so-called "naïve view." However, as Topál goes on to address, domestication research confounds this dismissal: "growing evidence regarding dogs' communication skills and other social-cognitive abilities have aroused a great deal of interest among cognitive ethologists and led to a radical change in our attitude toward this 'naïve view'," and to note the social competence of dogs in their pedagogical receptivity, making them especially relevant models for human behaviour. See Topál J (2009) Understanding the Dog: What Is It Like to Be a Human Creation?, *Journal of Veterinary Behavior*, 4, 45. Brian Hare notes: "The days of dogs being considered artificially created animals for use in conditioning studies have given way to the recognition of the dog's rich social life requiring it to adapt to the most complex primate of all." See Hare B (2008) The Dog: A Biologist's Best Friend, *Current Biology*, 18(13), R543–R544: p. R544. These aspects are explored further, particularly in Chapter 2, "The imitation of domestication"; Chapter 8, "Pack fiction"; and Chapter 10, "Shared interests".
54 For instance, in relation to the developing research on animal culture, Laland and Galef identify obstacles which, although not expressly attributed as such, are notably consistent with an underlying narrative of human exceptionalism: "researchers disagree over whether human culture and animal cultures are fundamentally different or fundamentally similar (or perhaps more accurately, in what ways human and animal cultures are similar to or different from one another)." See Laland KN & Galef BG (2009) Introduction, in Laland KN & Galef BG (eds.) *The Question of Animal Culture*, Harvard UP, Cambridge, MA, 1–18: p. 9. The immediate question is why such cultures should be similar? Why

is similarity a measure of culture other than if the presumption of human exceptionalism as the benchmark remains firmly in place.
55 Galef B (1992) The Question of Animal Culture, *Human Nature*, 3(2), 157–178: "Some feel (and I confess that this is my own bias) that it is probably best for scientists to be conservative" (158). In their introduction to their volume on animal culture, Laland and Galef explain: "A large part of the controversy concerns the kinds of evidence sufficient to establish that differences in the behaviour of geographically separate populations of a species result from social learning rather than from genetic differences between populations or differences in the way diverse ecologies shape behavioural development of individuals. Here researchers differ in the degree to which they are willing to rely on circumstantial evidence and plausibility arguments, and laboratory experimentalists and field researchers often take different sides" in Laland KN & Galef BG (2009) Introduction, in Laland KN & Galef BG (eds.) *The Question of Animal Culture*, Harvard UP, Cambridge, MA, 1–18: p. 9. For instance, in a review of recent research on imitation and social learning in young banded mongooses, Bennett Galef notes these obstacles to research in animal cultures: "because the ethnographic method rests solely on observation, it provides only indirect evidence that differences in the behavioural repertoires of sub-populations of a species result from the social transmission of behaviors between individuals . . . the possibility always exists that any potentially traditional behaviour identified using the ethnographic method reflects some as-yet undiscovered differences in either the environments that groups occupy or in their genetic compositions, rather than social transmission within groups. See Galef BG (2010) Animal Traditions: Experimental Evidence of Learning by Imitation in an Unlikely Animal, *Current Biology*, 20(13), R555–R556: p. R555. See further the report of the study: Müller CA & Cant MA (2010) Imitation and Traditions in Wild Banded Mongooses, *Current Biology*, 20(13), 1171–1175.
56 Burkhardt RW, Jr (2008) Dilemmas in the Constitution of and Exportation of Ethological Facts, Working Papers on The Nature of Evidence: How Well Do 'Facts' Travel?, London School of Economics, 32/08.
57 Gibson J (2014) *The Logic of Innovation*, Ashgate, Aldershot, 38–44, and *passim*.
58 See further the discussion of Hohfeld's approach in Resocialisation.
59 Deleuze G & Guattari F (1980/[1987]) *A Thousand Plateaus: Capitalism and Schizophrenia*, B Massumi (trans.), U of Minnesota P, Minneapolis, 239–240. Bruno Latour notes in Tarde's approach to social theory, "that the nature/society divide is irrelevant for understanding the world of human interactions," and "that the micro/macro distinction stifles any attempt at understanding how society is generated." See Latour B (2002) Gabriel Tarde and the End of the Social, in Joyce P (ed.) *The Social in Question: New Bearings in History and the Social Sciences*, Routledge, London, 117–132: p. 118.
60 Allee WC (1945) Social Biology of Subhuman Groups, *Sociometry*, 8(1), 21–29: p. 24.
61 Tarde G (1890/[1903]) *The Laws of Imitation*, EC Parsons (trans.), Henry Holt & Co, New York, 371.
62 The nature of property in animals, together with considerations over animal rights, welfare and autonomy, including authorship and ownership, is examined in much more detail in Gibson J (forthcoming) *More Than Human Intellectual Property: Animal Authors and Human Machines*, Routledge, London.
63 Candea M (2016) Revisiting Tarde's House, in Candea M (ed.) *The Social after Gabriel Tarde: Debates and Assessments*, 2nd ed., Routledge, London, 1–27: p. 3.

64 Latour B (2002) Gabriel Tarde and the End of the Social, in Joyce P (ed.) (2002/[2012]) *The Social in Question: New Bearings in History and the Social Sciences*, Routledge, London, 117–132: p. 120.
65 Deleuze G & Guattari F (1980/[1987]) *A Thousand Plateaus: Capitalism and Schizophrenia*, B Massumi (trans.), U of Minnesota P, Minneapolis, 219.
66 Candea M (2016) Revisiting Tarde's House, in Candea M (ed.) *The Social after Gabriel Tarde: Debates and Assessments*, 2nd ed., Routledge, London, 1–27: p. 2.
67 Davis MM (1906) *Gabriel Tarde: An Essay in Sociological Theory*, Columbia University Dissertation, New York, 5.
68 Giddings FH (1903) Introduction, in Tarde G (ed.) (1890/[1903]) *The Laws of Imitation*, EC Parsons (trans.), Henry Holt & Co, New York, iv.
69 Davis MM (1906) *Gabriel Tarde: An Essay in Sociological Theory*, Columbia University Dissertation, New York, 5.
70 Tarde G (1890/[1903]) *The Laws of Imitation*, EC Parsons (trans.), Henry Holt & Co, New York, 371.
71 Tarde G (1899) *Social Laws: An Outline of Sociology*, HC Warren (trans.), Macmillan, New York, 48 note 1. Bruno Latour notes: "Yes, I know, Tarde was not as lucky as Leibniz: his monadology did not transform sociology as much as the infinitesimal calculus transformed mathematics. But history is still young and if nature stops bifurcating, Tarde's innovation might still come true." See Latour B (2008) *What Is the Style of Matters of Concern?*, Van Gorcum, Amsterdam, 9.
72 Deleuze and Guattari refer to Tarde as inventing microsociology in Deleuze G & Guattari F (1980/[1987]) *A Thousand Plateaus: Capitalism and Schizophrenia*, B Massumi (trans.), U of Minnesota P, Minneapolis, 218–219.
73 First introduced in Gibson J (2014) *The Logic of Innovation*, Ashgate, Aldershot, 38–44.
74 Latour B (2008) *What Is the Style of Matters of Concern?*, Van Gorcum, Amsterdam, 4.
75 Margaret Floy Washburn studied with Edward Bradford Titchener, being his first doctoral student. She became the first woman to achieve a PhD in psychology in 1894. See Dallenbach KM (1940) Margaret Floy Washburn 1871–1939, *The American Journal of Psychology*, 53(1), 1–5.
76 To this intellectual biography I would add the early mid-twentieth-century scientists who continued to push enquiry into cooperation as a fundamental characteristic of evolution and the value of interdisciplinarity in furthering understanding of human (and other animals) societies, particularly Warder Clyde Allee who emphasised sociology in his own work. While it is beyond the scope of the present work to track meticulously the entire intellectual history, an attempt has been made to acknowledge some key figures in the sociability of law, sociology, anthropology, philosophy, and science throughout. For further discussion of the development of an affective science in ethology, please see Gibson J (forthcoming) *More Than Human Intellectual Property: Animal Authors and Human Machines*, Routledge, London.
77 Tarde G (1890/[1903]) *The Laws of Imitation*, EC Parsons (trans.), Henry Holt & Co, New York, 89–90.
78 Latour B (2002) Gabriel Tarde and the End of the Social, in Joyce P (ed.) *The Social in Question: New Bearings in History and the Social Sciences*, Routledge, London, 117–132: p. 117.
79 Burkhardt RW, Jr (2008) Dilemmas in the Constitution of and Exportation of Ethological Facts, Working Papers on The Nature of Evidence: How Well Do 'Facts' Travel?, London School of Economics, 32/08: 4.
80 Sir Alexander Morris Carr-Saunders (1886–1966) was also the fifth Director of the London School of Economics 1937–1956: Blacker CP and DVG (1966) Obituary: Sir Alexander Carr-Saunders, *Population Studies*, 20(3), 365–369.

81 As one review contemporary with its publication noted, the book addresses "a theme the perennial urgency of which has been clearly demonstrated by recent European events." See Rudlin WA (1934) Review: *The Professions* by AM Carr-Saunders and PA Wilson, *The Economic Journal*, 44(174), 322–324: p. 322.
82 Carr-Saunders AM & Wilson PA (1933), *The Professions*, Clarendon Press, Oxford, 497–498.
83 Kocourek A (1917) The Nature of Interests and Their Classification, *American Journal of Sociology*, 23(3), 359–368: p. 362.
84 Haraway D (2008) *When Species Meet*, U of Minnesota P, Minneapolis, 133.
85 Deleuze G & Guattari F (1980/[1987]) *A Thousand Plateaus: Capitalism and Schizophrenia*, B Massumi (trans.), U of Minnesota P, Minneapolis, 219.
86 Kocourek A (1917) The Nature of Interests and Their Classification, *American Journal of Sociology*, 23(3), 359–368: p. 359.
87 See in particular Morgan LH (1877) *Ancient People, or Researches in the Line of Human Progress, from Savagery through Barbarism to Civilization*, Charles H Kerr & Co, Chicago. See further the update to evolutionary theories of property in the context of the evolution of social institutions, in Earle T (2000) Archaeology, Property, and Prehistory, *Annual Review of Anthropology*, 29, 39–60. See further Krier JE (2009) Evolutionary Theory and the Origin of Property Rights, *Cornell Law Review*, 95(1), 139–159.
88 For instance, see Davidson DS (1928) The Family Hunting Territory in Australia, *American Anthropologist*, 30(4), 614–631. Davidson notes: "Until comparatively recent years, there has been a general supposition that so-called primitive man held no concept of real property ownership. . . . It has been maintained that it was impossible for people who were constantly on the move in search of game, upon which they were dependent for a food supply, to come to regard any part of the terrain over which they wandered, as belonging exclusively to any one group, let alone to any one individual" (614).
89 Morgan LH (1877) *Ancient People, or Researches in the Line of Human Progress, from Savagery through Barbarism to Civilization*, Charles H Kerr & Co, Chicago. A contemporary of Marx and Engels, Morgan's influence on their work has been widely acknowledged in the literature, particularly his evolutionary theory of property. See Shaw WH (1984) Marx and Morgan, *History and Theory*, 23(2), 215–228. See the more detailed discussion of "communism" in so-called primitive societies in Predatory Drift.
90 Morgan LH (1877) *Ancient People, or Researches in the Line of Human Progress, from Savagery through Barbarism to Civilization*, Charles H Kerr & Co, Chicago, 5–6.
91 Morgan LH (1877) *Ancient People, or Researches in the Line of Human Progress, from Savagery through Barbarism to Civilization*, Charles H Kerr & Co, Chicago, 579.
92 Ingold T (2000) *The Perception of the Environment: Essays in Livelihood, Dwelling and Skill*, Routledge, London, 77–78.
93 For example, see Hallowell AI (1949) The Size of Algonkian Hunting Territories: A Function of Ecological Adjustment, *American Anthropologist*, 51(1), 35–45.
94 Davidson DS (1928) Family Hunting Territories of the Tribes of Tierra del Fuego, *Indian Notes*, 5(1), 395–410: pp. 305–396. See further the work of Frank G Speck and the demonstration of property rights in hunting grounds: Speck FG (1914–1915) The Basis of American Indian Ownership of the Land. University of Pennsylvania Faculty, Public Lectures, 181–196; Speck FG (1926) Land Ownership among Hunting Peoples in Primitive America and the World's Marginal Areas. Proceedings, Twenty-Second International Congress of Americanists, 323–332. This relationship between cultural and social organisation,

territory and property, is explored in greater detail in Chapter 4, "Marking territory."
95 Hallowell AI (1949) The Size of Algonkian Hunting Territories: A Function of Ecological Adjustment, *American Anthropologist*, 51(1), 35–45.
96 See in particular the chapters in the Space Age.
97 Krier JE (2009) Evolutionary Theory and the Origin of Property Rights, *Cornell Law Review*, 95, 139–159: p. 158.
98 Tarde G (1890/[1903]) *The Laws of Imitation*, EC Parsons (trans.), Henry Holt & Co, New York, 125–126.
99 This relationship between the rise of agriculture and the development of new systems of property rights in relation to settled territories is long established in the literature. For example, see the discussion in Herskovits MJ (1952/[1940]) *Economic Anthropology*, Alfred A Knopf, New York: Part IV, Property. For a discussion of property in hunting territories see Hallowell AI (1949) The Size of Algonkian Hunting Territories: A Function of Ecological Adjustment, *American Anthropologist*, 51(1), 35–45; Davidson DS (1928) The Family Hunting Territory in Australia, *American Anthropologist*, 30(4), 614–631; and more recently in Krier JE (2009) Evolutionary Theory and the Origin of Property Rights, *Cornell Law Review*, 95(1), 139–159. For recent discussions on the relationship between agricultural development and property, see further: Bowles S & Choi J-K (2013) Coevolution of Farming and Private Property during the Early Holocene, *PNAS*, 110(22), 8830–8835; Orton D (2010) Both Subject and Object: Herding, Inalienability and Sentient Property in Prehistory, *World Archaeology*, 42(2), 188–200; Earle T (2000) Archaeology, Property, and Prehistory, *Annual Review of Anthropology*, 29, 39–60.
100 Bowles S & Choi J-K (2013) Coevolution of Farming and Private Property during the Early Holocene, *PNAS*, 110(22), 8830–8835: p. 8830. The authors note: "This Holocene revolution was not sparked by a superior technology. It occurred because possession of the wealth of farmers – crops, dwellings, and animals – could be unambiguously demarcated and defended. This facilitated the spread of new property rights that were advantageous to the groups adopting them" (8830). This relationship between territory and the value of "defence" with respect to property is discussed in greater detail in Chapter 4, "Marking territory."
101 The authors explain: "We propose that the new property rights and the new way of making a living coevolved, neither being viable alone but each providing the conditions permitting the advance of the other. This coevolution hypothesis is based on two empirically motivated premises: that farming required a novel system of property rights, and that (in the absence of exceptional circumstance) this system of farming-friendly property rights was not viable in an economy based on wild plant and animal species." See Bowles S & Choi J-K (2013) Coevolution of Farming and Private Property during the Early Holocene, *PNAS*, 110(22), 8830–8835: p. 8830.
102 The relationship between communalism and private property, as traced through the anthropological and other literature, is explored in greater detail in Chapter 10, "Shared interests".
103 See the discussion in Gibson J (2008) The Law of the Land, in Graber CB & Burri-Nenova M (eds.) *Intellectual Property and Traditional Cutlural Expressions in a Digital Environment*, Edward Elgar, Cheltenham, 182–201.
104 Mead M (1961) Some Anthropological Considerations Concerning Natural Law, *Natural Law Forum*, 6, 51–64.
105 Tarde G (1890/[1903]) *The Laws of Imitation*, EC Parsons (trans.), Henry Holt & Co, New York, 125–126.

106 Tarde G (1890/[1903]) *The Laws of Imitation*, EC Parsons (trans.), Henry Holt & Co, New York, 277.
107 Briffault R (1931) *The Mothers: The Matriarchal Theory of Social Origins*, Macmillan, New York, 99.
108 See for instance the discussion in relation to fashion production in Gibson J (2014) *The Logic of Innovation*, Ashgate, Aldershot, Chapter 4 (Taste).
109 Hall AJ (2010) *Earth into Property: Colonization, Decolonization and Capital*, McGill-Queen's UP, Montreal-Kingston, 231–232. See further the legacy in Bassin M (2003) Between Realism and the 'New Right': Geopolitics in Germany in the 1990s, *Transactions of the Institute of British Geographers*, 28(3) 350–366.
110 Mosse GL (1966) The Genesis of Fascism, *Journal of Contemporary History*, 1(1), 14–26: p. 16.
111 Tarde G (1890/[1912]) *Penal Philosophy*, R Howell (trans.), Little, Brown, and Co, Boston, 103.
112 Tarde G (1890/[1912]) *Penal Philosophy*, R Howell (trans.), Little, Brown, and Co, Boston, 103.
113 Axelrod R (1984) *The Evolution of Cooperation*, Penguin, London.
114 Trivers RL (1971) The Evolution of Reciprocal Altruism, *Quarterly Review of Biology*, 46(1), 35–57.
115 Clancy K (2017) Survival of the Friendliest, *Nautilus*, 23 March.
116 Scientific Serials, Memoirs of the St Petersburg Society of Naturalists, *Nature*, 17 March 1881, 474.
117 Kropotkin P (1902) *Mutual Aid: A Factor in Evolution*, McClure Phillips & Co, New York.
118 Allee WC (1945) Social Biology of Subhuman Groups, *Sociometry*, 8(1), 21–29: p. 25.
119 Harman O (2011) *The Price of Altruism*, Vintage, London, 124.
120 Schwartz B (1993) Why Altruism Is Impossible . . . and Ubiquitous, *Social Service Review*, 67(3), 314–343: p. 314.
121 Trivers RL (1971) The Evolution of Reciprocal Altruism, *Quarterly Review of Biology*, 46(1), 35–57: p. 35.
122 Allee WC (1943) Where Angels Fear to Tread: A Contribution from General Sociology to Human Ethics, *Science*, 97(2528), 517–525: p. 524.
123 Allee WC (1943) Where Angels Fear to Tread: A Contribution from General Sociology to Human Ethics, *Science*, 97(2528), 517–525: p. 524. Allee notes elsewhere: "Each advance in complexity of metazoan individuals came from the natural selection of an increased ability in natural cooperation on the part of the evolving stock; the greater natural cooperation came first, and then it was selected." See Allee WC (1945) Social Biology of Subhuman Groups, *Sociometry*, 8(1), 21–29: p. 23.
124 April–May 1942. Cited in Leonard RJ (1995) From Parlor Games to Social Science: Von Neumann, Morgenstern, and the Creation of Game Theory 1928–1944, *Journal of Economic Literature*, 33(2), 730–761: p. 730.
125 Deleuze G & Parnet C (1977/[1987]) *Dialogues*, H Tomlinson & B Habberjam (trans.), Columbia UP, New York, 14.
126 Mills DS et al. (2010) *The Encyclopedia of Applied Animal Behaviour and Welfare*, CAB International, Wallingford, OX, 488.
127 Agassi J (1989) The Role of the Philosopher among the Scientists: Nuisance or Necessity?, *Social Epistemology*, 3(4), 297–309.
128 Burkhardt RW, Jr (2008) Dilemmas in the Constitution of and Exportation of Ethological Facts, Working Papers on The Nature of Evidence: How Well Do 'Facts' Travel?, London School of Economics, 32/08: 3.

Part I

Domestication, the stone age

> All philosophy hitherto has been based on the verb *Be*, the definition of which was the philosopher's stone, which all sought to discover . . . if it had been based on the verb *Have*, many sterile debates and fruitless intellectual exertions would have been avoided.
> Gabriel de Tarde, *Monadology and Sociology*, 1895

> Sitting back, he put his fingertips together, and said, "You offer gold, believing I hold the secret of the philosopher's stone, which turns base metals into gold. It's not gold I seek. If it's gold you're interested in, you'll never be a disciple of mine."
>
> "I don't care about gold," the other man answered. "These coins are but a token of my willingness to work. I want you to teach me the Grand Secret. I want to follow by your side the path that leads to the stone."
>
> "The path is the stone," Paracelsus said slowly. "The stone is the point of departure. If you don't understand these words you have not even begun to understand. Each step along the path is the destination."
> Jorge Luis Borges, Paracelsus and the Rose, 1983

> In this sense, the stone is free.
> Jean-Luc Nancy, *The Experience of Freedom*, 1988

Chapter 1

Canis familiaris – the invention of domestication

> The first animal, the first natural being which appealed to the savage's curiosity, opened out a new world to him, a world outside of his family, or, rather, made a new opening for him into that world which the never-ending growling of savage creatures had never allowed him wholly to ignore. Seen through his dreams or fears, either the commonplace of the terrible animal revealed to him something outside of himself or his people that was worthy of his interest. This animal, then this stranger, whose prestige he feels and yields to, tears him away from the exclusive prestige of his divine ancestors and despotic master.
>
> Tarde G (1890/[1903]) *The Laws of Imitation*, EC Parsons (trans), Henry Holt & Co, New York, 275–76

That dog – in moving in with humans many, many thousands of years ago – became a member of the house that dog created. That dog went "inside" to motivate the enlargement outwards, to the exterior, the outland, the reason of society. Ever since, dogs everywhere bring things out into the open.

What is domestication?

> Domestication is the process of enfolding a species into human society.[1]

As the story goes, domestication is defined as the process of appropriating plant and animal species within the human animal's social and environmental development – the enfolding of nature into society. But the language of enfoldment is all at once intriguing and complicating. Enfolding into society encounters prospects of dominance and submission[2] and, although not used in the diminished sense of the "dominance" concept deployed to great damage in everyday training discourse,[3] the conventional domestication narrative arguably attenuates or utterly abrogates any notion of other animal subjectivities. It is also a narrative that presumes a human animal intentionality through the emphasis on theories such as "taming" and "selecting" and "controlling" the natural world,[4] seemingly obscuring the suggestion of "Unconscious Selection" set out in Darwin's original treatise.⁵ As Tim Ingold explains: "It follows that when we speak of production and domestication as interventions in nature, as we are inclined to do, humanity's transcendence of the natural world is already presupposed."⁶ For instance, an emphasis on an interpretation of conditioning in domestication,⁷ rather than any attribution of social cognition or intentionality on the part of the domesticates,⁸ continues to mark the research field.⁹ As Helen Leach has noted, parallels in morphological changes between humans and other animals through a process of potential co-domestication have sometimes been obscured by the dominant narrative: "The long-established paradigm of human control over domestication through artificial selection has meant that parallelism in these changes is seldom noted and few inclusive explanations have been attempted since the early 1900s."¹⁰ This in itself belies a persistent exceptionalism applied to human animals, even in the literature of domestication science, in what may be described as "scholarly reluctance to entertain the notion of human domestication in other than a social or an ideological sense."¹¹ Indeed, the domestication narrative is thus inextricably interwoven with the narrative of civilisation and human exceptionalism.¹²

But in fact, despite the resilience of the "enfolding" definition, there is some considerable diversity in approaches to defining domestication within the research literature that is perhaps sometimes not as apparent in the popular discourse. Zooarchaeologist Melinda Zeder, notes: "There is a surprising lack of consensus on how to define domestication. Beyond agreeing that it involves a relationship between a domesticator and a domesticate, there is little agreement on what this relationship entails or how and when it results in the creation of a domesticated plant or animal."¹³ Even in lamenting the lack of agreement on definitions, Zeder still, arguably unwittingly, adopts the language of the "creation" of a domesticated animal. Zeder's own definition is much more comprehensive in its approach to the kind of shared intentionalities that are explored throughout this chapter: "Domestication is a sustained multigenerational, mutualistic relationship in which one organism assumes a significant degree of influence over the reproduction and care of another organism in order to secure a more predictable supply of a resource of interest, and through which the partner organism gains advantage over individuals that remain outside this relationship, thereby benefitting and often increasing the fitness of both the domesticator and the target domesticate."¹⁴

Zeder also notes that one of the more common definitions of domestication is "from the perspective of the domesticator, emphasizing the role of humans in separating a target domesticate from free-living populations and assuming mastery over all aspects of its life cycle."¹⁵ Indeed, she observes elsewhere that such definitions emphasising the role of the human animal present domestication as "a process in which humans deliberately and with forethought assume control over the domesticate's movement, feeding, protection, distribution, and, above all, its breeding – directed at achieving specific clearly identified goals."¹⁶ In other words, domestication assumes the economy of a causal, linear narrative where "Domesticates within this perspective are usually characterized in economic terms as productive capital."¹⁷ Not only does such an approach foreground human intentionality and "authorship" of the domesticate, but also it continues the narrative of selection and separation in the inside and outside of society and nature. The animal is brought inside. But in fact did that dog bring the human outside?

This perspective is also consistent with the idea of the animal as resource: "Domesticates within this perspective are usually characterized in economic terms as productive capital."[18] In explaining the meaning behind the title of her work on domestication, *The Walking Larder*, Juliet Clutton-Brook argues, "the provision of food is by far the most important function of animals in all human societies, and while they are alive the animals are almost always on the move. Like wolves, humans roam over huge home ranges; they must have protein to eat but they are compulsive travellers who are always searching to widen their territories and find new resources."[19] Thus, the relationship is established as always already one of predation, acquisition, and utilisation of those without home, without property, and "always on the move." While the human animal as "compulsive traveller" is acquiring territory, the animal is constructed as "on the move," indeed, "on the run" from human intentionality. Tim Ingold describes this retreat as a shift in relationship from trust to domination through the domestication process: "the transition in human-animal relations that in western literature is described as the domestication of creatures that were once wild, should rather be described as a transition from trust to domination."[20] Similarly, Nerissa Russell argues that the essence of domestication is "converting animals into property."[21] These views are consistent with the predatory drift explored in the present work, from the sociable territories of that first domestication through to the dominion of rivalrous conflict; but they concede an object-led approach to property and to rights, a discursive ambiguity of property rhetoric that must be addressed by restoring attention to the relations within the law.

An ancient paradox

Who came first, the dog or the pet?

Chickens or eggs, eggs or chickens, causes or effects, the domestication story is perhaps the most compelling challenge to the paradox of causality and indeed the agents of history and innovation.

Did domestication produce the dog? Or did that dog invent domestication? This is a question that preoccupies not only the popular literature but also science.

Even though the earlier view of domestication in the scientific literature as that of capture and taming has ceded to the current view of habituation[22] or even "apprenticeship,"[23] the overwhelming cultural impact of the domestication narrative persists as a relationship of dominion and submission, of human exceptionalism and accidental tourist. For dogs, this is seen nowhere more clearly than in contemporary training discourse and popular culture. Indeed, in that context, the myths of domestication become a serious welfare issue.[24] The domesticated animal submits to the constraints and expectations of the human environment, and the human maintains a prospect of guardianship, oversight, and authorship of the domesticated species, not only through suggestions of historic selection and processes of "taming" but also through breeding and further differentiation of the species into more and more divisions. The clamorous mythologies of domestication drown out the science and no doubt fuel this discourse and limitation of the subjectivity of the more-than-human author/artist/inventor in far-reaching ways.[25] Both deafening and deafened to the science.

To fold and enfold introduces the relationships of "having" and possession that continue to characterise the human-dog dyad, not only in terms of a possessory-like "authorship" of that dog's life, behaviour, and abilities but also in terms of the persistence of a "dominance" paradigm right through to the articulation of the welfare and well-being of animals within a property framework. At the same time, however, that "having" is constitutive of the self and selves communicating in that relationship: "If having seems to indicate being, being surely implies having. Being, that hollow abstraction, is never conceived except as the *property* of something, of some other being, which is itself comprised of *properties*, and so on to infinity."[26] Turtles all the way down.

This is not to deploy a banal and treacherously bourgeois notion of property as self but rather to understand the taking and having of perspectives as the necessary social tie that prefigures society. In other words, the fold is also a doubling, an intimacy, and a proximity that confounds conventional domestication stories and questions the stewardship from which other social inventions arise: "as long as the outside is folded an inside is coextensive with it, as memory is coextensive with forgetting."[27] To domesticate is to cause to be a home, to create a household, to make duties.[28] This is *Umwelt*, the abode of ethics.[29] At the same time, then, domestication provides for settling and place, the very basics of future agricultural enterprises and notions of property. Thus, when that first dog came inside, domestication opened humans to a world outside their kin, outside their family,[30] and to a cavalcade of innovation thereafter. The domestication story is, to all intents and purposes, a boundary story that knows no bounds:

> If Descartes did not know how to get through the labyrinth, it was because he sought its secret of continuity in rectilinear tracks, and the secret of liberty in a rectitude of the soul. He knew the inclension of the soul as little as he did the curvature of matter. A "cryptographer" is needed, someone who can at once account for nature and decipher the soul, who can peer into the crannies of matter and read into the folds of the soul.[31]

A cryptographer is needed for this story of canine innovation, the ultimate invention, of animal authors, of creaturely creativity. And the cryptographer is that dog.

Whither domestication?

> Once again we are in a knot of species coshaping one another in layers of reciprocating complexity all the way down. Response and respect are possible only in those knots, with actual animals and people looking back at each other, sticky with all their muddled histories.[32]

To where and to whom are we bound?

The invention of domestication is perhaps the most important invention in human history. In his startling work of nineteenth-century sociological curiosity, Gabriel Tarde imagined the fundamental place of domestication in human history: "It is difficult for us to imagine how necessary genius and exceptional circumstances were for the development of the simplest ideas. To tame and make use of harmless indigenous animals, instead of merely hunting them, would seem at first to be the most natural, as well as the most fruitful, of initiatives, an inevitable initiative, in fact."[33] And indeed, it is an invention: "[T]his idea was far from being an inevitable one."[34] But whose invention? Accidental or on purpose? Whose accident? Whose purpose?

Tarde notes, "The domestication of the horse depended upon some individual accident," as perhaps all good ideas do. However, the horse was not the first domesticated animal. Domestication had been invented far sooner than that. And to all intents and purposes, it was no accident, at least not on the part of the ingenious animal who took that first initiative.[35] That the humans took long enough to pay attention is perhaps the more fortuitous element of this tale. "Now, can we imagine humanity without these prime inventions!" How indeed!?

Domestication provided for "home," for territory, for place. It was the fundamental premise upon which further imitation and enterprise was based. If we are to talk about the very first domestication then, society did not create the process; the process created society.[36] It gave humans reason and capacity to stand still, to grow food, to nurture, to civilise.

But who domesticated whom? When it comes to the traditional story, Donna Haraway notes, "There are other ways to think about domestication that are both more historically accurate and also more powerful for addressing past and present brutalities and for nurturing better ways to live in multispecies sociality."[37] And that revision of the popular mythologies of domestication comes from science itself. Domestication science is itself a source for a much more creative and ethical understanding of the human-dog relationship through domestication and indeed for the production of animal subjectivity in contemporary circumstances of legal and welfare frameworks. Such an "enfolding" is indeed a "having," not necessarily on the part of the human but on the part of the domesticator. But who is the domesticator? Despite the rhetoric, things may not be entirely as they seem. Who domesticated whom? It would be an anathema to the quality of property relations to misattribute the author.

When it comes to understanding what dogs bring to the social history of property, this picture of domestication as enfolding that dog into society is arguably putting the cart before the horse, the plough before the ox, the yarn before the sheep, as it were. What is really needed in this story is the nest before the hen. It was not so much humans that invited dogs into their home; it was dogs who denned some humans.[38]

But first, some history.

A brief history of a long time

There is considerable dispute over the period of time since dogs first became domesticated, and there is some dispute over how, but there is practically no dispute that dogs were the first animals to be domesticated.[39]

Recent research claims that dogs split from wolves 40,000 years ago,[40] much earlier than previous findings, with domestication as early as 32,000 years ago,[41] suggesting quite a different scenario from the persistent myth of "tamed wolves." While other research suggests more conservative findings of 16,000–17,000 years ago,[42] this research is still consistent with the earlier separation timeline. There had been earlier hypotheses that the separation of dogs from wolves was even earlier, dating back more than 100,000 years;[43] however, these have been subsequently refuted or, at best, not as yet validly confirmed.[44] What is important to note, however, is that the popular genealogy story for wolves and dogs has been somewhat dismantled by recent research into the divergence of dogs and wolves, notwithstanding the variations in theories on when this divergence might have commenced.[45]

The uncertainty over the principal dates for domestication appears also to reflect a lack of consensus on the actual process or course of domestication itself; indeed, a lot of this disagreement is actually focused on the period of time required for domestication. Along with persistent uncertainty as to the evolutionary and morphological changes involved, this emphasis on time reflects the sense of purpose or intervention required for domestication. Indeed, the typical narrative, with the human at the centre, selecting and taming wolves, no doubt guided much of the earlier questions that led enquiries and influenced research design. But this anthropocentric perspective on domestication has since been put into question within the scientific discourse and research.[46] Nevertheless, even with revisions to this model, the dominant research discourse continues to account for domestication as "a special case of evolution where humans drive the process."[47]

The older dates, which seem to be increasingly confirmed by accumulating research data,[48] albeit with some continuing scientific dissensus,[49] point to a lengthy process or perhaps even indicate that knowledge is moving towards compiling a story of domestication as one arriving much earlier and involving prehistoric dogs. In contrast to the earlier commencement timelines, the estimations of a later date are not merely concerning a later "commencement" of the process but rather a theory of domestication as something that may have been quite rapid, and, indeed, may even have been a process of self-domestication or co-domestication rather than purposeful selection towards the objective of domestication.[50] That dog, 30,000–40,000 plus years ago, may have precipitated quite an astounding inventive event rather than a more protracted process.[51] Indeed, adherence to the notion of "process" and attributing to humans the credit becomes a little illogical: "Darwinian evolutionary theory . . . posits that evolution first happens through the marginal before imposing itself on the species, something classical ethology had forgotten but that cognitive ethologists are insisting on more and more as they focus on animal inventions and how these inventions spread."[52]

An emerging consensus on an emphasis on the concept of co-evolution might be seen to acknowledge the cooperation involved and usher in a narrative of mutual benefit and socialisation,[53] but it nevertheless conceals any intentionality on the part of the canids.

This is clear in the way in which Greger Larson[54] tells the story of co-evolution: "It's likely to have been co-evolution. At first a pack of wolves got close to humans, then humans got used to the wolves and, finally, there would have been *something more intentional on the part of people*."[55] This scenario appears to underestimate the wolves quite considerably, finding intention only on the part of the humans and only after they starting imitating what the wolves had shown them. The story of invention does not conflict with the scenario presented here; it is simply a difference in perspective on what constituted the decision of the wolves to "get close." And this is where the research on their social structures and cooperative behaviour is significant. Despite the ethology presenting a luminous example of invention, the efforts to discount it form part of the linguistic scaffolding for research. As Larson himself notes elsewhere, "dog domestication could have started when wolf populations were attracted to the waste products generated by human camps . . . animals that were naturally wary of humans were nonetheless attracted to the niche that humans created, and *the ability to take advantage of the human-created resources was the first step leading to domesticated animals.*"[56] While this is slightly different from the model of pastoral apprenticeship discussed later in this chapter, it still places the initiative firmly with the wolves.

On the other hand, in the discourse of self-domestication (or even co-domestication), some purposive effort is imputed on the part of the wolves. Arguably, however, scientific enquiry and the surrounding discourse continue to defy notions of actual initiative and inventiveness on the part of the dogs themselves, preferring to explain the relationship in terms of opportunity, suitability, and habituation. However, domestication, if that is who you really are, becomes a little more intriguing as our tale continues, with respect to the mutual shares in this revolutionary invention.[57]

Timetables aside, what is unanimously accepted is that the dog is the first domesticated animal,[58] several thousands of years before domestication of livestock:[59] "the meeting of wolves and modern humans predates, by far, anything that could be considered a human habitation in the form of a *domus*. . . . Canids' use of dens dates back further. Consequently, instead of domestication, we should talk about 'cubilation' . . . and wonder who cubilicated whom."[60]

Long before the idea of settling, or taming, or agriculture, or property . . . who other than a dog to grab the ball and run with it? What a surprise domestication turns out to be.

> Conceive, indeed, of the immense and beneficent change which was wrought when, in the midst of some small human colony, which lacked all forms of industry or agriculture and all means of supply but the bow and harpoon, some savage genius dreamed of domesticating a dog, a sheep, a reindeer, a cow, an ass, or a horse. What do all our modern inventions amount to in comparison with this capital invention of domestication?[61]

Thus, according to Tarde, domestication made possible the later innovations of agriculture, territory, and ultimately property,[62] and indeed further domestication.[63] In other words, domestication, in every sense of the word, provided for "home" and thus territory and place in order to constitute settled agricultural enterprise, the very basis for the early conceptualisations of property. The first dog, who brought the human "outside" with that original invention of domestication, is indeed a very important historical figure. If we are to talk about the very first domestication, then society did not create the process. It was not about enfolding the first animal into society. Indeed, the process created society, the process enlarged human potential out into the open. It gave humans reason and capacity to stand still, to grow food, to nurture, to civilise.

Domestication made it happen. But who made domestication?

Who domesticated whom? Indeed, who "rescued" whom? That dog. Every time.

Opportunity makes a thief

Following the usual deterministic inferences, the scavenger theory of domestication is presented less as initiative and more in terms of "nuisance." But what an important development a nuisance can be. Nevertheless, scavenging of ancient canids is often constructed as opportunistic from a purely adaptive and functional perspective. It may even be referred to colloquially as "cunning," a biologically determined stereotype that pervades training and popular discourse. But is it not more interesting to think about the ingenuity, the initiative, the reconfiguring of territory? That is, is it not more responsible to recognise invention? Instead of merely dismissing the domestication story as scavenging from humans, a nuisance, is it not more useful to think about the way in which the dogs began assembling humans together? Scrapping them together, as it were? Indeed, one cannot trespass where there is no territory. Just as one cannot contract where there is no bond. So, who shepherded whom? The fascinating story here is not one that may be summarised as lowly opportunism, but one that should be expanded to the inventiveness of the dogs' pastoralism of the humans themselves. The dogs did not hunt the humans – the dogs farmed them.

And what of the modern scavenger? The dog who runs off with a picnic, the fan who creates a meme? Is the consumer a farmer or a hunter? A shepherd or a scavenger? Is this a battle for control, or is this a relationship of wits? Is this a cunning acquisition, or is this simply a case of canid boredom?[64] For the picnic invader, the human is already implicated in the discussion, situated within the dog's performance zone, incorporated into the dog's abundant excess of embodied communication as they gallop through the circle. In this scavenging is it not possible to recognise the emergent, creative transformation of scraps into sociality? Thus, for the viral meme, the question is not the scavenging but the quality of the association, the quality of the "implication," and the attribution of the producers in that relation.

Indeed, in many promising ways, scavenging actually entails shepherding. An early use of the word scavenger attended to this notion of keeping order. This office was usually held by a churchwarden or similar and was a respectable appointment.[65] Scavenging is propelled by attentiveness – to look and to look after.[66] Scavenging is combining, removing, retooling – scavenging is a productive intrusion, a "fruitful interference."[67] Scavenging is innovative.

It is notable also that an intriguing historic word with a shared etymology, scavage, also referred to an ancient toll imposed by the Corporation of London and other towns upon stranger merchants offering goods for sale within their precincts.[68] In what operates like an early form of territory making, the toll was an interesting shift in perspective on the scavenging of the wares "discarded" for sale by the merchant, with the implication of the merchant in a system of mutual interests and benefits. The management of the commercial enlargement of the social circle through the toll is a modest landmark, as it were, in trade relationships in municipal Britain.

There is much to learn from the dog domestication story to inform contemporary views of "scavengers" of property – the copyists, the mashups, the remixes, the users themselves – sampling morsels of knowledge and representing them in creative, embodied relations. Rather than trespassers and scavengers, are they more aptly understood as farmers? The challenge ahead is how to reconcile these imitative approaches to production without forgetting that fundamental relationship.

Self-domestication

In his 1865 paper, The Domestication of Animals, Sir Francis Galton declared:

> I cannot believe it to have been the result of a preconceived intention, followed by elaborate trials, to administer to the comfort of man. Neither can I think it arose from one successful effort made by an individual, who might thereby justly claim the title of benefactor to his race; but, on the contrary, that a vast number of half-unconscious attempts have been made throughout the course of ages, and that ultimately, by slow degrees, after many relapses, and continued selection, our several domestic breeds became firmly established.[69]

Yes, perhaps not the result of human preconceived intention, but domestication certainly was no accident. And the vast number of half-unconscious attempts? No doubt a proliferation of imitations of that fortuitous canine invention.[70]

As the "self" of this equation, humans are regularly credited with "self-domestication" and indeed with intentionality with respect to the selection and domestication of early canids.[71] However, with the self-domestication hypothesis of dog domestication,[72] the authorship of this original invention rests with that dog. It was the dogs, as it were, who domesticated the "self," ushering it into being through a complex and necessary social bond upon which the civility and sociability of the "self" was premised.[73]

Therefore, the theory of self-domestication potentially restores attention to the intentionality of that dog. At the same time, self-domestication is viewed as a two-stage process, thus incorporating human intentionality in a commensal pathway[74] in what amounts to a significant account of sociability and cooperation at the heart of human development. In this way, self-domestication also emerges as an example of interspecies perspective-taking, an awareness of the other and another, in a mutually constitutive way.[75] That first domestication starts with making kin but as will be seen through the predatory drift of the Machine Age, property discourse makes a stranger of that dog.

Or perhaps humans had no choice in the matter, effects rather than causes: "Isn't it strange that, our being such an intelligent primate, we didn't domesticate chimpanzees as companions instead? Why did we choose wolves even though they are strong enough to maim or kill us?"[76] Such a question toys with the common everyday presumption that humans knew what they were doing and acted purposefully and intentionally when it came to the first domestication. However, the story plays out much more as one "with emphasis on companionship rather than human superiority."[77] Notably, in this context, there is little evidence that humans were ever prey for wolves. The relationship appears to have been more one of chasing and control, than predation, which appears more as a presumption of early "savage" life than a reality of the early human-dog relationship.[78]

The invention of domestication

> What do all our modern inventions amount to in comparison with this capital invention of domestication? This was the first decisive victory over animality. Now, of all historic events, the greatest and the most surprising is, unquestionably, the one which alone made history possible, the triumph of man over surrounding fauna.[79]

The language of taming is tenacious in its persistence in everyday discourse on dogs and their training,[80] and the presumption of human authority in respect of the dog's history, domestication, and destiny is ubiquitous.[81] Dogs are considered to be "bred for" and "designed for" a particular function[82] and for a dog – defined as it is to be enslaved by its instinct – to live a life without that "purpose" (rhetoric used particularly in the defence of hunting) is to live a compromised life. With no intention at all, dogs are "mechanomorphized,"[83] rendered mere biological chattels at the mercy of their instincts.

The adherence to this belief in a kind of engineering of the canine "machine" on the part of the human is necessarily unsettled by attention to the domestication story. As the evidence accumulates, the story is far from a fable of the brave and ingenious human taming[84] the wild and ignorant dog. Indeed, what is beginning to emerge is a story of a domestication process precipitated not by taming but by the human following that dog, learning from that dog, being apprenticed to that dog.[85] This disrupts the mythology of animals as property, at least in terms of what prompted humans onto the course of domestication, and causes one to hesitate more generally over the common conceptions of proprietary-like models emerging from domestication, pastoralism, and agriculturalism, more broadly speaking.

Indeed, the refutation of the basic taming theory in the domestication of dogs restores the view of domestication as primarily the making of "home" rather than the rendering of animal objects. That is, domestication is the settling and recognising of place and its link to family identity, including interspecies kin, through what is arguably a much more cooperative relationship from the outset. In this way dogs presented to humans the vital and social benefits to be had from territory, pastoralism, and cooperation – techniques which humans then began to imitate in relation to other species. That first domestication then is a kind of precondition for the ultimate development of property and conventional notions of proprietary-like relationships; but nevertheless, it breaks free from the chains of property as a kind of deterministic model, property at the will of biological determinism, as it were, with proprietary relations reconfigured as something dynamic, interactive, and embodied. In other words, property is not necessarily a given, not necessarily common knowledge or common sense. Thus, the development of property is cross-cultural and cross-species.

In this respect, the relationship between domestication, the making of territories, and the negotiation of shared spaces is important. Early models of pastoralism were key developments in the establishment of agricultural communities and early human societies.[86] Indeed, the theory of domestication as a kind of apprenticeship is compelling as a story of invention, but the apprenticeship is not of that dog to the human but rather of the human to that dog in the ways of pastoralism. Wolfgang Schleidt and Michael Shalter suggest a theory of domestication based upon that dog's superior abilities at sharing overlapping territories and pastoral spaces: "among mammals, Eurasian Wolves can be viewed as the first true pastoralists, ahead of human pastoralists by tens of thousands, hundreds of thousands of years."[87] As the authors note further, "canids became herd followers, exploiting an ecological niche that anticipated early forms of pastoralism."[88] Building upon this earlier work, the authors hypothesise that early canids invented an early form of pastoralism in the form of a rudimentary herd management as an alternative to conventional forms of predation,[89] suggesting that through cooperation with these early canids, humans imitated pastoralism from the canid model.[90] Thus, when speaking of the intelligence required of species to submit to domestication, it seems that human animals are indeed a fundamental example of the "cognitive abilities of the kind that permit this enfolding."[91]

Domestication is not simply a story of a biological machine, a story of adaptation and function, of survival and reproduction, or even of a social contract: "We ceased long ago to believe in Rousseau's 'social contract.'"[92] It is a social story of dynamic relations.[93] It is a story of canine invention.[94]

Whither that dog?

Whither the hunter, whither the farmer, whither that dog?

From the mythology of the ancient hunter to the passivity of that dog as scavenger, what is now emerging from the evidence is that dog as inventor. From early pastoral territories through to the introduction of the basic conditions for agriculture and society itself, that dog is a central figure.

The figure of the predatory wolf or dog has been disrupted. There is little to no evidence that wolves and dogs hunted humans[95] or even that their early relationship was one of hunting companions.[96] Rather than an antagonistic relationship of hunter and hunted, there is instead a narrative of sharing, of pastoralism, of Lorenz's farmer:[97]

> What Lorenz is trying to build is indeed an ethos, a goose's ethos, but it is still more an ethos pervaded with humans, an ethos for which the 'natural conditions' are, in an undetermined manner, of the nature of the animal and of the nature of the one who questions him, an ethos where 'natural condition' never means neutral condition . . . This device clearly discloses itself as a 'domesticating device' when Lorenz uses his own body as a tool for knowing, as a tool for asking questions, as a means to create a relation that provides new knowledge.[98]

Unlike the presumed indifference of the observer and the observed in the traditional models of scientific observation, and indeed in the early renditions of domestication, here is a mutual becoming, a cooperation of bodies in the pastoral space, an attachment. It is a dual (becoming), not a duel. The human is at once an element in the story of the dog's domestication.[99] Not an author, but an interpreter; not an inventor, but an imitator. Rather than the logical duel of model and copy,[100] the human is the copyist, the imitator. The becoming is doubled.

And so, did that dog invent taming? Instead of annihilating the other through hunting, suddenly a cooperative, co-existing world of pastoral care, territory, and ultimately taming proved to be ingenious: "To tame and make use of harmless indigenous animals, instead of merely hunting them, would seem at first to be the most natural, as well as the most fruitful, of initiatives, an inevitable initiative, in fact."[101]

Notably, although that first dog to share a table with humans,[102] as it were, was a hunter just like the humans, this is not considered the reason for the early relationship.[103] Indeed, it was more likely a reason to have avoided each other. Perhaps even more importantly, there is little evidence if any that the relationship between human and dog was ever one of predator and prey; rather, it was one of mutual attention and regard. As Tarde explains, without defences or weapons or territory, "The chase of man is . . . the first international relation."[104] Indeed, the dog was neither prey nor predator. The most likely prey of the ancient human were humans themselves.[105] But it is not the predatory chase that Tarde perhaps imagined as such, but the following, the imitation of innovation, imitation as innovation.

Donna Haraway vividly entertains this comradery as "messmates at table": "Messmates at table are companions. Comrades are political companions."[106] And indeed, domestication was perhaps the first political relationship to found all others. Rather than a conflict of chasing and taming, of victor and conquered, domestication is arguably a relation of mutual consent and purpose. This depiction also resonates with the scavenger theories of dog domestication, where dogs scavenged the scraps of human activities.[107] While the scavenger theory does provide for a theory of self-domestication, it perhaps does not account for some of the extraordinary transformations for both humans and dogs through the process of domestication. In contrast, as will be discussed, the pastoral relationship presents a compelling narrative of inventiveness and social change.

The scavenger theories of accidental domestication may seem to upset this property relationship, suggesting a more chance encounter, as it were.[108] However, this suggests once again an assumption of that dog as purposeless wanderer rather than intentional gatherer. Further, in its negotiation of shared space, the scavenger relationship is also still a style of shepherding.[109] And what is perhaps even more persuasive is the nature of this scavenging relationship itself, demonstrating a management of resources that is both sociable and at the same time non-competitive.

In this way, both the pastoral and scavenger models present a sociability that is absent in the kind of agonistic model that circulates today, particularly through newspaper reporting of human-dog conflict as well as through popular dog training discourse that deploys a narrative of domestication and pack theory that simply is a mythology.[110] Indeed, it is in more recent times that the relationship between human and dog has shifted to one of hunter and hunted, as it were, of dominance and submission, of training and compliance. The behaviour of wolves themselves has also changed and evolved in response to the changed attention of and relationship with humans. Once cohabitant, now hunted: "[A]s dogs adapted to live in close association with humans, wolves must have adapted over the past 20,000 years to humans carrying lethal armament. Thus, the wolves of Yellowstone Park, today, we accept as typical for Canis lupus, most likely are very different in behaviour and genetic makeup from the wolves who first immigrated into this area after the Laurentide Ice Sheet receded."[111]

The joy of invention

The joy, the passions of that dog's invention – it is never the work of domestication; it is the joy of invention. The dog is not a labourer; the dog is ingenious.[112]

Far from a story of domination, the invention of domestication is a truly dogged tale. Indeed, to see it any other way is to credit the human in ways that only humans can: "Taking themselves to be the only actors, people reduce other organisms to the lived status of being merely raw material or tools. The domestication of animals is, within this analysis, a kind of original sin separating human beings from nature."[113] Instead, this is a story of the dog that wags the tale. Far from an "affectional slave,"[114] it will become clear that dogs initiated the sociability of property relations. The dogs came to play.

It is perhaps in the imitation and re-imitation of domestication that the story became re-invented. And the original "intention," as it were, was obscured, as in the following chapter we will, somewhat ironically, see.

Notes

1 Mills DS et al. (eds.) (2010) *The Encyclopedia of Applied Animal Behaviour and Welfare*, CAB International, Wallingford, OX, 184. This relationship between domestication and society is important, not merely in terms of the definition but rather with respect to human-animal sociality. This interspecies sociality is intrinsic to emerging property relations, as developed throughout; however, it is also integral to the methodology itself. See further the discussion a social approach to animals in prehistory in Orton D (2010) Both Subject and Object Herding, Inalienability and Sentient Property in Prehistory, *World Archaeology*, 42(2), 188–200.

2 Emma Power notes critically, "Domestication is a key process through which humans have claimed dominance over nature." She describes this perspective as understanding domestication as the process through which 'wildness' . . . was brought *in* and re-made in the image of human culture through selective breeding and incorporation into human social structures" (emphasis added). Power instead contends that domestication is "an experimental, contingent, and contestable process that draws in culture and nature, human and nonhuman, mind and body, and that frequently exceeds human control and intentionality." See Power ER (2012) Domestication and the Dog: Embodying Home, *Area*, 44(3), 371–378: p. 378. See further, Clark N (2007) Animal Interface: The Generosity of Domestication, in Cassidy R & Mullin M (eds.) *Where the Wild Things Are Now: Domestication Reconsidered*, Berg, Oxford, 49–70.

3 The impact of misunderstandings about domestication origins and group behaviour is discussed in more detail in Chapter 8, "Pack fiction," and in the context of training discourse; see in particular Chapter 10, "Shared interests."

4 David Orton notes a history of "appropriation" in relation to the definition of domestication, whereby "domestication is a process of appropriation, and domesticates are set apart from wild animals by their status as property." See Orton D (2010) Both Subject and Object Herding, Inalienability and Sentient Property in Prehistory, *World Archaeology*, 42(2), 188–200: p. 190. See further Ducos P (1978) Domestication Defined and Methodological Approaches to Its Recognition in Faunal Assemblages, in Meadow RH & Zeder M (eds.) *Approaches to Faunal Analysis in the Middle East*, Peabody Museum, Cambridge, MA, 53–56, where the author notes the relationship between domestication and the integration of animals within human-animal social and economic structures, including as subjects of ownership and trade. See further the review of the language of domestication and the dog in Power ER (2012) Domestication and the Dog: Embodying Home, *Area*, 44(3), 371–378.

5 Darwin C (1859/[2008]) *On the Origin of Species*, Oxford UP, Oxford: "At the present time, eminent breeders try by methodical selection, with a distinct object in view, to make a new strain or sub-breed, superior to anything existing in the

country. But, for our purpose, a kind of Selection, which may be called Unconscious, and which results from every one trying to possess and breed from the best individual animals, is more important" (29). See further Helen Leach on the discussion of unconscious selection in Leach HM (2007) Selection and the Unforeseen Consequences of Domestication, in Cassidy R & Mullin M (eds.) *Where the Wild Things Are Now: Domestication Reconsidered*, Berg, Oxford, 71–99. On human intentionality in domestication, compare the work of David Rindos, who has explored the scope of unconscious selection and questioned human intentionality as characterised in the process of domestication: "The notion of intentionality has pervaded the study of domestication and the origin of agricultural systems. Natural scientists have ignored, in large part, the mechanistic process that might underlie agricultural evolution because (as the unstated reasoning goes), if crops and agricultural systems are ultimately derived from individual or cultural choice or decision making, they are beyond the ken of the evolutionary biologist." See Rindos D (1984) *The Origins of Agriculture: An Evolutionary Perspective*, Academic Press, San Diego, 2.

6 Ingold T (1994) From Trust to Domination: An Alternative History of Human-Animal Relations, in Manning A & Serpell J (eds.), *Animals and Human Society: Changing Perspectives*, Routledge, London, 1–22: p. 4. Elsewhere Ingold notes that most histories of human development in relation to the environment can be characterised by the terms collection and production: "there are basically just two ways of procuring a livelihood from the natural environment, conventionally denoted by the terms *collection* and *production*. The distinction between them was first coined by Friedrich Engels. In a note penned in 1875, Engels pointed to production as the most fundamental criterion of what he saw as a kind of 'mastery' of the environment that was distinctly human." See Ingold T (2000) *The Perception of the Environment: Essays in Livelihood, Dwelling and Skill*, Routledge, London, 77–78. It is notable, as noted in the introductory chapter, that this distinction is attributed to work by Friedrich Engels in the nineteenth century, and further, that it has much in common with the evolutionary theory of social development of the nineteenth century, identified mainly with the work of Lewis Henry Morgan, a great influence on Karl Marx and Friedrich Engels. This relationship between domestication theories and evolutionary theory is considered further in Chapter 2, "The imitation of domestication." On language and domestication, see further the discussion in Orton D (2010) Both Subject and Object Herding, Inalienability and Sentient Property in Prehistory, *World Archaeology*, 42(2), 188–200. See further the useful historical review of the relationship between science, evolutionary theory, and late-nineteenth and early-twentieth century socialist thought in Pittenger M (1987) Science, Culture and the New Socialist Intellectuals before World War I, *American Studies*, 28(1), 73–91.

7 For instance, see Udell MAR et al. (2008) Wolves Outperform Dogs in Following Human Social Cues, *Animal Behaviour*, 76, 1767–1773.

8 For instance, see Miklósi A & Soporoni K (2006) A Comparative Analysis of Animals' Understanding of the Human Pointing Gesture, *Animal Cognition*, 1, 113–121; Hare B & Tomasello M (2005) Human-Like Social Skills in Dogs?, *Trends in Cognitive Science*, 9, 439–444; Miklósi A et al. (2003) A Simple Reason for a Big Difference: Wolves Do Not Look Back at Humans, But Dogs Do, *Current Biology*, 13, 763–766; Hare B et al. (2002) The Domestication of Social Cognition in Dogs, *Science*, 298, 1634–1636.

9 See further the division set out in a *New Scientist* article on research promoting the conditioning theory, where Clive Wynne (advocate for conditioning theories)

described alternative theories of cognitive skills as overlooking the obvious: "Researchers who argue for a dog 'theory of mind' are overlooking this obvious explanation." On the other hand, Brian Hare, an advocate for more credit to the dog, gave a response in the same article: "I think there is so much data from other labs pointing to the previous finding of dogs being unusually skilled at using human cues that it will take extraordinary findings to argue against it." See Callaway E. (2008) Wolves Make Dog's Dinner Out of Domestication Theory, *New Scientist*, September. An interesting corollary to this is the human history of animism and animal idolatry and the impact on power on social relations between humans and animals, discussed further in Part 3, "Dominion, the machine age."

10 Leach HM (2003) Human Domestication Reconsidered, *Current Anthropology*, 44(3), 349–360: p. 349.
11 Leach HM (2003) Human Domestication Reconsidered, *Current Anthropology*, 44(3), 349–360: p. 356. In this article, Leach provides a compelling and concise history of the language of domestication, demonstrating the scholarly traditions of reluctance and exceptionalism throughout.
12 Indeed, in *Roget's Thesaurus*, the first synonym for civilise is humanise.
13 Zeder MA (2015) Core Questions in Domestication Research, *PNAS*, 112(11), 3191–3198: p. 3191.
14 Zeder MA (2015) Core Questions in Domestication Research, *PNAS*, 112(11), 3191–3198: p. 3191.
15 Zeder MA (2015) Core Questions in Domestication Research, *PNAS*, 112(11), 3191–3198: p. 3191.
16 Zeder M (2012) The Domestication of Animals, *Journal of Anthropological Research*, 68(2), 161–190: p. 162.
17 Zeder M (2012) The Domestication of Animals, *Journal of Anthropological Research*, 68(2), 161–190: p. 162. This relationship between domestication and an emerging property narrative in terms of the management of resources is notable in the context of economic theories of property. In the model offered by Harold Demsetz that continues to influence law and economics scholarship, there is adherence to this idea of the inextricable link between settlement and property: "the emergence of new property rights takes place in response to the desires of the interacting persons for adjustment to new benefit-cost possibilities." See Demsetz H (1967) Toward a Theory of Property Rights, *The American Economic Review*, 57(2), 347–359: p. 350. See further the revision in Demsetz H (2002) Toward a Theory of Property Rights II: The Competition between Private and Collective Ownership, *The Journal of Legal Studies*, 31(S2), S653–S672. In relation to the perfect-competition model of neoclassical economics, Demsetz notes: "There is an implicit part of the supporting substructure that relates to conditions of ownership. Supplies of and demands for goods, the price-determining market conditions that derive from the perfect-competition model, reflect private-ownership institutional arrangements in their customary applications. More than this, to support perfect competition, all scarce resources should be private, unambiguously, and securely owned" (S654). He goes on to qualify this: "That perfect private ownership is unrealizable, as is perfect competition, does not imply that the concept lacks usefulness" (S654, note 4). This relationship between early agriculture and emerging property models is considered in further detail in Chapter 2, "The imitation of domestication."
18 Zeder M (2012) The Domestication of Animals, *Journal of Anthropological Research*, 68(2), 161–190: p. 162.

19 Clutton-Brock J (1989/[2015]) Introduction, in Clutton-Brock J (ed.) (1989/[2015]) *The Walking Larder: Patterns of Domestication, Pastoralism, and Predation*, Routledge, London, 1–3: p. 2.
20 Ingold T (1994) From Trust to Domination: An Alternative History of Human-Animal Relations, in Manning A & Serpell J (eds.) *Animals and Human Society: Changing Perspectives*, Routledge, London, 1–22: p. 18. Compare Armstrong Oma K (2010) Between Trust and Domination: Social Contracts between Humans and Animals, *World Archaeology*, 42(2), 175–187.
21 Russell N (2002) The Wild Side of Animal Domestication, *Society & Animals*, 10(3), 285–302: p. 290.
22 Clutton-Brock J (2017) Origins of the Dog: The Archaeological Evidence, in Serpell J (ed.) *The Domestic Dog: Its Evolution, Behavior and Interactions with People*, 2nd ed., Cambridge UP, Cambridge, 7–21: p. 9.
23 Schleidt WM & Shalter MD (2018) Dogs and Mankind: Coevolution on the Move: An Update, *Human Ethology Bulletin*, 33(1), 15–38; Schleidt WM & Shalter MD (2003) Co-Evolution of Humans and Canids: An Alternative View of Dog Domestication: *Homo Homini Lupus?*, *Evolution and Cognition*, 9(1), 57–71; Schleidt WM (1998) Is Humaneness Canine?, *Human Ethology Bulletin*, 13 (4), 7–20: p. 19.
24 The relationship between myth-making and training welfare is explored in detail in Chapter 8, "Pack fiction."
25 For instance, in the area of animal intentionality and creativity, especially as interpreted through traditional parameters of intellectual property, these questions have raised some startling issues. See Gibson J (forthcoming) *More Than Human Intellectual Property*, Routledge, London.
26 Tarde G (1893/[2012]) *Monadology and Sociology*, T Lorenc (trans.), Re-Press, Melbourne, 52. A similar perspective upon "having" as the fundamentally relational character of rights is found also in Hohfeld's scheme. See further the discussion in Chapter 4, "Marking territory" as well as the more extended consideration in Chapter 11, "Resocialisation."
27 Deleuze G (1988/[1986]) *Foucault*, S Hand (trans.), U of Minnesota P, Minneapolis, 108.
28 *The Complete Oxford English Dictionary*.
29 Gibson J (2014) *The Logic of Innovation*, Ashgate, Aldershot, 38. This notion of domestication is related to the relational character of use (26) and the distinctly sociable nature of familiar production (38). See further the discussion in the chapters in Part 4, "Altruism, the social age," particularly "*Res familiaris.*"
30 Schleidt and Shalter argue that the humans acted in a kind of apprenticeship role, adopting the wolf pack algorithm that took them outside their immediate kin or family and introduced them to cooperation and the sharing of risk. See Schleidt WM & Shalter MD (2003) Co-Evolution of Humans and Canids: An Alternative View of Dog Domestication: *Homo Homini Lupus?*, *Evolution and Cognition*, 9(1), 57–71: p. 68. See further the discussion later in Chapter 2, "The imitation of domestication," whereby imitation itself also comes to be an innovating and civilising force. This is related to Tarde's depiction of the enlargement of the social circle from family through to outside; that is, the invention of society. If dogs encouraged humans to move outside the family, then the relationship between the intentionality of strictly human animals and the development of society becomes somewhat more complicated.
31 Deleuze G (1988/[1993]) *The Fold: Leibniz and the Baroque*, T Conley (trans.), U of Minnesota P, Minneapolis, 3.
32 Haraway D (2008) *When Species Meet*, U of Minnesota P, Minneapolis, 42.

33 Tarde G (1890/[1903]) *The Laws of Imitation*, EC Parsons (trans.), Henry Holt & Co, New York, 46.
34 Tarde G (1890/[1903]) *The Laws of Imitation*, EC Parsons (trans.), Henry Holt & Co, New York, 46.
35 Indeed, a curious contemporary "domestication" narrative is that of an emu who followed some drovers back to a remote cattle station in rural Queensland, Australia. He has stayed on living with the family and reportedly even participates in the pastoral territory-making of mustering. It is notable that Fred Jones, a professor of ecology at Griffith University, attributes the behaviour to sociability and to the need for family (potentially having lost his family group) and speculates that it is his intelligence that led him to stay on with the human family. See further Groves M (2019) Fred the Emu Adopts Farming Family and Helps Out with the Mustering, *ABC News*, 6 February. The family even suggests that the emu chose his own name: "When the family's six children began calling out names to the animal – which up until that point was simply referred to as 'the emu' – Fred was just the one that caught his attention" (Quested V (2019) Six Kids and an Emu: The Unlikely Aussie Pet That Adopted a Queensland Family, *10 Daily News*, 25 March).
36 Tarde G (1890/[1903]) *The Laws of Imitation*, EC Parsons (trans.), Henry Holt & Co, New York, 277. See also the discussion in relation to the domestication of plants in Stetter MG et al. (2017) How to Make a Domesticate, *Current Biology*, 27, R896–R900: "The Neolithic Revolution brought about the transition from hunting and gathering to sedentary societies, laying the foundation for the development of modern civilizations. The primary innovation that facilitated these changes was the domestication of plants and animals." (R896).
37 Haraway D (2008) *When Species Meet*, U of Minnesota P, Minneapolis, 207.
38 As Schleidt and Shalter note: "While canids are known to dig their own dens, and some of such dens may have been used by many generations, even over hundreds of years, humans are apparently the only primates to make use of caves, and their association with dogs predates the construction of permanent houses by thousands of years. Is it not absurd to talk about the 'domestication' of dogs by humans who had not yet any permanent domiciles ('domus')?" See Schleidt WM & Shalter MD (2003) Co-Evolution of Humans and Canids: An Alternative View of Dog Domestication: *Homo Homini Lupus?*, *Evolution and Cognition*, 9(1), 57–71: p. 65. See further the discussion on page 66 and the concept of "cubilication" as opposed to domestication.
39 Larson G et al. (2012) Rethinking Dog Domestication by Integrating Genetics, Archeology, and Biogeography, *PNAS*, 109, 8878–8883.
40 Skloglund P et al. (2015), Ancient Wolf Genome Reveals an Early Divergence of Domestic Dog Ancestors and Admixture into High Latitude Breeds, *Current Biology*, 25, 1515–1519. See further Botigué LR et al. (2017) Ancient European Dog Genomes Reveal Continuity since the Early Neolithic, *Nature*, 18 July on a possible single origin. See also the discussion in Slezak M (2015) Ancient DNA Suggests Dogs Split from Wolves 40,000 Years Ago, *New Scientist*, 21 May. See further the work in Savolainen P et al. (2002) Genetic Evidence for an East Asian Origin of Domestic Dogs, *Science*, 298, 1610–1613, detailing a possible single origin for domestic dogs in East Asia between 15,000 and 40,000 years ago.
41 Germonpré M et al. (2015) Fossil Dogs and Wolves from Palaeolithic Sites in Belgium, the Ukraine and Russia: Osteometry, Ancient DNA and Stable Isotopes, *Journal of Archaeological Science*, 36, 473–490, where the authors argue there is evidence from a Belgium dig of the presence of Paleolithic dogs as early as 31,700 BP, suggesting that domestication had already commenced by then

if not sooner. See further, Germonpré M et al. (2017) Palaeolitihic and Prehistoric Dogs and Pleistocene Wolves from Yakutia: Identification of Isolated Skulls, *Journal of Archaeological Science*, 78, 1–19; Germonpré M et al. (2014) Paleolithic Dogs and Pleistocene Wolves Revisited: A Reply to Morey, *Journal of Archaeological Science*, 54 (2015), 210–236; Pionnier-Capitan M et al. (2011) New Evidence for Upper Paleolithic Small Domestic Dogs in South-Western Europe, *Journal of Archaeological Science*, 38, 2123–2140; Thalmann O et al. (2013) Complete Mitochondrial Genomes of Ancient Canids Suggest a Curopean Origin of Domestic Dogs. *Science*, 342, 871–874. See further the work on Predmostí, a Gravettian site in the Czech Republic, dating to around 24,300 BP to 27,000 BP in two layers, which provides evidence of Paleolithic dogs and Pleistocene wolves: Germonpré M et al. (2015) Large Canids at the Gravettian Predmostí Site, the Czech Republic: The Mandible, *Quaternary International*, 359–360, 261–279; Germonpré M et al. (2012) Paleolithic Dog Skulls at the Gravettian Predmostí Site, the Czech Republic, *Journal of Archaeological Science*, 39, 184–202. See further the discussion in Barras C. (2013) Wolves Turned into Dogs by European Hunter-Gatherers, *New Scientist*, November. There is also evidence of "training" in the form of "sled dogs" which researchers believed could have been in use as early as 15,000 years ago in Siberia: Pitulko VV & Kasparov AK (2017) Archaeological Dogs from the Early Holocene Zhokhov Site in the Eastern Siberia Arctic, *Journal of Archaeological Science Reports*, 13, 491–515.

42 Morey DF (2014) In Search of Paleolithic Dogs: A Quest with Mixed Results, *Journal of Archaeological Science*, 52, 300–307. See further Morey DF & Jeger R (2015) Paleolithic Dogs: Why Sustained Domestication Then?, *Journal of Archaeological Science: Reports*, 3, 420–428; Drake AG et al. (2015) 3D Morphometric Analysis of Fossil Canid Skulls Contradicts the Suggested Domestication of Dogs during the Late Paleolithic, *Scientific Reports: Nature*, 5, 1–8.

43 Ruvinsky A & Sampson J (2001) *The Genetics of the Dog*, CAB International, Wallingford, OX, ix. See further the work of Robert Wayne and Carles Vilà which identifies a possible separation between wolves and dogs over 100,000 years ago. They argue, "early domestic dogs may not have been morphologically distinct from their wild relatives," and that further changes to the dog may not have occurred until after domestication and after humans started to adopt more permanent settlements, around 10,000 to 15,000 years ago. In other words, there was further, and possibly selective, breeding, but this is nevertheless well after the first domestication. And indeed, this process may have had an impact on the development of the modern wolf as well, through the continued exchange of genes between wolves and dogs. See Vilà C et al. (1997) Multiple and Ancient Origins of the Domestic Dog, *Science*, 276, 1687–1689. See further Schleidt WM (1998) Is Humaneness Canine?, *Human Ethology Bulletin*, 13(4), 14–20: p. 16, where the author describes the findings as "an amazing temporal and geographical coincidence between the emergence of mankind and dogkind, between hominization and canisization."

44 The interpretation of the evidence for a date of 135,000 years has subsequently been discredited as problematic and flawed. Nevertheless, there is still considerable consensus on the date of the first emergence to be around 35,000 years ago, still well before the date of domestication for any other animal. See Clutton-Brock J (2017) Origins of the Dog: The Archaeological Evidence, in Serpell J (ed.) *The Domestic Dog: Its Evolution, Behavior and Interactions with People*, 2nd ed., Cambridge UP, Cambridge, 7–21: p. 9.

45 Freedman AH et al. (2014) Genome Sequencing Highlights the Dynamic Early History of Dogs. *PLoS Genetics*, 10(1), e1004631: "[W]e infer that dogs diverged from the sampled wolf populations at about the same time these wolf populations diverged from each other. Additionally the greater difference between estimated divergence times in our original analysis provides some support for our initial assumption that dogs and wolves form sister clades." (7). Schleidt and Shalter review and synthesise the recent data to argue that the separation between wolves and dogs was so early that it is unlikely that humans had a hand to play. See Schleidt WM & Shalter MD (2018) Dogs and Mankind: Coevolution on the Move: An Update, *Human Ethology Bulletin*, 33(1), 15–38.
46 Clutton-Brock J (2017) Origins of the Dog: The Archaeological Evidence, in Serpell J (ed.) *The Domestic Dog: Its Evolution, Behavior and Interactions with People*, 2nd ed., Cambridge UP, Cambridge, 7–21: p. 9.
47 Agnvall B et al. (2018) Is Evolution of Domestication Driven by Tameness? A Selective Review with Focus on Chickens, *Applied Animal Behaviour Science*, 205, 227–233.
48 Botigué LR et al. (2017) Ancient European Dog Genomes Reveal Continuity since the Early Neolithic, *Nature*, 18 July.
49 Guarino B (2017) Your Dog's Ancestor Came from a Group of Wolves 40,000 Years Ago, Study Says, *The Washington Post*, 18 July.
50 Morey DF & Jeger R. (2015) Paleolithic Dogs: Why Sustained Domestication Then?, *Journal of Archaeological Science: Reports*, 3, 420–428.
51 James A Serpell describes domestication as "a process rather than an event," attributing not inconsiderable purpose on the part of the human contribution. See Bekoff M (ed.) (1998) *Encyclopedia of Animal Rights and Animal Welfare*, Fitzroy Dearborn Publishers, London, 136.
52 Baratay É (2015) Building an *Animal* History. S Posthumus (trans.), in Mackenzie L & Posthuman S (eds.) *French Thinking about Animals*, Michigan State UP, East Lansing, MI, 3–14: p. 13.
53 For a discussion of this concept specifically in relation to dogs see Schleidt WM & Shalter MD (2003) Co-Evolution of Humans and Canids: An Alternative View of Dog Domestication: *Homo Homini Lupus?*, *Evolution and Cognition*, 9(1), 57–71: p. 66: "From a biologist's vantage point, the intertwining process of canization makes sense only if viewed as coevolution." See further, Schleidt WM & Shalter MD (2018) Dogs and Mankind: Coevolution on the Move: An Update, *Human Ethology Bulletin*, 33(1), 15–38; Pierotti R & Fogg BR (2017) *The First Domestication: How Wolves and Humans Coevolved*, Yale UP, New Haven. For a wider discussion of the concept of co-evolution see O'Connor TP (1997) Working on Relationships: Another Look at Animal Domestication, *Antiquity*, 71, 149–156. For a discussion in relation to the concept of niche construction see Smith BD (2006) Niche Construction and the Behavioral Context of Plant and Animal Domestication, *Evolutionary Anthropology*, 16, 118–199.
54 Larson is Director of the Palaeogenomics and Bio-Archaeology Research Network (Palaeo-BARN). Palaeo-BARN is a Wellcome Trust Research Network based at Oxford University, where Greger Larson is Professor in the School of Archaeology.
55 Greger Larson quoted in Hirschler B (2016) How Dogs Became Man's Best Friend: Twice over, *Reuters*, 2 June (emphasis added).
56 Larson G & Burger J (2013) A Population Genetics View of Animal Domestication, *Trends in Genetics*, 29(4), 197–205 (emphasis added).
57 There is considerable scientific consensus on the significance of the relationship between humans and early canids and that this relationship is inextricably bound

up with the success of canine domestication. See further Germonpré M et al. (2013) Paleolithic Dogs and the Early Domestication of the Wolf: A Reply to the Comments of Crockford and Kuzmin (2012), *Journal of Archaeological Science*, 40, 786–792, in which the authors posit a possible relationship between early domestication and the Paleolithic dogs and the later wolf domestication, suggesting a possible contribution from early "pet" dogs to the wolf itself.

58 Mills DS et al. (2010) *The Encyclopedia of Applied Animal Behaviour and Welfare*, CAB International, Wallingford, OX, 184; Clutton-Brock J (2017) Origins of the Dog: The Archaeological Evidence, in Serpell J (ed.) *The Domestic Dog: Its Evolution, Behavior and Interactions with People*, 2nd ed., Cambridge UP, Cambridge, 7–21. See also further the discussion in Germonpré M et al. (2017) Palaeolitihic and Prehistoric Dogs and Pleistocene Wolves from Yakutia: Identification of Isolated Skulls, *Journal of Archaeological Science*, 78, 1–19.

59 Schleidt WM (1998) Is Humaneness Canine?, *Human Ethology Bulletin*, 13(4), 14–20: p. 15.

60 Schleidt WM & Shalter MD (2003) Co-Evolution of Humans and Canids: An Alternative View of Dog Domestication: *Homo Homini Lupus?*, *Evolution and Cognition*, 9(1), 57–71: p. 66. See also the earlier discussion of this point in Schleidt WM (1998) Is Humaneness Canine?, *Human Ethology Bulletin*, 13(4), 14–20: "Reconsideration of past and current concepts of domestication has become unescapable. Even the term 'domestication' sounds now absurd, since the meeting of wolves and AMHs [Anatomically Modern Humans] predates by far anything that could be considered a human habitation in the form of a 'domus'. Canids' use of dens dates back much further; we may instead want to talk about 'cubilication' and wonder who cubilicated whom." (16).

61 Tarde G (1890/[1903]) *The Laws of Imitation*, EC Parsons (trans.), Henry Holt & Co, New York, 276–277.

62 The domestication of the dog long predates the first use of the sickle in agriculture, which occurred around 8,000 years ago, a date which continues to be accepted as the first cropping (wheat) and an indication of the first permanent settlement of humans along with their domestication and keeping of animals. See Zeuner FE (1963) *A History of Domesticated Animals*, Harper & Row, New York, 30.

63 The dog was not only the first domestic animal but also the only animal to be domesticated before settled agriculture: Frantz LAF et al. (2016) Genomic and Archaeological Evidence Suggests a Dual Origin of Domestic Dogs, *Science*, 352, 1228–1231. This is significant because it means that all other domestications occurred in the context of the agricultural enterprise, a point discussed in greater detail in Chapter 2, "The imitation of domestication." See further, Larson G et al. (2012) Rethinking Dog Domestication by Integrating Genetics, Archeology, and Biogeography, *PNAS*, 109(23), 8878–8883.

64 Scavenging, bin trawling, and counter-surfing are commonly described and maligned in the dog training literature in terms of the dog's motivation, including the myth that the dog is seeking to assert "dominance" through the control of the food. An interesting response to this is in "Dominance Myths and Dog Training Realities" published by The Association of Professional Dog Trainers – in fact, maybe your dog is just bored.

65 Scavengers were respectably paid in order to "sub-contract" to paupers to attend to the cleaning. 1835 App. Munic. Corpor. Rep. i. 172 (Aberystwith). See further: *The Complete Oxford English Dictionary*.

66 The word "scavenger" comes from scavage (also scawage, skawage, skavage) from *escauwage*, to inspect, and *scauwen* (Flemish), to show. *The Complete Oxford English Dictionary*.

67 Tarde G (1890/[1903]) *The Laws of Imitation*, EC Parsons (trans.), Henry Holt & Co, New York, 382.
68 The toll was eventually prohibited in 1503 pursuant to the Scavage Act 1503 c. 8. The stranger merchant will be revisited in Chapter 9, "Wild abandon."
69 Galton SF (1865) The First Steps towards the Domestication of Animals, *Transactions of the Ethnological Society*, 3, 122–138: p. 138.
70 Richard Bulliet proposes that the domestication of cats and dogs "occurs without human deliberation." Thus, it is a self-domestication and "Since there is no human deliberation, that is to say, no decision to engage in a conscious process of domestication, the same scenario could occur in more than one settlement." In other words, the "success" is largely down to the motivation of the dogs and cats and "may not in all cases have resulted from purposeful human activity." See Bulliet RW (2005) *Hunters, Herders, and Hamburgers: The Past and Future of Human-Animal Relationships*, Columbia UP, New York, 89.
71 This is sometimes referred to as the human-selection domestication scenario or the "directed pathway": see Marshall-Pescini et al. (2017) Integrating Social Ecology in Explanations of Wolf-Dog Behavioural Differences, *Current Opinion in Behavioral Sciences*, 16, 80–86.
72 Coppinger R & Coppinger L (2016) *What Is a Dog?*, U of Chicago P, Chicago. See further the discussion of the commensal pathway in Larson G & Fuller DQ (2014) The Evolution of Animal Domestication, *Annual Review of Ecology, Evolution, and Systematics*, 45, 115–136: pp. 117–119; and in Marshall-Pescini et al. (2017) Integrating Social Ecology in Explanations of Wolf-Dog Behavioural Differences, *Current Opinion in Behavioral Sciences*, 16, 80–86.
73 The relationship between domestication and the constitution of humanity is explored further in "Part 1, Domestication, the stone age."
74 Marshall-Pescini et al. (2017) Integrating Social Ecology in Explanations of Wolf-Dog Behavioural Differences, *Current Opinion in Behavioral Sciences*, 16, 80–86.
75 See further the discussion in Pierotti R & Fogg BR (2017) *The First Domestication: How Wolves and Humans Coevolved*, Yale UP, New Haven, in which the authors emphasise a history of cooperation and interaction towards co-evolution, as distinct from a narrative of rivalry and competition.
76 Schleidt WM & Shalter MD (2003) Co-Evolution of Humans and Canids: An Alternative View of Dog Domestication: *Homo Homini Lupus?*, *Evolution and Cognition*, 9(1), 57–71: p. 57.
77 Schleidt WM & Shalter MD (2003) Co-Evolution of Humans and Canids: An Alternative View of Dog Domestication: *Homo Homini Lupus?*, *Evolution and Cognition*, 9(1), 57–71: p. 57.
78 See further Pierotti R & Fogg BR (2017) *The First Domestication: How Wolves and Humans Coevolved*, Yale UP, New Haven.
79 Tarde G (1890/[1903]) *The Laws of Imitation*, EC Parsons (trans.), Henry Holt & Co, New York, 277.
80 See further the discussions in Chapter 8, "Pack fiction"; and Chapter 9, "Wild abandon."
81 On the dominion of human beings as central to religious doctrine, see Haraway D (2008) *When Species Meet*, U of Minnesota P, Minneapolis, 245: "In this feast, there are no companion species, no cross-category messmates at table. There is no salutary indigestion, only licensed cultivation and husbandry of all the earth as stock for human use."
82 See, for example, the UK Kennel Club's Fit for Function campaign. www.thekennelclub.org.uk/health/fit-for-function/ While this campaign is a conscientious

attempt to address welfare issues by seeking to help prospective purchasers select a breed suitable for their lifestyle, it is nevertheless completely complicit in the notion of breed and instinct-driven behaviour, fitting dogs to environments, and doing little to address public attitudes to the converse, the dog's well-being within the family."

83 Huxley J (1952) Foreword, in Lorenz KZ *King Solomon's Ring: New Light on Animal Ways*, M Kerr Wilson (trans.), Methuen & Co, London, 9–13: p. 11.
84 See further the discussion of the discourse of "taming" in Chapter 9, "Wild abandon".
85 Kari Weil notes: "to realize that historical agency should not be regarded only in terms of human intention has been crucial to recent reexaminations of the process of domestication and the role of humans and animals alike." Weil K (2012) *Thinking Animals: Why Animal Studies Now?*, Columbia UP, New York, 57. See further the discussion in "Part 1, Domestication, the stone age" with respect to social competence and fairness.
86 For a discussion of the role of pastoralism in domestication and in expanding society in early modern humans, see McClure SB (2015) The Pastoral Effect, *Current Anthropology*, 56(6), 901–910.
87 Schleidt WM & Shalter MD (2003) Co-Evolution of Humans and Canids: An Alternative View of Dog Domestication: *Homo Homini Lupus?*, *Evolution and Cognition*, 9(1), 57–71: pp. 66–67.
88 Schleidt WM & Shalter MD (2003) Co-Evolution of Humans and Canids: An Alternative View of Dog Domestication: *Homo Homini Lupus?*, *Evolution and Cognition*, 9(1), 57–71: p. 70.
89 Schleidt WM & Shalter MD (2018) Dogs and Mankind: Coevolution on the Move: An Update, *Human Ethology Bulletin*, 33(1), 15–38: pp. 27–28.
90 Schleidt WM (1998) Is Humaneness Canine?, *Human Ethology Bulletin*, 13(4), 14–20: pp. 16–17.
91 Mills DS et al. (2010) *The Encyclopedia of Applied Animal Behaviour and Welfare*, CAB International, Wallingford, OX, 184.
92 Tarde G (1890/[1903]) *The Laws of Imitation*, EC Parsons (trans.), Henry Holt & Co, New York, 371.
93 In reviewing critique contemporary with Tarde's influence on sociology in the United States, Ruth Leys notes: "Imitation-suggestion thus became the unifying concept for a newly professionalizing American sociology committed to abandoning contractual, utilitarian, and biological models of society in order to place the study of the relation of self to other on a new, psychological foundation." Leys R (1993) Mead's Voices: Imitation as Foundation, or, the Struggle against Mimesis, *Critical Inquiry*, 19(2), 277–307: p. 279.
94 Hare B & Woods V (2013) We Didn't Domesticate Dogs: They Domesticated Us, *National Geographic News*, 3 March.
95 Compare the pastoral relationship in Schleidt WM & Shalter MD (2018) Dogs and Mankind: Coevolution on the Move: An Update, *Human Ethology Bulletin*, 33(1), 15–38.
96 Schleidt WM & Shalter MD (2003) Co-Evolution of Humans and Canids: An Alternative View of Dog Domestication: *Homo Homini Lupus?*, *Evolution and Cognition*, 9(1), 57–71: p. 67.
97 See further the discussion of Tinbergen (scientist as hunter) and Lorenz (scientist as farmer) in Burkhardt RW, Jr (2005) *Patterns of Behavior: Konrad Lorenz, Niko Tinbergen, and the Founding of Ethology*, U of Chicago P, Chicago, 10–11, 188, 474–475 in particular.
98 Despret V (2004) The Body We Care For: Figures of Anthropo-zoo-genesis, *Body & Society*, 10(2–3), 111–134: p. 129.

99 As Despret notes, "Lorenz takes the mother's place, and becomes all at once a variable of the experiment." Despret V (2004) The Body We Care For: Figures of Anthropo-zoo-genesis, *Body & Society*, 10(2–3), 111–134: p. 129.
100 See Tarde's concept of the logical duel of models competing for supremacy, similar to the rivalrous notion of property (and intellectual property): Tarde G (1890/[1903]) *The Laws of Imitation*, EC Parsons (trans.), Henry Holt & Co, New York, 154–158 in particular.
101 Tarde G (1890/[1903]) *The Laws of Imitation*, EC Parsons (trans.), Henry Holt & Co, New York, 56.
102 See Donna Haraway's discussion of companion species as "messmates at table" in Haraway D (2008) *When Species Meet*, U of Minnesota P, Minneapolis, 17–18, 208.
103 Schleidt WM & Shalter MD (2018) Dogs and Mankind: Coevolution on the Move: An Update, *Human Ethology Bulletin*, 33(1), 15–38.
104 Tarde G (1890/[1903]) *The Laws of Imitation*, EC Parsons (trans.), Henry Holt & Co, New York, 377.
105 As Tarde notes, "This undoubtedly is the reason why, in prehistoric coves, we never find among their flint implements any complete animal skeleton, not even those of cave bears." Tarde G (1890/[1903]) *The Laws of Imitation*, EC Parsons (trans.), Henry Holt & Co, New York, 273 note 1.
106 Haraway D (2008) *When Species Meet*, University of Minnesota Press, Minneapolis, 17.
107 Clutton-Brock J (2017) Origins of the Dog: The Archaeological Evidence, in Serpell J (ed.) *The Domestic Dog: Its Evolution, Behavior and Interactions with People*, 2nd ed., Cambridge UP, Cambridge, 7–21: p. 9.
108 This is discussed in more detail in Chapter 9, "Wild abandon."
109 As discussed in Chapter 2, "The imitation of domestication."
110 See in particular the discussion in Chapter 3, "Socialisation"; and Chapter 8, "Pack fiction."
111 Schleidt WM & Shalter MD (2018) Dogs and Mankind: Coevolution on the Move: An Update, *Human Ethology Bulletin*, 33(1), 15–38: pp. 15–16.
112 Tarde G (1902/[2007]) Economic Psychology, A Toscano (trans.), *Economy and Society*, 36(4), 614–643: pp. 617, 640.
113 Haraway D (2008) *When Species Meet*, U of Minnesota P, Minneapolis, 206.
114 Haraway D (2008) *When Species Meet*, U of Minnesota P, Minneapolis, 206.

Chapter 2

The imitation of domestication

> In the beginning of societies, the art of chipping flint, of domesticating dogs, of making bows, and, later, of leavening bread, of working bronze, of extracting iron, etc., must have spread like a contagion; since every arrow, every flake, every morsel of bread, every thread of bronze, served both as model and copy.
>
> Tarde G (1890/[1903]) *The Laws of Imitation*, EC Parsons (trans), Henry Holt & Co, New York, 17
>
> The animal origin of man implies the animal origin of human society.
>
> Briffault R (1931) *The Mothers: The Matriarchal Theory of Social Origins*, Macmillan, New York, 1

If the "capital invention" of domestication is indeed the turning point in human history towards socialisation, civilisation, and humanity, then surely this happened at the feat of that dog, so to speak. And it spread.

As revealed in the previous chapter, mounting research has assembled a major disruption to the traditional story of the domestication of the dog and the extent to which humans proposed the idea in the first place. Indeed, with the revision of the taming narrative and the compelling evidence for self-domestication, or even co-domestication at best, was the human "invention" of domestication just an accident or a thoughtful copy? If an accident, it was not an inevitable one. Far from it. The notion of accident is perhaps just another deferral of the intentionality of all other animals, along with instinct.[1]

It was no accident. It was an ingenious idea. That is, rather than simply explaining it as opportunistic habituation, surely the initiative taken suggests an important enterprise and inventiveness on the part of the dog? There is much to be learned from the domestication story. The actual material of the story does not change at all; it is just a question of perspective on the capacity of the humble dog. It is simply to credit this event with an intentional and purposive life rather than contrive a domestication story of that dog conscripted by biological determinism alone.

The wild goose and the tame egg

The proverb of the wild goose and the tame egg is reputedly about the predictability or inevitability of things. It is the story of biological determinism, of beings controlled and directed by their environment. It is the all-to-familiar chorus that responds to any notion of animal creativity and consciousness. The accolade of creative, or innovative, or inventive is a powerful tool of human exceptionalism. The anxiety and self-consciousness with which animals are denied creative purpose is instructive not only in terms of the constructed nature of human uniqueness but also in asking all other animals for answers that are almost never required of human animals.

The discourse of human exceptionalism, however, introduces as well a passion for differentiation and division, a predetermination that underpins and circulates through proprietary systems. Were human animals apprentices to pastoralists? Or were they unwitting victims of scavenging trespassers? Or is it none of the above? It is all in the presumption. Far from an inevitable idea, domestication is the story of the wild goose that indeed laid the tame egg.

This idea was far from an inevitable one

The social and cultural influence of the domestication narrative is starting to emerge. Domestication, it seems, is at the very heart of the ideology of human exceptionalism, but as Tarde notes, "this idea was far from being an inevitable one."[2] Who really cracked the egg of Columbus?[3] Throughout the popular literature and idiom, the story of canine domestication may seem to be accepted as an inevitability of instinct and biology, supported by the paradigm of human exceptionalism that continues to put the human at the centre of domestication. But far from the human playing a central and intentional role, the humans presented an opportunity to be exploited, and canine domestication is a considerable accomplishment of self-domestication. And it is the first domestication. The kind of underestimation of that dog in this regard, tracked in the previous chapter, continues to characterise a lot of contemporary enquiry into animal consciousness and creativity more widely. But what of the human if that dog had never wandered into the fold? The invention of domestication was not obvious – *this idea was far from an inevitable one*.

And if the notion of cooperating, socialising, domesticating did indeed present a solution that was simply reasonable, adaptive, and functional, this does not coerce a conclusion that the dogs were driven to it simply by biology alone. There is much at play in domestication. And indeed, what is invention if not opportunity and the proposal of a solution or an improvement? This wondrous idea of domestication – *this idea was far from an inevitable one*.

Giving credit where credit is due then rather than concealing it behind a discourse of biological incarceration, if dogs invented domestication, to what extent is domestication responsible for the qualities of compassion, caring, and indeed "humanity" in the modern human? Did dogs socialise humans? Did dogs invent humaneness?[4]

If dogs invented domestication, did humans merely go on to imitate the process in respect of other species in order to develop and disseminate that original invention in a multitude of generic imitations? Is domestication the original story of plagiarism? Indeed, is property properly plagiaristic? In intellectual property vernacular, is property theft?

Adaptation

> What do all our modern inventions amount to in comparison with this capital invention of domestication? This was the first decisive victory over animality.[5]

Tarde's laudatory statement on domestication has more in common with the scientific definition than at first it might appear. Tarde is arguably influenced by the time in which he is writing and the intense interest in Darwin's theories and in the subsequent application to social evolution.[6] In this respect, domestication as the process of "enfolding a species into human society" is a kind of process of adaptation, and indeed Tarde is expressing a similar kind of "evolutionary" relationship between invention and adaptation in his own sociology.[7] In so doing, Tarde explains that the observation of adaptation is not an explanation: "It would be erroneous to think, however, that because we had shown the adaptation of living or social types to external phenomena we had thereby explained them."[8] Indeed, through the sociability of interferences and interactions of imitation and repetition, Tarde sees genuine innovation through the production of difference: "Repetition, opposition, and adaptation, I repeat, are the three keys which science employs to open up the arcana of the universe. She seeks, before all else, not the mere causes, but the laws that govern the repetition, opposition, and adaptation of phenomena."[9]

Tarde explicitly distinguishes the work of Darwin as investigating not the laws of adaptation, as it were, but rather the "phenomena of life from the standpoint of repetitions and oppositions."[10] In this the very "innovation" in imitation begins to take shape, not as reproduction but as production. Repetition garners innovation, opposition is productive contact,[11] and imitation is the stuff of cultural development.[12]

> The encounters between men have not only served this propagation of discoveries or inventions spontaneously born in the most talented individuals confronted with nature. They have served especially to elicit discoveries and inventions of a higher degree which – allowing for the perception of nature through the characteristic sentiments of social life, loves and hatreds, adorations and execrations, sorrows and angers, sympathies and antipathies, through the refracting lenses of words and dogmas, of languages and religions, of philosophical theories and scientific concepts – provide desire with a crowd of wholly new objects, pursued through entirely new avenues of activity.[13]

Imitation must encompass difference; that is, it serves "both as model and copy," and through that difference innovation continues to thrive. Imitation thus becomes a productive enterprise. Tardean opposition and competition are not merely adversarial but rather incorporate a kind of prosociality that is somewhat obscured in modern predatory proprietary models: "*Competition* is an ambiguous word which signifies at once, or in turn, *joint action* and *contest*."[14] Indeed, in the original French text, Tarde uses the word *concurrence* throughout, which more completely encompasses the conjugation of meanings.[15] This duality is identified also in Darwin's theory of natural selection and the interference of both competition and cooperation,[16] as well as in Spencer's explanation of altruism as a fundamental relation with egoism rather than an incompatible and exclusive antagonism,[17] both of whom were significant influences in Tarde's sociology.

Thus, in reviewing this first "capital invention" in the context of adaptation, the relationship between sociality and innovation becomes more complex and enriched within the domestication narrative. But precisely whose decisive victory is a different matter.

Pastoral care

A story of pastoralism and apprenticeship in canine domestication history has started to emerge. In presenting a story of the wolf pack pastoral system, the Austrian ethologist Wolfgang Schleidt and his collaborator Michael Shalter tell a story of the humans following and learning from the wolves in a relationship of teacher and student. It is a story not of the humans conquering the wolves but of the wolves calling to attention the humans – a social call, as it were. *That dog looks back.*

As discussed in the previous chapter, domestication was instrumental in the development of human society. Pursuing this relationship through domestication science, modern human society arguably has arisen out of the relationship between dogs and humans, one that motivated the human towards settlement and pastoralism and ultimately to the production of a cultivated, agricultural society: "*it is the town that invents agriculture.*"[18] Indeed, it is through the very imitation of domestication towards the implication of a kind of economy that domestication describes the economy implicit in mimesis. The imitation of domestication facilitated the first economy in private property, in which the domesticates themselves embody the currency: "Cattle were the most precious part of spoil, the most coveted kind of treasure, and the first form of money."[19]

In disputing the view of classical anthropology that property did not exist in so-called primitive or nomadic societies, the anthropologist Bronislaw Malinowski notes that not only enforcement ("by belief and magic, as well as by secular sanctions"[20]) but also the very act of "stealing" means that property always already persists in early societies: "[S]tealing presupposes the existence of private property. Private property again, as the legally defined, exclusive right to use and to consume tools and goods respectively, is essential, and without such a principle there would occur a chronic chaos and disorganization even in the simplest activities of primitive man."[21]

In other words, domestication facilitated wider and more systematic economic relationships. But in imitating the domestication initiated by that dog, humans could do little more than continue to testify to the foresight and generosity of that early domestication relationship. In this way, the "inventiveness" of early human society was really facilitated by that dog, by the patronage of that dog.

The wolf pack itself, contrary to the persistence of popular stereotypes, is not a simple system of rectilinear hierarchies, conflicts, and confrontations but an assemblage of cooperation and the sharing of risk.[22] In adopting the wolf pack algorithm, arguably this took the early humans outside their immediate family circle, enlarging their family, enlarging their community of kin. Thus was born an aspiration towards the open.[23] Where once the family was the primary or even the sole social group, this comes to be stirred and scrambled, opened out to wider influences. As Tarde explains, this enlargement brings with it the early cooperative and collaborative bases for social structures:

> [I]n the beginning the family, or the pseudo-family that grew up by the side of it, was the only social group, and that every subsequent change resulted in lessening its importance in this respect by constituting new and more ample groups which were formed artificially, at the expense of the social side of families, and which reduced them to mere physiological expressions; but that, finally, such dismembered families tended to aggregate into a kind of enlarged family that was both natural and social like the original family, except that the physiological characteristics, which were transmitted through heredity, existed mainly to facilitate the transmission through imitation of the elements of civilisation, and not *vice versa*.[24]

As well as the cooperation towards common objectives, it is proposed that the very elements of compassion, equity, and acknowledgement of the other, so prized by humans as a part of their self-composed exceptionalism, may indeed have come from these first interspecies cultural transmissions. In this way, the early dog not only domesticated itself but also domesticated the humans, as it were, through this cultural expansion, "*both natural and social like the original family.*"[25] For Tarde, this process is part of the development and ongoing enlargement of society. Through that "capital invention of domestication . . . which alone made history possible,"[26] dogs set the play.

Calling to attention

Human attentiveness no doubt underpinned the capacity for humans to adapt and recruit new species to their emerging society, but to what were they paying attention in the first place? An accident, a mechanism, an idea? While it is accepted that "a major modification of the human organism, namely its ability to pay attention, occurred when a major cultural innovation, domestication, was adopted,"[27] from what (or whom) did this idea arise?

Indeed, the language of adoption is apt. Domestication was indeed adopted, and it was adopted into the family of the nascent "household"[28] that preceded modern civilisations. It was adopted by example – an example set by dogs. From the wealth of research in domestication science and archaeological anthropology, it seems clear that the domestication of humans preceded the development of agriculturalism and the domestication of other species: "[D]omestication can be conceived of as an independent innovation and even . . . the domestication of plants and animals follows the domestication of human beings and is inspired by it."[29]

Although it is now established and widely accepted that the first domestication was that dog, and that dog's domestication story itself is also becoming more commonly accepted as a story of co-evolution or co-domestication with humans rather than a simple domination over ancient dogs, a presumption of human intentionality nevertheless persists. Where co-domestication introduces greater purposive capacity on the part of the canids, as distinct from the co-evolution model, nevertheless it still proposes a model of calling in the dogs. What or who summoned the humans? Is the concept of co-domestication really plausible for such a metamorphosis in human society? Or were the humans led? Following the discussion in the previous chapter, it would seem that hasty conclusions as to the progression of domestication betray a presumption of initiative solely on the part of the human animals: *this invention was far from an inevitable one.*

The theory of self-domestication is compelling in situating what is a remarkable transformation in human behaviour, diet, movements, and geographies – shifting from a wandering forager to a focused and territorial pastoralist and hunter, and ultimately to a settled and "industrious" agriculturalist: "The traditional myth of man the Ice age hunter as 'the mighty top carnivore' and keystone species has been eroded by mounting evidence."[30] Humans were instead not the centre, the umbilicus of biological life, but at the fringe, the periphery, "surviving on the southern fringes of the mammoth step due to the association with their dogs."[31]

In this way, the domestication of human beings themselves was inspired by the ingenious canine invention of dog societies. This proposition is controversial only if one adheres to an unprincipled human exceptionalism.

The body politic

> At that time I still knew hardly anything of the creative gift for music with which the canine race alone is endowed, it had naturally enough escaped my but slowly developing powers of observation. . . . They did not speak, they did not sing, they remained generally silent, almost determinedly silent; but from the empty air they conjured music. Everything was music, the lifting and setting down of their feet, certain turns of the head, their running and their standing still, the positions they took up in relation to one another . . . and none made a false move, not even the last dog, though he was a little unsure, did not always establish contact at once with the others, sometimes hesitated, as it were, on the stroke of the beat, but yet was unsure only by comparison with the superb sureness of the others, and even if he had been much more unsure, indeed quite unsure, would not have been able to do any harm, the others, great masters all of them, keeping the rhythm so unshakably.[32]

The hypothesis of two separate domestication events, one in East Asia and the other in Europe,[33] does not undermine this theory of canid invention; in fact in some ways it compounds the evidence for a canid invention: "likeness between artistic products is no proof at all of consanguinity, it points only to a contagion of imitation."[34] In other words, the "first" domestication did not arise from an unprecedented social initiative of humans, twice, but rather from the established participatory and reciprocal community structures of the more advanced canid societies. More recent studies, although not conclusive, suggest that the domestication "event" was actually a once-only affair.[35] However, whether once or twice, it is generally agreed that early canids initiated things by moving closer to humans, scavenging scraps, and so on: "While the humans did not initially gain any kind of benefit from this process, over time they would have developed some kind of symbiotic relationship with these animals, evolving into the dogs we see today."[36] In other words, following this theory, only the dogs were to gain from that initial contact; the benefit to humans came only after that initial socialisation, that first entanglement. This is the concept of embodiment,[37] that defiance of Cartesian separation of mind and body, of the exceptional human and the machinic animal. Language is embodied, and the body is language. Notably, as the visual becomes prioritised as the primary sense,[38] through to property and the reduction of the sociality of property to things (and thingness), the resistance to this embodiment in favour of a Cartesian dualism is instrumental in predatory discourse.

However, in the revision of the domestication event, communication is materially embodied, a physically engaged experience, inter-relational and interconnected. It is situated:[39] that is, it is social and specific rather than general and dislocated; it is implicated and cooperative rather than unanswerable and adversarial ("beyond my control"[40]). Whereas the predatory drift in property particularises a model of property that relies not on sociality, has no need of manners, disavows accountability other than to the self, and is entirely premised upon the "struggle for life" that characterises a competitive, rivalrous view of development, instead, the situatedness and the constitution of one's individual world in relation to another characterises the domestication story of association and the cartography of social life.[41] Domestication as such was indeed the ultimate communicative relationship. And in the domestication story, the initiative for that embodied communication[42] seems to rest entirely with the dogs. As Barbara Smuts explains: "Meaning in interactions like these does not reside in the specific behaviors shown, nor does the interaction refer to something "out there" in the world. Rather, meaning is mutually constituted, literally embodied as two individuals behaviors ("the parts") combine to create something new ("the whole")."[43]

The dog domestication story is thus a particularly historic communication between humans and other animals, the first "contact zone," to use Donna Haraway's insight, the first mapping of human social life, the first "mortal worldmaking entanglement."[44] Domestication does indeed make worlds. And this contact was creative, inventive, and intentional. *Everything was music*: "The whole of the refrain is the being of sensation."[45]

This brings to mind a personal experience with such embodied communication and imitation – between Jeff the Border Terrier and Howard the Parson Russell Terrier and a toddler boy in the park. Jeff and Howard were playing in the longer green grass, quite lush from recent rain. They were seemingly oblivious to a little toddler boy who was quite fascinated by their play, running and sniffing, running and sniffing. The little boy was with his parents, and he started to wobble towards the two terriers (walking seemed to be a recent skill), and his father followed closely. Still the two terriers kept on sniffing and playing without much regard for the stranger. Then the two terriers started running back and forth and up and down the little hill. The little boy started to try to run after them, at which point he fell over. Jeff immediately stopped, ran back to the little boy, sniffed and stood with him until he stood up again. Then Jeff and Howard started rolling in the green grass, and the little boy, by this time utterly captivated by his little terrier shepherds, started imitating them, rolling away in the grass as well. And together the three of them, legs in the air, rolled and rolled.

This characterisation of embodied communication as a performative interaction resonates with Gabriel Tarde's associative sociology, as distinct from society as a discrete phenomenon: "Heterogeneity, not homogeneity, is at the heart of things."[46] Embodied communication conveys the inextricability in social relations that characterises Tarde's social and physical cartography.[47] Tarde addresses instead the concept of sociality as a dynamic and imitative association: "A society is always in different degrees an association, and association is to sociality, to *imitativeness*, so to speak, what organisation is to vitality, or what molecular structure is to the elasticity of the ether."[48] Society is thus an interactive and dynamic sociality, according to Tarde: "This social tie may be weak and inadequate, but it gains in strength as other common traits, all originating in imitation, are added to it."[49] In this way imitation is not only a mutual accountability but also ultimately a source of innovation and development, and society is a dynamic assemblage:[50] "Our interaction communicated desires, expressed emotion, invoked a playful mood, and accomplished a mutually satisfying goal: afterwards, we could each settle comfortably into our respective modes, separate but still very much connected. If you ask what our interaction was about, the best answer is that it was about *us*."[51]

Sympathetic properties

This situated and embodied communication as the constitution of self is instrumental in understanding sympathy and the development of "humanity" of humans.[52] It is at once a kind of perspective-taking and reciprocal accountability – the forces of attraction of the social, as it were: "Sympathy is certainly the primary source of sociability and the hidden or overt soul of every kind of imitation, even of imitation which is envious and calculating, even of imitation of an enemy. Only, it is certain that sympathy itself begins by being one-sided instead of mutual."[53]

This accountability in situated and embodied communication can also be recognised in the work of Henri Bergson, particularly in his discussion of the relationship between predator and prey, between hunter and hunted. This is especially so in his consideration of the Ammophila and the caterpillar in *Creative Evolution*, in an attempt to negotiate the question of animal intelligence. There, instinct becomes a kind of embodied communication through the capacity of sympathy but not in order to delineate instinct but rather to imbue it with intelligence; that is, an embodied communication.

The theory of instinct and the biological determinism that attends it resonates with the Cartesian reduction of animals to mere automata. And indeed, in the way in which economic modelling attempts to define and prepare the exacting conditions for a predictable creativity and innovation, there is much in agreement with an extreme or radical behaviourism perspective.

As Tarde declares, "Nothing, however, is less scientific that the establishment of this absolute separation, of this abrupt break, between the voluntary and the involuntary, between the conscious and the unconscious. Do we not pass in insensible degrees from deliberate volition to almost mechanical habit?"[54] To underestimate an animal through the presumed yet contrived objectivity of this separation, this duality, is to secure an ongoing justification for that animal's enforced silence and a platform for the shouting of human exceptionalism. This artificial separation is utterly rejected by Tarde: "matter is mind, nothing more."[55] In other words, these flows of belief and desire persist and proliferate through imitation, unsettling the configuring of poles of production and consumption: "*Imitation is the propagation of a flow; opposition is binarization, the making binary of flows; invention is a conjugation or connection of different flows . . .* Infinitesimal imitation, opposition and invention and therefore like flow quanta marking a propagation, binarization, or conjugation of beliefs and desires."[56]

For Bergson, these flows of beliefs and desires are what he understands as intuition: "Instinct is sympathy. . . . But it is to the very inwardness of life that *intuition* leads us – by intuition I mean instinct that has become disinterested, self-conscious, capable of reflecting upon its object and of enlarging it indefinitely."[57] Bergson notes that "if we suppose a *sympathy* . . . between the Ammophila and its victim" then this "teaches it from within, so to say, concerning the vulnerability of the caterpillar."[58] This sympathy is not engaged through an objective stance but rather through an inextricable relation: "This feeling of vulnerability might owe nothing to outward perception, but result from the mere presence together of the Ammophila and the caterpillar, considered no longer as two organisms, but as two activities. It would express, in a concrete form, the *relation* of the one to the other."[59] For Bergson, this effort is made possible by a sense of beauty, an aesthetic faculty:

> The intention of life, the simple movement that runs through the lines, that binds them together and gives them significance, escapes it. This intention is just what the artist tries to regain, in placing himself back within the object by a kind of sympathy, in breaking down, by an effort of intuition, the barrier that space puts up between him and his model. It is true that this aesthetic intuition, like external perception, only attains the individual. But we can conceive an inquiry turned in the same direction as art, which would take life *in general* for its object.[60]

This is also a kind of property on the move, territories that are marked by mobilities rather than boundaries, a relational approach to property. Indeed, this substantiality of mobile territoriality and property in movement is arguably what defeated classical anthropology when it came to recognising the property in nomadic and primitive societies.[61] Thus, territory and property in territory comes to be recognised as a co-constituted space, through the tracks and the paths and the many points of contact: *The path is the stone.*

The embodied communication between ancient canids and humans, through the careful social cartography and cooperation within territory, an aesthetic and fleshly network, belies a sense of the aesthetic through the social: "This is not synesthesia in the flesh but blocs of sensations in the territory – colors, postures, and sounds that sketch out a total work of art. . . . The whole of the refrain is the being of sensation. Monuments are refrains. In this respect art is continually haunted by the animal."[62]

Property on the move. Is this possible?

How might it be possible to manage the landmarks and milestones and monuments of territory that begin to map a social property, rather than secrete the things that trace it out? The network is a thing of beauty. Art is haunted by the animal, the ghost in the Cartesian machine: "The artist: the first person to set out a boundary stone, or to make a mark."[63]

And in that sympathetic moment, that dog made artists of us all.

A network of possibilities

> This is not an appeal to mystery, but rather to the profound and underappreciated ability to affirm a beyond to the horizon of facts and not to misjudge, at least, what one cannot know. If to affirm the unknown is to use our ignorance, to deny the unknown is to be ignorant twice over.[64]

It would seem that sociality is indeed a networked production. And dogs, like Tarde, appear to have been the original "thinkers of networks."[65]

From that original "capital invention" the possibilities were opened up for society, for agriculture, for the arts. Through domestication, humans began to map their relationships with other species and were introduced to sedentary society. The constitution of "home territories," as it were, was a civilising moment: "The animals with territory (for there are animals without territory) are prodigious. Because constituting a territory is nearly the birth of art."[66] Gabriel Tarde lauds domestication as "of all historic events, the greatest and the most surprising . . . the one which alone made history possible."[67] The surprise is not for us, however; the surprise was for those early humans, as they found themselves set in the social sights of some ingenious canids. It was very surprising indeed.

In the establishment of a home and place came a most extraordinary metamorphosis of humans, as it were, into a world of imitation, into society. After all, *society is imitation*:⁶⁸

> This influence is much greater and more farspread than we suppose. It is not only the related and even the unrelated individuals of the same species who copy one another . . . individuals of different species as well borrow both the useful and the unmeaning peculiarities of one another. Here we see the deep-seated desire to imitate for the sake of imitation, the desire which is the original source of all our arts. . . . Not many only, but every animal, reaches out according to his degree of mentality to a social life as the *sine qua non* of mental development.⁶⁹

It is in this creation of "home" that the possibility for art is found; indeed, "Perhaps art begins with the animal, at least with the animal that carves out a territory and constructs a house."⁷⁰ Domestication transformed social relations for humans and dogs alike. Importantly, it was through the domestication process that transformative conceptions of territory were innervated: "the territory implies the emergence of pure sensory qualities, of sensibilia that cease to be merely functional and become expressive features, making possible a transformation of functions."⁷¹ But for dogs, would there be art for dogs?

Imitation apprenticeship

Through apprenticeship in the pastoralism of early canids, the conditions for imitation became possible. In view of this apprenticeship model, Schleidt and Shalter propose co-evolution as "a good alternative hypothesis to the current theories of domestication with man conquering beasts, including wolves, through cognitive superiority and to the bootstrapping theory of hominization with man domesticating himself."⁷² In many ways, the idea of co-evolution does indeed usher in the kind of sociality that is seen here, but it does not give credit to the inspiration of the initiative to domesticate. It is more clearly a case of the dogs intruding, trespassing, making a nuisance of their ideas in order to provoke an imitation of settlement on the part of the humans:

> [E]very invention and every discovery consists in the interference in somebody's mind of certain old pieces of information that have generally been handed down by others. What did Darwin's thesis about natural selection amount to? To having proclaimed the fact of competition among living things? No, but in having for the first time combined this idea with the ideas of *variability* and *heredity*. The former idea, as it was proclaimed by Aristotle,

remained sterile until it was associated with the two latter ideas. From that as a starting point, we may say that the generic term, of which invention is but a species, is the fruitful interference of repetitions.[73]

Is this not then a case of dogs civilising humans, giving them the material for that extraordinary imitation which would become the foundations for society? "Society is imitation."[74] Far from a tale of humans conquering beasts, as it were, it is to bring domestication to the conquered human, to associate with them, domesticating them (or "civilising"[75] them) in the process: "war is much more of a civiliser for the conquered than for the conqueror, for the latter does not deign to learn from the former, whereas the former submits himself to the ascendency of victory and borrows from his enemy a number of fruitful ideas to add to his national store."[76] The myth of the conqueror, the all-dominating human, the exceptional being, is at least under question, and at most in the undergrowth.[77] Remarkable innovation comes not from conflict but from association and the home, the niche, the household[78] of familiar production, not calls to war and dominion: "These calls stimulate invention, but it is not that they engender the invention itself. How much more often does it happen that they kill the germ of an idea! Invention had peace, love, family, or professional fraternity for a cradle."[79] And thus domestication was bound forever to repeat itself: "it is seldom than an inventor does not climb up several obscure rungs in such a ladder before reaching the illustrious step."[80]

The invention of society

> The movement of the swimmer does not resemble that of the wave, in particular, the movements of the swimming instructor which we reproduce on the sand bear no relation to the movements of the wave, which we learn to deal with only by grasping the former in practice as signs. That is why it is so difficult to say how someone learns. . . . We learn nothing from those who say: 'Do as I do'. Our only teachers are those who tell us to 'do with me', and are able to emit signs to be developed in heterogeneity rather than propose gestures for us to reproduce.[81]

Society is imitation.[82] Imitations are creative in as much as the social production between them; they are embodied, communicative relations: "If we observe that there is a social relation between two living beings, there we have imitation in this sense of the word."[83] Whether we approach domestication from the perspective of the pastoral apprenticeship model or the scavenger model, the relationship between humans and ancient canids was not a relationship of dominion – *do as I do*. Rather, this was an introduction in the form of sociality – *do with me* – an ensemble, an assemblage.[84] In this way, a genuine physical, geographical, and cultural transformation was set in creative play, like a dog dropping a ball at your feet.

In contrast to the co-evolution narrative and the emphasis on biology driving certain behaviours entirely concerned with reproduction and survival, the kind of abbreviation and reduction of the "absolutely arbitrary" theories of "spontaneous appearance" against which Tarde rallies,[85] this is a story of choice, of creative freedom, of innovation. And whether dogs were largely recognised as scavengers or as pastoralists, they had the attention of the humans. And those humans had a choice. Rather than an accidental opportunity, domestication is a narrative of initiative arguably led by that dog. Indeed, the social competence[86] and social morality[87] of that dog cannot be explained by domestication. These are principles that dog brought to the cave. Nevertheless, through tales of "selection," the human animals continue to try to circumscribe that initiative with a human-led intentionality. At the very least, this is a tale of two halves.

While invention may be individualised – not only in terms of the narratives of creative genius but also in terms of its definition as species-specific, in law and in biology and popular culture – this is perhaps an unduly artificial construction, even an arbitrary one, far from the associative genius of its production:

> The laws of invention belong essentially to individual logic; the laws of imitation belong in part to social logic. Moreoever, just as imitation does not fall exclusively within social logic, but depends upon extra-logical influence as well, is it not obvious that invention itself is produced mentally, through conditions which are not alone the apparition of the premises in the mind of which it is the logical conclusion, but which are also other associations of ideas, called inspiration, intuition, genius?[88]

Domestication is thus the story of imitation as a potent tale of interference and innovation. Is there perhaps no greater interference in the discourse of production and consumption in the practices of innovation and creativity, in the rules of intellectual property, than the dogged tale of domestication? It is the tale that wags. And wags. And that dog authored the tale.

The rigid denial of animal creativity, through biological and indeed social narratives, continues to dog, as it were, investigations into animal consciousness, emotions, and self-awareness. However, the interference of the denials continues to innervate the proliferation of imaginative responses to animal creativity.[89] Similarly, the construction and recognition of creativity continues to presume strict rules of cause and effect in the way in which the concept is interpreted in intellectual property laws and their application: as though inventions are regular; as though the fruitful interferences can be not only foreseen but also encouraged and facilitated; as though nothing is accidental. Indeed, we are still led to believe the myth that intellectual property is based upon a plausible and predictable system of incentives and rewards, that this is actually good law and good social policy:

> However numerous may be the different kinds of things which are repeated, if we suppose that the centres of these repetitive radiations, otherwise known as inventions or the biological or physical analogues of inventions, be

regularly placed, their interferences may be foreseen; and these interferences or new centres will themselves present as much regularity in their disposition as did the primary centres. In such a universe, everything, however complex it might be, would be regular; nothing would either be or seem accidental.

But what if . . .

[O]n the contrary we assume that the primitive centres are irregular in position, the position of the secondary centres will also be unordered and their irregularity will equal that of the primary centres. Thus, there will never be in the world anything but *the same quantity of irregularity*, so to speak, only it will appear under the most changing forms. Let me add that, in spite of all, these changing forms must have a certain indefinable likeness. The original irregularity is reflected in its enlarged copies, the derived irregularities. From this I conclude that, although the idea of Repetition dominates the whole universe, it does not constitute it. For the bottom of it, I think, is a certain sum of innate, eternal, and indestructible diversity without which the world would be as monotonous as it is vast.[90]

The case of the egg of Columbus: *This idea was far from an inevitable one.*

Catch me if you can

'I am looking for friends. What does "tame" mean?'

'It is something which is too often forgotten,' said the fox. 'It means to establish ties . . .'

'"To establish ties"?'

'That's right,' said the fox. 'To me, you are still just a little boy like a hundred thousand other little boys. And I have no need of you. And you have no need of me, either. To you, I am just a fox like a hundred thousand other foxes. But if you tame me, we shall need one another. To me, you will be unique. And I shall be unique to you.'

'I'm beginning to understand,' said the little prince. 'There is a flower . . . I think she has tamed me.'

. . .

'I beg of you . . . tame me!' he said.

'Willingly,' the little prince replied, 'but I haven't got much time. I have friends to discover and a lot of things to understand.'

'One can only understand the things one tames,' said the fox. 'Men have no more time to understand anything. They buy ready-made things in the shops. But since there are no shops where you can buy friends, men no longer have any friends. If you want a friend, tame me!'

'What should I do?' asked the little prince.

'You must be very patient,' replied the fox. 'First you will sit down at a little distance from me, like that, in the grass. I shall watch you out of the corner of my eye and you will say nothing. Words are a source of misunderstandings. But every day, you can sit a little closer to me . . .'[91]

Catch me if you can.
Saint-Exupéry's story of the fox and the little prince offers intriguing insight into the domestication story. The fox tamed the little prince, called to him, interpellated him in the process, tying them both in knots. The prince then imitated the fox, tamed the fox, and went off then to tame his rose: "'And it is she I have listened to complaining or boasting or sometimes remaining silent. Because she is my rose.'"[92] And thus property blooms.

Thus, the suggestion from ancient dogs has been imitated over and over again by human animals in the development and proliferation of companion species and livestock, including the problematic incorporation of so-called "exotic species" into the companion bracket as pets. To all intents and purposes, that original invention of domestication has gone viral. It has spread like contagion, with repeated contact and association.[93] The dogs took the first initiative, "and the contagion of imitation does the rest":[94]

> In the beginning of societies, the art of chipping flint, of domesticating dogs, of making bows, and, later, of leavening bread, of working bronze, of extracting iron, etc., must have spread like a contagion; since every arrow, every flake, every morsel of bread, every thread of bronze, served both as model and copy . . . Every *social thing*, that is to say, every invention or discovery, tends to expands [sic] in its social environment, an environment which itself, I might add, tends to self-expansion, since it is essentially composed of like things, all of which have infinite ambitions.[95]

The remarkable invention is then spread through use, where use in itself is a kind of contagion and at the same time an assurance of the invention itself: "You own your discoveries and inventions all the more, it seems, to the extent that you have propagated them by conversation and discourse."[96] Conversation itself thus becomes a "factor of production."[97] In his comments on the productivity to be found in idle conversation, Tarde, perhaps unwittingly, certainly not inevitably, prefigures the models deployed today by social media platforms in order to produce revenue.[98]

Invention both emerges within, and is constituted by, imitation and use. Regulatory frameworks that co-opt this use and celebrate this alliance, such as available exceptions rather than oppressive limitations, are likely to be the most successful at in fact enforcing the integrity of the work in the first place: "Usage is the most despotic and the most circumstantial of governments, the most rigorous and the best-obeyed kind of legislation."[99]

Indeed, in a digital environment, the mechanism for fair play is perhaps not to be found in further differentiation of space and territory but in the ritual of use and the manners of that use: "those thousand and one traditional or recently established habits which regulate private conduct, not abstractly and from a distance, like law, but close at hand and in every detail, and which include all the artificial wants, all the tastes and distastes, and all the peculiarities of morals and manners which characterise a given country or a given period."[100] Indeed, it is through use that the greatest tool of harmonisation is undoubtedly to be found, whereby habits spread out through usage: "In this sense, usage, like government and law, is connected with religion. It is an offshoot of ritual."[101]

In tune

> 'Men have forgotten this basic truth,' said the fox. 'But you must not forget it. For what you have tamed, you become responsible forever. You are responsible for your rose.'[102]

In the domestication story, the "scavenger" in fact instigated one of the greatest feats of knowledge transfer of all time.[103] Contemporary efforts at further differentiation and division of property, and the greater complication of rights to access resources, would do well to consider canid domestication as a model for reform. *Do with me.*[104]

In the distance from domestication to property, the "taming" has become more and more concerned with a relationship of dominance, of *do as I do*, not *do with me*. The superior model of property relations has been compromised and forgotten. Vinciane Despret speaks of this original domestication relationship as one of attunement and, as such, one that creates the creative. In this remarkable embodied relation between dog and human, the human is "made" to "invent" domestication through further and further imitation. Domestication makes its mark:

> With the notion of 'availability' the signs that mark the world and that mark the subject are redistributed in a new way. Both are active and both are transformed by the availability of the other. Both are articulated by what the other 'makes him/her make'. This is, in my opinion, the most interesting characteristic of the practices that may be defined as practices of domestication, the practices that allow themselves to be pervaded by humans: they are practices that create and transform through the miracle of *attunement*.[105]

In this way, domestication is the ultimate and precipitative creative event. It makes its mark. It calls it into being. It sets up house: "It is the mark that makes the territory."[106] This call, just like that of the fox, just like that of the rose, of the book, of the painting, interpellates and inscribes humans within a relationship of ethical responsibility and shared vulnerability, shared interests.[107] That responsibility will never go away. This responsibility has much in common with the notion of trust that Tarde recognises in the loan, as distinct from the antagonism and exchange of favours that he describes in the relationship of trade.[108] Attunement, trust, this is the "basic truth" of domestication. Today, where is the trust in property? Where is the trust in the consumer? In contemporary property relations, including those found in intellectual property, the model is concerned almost exclusively with consumption, despite the primary and fundamental importance of association. This rings true through the contrived scarcity of property and the literal and material interpretation of the knowledge entity:

> There is another notion of which we have yet to speak, and of which we will simply say that it hardly has any possible application outside of the economic domain; it is therefore, from our current standpoint, the least important of all, despite the fact that economists include it in one of the three or four great divisions of their science: *consumption*. One consumes riches, that is, in order to employ them one must destroy them with greater or lesser speed; and perhaps one could also say that one consumes a power by exercising it, or abusing it; but does one consume one's glory, or even one's credit? Does one consume one's beliefs by thinking about them or the masterpieces that one admires by looking at them? On the contrary, there are two ideas that economists use in a far too restricted manner, those of alliance and struggles, of *adaptation* and *opposition*, ideas which are eminently capable of being generalised. Economists only deal with opposition in terms of the competition between productions or consumptions, and they neglect the hidden and continuous opposition of products which plays a crucial economic role, and they pay no mind either to the invisible alliances of products, to their fecund adaptations.[109]

The principle of scarcity arguably underpins modern conceptualisations of property (importantly, property as a whole, not merely within intellectual property discourse[110]). And as we will see, this "capital structure," as it were, of the asymmetrical contract circulates throughout not only the development of property jurisprudence and the concept of control[111] but also observations of animal behaviour and territory and the very presumptions underpinning the discourse of human exceptionalism.

In summary, conventional approaches to property interpret rights based upon a kind of scarcity or as part of the mechanism that manages scarcity. In this way, property rights are not only and simply a mechanism to exclude and thus generate scarcity but also a response premised upon the very presumption of scarcity itself. This link between scarcity and property rights can be traced to very early considerations of property and justice. Before John Stuart Mill and Adam Smith, the seemingly obligatory figures in contemporary property education, the philosopher David Hume, writing in the early eighteenth century, identified a relationship between scarcity and property rights and, perhaps more strikingly, the integral role this asymmetry[112] plays in the exchange of objects:

> [T]hese are intended as a remedy to some inconveniences, which proceed from the concurrence of certain *qualities* of the human mind with the *situation* of external objects. The qualities of the mind are *selfishness* and *limited generosity*. And the situation of external objects is their *easy change*, join'd to the *scarcity* in comparison of the wants and desires of men.[113]

What is forgotten in this rendering is the potential alliance between products, but as Tarde explains, "a product allies itself to all the previous products that it utilises."[114] There is a kind of sociality that insists through knowledge that is obscured to an extent through its complex differentiation within property: "There is no book, considered as a teaching, which is not made with other books, often given in the bibliography, and among which there are some which one can say that it is made *for* them, because it confirms and completes them."[115] Knowledge products may become tools of other knowledge products. Consumers may be tools of producers. Producers are tools of consumers, of other producers: "There is no product that is not or cannot become the auxiliary of another, the *tool* of another. The distinction between tool and product possesses a merely superficial or relative truth."[116] *Everywhere is music.*

This sociality of knowledge is the "basic truth" of creativity. These alliances are the flavour of property. However, the basic truth has been forgotten: "'But you must not forget it. For what you have tamed, you become responsible forever. You are responsible for your rose.'"[117]

It is time to recover our social life.

Notes

1 See further the discussion of instinct and learning in Chapter 10, "Shared interests."
2 Tarde G (1890/[1903]) *The Laws of Imitation*, EC Parsons (trans.), Henry Holt & Co, New York, 46.
3 This refers to the legend that Columbus, upon being told that his discoveries were perhaps inevitable, challenged his audience to standing an egg on its narrow end. After their many failed attempts, Columbus surprised his audience by tapping the egg gently, flattening the tip, and successfully standing the egg on its narrow end. The story shows that a brilliant and far from inevitable idea may seem easy and inevitable after the fact.
4 Schleidt WM (1998) Is Humaneness Canine?, *Human Ethology Bulletin*, 13(4), 7–20. See further the discussion in Schleidt and Shalter (2018): "To what extent and in which respect the behavior of wolves influenced human behavior, and vice versa, remains in the dark. Among primates, human sociality and parental behavior are amazingly similar to that of social canids. Dogs as companions have found their place in the human social network like no other species. Details are still lacking." Schleidt WM & Shalter MD (2018) Dogs and Mankind: Coevolution on the Move: An Update, *Human Ethology Bulletin*, 33(1), 15–38.

5 Tarde G (1890/[1903]) *The Laws of Imitation*, EC Parsons (trans.), Henry Holt & Co, New York, 277.
6 Franklin H Giddings, in his introduction to Tarde's *Laws of Imitation*, notes Tarde's universal sociology of microphenomena and the relationship to adaptation and invention: "This process is a logic, a synthesis of repetitions. It includes adaptation, invention, and organisation." See Giddings FH (1903) Introduction, in Tarde G (1890/[1903]) *The Laws of Imitation*, EC Parsons (trans.), Henry Holt & Co, New York, iii–vii: p. vi.
7 Arguably, European patent law also betrays a kind of adaptation definition of invention, in that inventive step is interpreted through what is known as the "problem-solution" approach. See European Patent Office, Guidelines for Examination, G-VII-5.
8 Tarde G (1890/[1903]) *The Laws of Imitation*, EC Parsons (trans.), Henry Holt & Co, New York, 141.
9 Tarde G (1899) *Social Laws: An Outline of Sociology*, HC Warren (trans.), Macmillan, New York, 7.
10 Tarde G (1899) *Social Laws: An Outline of Sociology*, HC Warren (trans.), Macmillan, New York, 8 note 1.
11 Contact is especially important in that it challenges the summative explanation of similar innovations in different cultures as "spontaneous," (i.e., "inevitable" and thus not innovative) (Tarde G (1890/[1903]) *The Laws of Imitation*, EC Parsons (trans.), Henry Holt & Co, New York, 325). The concept of culture contact becomes more common in early twentieth-century anthropology, following the work of late nineteenth-century anthropologists and ethnologists, such as Joseph Jacobs: "But if England is in culture-contact, mediate or immediate, with countries where junior right exists, it becomes a race between independent origin and borrowing; and to assume independent origin is to bet against the bank of Time with its unlimited means." See Jacobs J (1893) The Folk, *Folklore*, 4(2), 233–238: p. 236.
12 Imitation and social learning is an important area of ethological research into the concept of culture in animal societies, and the practice of overimitation as a particularly acute example of affiliative behaviour and cultural awareness. See the detailed discussion in "Part 4, Altruism, the social age."
13 Tarde G (1902/[2007]) Economic Psychology, A Toscano (trans.), *Economy and Society*, 36(4), 614–643: p. 638.
14 Tarde G (1899) *Social Laws: An Outline of Sociology*, HC Warren (trans.), Macmillan, New York, 116.
15 Tarde G (1899) *Social Laws: An Outline of Sociology*, HC Warren (trans.), Macmillan, New York, 116 translator's footnote 1: "the French word *concurrence*, which the author uses, means both competition and concurrent action." See Tarde G (1898) *Les lois Sociales: esquisses d'une sociologie*, Félix Alcan, Paris, 92.
16 The nature of cooperation in natural selection is explored in more detail in Chapter 10, "Shared interests."
17 In his 1892 treatise, *Principles of Ethics*, Spencer declares: "If we define altruism as being all action which, in the normal course of things, benefits others instead of benefiting self, then, from the dawn of life, altruism has been no less essential than egoism. Though primarily it is dependent on egoism, yet secondarily egoism is dependent on it" (§75). Although Spencer emphasises the fundamental value of egoism as self-protection (§68), echoing the individualistic approach to survival of the fittest discourse, the relationship is nevertheless mutually constitutive and essential.
18 Deleuze G & Guattari F (1980/[1987]) *A Thousand Plateaus: Capitalism and Schizophrenia*, B Massumi (trans.), U of Minnesota P, Minneapolis, 481.

19 Tarde G (1890/[1903]) *The Laws of Imitation*, EC Parsons (trans.), Henry Holt & Co, New York, 277.
20 Malinowski B (1944) *A Scientific Theory of Culture and Other Essays*, U of North Carolina P, Chapel Hill, 194. Malinowski's anthropology is considered further in later chapters, particularly Chapter 4, "Marking territory"; and Chapter 7, "Predatory drift."
21 Malinowski B (1944) *A Scientific Theory of Culture and Other Essays*, U of North Carolina P, Chapel Hill, 194.
22 See further the discussion of the mythologies and misconceptions surrounding "pack theory" in popular training discourse, and the attending welfare issues, in Chapter 8, "Pack fiction."
23 Schleidt WM & Shalter MD (2003) Co-Evolution of Humans and Canids: An Alternative View of Dog Domestication: *Homo Homini Lupus?*, *Evolution and Cognition*, 9(1), 57–71: p. 68.
24 Tarde G (1890/[1903]) *The Laws of Imitation*, EC Parsons (trans.), Henry Holt & Co, New York, 287.
25 Tarde G (1890/[1903]) *The Laws of Imitation*, EC Parsons (trans.), Henry Holt & Co, New York, 287.
26 Tarde G (1890/[1903]) *The Laws of Imitation*, EC Parsons (trans.), Henry Holt & Co, New York, 277.
27 Wilson PJ (2009) *The Domestication of the Human Species*, Yale UP, New Haven, xi.
28 This comes from the work of Gabriel Tarde (discussed further below), who saw the creation of home and settlement (through domestication) as the precursor to society. Tarde uses the term "household" to explain the kind of productive associations that are "family" (over and beyond actual circles of heredity) and to which he attributes the origin of the social group. See in particular the discussion in Tarde G (1969) *On Communication and Social Influence*, TN Clark (ed.), U of Chicago P, Chicago, 129–131.
29 Wilson PJ (2009) *The Domestication of the Human Species*, Yale UP, New Haven, 3.
30 Schleidt WM & Shalter MD (2018) Dogs and Mankind: Coeevolution on the Move: An Update, *Human Ethology Bulletin*, 33(1), 15–38.
31 Schleidt WM & Shalter MD (2018) Dogs and Mankind: Coeevolution on the Move: An Update, *Human Ethology Bulletin*, 33(1), 15–38.
32 Kafka F (1992/[1922]) Investigations of a Dog, Muir W & Muir E (trans.), in Glatzer NN (ed.) *Kafka: The Complete Short Stories*, Minerva, London, 278–316: p. 281.
33 Frantz LAF et al. (2016) Genomic and Archaeological Evidence Suggests a Dual Origin of Domestic Dogs, *Science*, 352, 1228–1231. See further the reports of the research in Hirschler B (2016) How Dogs Became Man's Best Friend: Twice over, *Reuters*, 2 June; Blakemore E (2016) Ruff News: Man's Best Friend May Have Been Domesticated Twice, *Smithsonian*, 2 June.
34 Tarde G (1890/[1903]) *The Laws of Imitation*, EC Parsons (trans.), Henry Holt & Co, New York, 99.
35 Botigué LR et al. (2017) Ancient European Dog Genomes Reveal Continuity since the Early Neolithic, *Nature*, 18 July. See further the report in Guarino B (2017) Your Dog's Ancestor Came from a Group of Wolves 40,000 Years Ago, Study Says, *The Washington Post*, 18 July.
36 Krishna R Veeramah, one of the authors of the study, quoted in Daley J (2017) New Study Has a Bone to Pick with Dog Domestication Findings, *Smithsonian*, 19 July.
37 In psychology the concept of embodiment largely refers to the constitution of human cognition through physical environmental interactions, including morphological, sensory, and motor systems, and is particularly influenced by

phenomenology and the critique of Cartesianism. In relation to language and communication, embodiment is emerging as a growing area of research: Glenberg AM & Kaschak MP (2002) Grounding Language in Action, *Psychonomic Bulletin & Review*, 9, 558–565; Pulvermuller F (2005) Brain Mechanisms Linking Language and Action, *Nature Reviews Neuroscience*, 6, 576–582.

38 See further the discussion in Chapter 6, "Separation anxiety." See also the discussion of radical behaviourism and the emphasis on the physically observable, through to the shift to embodied cognition, in Chapter 10, "Shared interests."

39 On situatedness in cognition and communication see: Barsalou LW (2008) Grounded Cognition, *Annual Review of Psychology*, 59, 617–645; Barsalou LW (2016) Situated Conceptualization: Theory and Applications, in Coello Y & Fischer MH (eds.) *Foundations of Embodied Cognition, Volume 1: Perceptual and Emotional Embodiment*, Psychology P, East Sussex, 11–37; Da Rold F (2018) Defining Embodied Cognition: The Problem of Situatedness, *New Ideas in Psychology*, 51, 9–14.

40 See Chapter 10, "Shared interests," with respect to cooperative behaviour and incentives to altruism and the discussion in Roch SG & Samuelson CD (1997) Effects of Environmental Uncertainty and Social Value Orientation in Resource Dilemmas, *Organizational Behavior and Human Decision Processes*, 70(3), 221–235: p. 230.

41 It is in this respect that the early twentieth-century jurisprudence of Wesley Newcomb Hohfeld recasts property relations through the prism of sociality, as explored in greater detail in "Part 4, Altruism, the social age" (particularly Chapter 11, "Resocialisation").

42 The concept of embodied communication has been explored in detail in relation to animals in the work of anthropologist and psychologist, Barbara Smuts, work which has been especially influential in reviewing interspecies communication and animal languages. See in particular Smuts B (2007) Embodied Communication in Non-Human Animals, in Fogel A et al. (eds.) *Human Development in the Twenty-First Century*, Cambridge UP, Cambridge, 136–146.

43 Smuts B (2007) Embodied Communication in Non-Human Animals, in Fogel A et al. (eds.) *Human Development in the Twenty-First Century*, Cambridge UP, Cambridge, 136–146: p. 137.

44 Haraway D (2008) *When Species Meet*, U of Minnesota P, Minneapolis, 4.

45 Deleuze G & Guattari F (1991/[1994]) *What Is Philosophy?*, H Tomlinson & G Burchill (trans.), Verso, London, 184. See further the discussion in Chapter 4, "Marking territory." The creativity and authorship of animals is considered further in Gibson J (forthcoming) *More Than Human Intellectual Property*, Routledge, London.

46 Tarde G (1890/[1903]) *The Laws of Imitation*, EC Parsons (trans.), Henry Holt & Co, New York, 71.

47 As Tarde notes, this emphasis on individuality obscures the true genius of associative encounters: "In its age-long effort to interpret everything outside us in terms of mechanism, even those things which most break forth with accumulated signs of genius, namely living beings, our mind as it were blows out all the lights of the world for the sole benefit of its own little spark." See Tarde G (1893/[2012]) *Monadology and Sociology*, T Lorenc (trans.), Re-Press, Melbourne, pp. 22–23.

48 Tarde G (1890/[1903]) *The Laws of Imitation*, EC Parsons (trans.), Henry Holt & Co, New York, 69–70.

49 Tarde G (1890/[1903]) *The Laws of Imitation*, EC Parsons (trans), Henry Holt & Co, New York, 68.

50 Deleuze and Guattari channel Tarde's imitative sociality in their concept of assemblage (*agencement*) in *A Thousand Plateaus*. The original French term, *agencement* (literally layout), is enticing in this context in that it points to the

spread and cartography of the kind of imitative sociality that Tarde is imagining. The collective and network character of the assemblage and its emergent potential resonate very familiarly and seductively with Tarde's approach.

51 Smuts B (2008) Embodied Communication in Non-Human Animals, in Fogel A et al. (eds.) *Human Development in the Twenty-First Century: Visionary Ideas from Systems Scientists*, Cambridge UP, Cambridge, 136–146: p. 137.
52 The critical concept of sympathy is explored in more detail in Chapter 3, "Socialisation".
53 Tarde G (1890/[1903]) *The Laws of Imitation*, EC Parsons (trans.), Henry Holt & Co, New York, 79 note 8. As Tarde explains, sympathy is the reciprocal dimension of which prestige is the unilateral substrate: "If, then, I have put prestige, and not sympathy, at the foundation and origin of society, it is because, as I have said before, the unilateral must have preceded the reciprocal." (79). This is notable in the context of Tarde's emphasis on the later reciprocal innovation of the social contract and, with that, the understanding of the social as territorial and ultimately towards the predatory drift of property. Indeed, Andrea Brighenti argues that "every type of social tie can be imagined and constructed as territorial": Brighenti A (2006) On Territory as Relationship and Law as Territory, *Canadian Journal of Law and Society/Revue Canadienne Droit et Société*, 21(2), 65–86: pp. 66–67. This argument is especially meaningful when considered in the context of early pastoral relations and the domestication narrative anatomised in the previous chapter, particularly the way in which these early interspecies relationships to territory are ultimately transformed through the predatory drift of contemporary property structures. This is discussed in greater detail in Chapter 4, "Marking territory"; and Chapter 7, "Predatory drift."
54 Tarde G (1890/[1903]) *The Laws of Imitation*, EC Parsons (trans.), Henry Holt & Co, New York, xiii.
55 Tarde G (1893/[2012]) *Monadology and Sociology*, T Lorenc (trans.), Re-Press, Melbourne, 15.
56 Deleuze G & Guattari F (1980/[1987]) *A Thousand Plateaus: Capitalism and Schizophrenia*, B Massumi (trans.), U of Minnesota P, Minneapolis, 219.
57 Bergson H (1907/[1944]) *Creative Evolution*, A Mitchell (trans.), Random House, New York, 194.
58 Bergson H (1907/[1944]) *Creative Evolution*, A Mitchell (trans.), Random House, New York, 191.
59 Bergson H (1907/[1944]) *Creative Evolution*, A Mitchell (trans.), Random House, New York, 191.
60 Bergson H (1907/[1944]) *Creative Evolution*, A Mitchell (trans.), Random House, New York, 194.
61 This is discussed again in greater detail in Chapter 4, "Marking territory."
62 Deleuze G & Guattari F (1991/[1994]) *What Is Philosophy?*, H Tomlinson & G Burchill (trans.), Verso, London, 184. See further discussion of territory, sociality, and creativity in "Part 2, Territory, the space age." The creativity and authorship of animals is considered further in Gibson J (forthcoming) *More Than Human Intellectual Property*, Routledge, London.
63 Deleuze G & Guattari F (1980/[1987]) *A Thousand Plateaus: Capitalism and Schizophrenia*, B Massumi (trans.), U of Minnesota P, Minneapolis, 316.
64 Gabriel Tarde in Tarde G & Durkheim É (2008) The Debate between Tarde and Durkheim, EV Vargas et al. (script), A Damle & M Candea (trans.), *Environment and Planning D: Society and Space*, 26, 761–777: p. 775.
65 Bruno Latour describes Tarde as "a thinker of networks before their time." See Latour B (2001) Gabriel Tarde and the End of the Social, *Soziale Welt: Zeitschrift für Sozialwissenschaftliche Forschung und Praxis*, 52, 361–81: p. 362.

66 Gilles Deleuze in interview with Claire Parnét. *L'abécédaire de Gilles Deleuze*, Pierre-André Boutang and Michel Pamart (dir), 1996. Transcript D Hurth (trans.).
67 Tarde G (1890/[1903]) *The Laws of Imitation*, EC Parsons (trans.), Henry Holt & Co, New York, 277.
68 Tarde G (1890/[1903]) *The Laws of Imitation*, EC Parsons (trans.), Henry Holt & Co, New York, 74.
69 Tarde G (1890/[1903]) *The Laws of Imitation*, EC Parsons (trans.), Henry Holt & Co, New York, 67 note 1.
70 Deleuze G & Guattari F (1991/[1994]) *What Is Philosophy?*, H Tomlinson & G Burchill (trans.), Verso, London, 183.
71 Deleuze G & Guattari F (1991/[1994]) *What Is Philosophy?*, H Tomlinson & G Burchill (trans.), Verso, London, 183.
72 Schleidt WM & Shalter MD (2003) Co-Evolution of Humans and Canids: An Alternative View of Dog Domestication: *Homo Homini Lupus?*, *Evolution and Cognition*, 9(1), 57–71: p. 69. See further Schleidt WM (1998) Is Humaneness Canine?, *Human Ethology Bulletin*, 13(4), 7–20; Schleidt WM & Shalter MD (2003) Co-Evolution of Humans and Canids: An Alternative View of Dog Domestication: *Homo Homini Lupus?*, *Evolution and Cognition*, 9(1), 57–71: p. 67: "a group of Neanderthals could have eased their way into the thriving business of wolf pastoralists, at first only as junior partners, and have shared the plenty of those large reindeer herds without raising the level of intra-pack social friction."
73 Tarde G (1890/[1903]) *The Laws of Imitation*, EC Parsons (trans.), Henry Holt & Co, New York, 382.
74 Tarde G (1890/[1903]) *The Laws of Imitation*, EC Parsons (trans.), Henry Holt & Co, New York, 74.
75 In particular, once more likely to hunt each other rather than larger animals, such as wolves, domestication likely diminished cannibalism with the presentation of alternative food sources. For instance, on cannibalism behaviour, including endocannibalism (i.e., within the family group itself) see Patou-Mathis et al. (2018) The Evidence from Vindija Cave (Croatia) Reveals Diversity of Neandertal Behaviour in Europe, *Quarternary International*, 23(6), 314–326.
76 Tarde G (1890/[1903]) *The Laws of Imitation*, EC Parsons (trans.), Henry Holt & Co, New York, 368.
77 Schleidt WM & Shalter MD (2018) Dogs and Mankind: Coeevolution on the Move: An Update, *Human Ethology Bulletin*, 33(1), 15–38. There is accumulating evidence that, contrary to the figure of the mighty hunter, early humans were omnivorous and survived primarily on a vegetarian diet and foraging. See Fiorenza L et al. (2015) To Meat or Not to Meat? New Perspectives on Neandertal Ecology, *American Journal of Physical Anthropology*, 156(S59), 43–71; Hardy K et al. (2015) The Importance of Dietary Carbohydrate in Human Evolution, *The Quarterly Review of Biology*, 90(3), c251–c268. See further Estalrrich A et al. (2017) Dietary Reconstruction of the El Sidrón Neandertal Familial Group (Spain) in the Context of Other Neandertal and Modern Hunter-Gatherer Groups: A Molar Microwear Texture Analysis, *Journal of Human Evolution*, 104, 13–22.
78 Tarde G (1969) *On Communication and Social Influence*, TN Clark (ed.), U of Chicago P, Chicago, 129–131.
79 Tarde G (1969) *On Communication and Social Influence*, TN Clark (ed.), U of Chicago P, Chicago, 81.
80 Tarde G (1890/[1903]) *The Laws of Imitation*, EC Parsons (trans.), Henry Holt & Co, New York, 381.

81 Deleuze G (1968/[1994]) *Difference and Repetition*, P Patton (trans.), Columbia UP, New York, 23.
82 Tarde G (1890/[1903]) *The Laws of Imitation*, EC Parsons (trans.), Henry Holt & Co, New York, 74. Sergio Tonkonoff notes: "Tarde called imitation a type of social bond in which someone offers him or herself, voluntarily or involuntarily, as a model, and someone else, consciously or unconsciously, copies him or her." Tonkonoff S (2017) *From Tarde to Deleuze and Foucault: The Infinitesimal Revolution*, Palgrave Macmillan, Cham, Switzerland, 29.
83 Tarde G (1890/[1903]) *The Laws of Imitation*, EC Parsons (trans.), Henry Holt & Co, New York, xiv.
84 See further the discussion in Gibson J (2006) *Creating Selves: Intellectual Property and the Narration of Culture*, Ashgate, Aldershot, 138–139.
85 Tarde G (1890/[1903]) *The Laws of Imitation*, EC Parsons (trans.), Henry Holt & Co, New York, 325.
86 Udell MAR et al. (2008) Wolves Outperform Dogs in Following Human Social Cues, *Animal Behaviour*, 76, 1767–1773: "domestication is not a prerequisite for human-like social cognition in canids" (1767). The authors conclude: "Our results clearly show that wolves, given proper socialization and daily experience with humans, are not only capable of following a human cue, but in some cases outperform domestic dogs. . . . This finding shows that domestication alone cannot be responsible for an individual's untrained sensitivity to human cues" (1771).
87 Essler JL et al. (2017) Domestication Does Not Explain the Presence of Inequity Aversion in Dogs, *Current Biology*, 27, 1861–1865.
88 Tarde G (1890/[1903]) *The Laws of Imitation*, EC Parsons (trans.), Henry Holt & Co, New York, 382.
89 See further the more detailed examination of animal creativity in the context of intellectual property in Gibson J (forthcoming) *More Than Human Intellectual Property: Animal Authors and Human Machines*, Routledge, London.
90 Tarde G (1890/[1903]) *The Laws of Imitation*, EC Parsons (trans.), Henry Holt & Co, New York, 382–383.
91 Saint-Exupéry A de (1943/[1995]) *The Little Prince*, I Testot-Ferry (trans.), Wordsworth, London, 76–79.
92 Saint-Exupéry A de (1943/[1995]) *The Little Prince*, I Testot-Ferry (trans.), Wordsworth, London, 82.
93 Responding to contagion and imitation in Tarde, Vinciane Despret utilises this approach in an analysis of the constitution of animal celebrity in social media and the engagement of the public in welfare discourse. See Despret V (2016) *What Would Animals Say If We Asked the Right Questions?*, Buchanan B (trans.) Minnesota UP, Minneapolis, 195–201. This can be seen also in her discussion of interspecies transplants or xenotransplants, which she describes as "a process of co-opting strangers." (191).
94 Tarde G (1890/[1903]) *The Laws of Imitation*, EC Parsons (trans.), Henry Holt & Co, New York, 4 note 1.
95 Tarde G (1890/[1903]) *The Laws of Imitation*, EC Parsons (trans.), Henry Holt & Co, New York, 17.
96 Tarde G (1902/[2007]) Economic Psychology, A Toscano (trans.), *Economy and Society*, 36(4), 614–643: p. 616.
97 Latour B & Lepinjay VA (2009) *The Science of Passionate Interests*, Prickly Paradigm Press, Chicago, 2.
98 See the discussion in Latour B & Lepinjay VA (2009) *The Science of Passionate Interests*, Prickly Paradigm Press, Chicago, 2.

99 Tarde G (1890/[1903]) *The Laws of Imitation*, EC Parsons (trans.), Henry Holt & Co, New York, 322.
100 Tarde G (1890/[1903]) *The Laws of Imitation*, EC Parsons (trans.), Henry Holt & Co, New York, 322.
101 Tarde G (1890/[1903]) *The Laws of Imitation*, EC Parsons (trans.), Henry Holt & Co, New York, 322.
102 Saint-Exupéry A de (1943/[1995]) *The Little Prince*, I Testot-Ferry (trans.), Wordsworth, London, 82.
103 Schleidt WM & Shalter MD (2003) Co-Evolution of Humans and Canids: An Alternative View of Dog Domestication: Homo Homini Lupus?, *Evolution and Cognition*, 9(1), 57–72. The authors note: "Within this process of coevolution, technology transfer and diversification began to thrive" (68).
104 Deleuze G (1968/[1994]) *Difference and Repetition*, P Patton (trans.), Columbia UP, New York, 23.
105 Despret V (2004) The Body We Care For: Figures of Anthropo-zoo-genesis, *Body & Society*, 10(2–3), 111–134: p. 125. Attunement is also linked to empathetic behaviour, discussed in more detail in Chapter 10, "Shared interests."
106 Deleuze G & Guattari F (1980/[1987]) *A Thousand Plateaus: Capitalism and Schizophrenia*, B Massumi (trans.), U of Minnesota P, Minneapolis, 315.
107 Kari Weil notes, "Like art, animals call us (pace Levinas) to witness our own and the other's time-bound, vulnerable existence." See Weil K (2012) *Thinking Animals: Why Animal Studies Now?*, Columbia UP, New York, 126.
108 Latour B & Lepinjay VA (2009) *The Science of Passionate Interests*, Prickly Paradigm Press, Chicago, 37–38. See further the discussion of the relationship between debt and morality in Gibson J (2014) *The Logic of Innovation*, Ashgate, Aldershot, 78.
109 Tarde G (1902/[2007]) Economic Psychology, A Toscano (trans.), *Economy and Society*, 36(4), 614–643: p. 620.
110 See further the discussion in Faraci D (2014) Do Property Rights Presuppose Scarcity?, *Journal of Business Ethics*, 125(3), 531–537: p. 539. David Faraci describes what he calls "the need to divorce the debate over this thesis (of scarcity) from the debate of Intellectual Property (IP) rights (the area where it is most frequently applied)" (531).
111 The concept of control is explored in more detail in Chapter 7, Predatory drift"; and Chapter 8, "Pack fiction." In relation to the development of control in the context of the scarcity thesis of Hume and Rawls, see Xenos N (1987) Liberalism and the Postulate of Scarcity, *Political Theory*, 15(2), 225–243. Nicholas Xenos notes that Rawls's position is "that people existing in a scarce environment must find some authoritative basis for the allocation of goods, and this takes him to the economic rationality of the neoclassical scarcity postulate to work out his theory of justice" (237). Indeed, scarcity is the underlying value coordinating the discourse of evolution and natural selection (through competition for resources, for mates and reproduction, and so on) as well as theories of domestication (such as the scavenger hypothesis), right through to its role as an organising principle of contemporary property discourse.
112 See also the discussion of the so-called bourgeois strategy as an evolutionarily stable strategy in Maynard Smith J (1982) *Evolution and the theory of Games*, Cambridge UP, Cambridge, 22.
113 Hume D (1739–1740/[1969]) *A Treatise of Human Nature*, Penguin, London, Book III, Sect II. See further the discussion in Xenos N (1987) Liberalism and the Postulate of Scarcity, *Political Theory*, 15(2), 225–243. Hume's approach is resonant with the contractarian approach identified with Thomas Hobbes and

his concept of desire that underpins proprietary-like motivations. See further Hobbes T (1651/[1909]) *Hobbes's Leviathan*, Clarendon Press, Oxford. On the Contractarian approach in Hume see Gauthier D (1979) David Hume, Contractarian, *The Philosophical Review*, 88(1), 3–38. This central device of the social contract in the contractarian approach betrays a reliance on an original social contract, an "original" relationship identified as a mythic device by Tarde in his rejection of the social contract as the fundamental social relationship.

114 Tarde G (1902/[2007]) Economic Psychology, A Toscano (trans.), *Economy and Society*, 36(4), 614–643: p. 621. Tarde provides an insightful example based upon wheat, as translated and cited by Latour and Lepinjay: "Before the broadening of the markets and the institution of Stock Exchanges, there were no forward sales to tyrannically fix the price of wheat. But was the price of wheat, under the Ancien Regime for example, determined by the real insufficiency or overabundance of wheat in a given region, or at a given time? No. At that time, when people were very ill-informed, when one knew only the harvest of one's own village, abundance or scarcity was judged based on the amount of wheat brought into the market hall of the little neighbouring town. It was enough for a few monopolizers (for there were indeed such people then, just as today there are big bankers who play on the Stock Markets), to drain the harvests of one or two towns, or to stock their own harvest (in the case of large landowners), to create the appearance of an entirely artificial scarcity, which resulted nonetheless, as if it had been real, in a prodigious hike in the price of wheat." See Latour B & Lepinjay VA (2009) *The Science of Passionate Interests*, Prickly Paradigm Press, Chicago, 62.

115 Tarde G (1902/[2007]) Economic Psychology, A Toscano (trans.), *Economy and Society*, 36(4), 614–643: p. 621.

116 Tarde G (1902/[2007]) Economic Psychology, A Toscano (trans.), *Economy and Society*, 36(4), 614–643: p. 621.

117 Saint-Exupéry A de (1943/[1995]) *The Little Prince*, I Testot-Ferry (trans.), Wordsworth, London, 82.

Chapter 3
Socialisation

> Dogs who make no reply to the greeting of other dogs are guilty of an offense against good manners which the humblest dog would never pardon any more than the greatest. Perhaps they were not dogs at all? But how should they not be dogs? Could I not actually hear on listening more closely the subdued cries with which they encouraged each other, drew each other's attention to difficulties, warned each other against errors; could I not see the last and youngest dog, to whom most of those cries were addressed, often stealing a glance at me as if he would have dearly wished to reply, but refrained because it was not allowed? But why should it not be allowed, why should the very thing which our laws unconditionally command not be allowed in this one case?
>
> Kafka F (1931/[1992]) Investigations of a Dog, W Muir & E Muir (trans), in Kafka F (1992) *Kafka: The Complete Short Stories*, Minerva, London, 278–316: p. 283

There is a cartoon by Dave Coverly, creator of the Speedbump cartoon panel, which depicts an adult wolf and a wolf cub rifling through a backpack that has been left behind in the woods. There is a plastic bottle on the ground, apparently discarded by the wolf cub as they searched through the bag. The adult wolf says to the wolf cub, "Hey, don't just throw that on the ground! What were you raised by, people?" In other words, civility comes from the canids. As this chapter will explore, this cartoon may well fit into the "funny because it's true" category.

In the previous chapters of the Stone Age, the "property" relations of domestication have emerged as inherently social, mutually constitutive, productive, and reproductive. As the previous chapters have tracked, domestication itself was not only facilitated by a mutual interest in the human-dog bond but also arguably attended by behaviours and customs indicative of a familial bond. To domesticate is to make home, to make family.

The definition of the process of socialisation in animal behaviour is curiously similar to that provided for domestication:[1] "Socialisation is the process by which animals adopt the behaviour patterns appropriate to the social environment in which they live, allowing them to coexist/interact with other individuals."[2] Once again it is a process through which animals assimilate with the largely human constraints of their social environments, the expectations of society, as it were. In many respects, the conventional language of taming and "manners" infuses the popular dog training discourse on the concept of socialisation. Socialisation, therefore, is about achieving the result of acceptable behaviour, folding into society. Unfortunately, in some respects, this invites contentious departures from good welfare in finding ways to achieve that result rather than focusing on the enrichment of the process: "the ways that dogs are produced as 'domestic' bodies . . . being disciplined in new ways that reflect changing social, cultural and economic imperatives around homemaking and pet-keeping that have emerged across post-industrial nations since the 1980s. In this context a disciplined dog is part of the performance of respectable middle-class identities."[3]

In other words, a conscientious approach focused on enforcing the ends may miss the many opportunities presented by the means. In some respects, this perverse view of socialisation as a result as distinct from a process is part of the predatory drift of property, examined in more detail in later chapters,[4] as manifest through dog ownership. The understanding of socialisation is at the same time habituation, to make habits, to adjust, and to accustom to social institutions and norms. However, through the lens of a predatory property model, there is an implied link between socialisation and the enforcement of those norms. Indeed, in dog training discourse socialisation is very much a part of that assimilation and indeed adhering to social rules.[5] It is thus implied that an unsocialised dog is consequently an aberrant misanthrope to be made subject to the coercive nature of society through further training or rehabilitation.[6] The popular discourse on owners and "inappropriate social behaviour" reinstates the centrality of ownership within the dominant property system less in terms of its social and legal relations and more as the kind of authoritative parameter within which to contain that unruly dog. In other words, the socialisation of dogs becomes a scandal of public order.[7]

However, this drift in property discourse is a significant departure from the kind of social relations presented through socialisation. As will be considered in the chapters in the Machine Age, the nature of ownership has become distorted and at the same time attenuated. As the *fin de siècle* German jurist, Rudolf von Jhering, asserts, property is fundamentally social and thus responsible; the notion of the owner's absolute dominion is simply a matter of belief, not of law:

> Jurists and laymen agree in the view that the essence of property consists in the unlimited control of the owner, and that every restriction is essentially an encroachment upon it, which is incompatible with the idea of the institution. How is this? My view is that this conception is fundamentally wrong. The relation of property to society is subject to the same conditions as that of the family.[8]

This proprietary-like approach to relationships is ubiquitous, and yet even in interpreting behaviour this has been erroneous, or at best misleading.[9] Both the sociology of Tarde and the work of domestication science uncover the somewhat machined moves, as it were, from the family as the original social unit to the contentious and indeed constructed properties of today. Similar property-led presumptions have also influenced early research in wolves. Instead of studying families, wolves were studied as contrived "packs," placing a group of wolves previously unknown to each other in a situation wholly unfamiliar. The result was anxiety, fear, and aggression. Despite being discredited decades later and revised with the current wisdom of the stable wolf family, this mythology of the wolf pack continues to influence dog behaviour and training discourse. The legitimacy of property models has similarly relied upon the contrived pack, the populist notion of the public, and the scope of property rights (from land through to intellectual property) comes to be understood not through its relations but through its enforcement, in defiance of the creative sociability of the original canine model presented in that first domestication.[10] This is what may be termed the "predatory drift" in property.[11]

This emphasis on an enforceable behavioural paradigm, as it were, is especially interesting in the context of the historical development of western conventions of rivalrous property. Domestication science provides a radical repositioning on the very nature of proprietary rivalry. Rather than a logical approach to survival, dominant property paradigms emerge as a kind of drift away from the sociability of the earlier models presented in canine domestication, the very basis upon which settlements were built. Rather than the conventional wisdom of "survival of the fittest", a competitive "free trade" of domestication success, a wholesale battle for settlement, a warring marketplace of intellectual properties, instead a sociable model of property becomes startlingly meaningful. It's not business. It is personal.

No things attached

Throughout the training literature there are frequent references to "critical periods" for socialisation, which owe much to Konrad Lorenz and theories of imprinting.[12] However, the socialisation concept also draws upon theories of attachment for its definition.[13] While imprinting is understood to be a rapid and mechanistic event of innate behaviour, attachment is a longer and extended process of social bonding and enlargement:[14] *A bond of slow formation*.[15] This inextricability of imprinting and attachment, otherwise distinct and separate in terms of the binarisation of instinct and intelligence, recalls the intuition of Henri Bergson and his interest in the interaction between instinct and intelligence: "such a doctrine does not only facilitate speculation; it gives us also more power to act and to live. For, with it, we feel ourselves no longer isolated in humanity, humanity no longer seems isolated in the nature that it dominates."[16] This intercommunication of imprinting and attachment is appealing in its resonance with Tarde's anti-Cartesianism; that is, socialisation introduces reciprocity, the joy of social bonds, of sociable property, beings no longer isolated by things but enthralled in conversation.

Where conventional property models are rivalrous and isolating, attachment grows and thrives through recognition and, importantly, attribution. The value of attribution in a sociable property model is discussed in more detail later,[17] but attribution is integral to a sociable property model in that it recognises beings, parties within social and legal relations, and motivates ongoing socialisation. That reciprocity and respect is unshackled from things and inheres in the relations between beings, between partners; attribution is thus a manifestation or accountability of that recognition and a fundamental value of sociability. Lack of recognition – lack of socialisation, as it were – results in loss of motivation, apprehension, fearfulness and possibly even aggression. Attribution is thus key to an incentive to contact, to participate, to create. In this way, socialisation brings to the fore Tarde's emphatic, "matter is mind, nothing more."[18]

These same theories of attachment have been suggested to provide further insight into the domestication process itself,[19] introducing an interesting perspective upon bonds between scavengers. As discussed earlier, this interaction between attachment, domestication, and socialisation is quite simply touching: "Lorenz uses his own body as a tool for knowing, as a tool for asking questions, as a means to create a relation that provides new knowledge."[20]

The importance of these bonds of attachment to a sociable property is that this reciprocity introduces correlative respect and responsibilities.[21] From a biological point of view, these can be recognised not only in relationships of cooperation but also, and perhaps more notably, in altruistic behaviour. Indeed, as will emerge throughout the discussion, the correlative structure of sociability is indeed harnessed through the developing concept of shared interests.[22]

In the process of domestication and enculturation, what came first? The dog or the pet? In other words, to what extent can the bases for the qualities of compassion, caring, and indeed "humanity" in the modern human be found in that first domestication?

Pet, me

There is evidence that the kind of care and attachment characteristic of a human-pet relationship is not in fact a recent development but is indeed apparent in the relationships between ancient humans and dogs. Curiously, it appears that dogs created petkeeping in what was perhaps the first genuine social enlargement of the human family, considerably earlier than the narrative of bourgeois Victorian pet-keeping might have us believe.[23] Indeed, the presumption that pet-keeping is a middle-class and ostensibly Victorian phenomenon is in and of itself further evidence of the predatory drift in property from the sociality of interspecies relations to the commodification of the dog as property. Arguably, this sort of reckoning within predatory property of that dog's history is complicit in the anthropodenial and exceptionalism that forgoes a wider understanding of personhood,[24] as well as the over-simplification of nomadic and traditional societies: *Terra nullius*. In other words, this interpretation feeds into the classical anthropological perspective upon so-called primitive societies as without property, without law, without society.[25] To all intents and purposes, as it were, dogs humanised humans. The pet is an entirely social and proliferative relationship and one that has existed for thousands of years, long before the Victorians. It was humans that turned these relationships into economies of property.[26]

A significant piece of evidence of the ancient pet relationship comes from the remains of the Bonn-Oberkassel dog who lived around 14,000 years ago.[27]

Subsequent examination of the remains has shown that this dog died of canine distemper, a very serious disease today, and with a very high mortality even if treated. In this particular case, obviously without the availability of resources of modern veterinary medicine, the dog died at 27–28 weeks. Its human companions subsequently gave the deceased dog a burial.

As the authors of the study explain, canine distemper is a prolonged illness, usually of several weeks. In this case the dog suffered three disease bouts in a very short life, and so the human companions must have been caring for this dog quite intensively.[28] Indeed, without intensive care the dog would have likely died much earlier, most likely when first afflicted. Further, the Bonn-Oberkassel dog was a very young dog, and so any notion that its value was purely utilitarian is unconvincing: "the inferred supportive care probably was due to compassion or empathy, without any expectation of reciprocal utilitarian benefits. We suggest that the Bonn-Oberkassel dog provides the earliest known evidence for a purely emotion-driven human-dog interaction."[29] As the researchers state, these findings "provide evidence that early dogs may have been regarded and treated as a pet . . . from their very beginning, already in the Pleistocene."[30]

Archaeological evidence from the Cis-Baikal region of Siberia also shows that dogs were given formal burials, very similar to those of humans, as soon as cemeteries themselves were established over 8000 years ago.[31] While animistic systems do recognise animals other than humans as having souls,[32] unlike Cartesian characterisation of animals as machines, animal souls are understood as cycling through the species itself, as distinct from the individual.[33] This is consistent with the language of commodification and generalisation that attends "the" animal, whether by species, breed, or region. Rather than an individual, considerations are generalised at all times to the group and this emphasis is persistent in animal-related discourse right through to the way in which the law attempts to negotiate questions of welfare and suffering, calculated at the level of the group.

However, there is evidence that in animistic systems, dogs, like humans and in contrast to most other species, are recognised as having souls unique to the individual.[34] Indeed, dogs are persons.[35] This is perhaps the kind of cryptography necessary in order to navigate the labyrinth of interspecies subjectivities. Once again, a cryptographer is needed, "someone who can at once account for nature and decipher the soul, who can peer into the crannies of matter and read into the folds of the soul.[36]

And once again, that dog is our cryptographer.

The invention of morality

As seen in earlier discussions, the theory of self-domestication is a significant expansion of canine social accountability, introducing a sense of morality, but not in the sense of an "all too human" morality. Rather, this is a morality of sociality, "herd morality," if you like, to introduce Nietzsche's interrogation of morality and domestication: "Morality is herd instinct in the individual."[37] But for Nietzsche, and in contrast to the popular discourse on domestication, this is not a morality of dominion, but one of cooperation; the cooperative family as distinct from the mythology of the aggressive pack.[38] It is the process of domestication, the family, the making of the household. The first domestication in many ways set forth this household-making sociality, constituting the first interactions with morality for humans. Indeed, this concept of "family" is a precondition for the kind of "social contract" imagined for an enlarging society. The family (not merely in the biological sense) is integral to the constitution of moral and accountable relations within that sociality and draws much from a greater understanding of such groups in animal assemblages as well.

Interestingly, Nietzsche draws upon the fraught concept of the pack to describe the actions of conquerors, "some pack of blond beasts of prey,"[39] in stark contrast to the "family" imagined through the discourse of domestication. In other words, the conquerors illuminate the predatory drift into the warring narrative of competition, departing from the cooperative sociability of herd morality. This sociability resonates with the contemporary scientific knowledge of the wolf pack, not as a bundle of aggression and confrontation as it is often misused in popular culture,[40] but rather as a "family."[41] The "pack" is not an agonistic and uncertain group, competing for resources, cowering before the mythical "alpha,"[42] it is a dynamic and functioning family:

> Rather than viewing a wolf pack as a group of animals organized with a "top dog" that fought its way to the top, or a male-female pair of such aggressive wolves, science has come to understand that most wolf packs are merely family groups formed exactly the same way as human families are formed.[43]

Dynamics within the group are cultural, social, embodied; they are not merely innate, biological, inherited.[44] In other words, the "pack," more meaningfully understood, is a cultural assemblage, not merely a biological one.[45] It is not a question of fighting for and maintaining a dominance hierarchy; it is a dynamic of contribution. There simply is no pack hierarchy, as such, in the popular sense of the term.[46] However, there is a sense of herd morality: "Inasmuch as ever since there have been human beings there have also been human herds (family groups, communities, tribes, nations, states, churches), and always very many who obey compared with the very small number of those who command."[47]

But where Nietzsche expressed disquiet with a weakening through herd morality, perhaps more recent cognitive ethology and wolf behaviour research might have changed his mind. Rather than seeing a moral framework of obedience as a need "by now innate as a kind of *formal conscience* which commands," instead of a rigid and enforceable hierarchy, there is an ongoing and embodied sociality. At least in terms of "herd morality," the concept can be recuperated in very productive ways. This familial alliance is emerging as an important way in which to understand the construction of sociality, from domestication right through to societies of data collection.

Darwin similarly deciphers a link between morality and a familial sociality: "The development of the moral qualities is a more interesting problem. The foundation lies in the social instincts, including under this term the family ties."[48]

The "social instincts," as Darwin calls them, are the fabric of this sociality: "Animals endowed with the social instincts take pleasure in one another's company, warn one another of danger, defend and aid one another in many ways. These instincts do not extend to all individuals of the species, but only to those of the same community."[49]

Self-domestication, the making of kin, the making of community, therefore ushers in a sense of morality. Domestication implies a sense of moral kinship through the very process itself. There is every opportunity to wonder at the possibility of a kind of moral kinship through domestication, largely through the very initiative itself, and the "herd instinct" of those dogs that scavenged that contact and that reciprocal accountability. The dogs came to play. And yes, they were friendly.

A game that two can play

> They are playing a game. They are playing at not playing a game. If I show them I see they are, I shall break the rules and they will punish me.
>
> I must play their game, of not seeing I see the game.[50]

Tarde notes Sir Francis Galton's hypothesis, "the domestication of animals as a consequence of playing with them."[51] *Do with me*, as it were. And what is play if not the most accomplished performance of sociability? Notably, Georg Simmel, a contemporary of Tarde, was similarly enthusiastic about the "good form" of sociability inherent in these kinds of spontaneous interactions:

> It is no mere accident of language that all sociability, even the purely spontaneous, if it is to have meaning and stability, lays such great value on form, on good form. For "good form" is mutual self-definition, interaction of the elements, through which a unity is made; and since in sociability the concrete motives bound up with life-goals fall away, so must the pure form, the free-playing, interacting independence of individuals stand out so much the more strongly and operate with so much the greater effect.[52]

As Simmel declares, "Sociability is, then, the play-form of association."[53] Through play, through this exuberant association, the ultimate moral framework for sociability is mobilised, and it is mobilised with joy. Play is creative and transformative, an art in and of itself, art "continually haunted by the animal," perhaps.[54] The play of association is that which motivated and sustained domestication, that which ushered humans into the open, through the superior sociability of that dog. Indeed, this sociability is quite emphatically the affinity of art and play, the alliance of joy and invention: "And what joins art with play now appears in the likeness of both to sociability."[55] As Simmel surmises, play is a performance of "symbolic significance which distinguishes it from pure pastime. And just this will show itself more and more as the essence of sociability . . . sociability (and the more it approaches pure sociability) takes on a symbolically playing fullness of life and a significance which a superficial rationalism always seeks only in the content."[56]

Simmel's approach to sociability through a series of relations in many ways reciprocates Hohfeld's approach to legal relations, always already between two beings, *in personam*: "Instead of starting from isolated actors or from the hyper-existence of society, methodologically Simmel begins with a theory of relations. As the basic unit of social relations, he takes the dyad, the being-with of two individuals, I and you. As a result, Simmel avoids assuming the pre-existence of society as a hypostasized, self-sustaining generality and is able to grasp the social in its nascence, its becoming."[57] In focusing on the interaction as distinct from the object, the crucial ethical and welfare dimension to sociable property is also manifest.[58] These basic units of social and legal relations will become significant in the fundamental socialisation of the legal and economic model of property pursued throughout this present discussion.[59] Sociable property is always already in communication, in play. And the roles within it are necessarily dynamic, intersubjective, and in flux. Consumers may be producers may be owners and so on, and this is the necessary play in the law that is important to indulge in its resocialisation[60] towards an integrated approach to an ethological jurisprudence of property.

Play along with me for now.

Morality play

> Social evolution begins and ends with games and celebrations. It was in play that little by little man learned most of his types of work; development of even the most difficult and least profitable industries tends to make life happier.[61]

This sociability with the "fullness of life" and "good form" resonates with the concept of dog play as embodied morality and just performance. Ethologist Marc Bekoff has studied mammalian play for decades and has promoted attention to the social play in animals and its possible role in a sense of justice and morality, particularly through practices of reciprocity and cooperation.[62] In his extensive study of dog play, Bekoff has identified a repertoire of play language, so to speak, and the social expectations and functions that go with that language, such as sanctions against cheating or unfairness in play.[63] Further, the abundantly creative and transformative assemblage of dogs in play has been identified as demonstrating not only a type of social morality[64] but also innovation and novelty[65] on the part of dogs. Further, this creativity, reciprocity, and cooperation has been recognised in the relationship between humans and dogs in play.[66] A form of social morality emerges through and as a consequence of playing with dogs. And that dog and domestication brought that potential into the open.

Such impassioned play, however, should not be simply dismissed as discomposure and irresponsibility.[67] On the contrary, play ignites accountability and sociability through embodied communication, *the play of form*, as it were. Despite appearance, to play is not to do simply as one pleases, but rather, as we please. A certain suspicion of play as aimless, pointless, plastic, lawless belies not only pretensions to rationalism but also (populist) discourses of control: "Play isn't an idle waste of time. Play is essential for an individual's mental and physical well-being."[68] The notion of "play" within property is regarded with apprehension and as a route to licentiousness. Instead, what is proposed through a predatory property perspective is a system of rigid and enforceable boundaries – for property and for that dog. In other words, in this context "play" is set up in terms of competitiveness, doing as *one* pleases, not as *we* please. Indeed, Bekoff cautions against these kinds of purely functionalist interpretations, which are arguably underpinned by the assumptions that are fundamental to a predatory property approach: "It is important not to be a cognitive or a moral speciesist."[69] The interpretive emphasis on control within social and economic frameworks is entirely contrary to Tarde's view that "passion and reason, from age to age, progress hand in hand."[70] To play is an emergent and creative assemblage, not a dysfunctional mastery. It is the very basis for invention.

Intriguingly, this suspicion of play also resonates within certain approaches to dog training, especially those described as "balanced," which institute control and dominance frameworks at their core. Such training approaches support the use of aversive methods, including physical punishment.[71] This is in contrast to the communicative and principally non-aversive approaches to training with positive reinforcement (variously referred to as "positive" training, "force-free" training, "do no harm" training, and so on) recommended by animal welfare bodies[72] and by the scientific literature itself.[73] Indeed, the semantic strategy of the term "balanced" purports to align this approach to dog training with notions of justice, fairness, and, above all, dispassionateness. The explicit recommendations against affection[74] together with the general approach of dispassion belie the denial of not only any genuine sociability between human and dog but also the creativity and ingenuity of dogs themselves. Affections come last, and not as sociability but as reward: "affection that's *earned*."[75] Thus, this communicative aspect has no value in and of itself within this transaction, only as a value in exchange for "work." And through the same semantic strategy, in positioning aversive approaches as "balanced," this discourse positions communicative or "positive" approaches as therefore "unbalanced" (the lawlessness of play, as it were).[76]

Thus, in many ways, so-called "balanced training" is entirely and overtly unsociable. Almost always proceeding from a misinterpretation of the wolf family as an antagonistic and aggressive pack with a rectilinear dominance hierarchy, these approaches advocate human leadership in a contrived dominance hierarchy within the household. Notably, despite trainers characterising themselves as "pack leaders," so-called balanced training is anxiously self-conscious about any kind of anthropomorphic language or perceived humanising of dogs, once again invoking a human exceptionalist narrative in the training context. And perhaps not unsurprisingly, where physical punishment is used, dogs have been found to be less interactive both in play with other dogs and with the handler.[77] What might this say about the law's coercive force in property and the quality of sociability in intellectual property?

Such approaches are also frequently outspoken against the "chaos" of frenetic dog play,[78] declaring that it is not organised, or controlled, or managed by the human "pack leader."[79] Indeed, contrary to the scientific knowledge of the importance of socialisation with conspecifics, balanced trainers often recommend not allowing dogs to play with other dogs at all, other than those in their own household "pack," advocating that all they need is the human: "you are the reward."[80] Again, lack of undivided attention placed upon the human is deemed another "failure" on the part of the self-declared "pack leader." In a profoundly anthropocentric characterisation of the dog's world and an obsessive preoccupation with attention, this approach is not only misguided but also raises significant welfare issues. As well as the attenuation of opportunities to express normal behaviour and to socialise with conspecifics, this approach actually interferes with the dog's very means of communication and social life, their ability to participate in cultural doggish life. Recent research has compiled a "dictionary" of referential gestures used by dogs in communication and signalling intention with humans.[81] Such gestures include behaviours that are regularly reported as "unwanted" and "undesirable," such as jumping up. But as non-accidental, intentional communication, the inappropriate "correction" or frustration of these referential gestures could present a welfare issue.[82] In other words, so to speak, this kind of approach limits the dog's freedom of expression.

Notably, this kind of focus and differentiation that is seen in discourses of "control" and "balance" can be recognised in proprietary systems. This is the very language of property, the discourse of dominion. And in particular, the conduct of this training model shares much with the kinds of translations of real property into intellectual property frameworks; for example, the emphasis on trespass and access, the contrivance of artificial scarcity (in both time and space), the competition for attention, the social tie as market transaction.

In stark contrast to these pronouncements against social play to be found in some corners of the dog training world, play research in dogs has opened the world of dog play as a wellspring of canine fairness and moral justice, as well as creativity, expression and positive welfare. In particular, frenetic dog play, often affectionately referred to as zoomies,[83] is not only physically beneficial but also socially invigorating.[84] Zoomies are intellectual exercise – passionate interests, if you will.

How might these passionate interests serve the creativity of property? The notion of "play" within intellectual property frameworks themselves is a sociable accommodation within the law. Play as may be imagined through parody and quotation, for example, necessarily relies upon an effective and recognisable attribution. Indeed, this is fundamental to the interchange that is integral to the humour or tribute. However, such play and sociability within the intellectual property system is arguably becoming increasingly compromised by a growing anxiety and unsociability, as it were, between producers and consumers, often resulting in further division and differentiation through legislative intervention. Ironically, much of this has been caused by inadequate attribution, cheating at the game, and thus resulting in a disincentive for future social play. No one can do as they please. But through genuine sociable play, we can do as we all please.

Where is the joy?

There is something joyous about the domestication story. The sociability, the play, the passions of that dog's invention – the joy. The story is not one of work – it is never about the work of domestication; it is the joy of invention. The dog is not a labourer, the dog is an ingenious scavenger, retooling the remnants of that human family into a new sociality:[85]

> [T]he principle of sociability may be formulated thus: everyone should guarantee to the other that maximum of sociable values (joy, relief, vivacity) which is consonant with the maximum of values he himself receives. As justice upon the Kantian basis is thoroughly democratic, so likewise this principle shows the democratic structure of all sociability. . . . Sociability creates, if one will, an ideal sociological world, for in it – so say the enunciated principles – the pleasure of the individual is always contingent upon the joy of others; here, by definition, no one can have his satisfaction at the cost of contrary experiences on the part of others. In other forms of association such lack of reciprocity is excluded only by the ethical imperative which govern them but not by their own immanent nature.[86]

A just and legitimate framework, therefore, cannot be enforced by the "pack of blond beasts of prey" but rather will be legitimated through the joy of the familial affinities of play. It seems that the moral of this story, as it were, is to bring back the play in the moral and social and legal frameworks for innovation and intellectual property. Where is the joy?

Darwin declares that in the development of moral qualities, "the more important elements are love, and the distinct emotion of sympathy."[87] But where Nietzsche decries pity, sometimes aligned with sympathy, as egoistic and immoral, this sociable sympathy, as invited by dogs and imitated by humans, is perhaps the only morally robust society: "only the sociable is a 'society.'"[88]

In this sympathetic relationship borne from that dog's initiative, is there not to be found perhaps the greatest affinity between all members of a productive community? Dogs and humans alike. Let's listen.

A sympathetic ear

> This spirit of imitation, or sympathy of one animal with another . . . is perceivable in the voice, the habits, and actions.
>
> The voice of one animal calls forth that of another. . . . This mutual response is even sometimes irresistible.[89]

For dogs, socialisation is described in the literature as critical to producing a dog with a healthy sense of self and species identity,[90] social intelligence, and eloquence through contact with both conspecifics as well as members of other species (especially humans)[91] and the confidence to express that identity in an active social life. The process of socialisation necessarily introduces social bonds through imitation, a process of enculturation,[92] incorporating relationships of difference and repetition through embodied communications and through playful conversation. Enculturation through socialisation, as a form of social learning and transmission of traditions, accomplishes the type of cultural exchange that is premised upon a social bond created through prestige and curiosity in the first place, through imitation. And "This spirit of imitation" is the "sympathy of one animal with another."[93] At the core of attachment theory is this recognition of one's partner, this sociability, this sympathy: "Sympathy is certainly the primary source of sociability and the hidden or overt soul of every kind of imitation."[94] Nevertheless, this exchange of "cultures" agitates some trainers as best avoided, considering it beyond the kind of communication they are able to imagine on the part of the dog.[95] Ongoing research, however, would challenge this as somewhat of an underestimation, particularly through the kind of embodied communication understood in relations of empathy between dogs and humans.[96]

Socialisation may be understood then to be a compelling reconfiguration of the unilateralism that often characterizes the production and consumption relationship more generally, not only in the popular mythologies of taming and domestication but also in the discourses of creativity and innovation, and in the practical characterisation of these values within intellectual property frameworks. This unilateralism unravels in the story of invention and imitation, where production is retooled and alliances formed. Through a sympathetic ear, the processes of enculturation initiate an interspecies social and cultural exchange. As we have seen, the social contract is impossible without a prior social bond: "contract was a bond of slow formation." An attachment, if you will. It is irresistible to see this same dynamic in Jacques Derrida's account of subjectivity and intersubjectivities, acknowledging the same necessary and reciprocal translation as a fundamental condition of the social: "There is no contract possible – no social contract possible – without a translation contract."[97] Socialisation, that attachment, as it were, demands attention.

How did we become attached?

Is humaneness canine?

> Strangely, there are indications that such humaneness, which many admire and hold, at least in theory, to be the highest achievement of humanity, was invented millions of years ago by early canids. It is practiced to this very day by some of the descendents and honed to perfection by members of the pack-hunting canid species.[98]

Old Tim Yilngayari told about the dingo origins of humans on a number of occasions. . . . "In beginning, when we come out of that hole [in the earth] we had long nose like dog. . . . Mother and Father Dingo make Aboriginal. White children out of white dog; Dingo for Aboriginal."[99]

One of the most important myths in the Numic (Shoshone, Comanche, Piute, Ute) tradition is that Wolf served as benevolent creator figure.[100]

The twins, Romulus and Remus, were born to Rhea Silvia, were abandoned, nursed by a she-wolf, and then rescued and brought up by the royal shepherd Faustulus. On silver and bronze Roman coins of the third century BC we have representations of the wolf and the twins. . . . [T]he animal is looking back at her nurslings. This attentive aspect is characteristic of the representations of the wolf wherever she is met with the twins on the coinage.[101]

That dog looked back.
Dog domestication – by that dog – is by now compelling in the story of introducing the curiosity and intrigue that motivated humans forward into standing still. In other words, this "capital invention," as we have seen, provided the inscrutable invitation to the human to play. This sociability and exemplary demonstration of the benefits of cooperating, reciprocating, exchanging, and settling made modern civilisation possible. Konrad Lorenz speaks of "the gifts of domestication, to which we owe our humanity,"[102] but domestication was invented through the tenacity of that dog. It not only introduced a social bond upon which principles of exchange, of transfer, of property could come to terms, but also a social bond through which the very fundaments of cooperation and so-called "humanity" could be imitated. Humanity? Through domestication, dogs settled the matter.[103]

In understanding the potential of play for its qualities of moral justice and fairness, the framework for entrusting humans to the social structure, for inviting and commending them to the open, the story of domestication restores insight into contemporary models of property and the propertied. To that relationship, that is, the relationship pursuant to that original domestication invention, dogs brought significant proficiencies. And indeed continue to do so.

First, the introduction of a social bond brought with it a certain vulnerability, but this is not to be interpreted as a weakening with the "herd instinct," as considered elsewhere, but rather a capacity through sympathy in so far as it necessitates a certain perspective-taking on behalf of the partners in the bond.[104] *What are you looking at?* This perspective-taking cultivates a kind of self-consciousness, befriends a sense of shame, as well as a circle of vulnerability: "To them, virtue is what makes modest and tame: with it they make the wolf into a dog and man himself into man's best domestic animal."[105] The gaze of the dogs interpellated the humans, rendering them modest and indeed tame.

There is a considerable amount of scientific research into dogs and their gaze in relation to their social bonds and cognitive capacities that resonates with this importance of communicative looking. Dogs' advanced sensitivity and responsivity to human cues,[106] while previously considered to be human-like cognitive abilities acquired through domestication,[107] have more recently come to be thought of as having in fact pre-existed the domestication process.[108] These human-like qualities, as it were, likely pre-date humans. Are human-like qualities therefore indeed canine? In other words, dogs may indeed have human-like social skills; it is just the origination of these that might be more complicated. Dogs looked back.[109] But so did the humans.[110]

Second, dogs introduced the concept of territory, of mapping and marking out space, and of recognising and situating oneself within and in relation to that space. But this concept of territory is not banally rivalrous as it is commonly interpreted and developed. Instead, canine territory necessitates not only cooperation with each other but also cooperation with the environment. And in transforming that environment, through tracks and smells and pastoralism, dogs demonstrated the first opportunities for pastoral development to those early human "settlers"; and with that, the first opportunities for property.

Third, dogs introduced principles of reciprocity and accountability and thus moral justice in relation to the sociability of the household, the family, the domesticates. It is notable that many of the qualities associated with this sense of moral justice are considered to have pre-dated domestication. Indeed, these qualities are likely conditions for that first domestication. For example, inequity aversion is recognised in dogs, where dogs will react to a perceived unfairness.[111] This extends not only to unequal treatment between peers (such as where two dogs might be performing a task but only one is rewarded) but also arguably to the quality of the treatment in the individual case (for instance, whether the quality of the reward is perceived to match the effort the dog has made in performing a task).

Finally, dogs practise a sense of accountability through their reactions to deception, as well as through the process of social play, and the sanctions against cheating and unfairness, altruistic relationships, inequity aversion, and cooperation characterise the expansive social competence of dogs. Fairness, for dogs is simply common courtesy, as it were.

This polite sociality is both the precondition for and the counterpoint of contemporary property models. But courtesy has no place in modern property law.[112] So how can we teach some manners in property? Property is human, all too human.

Society may be going to the dogs. We can only hope.

Notes

1 Indeed, Ádám Miklósi describes dogs as somewhat prepared for socialization through their domestication. See Miklósi Á (2015) *Dog Behaviour, Evolution, and Cognition*, 2nd ed., Oxford UP, Oxford, 30.
2 Mills DS et al. (2010) *The Encyclopedia of Applied Animal Behaviour and Welfare*, CAB International, Wallingford, 567.
3 Power ER (2012) Domestication and the Dog: Embodying Home, *Area*, 44(3), 371–378: p. 371.

4 Please see "Part 3, Dominion, the machine age" for a more detailed explanation of this concept.
5 For instance, see the explanation in Donaldson J (1996/[2013]) *The Culture Clash*, Dogwise Publishing, Wenatchee, WA, 60.
6 For instance, the commercial for Ceva Animal Health's pheromone product, Adaptil, focused upon the unpleasantness of anxiety for the owner, not for the dog: "You wouldn't put up with unwanted behaviour from people, so why put up with it from your dog?" The commercial has since been taken off air in the UK due to lack of evidence. See further www.adaptil.com/us/Success-Stories/As-Seen-On-TV
7 Socialisation receives an inordinate amount of traffic in social media and blogs on dog training and ownership, especially the controversy of the "friendly dog," who seeks to greet. Not only is that dog considered a nuisance, but also a considerable number of comments from owners and trainers emphasise that they do not want their dog speaking with other people and dogs, they want their whole focus on them, reiterating the pack mythology that perpetuates significant welfare issues in dog training. See further the more-detailed discussion in Chapter 8, "Pack fiction").
8 von Jhering R (1913) *Law as a Means to an End*, Boston Book Company, Boston, 386.
9 See further the discussion in Chapter 8, "Pack fiction."
10 See further the discussion of the pack concept in Chapter 8, "Pack fiction"; and Chapter 7, "Predatory drift."
11 The concept of predatory drift is set out in full in Chapter 7 of the same name.
12 Lorenz K (1988/[1991]) *Here Am I: Where Are You? The Behavior of the Greylag Goose*, RD Martin (trans.), Harcourt Brace Jovanovich, New York. See further Lorenz K (1935) Der Kumpan in der Umwelt des Vogels. Der Artgenosse als auslösendes Moment sozialer Verhaltensweisen, *Journal für Ornithologie*, 83, 137–215: pp. 289–413.
13 Attachment theory is largely attributed to the work of John Bowlby in the late 1960s, although Mary Ainsworth was working on similar research at the time, looking particularly at factors affecting the quality of attachments. John Bowlby's research into maternal deprivation and children led him to propose that the failure to achieve a good bond with a parent can lead to fearfulness and lack of motivation towards further challenges as the child progresses: Bowlby, J (1969) *Attachment and Loss, Vol 1 Attachment*, Pimlico-Random House, London.
14 Mills DS et al. (2010) *The Encyclopedia of Applied Animal Behaviour and Welfare*, CAB International, Wallingford, OX, 37. See further Previde EP & Valsecchi P (2014) The Immaterial Cord: The Dog-Human Attachment Bond, in Kaminski J & Marshall-Pescini S (eds.) *The Social Dog: Behaviour and Cognition*, Academic Press, San Diego, 165–189.
15 Tarde G (1890/[1903]) *The Laws of Imitation*, EC Parsons (trans.), Henry Holt & Co, New York, 371.
16 Bergson H (1907/[1944]) *Creative Evolution*, A Mitchell (trans.), Random House, New York, 295.
17 See further the discussion of attribution in a sociable property model in Chapter 12, *Res familiaris*.
18 Tarde G (1893/[2012]) *Monadology and Sociology*, T Lorenc (trans.), Re-Press, Melbourne, 15.
19 Marshall-Pescini S & Kaminski J (2014) The Social Dog: History and Evolution, in Kaminski J & Marshall-Pescini S (eds.) *The Social Dog: Behaviour and Cognition*, Academic Press, London, 3–33: p. 18. See further, Topál J et al. (2005) Attachment to Humans: A Comparative Study on Hand-Reared Wolves and Differently Socialized Dog Puppies, *Animal Behaviour*, 70, 1367–1375.

20 Despret V (2004) The Body We Care For: Figures of Anthropo-zoo-genesis, *Body & Society*, 10(2–3), 111–134: p. 129. See earlier the discussion in Chapter 1, "*Canis Familiaris* - the Invention of Domestication."
21 These relations of correlatives become especially significant in later discussion of their interpretation through Wesley Newcomb Hohfeld's scheme in later chapters, particularly the more detailed discussion in Chapter 11, "Resocialisation."
22 See in particular the discussion in "Part 4, Altruism, the social age," especially the discussion of altruistic and empathetic behaviours in Chapter 10, "Shared interests," as well as Hohfeld's fundamental legal conceptions in Resocialisation, and the discussion of sociable property in Chapter 12, "*Res familiaris*".
23 For instance, dingoes in Holocene Australia were kept almost exclusively as pets, their value in hunting being questionable or even a hindrance. There is considerable evidence in Aboriginal social organisation of dingoes as pets, including burial ceremonies and a protected status within the group (including important symbolic associations as well as taboos in relation to eating or using parts of the dingo for adornment). See the discussion in Balme J & O'Connor S (2016) Dingoes and Aboriginal Social Organization in Holocene Australia, *Journal of Archaeological Science, Reports*, 7, 775–781. The authors note, "They were reared as pets . . . given lavish care," and benefited from grooming, feeding, even suckling, as well as considerable affection (777). See further the discussion of pet-keeping in Chapter 9, "Wild abandon."
24 A more detailed examination of the personhood issue with respect to animals is undertaken in Gibson J (forthcoming) *More Than Human Intellectual Property: Animal Authors and Human Machines*, Routledge, London, in relation to animal creativity and animal authorship.
25 See further Chapter 7, "Predatory drift."
26 Pet-keeping is discussed again in Chapter 9, "Wild abandon."
27 Janssens L et al. (2018) A New Look at an Old Dog: Bonn-Oberkassel Reconsidered, *Journal of Archaeological Science*, 92, 126–138.
28 Dental examinations showed that the first episode was at 19 weeks, with two further attacks between 19 and 23 weeks.
29 Janssens L et al. (2018) A New Look at an Old Dog: Bonn-Oberkassel Reconsidered, *Journal of Archaeological Science*, 92, 126–138: p. 135.
30 Janssens L et al. (2018) A New Look at an Old Dog: Bonn-Oberkassel Reconsidered, *Journal of Archaeological Science*, 92, 126–138: p. 127.
31 Losey RJ et al. (2011) Canids as Persons: Early Neolithic Dog and Wolf Burials, Cis-Baikal, Siberia, *Journal of Anthropological Archaeology*, 30, 174–189. In a study examining the remains of both dog and wolf burials, the researchers note that investigations into the skeleton of the Shamanka dog show that it likely lived in close contact with humans, enjoying a high level of intimacy and care over a prolonged period of years, and it was subsequently given human-like mortuary treatment: "These seem ideal circumstances in which a dog could become known as a quite human-like person. At the time of the dog's death, human bodies in this region of Siberia were placed in graves within formal cemeteries, sometimes in pits that already contained other bodies. This is precisely the treatment shown the dog at its death."
32 Eduardo Viveiros de Castro explains that "for Amerindians, animals are humans. This formulation condenses a nebula of subtly varied conceptions" and that this cycling of relations, as it were, defeats the mind body dualism (28). Indeed, anthropological understanding can arise only through relations, not through externalities (61). See further Viveiros de Castro E (2015) *The Relative Native: Essays on Indigenous Conceptual Worlds*, Hau Books, Chicago.

33 Losey RJ et al. (2011) Canids as Persons: Early Neolithic Dog and Wolf Burials, Cis-Baikal, Siberia, *Journal of Anthropological Archaeology*, 30, 174–189: p. 175.
34 Grøn O (2005) A Siberian Perspective on the North European Hamburgian Culture: A Study in Applied Hunter-Gatherer Ethnoarchaeology, *Before Farming*, 1, 1–29. The author notes: "[H]umans with their three souls are distinguished from animals, which have only two. But intelligent/clever animals (e.g., hunting dogs and bears) can have three souls and actually be equal to humans – which is why they can be buried in traditional graves of the type reserved for humans (this practice can still be observed). The border between humans and animals is flexible in a way our culture does not recognise." (page 4).
35 Losey RJ et al. (2011) Canids as Persons: Early Neolithic Dog and Wolf Burials, Cis-Baikal, Siberia, *Journal of Anthropological Archaeology*, 30, 174–189: p. 175.
36 Deleuze G (1988/[1993]) *The Fold: Leibniz and the Baroque*, T Conley (trans.), U of Minnesota P, Minneapolis, 3.
37 Nietzsche F (1882/[1974]) *The Gay Science*, W Kaufman (trans.), Vintage Books, New York, Book III, 116. It is useful to note at this point that groups of animals described as herds are usually prey animals, whereas the term "pack" is usually applied to predators. This distinction between predator and prey is very relevant in the predatory drift of property discourse, where the predator is the captor, as it were. See further the discussions in Chapter 7, "Predatory drift"; and Chapter 12, "*Res familiaris.*"
38 See further the discussion in Chapter 7, "Pack fiction."
39 Nietzsche F (1887/[1989]) *On the Genealogy of Morals and Ecce Homo*, W Kauffman (trans.), Vintage, New York: Second Essay, "Guilt," "Bad Conscience," and the Like, Section 17.
40 For example, see the highly produced television programmes of Cesar Millan as well as further examples available on his website, www.cesarsway.com
41 Packard JM (2003) Wolf Behavior: Reproductive, Social, and Intelligent, in Mech LD & Boitani L (eds.) *Wolves: Behavior, Ecology, and Conservation*, U of Chicago P, Chicago, 35–65: pp. 60–61; Mech LD (2008) Whatever Happened to the Term Alpha Wolf?, *International Wolf*, Winter, 4–8.
42 The background to the term Alpha is considered in detail in Pack Fiction.
43 Mech LD (2008) Whatever Happened to the Term Alpha Wolf?, *International Wolf*, Winter, 4–8: p. 5. See further Mech LD (1999) Alpha Status, Dominance, and Division of Labor in Wolf Packs, *Canadian Journal of Zoology*, 77(8), 1196–1203.

The concept of the "pack" and, in particular, the various popular misconceptions of the pack and the application of this (mis)behaviour to other group structures, is examined in detail in Chapter 8, "Pack fiction."

44 Mech LD (1999) Alpha Status, Dominance, and Division of Labor in Wolf Packs, *Canadian Journal of Zoology*, 77(8), 1196–1203. With his extensive field research of wolf packs *in situ*, David Mech has overturned the assumption that "alpha" status or dominance could be predicted, as though "rank is innate or formed early, and that some wolves are destined to rule the pack, while others are not" (1197).
45 Mech explains, "individual wolves do not have an inherent permanent social status, even though captive pups show physiological and behavioral differences related to current social rank." Mech LD (1999) Alpha Status, Dominance, and Division of Labor in Wolf Packs, *Canadian Journal of Zoology*, 77(8), 1196–1203: p. 1197.
46 Mech explains, "The concept, nature, and importance of the dominance hierarchy or pecking order itself in many species are in dispute. Similarly, in a natural wolf pack, dominance is not manifested as a pecking order and seems to have much less significance than the results of studies of captive packs have implied."

Mech LD (1999) Alpha Status, Dominance, and Division of Labor in Wolf Packs, *Canadian Journal of Zoology*, 77(8), 1196–1203: p. 1198.
47 Nietzsche F (1886/[1973]) *Beyond Good and Evil*, Penguin, London, 199.
48 Darwin C (1871/[2004]) *The Descent of Man, and Selection in Relation to Sex*, Penguin, London, 680.
49 Darwin C (1871/[2004]) *The Descent of Man, and Selection in Relation to Sex*, Penguin, London, 680.
50 Laing RD (1970/[2012]) *Knots*, Routledge, London, 1.
51 Tarde G (1969) *On Communication and Social Influence*, TN Clark (ed.), U of Chicago P, Chicago, 159.
52 Simmel G (1949) The Sociology of Sociability, EC Hughes (trans.), *American Journal of Sociology*, 55(3), 254–261: p. 255.
53 Simmel G (1949) The Sociology of Sociability, EC Hughes (trans.), *American Journal of Sociology*, 55(3), 254–261: p. 255.
54 Deleuze G & Guattari F (1991/[1994]) *What Is Philosophy?*, H Tomlinson & G Burchill (trans.), Verso, London, 184.
55 Simmel G (1949) The Sociology of Sociability, EC Hughes (trans.), *American Journal of Sociology*, 55(3), 254–261: p. 255.
56 Simmel G (1949) The Sociology of Sociability, EC Hughes (trans.), *American Journal of Sociology*, 55(3), 254–261: p. 255. The symbolic in play and symbolic thought in animals is explored in considerably more detail in relation to creativity, authorship and language in Gibson J (forthcoming) *More Than Human Intellectual Property*, Routledge, London.
57 Pyyhtinen O (2009) Being-with: Georg Simmel's Sociology of Association, *Theory, Culture & Society*, 26(5), 108–128: p. 121.
58 Later discussions explore this in relation to the beings within property models, including intellectual property models and the treatment of producers and consumers within relevant frameworks. This emphasis on the interaction and relationship, as distinct from the object as focus of value, is very relevant in terms of interspecies property relationships as well. For example, in farmed animal welfare there is increasing attention on the interaction between stockpersons and animals, rather than on purely external features such as toys or housing: Hemsworth PH & Coleman GJ (2010) *Human-Livestock Interactions: The Stockperson and the Productivity and Welfare of Intensively Farmed Animals*, 2nd ed., CAB International, Wallingford, UK. Similarly, recent research in laboratory animals has emphasised the importance of the research-animal relationship as a source of enrichment and positive welfare: LaFollette MR et al. (2018) Practical Rat Tickling: Determining an Efficient and Effective Dosage of Heterospecific Play, *Applied Animal Behaviour Science*, 208, 82–91; Panksepp J (2000) The Riddle of Laughter: Neural and Psychoevolutionary Underpinnings of Joy, *Current Directions in Psychological Science*, 9, 183–186.
59 This reciprocity is also recognised in Jean-Luc Nancy's *being-with* as well as Donna Haraway's exploration of *becoming-with* in relation to relations between humans and other animals. These concepts are considered in more detail in later chapters – see Chapter 9, "Wild abandon," as well as further discussion in Part 4, Altrusim, the social age."
60 See the further discussion of this resocialisation in the chapters in Part 4, Altrusion, The social age."
61 Tarde G (1969) *On Communication and Social Influence*, TN Clark (ed.), U of Chicago P, Chicago, 160.
62 Bekoff M (2001) Social Play Behaviour: Cooperation, Fairness, Trust, and the Evolution of Morality, *Journal of Consciousness Studies*, 8(2), 81–90. See further Dugatkin LA & Bekoff M (2003) Play and the Evolution of Fairness: A Game

Theory Model, *Behavioural Processes*, 60, 209–214; Bekoff M (2007) *The Emotional Lives of Animals*, New World Library, Novato CA, 100–101. See further the detailed treatment of moral behaviour in animals in Bekoff M & Pierce J (2009) *Wild Justice: The Moral Lives of Animals*, Chicago UP, Chicago.
63 Bekoff M (1995) Play Signals as Punctuation: The Structure of Social Play in Canids, *Behaviour*, 132(5/6), 419–429.
64 Bekoff M (2015) Playful Fun in Dogs, *Current Biology*, 25(1), R4–R7.
65 Bateson P (2015) Playfulness and Creativity, *Current Biology*, 25(1), R12–R16.
66 Mitchell RW (2015) Creativity in the Interaction: The Case of Dog-Human Play, in Kaufman AB & Kaufman JC (eds.) *Animal Creativity and Innovation*, Academic Press, London, 31–42. See further the enhancement of the bond in Rooney NJ & Bradshaw JWS (2002) An Experimental Study of the Effects of Play Upon the Dog-Human Relationship, *Applied Animal Behaviour Science*, 75, 161–176. For a more detailed discussion of play as a source of creativity and innovation in animals in relationship to authorship and intellectual property, see Gibson J (forthcoming) *More Than Human Intellectual Property: Animal Authors and Human Machines*, Routledge, London.
67 Bekoff M (2017) It's OK for Dogs to Engage in Zoomies and Enjoy FRAPs, *Psychology Today*, 26 September.
68 Bekoff M (2007) *The Emotional Lives of Animals*, New World Library, Novato CA, 100.
69 Bekoff M (2001) Social Play Behaviour: Cooperation, Fairness, Trust, and the Evolution of Morality, *Journal of Consciousness Studies*, 8(2), 81–90: p. 81.
70 Tarde G (1902/[2007]) Economic Psychology, A Toscano (trans.), *Economy and Society*, 36(4), 614–643: p. 631.
71 From physical punishments and rattle cans to shock collars, spray collars etc. Balanced trainers have also been very vocal in protesting against any proposed ban on shock collars in the UK, frequently advocating the devices as important for "remote" training, consistent with the unsociability of the methodology.
72 For example, see the RSPCA's advice to use positive only trainers, www.rspca.org.uk/adviceandwelfare/pets/dogs/training
73 Todd Z (2018) Barriers to the Adoption of Humane Dog Training Methods, *Journal of Veterinary Behavior*, 25, 28–34.
74 The approaches also include diminishing the place of affection. Millan actually cites affection as a cause of behavioural problems: "Usually, people accidentally create a misbehavior by giving too much affection." In his list of a dog's needs, he includes affection ("exercise, discipline, and then affection, in that order"), but when affection comes first it is for humans (hence the title of the article). See www.cesarsway.com/when-affection-comes-first/
75 See further www.cesarsway.com/the-importance-of-giving-your-dog-affection
76 See further the critique in Todd Z (2016) In Dog Training, Balance Is Off, *Companion Animal Psychology*, 17 August, www.companionanimalpsychology.com/2016/08/in-dog-training-balance-is-off
77 Ziv G (2017) The Effects of Using Aversive Training Methods in Dogs, *Journal of Veterinary Behavior*, 19, 50–60.
78 Compare Bekoff M (2017) It's OK for Dogs to Engage in Zoomies and Enjoy FRAPs, *Psychology Today*, 26 September.
79 For a full discussion of the development of the term, pack leader, see Chapter 8, "Pack fiction." The term is notoriously widely used by balanced trainers. Indeed, a quick internet search results in many websites incorporating the term in some way.
80 You Are The Reward www.cesarsway.com/you-are-the-reward
81 Worsley HK & O'Hara SJ (2018) Cross-Species Referential Signalling Events in Domestic Dogs (*Canis Familiaris*), *Animal Cognition*, 21, 457–465.

82 See further the discussion in Chapter 8, "Pack fiction"; and Chapter 10, "Shared interests."
83 Zoomies are defined as frenetic random activity periods (FRAPs), characterised by exuberant bursts of energy expended in high-speed running and play, for varying periods. See further Bekoff M (2017) It's OK for Dogs to Engage in Zoomies and Enjoy FRAPs, *Psychology Today*, 26 September.
84 Bekoff M (2017) It's OK for Dogs to Engage in Zoomies and Enjoy FRAPs, *Psychology Today*, 26 September.
85 Tarde G (1902/[2007]) Economic Psychology, A Toscano (trans.), *Economy and Society*, 36(4), 614–643: p. 617.
86 Simmel G (1949) The Sociology of Sociability, EC Hughes (trans.), *American Journal of Sociology*, 55(3), 254–261: p. 257.
87 Darwin C (1871/[2004]) *The Descent of Man, and Selection in Relation to Sex*, Penguin, London, 680.
88 Simmel G (1949) The Sociology of Sociability, EC Hughes (trans.), *American Journal of Sociology*, 55(3), 254–261: p. 255.
89 Thompson EP (1851) *The Passions of Animals*, Chapman & Hall, London, 315–316.
90 Mills DS et al. (2010) *The Encyclopedia of Applied Animal Behaviour and Welfare*, CAB International, Wallingford, OX, 567–568.
91 The process of socialisation with humans has been described in other species as a process of enculturation, raising the topic of interlocking cultural transformations. See Tomasello M and Call J (1997) *Primate Cognition*, Oxford UP, Oxford.
92 Mills DS et al. (2010) *The Encyclopedia of Applied Animal Behaviour and Welfare*, CAB International, Wallingford, OX, 217–218.
93 Thompson EP (1851) *The Passions of Animals*, Chapman & Hall, London, 315.
94 Tarde G (1890/[1903]) *The Laws of Imitation*, EC Parsons (trans.), Henry Holt & Co, New York, 79 note 8.
95 For example see Puppy Socialisation Classes: A Good Idea?, http://thedogownersclub.co.uk/puppy-socialisation-classes-any-good? Compare the results of a recent study which showed considerable welfare and behaviour advantages for puppies attending puppy classes: González-Martínez Á et al. (2019) Association between Puppy Classes and Adulthood Behavior of the Dog, *Journal of Veterinary Behavior*, in press.
96 See further the discussion of animal cultures in Chapter 10, "Shared interests."
97 Derrida J (1982/[1988]) *The Ear of the Other*, P Kamuf (trans.), U of Nebraska P, Lincoln, 125.
98 Schleidt WM & Shalter MD (2003) Co-Evolution of Humans and Canids: An Alternative View of Dog Domestication: *Homo Homini Lupus?*, *Evolution and Cognition*, 9(1), 57–71: p. 60.
99 Rose DB (1992/[2000]) *Dingo Makes Us Human: Life and Land in an Australian Aboriginal Culture*, Cambridge UP, Cambridge, 47, quoting Old Tim Yilngayari.
100 Pierotti R (2016) The Role of Myth in Understanding Nature, *Ethnobiology Letters*, 7(2), 6–13: p. 9.
101 Boyce AA (1954) The Foundation and Birthday of Rome: In Legend and History, *Archaeology*, 7(1), 9–14: pp. 12–13.
102 Lorenz K (1992/[1996]) *The Natural Science of the Human Species: An Introduction to Comparative Behavioral Research, The "Russian Manuscript" (1944–1948)*, A von Cranach (ed.), RD Martin (trans.), MIT Press, Cambridge, MA, 75.

103 Konrad Lorenz's conflicted position on domestication in his writings during Nazi occupation and arguably influenced by those conditions is discussed later in Chapter 8, "Pack fiction."
104 As Kari Weil notes, "shame not only may be a form of taming but may also preserve or give life." See Weil K (2012) *Thinking Animals: Why Animal Studies Now?*, Columbia UP, New York, 78.
105 Nietzsche F (1883/[1969]) *Thus Spoke Zarathustra*, Penguin, London, Of the Virtue that Makes Small, Section 2, 190.
106 For example, see Gâcsi M et al. (2013) Wolves Do Not Join the Dance: Sophisticated Aggression Control by Adjusting to Human Social Signals in Dogs, *Applied Animal Behaviour Science*, 145, 109–122.
107 Hare B & Tomasello M (2005) Human-Like Social Skills in Dogs?, *Trends in Cognitive Science*, 9, 439–444; Miklósi Á et al. (2003) A Simple Reason for a Big Difference: Wolves Do Not Look Back at Humans, But Dogs Do, *Current Biology*, 13, 763–766; Hare B et al. (2002) The Domestication of Social Cognition in Dogs, *Science*, 298, 1634–1636.
108 Udell MAR et al. (2008) Wolves Outperform Dogs in Following Human Social Cues, *Animal Behaviour*, 76, 1767–1773. See further Johnston AM et al. (2017) Uncovering the Origins of Dog-Human Eye Contact: Dingoes Establish Eye Contact More Than Wolves, But Less Than Dogs, *Animal Behaviour*, 133, 123–129.
109 Miklósi Á et al. (2003) A Simple Reason for a Big Difference: Wolves Do Not Look Back at Humans, But Dogs Do, *Current Biology*, 13, 763–766. See further Marshall-Pescini S et al. (2017) The Role of Domestication and Experience in 'Looking Back' towards Humans in an Unsolvable Task, *Nature*, 7, 46636.
110 Nagasawa M et al. (2015) Oxytocin-Gaze Positive Loop and the Coevolution of Human-Dog Bonds, *Science*, 383, 333–336.
111 Essler JL et al. (2017) Domestication Does Not Explain the Presence of Inequity Aversion in Dogs, *Current Biology*, 27, 1861–1865; Horowitz A (2013) Sensitivity to Unequal Rewards in the Domestic Dog: Quantity over Fairness, *Journal of Veterinary Behavior*, 8(4) e30–e31; Range F et al. (2009) Effort and Reward: Inequity Aversion in Domestic Dogs?, *Journal of Veterinary Behavior*, 4(2) 45–46.
112 Property "does not depend on another's courtesy." Greenberg D et al. (eds.), *Jowitt's Dictionary of English Law*, 5th edition, Sweet & Maxwell, London, 2019.

Part 2

Territory, the space age

> Everywhere there are starting points, intersections and junctions that enable us to learn something new if we refuse, firstly, radical distance, secondly the distribution of roles, and thirdly the boundaries between territories.
>
> Jacques Rancière, *The Emancipated Spectator*, 2008

Chapter 4

Marking territory

[A]lthough the matter is often an intricate one, and the rights of territory somewhat involved, there can, I think, be no question that territorial rights are established rights amongst the majority of species of animals. There can be no doubt that the desire for acquisition of a definite territorial area, the determination to hold it by fighting if necessary, and the recognition of individual as well as tribal territorial rights by others, are dominant characteristics in all animals. *In fact, it may be held that the recognition of territorial rights, one of the most significant attributes of civilisation, was not evolved by man, but has ever been an inherent factor in the life history of all animals.*
   Heape W, *Emigration, Migration and Nomadism*, W Heffer & Sons, Cambridge, 1931, p. 74 (emphasis added)

In the chapters of the Domestication Age, that first domestication emerged for the "capital invention"[1] that it is, providing for settlement and place, for localism and farming, and ultimately for the very foundations of property itself: "What do all our modern inventions amount to in comparison with this capital invention of domestication?"[2] And from this capital invention came the possibilities for pastoralism and agriculture and ultimately the very foundations for property itself. As Walter Heape asserts, in what is some of the earliest work on territory, these relations of home and territory substantiate the recognition of civilisation and society in animals, from which human civilisation is "built up."[3] Animals thus introduced humans to territory:

> The more one studies the motives which determine the various movements of animals, the more one is impressed with the almost universally instinctive recognition of "home" and the rights over home territory which they show and practice. It is indeed on this instinct that the claim for any degree of civilisation among animals must be based. Thus, it is of great interest to observe that in man, this instinct, exhibited with increased strength, which is, in reality, the foundation upon which all his civilisation is built up, is derived from identically the same instinct possessed by the lower animals, and both clearly recognised and almost universally respected by them.[4]

Arguably all systems of property derive from this early sociability within and between territories that began to be explored through imitation. From systems of communalism and stewardship, right through to more clearly possessory notions of real property in common law systems, this early marking of territory located that sociability in the relation between possession and being.

However, this early socialisation through territory is in the nature of territory as movement and interaction, rather than enclosures and discourtesy.[5] Territory is navigated through intentionality and communication rather than organised through a grammar of maps, facilitated through sociability rather than channelled along boundaries. In other words, that first domestication story is *a boundary story that knows no bounds*. It describes a territory that is interpreted through relations, not exclusions, through sociability, not socialisation regimes. Although he admits not dealing with it explicitly in his work on territory, Heape identifies the "sociability amongst animals of widely different natures" and describes "the sharing of home territory by quite distinct species which do not interfere with one another or which live upon quite different types of food. . . . The territory of the one may be included in the territory of the other without inconvenience to either and without engendering enmity between them."[6]

The marking of territory is thus inextricably bound with the determination of the relative rights of territory, the relations not only to territory but also to each element and being within that territory. In this way territory is based upon a sociability of manners, as it were, the reciprocity and cooperation of mutual respect. As later chapters will show, this is in contrast to the truculence of predatory drift in modern property systems, where property no longer relies on courtesy. This is arguably a departure, though not an inevitable one, as will be shown, from the early sociability in animal territories from which contemporary systems of property have been developed:

> The recognition of rights over a definite territory is one of the very first indications of the growth of civilisation in man. Where such rights are established, where ownership of territory is recognised, home life begins, and the foundation is laid for that change of temperament which leads to the transformation of the save into the civilised human being.[7]

What is perhaps not as immediately clear is the way in which these notions of real property are extrapolated to govern other relations as well through permutations of proprietary-like relationships; that is, other possibly obvious property models, such as intellectual property through to confidential information, through to understanding a kind of "predatory drift", as it were, in a range of social and communicative relationships. Notably, property discourse operates also within a kind of territory-making in a digital environment, not only in relation to actual intellectual property but also with respect to instrumental use of material in achieving some kind of affective relationship online, not unrelated to the value of attribution that imbues sociability. Indeed, it has become increasingly important to understand this in the context of the use and re-use of creativity in conflicts over memes and other "incidental" innovation in this "social life": that is, in familiar production.⁸ Marking of territory thus dominates the conceptualisation of relationships not only in real property but also through other relations of possession and exclusion. As the discussion moves through space to dominion, revisiting domestication and the creation of property from a sociable base makes the reinvigoration of sociable property models more reasonable but the predatory drift in property less acceptable.

In this chapter, we move from the socialisation of the early property foundations explored in Chapter 3, "Socialisation," and the introduction to the shifting sands of that sociability in contemporary property models to a characterisation of property in intellectual life. The role of domestication in territory and settlement is compelling, but what is the artefact of domestication in intellectual property? How might this early sociability reposition today's intellectual property vista?

Making marks

In his work on the psychology of property, Ernest Beaglehole attempted to decipher an acquisitive instinct⁹ as the foundation for all property: "How scientific is it, for instance, to speak of an instinct of property, the feeling and inclination for property, the proprietary appetite, or of an instinct of appropriation or of acquisition?"¹⁰ In part this coincides with the emphasis since Hobbes and Locke, and indeed earlier,¹¹ on property rights as natural rights, on property as enshrined in natural law. In combining this natural explanation of property with an understanding of evolutionary property as based in a combat for survival, "the struggle for life," the predatory drift of property is supposedly justified as "natural," when indeed, as will be explored in more detail in later chapters, it is a contrived social construction.

This theory of acquisitive instinct is one which arises in classical anthropology as well as in property jurisprudence, but it is not an uncontested zone. Alfred Irving Hallowell, arguably one of the earliest legal anthropologists, disputes this link between instinct and the scholarship on property as "natural rights":

> If property is a ubiquitous human institution it is easy to understand how it was that some eighteenth century thinkers came to include property in the general class of "natural rights." These thinkers did not mean that property rights were instinctive, that men were born with an "acquisitive instinct;" this was a much later doctrine, which along with other instinctivistic explanations of human conduct, scarcely merit serious consideration today. What was meant by the eighteenth century thinkers was that the individual as a member of society needed protection against any infringement of what were considered to be his fundamental rights as a human being.¹²

In other words, property is merely an instrument through which social relations are to be managed and sustained rather than an end in and of itself. Hallowell's interpretation of a Lockean property model is thus far more sociable than perhaps is the dominant reading. Indeed, in his work on so-called primitive laws of property, Hallowell foreshadows the later research on cooperation and reciprocity within evolutionary biology[13] in his comments on enforcement as more effective when social (internal) rather than coercive (external): "non-legal (i.e., moral and religious) sanctions may not only serve the same purpose as legal sanctions; under certain conditions they even seem to be more effective."[14] Indeed, recalling the previous discussion of social play and socialisation, Hallowell describes this kind of affinity as providing the motivation for cooperation, even in the seemingly self-interested paradigm of property: "My motivation is a function of the process of socialization that I have undergone. I have introcepted the fundamental values of my society. They have become part of me."[15]

The paradox is that while the rejection of property as an acquisitive instinct complicates the notion of property as a natural right, at the same time it also allows for exceptionalist narratives to deny an animal basis for property. Hallowell claims, quite wrongly, however, that "There are no social sanctions in animal societies and no attitudes comparable to human attitudes because there are no rights to be sanctioned."[16] Apart from the curious causality assumed on the basis of rights, Hallowell's presumptions are defeated by scientific evidence, as the discussions and examples throughout "Part 4, Altruism, the social age" will attest.[17] As we have already seen, even in social play, the imposition of sanctions is conscientiously applied to those who play unfairly. However, further evidence of social values can be seen in examples of inequity aversion, as well as altruistic and empathetic behaviours.

A further concept that is arguably fundamental to property and which has characterised discussions of animal territory is the notion of a kind of right to that particular territory on the basis of first possession, or the principle of prior residence: "members of many species – various spiders, insects, birds, and mammals, for example – commonly resolve territorial disputes by a simple rule: the resident always wins. The rule, deference to possession, is a product of biological evolution."[18] The effect of prior residence is also linked to the so-called bourgeois strategy[19] in animal societies, proposed as an "evolutionarily stable strategy" (ESS) by John Maynard Smith and George Price[20] in their theories of conflicts between animals and why such battles rarely lead to death. In such contests, prior residence or "ownership" may be respected in order to settle conflict: "It seems that ownership is typically taken as the arbiter."[21] At the same time, conflict is interpreted not merely as a battle but also as a source of information, of social contact.[22] Following this concept of stable evolutionary strategy, any kind of accumulation through the so-called acquisitive instinct would interfere with this ESS, both from this biological point of view, as well as from the socialisation perspective presented by Hallowell. Indeed, this view from evolutionary biology and the temperance of the "predatory drift" of property also resonates with Thorstein Veblen's evolutionary economics several decades earlier: "But this emulation could not run in the direction of an individual acquisition or accumulation of goods, or of a life consistently given to raids and tumults. It would be an emulation such as is found among the peaceable gregarious animals generally."[23]

What of the burrowing Iguana? "Unless previous work on a burrow in some degree establishes ownership, it is hard to see why a lizard would ever *start* digging a burrow, since only the lizard which finishes a burrow gains any payoff."[24] In terms of "authorship," the burrow is a curious problem. What of innovators and disseminators? How might the application of an ESS in the context of creativity models (and intellectual property frameworks) be useful here? When it comes to social media, there are many examples where sharing might obscure (or even delete) the credit of the original creator, and yet the "payoff" in terms of attention (such as likes, follows, and shares) is to be garnered by the imitators. Unless all that previous work on the burrow establishes ownership, why would such creativity persist other than as a gamble? It is proposed that attribution would achieve the necessarily stable strategy in order to support more burrows, more creativity, and more stable overlapping territories in such circumstances. In this way there is no need for contests between producers and consumers to be to the creative death. Rather, an understanding of the emergence of cooperation in these kinds of "territory" relationships is crucial to the sociability of familiar production.

The making of territory

The word "territory" started appearing in use as early as the fifteenth century,[25] originally referring to the lands around a particular domain. Notably, this perspective on territory is motivated by the making of territory through the establishment of domain, of making and keeping house, rather than in the sense of a fixed or "propertied" territory in connection to developing notions of rivalrous property.

From the seventeenth century and one of the first examples of conscientious ornithology comes what is also possibly the earliest reference to a proprietary notion of territory (even though the word territory is not explicitly used). Francis Willughby describes a territory-like behaviour in the Nightingale framed by notions of property: "It is proper to this Bird at his first coming (saith *Olina*) to occupy or seize upon one place as its Freehold, into which it will not admit any other *Nightingale* but its Mate."[26] One of the earliest explicit references to territory in the ethological context is from the eighteenth century in Oliver Goldsmith's multi-volume natural history, *A History of the Earth, and Animated Nature*, first published in 1774. Goldsmith notes:

> All birds, even those of passage, seem content with a certain district to provide food and centre in. The redbreast or the wren seldom leaves the field where it has been brought up, or where its young have been excluded; even though hunted it flies along the hedge, and seems fond of the place with an imprudent perseverance. The fact is, all these small birds mark out a territory to themselves, which they will permit none of their own species to remain in; they guard their dominions with the most watchful resentment; and we seldom find two male tenants in the same hedge together.[27]

Thus, at least as early as the eighteenth century, zoologists were establishing more systematic scholarship on the principle of territory in animal species which, although identifying defensive behaviours with respect to territory, nevertheless depended upon a definition borne out of the population itself, usually a particular species family. Territories in this way can overlap and encounter each other without necessarily rupturing territory or displacing sociable use of shared spaces.

Reportedly the first known use of the term "territoriality" comes much later in an article by Edward Payson Evans, "The Ethics of Tribal Society," published in 1894. Speaking of race relations in the United States, after the abolition of slavery, Evans introduces the concept of territoriality in order to understand not defensive boundary-making but rather the way in which people are bound in community. In many respects, Evans's concept of territory is much more concerned with the animal sociability of contact as quite distinct from the contemporary notion of territoriality and exclusion through property:

> The consciousness of what might be called common territoriality tends not only to bind together and to blend diverse races into that "unity of a people" which constitutes a nation, but also to attenuate and to loosen the social and political unions, which are based upon common descent, and finally ruptures them altogether.[28]

Rather than a concept of exclusion, the early concept of territoriality is possibly one of the original incarnations of sociability, as distinct from today's understanding of territoriality, both in animal behaviour and elsewhere, having become a character or attribution of "property" itself in the territoriality of territory.[29]

Despite this early interest in the relationship between animals (primarily birds) and boundaries, the territory concept took some time to gain its influence within the scientific community. Similarly, the attending concept of territoriality as a more recent concept did not gain currency until the early twentieth century, and again not in law but in the animal sciences and zoology.[30] Johann Bernard Theodor Altum published *Der Vogel und sein Leben* in 1868 (*The Bird and his Life*) and, although he is widely acknowledged as the founder of the theory of territory in birds,[31] his influence outside Germany was limited until some of his work appeared in a translation undertaken by Ernst Mayr and published in the Proceedings of the Linnaean Society of New York in 1935.[32] Writing in 1950, the cultural biologist Marston Bates claims that the concept did not really take hold until the first half of the twentieth century,[33] with the publication of Henry Eliot Howard's *Territory in Bird Life* in 1920.[34]

Mayr offers a definition of territory in that same piece, arguing that the concept of territory should not be muddied, as it were, by trying to ascertain the purpose. Rather, territory should be defined by its subjection to defence and nothing further: "*Territory is an area occupied by one male of a species which it defends against intrusions of other males of the same species and in which it makes itself conspicuous.*"[35] At the same time, the territory has itself been interpreted as a principle of defence. The noted ornithologist, Margaret Morse Nice, observes in 1941: "*The chief function of territory is defense – defense of the individual, the pair, the nest and young. In many cases it also serves to bring the pair together and to strengthen the bond between them.*"[36]

The importance of territory and territoriality to animal behaviour is thus largely attributed to the early twentieth-century work of Howard.[37]

> In a series of books culminated in his *Territory of Bird Life* of 1920, Howard described the instinct for the possession of 'territory' that he had found in warblers and other birds. The drive to claim and defend a clearly bordered portion of the landscape, he argued, was the controlling factor in the birds' social life . . . Beginning in the 1920s, many biologists followed his lead in making territoriality a central problem of ethology and animal behaviour studies."[38]

Although the emphasis on territory has lessened since research developments of the 1970s,[39] "territory and territoriality would remain critical parts of the ethologist's conceptual toolbox."[40]

What is remarkable about these early accounts, and indeed about Bates's review of Howard's founding research, is that the emerging significance of the concept of territory is aligned with a growing claim of a relationship to ownership: "The implications of the territory habit are considerable. . . . The owner of a territory defends it against all intruders of his own kind and the surplus population, the individuals that do not own territories, are left at great disadvantage."[41] Further, this relationship between ownership and territory is articulated through the expressive behaviour of animals. At the same time, the conspicuousness of an animal's aesthetic life (be it in song or plumage or otherwise) is similarly delimited by the concept of territory. As discussed above, Altum is credited with one of the earlier definitions of territory, in which he emphasises this concept of conspicuity as well as placing the male at the centre of territorial relations: "[T]erritory is an area occupied by one male of a species which it defends against intrusion of other males of the same species and in which it makes itself conspicuous."[42] Similarly, Howard also attaches importance to display, noting that "where territory is imperative, a male isolates himself, makes himself conspicuous, becomes intolerant of other males and exercises dominion over a definite area; and by thus establishing a territory secures ground which will supply his young with food."[43] Margaret Morse Nice observes, "An essential element of the territory system is the conspicuousness of the male."[44] However, this conspicuousness is not in terms of the male's identity, as it is often presented in popular accounts, but rather with respect to the function of territory. The male restricts his movements to an identifiable area all the while making himself as conspicuous as possible rather than taking refuge or hiding, as it were.[45] These early accounts of territoriality in birds identify territory as necessarily isolating, notwithstanding communal territories[46] or tribal territorial rights:[47] "The proximate end of the male's behaviour is isolation – how is it to be obtained? If, after having occupied a territory, the bird were to remain silent, it would run the risk of being approached by rivals; if, on the other hand, it were merely to utter the recognition call of the species, it would be attract them . . . the song, by conveying a warning, plays an important part in the whole scheme."[48] Ownership must be advertised, resources must be displayed.

In this way, territory is almost an explanation for the propertied object: "Territory implies in the male bird isolation, advertisement, fixation, and intolerance. Where these four aspects are not present, the bird does not truly hold territory."[49] That object is separate and identifiable; it is isolated. That object displays and advertises; it is brand. That object is fixed and exchangeable; it is commodity. That object is intolerant of intrusion; it is property.

Property thus understood is noticeably isolating, as distinct from the sociable rendition of pastoral territories and the relations of familiar production and *res familiaris*.[50] Authorship is thus also contrived as an isolation, with the traditional notions of the isolated, creative genius, carefully differentiated from the audience or consumer, and immune against co-creativity.[51] However, this predatory isolation is at odds with not only the sociability of territory but also the evolutionary strategy of cooperation and collective interests: "What actually makes human autonomy possible is not isolation but relationship."[52] Creative life in this sense is not for creating, but for owning and for warning. This comparative ethology of territory that was influencing an ecological sociology ultimately makes owners out of authors: "The robin bursting with song in the garden is not trying to impress his mate, nor is he the victim of mere exuberance, finding an outlet for accumulated *joie de vivre*. He is, rather, proclaiming the ownership of a territory, warning all stray robins that this area has been pre-empted and that no poaching will be allowed."[53] In this way, the robin's expression is interpreted entirely in the functionalist terms and language of ownership, invoking an economic model of creativity and deploying the language of property to correct "misinterpretations" of expressions of ownership as "mere exuberance."[54]

This early rendering of territorial behaviours in relation to the language of property belies the predatory drift of property discourse. Not only do these interpretations diminish the performative excess as "mere exuberance," rather than any creative intent, but also such interpretation relegates creativity itself to a property model of functional incentives and purposive results as applied to the human as well. Instead of making property out of art, as it were, animal territories assist in rethinking property as art:

> Can this becoming, this emergence, be called Art? That would make the territory a result of art. The artist: the first person to set out a boundary stone, or to make a mark. Property, collective or individual, is derived from that, even when it is in the service of war and oppression. Property is fundamentally artistic because art is fundamentally *poster, placard*. As Lorenz says, coral fish are posters. The expressive is primary in relation to the possessive; expressive

qualities, or matters of expression, are necessarily appropriative and constitute a having more profound than being. Not in the sense that these qualities belong to a subject, but in the sense that they delineate a territory that will belong to the subject that carries or produces them. These qualities are signatures, but the signature, the property name, is not the constituted mark of a subject, but the constituting mark of a domain, an abode.[55]

Notably, in one of the earliest systematic reviews of the developing concept of territoriality in animal sciences, Clarence Ray Carpenter, an American primatologist, accounted for territoriality not simply as physical space, or even as combined space, but rather in terms of primarily the behavourial (and arguably conceptual) dimension: "It is clear that those who have studied territoriality have attempted to conceptualize the behavior mainly in two ways: as a spatial or geographic phenomenon and as a behavioral phenomenon. It would seem advantageous to view territoriality primarily as a behavioral system which is expressed in a spatial-temporal frame of reference."[56] In this way, Carpenter interprets territoriality as a social phenomenon rather than purely a question of resources: "Territoriality is a social phenomenon involving flocks, pairs, groups, and herds. Thus it would seem that the 'perceptual-cognitive maps' or behavioral systems of animals, if and when they are charted, will more accurately represent territorial behavior than merely geographic or physical space maps . . . territoriality is of the nature of higher order, complex and dependent behavior systems."[57] Thus, territory is not always or even primarily about keeping others out; it may well be as much about fitting others in. The first comprehensive study of wolves similarly identified this kind of negotiation of overlapping space: "It appears that territory marking with urine, which above all is practiced by the pack, is not intolerant in character, but rather it represents a peaceful form of contact among neighbours."[58] Niko Tinbergen, although also incorporating defence into his understanding of territory, nevertheless links territory to sociality and tradition in his analysis in *The Herring Gull's World*. Tinbergen explains that territory for the Herring Gull is not a question of rivalrous space, or even geographical location, but rather it is the nature of sociable traditions and community: "Territory in the Herring Gull most certainly has nothing to do with the reservation of a nesting site either, as it has in hole-nesting birds. The number of nest-sites available is practically unlimited. It is only tradition that keeps a colony at its locality, and a growing colony expands into territory that was unoccupied before, simply because it was too far away from other resident gulls."[59] Thus, in some of the first comprehensive studies of the concept, territory was nevertheless recognised as relation, not merely boundary.[60]

Early attempts to recognise the relationship between the law and the environment, as well as law and geography, also approach ideas similar to this idea of territory as sociality, through the concept of "contact." One of the early formative influences on geography and law comes from the Welsh solicitor, Henry James Randall, who undertook a comprehensive study on the potential relationship between geography and various stages of human development and culture.[61] Although Randall's work has been criticised for its ethnocentrism and its colonialist perspective, it nevertheless identifies "contact" between civilisations as a catalyst for change and development, rather than attributing advancement to a specific type of geography or region. He calls this the difference between "Law in Isolation" and "Law in Contact".[62] Randall's interest in geography appears to be influenced also to a great degree by Darwinism and the accountability for a range of factors in influencing the evolution and development of the law: "It is obvious that the nature of these rules will be largely conditioned by the social structure of the particular society under observation, and that social structure in its turn will be conditioned by the external environment."[63] This relationship between law and the physical environment as a "culture contact" or acculturation is notable also in the context of early anthropology and the identification of land ownership as responsive to and in communication with the environment. This concept of contact between cultures resonates with Tarde's writings on travel and the way in which travel can provoke developments through these social relations of the coincidence and collision of ideas, frontiers not as boundaries but as relations of contact.

Thus, the art of animal territory is not in terms of territory as physical space and boundaries but in terms of producing space; that is, the relations of space, of making and keeping a home.

Covering territory

The influence of the natural sciences on the social sciences can be seen in the very translation of the concept of territory within other disciplines in the early twentieth century and the continuing influence of the concept in contemporary scholarship, including sociology, political history,[64] and indeed in law. Etienne Benson notes the interdisciplinary commonality in the term between the natural and social sciences: "They seem to be based, moreover, on a very similar model of territory."[65]

Comparative ethology has also informed some very critical early twentieth-century sociology on spatiality and territory, including Erving Goffman's exploration of territory and the social use of space within psychiatric institutions and prisons in his work, *Asylums*.[66] In his surveying of free places, group territories, and personal territory, Goffman draws upon ethological research (which he credits with a "restimulation" of work on the social use of space[67]) to understand a process of territory formation: "A continuum is involved, with a veritable home or nest at one extreme, and at the other a mere location or refuge site in which the individual feels as protected and satisfied as is possible in the setting."[68] The "sociable" nature of the territory of free place is arguably throughout Goffman's work where, "exclusiveness and sense of ownership were not involved."[69] At the same time, the mixed space of "group territory" is especially insightful in terms of the comparative ethology of that space: "a group of patients added to their access to a free place the proprietary right to keep out all other patients, except when properly invited. We can speak here of group territories."[70] What appears at first as an exclusion is arguably a sociable space ultimately navigated by manners and the "proper invitation", a space overlapping, as it were, with the sociable "proprietary" space of early territory relations. Thus, the identities and roles accommodated in that territory rely not on exclusion as such but rather on the manners or courtesy around the navigation and negotiation of boundaries; a meaningful entanglement, as it were.

Sociology in particular has had an especially productive relationship with the natural sciences in this area. Scholarship around territory in ecology was engaged within a particular area of study known as "the ecological school,"[71] and animal studies provided a rich source of scholarship[72] in what has been described as a comparative ethology in early twentieth-century sociology.[73] In many ways, however, this comparative ethology betrayed a preoccupation with finding what marked humans out as distinctive: "Fruitful areas of research comparable to those developed in comparative ethology might be, for example: territoriality . . . This expansion of orientation should lead to a better understanding of the non-cultural aspects of human social systems and in consequence to a sharper appreciation of the role of culture in human adaptation."[74] In doing so, the study of territory has itself betrayed a "predatory drift" towards an emphasis on boundaries and exclusions rather than on the sociability of encounters between bounds: "When . . . in 1939, Noble at a symposium in Washington casually referred to a territory as 'a defended area,' biology leaped at the phrase. Problems of function and motivation were relegated to pigeonholes. From that day to this, biology as a whole asks but one question of a territory: is it defended? Defense defines it."[75]

While it may be argued that the interpretation of territory in animal studies was influenced by the understanding of the territorial nation-state in human societies,[76] the very earliest relevant use of the concept appears to be in the observations of animals. But arguably, it is in the appropriation of territory in the study and arrangement of human societies that the concept becomes perverted through the process of "predatory drift," and it is this drift that might indeed influence the way in which territory studies have progressed in ethology and may sustain a contrived human exceptionalism in the studies of today. In this "territorial imperative," there is thus a construction of property as a moral imperative, an imperative not only of survival but also of that fundamental biological and social unit of survival, the family:

> [W]e must know that the territorial imperative – just one, it is true, of the evolutionary forces playing upon our lives – is the biological law on which we have founded our edifices of human morality. Our capacities for sacrifice, for altruism, for sympathy, for trust, for responsibilities to other than self-interest, for honesty, for charity, for friendship and love, for social amity and mutual interdependence have evolved. . . . Whether morality without territory is possible in man must remain as our final, unanswerable question.[77]

In other words, all of these "values" are premised upon a fundamental assumption of competition for resources, of conventional property. In this view, our morality presupposes property. And what might that say for our relationship with animals if empathy (underpinning efforts at conservation and compassion) is premised upon this predatory notion of property? From an investigation of tracks to a construction of borders, it is perhaps necessary to revisit the understanding of territory to which humans were perhaps first introduced through domestication and "to claim that similar concepts are used to explain human and animal behaviour because the two have common biological roots."[78]

Further, central to this concept of territory is the concept of scarcity, of resources over which battles must be waged and competitions won. Property thus based on this concept of territory is similarly premised upon a dynamic of scarcity, information asymmetry, or debt – that is, any kind of imbalance. But this is not to say that this is the inevitable reckoning of property, far from it. This is simply the predatory drift of the property model.

Defence defines it

> What is wrong with boundary imagery? . . . What is essential to the development of autonomy is not protection against intrusion but constructive relationship.[79]

The language of defence that is ubiquitous in territory discussions immediately characterises territory in terms of security, resonating with the language of new property and the link between security and liberty, with "the focus on boundaries as the means of comprehending and securing the basic values of freedom or autonomy."[80] In her examination of American constitutionalism, Jennifer Nedelsky identifies a comparable appeal to bounded space invoked in the language of privacy but cautions against the presumption that a rights-based discourse will restore personal autonomy: "I do not accept the position that we should simply remove the perversions of the original focus on property by replacing it with other rights to serve as boundaries."[81] Nedelsky describes the understanding of freedom and security in terms of these personal boundaries, or "bounded spheres," through which the individual's identity is a discrete shell, immune to collective interest. Even in my first studies in animal behaviour as a student, and the investigation of rank orders or hierarchies, I recall how we constructed those imaginary spheres and observed the chickens moving about within them while we counted the number of infractions or intrusions in order to measure relationships of rank; in other words, the measuring of relationships within territory according to interpretations of dominance.

The original work in these kinds of rank orders comes from observations in chickens published in 1922 by Thorleif Schjelderup-Ebbe[82] and came to be known in English as "pecking order." Although not regularly used in the scientific literature, the term "pecking order" continues to be preserved in the literature of management studies and economic theory.[83] The somewhat colloquial term is all but gone from animal studies apparently not appearing in any of the research literature since the 1980s. Granted, it has been largely replaced by "rank order," but importantly this term conveys more complex relationships of duties and obligations, as distinct from outright physical aggression and defence. The other favoured term is dominance hierarchy, but it too comes with various problems, raising difficulties by aligning rank with dominance as a kind of static term.[84] But as for pecking order, it appears to have been almost entirely appropriated by management theory and economics discourse, despite a lack of evidence for the viability of pecking order theory in practice.[85] Why are such renditions of social structure so resilient?

Pursuing this language of security and defence, the further characterisation of territory with the notion of dominance is significant. Dominance is a fraught concept in popular behaviour discourse and has escalated as a legal fiction in training language and even within breed-specific legislation.[86] Nevertheless, in the development of the territory concept, dominance has been pervasive throughout attempts at definitions. Gladwyn Kingsley Noble, the American zoologist whose fundamental definition of territory has been most regularly cited throughout the literature, interpreted dominance as the basic architecture of territory from the outset, at the same time identifying displays of dominance almost invariably in terms of resources, things, materiality: "Social dominance is directed toward objects with an uncanny eye for detail."[87] Beaglehole similarly identifies objects within the language of territorial defence and in a social context of aggression: "[T]his same principle of the use and control of property objects is equally a characteristic of animal, primitive and human societies and may be judged in all by the same objective standard of *defence against aggression*."[88]

The abrogation of property as simply the law of things is an unhelpful attenuation of property jurisprudence, and yet it is almost (and somewhat surprisingly) an omnipresence in the literature as a reassuring shorthand.[89] This object-based approach to territory reinforces interpretations through reckonings of ownership as a source of identity in a unilateral "to be" of property, as distinct from Tarde's reciprocal possession of *having*: "Here possession is reciprocal, as in the *intra-social* relation; but it can be unilateral, as in the *extra-social* relation of master to slave, or of the farmer to his cattle."[90] With the agonistic, boundary-making structure of "to be," where territory is a sphere of personal protection and security, the reciprocity of the intra-social is lost, and the links between ownership and identity as "to be" become more consolidated as fundamental questions of integrity: "Basically, property is conceived of as a part of the personality or self; it is a relation between the person and the thing. Something that the individual has touched or handled becomes imbued with a portion of his personality."[91]

Hohfeld indeed makes a very similar observation with respect to relations in law, as distinct from fixed identities in law, and laments the ambiguity in language and the expansive rhetoric of rights.[92] In support of this attention to relations and a greater clarity in the language of rights, duties, immunities, and so on, Hohfeld cites an 1877 decision in which the court stated: "The term *right* in civil society is defined to mean that which a man is entitled *to have*, or *to do*, or *to receive* from others within the limits prescribed by law."[93] That is, a right is not a fixed identity; it is articulated through a relation, always already an interaction between two beings. This has been obscured by the suggestion of absolute dominion in respect of ownership discourse and concepts. And the dominant discourse in rights reflects a similar emphasis on possessory and rivalrous conceptions of identity and freedom, as distinct from the sociability expressed through Tarde's concept of reciprocal possession and Hohfeld's very similar articulation of jural relations. As is becoming clear, through the inheritance of a kind of biological determinism not only in sociology, but also in many other fields, including anthropology, geography and law, the predatory drift in the discourse on territory becomes habitual.[94] Aggressiveness becomes territory's "kindred phenomenon."[95]

Thus, the concept of territory, as defined by defence and aggression, serves to instate and perpetuate human exceptionalism by presenting the wild state to which every animal cannot but return, always betrayed by their biology, enslaved by instinct, and uncivilised in their zoopathology, as it were. Just as so-called primitive societies have been relegated, separated, and exceptionalised as bewitched by custom, the discourse on the animal in property, of property, as property, is consistently captive in this perspective. But while the object-based analysis of property may serve the boundary-making discourse of human exceptionalism with the contrived freedom of human distinction, "That particular form of freedom would, I think, be radically transformed if we were to come to see ourselves as 'inseparable from all the other beings in the universe.'"[96]

Nevertheless, although early jurisprudence and anthropology largely dismissed so-called primitive property systems on the basis of the dominance of this unilateral model, some notable exceptions recognised the reciprocal sociable systems and dared to transform this perspective. Hallowell asserts: "Property as a social institution implies a system of relations between individuals."[97] And Edward Adamson Hoebel calls for a cross-cultural understanding of property on the basis of dynamic relations, drawing upon Hohfeld's jurisprudence.[98] Responding to the innovative work of another anthropologist, Bronislaw Malinowski, whose work is considered further in later discussion,[99] Hoebel explicitly details this fundamental relation of reciprocal possession: "[Malinowski] insisted that the key to law is reciprocity and its basic sanction the withdrawal of reciprocal services. . . . The lawyer who reads and digests the meat of the materials from primitive man will find himself orienting his legal thought in terms of law as a social device, *viz.* a means to an end, not an end in itself."[100] In such reciprocity is also found the law of social morality, as it were, of sanctions and rules: "[T]he same principle of mutuality supplies the sanction for each rule. There is in every act a sociological dualism: two parties who exchange services and functions, each watching over the measure of fulfilment and the fairness of conduct of the other."[101]

This sociological dualism is not only a quality of Tarde's laws of imitation but also, as will be shown in later chapters, a key articulation of Hohfeld's fundamental legal conceptions. Rather than property being conceived as a unilateral relation between a person and the thing, Hohfeld emphasises the reciprocal relations between two beings, in concert with Tarde's logical duel structure,[102] and Malinowski's mutuality. Hohfeld's noted respondent, Walter Wheeler Cook, explains Hohfeld's system in terms marvellously resonant with Tarde's monadological perspective: "He does not *own* the rights, etc., he *has* them; because he has them, he 'owns' in very truth the material object concerned."[103]

And relations move.

Movable property

> A nomadic people, wandering from place to place, is not associated in any sense with the soil; the tribe remains the same, but not the territory it occupies. With the beginning of agriculture and sedentariness this relation is reversed. The conception of a nation, nowadays, implies fixed or at least well-defined geographical boundaries. Changes may take place in the character of the inhabitants and in the constitution of the government as the result of emigration and revolution; individuals and families may disappear and be superseded by others of a different stock, but the nation remains, as it were, *adscripta glebæ* within certain territorial limits and is not destroyed by any admixture of foreign with native elements in the population.[104]

But what if territory moves?

Nineteenth-century accounts of so-called primitive nomadic groups gave limited credit to the social organisation around territory, almost invariably struggling to find concepts of property among nomadic hunters.[105] Much of this disregard of ownership within such societies was based upon a perception that such societies simply had no concept of individual ownership in the land: "This attitude has been current since the time of Lewis H. Morgan, who categorically assumed that such a characteristic was to be found only among peoples endowed with civilization, as he defined the term."[106]

Nevertheless, several early twentieth-century anthropologists began to question this simplified account of earlier civilisations and to critique the view of nomadic peoples as the "unrestricted wanderer."[107] In 1928, Daniel Sutherland Davidson explained the very clear property customs around territory among Australian indigenous people: "Although a constant nomad, however, and this point cannot be too strongly emphasized, the Australian is not the unrestricted wanderer which some would have us believe. Neither the tribe, the local group, the family, nor the individual move about from one part of the continent to the other wherever fancy happens to guide, for all are bound to certain customs and traditions which have the force of inviolable laws," and "there are well defined limits beyond which an individual and his family may not trespass."[108] As Davidson maintained, "The local group is a land-owning unit"[109] and "Boundaries of the local group territory are well known."[110] The laws are not only enforced but also clearly communicated to others: "among many of the hunting peoples individual ownership of land is not only a recognized principle, but in fact often a most outstanding culture characteristic."[111]

Even earlier accounts describe the ownership of territory as individual property, whereby the territory is "used in common" but further subdivided "each of which is the personal property of a single male."[112] The mutuality of "ownership," in the Australian context, as a circulation of obligations as distinct from static objects, is also recognised and considered in this early anthropological account: "The fundamentality of land ownership in Australia is further evinced in another connection, that of the deep regard which an Australian holds for his birthplace. In some parts of Australia, the native mind has developed the philosophy that not only does the land belong to the humans, but also that the humans likewise belong to the land."[113] This is notable also in the context of the flux of territorial properties, responding to changing conditions in environment and ecology in a kind of communicative relation between owner and land, as distinct from a static dominion over the land as object.[114]

In a review article highly critical of the methodological approach to studying hunter-gatherer territoriality, "where the hunting-gathering group under study is researched as if it were an archaic paleolithic societal form," Mathias Georg Guenther provides an interesting account of attempts in the literature to reconcile the mobile territories of a hunter-gatherer society with the modular property model characterised by its defence and exclusion. Guenther notes: "'[T]erritoriality' is poorly defined as an analytical category . . . it is treated as an independent, biological variable and not as a dependent, cultural variable that interacts with a number of other factors."[115] In critiquing a particular study of "hunter-gatherer territoriality," where the authors depict the !Ko Bushmen of the central Kalahari as aggressive and territorial, Guenther identifies in their research what is instead a kind of "group territory" model in order to accommodate encounters and indeed communications between territories through a kind of commons model:

> Heinz presents the !Ko as strongly territorial. Their ranges are "precisely demarcated", both conceptually and by land marks, so that a person from the wrong group "would not step over an imaginary line" and would never hunt on the wrong territory, not even obtain permission to do so. It is to be noted that in the case of the !Ko (as among the !Kung), the bands themselves are apparently not territorial (although the point is not clearly made since early in the article, on page 407, the band is said to be a territorial unit as well). . . . One inconsistency in Heinz' presentation of !Ko territoriality is that, despite their strictly demarcated boundaries, there are, nevertheless, "strips of no-man's land" between the territorial units on which members from neighbouring groups can hunt and gather. The existence of such tracts of common land seems inconsistent with rigid territoriality and

suggests, instead, not mutual exclusiveness but overlap of territories. That is, 'no-man's land' may, perhaps, be 'everyman's land' which blurs rather than defines inter-group boundaries. Upholding the notion that 'man is a territorial animal' Heinz may himself have committed a '*Beobachtungsfehler*' and presented an exaggerated picture of !Ko nexus-territoriality."[116]

Highlighting the link between the socio-political context for research and the potential for contrived environments and thus misleading influence upon scientific perspectives, Guenther goes further to critique the study's reliance upon colonial periods of research, neglecting the fact that "They were written in the late nineteenth and early twentieth centuries, a period when the white settlers encroached on the Bushmen."[117]

Methodologically, this is not dissimilar from the problems that arose from early wolf research where artificial groups were defined as "packs" and thus territoriality and aggression were identified as integral to pack behaviour. Guenther notes: "The aggressive, territorial Bushman is thus a product of a particular historical, acculturative situation, one in which hostile colonist neighbours encroach and are met in corresponding fashion, instilling in the natives aggressive ethos, and socio-political organization, and territorial closedness. . . . The pejorative stereotype presented in these nineteenth century writings goes back to the seventeenth century, the time of contact."[118] There is certainly nothing inevitably objective about biological determinism: "[S]ome accounts, consciously or not on the part of the authors, exaggerated these traits for ideological or political motives."[119]

Nevertheless, there have been notable challenges to this nature/culture divide in the territory concept in sociology,[120] and indeed in ethology itself, particularly motivated by developments in cognitive ethology. Importantly, this "zoological turn" in sociology is an enchanting precursor for the notion of the ethological jurisprudence that is emerging.[121]

And in walks that dog.

Notes

1. Tarde G (1890/[1903]) *The Laws of Imitation*, EC Parsons (trans.), Henry Holt & Co, New York, 277.
2. Tarde G (1890/[1903]) *The Laws of Imitation*, EC Parsons (trans.), Henry Holt & Co, New York, 277.
3. Heape W (1931) *Emigration, Migration and Nomadism*, W Heffer & Sons, Cambridge, 25.
4. Heape W (1931) *Emigration, Migration and Nomadism*, W Heffer & Sons, Cambridge, 25.
5. As introduced in Socialisation and explored further in the later chapter, Predatory Drift, property "does not depend on another's courtesy." Greenberg D et al. (eds.), *Jowitt's Dictionary of English Law*, 5th edition, Sweet & Maxwell, London, 2019.
6. Heape W (1931) *Emigration, Migration and Nomadism*, W Heffer & Sons, Cambridge, 29. Notably, Heape explains that where the rules of territory are

breached or violated is in the case of predators, the notion of absolute dominion in terms of predation. This becomes very relevant in the development of the concept of predatory drift in the Dominion Age as well as the discussion of ownership and "the captor" in *Res familiaris*. See further Brighenti A (2006) On Territory as Relationship and Law as Territory, *Canadian Journal of Law and Society/Revue Canadienne Droit et Société*, 21(2), 65–86: pp. 68–69.

7 Heape W (1931) *Emigration, Migration and Nomadism*, W Heffer & Sons, Cambridge, 24–25.
8 The concept of familiar production is introduced in detail in Gibson J (2014) *The Logic of Innovation*, Ashgate, Aldershot (see especially pp. 38–44), as well as discussed more fully in Chapter 12, "*Res familiaris.*"
9 Beaglehole E (1931) *Property: A Study in Social Psychology*, George Allen & Unwin, London. Ernest Beaglehole engaged in a conscientious study of acquisitiveness, although a presumed acquisitive instinct can be found in a range of much earlier anthropological sources. Heape, as seen in the quote opening this chapter, also refers to acquisition in relation to territory as a fundamental characteristic of all animals: Heape W (1931) *Emigration, Migration and Nomadism*, W Heffer & Sons, Cambridge, 74.
10 Beaglehole E (1931) *Property: A Study in Social Psychology*, George Allen & Unwin, London, 14.
11 See further the discussion in Long AA (1997) Stoic Philosophers on Persons, Property-Ownership and Community, *Bulletin of the Institute of Classical Studies*, 68, Aristotle and After, 13–31, where the author argues that Stoic doctrine on property and persons has certain shared notions with ideas developed by Locke and Hegel.
12 Hallowell AI (1942) The Nature and Function of Property as a Social Institution, *Journal of Legal and Political Sociology*, 1, 115–138: pp. 134–135.
13 See further the discussion of altruism and cooperation in Chapter 10, "Shared interests". On self-management, see also the work of Ruth Ostrom on the commons, discussed in Chapter 12, "*Rex familiaris.*"
14 Hallowell AI (1942) The Nature and Function of Property as a Social Institution, *Journal of Legal and Political Sociology*, 1, 115–138: p. 133.
15 Hallowell AI (1942) The Nature and Function of Property as a Social Institution, *Journal of Legal and Political Sociology*, 1, 115–138: p. 135.
16 Hallowell AI (1942) The Nature and Function of Property as a Social Institution, *Journal of Legal and Political Sociology*, 1, 115–138: p. 137.
17 See in particular the discussion in Chapter 10, "Shared interests."
18 Krier JE (2009) Evolutionary Theory and the Origin of Property Rights, *Cornell Law Review*, 95, 139–159: p. 152. See further the discussion of "dominance by those in possession" in Nice MM (1941) The Role of Territory in Bird Life, *The American Midland Naturalist*, 26(3), 441–487: p. 469.
19 For a comprehensive examination of the bourgeois strategy, see Maynard Smith J & Price GR (1973) The Logic of Animal Conflict, *Nature*, 246, 15–18; Maynard Smith J (1979) Game Theory and the Evolution of Behaviour, *Proceedings of the Royal Society of London*, 205(1161), 475–488.
20 George Price has become best known for his contributions to the science of altruism: Harman O (2011) *The Price of Altruism*, Vintage, London.
21 Maynard Smith J (1979) Game Theory and the Evolution of Behaviour, *Proceedings of the Royal Society of London*, 205(1161), 475–488: p. 481.
22 Maynard Smith J (1979) Game Theory and the Evolution of Behaviour, *Proceedings of the Royal Society of London*, 205(1161), 475–488.

23 Veblen T (1898) The Instinct of Workmanship and the Irksomeness of Labor, *American Journal of Sociology*, 4(2), 187–201: p. 196.
24 Maynard Smith J (1979) Game Theory and the Evolution of Behaviour, *Proceedings of the Royal Society of London*, 205(1161), 475–488: p. 47.
25 The Oxford English Dictionary provides the first use as 1432–40 in *Higden* (Rolls). What is particularly notable, as will also be explored in the present discussion, is that throughout the at times quite different meanings and applications of territory across a range of disciplines, the definitions nevertheless rely on common principles of exclusion and boundary making. See further the discussion of boundary metaphors in Nedelsky J (1990) Law, Boundaries, and the Bounded Self, *Representations*, 30, 162–189: p. 172.
26 Willughby F et al. (1678) *The Ornithology of Francis Willughby of Middleton in the County of Warwick, Esq*, John Martyn, London, 222. This sentence was added in the English edition by John Ray but did not appear in the original Latin edition of 1676. It is also notable, in the context of "creative property", that the sentence originally translated as "it ordinarily sings in its freehold." See the discussion in Nice MM (1941) The Role of Territory in Bird Life, *The American Midland Naturalist*, 26(3), 441–487: p. 442.
27 Goldsmith O (1824) *A History of the Earth, and Animated Nature, Volume II, Part Third, History of Animated Nature, Birds*, Henry Fisher: Caxton Press, London, 121. See further the later 1854 collection of Oliver Goldsmith's works: Goldsmith O (1854) *The Works of Oliver Goldsmith*, P Cunningham (ed.), John Murray, London, 352.
28 Evans EP (1894) The Ethics of Tribal Society, *Popular Science Monthly*, 44, 289–207: p. 305.
29 Compare the later work on human territoriality from Robert Sack, where the link between territoriality and power (towards predatory drift) is starting to dominate. In his concept of human territoriality, Robert Sack defines territoriality as "the attempt by an individual or group to influence, affect, or control objects, people, and relationships by delimiting and asserting control over a geographic area. This area is the territory." Sack clarifies further the nature of territorial encounter or contact that is integral to territory "Territoriality is an extension of action by contact. It is a strategy to establish differential access to people, things, and relationships. Its alternative is always nonterritorial action." See Sack RD (1983) Human Territoriality: A Theory, *Annals of the Association of American Geographers*, 73(1) 55–74: p. 56.
30 Carpenter CR (1958) Territoriality: A Review of Concepts and Problems, in Roe A & Simpson GG (eds.) *Behavior and Evolution*, Yale UP, New Haven, 224–250. See further William H Burt, writing in 1949: "It is fairly well agreed, I believe, among those who are competent to judge, that territoriality does exist as a part of the behavioristic pattern of many kinds of animals (birds, mammals, reptiles, fishes, and some invertebrates). If this is true, and we shall for the moment assume that it is, what might be its biological significance?" Burt WH (1949) Territoriality, *Journal of Mammalogy*, 30(1), 25–27: p. 25. Territoriality was accepted as a biological phenomenon, once again defining the animal purely in terms of perpetuating the species: "If success of a species of mammal be defined as longevity in time (either by the species or by its descendents), it probably is advantageous for individuals to possess a territorial trait . . . Whatever may be the biological implications of territoriality, and there probably are many, we can say with certainty that it is a potent factor which serves as a kind of governor in preventing over-population." (26–27).

31 Alongside the work of Eliot Howard, most notably in *Territory in Birdlife*, published in 1920. See the discussion in Nice MM (1941) The Role of Territory in Bird Life, *The American Midland Naturalist*, 26(3), 441–487: p. 441.
32 Mayr E (1935) Bernard Altum and the Territory Theory, *Proceedings of the Linnaean Society of New York*, 45–46, 24–38.
33 Bates M (1990/[1950]) *The Nature of Natural History*, Princeton UP, Princeton, 157: "The history of science is full of illustrations of the futility of being ahead of the times. The general acceptance of an idea depends on a receptive mental environment among the scientific community, on the ripeness of the time."
34 Howard HE (1920) *Territory in Bird Life*, EP Dutton & Co, New York.
35 Mayr E (1935) Bernard Altum and the Territory Theory, *Proceedings of the Linnaean Society of New York*, 45–46, 24–38: p. 31.
36 Nice MM (1941) The Role of Territory in Bird Life, *The American Midland Naturalist*, 26(3), 441–487: p. 470.
37 Howard was in fact an amateur naturalist, being the director of a steelworks, but is credited with demonstrating the importance of fieldwork to the development of ethology: Burkhardt RW, Jr (2005) *Patterns of Behavior: Konrad Lorenz, Niko Tinbergen, and the Founding of Ethology*, U of Chicago P, Chicago, 92.
38 Benson E (2014) The Biopolitics of the Border, *RCC Perspectives: The Edges of Environmental History*, 81–86: p. 81.
39 Indeed, the concept had become so dominant in behaviour studies that territory became a fundamental starting point of analysis. In 1933, the ornithologist, Margaret Morse Nice, stated: "Howard's great service was emphasis. He has captured the imagination of the bird students of the world and the latter are in danger of going territory-mad. Every one now scoffs at the former notion of males battling over the females and it is the fashion to consider that every single bird must have a territory, be it never so small or undefended." See Nice MM (1933) The Theory of Territorialism and Its Development, *Fifty Years' Progress of American Ornithology, 1883–1933*, American Ornithologists' Union, Lancaster PA, 89–100: p. 90.
40 Benson E (2014) The Biopolitics of the Border, *RCC Perspectives: The Edges of Environmental History*, 81–86: p. 82.
41 Bates M (1990/[1950]) *The Nature of Natural History*, Princeton UP, Princeton, 157.
42 Cited in Carpenter CR (1958) Territoriality: A Review of Concepts and Problems, in Roe A & Simpson GG (eds.) *Behavior and Evolution*, Yale UP, New Haven, 224–250: p. 225. In his persistently influential review of the concept, primatologist, Clarence Ray Carpenter, notes the importance of Altum's influence in territory studies.
43 Howard HE (1929) *An Introduction to the Study of Bird Behaviour*, Cambridge UP, Cambridge, 63.
44 Nice MM (1933) The Theory of Territorialism and Its Development, *Fifty Years' Progress of American Ornithology, 1883–1933*, American Ornithologists' Union, Lancaster PA, 89–100: p. 95.
45 Howard HE (1929) *An Introduction to the Study of Bird Behaviour*, Cambridge UP, Cambridge, 63.
46 For example, rookeries, which establish community through the operation of defined communal territories: "A community, however, in the true sense of the word, is a collection of individuals brought together, not primarily as a result of shortage of breeding ground, but in consequence of advantages of communal ownership over individual ownership. A rookery is an example of a true community." Howard HE (1920) *Territory in Bird Life*, EP Dutton & Co, New York, 202. See further the discussion from Ernest Thompson Seton of nurseries

of particular species as a "home region" or "home range" in, for example, Seton ET, *Life-Histories of Northern Mammals: Volume 1, Grass-Eaters*, Charles Scribner's Sons, New York City, 1909.
47 Heape W (1931) *Emigration, Migration and Nomadism*, W Heffer & Sons, Cambridge, 74.
48 Howard HE (1920) *Territory in Bird Life*, EP Dutton & Co, New York, 147–148.
49 Nice MM (1933) The Theory of Territorialism and Its Development, *Fifty Years' Progress of American Ornithology, 1883–1933*, American Ornithologists' Union, Lancaster PA, 89–100: p. 98.
50 Jennifer Nedelsky identifies a similar effect of isolation in the United States constitutional protection of liberty through the links to property: "The perverse quality of this conception is clearest when taken to its extreme: the most perfectly autonomous man is the most perfectly isolated." See Nedelsky J (1990) Law, Boundaries, and the Bounded Self, *Representations*, 30, 162–189: p. 167.
51 Gibson J (2006) *Creating Selves*, Ashgate, Aldershot, 109. See further the discussion of territory and classes of authorship, 64–66.
52 Nedelsky J (1990) Law, Boundaries, and the Bounded Self, *Representations*, 30, 162–189: p. 169.
53 Bates M (1990/[1950]) *The Nature of Natural History*, Princeton UP, Princeton, 156.
54 Recent research has detailed many examples of not only pleasure but also novelty and originality in bird song. See for example the extensive work of Gisela Kaplan: Kaplan G (2009) Animals and Music: Between Cultural Definitions and Sensory Evidence, *Sign System Studies*, 37(3/4), 75–101: Kaplan G (2015) *Bird Minds: Cognition and Behaviour of Australian Native Birds*, CSIRO, Clayton South, VIC; Kaplan G & Rogers LJ (2007) Elephants That Paint, Birds That Make Music: Do Animals Have an Aesthetic Sense? in Read CA (ed), *Cerebrum 2007: Emerging Ideas in Brain Science*, Dana Foundation Press, New York, 1–14.
55 Deleuze G & Guattari F (1980/[1987]) *A Thousand Plateaus: Capitalism and Schizophrenia*, B Massumi (trans.), U of Minnesota P, Minneapolis, 316.
56 Carpenter CR (1958) Territoriality: A Review of Concepts and Problems, in Roe A & Simpson GG (eds.) *Behavior and Evolution*, Yale UP, New Haven, 224–250: p. 228.
57 Carpenter CR (1958) Territoriality: A Review of Concepts and Problems, in Roe A & Simpson GG (eds.) *Behavior and Evolution*, Yale UP, New Haven, 224–250: pp. 229–230. Intellectual property rules present a curious inflection of this relationship, in that the object is indeed tied to territory, but territory persists where the object does not. In other words, a trade mark will be registered and exist within a territory, but outside that territory as far as the law is concerned, the trade mark will not exist, even though the sign does, confounding to an extent the object-based approach to territory, and reaffirming the behavioural and social interpretation, even in the context of explicit legal rules of territory.
58 Schenkel R (1947) Ausdrucks-Studien an Wölfen: Gefangenschafts-Beobachtungen, *Behaviour*, 1(2), 81–129: pp. 84/86.
59 Tinbergen N (1960/[1971]) *The Herring Gull's World: A Study of the Social Behaviour of Birds*, Harper Torchbook, New York, 94.
60 See Chapter 8, "Pack fiction" for a more comprehensive discussion of this particular wolf study, as well as the legacy of wolf research, where the problems and the impact of presumptions and mythologies arising from that early wolf research is considered in more detail. See also the discussion of smell and space in Chapter 6, "Separation anxiety."
61 Randall HJ (1918) Law and Geography, in A Kocourek & JH Wigmore (eds.) *Evolution of Law, Select Readings on the Origin and Development of Legal*

Institutions: Volume III, Formative Influences of Legal Development, Little Brown & Co, Boston, 198–214. This early legal geography is significant for the emphasis on the relationship between spatial character, movement, geography, and the marking of territory, as will become clearer in the discussion of landmarks in Chapter 5, "Resource guarding."

62 Randall HJ (1918) Law and Geography, in A Kocourek & JH Wigmore (eds.) *Evolution of Law, Select Readings on the Origin and Development of Legal Institutions: Volume III, Formative Influences of Legal Development*, Little Brown & Co, Boston, 198–214: p. 204. See further the comments on Randall's work in Cairns H (1941) *The Theory of Legal Science*, U of North Carolina P, Chapel Hill, 117.

63 Randall HJ (1918) Law and Geography, in A Kocourek & JH Wigmore (eds.) *Evolution of Law, Select Readings on the Origin and Development of Legal Institutions: Volume III, Formative Influences of Legal Development*, Little Brown & Co, Boston, 198–214: p. 203.

64 For instance, see Sassen S (2006) *Territory, Author, Rights: From Medieval to Global Assemblages*, Princeton UP, Princeton.

65 Benson E (2014) The Biopolitics of the Border, *RCC Perspectives: The Edges of Environmental History*, 81–86: p. 82.

66 Goffman E (1961) *Asylums: Essays on the Social Situation of Mental Patients and Other Inmates*, Anchor Books-Doubleday, New York.

67 Goffman E (1961) *Asylums: Essays on the Social Situation of Mental Patients and Other Inmates*, Anchor Books-Doubleday, New York, 227 note 80.

68 Goffman E (1961) *Asylums: Essays on the Social Situation of Mental Patients and Other Inmates*, Anchor Books-Doubleday, New York, 243–244.

69 Goffman E (1961) *Asylums: Essays on the Social Situation of Mental Patients and Other Inmates*, Anchor Books-Doubleday, New York, 239.

70 Goffman E (1961) *Asylums: Essays on the Social Situation of Mental Patients and Other Inmates*, Anchor Books-Doubleday, New York, 239.

71 See McKenzie RD (1924) The Ecological Approach to the Study of the Human Community, *American Journal of Sociology*, 30(3), 287–301. In this context it is useful also to note the principle of commensalism, derived from biology, as applied in the social sciences and, in particular, the study of shared use of space in plant communities: "The majority of individuals of a plant-community are linked by bonds . . . bonds that are best described as *commensal*. The term commensalism is due to Van Beneden, who wrote 'Le commensal es simplement un compagnon de table'; but we employ it in a somewhat different sense to denote the relationship subsisting between species which share with one another the supply of food material contained in soil and air, and thus feed at the same table." Park RE & Burgess EW (1921) *Introduction to the Science of Sociology*, U of Chicago P, Chicago, 175. This resonates strongly with the work of Donna Haraway and the notion of "messmates at table" developed in Haraway D (2008) *When Species Meet*, U of Minnesota P, Minneapolis.

72 Ardrey R (1967) *The Territorial Imperative*, Collins, London.

73 Tiger L & Fox R (1966) The Zoological Perspective in Social Science, *Man*, 1, 75–81.

74 Tiger L & Fox R (1966) The Zoological Perspective in Social Science, *Man*, 1, 75–81: p. 80.

75 Ardrey R, *The Territorial Imperative*, Collins, London, 1967, 210. See further the review of territory by ornithologist Margaret Morse Nice and the central nature of defence in the various uses of the concept, in Nice MM (1941) The Role of Territory in Bird Life, *The American Midland Naturalist*, 26(3), 441–487: "Noble's definition (1939) that a "territory is any defended area' is in

my opinion the most satisfactory because it is so simple and inclusive" (441). An interesting aside to this organising principle of "defence" that underpins notions of territoriality in ethology is the etymology of the English word itself. Andrea Brighenti notes that as well as the generally accepted origins in *terra* ("dry land") the root *tĕrrere*, meaning "to frighten", is also a possible origin: "Following this second hypothesis, territory is 'a place from which people are warned off'. From this point of view, the very origin of the term seems to reveal a functional dimension within which territories arise." See Brighenti A (2006) On Territory as Relationship and Law as Territory, *Canadian Journal of Law and Society/Revue Canadienne Droit et Société*, 21(2), 65–86: p. 67. Brighenti also identifies a link in ethology between territoriality and the study of aggression: Brighenti AM (2010) On Territorology, *Theory, Culture & Society*, 27(1), 52–72.
76 Benson E (2014) The Biopolitics of the Border, *RCC Perspectives: The Edges of Environmental History*, 81–86: p. 83.
77 Ardrey R, *The Territorial Imperative*, Collins, London, 1967, 351.
78 Benson E (2014) The Biopolitics of the Border, *RCC Perspectives: The Edges of Environmental History*, 81–86: p. 83. Benson notes: "One can therefore argue that territory was central to diplomacy and to ethology in the twentieth century because it is central to the lives of humans and many other kinds of animals. It simply took the flourishing of biological science in the twentieth century to make that fact clear." (83–84).
79 Nedelsky J (1990) Law, Boundaries, and the Bounded Self, *Representations*, 30, 162–189: p. 168. Nedelsky continues: "What is essential to the development of autonomy is not protection against intrusion but constructive relationship. The central question for inquiries into autonomy (legal or otherwise) is then how to structure relationships so that they foster rather than undermine autonomy. The boundary metaphor does not direct our attention to this question. Instead it invites us to imagine that the self to be protected is in some crucial sense insular and that what is most important to the preservation of such a self is drawing boundaries around it that will protect it from invasion (or at least that is the most crucial thing the law can do). (pages 168–169).
80 Nedelsky J (1990) Law, Boundaries, and the Bounded Self, *Representations*, 30, 162–189: p. 162.
81 Nedelsky J (1990) Law, Boundaries, and the Bounded Self, *Representations*, 30, 162–189: p. 168.
82 Schjelderup-Ebbe T (1922) Beiträge zur Sozialpsychologie des haushuhns/ Contributions to the Social Psychology of the Domestic Chicken, *Zeitschrift für Psychologie*, 88, 225–252, M Schleidt & WM Schleidt (trans.), in Schein MW (ed.) (1975) *Social Hierarchy and Dominance*, Dowden, Hutchinson & Ross, Stroudsburg, PA, 7–49. On the derivation of the term itself, see further Perrin G (1955) "Pecking Order" 1924–54, *American Speech*, 30(4), 265–268.
83 Some recent examples: Zeiden R et al. (2018) Do Ultimate Owners Follow the Pecking Order Theory?, *The Quarterly Review of Economics and Finance*, 67, 45–50; Fuxiu Jiang et al. (2017) A Pecking Order of Shareholder Structure, *Journal of Corporate Finance*, 44, 1–14; Allini A et al. (2018), Pecking Order and Market Timing Theory in Emerging Markets: The Case of Egyptian Firms, *Research in International Business and Finance*, 44, 297–308.
84 Further, dominance has been taken to mean both a "property" (quality) and an action to the detriment of precision in welfare and training discourse. On this question of language, the British jurist, Sir Thomas Erskine Holland, notes a

similar problem in relation to the various meanings of the term "right": "This simple meaning of the term 'a right' is for the purposes of the jurist entirely adequate. It has, however, been covered with endless confusion owing to its similarity to 'Right'; an abstract term formed from the adjective ' right,' in the same way that 'Justice' is formed from the adjective 'just.' Hence it is that Blackstone actually opposes 'rights' in the sense of capacities, to 'wrongs' in the sense of 'unrighteous acts.' . . . If the expression of widely different ideas by one and the same term resulted only in the necessity for these clumsy periphrases, or obviously inaccurate paraphrases, no great harm would be done; but unfortunately the identity of terms seems irresistibly to suggest an identity between the ideas which are expressed by them." This difficulty occurs not only in the combination of dominance and hierarchy but also in the language of property and ownership, of law and rights, and so on. See Holland TE (1916) *Jurisprudence*, 12th ed, Clarendon Press, Oxford, 84–85. In his endeavour to address the precision in legal language, Hohfeld calls this "the principle of linguistic contamination." See Hohfeld WN (1917) Fundamental Legal Conceptions as Applied in Judicial Reasoning, *The Yale Law Journal*, 26(8), 710–770: p. 716. The concepts of dominance, territorial behaviour, and hierarchy are examined in more detail in Chapter 8, "Pack fiction."
85 Seifert B & Gonenc H (2008) The International Evidence on the Pecking Order Hypothesis, *Journal of Multinational Financial Management*, 18(3), 244–260; Frank MZ & Goyal VK (2003) Testing the Pecking Order Theory of Capital Structure, *Journal of Financial Economics*, 67(2), 217–248.
86 See further the review of legislation in Cooke F (2017) Canine Aggression and the Law: An International Perspective," Mills DS & Westgarth C (eds.) *Dog Bites: A Muiltidisciplinary Perspective*, 5m Publishing, Sheffield, 191–204.
87 Noble GK (1939) The Role of Dominance in the Social Life of Birds, *The Auk*, 56(3), 263–273: p. 269.
88 Beaglehole E (1931) *Property: A Study in Social Psychology*, George Allen & Unwin, London, 16 (emphasis added).
89 For instance, in a comment on the American Law Institute's 1937 Restatement of Law of Property of the Property, John P Maloney notes, "The Restatement uses the word 'property' to denote legal relations between persons with respect to a thing," but in the very next paragraph also notes that "the Hohfeld system of terminology has been adopted almost *in toto*." See Maloney JP (1937) Restatement of the Law of Property, *St John's Law Review*, 12, 1–21: p. 7. Compare the "distinct sense of disappointment" in the quest for terminology in the Restatement, conveyed by William R Vance in his comment on the same edition of the document, where he argues, "Lawyers and judges do not in fact understand the Hohfeld system, and one suspects that even the restaters have their difficulties with it." See Vance WR (1937–1938) Restatement of the Law of Property, *U of Pennsylvania Law Review*, 86, 173–188: pp. 174, 175. Vance goes on to argue: "The plan of the *Restatement* is based upon the misconception that 'the law' is static and capable of formulary statement; that it is subject to still photography" (178). He rejects the value of restating the "black letter rules" with no anthropology, as it were, of the law: "The black letter rules have no literary merit, and as declarations of law, supported only by their own authority, they are absurd" (188).
90 Tarde G (1893/[2012]) *Monadology and Sociology*, T Lorenc (trans.), Re-Press, Melbourne, 54.
91 Cairns H (1931) Law and Anthropology, *Columbia Law Review*, 31(1), 32–55: p. 43.
92 Hohfeld WN (1913) Some Fundamental Legal Conceptions as Applied in Judicial Reasoning, *Yale Law Journal*, 23(1), 16–59: p. 31 note 29.

93 *Atchison & Neb. R. Co. v Baty* (1877), 6 Neb., 37, 40.
94 Indeed, Andrea Mubi Brighenti notes that "the term itself sounds uncanny and slightly arcane among social scientists, probably because it is generally associated with biological and ethological determinism." See Brighenti AM (2010) On Territorology: Towards a General Science of Territory, *Theory, Culture & Society*, 27(1), 52–72: p. 52.
95 Guenther MG (1981) Bushman and Hunter-Gatherer Territoriality, *Zeitschrift für Ethnologie*, 106(1/2), 109–120: p. 109.
96 Nedelsky J (1990) Law, Boundaries, and the Bounded Self, *Representations*, 30, 162–189: p. 183. Nedelsky also traces a practice of boundary-making in relation to children (171–176), of which much of this can be seen also in dog training discourse, particularly in the perversely anti-social discourse of so-called balanced training. While it is beyond the scope of the present discussion to review this in detail, the notion of "practicing separateness," as set out by Nedelsky, is certainly echoed in training discourse (172). Terms such as "safe space" (applied in the use of crates or cages for dogs), setting boundaries (particularly applied during socialisation, and in relation to communication behaviours such as jumping up, or in disputes over furniture or rooms in the house), aversive training and apprehension around strangers, an emphasis on the human as "pack leader" with a concurrent lessening of control or autonomy on the part of the dog, suggested as a kind of "freedom" for the dog, and many more examples, all contribute to a language of separation and exceptionalism, of control and subjection, and, above all, convenience. As Nedelsky notes, this is at odds with values of attunement and sociability (175). Incentives, aversives, positive reinforcement, and the language of consequences are all considered in more detail in Chapter 10, "Shared interests."
97 Hallowell AI (1942) The Nature and Function of Property as a Social Institution, *Journal of Legal and Political Sociology*, 1, 115–138: p. 119.
98 Hoebel EA (1942) Fundamental Legal Concepts as Applied in the Study of Primitive Law, *Yale Law Journal*, 51, 951–966.
99 See Chapter 7 "Predatory drift" in "Part 3, Dominion, the machine age."
100 Hoebel EA (1946) Law and Anthropology, *Virginia Law Review*, 32(4), 835–854: p. 851.
101 Malinowski B (1926) *Crime and Custom in Savage Society*, Harcourt Brace & Co, New York, 26.
102 Tarde G (1890/[1903]) *The Laws of Imitation*, EC Parsons (trans.), Henry Holt & Co, New York, 154–173.
103 Cook WW (1919) Hohfeld's Contributions to the Science of Law, *The Yale Law Journal*, 28(8), 721–738: pp. 729–730.
104 Evans EP (1894) The Ethics of Tribal Society, *Popular Science Monthly*, 44, 289–207: p. 304.
105 For instance, see the evolutionary property model of Lewis Henry Morgan, which found favour with Karl Marx and Joseph Engels because of the communitarian models of ownership in early civilisations: Morgan LH (1877) *Ancient People, or Researches in the Line of Human Progress, from Savagery through Barbarism to Civilization*, Charles H Kerr & Co, Chicago.
106 Davidson DS (1928) Family Hunting Territories of the Tribes of Tierra del Fuego, *Indian Notes*, 5(1), 395–410: pp. 395–396. See further the work of Frank G Speck and the demonstration of property rights in hunting grounds: Speck FG (1914–1915) The Basis of American Indian Ownership of the Land. University of Pennsylvania Faculty, Public Lectures, Philadelphia, 181–196; Speck FG (1926) Land Ownership among Hunting Peoples in Primitive America and the

World's Marginal Areas. Proceedings, Twenty-second International Congress of Americanists, Rome, 323–332.
107 Davidson DS (1928) The Family Hunting Territory in Australia, *American Anthropologist*, 30(4), 614–631.
108 Davidson DS (1928) The Family Hunting Territory in Australia, *American Anthropologist*, 30(4), 614–631: p. 617.
109 Davidson DS (1928) The Family Hunting Territory in Australia, *American Anthropologist*, 30(4), 614–631: p. 618. Davidson goes on to qualify this assertion further by noting, "In many parts of Australia, however, the local group itself is not the primary land-owning unit . . . the local group is itself no more than a large paternally related family. . . . In parts of Australia, apparently for the most part in most regions except in central and northwest Australia, there are many reports to show that the land of the local group is divided among the individual families which compose its membership. . . . It seems clearly evident to me that, whether a family or an individual is spoken of as possessing ownership of a district, the same meaning is inferred" (619).
110 Davidson DS (1928) The Family Hunting Territory in Australia, *American Anthropologist*, 30(4), 614–631: p. 619.
111 Davidson DS (1928) Family Hunting Territories of the Tribes of Tierra del Fuego, *Indian Notes*, 5(1), 395–410: p. 395.
112 Curr EM (1886) *The Australian Race: Its Origin, Languages, Customs, Place of Landing in Australia and the Routes by Which It Spread Itself over the Continent*, John Ferres Government Printer, Melbourne, 64. See further the discussion in Davidson DS (1928) The Family Hunting Territory in Australia, *American Anthropologist*, 30(4), 614–631.
113 Davidson DS (1928) The Family Hunting Territory in Australia, *American Anthropologist*, 30(4), 614–631: p. 626 Davidson notes further the "keen respect for property boundaries, outside of which a native is afraid to wander, which has been retained in the face of European influence, certainly serves to emphasize the importance which this concept must have played in the mind of the aboriginal Australian" (627). See also Gibson J (2005) *Community Resources*, Ashgate, Aldershot, Chapter 7.
114 Hallowell AI (1949) The Size of Algonkian Hunting Territories: A Function of Ecological Adjustment, *American Anthropologist*, 51(1), 35–45.
115 Guenther MG (1981) Bushman and Hunter-Gatherer Territoriality, *Zeitschrift für Ethnologie*, 106(1/2), 109–120: p. 115.
116 Guenther MG (1981) Bushman and Hunter-Gatherer Territoriality, *Zeitschrift für Ethnologie*, 106(1/2), 109–120: p. 109, citing Heinz HJ (1972) Territoriality among the Bushmen in General and the !Ko in Particular, *Anthropos*, 67, 404–416. Recall also the account of the rookery in Henry Eliot Howard's study of territory in birds.
117 Guenther MG (1981) Bushman and Hunter-Gatherer Territoriality, *Zeitschrift für Ethnologie*, 106(1/2), 109–120: p. 113.
118 Guenther MG (1981) Bushman and Hunter-Gatherer Territoriality, *Zeitschrift für Ethnologie*, 106(1/2), 109–120: pp. 113–114. See further the discussion in Chapter 8, "Pack fiction."
119 Guenther MG (1981) Bushman and Hunter-Gatherer Territoriality, *Zeitschrift für Ethnologie*, 106(1/2), 109–120: p. 114.
120 Sauvet G (2019) The *Lifeworld* of Hunter-Gatherers and the Concepts of Territory, *Quarternary International*, 503, 191–199: "Territory is an abstract, culturally encoded, notion that can take different forms in sedentary and nomadic populations" (191). See further Sack RD (1986) *Human Territoriality: Its Theory and History*, Cambridge UP, Cambridge. Robert Sack counters

Ardrey's "territorial imperative" with the concept of territory as strategy (with its attending imputation of intentionality and cognitive capacity): Sack RD (1983) Human Territoriality: A Theory, *Annals of the Association of American Geographers*, 73(1), 55–74. Andrea Brighenti notes that "biologists have supported in large majority the instinct thesis . . . while social scientists have mostly opposed it": Brighenti A (2006) On Territory as Relationship and Law as Territory, *Canadian Journal of Law and Society/Revue Canadienne Droit et Société*, 21(2), 65–86: p. 67. However, the extent to which this refutation of biological determinism is in part motivated by an attachment to human exceptionalism rather than an emancipation of animal personalities, as it were, is unclear. Indeed, Andrea Brighenti notes, "the rejection of ethological insights entails the opposite risk of hyperrationalist anthropocentric exceptionalism" (69–70).

121 See further the discussion in Lyman SM & Scott MB (1967) Territoriality: A Neglected Sociological Dimension, *Social Problems*, 15(2), 236–249, where the author notes an extension of ecological thinking to "a truly *interactional* dimension." (page 237, note 1), recognising in particular the hugely significant work of Erving Goffman (Goffman E, *Asylums*, Doubleday, New York, 1961).

Chapter 5

Resource guarding

> Every territory, every habitat, joins up not only its spatiotemporal but its qualitative planes or sections: a posture and a song for example, a song and a color, percepts and affects. And every territory encompasses or cuts across the territories of other species, or intercepts the trajectories of animals without territories, forming interspecies junction points.
> Deleuze G & Guattari F (1991/[1994]) *What is Philosophy?*
> H Tomlinson & G Burchill (trans), Verso, London, 185

We are looking for the tracks, not the lion.
  Interpreting the defence of territory in terms of an implied defence of resources within the territory, that is, in respect of things or possessions, as distinct from relations, influences animal behaviour literature in relation to an economic theory of territoriality.[1] In other words, territoriality is considered in terms of the consequences or costs, and so an emergent theory of respect of possession has become influential. This is sometimes referred to as the resource defence in animal behaviour literature; however, it has been translated to "resource guarding" in dog training discourse, a subtle semantic shift which should not go unnoticed.[2] Once again, the creeping mythology of the warring dog appears.[3]
  In this analysis, the "mine" of territoriality becomes solely a question of utility based upon a classic cost-benefit analysis rather than a prosocial communication. However, learning can also be social and, in respect of objects or resources, training discourse disturbs the narrative of instinctual enslavement. Over half a century ago, Alfred Irving Hallowell identified this as the distinguishing feature between humans and other animals – namely, that property was a social system and that human individuals were capable of learning in relation to objects but other animals were not:

> [W]hile rights, duties, powers and privileges are of the very essence of the human social order, because it is an order based on *learned* roles, the opposite is true in the case of animals. Lacking social sanctions, therefore, the behavior of animals is motivated in quite different terms from that of human beings. The individual animal cannot take the attitude of other animals because he has not been socialized in terms of common traditional animals. Consequently, an individual animal, or group of animals, must be

prepared to meet any threat to food, nest or territory by the exertion of physical force. A dog will fight any other dog who tries to take his bone. No other remedy is possible, for this is the inevitable result in circumstances where there is no institutionalization of claims to objects of value.[4]

Yet the earlier discussion of the process of socialisation, together with social play and other kinds of "moral" behaviour, seems to confound this assertion by Hallowell. Similarly, research on perspective-taking and other empathetic behaviour has produced evidence of such social awareness on the part of many species, including that dog, both with members of their own[5] as well as other species.[6] Further, training in relation to resource guarding (whether from the mother or from a human guardian) is arguably precisely this kind of social learning that underpins a sociable property system.[7] And finally, the assumption of the struggle for life as the core value of all animal societies and their development is not only an impoverished view but also arguably an inaccurate one, as later discussions will explore in more detail.[8]

And what of the sociality through territory that has been identified across a range of species? Indeed, defence in and of itself can become a social affair. For example, this is seen in insect colonies in what is termed resource-defence sociality, with cooperation towards the protection of the home.[9] Further, what of the tolerance communicated through animal territories that has been identified across a range of species, including the *Canis* genus? Rather than an identity or trait of "guarding" that goes with a mythical and rigid hierarchy, as it is implied in dog training discourse,[10] is this possession rather more clearly indicated by a dynamic relation of challenge and potential? Of contact through space rather than exclusion from place?

Canine research in this area investigates a more dynamic relation in terms of the concept of resource-holding potential,[11] one that is varied and personal: "The resource-holding potential is determined by fighting ability, information about the disputed resource, and motivation to invest in the contest."[12] Importantly, this kind of agonistic behaviour also has an affiliative dimension in that dogs will adjust their behaviour to friendly human signals,[13] reaffirming the kind of positive reinforcement model of shared interests proposed for property relations in later discussion.[14] Further, resource-holding potential emphasises more clearly the behaviours associated with display, or advertising traits or signals, rather than a rigid and hierarchical relationship of aggression. A display of resource-holding potential is a source of information, and in many respects a prosocial one at that, a social communication rather than an inevitable conflict.

To speak of resource defence or resource guarding is to speak of things and thus to translate this back into the "being" of that dog. That is, it becomes part of that dog's identity – to take a Tardean approach to dog training discourse, this is the problem of a discussion of "being" in training (a rigid trait) as distinct from "having" (in terms of properties and dynamic relations), and it does not tally with biological realities. In contrast to these static positions, to communicate resource-holding potential is to maintain the emphasis on sociability and relations. Thus, the challenge for property theory is how this might be translated within a commercial context. This is not an inconsequential shift in perspective on property and, in particular, on intellectual property. Display, and the attention to that "conspicuous" attribution through that display, as distinct from guarding and the defence of objects and place, is an important transformation of a fundamental perspective upon property.

What does it mean to move from defence to display?

The path is the stone

> Among the Yurok Indians of California, as typical of a less specifically organized people, the "court" was less definite but it was nevertheless there. An aggrieved Yurok who felt he had a legitimate claim engaged the services of two non-relatives from a community other than his own. The defendant did likewise. These persons were called "crossers" because they crossed back and forth between the litigants. The litigants did not face each other in the dispute. After hearing all that each side offered in evidence and argument, the "crossers" rendered a judgment on the facts. If the judgment was for the plaintiff, they rendered a decision for damages according to a well-established scale that was known to all. For their footwork and efforts each received a piece of shell currency called a "moccassin." Here again we have a court.[15]

This form of justice is remarkable for its difference from the conventional adversarial model in common law. The tracks themselves are the mark of justice, achieved not through combat but through the crossing, back and forth towards convergence.[16] The crossers traverse the space between mapping the jural relations, the intra-sociality of the dispute, in a physically communicative performance of justice. The moccasin "literally compensates for the footwork involved in adjudicating the case."[17] Footwork serves justice. Tracks make the work of territory. They make the author visible, "stories written in footprint code."[18] Tracks are thus the image of law – movement, relations, and use, rather than tracing static objects.

In a departure from the usual picture books depicting the likenesses of animals, Nikolaas Tinbergen collaborated on several occasions with Eric Ennion, the former medical practitioner and accomplished wildlife artist, to bring the stories of animal territories and tracks to a more general audience[19] as well as to children.[20] In a way perhaps not possible through a photographic copy of the animal, the tracks set out that "noise" in animal representations, echoing the absent animal. Instead of the animal's likeness, we can see the animal's difference, as it were: "Having established who was there, the next problem is when and then why. Tracks may provide information obtainable in no other way about what actually happened."[21] Further, tracks evoke the movement of territory, the sociality of territorial relations: "But remember that tracks are as a rule short-lived and often hard to see."[22]

> After a hard night's work a Hedgehog trots home as the sun rises over the crest of the dunes. It will sleep through the day curled up under a tuft of marram grass where few will notice it. But it has left a record of its night's activities printed in the sand for anyone who cares to follow it.[23]

At the same time, the authors follow the tracks, taking their perspectives, co-constituting the territorial space with their collaborators, "revelling in the patterns of light and shade."[24] Thus, while following the animals, the authors are mapping their own microsociology of intra-social relations, of interspecies relations, of shared and overlapping territories:

> A Stoat, gracefully undulating along, has left its characteristic fourfold prints alongside a Hedgehog's. Both were following the same route towards a gull colony in the dunes to take their toll of chicks. Above them a Skylark crosses from right to left, its miniature crow-prints linked by claw scratches caused by the dragging of the bird's middle toes. An unknown insect, entering by one of the hedgehog prints, seems to have tunneled under the sand.[25]

The path is the monument, the landmark, creating space as a dynamic relation of overlapping and coexistent territories, rather than tracing static boundaries.

It is the tracks we are in search of, not the lion. The path is the stone.

Monumental problems?

> The territorial boundaries, so real to the birds, are invisible to us.[26]

> If they met at the boundary between their two territories, where the issues were even, neither group attacked. . . . [E]very now and then they lifted a leg and urinated – planting a 'scent flag' as it can be called, for this is a means of staking out a territory and advertising it by smell.[27]

Where conventional representations of property rely upon external boundary-making and enforcement, these animal territories are mobile and emergent, created and maintained through sociability, through making spaces rather than tracing and trading places. Space is thus generated through that sociality, inside looking out. Recalling the discussion of nomadic territories in the previous chapter, territory is sustained through that sociality whereby space is both mobile and yet territorial. Indeed, it is this very social mobility, so to speak, that substantiates territory from the organisation of hunter-gatherer societies through to agriculture. The sociability of animal territory unsettles, so to speak, the assumptions of a causal progression of technological development through to the commitment of settlement. To presume this narrative is to accept the fiction of predatory drift. As will be shown in later chapters, the predatory drift in territory and property relations fixes place and jural relations (through appealing to the prey of the object-based approaches to rights) in order to trace and govern seamlessly, as it were. However, in the sociability of those first pastoral encounters, the justice of space is co-constituted through that pastoral sociality, crossed back and forth. In order to serve justice, to make territory, one must move. Literally.

Animal territory is thus "seen" through landmarks and invisible monuments that establish contact and belonging as much as they signal boundaries. Recalling Rudolf Schenkel's earliest wolf studies, marking territory "represents a peaceful form of contact among neighbours."[28] And in terms of the family group, as one researcher puts it: "Wolves that pee together stay together."[29] In many respects, the sociability of animal territories is the kind of remarkable and aspirational space that could facilitate relations in the digital market and yet continues to be somewhat out of reach in this context. The anthropocentric understanding of landmarks as that of an ordinarily physical mark, one which defines place and points to exclusion, dominates approaches to the enforcement of property in contemporary frameworks. What is recognised as a landmark, both in law and in territory studies, is almost invariably the physical environment, the physical object, rather than the relation with space (through smell, sound, and similar).[30] And once again, *defence defines it*.

What is interesting about the various developments in the concept of territory is that almost invariably the convergence is in the nature of the relationship between dominion and space.[31] In other words, the way in which territory is predominantly understood is in line with the concept of "predatory drift" in the property model being developed in the present discussion. This language informs the very nature of the perspective upon dog behaviour itself, not only in terms of the contrivance of predatory drift but elsewhere in the notions of territory marking (or is it just leaving a message?) and resource guarding (or is it display?). Thus, much of the training and behaviour discourse itself bears the history of its inflection with the predatory drift of the property model.[32] Consistent with this is the adherence to a flawed and contrived notion of pack behaviour and competition,[33] and the wild abandon, as it were, of everything else. In the process, territory is translated from the milieu of tracks in the first domestication relationship through to the stratification of space via boundaries and limits. But what of intangible space? How might this upset things, so to speak?

Making space

> The animals with territory (there are animals without territory) are prodigious. Because constituting a territory is nearly the birth of art.[34]

As the story progresses, from that first domestication, what is emerging is a story of invention that is especially fascinating also for its inextricable ties with territory-making as a tale of social as well as physical cartography. This interspecies pastoral sociability is also decidedly triadic in structure, fulfilled not only by the relationship between those early humans and that dog but also with the grazing herds that cooperate within that space, as it were, contributing to the production of a social and arguably "legal" territory in those earliest societies. As will be shown in later discussions, this is an important dynamic of the fuller jural relations of Hohfeld's resocialisation of property.[35]

This notion of cooperation through domestication events is important, and it is quite different from the "red in tooth and claw"[36] Hobbesian narrative[37] and the persuasive refrain of "survival of the fittest" that have come to dominate popular discourse on innovation, property, and competition. In contrast, the pastoral theory of domestication is a compelling narrative of the manner in which concepts of property, and "owning" territory as both a management of and a familiarity with an area, were introduced to humans through sociability rather than conflict.

Writing also at a time of increasing interest in eugenics, it is in this respect that Tarde's sociology engages with evolutionary theory not as a rejection of Darwinism but rather as a critique of the proposed mechanism of competition and the emphasis on selection and dominion as a violent conflict:[38] "for Tarde it was association, harmonization and conjunction which came first."[39] Spencer's social evolution or social Darwinism was challenged by Tarde as overly deterministic rather than genuinely social:[40] "[I]t is not as true as it has been said to be that the fight for life, the radical hostility of beings and of their elements, is the first and fundamental principle of the Universe."[41] Tarde's theory of imitation, both creative and affective, tributary and innovative, resonates with the "mystery" in traditional selection narratives posed by reciprocal altruism in the "natural" world:[42] "The Darwinian idea of 'survival of the fittest' is a cornerstone of evolutionary theory, providing a framework to understand the principles of selection. In this context, cooperation – that is, any behavior where individuals interact to enhance the fitness of the population – should rarely occur: why should individuals work together if the ultimate goal is simply to increase one's own individual fitness?"[43] The Cartesian divide between nature and culture is thus confounded by this appeal to the social. The selfish individual is, after all, an anathema to the cooperation of the collective interest and evolutionary development. All at once the interpretation of the canine nature of humaneness, that first encounter, is not only remarkable but also fundamental. What a nuisance!

Through harmony, rather than a kind of evolutionary competition, an entirely new perspective emerges not only on the development of society but also on the nature of property relations and possession: how that might be displayed, as distinct from guarded; how property might be reputational (and indeed social), as distinct from purely rivalrous (and individualistic); a relation of potential emulation, as distinct from opposition. With this comes a renewed interest in the individual, but the individual as a social being. Indeed, cooperation was something early evolutionary theory struggled to understand and even dismissed, coerced by the fundamental evolutionary principle of "the struggle for life and the survival of the fittest." However, in the decades after Tarde's publications, the focus on cooperation increased, and, through theories of kinship and reciprocation,[44] science started to converge with Tarde's universal sociology: "Many of the benefits sought by living things are disproportionally available to cooperating groups . . . this statement, insofar as it is true, lays down a fundamental basis for all social life."[45]

This kind of multispecies cooperation can be recognised in the sociability of territories in that first domestication, from the strategic opportunities to share and coexist, through to the pastoral sociability of co-constituted territories.[46] As Kelly Donati states, "Agriculture is always a more-than-human endeavour,"[47] and indeed that first domestication event shows that to be more extensive than might have been thought. Rather than a relationship of domination, a more complex interaction of sociability was necessarily the basis for domestication: "it is the convivial entanglements of social reproduction that enable the work of living to get done."[48] Drawing upon Charles Fourier's nineteenth-century concept of "industrial attraction,"[49] Donati argues that this, "re-imagines processes of domestication from a relation of domination and mastery to one of mutualism and sociality."[50] Rather than a narrative of pure conquest, that first domestication is a story of cooperation. As later discussions will show, the "wild abandon" with which animals are distinguished as noble, exotic, untrammelled others, is part of a mechanism of human exceptionalism that sustains the distance. When animals recognise reciprocity, they "reach out."[51]

In this way, participation and sociality are enriched as incentives in their own right; the motivation and the sustenance of familiar production comes from sociability itself. Fourier's mention of an economy of incentives is notable in this respect; that is, this suggests an economy not of products, as such, but of the motives themselves: "The variety of enticements that the armies offer to young people means that they assemble spontaneously at the first call for volunteers, and admission to their ranks, as I have said, becomes a privilege won by the trials they go through. This method of raising armies thus achieves the two aims I have spoken of, industrial attraction and economy of incentives."[52] This is an economy of "passionate interests,"[53] of the innovation through imitation. This resonates strongly with the concept of shared interests being developed here. Value inheres not in the product, but in the motives to share, to acknowledge, to talk about, and so on. The commons, as it were, thus nourishes and governs itself.[54] But this economy of incentives has been disqualified and replaced by objects seemingly willed by incentives of false premises and unanchored conclusions.

Works of art

> If they met at the boundary between their two territories, where the issues were even, neither group attacked. . . . [E]very now and then they lifted a leg and urinated – planting a 'scent flag' as it can be called, for this is a means of staking out a territory and advertising it by smell.[55]

In studies of animal navigation, an anthropocentric view of landmarks appears to persist. That is, although there is considerable investigation of the use of sound and smell in navigation,[56] when it comes to landmarks and the alteration of (or work upon) the environment, there is an assumption that landmarks themselves are always visual[57] or involve a visual transformation of the environment. In other words, the history of landmarks in animal as well as human art history is presumed to be visual. But while the concept of landmark in the visual sense is well established in behaviour science,[58] is this emphasis on the visual appropriate or even comprehensive?

This very subject arose in an engaging Twitter exchange between science researchers that throws light on these same concerns. In the original tweet, one researcher relayed a question from a student as to whether animals ever modified their environment in order to construct a landmark cue (the example provided was piling rocks).[59] In the subsequent thread of replies, the first response suggested that perhaps landmarks may not be "so overt," that indeed many species construct mental maps by scent. Yet another asked, "Why can't a landmark be a smell?" At this point the distinction was made between olfactory cues as something generated by the animal as opposed to a physical modification of the environment through, for example, moving rocks, thus seemingly resolving the notion that scent can modify a landscape.[60] What appeared to remain outstanding at this point is why the thread was so quick (and so motivated) to consider scent marking as other than physical modification of the environment? Is this anthropocentric view on scent simply wrong? Why should the marking of a territory, the establishment of a landmark, the rendering of an invisible sculpture, be defined only through viewpoints that are relevant to humans?[61] And why should such viewpoints explain those landmarks in terms of function alone? Where is the art in that?

It is interesting to note how this discussion maps onto the emphasis in aesthetics on a sense hierarchy, with the so-called higher senses recognised for their "structural complexity . . . required to sustain our attention over time."[62] This hiding of the scent is part of the forgetting towards a "complete" property system. As Alain Corbin notes, scent is a diminished artefact of a representationalist approach to property, of Platonic ideals of originals and copies: "Unlike the senses of hearing and sight, valued on the basis of a perpetually repeated Platonic prejudice, olfaction is also relatively useless in civilized society."[63] Notably, anyone who has walked with a dog can attest to the way in which a scent can certainly sustain attention (to the extent that it may halt the walk completely) and the way in which scents can maintain their monumentalism for weeks and months (with the same spots in the park demanding attention with every new visit).[64] In taking the perspective of what might be monumental to that dog, a fuller consideration of the aesthetic sense begins to emerge.[65] Indeed, in this way smell is recognised as conspicuous, a display of resources: "Like natural features in appropriate conditions, these constructions may allow intruders to recognize areas that are more costly to use."[66]

What is perhaps more significant, however, is the way in which nonvisual landmarking might expand the more static concept of territory, and indeed property, in terms of its spatial and thing-like limits. An appreciation for invisible sculptures in animal landmarks may facilitate a way into understanding mutualistic relationships of property in human societies as well. In other words, the landmark defines not only the "owner's" boundary but also the "user's" in that the owner equally cannot impose upon the user's "space." While territorial landmarks may present a physical obstacle, or a conspicuous obstacle may be marked, the relationship to the landmark has been interpreted as not necessarily a physical barrier (in fact a conspicuous landmark may even inhibit defence by obscuring vision) but rather as an arbitrary cue.[67] Indeed, through convention,[68] the landmark facilitates communication across boundaries as distinct from defensive boundary-making[69] in ways consistent with the concept of shared interests in a sociable property being developed in the present work.[70]

From the understanding of the convention of landmarks and the lessening or even elimination of disputes between animal species,[71] together with an expansion of the meaning of "conspicuousness" for the purposes of those conventions, there is potential to explore more imaginatively and innovatively what might constitute a landmark for the purposes of solutions to disputes in a digital environment. Instead of just the obstacles of producers, how might such an environment recognise and value the landmarks of consumers? Such effective landmarking could be relevant not only to the question of resources in such environments[72] but also to the public interest in participation, collaboration, and indeed innovation in such environments.

A scent of the aesthetic

> Clearly there are in the mind no objects or events – no pigs, no coconut palms, and no mothers. The mind contains only transforms, percepts, images, etc., and rules for making these transforms, percepts, etc. in what form these rules exist we do not know, but presumably they are embodied in the very machinery which creates the transforms. . . . In any case, it is nonsense to say that a man was frightened by a lion, because a lion is not an idea. The man makes an *idea* of the lion.[73]

The persistent perspective directing the emphasis on the visual is arguably the same as that which propels the drift in property relations, from domestication to contestation, from making home to making war, and this relates to the relentless preoccupation with fixed identity and being: *to be*. In other words, in the way in which being or identity is presumed to be consistent, something which can be "found", the preoccupation with duration and permanence similarly infuses the concept of property, including intellectual property. Smell with its impermanent, promiscuous, wandering whimsy is the antipathy of a seemingly complete and resolute property system. Instead, over time, literally, civilisation and its attending "properties" became endorsed through impressions of permanence, repeatability, resilience: "Transitory goods are deceitful and minor. As a result, the fine arts, whose material agent is (quasi-)permanent, had to slide almost naturally into the center of aesthetics. Later on, the theory of music, theatre and other performing arts emphasized the value of the transitory, and permanent material objects have been replaced by repeatable performances of the same work of art."[74]

Smell indicates what is elsewhere – a memory, the object, the author, the value. In that elsewhere is perhaps the repeatability that can suggest the "fixation" for the purposes of property, the *res familiaris*. This is a question for later discussion.[75] For now it is important to see the way in which smell produces a having that is somehow and something altogether different, moving away from the universal subject of stable properties, of fixed objects, of static relations, to a scent of the aesthetic, the so-called aesthetic of the secondary senses, a productive sociality in commons.

> Between us and them, at first sight, there isn't much difference: we're all made the same way, and besides, what's the point of standing there staring? Odor, that's what each of us has that's different from the others. The odor tells you immediately and certainly what you need to know. There are no words, there is no information more precise than what the nose receives.[76]

Indeed, what is the point of standing there staring when there is so much to smell? It is no coincidence that in a land of fences and a museum of objects "space has a bad odour for many property scholars."[77]

What of art?

The sweet smell of territory

> The animals with territory (there are animals without territory) are prodigious. Because constituting a territory is nearly the birth of art.[78]

It is perhaps no accident that the object of taming in Saint-Exupéry's *Le Petit Prince* is a rose. The rose, a symbol of attraction,[79] represents at first instance the sociality of domestication, of the process of coming together into a society. Smell is thus a sensation of connectedness, as well as potential boundaries; that is, above all, it is a sensation of relatedness. But the rose is also "a symbol of visual and olfactory perfection,"[80] and itself a figure of the predatory drift of the visual[81] at the expense of the olfactory:

> During the Enlightenment, however, roses came to be laid out in their own flower beds and to be valued more for their visual appearance. Roses were bred to perfect their colour and form and this had the unintended consequence of breeding the scent right out of certain varieties, as the modern period progressed . . . smell was demoted by the likes of Darwin and Freud to the rank of being the most animalistic of the senses (where once it had been the most spiritual). The history of the rose provides a good illustration of shifting sensory priorities – in the instance case, from essence to appearance.[82]

The use of smell to traverse home ranges and various territories, both in terms of marking and in terms of navigating, is identified in a diverse range of animal species. For example, olfactory navigation and memory have been identified and studied in various species of nematodes,[83] worms,[84] insects,[85] spiders,[86] birds,[87] and mammals[88] (including dogs[89] and even humans[90]).

Smell is thus both a vehicle of individual agency as well as a landmark of territory and a monument of community.

Scent is communicative and social, and notably the way in which mammals deploy smell for marking territory is largely through the making of tracks rather than through the demarcation of limits: "Individuals scent mark throughout their home ranges rather than just on borders."[91] In other words, contrary to the boundary-making model of territory that is the hallmark of the predatory drift of property, animal territories are perhaps more closely aligned with Deleuze and Guattari's concept of milieu. In many respects, animal territories are the "musical model" of Deleuze and Guattari's smooth space: "The smooth is the continuous variation, continuous development of form; it is the fusion of harmony and melody in favor of the production of properly rhythmic values, the pure act of the drawing of a diagonal across the vertical and the horizontal."[92] This is indeed resonant with the response to smell as impermanent, undefined, transient, and so on: "Everything about 'smell' appears not as a well-defined and self-contained domain, but as strands across a spectrum of human endeavors and academic inquiries whose central concerns are often not primarily olfactory."[93] In other words, the "territory" model throughout ethology is perhaps not territory at all; it is milieu. Rather than boundaries, animal territories, as distinct from the dominant concept of territory, are the between.[94]

> Still, we do not yet have a *Territory*, which is not a milieu, not even an additional milieu, nor a rhythm or passage between milieus. The territory is in fact an act that affects milieus and rhythms, that "territorializes" them. The territory is the product of a territorialization of milieus and rhythms. It amounts to the same thing as when milieus and rhythms become territorialized, and what the difference is between a nonterritorial animal and a territorial animal. A territory borrows from all the milieus; it bites into them, seizes them bodily (although it remains vulnerable to intrusions). It is built from aspects of portions of milieus. It itself has an exterior milieu, an interior milieu, an intermediary milieu, and an annexed milieu. It has the interior zone of a residence or shelter, the exterior zone of its domain, more or less retractable limits or membranes.[95]

In other words, territory is indeed part of the process of domestication, but the bounded places we have come to understand and use to represent territory are perhaps some way from the productive sociality of animal territories.

> There is a territory precisely when milieu components cease to be directional, becoming dimensional instead, when they cease to be functional to become expressive. There is a territory when the rhythm has expressiveness. What defines the territory is the emergence of matters of expression (qualities). Take the example of color in birds or fish: color is a membrane state associated with interior hormonal states, but it remains functional and transitory

as long as it is tied to a type of action (sexuality, aggressiveness, flight). It becomes expressive, on the other hand, when it acquires a temporal constancy and a spatial range that make it a territorial, or rather territorializing, mark: a signature. The question is not whether color resumes its functions or fulfills new ones in the territory. It is clear that it does, but this reorganization of functions implies first of all that the component under consideration has become expressive and that its meaning, from this standpoint, is to mark a territory.[96]

This is evident in the study of landmarks in ethology, where landmarks are understood not merely in terms of function (for example, shelter) but in terms of having no functional value beyond their value as a landmark, a monument, a boundary.[97] In other words, this is the exuberance and expression of marking, where the landmark is not primarily about its possible functions for survival but rather the landmark is expressive: "Functions in a territory are not primary; they presuppose a territory-producing expressiveness."[98] Thus, in this sense the landmark is not interpreted as an object of property, but rather as an expression, the value of which is elsewhere other than in the object itself: *res familiaris*.[99] In a purely functional analysis in discussions of territory, the landmark would be reduced to milieu, sustaining a discourse of human exceptionalism where the mark is subject to a functional reductionism in its interpretation. However, in a review of territory in terms of expression, the art of territory emerges. Thus, contrary to a traditional behaviour account of territory, where defence defines it, emerging is a territory of pure expression. According to Deleuze and Guattari, "The territory is not primary in relation to the qualitative mark; it is the mark that makes the territory."[100] Thus, the marking of territory is relational and abundant; it is expressive, while the territory itself is a product of territorialization: "Territorialization is an act of rhythm that has become expressive, or of milieu components that have become qualitative. The marking of a territory is dimensional, but it is not a meter, it is a rhythm."[101] Thus, the presumption of aggression and defence at the heart of territory is not sustainable:

> That is why we cannot accept a thesis like Lorenz's, *which tends to make aggressiveness the basis of the territory:* the territory would then be the product of the phylogenetic evolution of an instinct of aggression, starting at the point where that instinct became intraspecific, was turned against the animal's own kind. A territorial animal would direct its aggressiveness against members of its own species; the species would gain the selective advantage of distributing its members throughout a space where each would have its own place. This ambiguous thesis, which has dangerous political overtones, seems to us to have little foundation. It is obvious that the function of aggression changes pace when it becomes intraspecific. But this reorganization of the function, rather than explaining the territory, presupposes it. . . . Can this

becoming, this emergence, be called Art? That would make the territory a result of art. The artist: the first person to set out a boundary stone, or to make a mark.[102]

If we cannot yet see it, what if we can smell it?

Notes

1 For example, see Gill F & Wolf LL (1975) Economics of Feeding Territoriality in the Golden-Winged Sunbird, *Ecology*, 56, 333–345.
2 Jacobs et al. provide the following definition: "Canine resource guarding (RG) describes the behaviour used by a dog to achieve or maintain control over an item of perceived value." See Jacobs JA et al. (2017) Ability of Owners to Identify Resource Guarding Behaviour in the Domestic Dog, *Applied Animal Behaviour Science*, 188, 77–83: p. 83. See further Jacobs JA et al. (2018a) Factors Associated with Canine Resource Guarding Behaviour in the Presence of Dogs: A Cross-Sectional Survey of Dog Owners, *Preventive Veterinary Medicine*, 161, 134–142; Jacobs JA et al. (2018b) Factors Associated with Canine Resource Guarding Behaviour in the Presence of People: A Cross-Sectional Survey of Dog Owners, *Preventive Veterinary Medicine*, 161, 143–153. See also the discussion of resource guarding and conflict mitigation behaviours as a response to stress in Kuhne F (2016) Behavioural Responses of Dogs to Dog-Human Social Conflict Situations, *Applied Animal Behaviour Science*, 182, 38–43; and the relationship between "resource guarding" and imputations of "spite" in Ha JC & Campion TL (2019) *Dog Behavior: Modern Science and Our Canine Companions*, Academic Press, Amsterdam, 101. The term "object guarding" is also sometimes used, more usually in the scientific literature. For example, see Pfaller-Sadovsky N et al. (2017) It Is Mine! Using Clicker Training as a Treatment of Object Guarding in 4 Companion Dogs (*Canis Lupus Familiaris*), *Journal of Veterinary Behavior*, 22, 57–65.
3 Thus, behaviour discourse itself bears the history of its inflection with the predatory drift of the property model. On this question of resources and display it is interesting to note this predatory drift in behaviour discourse right through to persistent training models, which continue to be popular despite considerable evidence of their negative impact on welfare and learning (see the fuller discussion in Chapter 10, "Shared interests"). It is noteworthy that Karen Pryor makes this link between display, dominance, and training in her book, *Don't Shoot the Dog*. Pryor notes: "Punishing is also reinforcing for the punisher because it demonstrates and helps to maintain dominance. . . . This in fact may be the main motivation behind our human tendency to punish: establishing and maintaining dominance. The punisher may be primarily interested not in behaviour but in being proved to be of higher status." See Pryor K (2002) *Don't Shoot the Dog! The New Art of Teaching and Training*, Rev ed., Ringpress, Dorking, 108. See further the discussion in Chapter 7, "Predatory drift" and in particular the discussion of dominance and punishment in Chapter 8, "Pack fiction".
4 Hallowell AI (1942) The Nature and Function of Property as a Social Institution, *Journal of Legal and Political Sociology*, 1, 115–138: p. 137.
5 Bonanni R et al. (2010) Effect of Affiliative and Agonistic Relationships on Leadership Behaviour in Free-Ranging Dogs, *Animal Behaviour*, 79, 981–991.
6 Duranton C & Gaunet F (2015) *Canis Sensitives*: Affiliation and Dogs' Sensitivity to Others' Behaviour as the Basis for Synchronization with Humans?, *Journal of Veterinary Behavior*, 10, 513–524.

7 As discussed in more detail in "Part 4, Altruism, the social age," through cooperation, affiliative learning and other empathetic behaviours, such as reciprocal altruism, this simple separation between human and other animals in relation to property is not easily sustained.
8 See in particular the discussion of cooperation and reciprocal altruism in Chapter 10, "Shared interests."
9 Costa JT (2019) Social Evolution in "Other" Insects and Arachnids, in Choe JC (ed.) *Encyclopedia of Animal Behavior: Volume Four*, 2nd ed., Academic Press, Amsterdam, 617–631: pp. 623–634.
10 For instance, see the work of Bradshaw JWS et al. (2009) Dominance in Domestic Dogs: Useful Construct or Bad Habit, *Journal of Veterinary Behavior*, 4, 135–144. For further discussion of the problematic interpretation of dominance and cultural mythology of pack theory, see Chapter 8, "Pack fiction."
11 Parker GA (1974) Assessment Strategy and the Evolution of Animal Conflicts, *Journal of Theoretical Biology*, 47, 223–243. Ha and Campion note that Parker's model makes it possible "to disambiguate one's ability to physically defend a resource from one's motivation to persevere in this altercation. Parker's work focusing on behavioural ecology was pivotal in this paradigm shift from viewing evolution primarily in 'species survival' terms to more gene-centric ones, with a focus on individuals and their relatives." See Ha JC & Campion TL (2019) *Dog Behavior: Modern Science and Our Canine Companions*, Academic Press, Amsterdam, 170.
12 Miklósi Á (2015) *Dog Behaviour, Evolution, and Cognition*, 2nd ed., Oxford UP, Oxford, 238.
13 Miklósi Á (2015) *Dog Behaviour, Evolution, and Cognition*, 2nd ed., Oxford UP, Oxford, 239: "Importantly, this guarding behaviour was continuously under control of human signalling. Dogs stopped guarding when the experimenter reverted to friendly behaviour." See further Gácsi M et al. (2013) Wolves Do Not Join the Dance: Sophisticated Aggression Control by Adjusting to Human Social Signals in Dogs, *Applied Animal Behaviour Science*, 145, 109–122.
14 See "Part 4, Altruism, the social age."
15 Hoebel EA (1946) Law and Anthropology, *Virginia Law Review*, 32(4), 835–854: p. 842. Hoebel notes elsewhere, the moccasin "literally compensates for the footwork involved in adjudicating the case."
16 See further the discussion in Hoebel EA (1954) *The Law of Primitive Man: A Study in Comparative Legal Dynamics*, Harvard UP, Cambridge, MA, 24–25.
17 Hoebel EA (1942) Fundamental Legal Concepts as Applied in the Study of Primitive Law, *Yale Law Journal*, 51, 951–966: p. 959.
18 Ennion EAR & Tinbergen N (1967) *Tracks*, OUP, Oxford, 5.
19 Ennion EAR & Tinbergen N (1967) *Tracks*, OUP, London; Tinbergen N & Falkus H (1970) *Signals for Survival*, E Ennion (illus.), Clarendon Press, Oxford.
20 Allen G & Denslow J (1975) *Tracks and Signs (Clue Books)*, N Tinbergen & EAR Ennion (illus.), OUP, Oxford.
21 Ennion EAR & Tinbergen N (1967) *Tracks*, Oxford UP, London, 16.
22 Ennion EAR & Tinbergen N (1967) *Tracks*, Oxford UP, London, 5.
23 Ennion EAR & Tinbergen N (1967) *Tracks*, Oxford UP, London, 5.
24 Ennion EAR & Tinbergen N (1967) *Tracks*, Oxford UP, London, 5.
25 Ennion EAR & Tinbergen N (1967) *Tracks*, Oxford UP, London, 10.
26 Tinbergen N & Falkus H (1970) *Signals for Survival*, E Ennion (illus.), Clarendon Press, Oxford, 15.
27 Tinbergen N (1958) *Curious Naturalists*, Doubleday, New York, 31.
28 Schenkel R (1947) Ausdrucks-Studien an Wölfen: Gefangenschafts-Beobachtungen, *Behaviour*, 1(2), 81–129: pp. 84/86.

29 Russell J Rothman quoted in Mech LD (ed.) (2000) *The Wolves of Minnesota: Howl in the Heartland*, Voyageur Press, Stillwater, MN, 71.
30 Davidson DS (1928) The Family Hunting Territory in Australia, *American Anthropologist*, 30(4), 614–631. Davidson also notes that a lack of artificial marking of boundaries in indigenous Australian hunting territories does not negate the existence of landmarks and boundaries (620). See further Curr EM (1886) *The Australian Race, Volume I*, Australian Government Publication, Melbourne: "The boundaries of these portions are known but not with any precision, and I have never heard of an instance of their being artificially marked, as some writers have asserted in general terms. Had they been so, the fact must have attracted attention. A little consideration will show also that the very frequent markings which would have been necessary on each fresh subdivision of the land amongst a family on the death of a father would have been laborious, and of no practical use" (64).
31 Brighenti interprets this dominance model, explored in more detail in "Part 3, Dominion, the machine age," as one premised upon ownership (that is, upon an object-based model of unilateral relations between an individual and a thing). Brighenti notes, "The fact that we tend to frame the basic territorial form as 'property' is revealing of the current dominant model of property rights, which is of course ownership." See Brighenti AM (2010) Lines, Barred Lines: Movement, Territory and the Law, *International Journal of Law in Context*, 6(3), 217–227: p. 217.
32 On this question of resources and display it is interesting to note this predatory drift in behaviour discourse right through to persistent training models, which continue to be popular despite considerable evidence of their negative impact on welfare and learning. See Bain M (2019) Overview of Animal Training: A Welfare Perspective, in Chun Choe J (ed.) *Encyclopedia of Animal Behavior*, Vol. 1, 2nd ed., Academic Press, Amsterdam, 203–213. It is noteworthy that Karen Pryor makes this link between display, dominance, and training in her book, *Don't Shoot the Dog*. Pryor notes: "Punishing is also reinforcing for the punisher because it demonstrates and helps to maintain dominance. . . . This in fact may be the main motivation behind our human tendency to punish: establishing and maintaining dominance. The punisher may be primarily interested not in behaviour but in being proved to be of higher status." See Pryor K (2002) *Don't Shoot the Dog! The New Art of Teaching and Training*, Rev ed., Ringpress, Dorking, 108. See further the discussion in Chapter 7, "Predatory drift" and in particular the discussion of dominance and punishment in Chapter 8, "Pack fiction."
33 For a more comprehensive analysis of these concepts and issues, see Chapter 8, "Pack fiction." For a more detailed account of predatory drift, see Chapter 7, "Predatory drift."
34 Deleuze G (1994–1995) A comme animal/A as in Animal. Dominique Hurth (trans.). Transcription of the first part (first letter of the ABC) of the eight-hour series of interviews between Gilles Deleuze and Claire Parnet, filmed by Pierre-André Boutang in 1988–1989. Broadcast on Arte between November 1994 and Spring 1995.
35 Hohfeld's fundamental conceptions and the potential for resocialising property, in a manner of speaking, are considered in greater detail in "Part 4, Altruism, the social age," in particular, see Chapter 11, "Resocialisation." For a further exploration of the triadic structure of property and the reappearance of that dog, see Chapter 12, "*Res familaris.*"
36 Tennyson A (1850) *In Memorium AHH*, Edward Moxon, London, Canto 56.
37 "[T]he natural state of men, before they entered into society, was a mere war, and that not simply but a war of all men against all men." Hobbes T (1642/[1949]) *De Cive or the Citizen*, Appleton-Century-Crofts, New York, I, 12.

38 Citing the analysis of Jean Milet, Matei Candea notes: "Milet particularly highlights the fact that Tarde refused the primacy of 'the struggle for life' as a motor of history." See Candea M (2016) Revisiting Tarde's House, in Candea M (ed.) *The Social after Gabriel Tarde: Debates and Assessments*, 2nd ed., Routledge, London, 1–27: p. 3. See further, Milet J (1970) *Gabriel Tarde et la philosophie de l'histoire*, Vrin, Paris. See also Milet J (1972) Gabriel Tarde et al. psychologie sociale, *Revue française de sociologie*, 13(4), 472–484.
39 Candea M (2016) Revisiting Tarde's House, in Candea M (ed.) *The Social after Gabriel Tarde: Debates and Assessments*, 2nd ed., Routledge, London, 1–27: p. 3.
40 Tarde G (1884) Darwinisme naturel et Darwinisme social, *Revue Philosophique de la France et de l'Étranger*, 17, 607–637.
41 Tarde G (1890/[1912]) *Penal Philosophy*, R Howell (trans.), Little, Brown, and Co, Boston, 103.
42 Reciprocal altruism is explored in more detail in "Part 4 Altruism, the social age", particularly in Chapter 10, "Shared interests."
43 Asfahl KL & Dandekar AA (2018) Social Evolution: Selection on Multiple Cooperative Traits Optimizes Cost-Benefit Relationships, *Current Biology*, 28, R737–R759: p. R737.
44 See in particular the work of the British evolutionary biologist, William Donald Hamilton, and genetic approaches to kinship and social behaviour: See further the work on reciprocal altruism by Robert Trivers. See also George Robert Price's approach to altruism and his development of Hamilton's work on kin selection. Cooperative and collective sociality was also a specific focus of some early twentieth-century biology, arguably influenced by sociology (and in Allee's case specifically accounting for sociological approaches), providing important legacies for later theories in altruism and collective behaviour. See in particular the foundational work of Warder Clyde Allee on cooperation and the development of the so-called Allee effect and the benefits of collective, social living as distinct from rivalrous individuality. See further the collection, Courchamp F et al. (2008) *Allee Effects: In Ecology and Conservation*, Oxford UP, Oxford. Collective and cooperative behaviour is examined in more detail in "Part 4, Altruism, the social age" towards the concepts of shared interests and familiar production, and the *res familiaris* approach to modern property relations.
45 Axelrod R & Hamilton WD (1981) The Evolution of Cooperation, *Science*, 211(4489), 1390–1396: p. 1391. Cooperation, mutualism and reciprocal altruism are discussed in more detail in the Chapter 10, "Shared interests."
46 For an excellent analysis of this sociability of space in the context of potential human-wildlife conflict, see Ojalammi S & Blomley N (2015) Dancing with Wolves: Making Legal Territory in a More-Than-Human World, *Geoforum*, 62, 51–60. In this article the authors analyse the relationships between wolves, humans, and sheep through a case study in southwest Finland, "in an attempt to treat the animal not merely as an object in legal space, but also as an agent of its production" (51). See further the relation between herders and herd in Lorimer H (2006) Herding Memories of Humans and Animals, *Environment and Planning D: Society and Space*, 24, 497–518, in which the author considers the "diverse geographies that coexisting humans and animals create" (497).
47 Donati K (2019) 'Herding Is His Favourite Thing in the World': Convivial World-Making on a Multispecies Farm, *Journal of Rural Studies*, 66, 119–129: p. 119.
48 Donati K (2019) 'Herding Is His Favourite Thing in the World': Convivial World- Making on a Multispecies Farm, *Journal of Rural Studies*, 66, 119–129: p. 122.

49 Fourier C (1808/[1996]) *The Theory of the Four Movements*, I Patterson (trans.), Cambridge UP, Cambridge.
50 Donati K (2019) 'Herding Is His Favourite Thing in the World': Convivial World-Making on a Multispecies Farm, *Journal of Rural Studies*, 66, 119–129: p. 122.
51 Donati K (2019) 'Herding Is His Favourite Thing in the World': Convivial World-Making on a Multispecies Farm, *Journal of Rural Studies*, 66, 119–129: p. 122.
52 Fourier C (1808/[1996]) *The Theory of the Four Movements*, I Patterson (trans.), Cambridge UP, Cambridge, 176.
53 Tarde G (1902/[2007]) Economic Psychology, A Toscano (trans.), *Economy and Society*, 36(4), 614–643: pp. 631–632. See also Latour B & Lepinjay VA (2009) *The Science of Passionate Interests*, Prickly Paradigm Press, Chicago.
54 See the more detailed consideration of the commons in Chapter 12, "*Res familiaris*," where the concept of familiar production is also expanded.
55 Tinbergen N (1958) *Curious Naturalists*, Doubleday, New York, 31.
56 Studies of insect navigation, however, suggest that whole scenes are recognised in terms of their spatial arrangement, as distinct from the monumentalisation, as it were, of individual landmarks. See further Wystrach A & Graham P (2012) What Can We Learn from Studies of Insect Navigation?, *Animal Behaviour*, 84, 13–20; Baddeley B et al. (2012) A Model of Ant Route Navigation Driven by Scene Familiarity, *PLoS Computational Biology*, 8, e1002336. See further: Zeil J et al. (2003) Catchment Areas of Panoramic Snapshots in Outdoor Scenes, *Journal of the Optical Society of America A: Optics Image Science and Vision*, 20, 450–469; Möller R & Vardy A (2006) Local Visual Homing by Matched-Filter Descent in Image Distances, *Biological Cybernetics*, 95, 413–430. This points towards the experience and experimentation within the scene itself. That is, rather than focusing upon and valorising specific objects, the approach is one of the animal's mise-en-scène, their *Umwelt*. Indeed, any notion of insects recognising scenes through individual objects is considered illogical in terms of the survival costs: "we can wonder why animals would accept the processing cost of isolating and recognizing individual objects for navigational purposes, when simple egocentric views can encompass the overall structure and layout of a scene and underpin economical and robust navigation." Further, in the Wystrach & Graham study, the authors go on to consider that the assumption of individual landmarks that exists in vertebrate literature should be reconsidered in the light of insect studies (18). However, this view is not in terms of a broadened understanding of perception, but rather, in terms of survival "costs". Once again, the assumption of the animal's environmental experience is that it is purely in terms of survival and reproduction. What about the animal's environment could possibly be monumental under those conditions?
57 For instance, see Bennett ATD (1996) Do Animals Have Cognitive Maps?, *The Journal of Experimental Biology*, 199, 219–224: "I will consider that 'landmarks' can only be perceived *visually* by animals." (219). See further the discussion in Spetch ML & Kelly DM (2006) Comparative Spatial Cognition: Processes in Landmark- and Surface-Based Place Finding, in Wasserman EA & Zentall TR (eds.) *Comparative Cognition: Experimental Explorations of Animal Intelligence*, Oxford UP, Oxford, 210–228. Tinbergen's transformational approach is where an animal is trained to locate food hidden in relation to a specific arrangement of distinct landmarks, and then those landmarks are moved in order to assess the way in which animals might process space (including distance and direction). This approach was utilised by Sylvain Fiset to study distance and landmarks in dogs, demonstrating landmark-based spatial memory and cognition in domestic

dogs: Fiset S (2009) Evidence for Averaging of Distance from Landmarks in the Domestic Dog, *Behavioural Processes*, 81, 429–438. See further Tinbergen N (1972) *The Animal in Its World: Volume I, Field Studies*, Harvard UP, Cambridge.
58 Chan E et al. (2012) From Objects to Landmarks: The Function of Visual Location Information in Spatial Navigation, *Frontiers in Psychology*, 3(304), 1–11. For instance, see also Bennett ATD (1996) Do Animals Have Cognitive Maps?, *The Journal of Experimental Biology*, 199, 219–224, where the author explicitly limits the discussion to the visual: "I will consider that 'landmarks' can only be perceived *visually* by animals" (219).
59 Tweet from @Alyssaarre 12 September 2018, 17:58 GMT+1.
60 Of course, scent-making may be accompanied by flamboyant or expressive behaviour, such as ground scratching or demonstration marking (see further Bekoff M (1979) Ground Scratching by Male Composite Dogs: A Composite Signal, *Journal of Mammalogy*, 60(4), 847–848). However, for the purposes of the present example, the focus is on the seemingly "intangible" nature of the landmark through scent. These performances are considered further in Chapter 6 "Separation anxiety."
61 This question is expanded further in relation to smell and "works" in the Chapter 6, "Separation anxiety," through Alexandra Horowitz's concept of the olfactory mirror.
62 Diaconu M (2006) Reflections on an Aesthetics of Touch, Smell and Taste, *Contemporary Aesthetics*, 4, 1–10: p. 2; Classen C (1993) *Worlds of Sense: Exploring the Senses in History and across Cultures*, Routledge, London, 3–4.
63 Corbin A (1982/[1994]) *The Foul and the Fragrant: Odour and the Social Imagination*, Picador, London, 6. Also of note in this invalidation of smell is the theory of "object failure" in relation to olfactory objects (and indeed other objects), which is defined as "the failure of an experience to present objects accurately" (Batty C (2010) What the Nose Doesn't Know: Non-Veridicality and Olfactory Experience, *Journal of Consciousness Studies*, 17(3–4), 10–17: p. 10). Batty describes this disengagement and "nonrepresentational" account of smell as putting olfactory experience in error and the proponents of such approaches to smells as "error theorists" (see Batty C (2011) Smelling Lessons, *Philosophical Studies*, 153(1), 161–174: p. 169). Batty clarifies thus: "Although olfactory experience does not present us with particular objects, olfaction clearly constitutes an informational system. Olfaction has this in common with vision as well as the other sense modalities" (170). See further Batty C (2009) What's That Smell?, *The Southern Journal of Philosophy*, 47(4), 321–348. Smell is discussed further in Chapter 6, "Separation anxiety."
64 For a comprehensive and entertaining account of the dog walk, including the impact of smells, see Horowitz A (2013) *On Looking: About Everything There Is to See*, Simon & Schuster, London.
65 This can be seen in other priorities in terms of questions posed as a measure of intelligence and the anthropocentrism of what those questions may be (such as the mirror test for self-awareness, pointing and the gaze, trainability, and so on). See Waal F de (2016) *Are We Smart Enough to Know How Smart Animals Are?*, Granta, London, Chapter 8. See further the excellent analysis of this in Despret V (2012/[2016]) *What Would Animals Say If We Asked the Right Questions?*, B Buchanan (trans.), U of Minnesota P, Minneapolis.
66 Heap S et al. (2012) The Adoption of Landmarks for Territorial Boundaries, *Animal Behaviour*, 83, 871–878: p. 876.
67 In other words, "conspicuous landmarks allow conventional solutions to the problems of territory division": Mesterton-Gibbons M & Adams ES (2003)

Landmarks in Territory Partitioning: A Strategically Stable Convention?, *The American Naturalist*, 161(5), 685–696: p. 685.

68 Heap S et al. explain: "[L]andmarks may be used as a convention that allows a cost-effective way for boundaries to be established, assuming that boundary formation is normally a costly process. . . . For the clear-boundaries hypothesis, individual benefit unilaterally, in that any individual that adopts a landmarked boundary will experience some benefit. In contrast, the landmarks-as-convention hypothesis stipulates that settlers must mutually adopt the same landmark for their boundary in order for either to benefit." See Heap S et al. (2012) The Adoption of Landmarks for Territorial Boundaries, *Animal Behaviour*, 83, 871–878: p. 874.

69 In a comparison of the unilateral benefits of the clear-boundaries model and the mutual arrangements of the landmarks-as-convention model, Heap S et al. outline in fact what may be identified as elements of the kind of "shared interests" in the sociable property model being developed in the present discussion: see Heap S et al. (2012) The Adoption of Landmarks for Territorial Boundaries, *Animal Behaviour*, 83, 871–878.

70 The clear-boundaries hypothesis quite noticeably coincides with the notions of permanence, stability and durability that attach to property models (from real property to intellectual property). It is a landmark model based upon spatial awareness. However, in the landmarks-as-convention hypothesis, boundary-making becomes not only arbitrary but also secondary to the expressiveness of territory. Through convention, the use of space arguably is not only more efficient, but also more social. See further the discussion in Heap S et al. (2012) The Adoption of Landmarks for Territorial Boundaries, *Animal Behaviour*, 83, 871–878.

71 Mesterton-Gibbons M & Adams ES (2003) Landmarks in Territory Partitioning: A Strategically Stable Convention?, *The American Naturalis*, 161(5), 685–697.

72 Heap S et al. (2012) The Adoption of Landmarks for Territorial Boundaries, *Animal Behaviour*, 83, 871–878: "animals can invest less in defence over landmarked boundaries that are visually conspicuous than nonlandmarked boundaries," and "Reduced investment in territory defence may have a suite of other benefits to a resident, such as an increased ability to invest in exploitation of the territory" (874).

73 Bateson G (1972/[2000]) *Steps to an Ecology of Mind*, U of Chicago P, Chicago, 271.

74 Diaconu M (2006) Reflections on an Aesthetics of Touch, Smell and Taste, *Contemporary Aesthetics*, 4, 1–10: p. 7.

75 See the Chapter 12, "*Res familiaris*," in particular for a discussion of the opportunity to capture value in relations (notably including sharing) as distinct from objects.

76 Calvino I, The Name, the Nose, in *Under the Jaguar Sun*, W Weaver (trans.), Vintage, London, 1993/[1986], 72.

77 Blomley N (2016) The Territory of Property, *Progress in Human Geography*, 40(5) 593–609: p. 595.

78 Deleuze G (1994–1995) A comme animal/A as in Animal. Dominique Hurth (trans.). Transcription of the first part (first letter of the ABC) of the eight-hour series of interviews between Gilles Deleuze and Claire Parnet, filmed by Pierre-André Boutang in 1988–1989. Broadcast on Arte between November 1994 and Spring 1995.

79 Largey GP & Watson DR (1972) The Sociology of Odors, *American Journal of Sociology*, 77(6), 1021–1034: p. 1024. See further the history of the rose in

Classen C (1993) *Worlds of Sense: Exploring the Senses in History and Across Cultures*, Routledge, London, Chapter 1.
80 Howes D (2013) The Social Life of the Senses, *Ars Vivendi Journal*, 3, 4–23: p. 10.
81 The emphasis on the visual, explored and sustained throughout philosophy and other disciplines, is widely documented. See for example Batty C (2011) Smelling Lessons, *Philosophical Studies*, 153(1), 161–174.
82 Howes D (2013) The Social Life of the Senses, *Ars Vivendi Journal*, 3, 4–23: p. 10.
83 Tanimoto Y & Kiimura KD (2019) Neuronal, Mathematical, and Molecular Bases of Perceptual Decision-Making in *C. elegans*, *Neuroscience Research*, 140, 3–13.
84 Kaplan HS & Zimmer M (2018) Sensorimotor Integration for Decision Making: How the Worm Steers, *Neuron*, 97(2), 258–260.
85 Freas CA et al. (2019) Experimental Ethology of Learning in Desert Ants: Becoming Expert Navigators, *Behavioural Processes*, 158, 181–191; Buehlmann C et al. (2015) Desert Ants Use Olfactory Scenes for Navigation, *Animal Behaviour*, 106, 99–105; Steck K (2012) Just Follow Your Nose: Homing by Olfactory Cues in Ants, *Current Opinion in Neurobiology*, 22(2), 231–235; Mercier D et al. (2018) Olfactory Landmark-Based Communication in Interacting Drosophila, *Current Biology*, 28(16), 2624–2631.e5; Gaudry Q et al. (2012) Smelling on the Fly: Sensory Cues and Strategies for Olfactory Navigation in Drosophila, *Current Opinion in Neurobiology*, 22(2), 216–222. Reinhard J et al. (2004) Olfaction: Scent-Triggered Navigation in Honeybees, *Nature*, 427, 411; Menzel R (2009) Learning and Memory in Invertebrates: Honey Bee, in LS Squire (ed.) *Encyclopedia of Neuroscience*, Academic Press, Cambridge, MA, 435–439.
86 Wiegmann DD (2019) Nocturnal Navigation by Whip Spiders: Antenniform Legs Mediate Near-Distance Olfactory Localization of a Shelter, *Animal Behaviour*, 149, 45–54.
87 Wallraff HG (2014) Do Olfactory Stimuli Provide Positional Information for Home-Oriented Avian Navigation?, *Animal Behaviour*, 90, 31–36; Wallraff HG (2004) Avian Olfactory Navigation: Its Empirical Foundation and Conceptual State, *Animal Behaviour*, 67(2), 189–204; Grubb TC (1974) Olfactory Navigation to the Nesting Burrow in Leach's Petrel (*Oceanodroma Leucorrhoa*), *Animal Behaviour*, 22(1), 192–202.
88 Campbell-Palmer R & Rosell F (2011) The Importance of Chemical Communication Studies to Mammalian Conservation Biology, *Biological Conservation*, 144, 1919–1930.
89 Horowitz A (2016) *Being a Dog: Following the Dog into a World of Smell*, Simon & Schuster, London, 77–78.
90 Bao X et al. (2019) Grid-Like Neural Representations Support Olfactory Navigation of a Two-Dimensional Odor Space, *Neuron*, 102(5), 1066–1075e.
91 Krofel M et al. (2017) Does Human Infrastructure Shape Scent Marking in a Solitary Felid?, *Mammalian Biology*, 87, 36–39: p. 36.
92 Deleuze G & Guattari F (1980/[1987]) *A Thousand Plateaus: Capitalism and Schizophrenia*, B Massumi (trans.), U of Minnesota P, Minneapolis, 478.
93 Rindisbacher HJ (2015) What's This Smell? Shifting Worlds of Olfactory Perception, *KulturPoetic*, 15(1), 70–104: p. 84. Rindisbacher notes: "the very deficiencies encourage, in fact, require, linguistic creativity" (84). Curiously enough, Rindisbacher also refers to the "emerging literary territory" of olfactory fiction (88). He defines olfactory writing not as the mere use of smell in fiction, but where smell is so significant it is part of the plot itself.

94 Brian Massumi notes: "In French, *milieu* means "surroundings," "medium" (as in chemistry), and "middle." In the philosophy of Deleuze and Guattari, "Milieu" should be read as a technical term combining all three meanings." See the Notes on the Translation and Acknowledgements in Deleuze G & Guattari F (1980/[1987]) *A Thousand Plateaus: Capitalism and Schizophrenia*, B Massumi (trans.), U of Minnesota P, Minneapolis, xvi–xix: p. xvii. And in animal behaviour studies, territoriality arises from other benefits: "Functionally, territoriality provides individuals with the benefits of having exclusive or priority access to resources within a given space (e.g. food, mates, shelter). Thus territoriality will evolve when these benefits outweigh the costs of maintaining dominance in the area through aggression and display" Heap S et al. (2012) The Adoption of Landmarks for Territorial Boundaries, *Animal Behaviour*, 83, 871–878: p. 871. In other words, even in animal behaviour the notion of territory is accepted as presupposed by the milieu, even if the popular discourse of territory comes to express a somewhat over-simplified account.

95 Deleuze G & Guattari F (1980/[1987]) *A Thousand Plateaus: Capitalism and Schizophrenia*, B Massumi (trans.), U of Minnesota P, Minneapolis, 314.

96 Deleuze G & Guattari F (1980/[1987]) *A Thousand Plateaus: Capitalism and Schizophrenia*, B Massumi (trans.), U of Minnesota P, Minneapolis, 315.

97 For instance, in their review of the use of landmarks in territory, Heap S et al. state: "We consider landmarks that do not constitute complete physical barriers to movement, but rather act as barriers owing to the consequences of crossing them. To avoid confounding landmarks with other types of territorial resource, we do not explicitly consider landmarks that provide or diminish reproductive and survival benefits (e.g. food, reproductive opportunities, improved visibility, shelter). We focus instead on landmarks that have no cost or value beyond their use as boundaries." See Heap S et al. (2012) The Adoption of Landmarks for Territorial Boundaries, *Animal Behaviour*, 83, 871–878: pp. 871–872.

98 Deleuze G & Guattari F (1980/[1987]) *A Thousand Plateaus: Capitalism and Schizophrenia*, B Massumi (trans.), U of Minnesota P, Minneapolis, 315.

99 See the discussion of this kind of "object" value in the chapter, *Res familaris*.

100 Deleuze G & Guattari F (1980/[1987]) *A Thousand Plateaus: Capitalism and Schizophrenia*, B Massumi (trans.), U of Minnesota P, Minneapolis, 315.

101 Deleuze G & Guattari F (1980/[1987]) *A Thousand Plateaus: Capitalism and Schizophrenia*, B Massumi (trans.), U of Minnesota P, Minneapolis, 315.

102 Deleuze G & Guattari F (1980/[1987]) *A Thousand Plateaus: Capitalism and Schizophrenia*, B Massumi (trans.), U of Minnesota P, Minneapolis, 315–316.

Chapter 6

Separation anxiety

> Territorial marks are readymades. And what is called *art brut* is not at all pathological or primitive; it is merely this constitution, this freeing, of all matters of expression in the movement of territoriality: the base or ground of art. Take anything and make it a matter of expression.
>
> Deleuze G & Guattari F (1980/[1987]) *A Thousand Plateaus: Capitalism and Schizophrenia*, B Massumi (trans), U of Minnesota P, Minneapolis, 316

> In human affairs smell has degenerated into an aesthetic side-show, a pivot for a luxury trade.
>
> British Medical Journal (1942) The Shape of a Smell, *British Medical Journal*, 2(4262), 315

The previous chapters in this age, the Space Age, have explored the way animal territories are articulated around relations rather than absolute dominion, guiding individuals through interactions rather than absolute exclusions. And in the previous chapter the monumental importance of smell was introduced in the context of landmarks and navigation. Smell both generates territory and eludes territory. From a property perspective, from the invisible boundaries of scent fences to the casual remarks of scent-marking, to the blank look of smell art, smell is a sensational challenge that commands much needed attention. Smell is loud, appetising, ticklish, and showy. Smell breathes much to be desired.

The challenge ahead is to consider how the use of scent, through marking territory and so on, can be interpreted alongside smell art and the treatment of smell within intellectual property in order to acquire further insight into the way in which humans were themselves introduced to property. Smell art is indeed exemplary for explaining a canine world of authorship and attribution and indeed for navigating the very treacherous terrain of intellectual property in "incomplete territories," including digital ones.

There is so much ground to cover. Let's make tracks.

Smell, a sense of self

They call me a scent artist.

I have tried to accept this over time, yet I feel I am more of a visual artist, who uses smell/scent as the main sense/medium to give meaning to the image, so that this image does not necessarily need to be visible.[1]

The smell becomes form and colour and when this comes to consciousness the result is visual smell.[2]

Marking creates an image of the marker, an image of that dog.[3]

The marker does not necessarily need to be visible or even present. We are looking for the tracks, not the lion. Marking is also not necessarily about possession and territory but may be a kind of pure expression, as it were.[4] Indeed, the ready equation of marking with territory (or even dominance) belies the drift of predatory discourse into the interpretation of scent-marking behaviour itself.[5] Scent-marking is a signature, that dog's freedom of expression,[6] communication at will, communication all over the place.

Whether that image of the marker is through ground scratching and other "visual components of behaviors used to deposit scent"[7] and mark space, or through the opportunity to identify and recognise sex in different markings,[8] or indeed the importance of the situation of the mark itself, scent is the illustrator.

Scent is a lot of things. As seen in previous chapters, scent is cooperative with landmarks, both in terms of navigation and communication. As well as an accumulation of scents on particular landmarks or monuments of importance,[9] the landmarks themselves are communicative not only in terms of presenting a possible obstacle (for example, the landmark may be chosen for its conspicuous presence) but also in terms of a so-called bourgeois strategy of animal ownership.[10]

However, as well as the expression in relation to a particular landmark, the scent mark creates an image of the marker not by accident but by intention. The position of the scent[11] and the frequency of the mark[12] create a physical image of the invisible pen.[13] Various mammals will adjust their posture when scent-marking in order to appear "bigger" to other individuals who might subsequently encounter their scent.[14] Dwarf mongooses have been found to do "handstand scent-marking" to achieve this;[15] brown bears will leave scent marks higher in trees to appear bigger;[16] and dogs are influenced by their size both in terms of how often they urinate[17] and how high.[18] Male dogs (particularly smaller dogs) tend to promote a particular image of themselves through a careful positioning of their deposit, raising their legs higher in order to achieve a higher mark[19] and thus suggesting a greater size.[20] In other words, dogs will use different postures in order to suggest their physical potential to their "readers." The imposture of posture.

Such marking is also concerned with participation (perhaps even more so than it is with territory, at least in the case of dogs), with scent-marking in public spaces being identified with sociability, greetings, and general communication:[21] "Smells are something more than a way of perceiving or understanding the world. They are a way of understanding and relating to the world, of engaging with the world."[22] Communication is not necessarily competitive; instead it is social and participatory. Indeed, this is fundamental to the sociable property of canine territories. Smells are connections, greetings, encounters. Thus, smell is not only a source of information but also a gesture of communication and participation. It is genuinely expressive. In other words, "territorial marking" or territorial demarcation is not all about territoriality.[23] That is, it is not necessarily about boundaries at all.

And what of the reader? The participation in smell is a remarkable, embodied performance. Rolling in a smell not only downloads that smell onto the enthusiast but also mashes up their smell with the existing work: "As a scent-mark gets the animal's scent on the ground, scent-rolling or -rubbing gets the ground's scent on the animal. Or, rather, the scent of whatever-it-is that they are rolling in."[24] Scent-rolling also artfully, as it were, challenges the otherwise arbitrary demarcation and separation of senses in that the engagement is both (and at least) haptic and olfactory all at once. This is truly performance art within the installation space, and, with that, scent becomes a mobile property. The dog literally picks it up and takes it away in a truly embodied communication. And at the same time, the scent transports the consumer, allowing them to be somewhere, back there, where they are not.

A range of theories have been offered to explain this exuberance. A common one is to interpret the behaviour again within the paradigm of boundary-making and territory, potentially skewed by the presumptions around predation and competition. In this theory, the dressing in smell is interpreted as a camouflage in order to stay safe when within another's environment.[25] Arguably a more compelling, more reasonable, and a more "sociable" theory, as it were, is the "popularity" theory.[26] And finally, there is the hedonic theory, the performative excess of unfettered joy and pleasure, a communication beyond mere survival or reproductive value, a pure expression: "it is simply pleasurable . . . the fragrance can be enjoyed later. New sources of smell are particularly interesting."[27] Art for dogs.

The significance of play and pleasure as metacommunicative expression will be considered again a little later in this chapter. But first, the importance of the popularity theory is that it really engages with the smell as social expression rather than defence. In other words, the smell invites contact rather than offends it. The smell is, quite literally, hospitable, despite what any human might think![28] Indeed, it could be argued that it still invites interspecies contact, even if that contact turns out to be a bath. Thus, contrary to the usual reasons for its disregard, smell is not immobile, smell is not inalienable, but it does require a "consumer" in order to be disseminated further. From a property perspective, this aspect is fascinating.

In this way, scent is genuinely inviting. Scent opens up a world of belonging for that dog, of making home. In other words, scent is not so much a beacon of exclusive territories, as perhaps often thought, but is rather a communication of managing different relations within overlapping territories.[29] Indeed, so-called scent fences often succeed whether physical barriers fail. In other words, these are systems of mutual respect, a property of "manners." On the other hand, physical barriers do not engage with nor depend upon a kind of mutual understanding, do not resonate meaningfully with an animal's ethology and ecology and, for those reasons and others, often fail. In this way smell presents a porous barrier that operates on a system of relations between beings and coexistence within a shared space. There is indeed much to be learned from the ways in which animals mutualise territories, as distinct from the system of objects and enforcement in conventional property frameworks. Thus, smell is to be understood, perhaps more importantly, in terms of familiarity and mutual understanding.[30] Scent-marking is indeed familiar production, *sniff large*.

Scent-marking is thus also intricately bound up with recognition of self, a sense of self, as it were.[31] In many respects, it is a kind of attribution, a biological metadata of every visitation by that olfactory author. Here am I, where are you? Whether in the marks in the ground or the scent left behind, smell provides a kind of imprint or signature upon the landscape. As with tracks, as with smells, the author makes her mark.

In order to test self-awareness in animals, researchers engage regularly in the testing of self-recognition and other self-directed activity most usually through a form of the mirror self-recognition test or MSR test. The MSR test was developed almost 50 years ago by Gordon Gallup as a means by which to determine empathic perspective-taking and self-awareness.[32] By measuring reactions to a mirror, such as self-recognition and using the mirror as a tool to achieve self-directed behaviour, researchers have attempted to gauge the level of self-awareness and the possession of self-image in various species. This research has also included the use of marks (the mirror mark test),[33] where a mark is applied to the animal in such a way that it can be seen only with a mirror in order to investigate whether the animal reacts to the mark by attempting to remove it through the use of the mirror as a tool.[34] However, these tests clearly privilege the visual over all other senses, as well as presume a priority of self-grooming and presentation, through a somewhat anthropocentric view of the animal's interests physiologically, ethologically, and otherwise.[35]

For dogs, and indeed other species, where olfaction is a much more important sense than vision, the traditional mirror test arguably asks all the wrong questions.[36] In a study of elephant cognition and the use of smell, the researchers note: "As the study of cognition in animals continues to grow as a field, it is becoming increasingly important that experimental designs become more species-specific. Research into the minds of animals should account of differences in sensory perspectives to ensure fair comparisons of cognitive capacity, rather than rely on approaches that are unfairly biased toward the primate-centric, visual perspective."[37]

In response to the traditional tests for self-awareness, Alexandra Horowitz has advocated what she calls an "olfactory mirror" in order to account for the way in which dogs use smell as a form of self-recognition.[38] Describing the meta-cognitive abilities of dogs, such as perspective-taking and thus an implied "sense of the distinction of 'self' and 'other,'" Horowitz calls for a test based upon olfaction, that is, the primary sense by which dogs acquire information: "Given the role of olfaction in dogs' social lives, olfactory stimuli are more ecologically relevant to the species than visual stimuli. . . . Dogs do, however, engage in bouts of olfactory investigation of conspecifics, and, too, of their own odours."[39] Smell creates and reflects the image, the self-image. Smell is thus a *looking-glass: the image does not need to be visible.*

The previous chapters in the Space Age have shepherded the dynamic territories of smell in sociable properties. But what does this sensory dimension of the image, this smelly boundary-making, tell us about the work and about intellectual property in particular and the "work" of art?

Unseen works

> Perhaps art begins with the animal, at least with the animal that carves out a territory and constructs a house.[40]

As we have seen, so to speak, smell carves out and marks that dog's territories, but not necessarily from the perspective of defence. Instead, smell tracks the artistry of contact, a territory of movement, familiarity, and sensation, as distinct from inaction, detachment, and distance. Scent marks make advances, leave word, make a mark, get in touch. Indeed, smell creates not only the landmarks, the monuments of a space, but also the makers, the markers, the authors of that space.

Smell both creates the landscape and yet is indecipherable from it, a source of anxiety for a property system obsessed with things and separation. It is perhaps not arbitrary that smell has been relegated to the extent that it has as a so-called lower sense:

> It is significant that the main European languages contain no names for the qualities of smells and we can refer to them only by metaphors, as is done in the perfumery trade, or by mentioning their source – the fragrance of a rose, the smell of violets, etc. The latter way does not work for complex and blended odours. There is need of a scientific and recognized vocabulary for naming the qualities of smells, but this could only be constructed if it became possible to classify smells systematically.[41]

This ranking of the senses also belies the enterprise of treating the senses as separable, discrete "things." David Howes notes that "one of the defining characteristics of modernity is the cultural separation of the senses into self-contained fields."[42] And the individual senses have also been subjected to a further categorical imperative, such as in the discrete reproducibility of colour in the Pantone system; but taste and smell have continued to elude (or to be ignored) in the campaign of sensory object-making, to their detriment for the purposes of intellectual property protection: "Even though the human sense of smell can distinguish hundreds of thousands of smells and in this regard is comparable to sight or hearing, in none of the world's languages does there seem to be a classification of smells comparable, for example, to colour classification."[43]

Almost none that is. Notably, the South American Quechua language, spoken largely in the Andes, has a sophisticated system of differentiation not only for smells but also for smelling actions and practices. In other words, there is an intentionality and an originality to smelling: "It is not only odour which is classified and thus expressed in different ways through language, but also the act of smelling. In English we use but one word to refer to both inhaling and emitting odours – namely, to smell. Other languages are a good deal more explicit."[44] However, the links between the depreciation of smell in humans and an emphasis on human exceptionalism, while seemingly celebrating the special olfactory skills of the spiritual (and "exotic") animal other, have also informed the agenda of racial discourse and colonial enterprise.[45] This presents a stark contrast to the sociability expressed through smell within animal territories; for humans, as Simmel maintains, "one can characterize the sense of smell as the dissociating sense."[46] However, this distancing is not only arbitrary, but also contrary and subject to a disquieting assumption. Smell in fact necessitates immediate intimacy: "By smelling something, we draw this impression or this radiating object more deeply into ourselves, in the centre of our being: we assimilate it, so to speak, by the vital process of breathing more intimately with ourselves than is possible with respect to an object by any other sense."[47] In many respects this is consistent with Simmel's sociology of visual interaction in that smell is a relationship of "mutual glances,"[48] of olfactory glances and memories. The dog looked back. Simmel just hadn't seen it yet.

These efforts at the depletion of the expressive value of the olfactory sense, together with the sociological deprecation of smell, form the context for its frequent disregard as a form of aesthetic expression. Smells and tastes and the "sensations" of expression have historically been reduced to crafts, forcing a distinction between high and low art traced along sensory lines and excommunicating smell, as it were, from the world of the aesthetic and public taste: "The fact that the chemical senses require material, molecular intake and their (artistic) creations are subsequently consumed in the process of perception makes them unsuitable, in the Enlightenment understanding of aesthetics, for being considered among the arts. Indeed, the culinary arts and perfumery have never fully transcended the status of mere *crafts*."[49]

The olfactory sense is indeed rarely regarded, as it were, as capable of producing art in the conventional aesthetic sense. Mădălina Diaconu argues that the recognition of an aesthetics of smell (and touch and taste) must overcome the challenges from the cultural and social traditions framing the interpretation of the senses. Diaconu explains, "Modern aesthetics regards sight and hearing as the only senses which were able to produce art," and while it is usually accepted that, "Touch, smell and taste might offer pleasant stimuli," they "can never achieve the status of art objects."[50] This resonates with Georg Simmel's assertion: "Smell does not form an object on its own, as do sight and hearing, but remains, as it were, captive in the human subject."[51] As we will see, this aesthetic hierarchy and the emphasis on the visual also informs the law's interpretation of art. What is a work? Does it smell?

Communication through scent-marking is also enticingly similar to the way in which information is gambled, exchanged, and lost in social media: "Scent marking, a common form of communication in mammals, is remarkably indirect: on individual places a mark in the environment that another individual might encounter, typically in the absence of the individual that placed the mark."[52] The author is invisible, and yet the message creates an image.

Smell is a meeting place, meeting again and again: "Once 'we' have met, we can never be 'the same' again."[53] Intimacy is also implicated through smell – intimacy in the engagement with the surrounding world and intimacy between beings (present or absent). This meeting again through the senses is thus a kind of "somatic attunement."[54]

Smell is a world of opening up, *Umwelt*, not the diminished world of representation to which much of our thought arguably has been reduced.[55] Michel Serres laments the studied "thingness" of language and culture, with the loss of this embodied communication and arguably the compassion of a more relational approach:

> It takes a body and senses to create a culture. Language or artificial intelligence produce a sub-culture, for want of a body. Through this imposed abstraction the sensible returns, a stubborn, infernal shadow, in images and language, but defigured by wasteful contempt. seated at the banquet, the statues and robots dream of lists and icons. . . . In bottles, around the lips, there lies culture. And, absolutely all things considered, knowledge: intelligence and wisdom. *Homo sapiens*: he who knows how to taste. Sagacious: he who knows how to smell. All of these things are vanishing under the weight of logic and grammar, dreary and insane when they deny themselves bodies.[56]

This embodied communication in relation to smell is important. One moves through and is framed by the world of smell; this is not an art of borders and fixation but an art of the *Umwelt*. The world of representation is always already a truncated viewpoint, an abbreviated position, an excised account: "Since we are not in a position to investigate the appearance-world of another subject, but only that part of our appearance-world surrounding it, we had better speak of the surrounding-world of the animal. It is only for the observer himself that the surrounding-world and the appearance-world are identical."[57] And yet it is a presumption of a privileged perspective upon this appearance-world that keeps property intact and deodorises the mutual olfactory gaze: "In contrast to political ideology, with its intellectual reductionism and simplification and the inadequacy of its approaches to reality, the study of smells requires that we observe and analyse the whole of reality, embracing its complexity and its incalculable abundance."[58] Indeed, roll in it, rub in it, and carry it away.

The American psychologist and one of the leading figures in the history of the field of visual perception, James Gibson, develops an ecological view of perception in which he speaks of the "meaningful environment,"[59] thus confounding the conventional attributions (and pretensions) of objectivity and reliability with respect to the visual: "the percept is never completely determined by the physical stimulus. Instead, the percept is something essentially subjective in that it depends on some contribution made by the observer himself. Perception goes beyond the stimuli and is superposed on sensations."[60] Perception is always already about relations, and this is an integral part of the revisioning of property from the perspective of sociability, towards a dynamic interpretation and resocialisation of property rights: "What the other animal affords the observer is not only behavior but also social interaction."[61]

This is not intended as a romanticisation of the animal other, far from it. Rather, it is an appeal to get moving. That dog and those unseen works of olfactory expression are an irrepressible provocation to the notions of the incorporeal work. The nature of smell, the unseen work, is an astonishing interrogation of intellectual property boundaries, of the nature of the work, and the intentionality of the author. Thus, smell presents an extraordinary opportunity to challenge the dominant narrative proposed by intellectual property and to agitate its separation anxiety. Intellectual property is indeed presented with many sensational challenges, but how might an ethological jurisprudence of intellectual property inform its interpretation of smell or olfactory art?

Making works of sense

> Epigraphs in an undecipherable language, half their letters rubbed away by the sand-laden wind: this is what you will be, *O parfumeries*, for the noseless man of the future.[62]

The shifting sands of smell are seemingly no foundation upon which to build the clear borders of contemporary western property models, particularly in the grips of the Machine Age and the predatory drift in the development of western property values. However, this predation by the visual is not inevitable. How can we make property more smelly?

Smell is seen, as it were, to consume its landscape, to be inseparable from its surroundings, to be indecipherable as a work: "the putative unity of the idea of landscape (which is largely a visual construct) in recognition of the heterogeneity of the means of perception."[63] At the same time, smell is not necessarily identified as transforming its medium, as doing work (as considered in the previous chapter in relation to landmarks). Property's pretence is at scarcity, but its mechanism is in reproducibility, and the immateriality of smell confounds this very architecture.[64] In other words, smell struggles both for recognition of any transformation of its medium while at the same time supposedly consuming it: "It has often been argued that touch, smell and taste cannot produce art because they deal with ephemeral stimuli and consume their objects."[65] Where is the evidence of "a work"?

While the visual has been emphasised in the cultural and intellectual history of the west, smell has been barely touched, so to speak:

> That sight and hearing, the two most highly valued senses in the West, are mediated by culture may perhaps be readily appreciated. The notion of 'the period eye' and 'the educated listener' are commonplace. To what extent,

however, can the senses of touch, taste and smell model and transmit cultural values? This is a subject that has been far less often considered, primarily because cognition is not usually associated with the 'lower' senses in modern culture. Indeed, one clear sign of the cultural importance of sight and hearing in our society is the sheer volume of academic and scientific work dedicated to the exploration of these senses compared to the vastly-reduced interest in the study of the other senses.[66]

And, indeed, the sheer volume of property incorporated in these senses is another clear sign compared to the almost irreconcilable differences with the other senses. The visual has also dominated the history of ethology and behaviourism and the "perceived" difficulty in entertaining ideas of animal consciousness and emotion.[67] John Broadus Watson, the "father" of radical behaviourism, sought to distinguish his field on the basis of the visual and avoid "the absurd terminology of Beer, Bethe, Von Uexküll, Nuel," proclaiming, "Psychology, as the behaviorist views it, is a purely objective, experimental branch of natural science which needs introspection as little as do the sciences of chemistry and physics."[68]

Georg Simmel, in his influential essay, 'Sociology of the Senses,' relegates the senses other than sight and hearing as secondary but nevertheless anticipates the importance of smell: "Compared with the sociological significance of sight and hearing, that of the lower senses is of secondary importance, although not so small in the case of smell as the peculiar vagueness and undevelopment of its impressions would erroneously lead us to assume."[69]

This historic and monumental emphasis on the visual recalls the landmark discussion in the previous chapter and the difficulty in comprehending the intention and purposive creativity in non-visual landmarks. Similarly, the emphasis on visual tests for self-awareness in animal behaviour research, with arguably less attention on other examples of self-image, as discussed earlier, begins to appear even more complicit with the emphasis on the visual in western culture.

Smell, the "lower sense," has historically been regarded as animalistic (you don't say) and unrespectable, deployed to mark out difference in discriminatory classist and racist discourse as well as discourses of gender and sexuality.[70] The so-called animalistic sense also becomes a mark of distinction (and indistinction) in human exceptionalism narratives. Dogs in particular are lauded for their superpowers of smell, but this often persists in popular discourse as an endorsement of their separation – aberrant and certainly not human. Thus, as seen (or not seen) with the non-visual landmarks, this kind of separation persists as a basis for claiming that smell has no meaning: "Aestheticians have also doubted that the so-called lower senses are able to achieve that structural complexity that would be required to sustain our attention over time. . . . This lack of reflection and complexity is responsible, as well, for the common belief that tactile and olfactory stimuli actually have no meaning and thus cannot release a process of perceptual contemplation and interpretation."[71] In other words, smell becomes relegated to purposes of survival, competition, "the struggle for life," and denied any intentional, communicative expression: "touch, smell and taste apparently do not contribute to a humanist perspective because they do not grasp the difference between man and animal."[72] François Laplantine is critical of this categorical imperative in the senses and its marginalisation of animal expression: "It is only in the Eurocentric Cartesian construction of distinct 'faculties' that the sensible is enclosed in a separate domain by relegating it to the side of instinct, drive, and impulse, that is, of animal life. In this perspective, and this perspective only, sensations are deemed to be devoid of psychological and *a fortiori* signification."[73] They have no meaning.

The mirror test? Lack of reflection indeed.

Sense-making requires work, it demands practice: "There is no difference in principle between attending to the sensory nature of a smell and enjoying good tone in musical performance or colour in painting. There are 'fragrance gardens' for the blind. . . . The appreciation of works of arts consists of a similar *kind* of heightened awareness through the exercise of a cultivated sensibility for more elaborately structured objects."[74] In this context, Waskul and Vanini speak of "somatic work,"[75] maintaining that, "In short, it is through somatic work that sensory meaning is made . . . people sense as well as make sense."[76] The work of the gaze is significant here; to wander, to stray, is anything but purposeless.[77]

Intellectual property is thus an immateriality in search of an object, a reason in search of an artefact (or the other way around?), a masterpiece in search of a meaning. When it comes to animal creativity, that's about the smell of it. The work? A smell by any other name would smell as sweet.

Making space for art

> And what joins art with play now appears in the likeness of both to sociability.[78]

In 2016 I took three dogs (Aubrey, Huw, and Jeff) to visit the Dominic Wilcox curated exhibition, Art for Dogs, in London.[79] The exhibition included several works by Wilcox as well as additional wall-based works by invited artists. These included scent works hung at nose level. Wilcox produced several interactive works, including *Cruising Canines*, an open-car-window simulator with a mechanical moving landscape combined with a scent-blowing fan blowing various olfactory "objects" into the air, including the smells of meat, fish, and footwear. Another work, *Watery Wonder*, was a fountain exhibit where water bowls were placed on artificial grass out of which fountains of water would spring and then bounce between each bowl. What was striking about the way in which the dogs experienced the entire landscape of the exhibit was the way in which they engaged with the individual works not as discrete forms but through experimentation in their use. The way the dogs "viewed" the works transformed the gallery space and the works themselves, as well as drew their human companions into the reshaping of the exhibits themselves. Many dogs also contributed to an impromptu work when one after the other they lay and overlay marks on a central supporting column. While there was no formal work for ground-marking or scent-rolling, the dogs nevertheless innovated and fashioned an alternative. It proved extremely popular and a genuinely participatory co-constitution of the artistic space.

One of the works, *Dinnertime Dreams*, was comprised of a giant 12-foot dog bowl of the dimensions of a small pond, filled with over 2000 large brown plastic balls (to resemble dog food). This particular work kindled enthusiastic play once one dog, our very own Jeff, initiated the interaction, first playing by himself, then with other dogs, and then with humans as well. The dogs played with each other in the ball pit, as well as opened up the play, inviting in the humans and other dogs moving around the exhibit. As the dogs played, they would usually send quite a few balls flying out of the pit, unfolding the work onto the other surrounding works and engaging the many humans as they ran to fetch balls and throw them back into the pit, not so much to preserve the integrity of the work but rather to participate. Everybody began to play, world to world, in a joyous *intersensorial relation*.[80]

Natasha Lushetich describes a similar interaction through the example of a child playing in leaves:

> The difference between the pre-formatting sensorial relationship to the world and the formatted one lies not only in the fact that a child will, for example, appreciate a pile of autumn leaves by jumping into it while an adult will, most likely, appreciate it by saying "Oh, the colours are so rich!" It also lies in the child's momentary transubstantiation into a pile of soft, rustling leaves, which will capture its textural, aural and olfactory "imprint" . . . the child's body will momentarily "become" the pile of leaves thus establishing an *intersensorial relation* with the matter it comes into contact with.[81]

This intersensorial relation of play was also incorporated in the vernissage for the 1942 group exhibit, *First Papers of Surrealism*, organised by Marcel Duchamp and André Breton. The opening of the exhibition included children playing, as well as an olfactory element, the smell of cedar, which was explained in the catalogue as associated with children's play:[82] "*Vernissage consacré aux enfants jouant, à l'odeur du cèdre.*"[83]

Duchamp also had played with expressions through smell a few years earlier in what is possibly one of the first examples of olfactory art. In the 1938 exhibition of surrealist artists, the Exposition Internationale du Surréalisme, the poet Benjamin Péret installed a coffee-roasting machine and filled the exhibit with the smell of fresh coffee.[84] Like smell, play is a work "finally unfinished."[85] Duchamp famously always referred to his work *Glass* (also known as *The Bride Stripped Bare By Her Bachelors, Even*) as unfinished.[86] Octavio Paz describes Duchamp's move away from traditional visual arts as his "negation of painting" and as "the beginning of his true *work*. A work without works: there are no pictures except the *Large Glass* (the great delay), the Readymades, a few *gestures*, and a long silence."[87] This "unfinished" nature of any work is a critical challenge for property frameworks, and it is a challenge that is presented inexhaustibly by smell art and by the play of sociability in various forms of collaborative unsettling of authorship, creative interruptions by the consumer, and the sociable territories of the digital.

Art stinks

> Surrealism is only trying to rejoin the most durable traditions of mankind. Among the primitive peoples art always goes beyond what is conventionally and arbitrarily called the "real."[88]

> To paraphrase John Barth, reality is a nice place to visit (philosophically), but no one ever lived there.[89]

One of the last things Charles Baudelaire composed before his death in 1867 was a short story, published in 1869,[90] entitled "Les Bons Chiens, á Joseph Stevens."[91] The story was dedicated to his friend Joseph Stevens, the Belgian animalier whose favourite subject was dogs. In the story, two of the "Bohemian artist dogs" admire a work of smell, "*l'oeuvre sans nom*" or "nameless artwork,"[92] "their magician's gaze fixed on the stove where *work without a name* simmers."[93] For Baudelaire's "four-legged philosophers"[94] (or "four-footed philosophers"[95]) their aesthetic is smell.

But is it art?

Fluxus is the name given to an international avant-garde or possibly Dadaist group or art movement (although members resisted pretensions towards either) that was created in the 1960s, reaching the height of its influence in the 1970s but still continuing today.[96] Some of the key proponents have included Joseph Beuys, George Brecht, and Yoko Ono, and the composer, John Cage;[97] however, the founding of Fluxus is largely attributed to George Maciunas, the Lithuanian-American artist who coined the name and imposed himself as chairman.[98] The name was first devised for the purposes of a magazine but ultimately became applied to the group itself.

In the founding Manifesto, Maciunas declares that the group will, "PROMOTE A REVOLUTIONARY FLOOD AND TIDE IN ART, promote living art, anti-art, promote NON ART REALITY to be fully grasped by all peoples, not only critics, dilettantes and professionals."[99] As such, Fluxus exhorts the unrepresentability of representation (the impossibility of an objective "appearance-world," the truncated view in the mirror, and so on): "The operative word *about*, like the word *of*, insists on the distance between object and user."[100] In other words, the sensation (*relation*), as distinct from the object (*thing*) is what is at stake: "Fluxkit makes an experience for the handler that *is* the sensation contained in it; the Fluxkit is not *about* the sensation."[101]

The most resilient traits or qualities shared by members of Fluxus are characterised by a resistance to notions of tradition and professionalism in the arts, as well as locating art mainly through events or happenings (*Aktions*), as distinct from the carefully curated work in traditional settings – in other words, in Maciunas's words, anti-art. In the second manifesto, Fluxmanifesto, Maciunas rails against the commodification of art:

> Fluxmanifesto on Fluxamusement – vaudeville – art? To establish artist's non-professional, nonparasitic, nonelite status in society, he must demonstrate own dispensability, he must demonstrate selfsufficiency of the audience, he must demonstrate that anything can substitute art and anyone can do it. Therefore this substitute art-amusement must be simple, amusing, concerned with insignificances, have no commodity or institutional value. It must be unlimited, obtainable by all and eventually produced by all. The artist doing art meanwhile, to justify his income, must demonstrate that only he can do art. Art therefore must appear to be complex, intellectual, exclusive, indispensable, inspired. To raise its commodity value it is made to be rare, limited in quantity and therefore accessible not to the masses but to the social elite.[102]

In many ways, with "works of art with no financial value as such,"[103] Maciunas is speaking out against a kind of predatory drift in art that moves towards an arbitrary scarcity and stratification of art and away from the sociable territories of a playful, useless, smelly, pure expression of "a bunch of jokers."[104]

Indeed, a rich ambrosia of olfactory art has emerged from the Fluxus movement. One of the most celebrated examples was a series of special chess sets by the Japanese artist, Takako Saito, referred to as *Fluxchess*,[105] and including the work, *Smell Chess*.[106] Saito produced sets to fascinate the range of senses, including smell. That these works were also intended to be played as games and the pieces "sampled" plays up the sociability of these pieces and the vital participation of the audience: "Saito's *Smell Chess* denies the sort of perception that corresponds to the game's requirement for logical and hierarchical manageability and in its place proposes olfactory perception which, contrarily to the game's purpose, erases 'discrete' spatio-temporal units and confuses boundaries."[107] The chess set still adheres to the rules of the game, but at once attention is drawn to the chess pieces themselves: "The white king is cardamom and the white queen is anise while the black pawns are made of black pepper, the black rooks of coriander, black knights of turmeric, black bishops of cumin, the black king of asafetida and the black queen of cayenne pepper."[108] This is not a piece about the game of chess. This is a game of chess.[109]

As such, smell art irritates the prospect for property, while navigating an expansion of aesthetic territories. As the Belgian artist, Guy Bleus, affirms: "So there are lots of possible kinds of communication often entirely unpredictable, because a specific personal reaction is involved but this fact increases the aesthetic adventure, the thrill of working with odours."[110]

Smell, a mile away

No longer just "an aesthetic side-show, a pivot for a luxury trade,"[111] olfactory art is now being promoted as precisely otherwise: "a true artistic medium rather than just a consumer product."[112] It is intriguingly paradoxical that the nature of smell, so resistant to the commodity model, has nevertheless been managed up until recently by its relegation as such.

For intellectual property, smell is all but incomprehensible according to current law, for all the reasons discussed – smell is impossible to separate, as it were, from the author, from the room, from each other, and from itself. Fundamentally, it is not possible to protect smell other than indirectly. Does that mean smell does not have an author? Does art have to be intellectual property? Duchamp's coffee smell could not be protected as a work, but the shape of the coffee pot might be; that is, not the sociability in the coffee, but the container, the boundary-maker. For property and intellectual property, it seems, paradoxically, that walls must be built if the work is to be seen.

This really points to the sociability of smell as "having," as a kind of reciprocal possession, as distinct from the boundary-making of property systems, including intellectual property. When it comes to intellectual property in a digital environment, however, very similar problems start to accrue. In the familiar production of social media platforms, the "having" is the primary motivation for the sociability through the work, not the being of the work. Indeed, in a very fundamental way, the basic form of intellectual property is at odds with a sociable reciprocal possession. But is it art?

A canine "smell art" demonstrates a kind of canine property, including the importance of attribution and acknowledgement, without the necessity for walls. In this respect, the negotiation of the "work" is not in terms of the value in and of itself but the value that is displaced and created in other settings. Nevertheless, attribution is always intact, and the relationship between the individual and the environment is always maintained. This is arguably at the heart of a functioning, sharing dynamic, as it were, while at the same time assuring the intellectual property delivered into that environment. That is, the crucial value that must be maintained is that of the haver, the attribution. With that assured, the value is in spreading one's "mark" – on a post, on the trees, in one's fur. Where human property has no need of courtesy, canine property depends upon it.

In fact, can possession be about art at all? If art is necessarily about sociability, expression, and communication, then the relations of property are arguably recuperated through this reciprocal possession – this rolling and scratching and marking.

One of the biggest threats to the sociability of intellectual property is not dissemination (perhaps that is obvious) but rather misattribution or no attribution at all. It is not possible to enjoy reciprocal possession if in fact sharing risks appropriating "identity" according to the same conventional model as that which sustains intellectual property paradigms in the first place.

In a way, the intellectual property environment needs some insight from the way in which animals share and overlap territories, with more manners rather than physical fences, effective attribution rather than managed dissemination.

There actually is a reality to smell, an objective physicality, but one that comes through the subjectivity of the users of the system. We need to relearn our sense of smell.

Get marking.

Notes

1 Cupere P de (2016) *Scent in Context: Olfactory Art*, Stockmans Publishers, Brussels, 9.
2 Ventós E (2011) The World of Smell, in ACTAR/Arts Santa Mònica (ed.) *Smell Colour: Chemistry, Art and Pedagogy*, ACTAR, Barcelona, 17–27: p. 24.
3 For a comprehensive account of the dog's "world of smell," see Horowitz A (2016) *Being a Dog: Following the Dog into a World of Smell*, Simon & Schuster, London. See further Galibert F et al. (2016) The Genetics of Canine Olfaction, *Journal of Veterinary Behavior*, 16, 86–93; Horowitz A et al. (2013) Smelling More or Less: Investigating the Olfactory Experience of the Domestic Dog, *Learning and Motivation*, 44, 207–217.
4 "Scent marking is an important aspect of olfactory communication in mammals": Ralls K (1971) Mammalian Scent Marking, *Science*, 171(3970), 443–449. See further the discussion of scent-marking in wolves, where marking does not denote a boundary as such, but rather certain "hot spots," either at the edge or in terms of the activity and value of that particular place: Zub K et al. (2003) Wolf Pack Territory Marking in the Białowieża Primeval Forest (Poland), *Behaviour*, 140(5), 635–648.
5 This is explored further in "Part 3, Dominion, the machine age," particularly in relation to the dominance myth and pack theories explored in Chapter 8, "Pack fiction."
6 The importance of sniffing as well as scent-marking as communication has been detailed in a number of studies. See for example, Duranton C & Horowitz A (2019) Let Me Sniff! Nosework Induces Positive Judgment Bias in Pet Dogs, *Applied Animal Behaviour Science*, 211, 61–66; Rezáč P et al. (2011) Factors Affecting Dog-Dog Interactions on Walks with Their Owners, *Applied Animal Behaviour Science*, 134, 170–176.
7 Bekoff M (1979) Ground Scratching by Male Domestic Dogs: A Composite Signal, *Journal of Mammology*, 60(4), 847–848.
8 Riach AC et al. (2017) Length of Time Domestic Dogs (*Canis Familiaris*) Spend Smelling Urine of Gonadectomised and Intact Conspecifics, *Behavioural Processes*, 143, 138–140.
9 Clapham M et al. (2013) The Function of Strategic Tree Selectivity in the Chemical Signaling of Brown Bears, *Animal Behaviour*, 85, 1351–1357. See further the discussion in Mesterton-Gibbons M & Adams ES (2003) Landmarks in Territory Partitioning: A Strategically Stable Convention?, *The American Naturalist*, 161(5), 685–697.
10 Mesterton-Gibbons M & Sherratt TN (2014) Bourgeois versus Anti-Bourgeois: A Model of Infinite Regress, *Animal Behaviour*, 89, 171–183; Mesterton-Gibbons M & Adams ES (2003) Landmarks in Territory Partitioning: A Strategically Stable Convention?, *The American Naturalist*, 161(5), 685–697. See

further the discussion of "prior-residence effect" and evolutionary game theory in Kokko H et al. (2006) From Hawks and Doves to Self-Consistent Games of Territorial Behavior, *The American Naturalist*, 167(6), 901–912. Dogs have also been shown to use landmarks such that their navigation is based upon recognition of an external cue, an allocentric orientation or external spatial awareness, rather than relying purely upon what is called egocentric orientation, which is navigation based upon their bodily position in space, thus demonstrating spatial memory. See further Fiset S (2009) Evidence for Averaging of Distance from Landmarks in the Domestic Dog, *Behavioural Processes*, 81, 429–438. See further the discussion in Gergely A et al. (2014) Dogs Are Able to Generalise Directional Acoustic Signals to Different Contexts and Tasks, *Applied Animal Behaviour Science*, 156, 54–61, where the authors demonstrated allocentric navigation with respect to sound. This is indeed potentially relevant to investigations of concept formation (same/different; above/below; etc). See the cautious discussion of this in Chittka L & Jensen K (2011) Animal Cognition: Concepts from Apes to Bees, *Current Biology*, 21(3), R116–R119. In relation to same/other differentiation in dogs through the use of smell, see Horowitz A (2017) Smelling Themselves: Dogs Investigate Their Own Odours Longer When Modified in an "Olfactory Mirror" Test, *Behavioural Processes*, 143, 17–24.
11 McGuire B et al. (2018) Urine Marking in Male Domestic Dogs: Honest or Dishonest, *Journal of Zoology*, 306, 163–170.
12 McGuire B & Bemis KE (2017) Scent Marking in Shelter Dogs: Effects of Body Size, *Applied Animal Behaviour Science*, 186, 49–55, identifies an influence of body size on chemical communication in terms of frequency: "small dogs communicate more frequently via scent marking than larger dogs" (49).
13 McGuire B et al. (2018) Urine Marking in Male Domestic Dogs: Honest or Dishonest, *Journal of Zoology*, 306, 163–170.
14 Alberts AC (1992) Constraints on the Design of Chemical Communication Systems in Terrestrial Vertebrates, *American Naturalist*, 139, S62–S89.
15 Sharpe LL (2015) Handstand Scent Marking: Height Matters to Dwarf Mongooses, *Animal Behaviour*, 105, 173–179; Sharpe LL et al. (2012) Handstand Scent Marking in the Dwarf Mongoose (*Helogale parvula*), *Ethology*, 118, 575–583.
16 Clapham M et al. (2013) The Function of Strategic Tree Selectivity in the Chemical Signaling of Brown Bears, *Animal Behaviour*, 85, 1351–1357.
17 McGuire B & Bemis KE (2017) Scent Marking in Shelter Dogs: Effects of Body Size, *Applied Animal Behaviour Science*, 186, 49–55.
18 McGuire M et al. (2018) Urine Marking in Male Domestic Dogs: Honest or Dishonest, *Journal of Zoology*, 306, 163–170.
19 McGuire B et al. (2018) Urine Marking in Male Domestic Dogs: Honest or Dishonest, *Journal of Zoology*, 306, 163–170: p. 166.
20 "Information gleaned from the chemical composition of scent marks may include individual identity, age, sex, reproductive state, and social status; and height of the mark may provide information on body size. One advantage of this indirect transfer of information is that individuals can evaluate one another while often avoiding potentially dangerous direct interactions": McGuire B & Bemis KE (2017) Scent Marking in Shelter Dogs: Effects of Body Size, *Applied Animal Behaviour Science*, 186, 49–55: p. 49. The authors note: "Most evidence, however, indicates a positive relationship between competitive ability and scent marking" (p. 49). See further Gosling LM & Roberts SC (2001) Scent-Marking by Male Mammals: Cheat-Proof Signals to Competitors and Mates, *Advances in the Study of Behaviour*, 30, 169–217; Hurst JL & Beynon RJ (2004)

Scent Wars: The Chemobiology of Competitive Signaling in Mice, *BioEssays*, 26, 1288–1298.
21 Horowitz A (2016) *Being a Dog: Following the Dog into a World of Smell*, Simon & Schuster, London, 19.
22 Ventós E (2011) The World of Smell, in ACTAR/Arts Santa Mònica (ed.) *Smell Colour: Chemistry, Art and Pedagogy*, ACTAR, Barcelona, 17–27: p. 19.
23 Ralls K (1971) Mammalian Scent Marking, *Science*, 171(3970), 443–449: "A common kind of marking is that which, since the classic paper by Hediger 1949, has been characterized as 'territorial marking.' This terminology implies that the marks serve to identify a territory, that is, a fixed area of land which the marking individual will defend against rivals of the same species. Such an interpretation is no doubt correct for some species, but it should not be assumed that all marking is territorial" (443). See further Hediger H (1968) *The Psychology and Behaviour of Animals in Zoos and Circuses*, Dover Publications, New York, 22–23; Hediger H (1959) *Wild Animals in Captivity*, Butterworths, London: "Territory may be represented as an area which is first rendered distinctive by its owner in a particular way and, secondly, is defended by it" (9).
24 Horowitz A (2016) *Being a Dog: Following the Dog into a World of Smell*, Simon & Schuster, London, 19.
25 Horowitz A (2016) *Being a Dog: Following the Dog into a World of Smell*, Simon & Schuster, London, 19.
26 Horowitz A (2016) *Being a Dog: Following the Dog into a World of Smell*, Simon & Schuster, London, 19–20.
27 Horowitz A (2016) *Being a Dog: Following the Dog into a World of Smell*, Simon & Schuster, London, 20.
28 Horowitz A (2016) *Being a Dog: Following the Dog into a World of Smell*, Simon & Schuster, London, 19–20.
29 For example, there are many examples of the use of scent in order to manage co-existing populations of human and animal species. In these cases, the "scent fence" has been a crucial part of conservation efforts where there is wildlife-human conflict. Through the use of scent, it is possible to manipulate territories and to change patterns of movement within those territories. See the review in Campbell-Palmer R & Rosell F (2011) The Importance of Chemical Communication Studies in Mammalian Conservation Biology: A Review, *Biological Conservation*, 144, 1919–1930, particularly p. 1922. See also the use of scent in species management in ways ranging from attraction of target species, to manipulation of mate choice, to deterrence, in Wyatt TD (2014) *Pheromones and Animal Behaviour: Chemical Signals and Signatures*, 2nd ed., Cambridge UP, Cambridge, 263–273. See further the example of Aiguafreda, near Barcelona in Spain, where wolf urine is used to deter wild boar from urban centres: Burgen S (2019) Town Near Barcelona Uses Wolf Urine to Keep Wild Boar Away, *Guardian*, 22 August. In other words, these are systems of mutual respect, "manners," rather than physical barriers which do not engage with nor depend upon a kind of mutual understanding and, for that reason, often fail.
30 Berns GS et al. (2015) Scent of the Familiar: An fMRI Study of Canine Brain Responses to Familiar and Unfamiliar Human and Dog Odors, *Behavioural Processes*, 110, 37–46.
31 Bekoff M (2001) Observations of Scent-Marking and Discriminating Self from Others by a Domestic Dog (*Canis Familiaris*): Tales of Displaced Yellow Snow, *Behavioural Processes*, 55, 75–79.
32 Gallup GG, Jr (1970) Chimpanzees: Self-Recognition, *Science*, 167, 86–87. See also Gallup GG, Jr (1975) Toward an Operational Definition of Self-Awareness,

in Tuttle RH (ed.) *Socioecology and Psychology of Primates*, Mouton, The Hague, 309–341. For an overview of the mirror self-recognition test and the mirror mark test see Vauclair J (1996) *Animal Cognition*, Harvard UP, Cambridge, MA, particularly 141–145. See also the discussion in Waal F de (2016) *Are We Smart Enough to Know How Smart Animals Are?*, Granta, London, particularly Chapter 8.

33 Gallup GG, Jr (1970) Chimpanzees: Self-Recognition, *Science*, 167, 86–87; see further Vauclair J (1996) *Animal Cognition*, Harvard UP, Cambridge, MA, 142–143.

34 Vauclair J (1996) *Animal* Cognition, Harvard UP, Cambridge, MA, 241–245.

35 For instance, see the critique in Bekoff M (2002) Animal Reflections, *Nature*, 419, 255.

36 Pongrácz P et al. (2017) Do You See What I See? The Difference between Dog and Human Visual Perception May Affect the Outcome of Experiments, *Behavioural Processes*, 140, 53–60. For instance, in relation to explosives detection, olfaction is considerably more important than vision: Gazit I & Terkel J (2003) Domination of Olfaction over Vision in Explosives Detection by Dogs, *Applied Animal Behaviour Science*, 82, 65–73. The possible inappropriateness of the mirror test leads to apparent "poor" performance on a test which arguably is almost irrelevant to the dogs: Howell TJ et al. (2013) Do Dogs Use a Mirror to Find Hidden Food?, *Journal of Veterinary Behavior*, 8, 425–430; Howell TJ & Bennett PC (2011) Can Dogs (*Canis Familiaris*) Use a Mirror to Solve a Problem?, *Journal of Veterinary Behavior*, 6, 306–312.

37 Plotnik JM et al. (2019) Elephants Have a Nose for Quantity, *PNAS*, 116(25), 12566–12571: p. 12569.

38 Horowitz A (2017) Smelling Themselves: Dogs Investigate Their Own Odours Longer When Modified in an "Olfactory Mirror" Test, *Behavioural Processes*, 143, 17–24.

39 Horowitz A (2017) Smelling Themselves: Dogs Investigate Their Own Odours Longer When Modified in an "Olfactory Mirror" Test, *Behavioural Processes*, 143, 17–24: p. 18. See further the response by Gallup GG.

40 Deleuze G & Guattari F (1980/[1987]) *A Thousand Plateaus: Capitalism and Schizophrenia*, B Massumi (trans.), U of Minnesota P, Minneapolis, 183.

41 Osborne H (1977) Odours and Appreciation, *British Journal of Aesthetics*, 17(1), 37–48: p. 43.

42 Howes D (2003) *Sensual Relations: Engaging the Senses in Culture and Social Theory*, U of Michigan P, Ann Arbor, 47.

43 Sperber D (1974/[1975]) *Rethinking Symbolism*, A Morton (trans.), Cambridge UP, Cambridge, 115. Sperber goes on to argue that smell is in and of itself "nothing for such a work to be about" and that it is only explicable (and thus possibly perceptible?) in its cause and effect, not in and of itself, as it were (115). Arguably this betrays a conceptual predatory drift towards a proprietary notion of the smell as object, as distinct from the sociable territories of olfactory monuments.

44 Classen C et al. (1994) *Aroma: A Cultural History of Smell*, Routledge, London, 112. The authors note in particular the example of South American language of Quechua, originating with the Incas and which continues to be spoken in the Andres, where there are specific olfactory terms for a range of activities in relation to olfaction, including smelling something, smelling something together as a group, and "to secretly sniff out what is being planned" (*Mucacumuni, mutqquimuni*). See Classen C et al. (1994) p. 112. See further the discussion in Diaconu M (2006) Reflections on an Aesthetics of Touch, Smell and Taste, *Contemporary Aesthetics*, 4, 1–10, on the impact on language of the socio-cultural

distinction between smell and the "exotic other" and smell and the "civilised" European: "smell and taste are embedded in particular sociocultural and symbolic systems that codify and regulate an individual's reaction to sensory stimuli in specific ways; correspondingly, aesthetic theory, too, should leave behind the idea of a universal subject" (2).

45 For instance, in a 1972 article, Gale Peter Largey and David Rodney Watson identify a "sociological approach to odors" contributing to differences in perception more widely, linking "foul smelling" to class and race prejudice and notions of "moral purity". See Largey GP & Watson DR (1972) The Sociology of Odors, *American Journal of Sociology*, 77(6), 1021–1034: "Much of the moral symbolism relevant to interaction is expressed in terms of olfactory imagery. An untrustworthy person may be described as a 'stinker,' a 'stinkoe,' or a 'stinkpot'. . . . In any case, particular odors, whether real or alleged, are sometimes used as indicants of the moral purity of particular individuals and groups within the social order, the consequences of which are indeed real" (1021–1022).

46 Simmel G (1907/[2000]) Sociology of the Senses, M Riter & D Frisby (trans.) in Frisby D & Featherstone M (eds.) *Simmel on Culture*, Sage, London, 109–120: p. 119. This kind of furtive interaction is explored further in Chapter 9, "Wild abandon."

47 Simmel G (1907/[2000]) Sociology of the Senses, M Riter & D Frisby (trans.) in Frisby D & Featherstone M (eds.) *Simmel on Culture*, Sage, London, 109–120: p. 119.

48 Simmel G (1921) Sociology of the Senses: Visual Interaction, in Park RE & Burgess EW (eds.) *Introduction to the Science of Sociology*, U of Chicago P, Chicago, 356–361.

49 Rindisbacher HJ (2015) What's This Smell? Shifting Worlds of Olfactory Perception, *KulturPoetic*, 15(1), 70–104: p. 73.

50 Diaconu M (2006) Reflections on an Aesthetics of Touch, Smell and Taste, *Contemporary Aesthetics*, 4, 1–10: p. 1.

51 Simmel G (1907/[2000]) Sociology of the Senses, M Riter & D Frisby (trans.) in Frisby D & Featherstone M (eds.) *Simmel on Culture*, Sage, London, 109–120: p. 118.

52 McGuire B & Bemis KE (2017) Scent Marking in Shelter Dogs: Effects of Body Size, *Applied Animal Behaviour Science*, 186, 49–55: p. 49.

53 Haraway D (2008) *When Species Meet*, U of Minnesota P, Minneapolis, 287. See further the discussion of the stranger in Chapter 9, "Wild abandon," and the nature of the encounter and shifting perspectives of belonging and exclusion.

54 Lushetich N (2014) *Fluxus: The Practice of Non-Duality*, Rodopi, Amsterdam, 116. The Fluxus art movement is considered in more detail later in this chapter.

55 "We are heirs to a civilization which is already intellectualized beyond the reaches of apprehension and is therefore stultified. We inhabit a culture where verbalization usurps the place of experience, where the photographic image is more real to us than reality, where we are no longer able to organize ourselves or our affairs and where mechanical devices remove us ever more completely from that direct contact with the environment, human and material, which can come only through the senses": Osborne H (1977) Odours and Appreciation, *British Journal of Aesthetics*, 17(1), 37–48: p. 47.

56 Serres M (1985[2008]) *The Five Senses: A Philosophy of Mingled Bodies*, Continuum, London, 234–235.

57 Uexküll J von (1920/[1926]) *Theoretical Biology*, Harcourt, Brace & Co, New York, 79. The term *Umwelt* has been translated variously throughout Uexküll's work, but most usually appears as "surrounding world" in early translations.

58 Ventós E (2011) The World of Smell, in ACTAR/Arts Santa Mònica (ed.) *Smell Colour: Chemistry, Art and Pedagogy*, ACTAR, Barcelona, 17–27: p. 19.
59 Gibson JJ (1979/[2015]) *The Ecological Approach to Visual Perception*, Psychology Press, New York.
60 Gibson JJ (1950) *The Perception of the Visual World*, Houghton Mifflin Company, Boston, 1. See further Gibson JJ (1979/[2015]) *The Ecological Approach to Visual Perception*, Psychology Press, New York. Gibson's work is considered further in Chapter 10, "Shared interests" in the context of the development of cognitive ethology.
61 Gibson JJ (1979/[2015]) *The Ecological Approach to Visual Perception*, Psychology Press, New York, 36.
62 Calvino I (1993/[1986]) The Name, the Nose, in *Under the Jaguar Sun*, W Weaver (trans.), Vintage, London, 67.
63 Howes D (2013) The Social Life of the Senses, *Ars Vivendi Journal*, 3, 4–23: p. 15.
64 This challenge is presented by other forms of "immaterial" works, such as performance art, where the object is consumed in the process of its production. See further Harris G (2019) What Am I Actually Buying?, *The Art Newspaper*, 29 August.
65 Diaconu M (2006) Reflections on an Aesthetics of Touch, Smell and Taste, *Contemporary Aesthetics*, 4, 1–10.
66 Howes D & Classen C (2014) *Ways of Sensing: Understanding the Senses in Society*, Routledge, London, 3. See further the discussion of "the hegemony of vision in Western culture" in Howes D (2003) *Sensual Relations: Engaging the Senses in Culture and Social Theory*, U of Michigan P, Ann Arbor, 45–49. Even in his 1907 essay, "Sociology of the Senses," Georg Simmel treats smell only briefly in comparison to the discussion of sight and hearing and does not deal with touch at all: "Among the individual sensory organs, the eye is destined for a completely unique sociological achievement." See Simmel G (1907/[2000]) Sociology of the Senses, M Riter & D Frisby (trans.) in Frisby D & Featherstone M (eds.) *Simmel on Culture*, Sage, London, 109–120: p. 111.
67 The emphasis on objectivity in radical behaviourism and the battle with cognitive ethology and theories of consciousness is considered in detail in Chapter 10, "Shared interests."
68 Watson JB (1913) Psychology as the Behaviorist Views It, *Psychological Review*, 20, 158–177.
69 Simmel G (1907/[2000]) Sociology of the Senses, M Riter & D Frisby (trans.) in Frisby D & Featherstone M (eds.) *Simmel on Culture*, Sage, London, 109–120: p. 117.
70 Howes D & Classen C (2014) *Ways of Sensing: Understanding the Senses in Society*, Routledge, London, 68–69. See further the discussion in Largey GP & Watson DR (1972) The Sociology of Odors, *American Journal of Sociology*, 77(6), 1021–1034: "One's olfactory identity is particularly associated with racial, class, and sexual identification" (1028).
71 Diaconu M (2006) Reflections on an Aesthetics of Touch, Smell and Taste, *Contemporary Aesthetics*, 4, 1–10: p. 2.
72 Diaconu M (2006) Reflections on an Aesthetics of Touch, Smell and Taste, *Contemporary Aesthetics*, 4, 1–10: p. 3.
73 Laplantine F (2015) *The Life of the Senses: Introduction to a Modal Anthropology*, J Furniss (trans.), Bloomsbury, London, 82.
74 Osborne H (1977) Odours and Appreciation, *British Journal of Aesthetics*, 17(1), 37–48: p. 41.

75 Waskul DD & Vannini P (2008) Smell, Odor, and Somatic Work: Sense-Making and Sensory Management, *Social Psychology Quarterly*, 71(1), 53–71.
76 Waskul DD & Vannini P (2008) Smell, Odor, and Somatic Work: Sense-Making and Sensory Management, *Social Psychology Quarterly*, 71(1), 53–71: p. 69.
77 See further the discussion in Chapter 9, "Wild abandon," particularly the consideration of Simmel's stranger. Sabido Ramos argues: "Simmel's sociological research of the senses is not only limited to what people can feel, but also how these sensitive experiences and feelings give place to *forms of socialization*. The Stranger is a *social form*, and he or she makes sense in its relation to others." Sabido Ramos O (2017) The *Senses* as a Resource of Meaning in the Construction of the Stranger: An Approach from Georg Simmel's Relational Sociology, *Simmel Studies*, 21(1), 15–41: p. 19.
78 Simmel G (1910/[1949]) The Sociology of Sociability, EC Hughes (trans.), *American Journal of Sociology*, 55(3), 254–261.
79 Full details of the exhibit and the individual works are available on the artist's website, http://dominicwilcox.com/portfolio/worlds-first-art-exhibition-for-dogs/. There is also a video of Dinnertime Dreams available at www.youtube.com/watch?v=b5dwcy0SfTg which shows Jeff and the interaction and play between exhibits, dogs, and humans.
80 Lushetich N (2014) *Fluxus: The Practice of Non-Duality*, Rodopi, Amsterdam, 118.
81 Lushetich N (2014) *Fluxus: The Practice of Non-Duality*, Rodopi, Amsterdam, 117–118.
82 Hopkins D (2014) Duchamp, Childhood, Work and Play: The Vernissage for *First Papers of Surrealism*, New York, 1942, *Tate Papers*, 22: p. 10.
83 "Opening devoted to children playing, to the smell of cedar": Breton A & Duchamp M (1942) *First Papers of Surrealism: Hanging by André Breton, His Twine Marcel Duchamp*, Coordinating Council of French Relief Societies, New York.
84 Kachur L (2001) *Displaying the Marvellous Marcel Duchamp, Salvador Dali, and Surrealist Exhibition Installations*, MIT Press, Cambridge, MA, 83.
85 Paz O (1968/[1990]) *Marcel Duchamp: Appearance Stripped Bare*, Arcade Publishing, New York, 3.
86 Duchamp M (1973) *The Writings of Marcel Duchamp*, M Sanouillet & E Peterson (eds.), Da Capo, New York, 135. There is a replica of *Glass* on exhibit in Tate Modern, London.
87 Paz O (1968/[1990]) *Marcel Duchamp: Appearance Stripped Bare*, Arcade Publishing, New York, 3. What Paz describes as Duchamp shift from the "painting-idea" to the "painting-painting" is reminiscent of the imperative in the Fluxus art movement to resist representational work: Higgins H (2002) *Fluxus Experience*, U of California P, Berkeley, 36–38. The Fluxus movement is discussed in more detail later in this chapter.
88 Breton A & Duchamp M (1942) *First Papers of Surrealism: Hanging by André Breton, His Twine Marcel Duchanp*, Coordinating Council of French Relief Societies, New York.
89 Sahlins M (1995) *How "Natives" Thinks: About Captain Cook, For Example*, U of Chicago P, Chicago, 204.
90 Baudelaire C (1869) *Le spleen de Paris, ou les cinquante petits poèmes du prose de Charles Baudelaire*, Émil-Paul, Paris, 169–175.
91 Joseph Stevens (1816–1892) was a Belgian animalier, an artist known for his realistic portrayal of animals and dogs in particular.
92 As translated by Anne Emmanuelle Berger. See Berger AE (2014) Reigning Cats or Dogs? Baudelaire's Cynicism, *Yale French Studies*, 125/126, 149–164: p. 157.

93 Baudelaire C (1869) Good Dogs, M Sorrell (trans.), in Baudelaire C (1869/[2010]) *Paris Spleen and Wine and Hashish*, Alma, Richmond, 98–101: p. 100. An earlier translation by Louise Varèse is: "who are watching with all a sorcerer's vigilance, a nameless concoction simmering on the lighted stove." See Baudelaire C (1869) The Faithful Dog, L Varèse (trans.), in Baudelaire C (1869/[1970]) *Paris Spleen*, New Directions, New York, 104–107: p. 106.
94 Baudelaire C (1869) Good Dogs, M Sorrell (trans.), in Baudelaire C (1869/[2010]) *Paris Spleen and Wine and Hashish*, Alma, Richmond, 98–101: p. 100.
95 Baudelaire C (1869) The Faithful Dog, L Varèse (trans.), in Baudelaire C (1869/[1970]) *Paris Spleen*, New Directions, New York, 104–107: p. 106.
96 Although the momentum of the first incarnation of Fluxus dissipated to an extent with the premature death of Maciunas in 1978, there are contemporary artists who continue to identify themselves as Fluxus artists today, including the Belgian artist, Guy Bleus (*The Thrill of Working with Odours*, 1978; *S:L:K = Scents:Locks:Kisses*, 2005), and Canadian artist Allan Revich (Revich A (2007) *Fluxus Vision*, Lulu, Toronto; see further Revich's Fluxus blog at www.digitalsalon.com). It is therefore inaccurate to think of it as a past movement (as it is sometimes described) as its influence continues today.
97 Lushetich N (2014) *Fluxus: The Practice of Non-Duality*, Rodopi, Amsterdam, 1–2. See further: Higgins H (2002) *Fluxus Experience*, U of California P, Berkeley; see also the material on Joseph Beuys in the writings of curator and critic, Harald Szeemann: Szeemann H (2018) *Selected Writings*, D Chon et al. (ed.), J Blower & E Tucker (trans.), Getty Research Institute, Los Angeles.
98 For further details of the founding and development of Fluxus, see the compelling biography of Maciunas: Kellein T (2007) *The Dream of Fluxus: George Maciunas: An Artist's Biography*, Edition Hansjörg Mayer, London.
99 George Maciunas (1963) *Fluxus Manifesto I* (emphases in original).
100 Higgins H (2002) *Fluxus Experience*, U of California P, Berkeley, 36.
101 Higgins H (2002) *Fluxus Experience*, U of California P, Berkeley, 36.
102 George Maciunas, *Fluxmanifesto*, 1971.
103 Kellein T (2007) *The Dream of Fluxus: George Maciunas: An Artist's Biography*, Edition Hansjörg Mayer, London, 9.
104 Kellein T (2007) *The Dream of Fluxus: George Maciunas: An Artist's Biography*, Edition Hansjörg Mayer, London, 9.
105 Lushetich N (2014) *Fluxus: The Practice of Non-Duality*, Rodopi, Amsterdam, 110–111.
106 Higgins H (2002) *Fluxus Experience*, U of California P, Berkeley, 43–45. The work is also sometimes referred to as *Spice Chess*.
107 Lushetich N (2014) *Fluxus: The Practice of Non-Duality*, Rodopi, Amsterdam, 137.
108 Lushetich N (2014) *Fluxus: The Practice of Non-Duality*, Rodopi, Amsterdam, 137.
109 This recalls the examination of representation as always already constrained within language in Gibson J (2014) *The Logic of Innovation*, Ashgate, Aldershot. With the assistance of Wittgenstein's language-game, "Language cannot be merely denotative, according to rules; it is meaning in practice, in use . . . meaning is a public affair" (182).
110 Bleus G (1978) *The Thrill of Working with Odours: Smell Manifesto*. Available at www.mailart.be/thrill.html
111 British Medical Journal (1942) The Shape of a Smell, *British Medical Journal*, 2(4262), 315.
112 Stamp J (2013) The First Major Museum Show to Focus on Smell, *Smithsonian*, 16 January.

Part 3

Dominion, the machine age

> In its age-long effort to interpret everything outside us in terms of mechanism, even those things which most break forth with accumulated signs of genius, namely living beings, our mind as it were blows out all the lights of the world for the sole benefit of its own little spark.
>
> Gabriel de Tarde, *Monadology and Sociology*, 1895

Chapter 7

Predatory drift

> People who cheat just don't know how to *play*. They treat a game as though it were serious.
>
> Bateson G (1972/[2000]) *Steps to an Ecology of Mind*, U of Chicago P, Chicago, 14

> D: Okay. But what about "not". Can the animal say, "I am not biting you"?
> F: ... If the animal is not biting the other, he's not biting it, and that's it.
> D: But he might be not doing all sorts of other things, sleeping, eating, running, and so on. How can he say, "It's biting that I'm not doing"?
> F: He can only do that if biting has somehow been mentioned.
> D: Do you mean that he could say, "I am not biting you" by first showing his fangs and *then* not biting?
>
> Bateson G (1972/[2000]) *Steps to an Ecology of Mind*, U of Chicago P, Chicago, 54

> It is of interest at this point to define more precisely what is meant by property. Property in its most general sense may be taken to mean the exclusive use, enjoyment and control of those things which are of value in so far as, directly or indirectly, they serve to satisfy the fundamental needs of the organism. It is private when these things are controlled by the individual; common when a number of individuals have several rights over things which, taken together, they hold, as a body, against other individuals ... [T]his same principle of the use and control of property objects is equally a characteristic of animal, primitive and human societies and may be judged in all by the same objective standard of defence against aggression.
>
> Beaglehole E (1931) *Property: A Study in Social Psychology*, Allen & Unwin, London, 15–16

Property, defence defines it.

There is a term that is often used in dog training discourse to describe an apparent moment when a dog, in the middle of playing, becomes allegedly confused or misinterprets the signals of another dog and suddenly starts to treat that dog as prey rather than play. In other words, the pure symbolic meta-communication of play – *as if biting* – becomes a literal communication of prey and predator – *I am biting*.

The term never seems to appear in the scientific literature, only in training literature:[1] "'Predatory drift' is another concept that I often hear, but that has no basis in animal behavior science. . . . I cannot find any reference to this concept in the animal behavior literature: there's no basis on which to think it would occur in the realm of modern animal behavior science."[2] Despite its circulation in popular dog training literature, it has been criticised by canine behaviour scientists as largely a fiction propelled by its memetic quality (similar to the circulation of "pack leader," "alpha" and related terms of the much-disputed dominance theory, as examined in the next chapter) and thus rapid and superficial cultural transmission in that context. An extensive search of the academic scientific literature reveals no references to the term at all (and indeed very few to instinctive or instinctual drift as well), demonstrating its lack of traction in research literature and practice.

Nevertheless, the concept seems to be derived from the theory of instinctive or instinctual drift proposed by Keller and Marian Breland in 1961,[3] although this is not attributed in the relevant literature. The Brelands, former students of BF Skinner, abandoned their studies to go and train animals for entertainment and became proprietors of Animal Behavior Enterprises. They are considered pioneers of humane animal training, using operant conditioning to train assorted species to perform various behaviours for public exhibition. However, during their training, they began to notice that after a while the animals became less willing to perform the behaviours for the reinforcement and began performing "instinctive" or innate feeding behaviours, even if the lack of performance of the conditioned response was costly in terms of physical effort and delayed reinforcement: "Here we have animals, after having been conditioned to a specific learned response, gradually drifting into behaviors that are entirely different from those which were conditioned."[4] Together they authored a paper proposing the concept of "instinctive drift": "The general principle seems to be that wherever an animal has strong instinctive behaviors in the area of the conditioned response, after continued running the organism will drift toward the instinctive behavior to the detriment of the conditioned behavior and even to the delay or preclusion of the reinforcement."[5]

In other words, where the conditioned response that is desired in training a raccoon is related to a behaviour in which there are other related instinctive behaviours, those instinctive behaviours will reemerge. For instance, a raccoon was trained to collect coins and put them in a piggy bank but subsequently began exhibiting behaviours associated with food retrieval instead (rubbing the coins together, keeping hold of the coins, and so on), despite ongoing positive reinforcement for the desired trained behaviour.[6] The animals were beginning to express natural behaviours associated with the same area of behaviour in which the Brelands identified the conditioned response. Thus, they attributed this to the hypothesis that "learned behavior drifts towards instinctive behavior."[7] However, was the raccoon simply innovating upon the conditioned response? Through boredom and frustration with the repetition of the conditioned response, were they simply trying something new?

And even if we accept the hypothesis of instinctive drift, the practice of translating this theory to play and predatory behaviour is arguably a misapplication of this theory within a wholly unrelated dynamic, resulting in a rather unhelpful and diminishing misinterpretation of canine creativity and communication through play. Whereas in the Brelands' theory the animals were being rewarded with food and then began to drift to perform other food-related behaviours (such as scratching, digging, and foraging), the relationship between play and predation is not analogous. Such a theory of predatory drift presumes that play is all about function and practising real-world skills and not about play for play's sake. It presumes there is simply no creativity or communicative value in play at all, and it presumes that it is almost entirely about rehearsing for the real thing.

Notably, the interpretation of these responses betrays another particular "drift" that is recognisable throughout the literature – that is, interpreting behaviours or responses as almost wholly constrained within the instinctual or predetermined species identity, or breed identity, rather than the possibility of innovation upon the tedium of the conditioned response. What both theories do have in common, however, is a presumption that animals are driven by reproduction, survival, and functional adaptation, and everything else is unthinkable within this supremely efficient model of the biological machine. It is indeed a curious coincidence perhaps that one of the most "successful" (qualified as it is a major welfare issue) memes in dog training discourse is that of the somewhat Huxleyan "alpha," from Aldous Huxley's dystopian novel, *Brave New World*, in which Huxley counters the eugenicist predeterminism of genetics (nature) with an emphasis instead on the environment (nurture).[8] As adopted by the proponents of dominance theory, the leadership hierarchy is an inescapable destiny of the dog's biology, enslaved by instinct and authored by selection – much more in keeping with the theories of Huxley's grandfather, Thomas, and brother, Julian, both figures in the eugenics movement.[9] While the propagation of pack and dominance theory, as well as the "alpha" concept, are considered in more detail in the following chapter, it is useful to recognise the legacy in biological predeterminism and social Darwinism.[10]

In this context, it is interesting to note that in training discourse, "predatory drift" is used in a sense of the drift as something of a reversion to instinct, an atavistic trait. In many respects this notion of drift resonates with the early criminology of Cesare Lombroso and his physiological model of the criminal type.[11] Against a background of the prevalence of social Darwinism, Tarde criticises Lombroso's analysis as an attempt "to interpret physiologically, and not socially, crime and the criminal."[12] In terms of the purported causality between instinct and drift, again there is a curious interplay with Lombroso's own explanation of motive in the atavistic "born criminal":[13]

> Lombroso seems to think that when we see an act of violence or fraud committed by an epileptic[14] or a madman preceded by a motive – however great may

be the disparity between the futility of the motive and the seriousness of the act, or, better still, between the temporary and accidental character expressed by this motive and the permanent character that is an essential part of the person – we cannot reasonably distinguish an act so committed from an analogous act committed by a criminal indisputably judged to be such. But this is an error.[15]

What is significant about the theory of instinctual drift, or the training discourse of predatory drift, or Lombroso's "criminal type," is that "motive" is arguably removed from the relationship, which becomes a narrative of biological mechanism and no more. What then of the motive? What then of the stimulus? Of the incentives? Of shared interests? The type (criminal type, breed type) is thus always already guilty and yet innocent, abandoned to biology.

Despite the obvious limitations in the context of training and behaviour, what is interesting about the concept of "drift" is the interpretation and assertion of boundaries, those of predatory and prey, and away from dynamic relations: "Our focus on boundary turns our attention away from relationship and thus away from the true sources and consequences of the patterns of power that property constitutes."[16] Nevertheless, by engaging in an ethological jurisprudence of these boundaries, the very flaws that impose a deterministic analysis also expose the fissures through which a relational value of property can be revived. Ultimately, property is a relation.

Predatory drift is thus a seemingly artificial narrative, contrived in part on the basis of a deterministic biologism when it comes to all sorts of potentially creative excess. It is a concept based upon an adherence to the animal as "hard-wired," instinctual machine rather than on the "common sense," as it were, of the sociability of territory introduced by domestication. If predatory drift is a misleading fiction, then why use it in this context? How might it be relevant to the discourse of property? First, recognised as a cultural construction in and of itself, it introduces the same flux into the accepted nature of property as almost natural and obvious. In other words, the survivalist rhetoric of healthy rivalry and competition that is integral to western property models and intrusive throughout popular discourse on human relations, emerges as a contrivance upon the early sociability. Second, it misunderstands even the earlier model of instinctual drift in that it assumes a causality between unrelated behaviours – territory and sociability on the one hand and predation and property on the other – as though all can be reduced to a unifying "feeding" instinct.

What could be meant then by interpreting human "drift" towards increasingly possessory models of relationships, away from the sociable property of the earliest domestication story? Possession, in this sense, is not about instinct or about function, but about being and sociability. What might the development of the modern system of property mean in terms of this theory of drift? And indeed, is the dominant, rivalrous property model a misapplication of proprietary relations, a convenient fiction of incentives and effects that reduces consumers and producers to a notion of predictable and "hard-wired" types?[17]

Property predators

> [T]he doctrine which found the justification of private property in the fact that it enabled the industrious man to reap where he had sown, was not a paradox, but, as far as the mass of the population was concerned, almost a truism. Property was defended as the most sacred of rights ... The proprietary rights – and, of course, they were numerous – which had their source, not in work, but in predatory force, were protected from criticism by the wide distribution of some kind of property among the mass of the population, and in England, at least the cruder of them were gradually whittled down.[18]

In terms of the theory of predatory drift in the context of dog training discourse, this is unashamedly a theory based upon the (flawed) premise of an animalistic narrative of return to instinct. This appears to be in contrast to the dominant property narrative that has informed anthropology and legal discourse for the past century, as explored in previous chapters, which presents property as a uniquely human quality and evidence of the morality and ethical values that are said to be specific to the species. Setting to one side the exceptionalist premise for one moment, property is thus attended by notions of the civilising, ethicalising human.[19] And yet arguably, while much of the scholarship openly discredits the early idea of acquisitive instinct as the basis for property (thereby opening the value to societies beyond the human while maintaining the biological determinism within which all other animals are contained in the discourse), notions of property are still underpinned by this "instinct", impliedly relying upon it for the assertion of property as immutable "natural law."[20] In other words, property discourse thus assumes a "natural" progression towards the rivalrous, competitive, combative model articulated around a prize of things, when in fact there are many other systems of property that are possible without appropriating the fantastic fiction of predatory drift and acquisitive instinct. While the chapters in the Space Age demonstrated the way in which territory has been conceived through an anthropocentric lens, in predatory drift there is the appropriation of biological processes in order to justify aggressive competition as somehow "natural": "What appears to be the biological fact of territory in bird life is in fact the cultural interpretation of animal behaviour in terms of the human concept of territory, while what appears to be the uniquely human institution of the nation-state is in fact the result of an ecological and evolutionary process common to birds and humans."[21]

Thus, if predatory drift is inaccurate or even incorrect, why would I want to co-opt this term in the context of property? Indeed, in many respects it is precisely for that reason. Identifying the artifice and mechanics of predatory drift within training discourse assists with the disruption and disturbance of its claimed inevitability and naturalness within property. Rather than obscuring and disguising the assumptions underpinning the analysis of dog behaviour, this is to detail and interrogate the emphasis on prey and predation in contemporary predatory discourse and in the law itself. First, it is useful to borrow the link with play, as surmised in dog training discourse, but to consider it not in terms of actual predatory behaviour but in terms of the changes in ways of motivating sociability: *to have and to hold*. Second, to reinterpret what is happening in instinctive drift, or predatory drift, arguably delivers significant insight into the modern perambulations of property, including intellectual property. Persistent in the prevailing discourse on intellectual property is an attachment to causality and the notion of incentives to create, and this has come to characterise effective models for creativity and innovation. However, these incentives largely arise from a rivalrous and territorial model of competition and predation in the creative economy. Third, the concept of predatory drift is also consistent with the currency of predation that characterises the dominant evolutionary and somewhat biologically deterministic economic model of "predatory capitalism." In other words, to the predators go the spoils, and at the same time creating a community of prey (the user, consumer, fan, animal, and so on).[22]

The evolutionary language of property is persistent in this manner of predatory discourse. Even the critics of predatory capitalism resort to the language of "relapse"[23] and even "drift"[24] to describe the state of capitalism. Presented as an inevitability of acquisitive instinct, it is thus explained by its advocates as both efficient and "natural." In the same way, predatory drift is imposed as a foregone conclusion upon the mechanised canine mind. Presented as an inevitability of instinct for which one must always be prepared, predatory capitalism has come to represent the purportedly obligatory necessity of modern economic organisation in service of a mythical "acquisitive instinct," all in the context of "natural selection" and the "fight for life." As the economist, James K Galbraith, asserts, "The metaphor of predation is evolutionary, and its origins are to be found in evolutionary economics."[25] Indeed the language of taming and domestication infuses the rhetoric of economists in response to these predatory narratives.[26] This is a drama of predator and prey. However, this narrative is not as simple as it is sometimes presented. As this and later chapters will show, a fundamental starting point might indeed be more productively that of harmony and cooperation, as basic values in the evolutionary system, and not the supreme value of conflict.

Thorstein Veblen's emphasis on evolutionary development is instrumental in this history of predatory capitalism, not necessarily with Veblen as the architect,[27] but rather as part of the Darwinian linguistic revolution in sociology and economics.[28] In the translation of natural selection into the evolutionary narratives of economics and property, however, the emphasis on a teleological explanation of competition, conflict, and struggle as the basis has led to the central thesis of predation as a fundamental value – *survival of the fittest*:

> [T]he institution of a leisure class has emerged gradually during the transition from primitive savagery to barbarism; or more precisely, during the transition from a peaceable to a consistently warlike habit of life. . . . [T]he community must be of a predatory habit of life (war or the hunting of large game or both); that is to say, the men who constitute the inchoate leisure class in these cases, must be habituated to the infliction of injury by force and stratagem.[29]

Veblen's analysis of the predatory phase of culture implies a similar kind of drift as that described in the context of dog behaviour, driven by the presumed evolutionary imperative of competition and survival. In this way, predation becomes a cultural habit, a learned behaviour, and an obligatory response to property: "The predatory phase of culture is attained only when the predatory attitude has become the habitual and accredited spiritual attitude for the members of the group; when the fight has become the dominant note in the current theory of life; when the common-sense appreciation of men and things has come to be an appreciation with a view to combat."[30] Such predatory behaviour and a culture of defence, as it were, "would be to make men industrious and frugal,"[31] that is, to continue to invest in their territory. However, as seen in the Space Age, animal territories, and particularly the use of landmarks as convention,[32] reduce this need for frugality and free up resources for participation and sociability in territory. Notably, this is something Veblen recognizes in that other economic forces may disturb or interrupt the perceived predatory drift of capitalism.[33] In this respect, the value of esteem (not dissimilar to Tarde's concept of prestige) is important in the context of the incentive to emulate: "When the community passes from peaceable savagery to a predatory phase of life, the conditions of emulation change. The opportunity and the incentive to emulation increase greatly in scope and urgency."[34]

The concept of esteem resonates with Tarde's notion of contact between cultures, including during conflict, as well as the kind of exchange that occurs in animal conflict and towards resolution.[35] What is especially important in this context is the way in which information might be exchanged during these adversarial encounters[36] and whether the contest in animal behaviour provides insight into the "drift" of property systems towards this predatory characterisation. While game theory suggests that the strategic move is that information would be withheld, animal behaviour shows that information is indeed transmitted. Animals are "honest" in their property, as it were, and indeed this can be a strategy towards achieving stability and resolving conflicts easily.[37] In other words, in Veblen's account, the predatory phase can be deciphered as otherwise than a unilateral "drift" towards atavistic traits. Even in Veblen's predatory capitalism, property is always in the first instance a matter of relations. Veblen's "predatory phase" is thus more sociable, as it were, than perhaps it first appears.

Nevertheless, in the displacement of this value of esteem and mechanism of emulation into objects, that relational quality is perhaps obscured and the "perfect system" of property is affected: "Aggression becomes the accredited form of action, and booty serves as *prima facie* evidence of successful aggression."[38] In the context of Veblen's account of predatory capitalism, the evidence for esteem is invariably the accumulation of objects of esteem: "The wealth or power must be put in evidence, for esteem is awarded only on evidence."[39] Indeed, Max Radin argues something very similar in his restatement of Hohfeld's jural relations: "As a matter of fact, the concept of power is an incident of what seems at the present time the one nearly essential element of property, more really essential than even the right of exclusion and of misuser. That is the right of 'alienating,' the *ius disponendi*. 'Alienation,' however, is a matter of power."[40] Once again, the thingness of static property hides the mutualistic and moveable qualities of property's sociability: "Private property no longer expresses the bond of personal dependence but the independence of a Subject that now constitutes the sole bond. This makes for an important difference in the evolution of private property: private property in itself relates to rights, instead of the law relating it to the land, things, or people. . . . And when capital becomes an active right in this way, the entire historical figure of the law changes."[41]

Thus, almost every aspect of daily life has come to be interpreted through or understood within the rhetoric of rivalrous property, including personal expression and freedom of expression. The predatory drift has swept away all forms of sociability in the momentum of the economy of the predator. In this way, property as conceived in this modern, institutionalised, predatory model always incorporates potentially conflicting rights; it is inherently and necessarily adversarial: "Property reflects the ways in which we resolve conflicting claims, visions, values, and histories."[42] In this way, innovation too is regarded not through sociable imitation but through a warring, combative competition: "[A]s soon as a similarity of works of art of monuments, of tombs, of mortuary relics, proves to them the action of one civilisation upon another, they at once conclude that wars or regular transactions of some kind must have occurred between them."[43] What remains to account is what other possible evidence of wealth and power might be accepted in a more sociable system.[44] But it is not a foredoomed narrative. It is possible to take flight rather than fight.

Writing during the second World War and just a few decades after the *fin de siècle* evolutionary theory of Veblen and the values of cooperation and sociability in Tarde, the ecologist Warder Clyde Allee states that an appeal to predation as a fundamental biological principle is a fallacious premise: "Those who assert that the whole trend of science is to lend support to the present war system in settling international disagreements are relying on a mistaken, outmoded phase of biological thought to bolster up a much older and unreasoned drive toward conflict."[45] In this context, it is useful to note the zooarchaeology of Nerissa Russell: "From World War II until the 1970s, the dominant model of human evolution was encapsulated in the phrase "Man the Hunter." . . . According to this view, it was hunting, the killing of animals, that made us human."[46] As well as the implications for the discourse of human exceptionalism, this perceived link between civilising imperatives and evolutionary impulses towards predation and competition resonates against the background of social Darwinism that introduced the "alpha."

Legal jurisprudence contemporary with Tarde's own work similarly rejects the notion of dominion as the fundamental value of property. As Rudolf von Jhering explains: "It is therefore not true that property involves in its "idea" the absolute power of disposition. Property in such a form society cannot tolerate and never has tolerated. The 'idea' of property cannot contain anything which is in contradiction with the 'idea' of society. This standpoint is a last remnant of that unhealthy conception of the Law of Nature which isolated the individual as a being all apart."[47] Indeed, the biological determinism of "survival of the fittest" is oversimplified to the point of fiction, not only in science but also as a legal fiction.

This basic premise sustaining the rivalrous and combative narrative of property is arguably "in contradiction with the 'idea' of society," in that it defies the always already in relation of the sociality of reciprocal possession.[48]

Colonialism and the "acquisitive instinct"

The fiction of predatory drift as an explanation for property principles is illustrated by early twentieth-century anthropological approaches to property: "Among the problems that exercised the minds of the earlier evolutionists who dealt with human society, that of property was one of the most important. Its influence in modern industrial civilization was potent; hence the evolutionary schematist naturally assumed that in the earliest phases of culture it had been nil."[49] In his influential 1924 work, *Social Organization*,[50] the British anthropologist and ethnologist, William Halse Rivers Rivers (better known as WHR Rivers), identifies in Melanesia and Africa "an early state of communal ownership of land and of certain kinds of property"[51] and that this is "ownership in which the common rights rest on kinship."[52] He goes on to identify a "primitive" stage in human development that he terms a "communistic stage" in all human civilisation in relation to property:

> If we accept, at any rate provisionally, the position that all human societies have passed through a communistic stage, with all its pervading group-sentiment, if not group-instinct, it becomes the task of the student to discover the mechanism of its transformation. We can now be sure that there has never been anything of the nature of a social contract, to which the acceptance of authority can be ascribed.[53]

The emphasis on a "communistic stage" as a kind of social or evolutionary progression is remarkable. There is a clear presumption of property as a kind of civilising tool and a tool of the civilised: "Among 'savages,' . . . property was inconsiderable."[54] Similarly, in relation to the animal subject, property or ownership is either presumed to be "inconsiderable" or, ironically, to be eradicated if it emerges in some sort of unwelcome "resource guarding." From an ethical perspective on training, this elimination of choice or control in terms of rights is notable and casts some intriguing light on the similar tensions in contemporary human property relations. In the same way, is the elimination of choice in respect of property liability today a potential welfare issue?

This early rendition of non-western civilisations in relation to property and, in particular, in relation to how they "transform," is especially useful in presenting not only the conflict of laws with respect to different property modalities but also the way in which predatory drift in property coincides with assumptions regarding property, traditional knowledge, and civilising development: "it is only the influence of the more enterprising members of another culture, endowed with qualities, material and mental, regarded as superior, which could change communistic and democratic societies with their powerful group-sentiment into individualistic and monarchical or aristocratically governed societies."[55]

The anthropologist, Bronislaw Malinowski,[56] whose work was introduced in previous chapters, was somewhat critical[57] of the summation of the various property relations as "communal" or "communism." Indeed, early explorations of law and anthropology were largely thwarted by the assumptions underpinning this predatory drift in the analysis of so-called primitive law: The exoticisation of the "noble savage" and the attending over-simplification of traditional and customary legal systems underplayed and in fact compromised the development of an anthropological jurisprudence: "Primitive law ceased to interest anthropologists . . . because they had an exaggerated idea of its perfection; it also ceased to attract attention because – and mistakenly – . . . it was apparently easily explained."[58] As Malinowski argues: "The savage is neither an extreme 'collectivist' nor an intransigent 'individualist' – he is, like man in general, a mixture of both."[59] In relation to Rivers's work on Melanesian property, particularly in respect of canoes, Malinowski explicitly rejects the "communistic" tag attached to so-called primitive property models:

> Nothing could be more mistaken than such generalizations. There is a strict distinction and definition in the rights of every one and this makes ownership anything but communistic. We have in Melanesia a compound and complex system of holding property, which in no way partakes of the nature of 'socialism' or 'communism'. A modern jointstock company might just as well be called a 'communistic enterprise.' As a matter of fact, any descriptions of a savage institution in terms such as 'communism', 'capitalism' or 'joint-stock company' borrowed from present-day economic conditions or political controversy, cannot but be misleading.[60]

Other contemporaries of Malinowski shared his criticism of the over-simplification of property models in traditional and local peoples: "These propositions are no longer tenable. In part they rest on ignorance of the ethnographic data, often on a failure to discriminate between moral and legal prescriptions."[61] Melville J Herskovits notes in *Economic Anthropology*:[62]

> It must thus be re-emphasized that the entire discussion of communism versus individualism, in so far as reference to "primitive" societies is concerned, seems to be but a kind of intellectual shadow-boxing. Verbalistic blows are dealt without command of adequate knowledge either of the actual forms taken by economic institutions of primitive groups, or of the significance of the terms 'socialistic' or 'communistic' or, indeed, even 'individualistic.'[63]

Others questioned the very nature of the distinction in the first place, interpreting many of the proprietary relations in so-called primitive societies as examples of private property. The anthropologist, Margaret Mead, writes: "[I]n spite of the widespread notions of primitive communism, there is no known culture without some institution of private property. The forms in which this is expressed may appear bizarre – the right to a name, or the right to certain forms of privacy such as the right to sleep without being awakened, or to eat without being spoken to – but the association of social identity with rights against the invasion of others is universal."[64] She notes further that such property systems are part of "a minimal culturally transmitted ethical code without which human societies were not viable."[65] This link between property and ethics as it is here enshrined in human anthropology has underpinned a discourse of human exceptionalism in relation to property. And this exceptionalism has been legitimated as intrinsically part of the evolutionary process. Julian Huxley, Conrad Waddington and other noted figures of evolutionary theory in the first half of the twentieth century arguably established the discourse of the uniquely human ethical animal. This "exceptional" ethical being is premised upon what is a distinctly causal and linear evolutionary narrative of "ethicizing"[66] beings, pronounced as "a real connection between evolutionary processes and man's ethical feelings."[67] And so the animal arguably has been not only objectified in conventional property discourse but also denied a moral and ethical life, a denial that is repeatedly defended on the basis of property rights and the attending intentionality. Thus, this evolutionary narrative becomes crucial to the construction of a natural law of property that is presented as explicitly and uniquely human: "'Natural law' might thus be defined as those rules of behavior which had developed from a species-specific capacity to ethicalize as a feature of those examples of such ethicalizing that appear in all known societies."[68]

As such, the construction of stages of civilisation seen in the work of Rivers and others is premised upon a supposed progression in property from communalism to competition, from savagery to predation,[69] that appears as an interpretive contrivance, a fictional dichotomy, not only in terms of the communities under observation in these studies but also with respect to the nature of property today. Examples of "practical communism"[70] in contemporary property abound, such as common land, rights of way and easements, and to an extent also the various limitations and exceptions applied in intellectual property. In a very general sense, these are examples of a kind of moral obligation rendered legal.

Malinowski thus offers an early anthropological definition of law in which the principles of prestige and reciprocity inhere: "Civil law, the positive law governing all the phrases of tribal life, consists . . . of a body of binding obligations, regarded as a right by one party and acknowledged as a duty by the other, kept in force by a specific mechanism of reciprocity and publicity inherent in the structure of their society."[71] In other words, this is a kind of property defence by landmarks of convention, as it were. In this way, it is possible to conceive of an accountability not only for so-called primitive law but also for supposed "advanced cultures" in a contemporary legal framework.[72]

This resonates with Hohfeld's analysis of the relationship between legal rights and equity just a few years earlier; that is, rather than a relationship of contest between private property and communalism:[73] "Use of the Hohfeldian fundamental concepts . . . keeps attention focused on the fact that all legal relations are relations between particular persons, and that this fact is primary in any understanding of law. Courts, constables and jails are secondary instruments, not fundamentals of a legal system, when set up as a system of imperatives or relations. They are the behavior-data from which a system is constructed."[74]

Bio-colonial determinism

This impact of nineteenth-century and early twentieth-century anthropology on the imperative of predatory property principles in the colonial context arguably is embedded in today's discourse on what is seemingly an intractable conflict over traditional knowledge.[75] The predatory and defensive territoriality of conventional property models is at odds with the sociality found in often complex traditional systems. As a result, some common misunderstandings of traditional knowledge persist, including: that traditional knowledge is simply communal, without any further explanation, understanding or insight; that protection of traditional knowledge is contrary to the mission of open knowledge as it seeks to close up that knowledge; and that defence defines the property (through defensive intellectual property).[76] This insistence on traditional knowledge systems as indiscriminately "communal" or "communistic" belies the predatory drift of discourse in these areas of debate. As previous discussion shows, anthropology has for some time cautioned against these kinds of discriminatory assumptions and generalising discourse. As noted earlier, anthropology has identified evidence of private property throughout various cultures and societies, which, although appearing in vastly diverse forms, nevertheless show a relationship between property and identity.[77] Indeed the resistance to recognising diverse approaches to private property belies a persistent colonialism in contemporary traditional knowledge protection debates.

What is particularly notable about this "history" of property in primitive and traditional law is that the first encounters through law and anthropology sought to deny intangible property in traditional societies.[78] And subsequently, in attempts to achieve protection in the context of contemporary intergovernmental discussions, the effort to force traditional knowledge through the similar predatory drift has framed intellectual property developments more generally, while at the same time criticising and even denying protection as an undesirable attempt to "lock up" or erect boundaries around knowledge. The international debates over traditional knowledge have frequently resorted to a dichotomy between custom (with the holders of knowledge reified as exotic, noble savages, enslaved by custom) and law. This has indeed been a persistent characterisation since the early encounters between law and anthropology. For instance, the anthropologist and one of the leading figures in the early development of an anthropological jurisprudence, Edward Adamson Hoebel, laments: "[T]he legal lie of primitive man has been treated less as unexplored than as non-existent. . . . In order to rationalize their neglect of law in the study of primitive society, a number of anthropologists have turned to an exaltation of custom. 'Custom is

King,' they cry. Custom is everything. Either there is no law because custom takes care of everything and the savage is its automatic slave, or law is by a strange act of sophistry merged in mere custom."[79] A mere slave to custom, the "savage" is rendered a legal mute in a way similar to the biological reductionism imposed upon the moral and social life of animals. The strategy is the same, an oppressive causality denies any autonomy or intentionality through a discourse of the "noble savage," the "spiritual other," the exotic.[80] As Hoebel notes: "Malinowski scoffed the benighted notion that the savage is the automatic slave of custom."[81] Similarly, Tarde offers the evidence of trading since the stone age as a curious obstacle to this colonialist rendering of the other: "But it does not seem to me to be proved, in spite of the prejudice to that effect which has become current, that the earliest savages were addicted to murder and theft on the largest possible scale . . . the most absolute improbity and inhumanity have eagerly been attributed to the people of the stone age, who nevertheless . . . Could not have been without all good faith, because they were given to trading outside their own territory."[82]

Rather than shoehorning cultures into a dominant predatory paradigm (not only ethnocentric but also anthropocentric, despite practices of possession, sanctions, and inequity aversion in animals[83]) through a contrived social and evolutionary narrative of predatory drift, with the establishment of rivalrous boundaries in the mythology of things, the opportunity to accommodate, opening up and bringing in, a more sociable perspective upon property as relations is not only legally exacting but also ethologically abundant towards a genuinely cross-cultural analysis and application of property: "When we try to understand the basic ideas underlying property and the family we find that the wealth and variety of forms anthropology exhibits compel us to define our concepts, if they are to possess validity, from the standpoint of all cultures. Either the definition must work in every community or it is insufficient."[84]

While animals are regularly marginalised through a biological determinism that obscures any cultural and social and indeed moral activity, similarly a kind of persistent colonial perspective upon the "traditional" belies a kind of cultural determinism in the sense of the determination of culture through biology, physiology, and environment. Malinowski himself identified this as the crucial turn, as it were, in the study of so-called "primitive law.": "The crucial problem in the study of primitive law turns round the concept of cultural determinism. Is man's organized and implemented behavior, that is culture, subject to laws in the scientific sense?"[85] But while a resistance to a kind of reductionist account of human culture has persisted across a range of disciplines, a resistance which is notably consistent with a discourse of human exceptionalism, early twentieth-century anthropology was actually attempting to render culture predictable, a scientific causality.[86] Instead of the concept of drift and instinctual drives to property seemingly blurring the distinction between the human and all other animals, this biological determinism has instead been recruited to endorse a similar kind of reductionist discourse that is wholly consistent with this predatory narrative of property and yet at the same time enshrines human exceptionalism in the distinction of a predatory imperialism, "the intentional controls invented by man."[87]

Importantly, what Malinowski, Hoebel, Lowie and others were advocating was an anthropological[88] and ethnographical[89] approach and indeed productive mutualism with the law, a genuinely transdisciplinary approach to property jurisprudence and arguably quite radical at the time. While Malinowski cautioned against the use of ownership in relation to traditional societies, it is not strictly in the sense of demarcating civilised and uncivilised worlds, but rather, in the sense of recognising the assumptions, cultural and social, that underpin the word "ownership."[90]

> Ownership, giving this word its broadest sense, is the relation, often very complex, between an object and the social community in which it is found. In ethnology it is extremely important not to use this word in any narrower sense than that just defined, because the types of ownership found in various parts of the world differ widely. It is especially a grave error to use the word ownership with the very definite connotation given to it in our own society. For it is obvious that this connotation presupposes the existence of very highly developed economic and legal conditions, such as they are amongst ourselves, and therefore the term 'own' as we use it is meaningless, when applied to a native society. Or indeed, what is worse, such an application smuggles a number of preconceived ideas into our description, and before we have begun to give an account of the native conditions, we have distorted the reader's outlook.[91]

Hoebel was identifying arguably this very colonialist dynamic when he explained in 1942: "the ethnology of law has been to a considerable extent a field of neglected opportunity for the anthropologist and study of law alike. Students of law, enchanted with the intricate mazes of their stately formal garden, have generally looked on the field of primitive law as an undomesticated and infertile wilderness. The prevailing pattern is to deny the existence of law in societies which succeed in settling disputes and claims with benefit of courts."[92] How clearly this resonates with the nature of the feral and the wild, and the marginalisation of the animal and traditional other in the predatory drift of property. The same kind of denial has been exercised throughout the development of ethology with respect to animal cognition and consciousness, as well as culture, morality, and justice. What might Hoebel have made of the "ethology" of law presented here?

This sociality of property is much more helpfully understood through use rather than defence, through cooperation rather than competition, an ethological jurisprudence of ownership. This brings the discussion back to the Iguana and the burrow. What is the incentive to build without achieving ownership of the burrow? Malinowski identifies these evolutionary mysteries of cooperation in the ownership of a Trobriand fishing canoe: "The only correct proceeding is to describe the legal state of affairs in terms of concrete fact. Thus, the ownership of a Trobriand fishing canoe is defined by the manner in which the object is made, used and regarded by the group of men who produced it and enjoy its possession."[93] In other words, not only the effort and investment in building the canoe but also the subsequent use of the canoe is relevant: "In using the craft, every joint owner has a right to a certain place in it and to certain duties, privileges, and benefits associated with it."[94] Thus, ownership is associated with identity but not in the sense of the conventional *to be* of wealth and display, but rather through the *having* of a participatory and productive use. Further, this use generates obligations and a mutual responsibility, such that owners collaborate in a genuine relationship of reciprocal possession:

> Thus on a close inquiry we discover in this pursuit a definite system of division of functions and a rigid system of mutual obligations, into which a sense of duty and the recognition of the need of co-operation enter side by side with a realization of self-interest, privileges and benefits. Ownership, therefore, can be defined neither by such words as 'communism' nor 'individualism', nor by reference to 'joint-stock company' system or 'personal enterprise', but by the concrete facts and conditions of use. It is the sum of duties, privileges and mutualities which bind the joint owners to the object and to each other.[95]

Ownership is thus not made meaningful through boundaries and defence, constraints and exclusions, as such, but through convergences and contact: *the ties that bind*. As Malinowski maintains, in these other models of ownership and property, "we are met by law, order, definite privileges and a well-developed system of obligations."[96] Hoebel similarly identifies the "significant legal behavior among primitives: that there is law in primitive societies in the same sense as in ours."[97]

Indeed, it is the predatory drift encouraged by dominant property discourse that provides for the adversarial and agonistic characterisation of various property conflicts,[98] from the discourse on Native Title in Australia[99] through to the incarnation of traditional knowledge protection as a threat to freedom of expression, and the perpetuation of "the illusion that law and custom are one among primitives."[100] And indeed, in the concept and contest of the commons.[101]

DAUGHTER: Daddy, what is an instinct?
FATHER: An instinct, my dear, is an explanatory principle.
D: But what does it explain?
F: Anything – almost anything at all. Anything you want it to explain.[102]

Notes

1 The concept was introduced by veterinarian, behaviourist and trainer, Ian Dunbar, and has been promoted widely in the lay literature by trainer, Jean Donaldson (Ha JC & Campion TL, xxii): see Donaldson J (2008) *Oh Behave! Dogs from Pavlov to Premack to Pinker*, Dogwise Publishing, Wenatchee, WA, 212–215; see further, Donaldson J (2004) *Fight! A Guide to Dog-Dog Aggression*, Dogwise Publishing, Wenatchee, WA.
2 Introduction in Ha JC & Campion TL (eds.) (2019) *Dog Behavior: Modern Science and Our Canine Companions*, Academic Press, London, xxii.
3 Breland K & Breland M (1961) The Misbehavior of Organisms, *American Psychologist*, 16(11), 681–684.
4 Breland K & Breland M (1961) The Misbehavior of Organisms, *American Psychologist*, 16(11), 681–684: p. 683.
5 Breland K & Breland M (1961) The Misbehavior of Organisms, *American Psychologist*, 16(11), 681–684: p. 684.
6 Breland K & Breland M (1961) The Misbehavior of Organisms, *American Psychologist*, 16(11), 681–684: p. 685.
7 Breland K & Breland M (1961) The Misbehavior of Organisms, *American Psychologist*, 16(11), 681–684: p. 684.
8 Huxley A (1932) *Brave New World*, Chatto & Windus, London.
9 For an extensive discussion of the relationship between the *fin de siècle* enthusiasm for evolutionary theories of society and the eugenics movement, see Turda M (2014) Biology and Eugenics, in Saler M (ed.) *The Fin-de-Siècle World*, Routledge, London, Chapter 29.
10 This link is also noteworthy in the social discourse on breed determinism, breed-specific legislation, and culpability according to physical "type" in dogs.
11 See Lombroso C (1876) *L'Uomo Delinquente*, Ulrico Hoepli, Milano. See further Lombroso C (1911) *Criminal Man, According to the Classification of Cesare Lombroso*, Lombroso-Ferrero G (ed.), GP Putnam's Sons, New York.
12 Tarde G (1890/[1912]) *Penal Philosophy*, R Howell (trans.), Little, Brown, and Co, Boston, 46.
13 Lombroso C (1911) *Criminal Man, According to the Classification of Cesare Lombroso*, Lombroso-Ferrero G (ed.), GP Putnam's Sons, New York: "The Modern, or Positive, School of Penal Jurisprudence . . . maintains that the antisocial tendencies of criminals are the result of their physical and psychic organisation, which differs essentially from that of normal individuals" (5).
14 Lombroso also hypothesised that a criminal impulse might emanate from an "epileptic constitution": Tarde G (1890/[1912]) *Penal Philosophy*, R Howell (trans.), Little, Brown, and Co, Boston, 238. This is startling in its link with similar explanations of sudden outbursts or aberrant behaviour from dogs, which are often hypothesised as seizures or "rage syndrome" (idiopathic aggression or episodic dyscontrol) often without systematic veterinary examination or rigorous investigation, leading to euthanasia. While earlier work suggested a physiological link (see Mugford RA (1984) Aggressive Behaviour in the English Cocker Spaniel, *The Veterinary Annual*, 24, 310–314), later work has shown idiopathic aggression to be more likely a behavioural problem: see further Hedhammar Å & Hultin-Jäderlund K (2007) Behaviour and Disease in Dogs, in Jensen P (ed.) *The Behavioural Biology of Dogs*, CABI, Wallingford, OX, 243–261: p. 260; Podberscek AL & Serpell JA (1996) The English Cocker Spaniel: Preliminary Findings on Aggressive Behaviour, *Applied Animal Behaviour Science*, 47, 75–89. In Våge J et al. (2008) Behavioral Characteristics of English Cocker Spaniels with

Owner-Defined Aggressive Behaviour, *Journal of Veterinary Behavior*, 3, 248–254, results pointed to the need for a clearer understanding of owner-defined aggression: "Owners have different expectations of their dogs and different opinions of their behaviour, thus creating different milieus for classification of behavioural phenotypes. . . . Nearly half of the aggressive dogs were euthanized as a result of unacceptable behaviour, which underlines the severity of the behavioural problem. We found no significant risk factors for euthanasia," and "The data also do not support an identical 'rage-like' phenotype" (253, 252). Compare the results in Amat M et al. (2009) Aggressive Behaviour in the English Cocker Spaniel, *Journal of Veterinary Behavior*, 4, 111–117, although there is no substantial exploration of the owner-dog dynamic. See further Pérez-Guisado J et al. (2006) Heritability of Dominant-Aggressive Behaviour in English Cocker Spaniels, *Applied Animal Behaviour Science*, 100, 219–227, where the researchers applied the Campbell test (Campbell WE (1972) A Behaviour Test for Puppy Selection, *Modern Veterinary Practice*, 12, 29–33) to 51 seven-week-old English Cocker Spaniel puppies and used this to determine a greater propensity for "dominance aggression." However, as others have argued, "Campbell tests were developed initially to help determine the main personality traits of a puppy. Many puppy temperament tests like the Campbell tests have been developed, but there is no evidence that they can predict adult behaviour accurately except maybe excessive fearful behaviour: Dalibard GH (2009) Parameters Influencing Service Dogs' Quality of Response to Commands: Retrospective Study of 71 Dogs, *Journal of Veterinary Behavior*, 4, 19–24: p. 20.
15 Tarde G (1890/[1912]) *Penal Philosophy*, R Howell (trans.), Little, Brown, and Co, Boston, 245.
16 Nedelsky J (2011) *Law's Relations: A Relational Theory of Self, Autonomy and Law*, Oxford UP, Oxford, 108.
17 See further the discussion of instinct in training discourse in Chapter 10, "Shared interests".
18 Tawney RH (1921) *The Acquisitive Society*, Harcourt Brace & Co, New York, 56–57.
19 Mead M (1961) Some Anthropological Considerations Concerning Natural Law, *Natural Law Forum*, 6, 51–64: p. 54. See further Waddington CH (1961) *The Ethical Animal*, Atheneum, New York, for the term "ethicising."
20 See the critique of acquisitive instinct in Hallowell AI (1942) The Nature and Function of Property as a Social Institution, *Journal of Legal and Political Sociology*, 1, 115–138: p. 134. Ruth Bunzel locates the impulse towards acquisition not within a so-called acquisitive instinct but in the "psychological compulsion" of institutions. See further Bunzel R (1938) The Economic Organization of Primitive Peoples, in F Boas (ed.) *General Anthropology*, Heath, Boston, 1938, 327–408: p. 356.
21 Benson E (2014) The Biopolitics of the Border, *RCC Perspectives: The Edges of Environmental History*, 81–86: p. 84. As Benson notes in relation to the world of Eliot Henry Howard, largely credited with the rise of territory in ethology, "He would have encountered the subjects of his research within a landscape that had already been thoroughly territorialised." (86).
22 Joseph Singer's explanation of the models of the rule of law and the marketplace interrogate a similar dynamic of predator and prey; in other words, the spoils are conferred upon predators, thus also producing prey, or "victims." While the model of the rule of law is interpreted as a kind of harmony of social contract, the model of the marketplace is predatory: "The model of the marketplace, on the other hand, characterizes life under the legal system as a process

of competition and struggle. This view is applicable not only to the economic realm, but to the realm of ideas and the realm of politics. The purpose of the marketplace is to choose winners and losers in the struggle for wealth, power and prestige. . . . The model of the marketplace is legitimated by the belief that the winners deserve to win and that the whole society is better off because of the individual striving that the marketplace generates. Nonetheless, power becomes concentrated in such a system. And along with the winners, such a system produces victims." See Singer JW (1982) The Legal Rights Debate in Analytical Jurisprudence from Bentham to Hohfeld, *Wisconsin Law Review*, 975–1060: p. 983. Singer states further, "While the classical jurists focused on the security and individual freedom offered by the rule of law, the modern critics focused on its victims. . . . The modern theory culminated in Wesley Hohfeld's famous article in 1913" (985). Hohfeld's work is considered in detail in the Social Age towards the proposal of the concept of shared interests.
23 Galbraith JK (2007) Taming Predatory Capitalism, in Rogers J et al. (2006) Taming Global Capitalism Anew, *The Nation*, 17 April: "After an entire century's struggle to escape from this phase, we've suffered a relapse. The predators are everywhere unleashed."
24 Seltzer LF (2012) Are You a Victim of Predatory Capitalism?, *Psychology Today*, 21 September: "[I]n this country today, we seem to have drifted toward a mutant (cancerous?) form of capitalism, or free enterprise. One that's under-regulated, dysregulated – or *both*."
25 Galbraith JK (2008) *The Predator State*, Free Press, New York, 126. There is a distinct biological rhetoric in some areas of economic discourse, infused as it is by a language of wildness, taming and domestication. For instance, Galbraith himself is included as a commentator in a special feature in *The Nation*, entitled Taming Global Capitalism Anew (Galbraith's section is titled, Taming Predatory Capitalism). See Rogers J et al. (2006) Taming Global Capitalism Anew, *The Nation*, 17 April.
26 For instance, see the special report in *The Nation*, Taming Global Capitalism, 17 April 2006, highlighting the characterising of capitalism as a wild predator to be civilised.
27 This particular teleological explanation of evolutionary economics, and indeed of property (as characterised by predatory drift) is not something Veblen necessarily advocated. Emilie Raymer notes that Veblen "criticized those who conflated Darwinism with teleological development, and argued that neither socialism nor any sort of perfected human beings were guaranteed." See Raymer EJ (2013) A Man of His Time: Thorstein Veblen and the University of Chicago Darwinists, *Journal of the History of Biology*, 46(4), 669–698: p. 672.
28 Emilie Raymer notes: "Veblen specified that society's 'growth' and 'development' was modelled on Darwinian natural selection." See Raymer EJ (2013) A Man of His Time: Thorstein Veblen and the University of Chicago Darwinists, *Journal of the History of Biology*, 46(4), 669–698: p. 672.
29 Veblen T (1899/[2007]) *The Theory of the Leisure Class*, Oxford UP, Oxford, 7.
30 Veblen T (1899/[2007]) *The Theory of the Leisure Class*, Oxford UP, Oxford, 19.
31 Veblen T (1899/[2007]) *The Theory of the Leisure Class*, Oxford UP, Oxford, 28.
32 Heap S et al. (2012) The Adoption of Landmarks for Territorial Boundaries, *Animal Behaviour*, 83, 871–878.
33 Veblen T (1899/[2007]) *The Theory of the Leisure Class*, Oxford UP, Oxford, 28.
34 Veblen T (1899/[2007]) *The Theory of the Leisure Class*, Oxford UP, Oxford, 16.
35 See further the discussion of prestige and esteem in the context of synchrony and social learning in the dog-human relationship in Chapter 10, "Shared interests."

36 Maynard Smith J (1979) Game Theory and the Evolution of Behaviour, *Proceedings of the Royal Society of London*, 205(1161), 475–488: pp. 481–482.
37 The nature of deception in animal cognitive studies, together with its links to creativity and honesty in production, is explored in Gibson J (forthcoming) *More Than Human Intellectual Property: Animal Authors and Human Machines*, Routledge, London.
38 Veblen T (1899/[2007]) *The Theory of the Leisure Class*, Oxford UP, Oxford, 17.
39 Veblen T (1899/[2007]) *The Theory of the Leisure Class*, Oxford UP, Oxford, 29.
40 Radin M (1938) A Restatement of Hohfeld, *Harvard Law Review*, 51(7), 1141–1164: pp. 1159–1160.
41 Deleuze G & Guattari F (1980/[1987]) *A Thousand Plateaus: Capitalism and Schizophrenia*, B Massumi (trans.), U of Minnesota P, Minneapolis, 453.
42 Underkuffler LS (2003) *The Idea of Property: Its Meaning and Power*, Oxford UP, Oxford, 11.
43 Tarde G (1890/[1903]) *The Laws of Imitation*, EC Parsons (trans.), Henry Holt & Co, New York, 48.
44 As Hoebel explains in his review of property in the Yurok Indians: "There is symbolic wealth in consumable goods, as well, but prestige comes from the goods whose value is largely fiduciary." Hoebel EA (1942) Fundamental Legal Concepts as Applied in the Study of Primitive Law, *Yale Law Journal*, 51, 951–966: p. 958.
45 Allee WC (1943) Where Angels Fear to Tread: A Contribution from General Sociology to Human Ethics, *Science*, 97(2528), 517–525: p. 524.
46 Russell N (2012) *Social Zooarchaeology*, Cambridge UP, Cambridge, 144–145. See also the notion of property in relation to species differences and the humanising of the family in Horwitz S (2012) How Capitalism and the Bourgeois Virtues Transformed and Humanized the Family, *The Journal of Socio-Economics*, 41, 792–795. Compare Aldred J (2019) *Licence to be Bad*, Allen Lane, London.
47 Jhering R von (1913) *Law as a Means to an End*, Boston Book Company, Boston, 389.
48 Later chapters will address this analysis of property through the (sociable) jural relations of Hohfeld's scheme. See in particular Chapter 11, "Resocialisation."
49 Lowie RH (1928) Incorporeal Property in Primitive Society, *Yale Law Journal*, 37(5), 551–563: p. 551.
50 Rivers WHR (1924/[1996]) *Social Organization*, Routledge, London. The work was published posthumously and is based upon a 1920 manuscript as well as lectures delivered in Cambridge in 1921 and 1922. After Rivers died suddenly in 1922, the final material was prepared by his doctoral student, William James Perry.
51 Rivers WHR (1924/[1996]) *Social Organization*, Routledge, London, 113–114.
52 Rivers WHR (1924/[1996]) *Social Organization*, Routledge, London, 114.
53 Rivers WHR (1924/[1996]) *Social Organization*, Routledge, London, 170.
54 Lowie RH (1928) Incorporeal Property in Primitive Society, *Yale Law Journal*, 37(5), 551–563. Lowie was responding to the work of Lewis H Morgan and his theory that there are three major periods – savagery, barbarism, and civilisation. See further page 551.
55 Rivers WHR (1924/[1996]) *Social Organization*, Routledge, London, 171.
56 Bronislaw Malinowski was a respected figure in the renewed interest in anthropological jurisprudence in the early twentieth century. See the words by his contemporary in Cairns H (1931) Law and Anthropology, *Columbia Law Review*, 31(1), 32–55: pp. 33–34.

57 This productive "encounter" between the two anthropologists is considered in some detail, along with the relevance of Hohfeldian principles in reconciling the perspectives, in Hoebel EA (1942) Fundamental Legal Concepts as Applied in the Study of Primitive Law, *Yale Law Journal*, 51, 951–966.
58 Cairns H (1931) Law and Anthropology, *Columbia Law Review*, 31(1), 32–55: p. 34.
59 Malinowski B (1926) *Crime and Custom in Savage Society*, Harcourt Brace & Co, New York, 56.
60 Malinowski B (1926) *Crime and Custom in Savage Society*, Harcourt Brace & Co, New York, 19.
61 Lowie RH (1928) Incorporeal Property in Primitive Society, *Yale Law Journal*, 37(5), 551–563: p. 552. See also Cairns H (1931) Law and Anthropology, *Columbia Law Review*, 31(1), 32–55: "Today the conception of primitive communism has been abandoned by legal historians and it has been found that real progress in the law lies in patiently working backwards towards the source of legal rules instead of beginning with a hypothesis and working forward, attempting at the same time to make each apparent advance conform with the hypothesis" (44). See further the discussion in Hallowell AI (1942) The Nature and Function of Property as a Social Institution, *Journal of Legal and Political Sociology*, 1, 115–138: pp. 125–130.
62 Originally published in 1940 under the title, *The Economic Life of Primitive Peoples*, here all references are to the 1952 re-edition as *Economic Anthropology*.
63 Merskovits MJ (1940/[1952]) *Economic Anthropology*, Alfred A Knopf, New York, 500.
64 Mead M (1961) Some Anthropological Considerations Concerning Natural Law, *Natural Law Forum*, 6, 51–64: p. 53.
65 Mead M (1961) Some Anthropological Considerations Concerning Natural Law, *Natural Law Forum*, 6, 51–64: p. 53.
66 A term used by Waddington through *The Ethical Animal* to describe the process of ethical development within the individual. See Waddington CH (1961) *The Ethical Animal*, Atheneum, New York. Waddington explains: "The process of turning the newborn infant into an ethicizing being is what I previously referred to by such phrases as 'the formation of the concept of the good'" (26).
67 Waddington CH (1961) *The Ethical Animal*, Atheneum, New York, 23.
68 Mead M (1961) Some Anthropological Considerations Concerning Natural Law, *Natural Law Forum*, 6, 51–64: p. 54.
69 Veblen T (1899/[2007]) *The Theory of the Leisure Class*, Oxford UP, Oxford.
70 Lowie RH (1928) Incorporeal Property in Primitive Society, *Yale Law Journal*, 37(5), 551–563: p. 552.
71 Malinowski B (1926) *Crime and Custom in Savage Society*, Harcourt Brace & Co, New York, 58 note 11. See further the discussion in Cairns H (1931) Law and Anthropology, *Columbia Law Review*, 31(1), 32–55: p. 38.
72 Huntington Cairns notes: "Anthropology has warned the jurist that his conception of law is perhaps egocentric, but it has shown him that with its aid he may be able to work out a conception of law that will be adequate for all social requirements." Cairns H (1931) Law and Anthropology, *Columbia Law Review*, 31(1), 32–55: p. 39. See further the approach to resocialising property through an emphasis on relations in Chapter 11, "Resocialisation."
73 As in the relationship of conflict between equity and common law identified in the "Langdell-Ames-Maitland" school of thought. See Hohfeld WN (1913) Some Fundamental Legal Conceptions as Applied in Judicial Reasoning, *Yale Law Journal*, 23(1), 16–59: pp. 16–18; Hohfeld WN (1917) Fundamental

Legal Conceptions as Applied in Judicial Reasoning, *The Yale Law Journal*, 26(8), 710–770: p. 769; Hohfeld WN (1913) The Relations between Equity and Law, *Michigan Law Review*, 537–571. See further, Cook WW (1919) Hohfeld's Contributions to the Science of Law, *The Yale Law Journal*, 28(8), 721–738: pp. 733–734; Cook WW (1917) The Alienability of Choses in Action: A Reply to Professor Williston, *Harvard Law Review*, 30(5), 449–485.
74 Hoebel EA (1946) Law and Anthropology, *Virginia Law Review*, 32(4), 835–854: p. 848.
75 See further the discussion in Gibson J (2005) *Community Resources*, Ashgate, Aldershot, particularly the setting out of the key issues in the introductory chapter.
76 See the discussion of defensive protection in Gibson J (2005) *Community Resources*, Ashgate, Aldershot, 141–149 in particular.
77 Mead M (1963) Some Anthropological Considerations Concerning Natural Law, *Natural Law Forum*, 6, 51–64: p. 53.
78 Hoebel EA (1942) Fundamental Legal Concepts as Applied in the Study of Primitive Law, *Yale Law Journal*, 51, 951–966; Lowie RH (1928) Incorporeal Property in Primitive Society, *Yale Law Journal*, 37(5), 551–563.
79 Hoebel EA (1946) Law and Anthropology, *Virginia Law Review*, 32(4), 835–354: p. 836.
80 This discourse of the "exotic other" is also recognised in popular impressions of animals as having exceptional sensory perception, not in terms of creativity or will but as in an acute environmental sensitivity, such as predicting storms, rendering them a kind of biological curiosity rather than an intentional agent.
81 Hoebel EA (1946) Law and Anthropology, *Virginia Law Review*, 32(4), 835–854: p. 853.
82 Tarde G (1890/[1912]) *Penal Philosophy*, R Howell (trans.), Little, Brown, and Co, Boston, 2.
83 See further the discussions in "Part 4, Altruism, the social age," as well as in Gibson J (forthcoming) *More Than Human Intellectual Property*, Routledge, London.
84 Cairns H (1931) Law and Anthropology, *Columbia Law Review*, 31(1), 32–55: p. 41.
85 Malinowski B (1942) A New Instrument for the Interpretation of Law: Especially Primitive, *The Yale Law Journal*, 51(8), 1237–1254: p. 1238.
86 This includes the work of Bronislaw Malinowski, who, in an article reviewing Llewellyn and Hoebel's *The Cheyenne Way*, argues, "culture is also largely determined by biological process within the human body and by the organic needs of man. Culture and its development again consist in technological invention, that is, in the discovery by man of natural laws and in their application to human ends." See Malinowski B (1942) A New Instrument for the Interpretation of Law: Especially Primitive, *The Yale Law Journal*, 51(8), 1237–1254: p. 1239. He continues: "The structure of economics, of the normative system, of organized recreation, and of magical and religious cults is also based on the human needs which are satisfied in each such activity. Human needs in turn are not arbitrary, but are based on physiology and environment, and also on the nature of those instrumentalities, physical, social, and psychological, which constitute culture. All the fundamental categories of human behavior are subject to the intrinsic determinism of culture" (1239). Malinowski sees the repetition of institutions as a similar indication of "the existence of order in culture" (1240). In a way this may seem to coincide with Tarde's account of imitation, but that is perhaps where the similarities end. Tarde cautions against the imperative to find

such ordered causality: "This, however, is the arduous task which the philosopher of history sets before himself and which he thinks that he cannot slur over if he is to do the work of a scholar. He will, therefore, wear himself out in trying to bring order out of disorder by discovering some law or reason for these historic chances and coincidences. He would do better to investigate how and why harmonies sometimes proceed from these coincidences and in what these harmonies consist." See, Tarde G (1890/[1903]) *The Laws of Imitation*, EC Parsons (trans.), Henry Holt & Co, New York, 10.
87 Cairns H (1941) *The Theory of Legal Science*, U of North Carolina P, Chapel Hill, 54.
88 Hoebel EA (1940) *The Political Organization and Law-Ways of the Comanche Indians*, American Anthropological Association, Menasha, WI, 45–48.
89 Hoebel EA (1942) Fundamental Legal Concepts as Applied in the Study of Primitive Law, *Yale Law Journal*, 51, 951–966: p. 952 (citing the work of German legal scholar and ethnologist, Joseph Kohler).
90 Equally, the discourse on rights is attended by similar problems, as introduced in earlier discussions.
91 Malinowski B (1922) *Argonauts of the Western Pacific*, Routledge and Kegan Paul, London, 116–117.
92 Hoebel EA (1942) Fundamental Legal Concepts as Applied in the Study of Primitive Law, *Yale Law Journal*, 51, 951–966: p. 951.
93 Malinowski B (1926) *Crime and Custom in Savage Society*, Harcourt Brace & Co, New York, 19.
94 Malinowski B (1926) *Crime and Custom in Savage Society*, Harcourt Brace & Co, New York, 20.
95 Malinowski B (1926) *Crime and Custom in Savage Society*, Harcourt Brace & Co, New York, 20–21.
96 Malinowski B (1926) *Crime and Custom in Savage Society*, Harcourt Brace & Co, New York, 21.
97 See Hoebel EA (1942) Fundamental Legal Concepts as Applied in the Study of Primitive Law, *Yale Law Journal*, 51, 951–966: p. 952.
98 As Hoebel remarks: "the most vexatious problems of primitive law – the drawing of the real shape of institutions said to be 'communistic' as against 'private', or to be 'corporeal' as against 'incorporeal.'" See Hoebel EA (1942) Fundamental Legal Concepts as Applied in the Study of Primitive Law, *Yale Law Journal*, 51, 951–966: p. 957. See further: "One of the fields of skirmish between the collectivist and the individualistically-minded anthropologists has been the identification of certain primitive property forms as either 'private' or 'communal.' . . . It seems likely that if his case had been put explicitly in Hohfeldian fundamental terms, his comprehensive grasp of the nature of property forms in primitive Melanesian society could not be grossly misconstrued, especially not by a student of law. For if a complex legal and social institution is reduced in clarity to its fundamental components, the vagary of gross catch-all concepts is banished. Confusion and useless argumentation go out with the catch-alls, for it is in the periphery of their fuzzy boundaries that all the fighting occurs" (961). Similar concerns are explored further in relation to the incorporeal, impermanent, intangible nature of some works, for example, smell, as well as other challenges to intellectual property in relation to the commons. See further the discussions in Chapter 6, "Separation anxiety"; and Chapter 12, "*Res familiaris.*"
99 A striking example of the impact of this predatory drift in property language in Australian native title discourse is an informal discussion I had at the University of Queensland with the Australian indigenous playwright, Eva Knowles Johnson,

who, in the pub following her presentation to a packed lecture hall, described a conversation she had with a neighbour in the late 1980s where the neighbour queried (to paraphrase), "Eva, why are you so upset about land rights? You own your own home." The language and discursive presumptions of property and of rights will always be instrumental in framing and characterising relationships as ones of conflict and in pre-determining to an extent the way in which those conflicts are resolved. As Jerrold A Long notes: "The often unchallenged assertion is the claim that the discussion is in fact about property rights. Once a particular property interest is characterized as a 'right,' the community's political capacity to regulate that property interest diminishes substantially." See Long JA (2012) Waiting for Hohfeld: Property Rights, Property Privileges, and the Physical Consequences of Word Choice, *Gonzaga Law Review*, 48(2), 306–364: p. 306. Long goes to argue that within the Hohfeldian system most so-called property rights are better understood as privileges and that the value of this is that the perspective is shifted away from the individual and onto the community (309). As Long states, "An accurate rhetorical landscape does not leave us with *less* property. It leaves us with *better* property. Consequently, it leaves us with better communities and landscapes (310–311).

100 Hoebel EA (1942) Fundamental Legal Concepts as Applied in the Study of Primitive Law, *Yale Law Journal*, 51, 951–966: p. 956.
101 See the discussion of the commons in *Res familiaris*.
102 Bateson G (1972/[2000]) *Steps to an Ecology of Mind*, U of Chicago P, Chicago, 38.

Chapter 8

Pack fiction

> Behavioral sciences of both human and nonhuman varieties continue to find anything but dominance and subordination hard to think about. Chicken knows that producing better accounts of animal doings, with one another and with humans, can play an important role in reclaiming livable politics.
>
> Haraway D (2008) *When Species Meet*,
> U of Minnesota P, Minneapolis, 271

The popular story of domestication is one of domination and mastery, apprehension and taming, enfolding the subordinated party into society so that it submits to its care.[1] Succumbing to the boundaries of property is thus presented as giving that animal their security and thus their "freedom."[2] According to the narrative of human exceptionalism, the wolf was domesticated into a "follower," a scavenger, or a consumer. The wolf was thus rendered property. Indeed, this perspective frames the designs of research questions themselves, where that dog's social competence is frequently attributed to the domestication narrative rather than the intentionality behind it.[3] In this way that dog is recollected, as it were, as a human creation.[4] But that first domestication is rewriting that story, presenting instead a cooperation and sociability that underpins not only the imitation through subsequent domestications, but also the nature of evolutionary development itself.

Telling fact from fiction

> Legal fictions are mistaken for objective legal truths and clear legal thinking becomes an unnecessarily arduous task.[5]

Some terms become repeated and imitated without question in the kind of "one-sided passive imitation of the somnambulist," as opposed to the mutual reciprocity of "our so-called waking life."[6] For the somnambulist, "all his power of belief and desire is concentrated on a single point."[7] Tarde's treatment of the concept of somnambulism, a kind of cultural hypnosis and mesmerism, a sleepwalking through life, provides insight into the institution and propagation of social and legal fictions. In this way, definitions are perpetuated by a belief system or dogma, bound through contagion and imitation, and sustained by coercion as social facts. As will be shown in the following discussion, such somnambulistic imitation results in the uncritical perpetuation of particular concepts or beliefs, such as that of the concept of "alpha" and the pack within dog training discourse: *a surprising fact at which nobody is surprised*.[8]

In the traditional sense, a legal fiction is something which is not true. For example, an easement, such as a right of way, is deemed to have been granted at a time forgotten in a document that was also forgotten. The fiction is a way of avoiding a situation where the long-standing enjoyment of something long since enjoyed, for which no original justification could be proven, could continue. Time immemorial is agreed as the commencement of the reign of Richard I (1189).[9] When time immemorial became too distant to substantiate, it became impossible to prove the original establishment of an easement, and so a fiction became the means by which to render it fact and property. Legal fictions are indeed, in the simplest sense, those constructed facts accepted by the court in order to be able to apply legal rules: "It is in property law, which always had a large substantive content, that major changes were made by legislation from the early days of the common law . . . the changes that ensued often went far beyond what was intended . . . one has only to look at reports and pleadings down to the nineteenth century to see that an important part must have been played by fiction."[10]

As in the following discussion of so-called pack or dominance theory, and the tenacity of the concept of alpha or pack leader, facts may be not only selective but also entirely constructed: "Experience in controversies such as these brings out the impossibility of learning anything from facts till they are examined and interpreted by reason; and teaches that the most reckless and treacherous of all theorists is he who professes to let facts and figures speak for themselves, who keeps in the background the part he has played, perhaps unconsciously, in selecting and grouping them, and in suggesting the argument *post hoc ergo propter hoc*."[11]

In a sense, what happens with these social facts and legal fictions, as it were, is what Jean-Luc Nancy describes as passing into right. That is, the discourse of pack and alpha becomes self-defining, self-fulfilling, and self-legitimating: "Jurisdiction is the fact of *saying* right."[12] In this sense, jurisdiction is the power to act, but that power is in and of itself a legal fiction: "the very notion of 'juridical discourse' borders on tautology."[13] Thus, Nancy identifies jurisdiction as a double structure: "On the one hand, it states the right of the case, thereby making it a case: it subsumes it, suppresses its accidental character."[14] In other words, "conceal what is going on."[15] A document is taken for the right, an object is taken for the property. Nancy's explanation is notably resonant with the language of drift, of a reversion to atavistic traits, *always relapse*: "The logic of the case is one of falling or sliding in on itself, a logic of falling back. In terms of the model established by right, the case, even the case that has already been judged, is always *lapse* and *relapse*."[16]

What is emerging is the contingent nature of property, or perhaps more significantly, the social nature of objectivity, of jurisdiction, of legal relations, always already *being-in-common*, a kind of nuisance prosociality in the law itself. Indeed, as seen in earlier discussions, any perspective on the facts is also situated and partial because the observer is always already implicated in the observation event:

> No matter what covenant guarantees that 'A is the observer' and 'B is the observed,' both function as observers; their compliance with this covenant itself implies both mutual awareness and self-observation. The fact that each of the two is therefore 'the observer' to himself and 'the observed' to the other, underlies all (so-called) disturbances which result from the fact that an experiment is performed. Awareness, hitherto treated as a 'nuisance' – or as 'noise' in terms of information theory – is a key datum of the life sciences, which reintroduces awareness even into experiments so constructed as to eliminate awareness.[17]

Indeed, that dog really is a nuisance.

The making of a myth

What is a pack animal? There are so few references to the term "pack" in the scientific behaviour literature that it is effectively not used. Where it is used it seems to be in other disciplines, such as sociology,[18] and often used in a misapplication of the now discredited theories arising from the earliest wolf literature. In the behaviour science literature, where it is rarely used, it is usually in in the use of the pack as "group," without any of the attending presumptions around hierarchies and leadership.[19] Indeed, in the reference literature, pack is either not defined at all[20] or is simply defined as a synonym for group.[21] Even before the earliest investigations into wolf behaviour, "pack" was used to imply a lower character as early as the 14th century,[22] or indeed a predatory purpose.[23] The remarkable thing about the group noun is the way in which it obscures the individual and at the same time identifies the group as acting all towards a singular purpose or function. That is, the act of naming a group according to an implied trait – such as a family of otters, a pride of lions, a skulk of foxes, a murder of crows, a school of fish, and, indeed, a pack of wolves – is somewhat complicit with an overarching biological narrative. At the same time, the group noun creates a set of objects, a group of things, and indeed these objects are often defined by place.[24] This is more explicit when dealing with examples such as a gallery of paintings, a library of books, a museum of artefacts, but the somewhat obsolete group noun for dogs, a kennel of dogs, also follows this pattern. The kennel group noun, albeit somewhat outdated, nevertheless implies home and domestication, whereas the replacement by "pack," a term ordinarily applied to undomesticated animals and most often predators,[25] is a curious predatory drift from that first domestication and that dog. Thus, with its use in other contexts, there is the attending literary flourish of "pack" that imbues it with further meaning.²⁶ The problem is that the term, "pack," comes with a lot of baggage, so to speak.

In many respects, Deleuze and Guattari somewhat recuperate the term in their own writings, departing from the link between pack and a simple linear hierarchy (the arborescent model) into which an individual is born, instead embracing pack as a cooperative system of relations (the rhizome): "The leader of the pack or the band plays move by move, must wager everything every hand, whereas the group or mass leader consolidates or capitalizes on past gains."²⁷ The static hierarchies imposed by constructions such as the pack in dominance theory, or the owner and visitor, or producer and consumer, and so on, arguably follow an arborescent model. However, the rich creativity of the genuinely rhizomatic pack is much more relevant to the realities of group-living canids: "A becoming-animal always involves a pack, a band, a population, a peopling, in short, a multiplicity."²⁸ In contrast, within the arborescent pack model of prevailing dominance theories, dogs are being over-trained or aversively trained with a resulting loss of spontaneity, loss of creativity, and certainly a loss of choice.²⁹ Are we seeing this same cult of obedience imposed on the kinds of productive socialities that might otherwise be achievable within the law?

The history of research into wolf dynamics and the extrapolation of the findings to the domesticated dog is a story in scientific myth-making. Arguably, many of the assumptions underpinning the miscalculations in the early research design resonate with the strict divide of human exceptionalism as the seat of culture and society, and all other animals as enslaved by instinct and biology. These assumptions led to some curious results in early wolf research that have unfortunately attained mythological status in the popular discourse, with alarming implications for canine welfare.³⁰ The results of early wolf research have an unfortunate legacy. The findings have long since been shown to have been a misleading interpretation of natural group behaviour in wolves because of the artificial group structure. The interactions of these "unfamiliar" wolves obscured the family and instead presented a hierarchical (and frequently combative) "pack." The influence of these conclusions over and beyond what was actually contained and observed within the study has generated a mythology of the dominance hierarchy in dogs, with the rhetoric of alpha, top dog, and pack leadership permeating all areas of popular culture.³¹ How did we get here?

Early wolf research notoriously ignored the "home" of wolves, the community and sociability within the wolf family group. This is especially apparent in the early research into wolf groups, where most research had been undertaken in captivity and on groups created by bringing together strangers: "These captive packs were usually composed of an assortment of wolves from various sources placed together and allowed to breed at will."³² The presumption was that pack formation had nothing to do with the individuals and everything to do with a programmed response to the seasons,³³ "implying some sort of annual assembling of independent wolves."³⁴ But everybody was a stranger, everybody belonged to someone or something else, outside this contrived "kin."

Follow the leader

In the 1940s, Rudolf Schenkel, a zoologist at the University of Basel in Switzerland, undertook research on wolf groups at the Basel Zoological Garden, leading to an influential study on expression in wolves.[35] In later work, Schenkel explicitly drew analogies between wolf and dog populations in relation to submission and dominance theories.[36] While the objectives of Schenkel's studies are notable for the emphasis on visual display and communication, the research design was fundamentally flawed because these were artificial groups, put together by the zoo rather than genuine family groupings.[37] Nevertheless, the observations on expression and faciality are still remarkable and significant in their emphasis on embodied communication and expression in captive wild animals. In almost all respects, the criticism of this study is more appropriately levelled at the interpretation and application of the results as a fixed and immutable representation of dominance and submission as objects, rather than relations within a particular and situated framework of stressors.[38] But it is the nature of these interpretations, with their readiness to narrate a story of aggression, competition and power, that is in itself significant. And it is these interpretations that have led to the problematic discourse of competition and pack leadership that permeates not only dog training discourse but also the predatory drift of social and commercial relationships more widely, including property.

In these studies, Schenkel described a linear hierarchy within the wolf pack and identified a lead wolf (*Leitwolf*[39]). Schenkel's research was then followed by David Mech in his landmark wolf studies of the 1960s and 1970s, including the publication of the influential book, *The Wolf*.[40] The term, "alpha wolf," although frequently attributed to Schenkel, was in fact introduced by Mech in 1966 in his study, *The Wolves of Isle Royale*.[41] Curiously, Mech attributes the term to Schenkel in this text,[42] although the denominations of alpha, beta, and omega appear nowhere in Schenkel's original study. Indeed, in Schenkel's study, the group is presented as somewhat less combative than the imagery implied by alpha status, and *Leitwolf* has much in common with the now preferred terms of breeder or parent wolf. Further, Schenkel's hierarchy model was not as rigid and exacting as would be suggested by the subsequent literature and mythology: "Social orders in wolf packs are by no means definitive and clear cut; they are far more equilibria among uninterrupted and interacting forces."[43]

Although Mech appears to have introduced the term in wolves, the term "alpha" had already been applied to captive canid groups for some time before Mech's studies, having been used in relation to a laboratory colony of prairie dogs a decade before.[44] The first use of alpha in relation to a primate appears to have been in the 1930s, but not as a marker of status. Alpha was actually the name of a captive female chimpanzee, the first to be born in the Yerkes Laboratories.[45] Somewhat ironically in the present context, she was described as "a timid creature of slightly below average intelligence,"[46] and elsewhere as "a docile creature used all her life to cooperating in psychological experiments."[47] The term alpha in relation to dominance hierarchies in primates does not seem to come into full circulation until the 1960s in the work of the Japan Monkey Center.[48] However, one of the very first times the term alpha was used in relation to status appears to have been not in groups of wolves but rather in the case of none other than the mouse.[49]

How and why, then, did the contemporary rhetoric of the alpha wolf become so dominant, so to speak, in popular culture, extrapolated as it has been to human status and machismo? The introduction of the term "alpha" in the studies of dominance hierarchies in wolves is informative in terms of the socio-cultural research context (although not so much in terms of the misleading behaviour observations). Alpha ends the conversation and any hope of "class mobility" within the animal society: "The point here is not so much the terminology but what the terminology falsely implies: a rigid, force-based dominance hierarchy."[50] Interestingly, early on in dominance studies, one scientist advocated the use of "alpha" in relation to macaque groups as a way to avoid the simple and incorrect idea of a literal linear hierarchy in movement of the group, implied by the term, leader:

> The word "leader" has a clearcut meaning in common English: one who leads or precedes another individual or a group and thus determined the direction of movement of the pair or larger group. . . . To speak of this animal as "the leader" and the subordinate males as "subleaders" is to give a misleading picture of social organization. Such an animal is definitely the alpha male in the dominance hierarchy, a general relationship, but his role in the leader-follower relationships of the band is much more special. He exercises some control over the movement of the band, and in special cases may take the lead, but in most cases the group is led by others.[51]

Significantly, in his earlier publications, Mech also extrapolates the pack mythology to incorporate the dog and human dynamic in the home, and in this way "dominance" and status began to characterise popular conceptions of the human-dog relationship: "Watch your pet dog. It dominates or submits to other dogs in the same way wolves do. Because you are an alpha member of your dog's pack, your dog submits to you. If it doesn't, you are in trouble!"[52] Similarly, Mech places the human at the head of the family "pack" in his advice elsewhere in the same book: "[T]he dog is essentially a juvenile wolf, dependent on and dominated by its owners who play the role of parents and older packmates."[53] In these earlier studies, Mech identifies constant assertiveness as an integral mechanism in wolf society,[54] implying a chronic anxiety about an artificial stability and a somewhat central role of combative rivalry as distinct from a cooperative society. In these same studies, Mech also emphasises the importance of leadership, although ostensibly as facilitating cooperation: "Beside privilege, the other aspect of dominance in wolves is leadership. This form of initiative probably is the more important of the two in the normal life of the pack, since cooperative ventures usually outnumber competitive ones."[55] However, the associated rhetoric of "top dog" and the constant battles for status have since become ubiquitous in inaccurate renditions of training in popular discourse and the translation of dominance and leadership into the human-dog relationship in dog training discourse has popularised the very inaccurate and biologically incorrect suppositions that come with a literal translation of the terminology, as warned against in the macaque example back in 1964.[56] Words matter.

Mech's work was followed by Erik Zimen in Italy and Germany, who, to an extent, reinforced the assumptions regarding a linear, combative hierarchy dominated by alphas through his study of similarly contrived and unnatural groups of unrelated wolves.[57] However, Zimen nevertheless introduced a language of democracy and sociality and later revised the antagonistic and linear hierarchical characterisation of pack relations as an oversimplification: "No member decides alone when an activity is to begin or end, or which way or at what speed the pack is to move, or exercises sole power of command in any of the other activities that are vital to the cohesion of the pack. *The autocratic leading wolf does not exist.*"[58]

The simple linear dominance model began to be disputed in the research, including by those originally identifying a strictly hierarchical structure. And both Mech[59] and Zimen[60] later qualified their earlier findings on the observation of captive groups: "Attempting to apply information about the behavior of unrelated captive wolves to the familial structure of natural packs has resulted in considerable confusion. Such an approach is analogous to trying to draw inferences about human family dynamics by studying humans in refugee camps. The concept of the alpha wolf as a "top dog" ruling a group of similar-aged compatriots is particularly misleading."[61] Mech notably advocates a change in terminology altogether,[62] and in his later publications, Mech has replaced "alpha" with "breeder"[63] to reflect more accurately the family structure of the pack. Indeed, Mech emphasises the family structure in later publications, describing the pack as nursery, and confounding the usual combative and warring cultural imagery of the pack: "the continued association of young wolves with their natal pack may simply be a way for the young to mature while still being subsidized by their parents."[64]

Mech has indeed spent the better part of his career revising his earlier conclusions and attempting to encourage the abandonment of the term, alpha.[65] Nevertheless, the mythology has persisted, the damage was done. *Many never looked back.*

A dominance paradigm

Thus, the model of simple linear hierarchies has been completely revised in the scientific literature, and yet, despite the identified problems in the research design and subsequent studies correcting the original assumptions, the mythology of pack leadership has embedded itself in popular dog training discourse. The characterisation of dogs as pack animals in a constant battle to dominate their humans to secure pack leadership is pervasive as a contest for resources and, indeed, for property.[66] Much of the (misplaced) advice on "becoming pack leader" follows a property-like model for evidence of prestige (as seen in Veblen's account of predatory capitalism). This includes references to a kind of esteem or prestige (for example, walking ahead) as well as to space (for example, setting boundaries on attention and place) and indeed resources (for example, eating first, controlling access to food, and so on).[67] This kind of so-called balanced training discourse arguably exposes a predatory drift not only in relation to the competition for resources that characterises the training paradigm, but also in relation to the presumption about dogs and other animals more generally as subjects of domination and control. Further, these beliefs continue to invade and thrive within dog training discourse, as well as arguably intruding upon the construction of research questions themselves. The extrapolation of an already incorrect paradigm to the human-dog relationship has resulted in serious welfare challenges in dog training. Melissa Bain notes the impact on welfare through the persistence of the alpha myth: "[Mech] presented the human family as equals with dogs, as if they are in a wolf pack, and owners were to act more 'wolf-like.' This led to the human construct of dominant gestures on behalf of dog trainers and owners, such as alpha-rolls and scruff shakes . . . Despite evidence to the contrary, some continue to view dogs as part of the human pack. In this paradigm, humans are told to be 'dominant' over their dog. Unfortunately, the use of these dominance constructs during training remains a persistent theme."[68]

As well as influencing a lot of dog training discourse today, with the attending welfare problems this raises,[69] this mythology of wolf behaviour and the associated pack discourse also continues to demonise the wild wolf[70] in ways that are often disastrous for individual welfare and conservation efforts:[71] "The issue is not merely one of semantics or political correctness. It is one of biological correctness such that the term we use for breeding wolves accurately captures the biological and social role of the animals rather than perpetuate a faulty view."[72] Indeed, if there is a pack mentality anywhere in any group, including humans, it does not demonstrate a refined social order. Rather, it is more appropriately understood as evidence of a lack of sociability between members, as can be seen regularly in social media storms.

Much of the aggression and expressions of dominance observed in that early research arose because of the artificial, indeed "unnatural" and most certainly unfamiliar, conditions in which these total strangers found themselves. The individuals subsist, but the group is a fiction. This is not the case of a number of sociable "fruitful interferences"[73] because there is no territory, no home into which to enter. Rather than a creative assemblage, this is a sterile and forced contact. Everybody is a stranger, no-one is kin. The group is earthbound with no territory, literal but with no story, worldly but with no world.

The other striking aspect about these early observations, particularly in the context of the literary background to the term, "pack," is the presumption that the wolves would simply come together to hunt, as though the pack were *a priori* a warring group before it had even formed. In other words, the construction of the "wolf pack" image betrays a kind of predatory drift that infuses the particular socio-political context for the research. This predatory drift assumes the same dynamic and the same pack rhetoric in economics, law, and so on, sustaining this problematic perspective as a fact of social evolution. Thus, recalling the popular uses set out at the beginning of this chapter, Schenkel's pack was seen as a seasonal convenience towards a particular purpose: "The pack formation starts with the beginning of winter. Chorus howling, joint wanderings and hunting, and fairly early rivalries concerning leadership and sexual partnership denote this period."[74] As Mech explains in his revision of the problematic pack mythology: "Several decades ago, before there were many studies of wolves under natural conditions, scientists interested in animal social behavior thought the wolf pack was a random assemblage of wolves that came together as winter approached in order to better hunt their large prey."[75]

What much of this predatory rhetoric ignores is the sociability of dominance, as it were, defining it instead as a static, fixed trait of an individual, instead of an important social interaction. As Simmel notes: "Nobody, in general, wishes that his influence completely determine the other individual. He rather wants this influence, this determination of the other, to act back upon *him*."[76] Dominance is not a trait but is always already relational. As Simmel observes, "the elimination of *all* independent significance of one of the two interacting parties annuls the very notion of society."[77] Indeed, the subject of scientific observation is perhaps more accurately that of the "dominance relationship" – always already two, social and sociable.[78] Dominance is actually invisible (and illogical) outside of a relation. A dog is not dominant, nor is a motive, but a relationship might be: "the use of the expression 'dominant dog' is meaningless, since 'dominance' can apply only to a relationship between individuals. Furthermore, the use of such terminology can lead to the application of training practices that can create anxiety in dogs about interactions with their owners."[79] In the context of this training paradigm, it is insightful to note as well Simmel's observation of speakers and their audience or teachers and their class: "The seemingly wholly passive element is in reality even more active in [these] relationships."[80]

Fundamentally, in human relationships, as well as in the wolf pack, there is an important plasticity: *The autocratic leading wolf does not exist*.[81] The observed has an effect on the observer,[82] the hypnotised an effect on the hypnotist.[83] That prosocial dog is a productive nuisance. Nevertheless, with the drift from sociability to the social contract, from territory to property, across diverse disciplines and sectors, the pack and dominance hierarchy concepts have become entrenched as motifs integral to predatory drift and the dominance paradigm. This perspective frames not only some areas of dog training but also the predatory model of economics and competition more generally. This can be seen in popular training literature and within the pervasive discourse of causality that characterises presumptions of dominance and submission in causal narratives of economics, innovation, and property, where the contribution of the other is frequently hidden despite the active mutuality in these relationships. Dominance, like property, is taken for the object itself, the sign taken for wonder, as it were; and in the process, the trespasser, the consumer, that dog, is an effect rather than a participant, always late to the party. But the despotic tyranny of the metaphor of wolf pack leader is simply a fiction; so why and how, from lone wolves to the wolves of Wall Street, has human behaviour become so easily and readily modelled upon it?

Signs taken for wonders

> Resistance is not necessarily an oppositional act of political intention, nor is it the simple negation or exclusion of the 'content' of another culture, as a difference once perceived. It is the effect of an ambivalence produced within the rules of recognition of dominating discourses as they articulate the signs of cultural difference and reimplicate them within the deferential relations of colonial power – hierarchy, normalization, marginalization, and so forth. For domination is achieved through a process of disavowal that denies the *différance* of colonialist power.[84]

Early wolf research demonstrates the relationship between science and the state, as it were, in that the behaviour was being interpreted through a particular historical and political lens. Once again, the observer is implicated in the construction of supposedly biological or natural laws. From science in the service of imperialism and colonisation in the late nineteenth and early twentieth centuries,[85] to the interpretation of biology through the lens of Nazi Germany,[86] to the self-reinforcing narrative of humans as "pack leaders" and "alphas" in the authoritarian mythology of pack theory today, biology has been continually compelled to provide questions to the answers always already desired.

By the mid-twentieth century, the "new biology" was the source of a biological determinism for human society,[87] not only for sustaining human exceptionalism but also for societal norms, including divisions and categorisations along racial and class lines. The fundamental point, however, was the continued mythologising and acceptance of certain theories that had since been disputed and revised in the literature. Just as we have the mythology of the pack and the alpha, similarly the notions of basic instincts in aggression and territorial dominion (and property) were propagated as justifications for the laissez-faire economics of a post-World War II period of regeneration.

Boria Sax examines the historical and political context of early wolf research, undertaken soon after the end of World War II and the defeat of Nazi Germany, and suggests a social and cultural influence in the interpretations of wolf behaviour that is consistent with a biological theory of social class: "In studying wolves, [Schenkel] was demythologizing them; nevertheless, the Nazi mystique comes through in his accounts of lupine behavior. Schenkel described in intricate detail cruel games played by dominant wolves, adding that the victim always belonged to another 'race of wolves' than the perpetrators."[88]

The significance of the socio-political context in which observations are undertaken is illustrated somewhat clearly by Konrad Lorenz's own work with wolves. In his subsequent observations, Lorenz concludes a clearly linear hierarchical structure, the explanation of which is disputed strongly by Schenkel.[89] Boria Sax argues: "[T]he enormous power of animal symbolism can direct and sometimes overwhelm observation. Lorenz described the canids according to the model of Nazi bureaucracy in which relationships were structured by unambiguous gestures of authority and submission. Both groups were conceived as strictly hierarchal within their society and ruthless toward those outside."[90] Social hierarchy: *defence defines it.*

Lorenz presents his theory of aggressive instinct as fact, but any traction it has achieved has been primarily in terms of the presentation and authorship (Lorenz's own prestige) and not in terms of subsequent investigation, which has gone on to refute the claim. Telling fact from fiction, as it were: "People who speak of 'the aggressive instinct' (few professional biologists are among them) are usually aggrieved and resentful when it is pointed out to them that there is no such thing."[91] Nevertheless, a claim of "aggressive instinct" has continued to be peddled as a justification for the status quo, that there is some sort of biologically determined basis for discrimination.[92] As seen in earlier discussions, this narrative has also been applied consistently to earlier population domestication stories of selection and taming, which persist in the popular discourse and in dog owner and trainer communities, despite their revision in the scientific literature. Indeed, one of the overwhelming aspects in common with much of this earlier domestication literature and the persistent popular account is that these theories do not take account of the dog's own equitable principles or social morality, as it were, and the accumulating evidence for empathetic and so-called moral behaviour for which domestication is not an explanation.[93] Indeed, with that first domestication and its subsequent imitation, that dog did invent humaneness.

The nature of predatory drift in today's economic and legal discourse is similarly apparent, particularly in economics and business management literature. In an explanation of a performance management exercise and team development, one such article refers to "a wolf pack on the hunt" and the "pack leader":[94] "The process of team development involves the traditional employment contract, training, and performance, all with the advice of their coaching staff. In this model, teams interact to become 'a wolf pack on the hunt.' . . . The pack leader has the full responsibility to perform the accepted project until completed or changed." And in another article, the metaphor continues in "the repositioning of the firm from sick puppy to a pack leader."[95] Further examples of the use of scientific misinformation, or the misuse of scientific information, come from systems design.[96] Arguably, part of the appeal in these contexts is the emphasis on group behaviour, but persistent is the underlying narrative of dominance and submission and a clear hierarchy. Dominance, in this context, is self-reinforcing.[97]

A pack of nobodies

> 'I don't know,' I cried without being heard, 'I do not know. If nobody comes, then nobody comes. I've done nobody any harm, nobody's done me any harm, but nobody will help me. A pack of nobodies. Yet that isn't all true. Only, that nobody helps me – a pack of nobodies would be rather fine, on the other hand. I'd love to go on an excursion – why not? – with a pack of nobodies. Into the mountains, of course, where else? How these nobodies jostle each other, all these lifted arms linked together, these numberless feet treading so close! Of course they are all in dress suits. We go so gaily, the wind blows through us and the gaps in our company. Our throats swell and are free in the mountains! It's a wonder we don't burst into song.'[98]

The pack is a fiction of convenience. When we look closely, we see nobody, and all we see is nobody. Such is the contrivance of representation that the somebody of this story of property, that dog, is out of the picture. And yet, those tracks, that nuisance, that nobody will always already be in the way. Recalling Simmel, "Nobody . . . wants this influence."[99] And that is what is needed. Property needs help from a pack of nobodies.

Notes

1 Tim Ingold argues that there is a move from trust to domination through domestication in the context of pastoral and agricultural systems. He regards the relationship between hunter-gatherers and animals as more sharing, although humans are still manipulating the relationship; while under pastoralism he sees the animal as having ceded control to the shepherd: "They are cared for, but they are not themselves empowered to care. . . . In short, the relationship of pastoral care, quite unlike that of the hunter towards animals, is founded on a principle not of trust but of domination." See Ingold T (1994) From Trust to Domination: An Alternative History of Human-Animal Relations, in Manning A & Serpell J (eds.) *Animals and Human Society: Changing Perspectives*, Routledge, London, 1–22: p. 16.

2 Nedelsky J (1990) Law, Boundaries, and the Bounded Self, *Representations*, 30, 162–189: p. 162. This is replicated in balanced dog training discourse, which premises the dog's "freedom" on relations of dominance, authority, and leadership. Indeed, Cesar Millan, referring to the five freedoms of animal welfare, explicitly interprets "freedom to express normal behaviour" in the context of discipline: "The key word in this freedom is 'normal,' and the key to normalcy is discipline. Dogs want to work for their food and affection, and they want to please their pack leaders. You can also use discipline to reinforce the calm energy state you achieve after exercise." See www.cesarsway.com/five-freedoms/

3 For instance, in a review of the literature supporting their comparative study of eye contact with humans of dogs, wolves, and dingoes, Johnston et al. maintain that, "behavioural research clearly demonstrates that dogs' tendency to make eye contact with humans has drastically changed over the course of domestication," however, this does not seem immediately clear without certain fundamental assumptions about the initial contact in the domestication context. See Johnston AM et al. (2017) Uncovering the Origins of Dog-Human Eye Contact: Dingoes Establish Eye Contact More Than Wolves, But Less Than Dogs, *Animal*

Behaviour, 133, 123–129: p. 123. The authors hypothesise that "the initial motivation for canids to initiate interspecific eye contact with humans evolved early in domestication, but the motivation to maintain prolonged eye contact with a familiar human may have evolved later" (127). But it is unclear how this supposition arises from the results other than through an assumption of a quality of degree of domestication between wolf, dingo, and dog, and an intentionality or "authoring" of the dog through domestication, rather than this prosociality being one of the drivers of co-domestication. Similarly, Brian Hare and colleagues, in their research on canid domestication, similarly maintain that the results support "the domestication hypothesis: that dogs' social-communicative skills with humans were acquired during the process of domestication." See Hare B et al. (2002) The Domestication of Social Cognition in Dogs, *Science*, 298, 1634–1636. Indeed, it is also possible to interpret the research on oxytocin-eye contact between dogs and humans feedback loop in this context: Nagasawa M et al. (2015) Oxytocin-Gaze Positive Loop and the Coevolution of Human-Dog Bonds, *Science*, 348, 333–336. That is, where eye contact triggers the release of oxytocin in both species, this does not occur in a wolf-human dyad, even where wolves have been hand-reared. Whether this is the result of domestication of the persistence of dogs' sociality, it is not convincing that an answer is certain in the research, but the presumption is always in favour of a "socialisation" of the dog through ongoing domestication (i.e., enfolding) within human society. This is not to deny the possible co-evolution of the human-dog bond, it is simply to indicate the kinds of presumptions with respect to human intentionality in the domestication process that may persist through research design and interpretation.

4 For a more critical perspective on this dominant view, see Topál J (2009) Understanding the Dog: What Is It Like to Be a Human Creation?, *Journal of Veterinary Behavior*, 4(2), 45.
5 Frank J (1949) *Law and the Modern Mind*, Stevens & Sons, London, 37.
6 Tarde G (1890/[1903]) *The Laws of Imitation*, EC Parsons (trans.), Henry Holt & Co, New York, 79.
7 Tarde G (1890/[1903]) *The Laws of Imitation*, EC Parsons (trans.), Henry Holt & Co, New York, 80.
8 Tarde G (1893/[2012]) *Monadology and Sociology*, T Lorenc (trans.), Re-Press, Melbourne, 15.
9 Statute of Westminster.
10 Milson SFC (2003) *A Natural History of the Common Law*, Columbia UP, New York, 26.
11 Marshall A (1925) *Memorials of Alfred Marshall*, AC Pigou (ed.), Macmillan, London, 167–168. See further the discussion in Burkhardt RW, Jr (2008) The Nature of Evidence: How Well Do "Facts" Travel? London School of Economics, Working Paper 32/08.
12 Nancy J-L (2003) *A Finite Thinking*, Stanford UP, Stanford, 154.
13 Nancy J-L (2003) *A Finite Thinking*, Stanford UP, Stanford, 154.
14 Nancy J-L (2003) *A Finite Thinking*, Stanford UP, Stanford, 155.
15 "Legal fictions, of their nature, conceal what is going on. They are a pretence. They represent an unacknowledged departure from existing principle. By resorting to the fiction of equating the value of a document as a chattel or piece of paper with the value of the rights embodied or recorded on it the courts concealed the reality." *OBG Limited (Appellants) v Allan* [2007] UKHL 21, [2008] 1 AC 1 at [228–229], per Lord Nicholls of Birkenhead.
16 Nancy J-L (2003) *A Finite Thinking*, Stanford UP, Stanford, 156.
17 See further Devereux G (1967) *From Anxiety to Method in the Behavioral Sciences*, Mouton & Co, The Hague, 31. And further, that position is anthropocentric, an interpretation through human priorities, questions and prejudice.

18 For example, see Holmberg T (2019) Walking, Eating, Sleeping: Rhythm Analysis of Human/Dog Intimacy, *Emotion, Space and Society*, 26–31: p. 28.
19 For example, see Rezac P et al. (2017) Factors Affecting Dog Jumping on People, *Applied Animal Behaviour Science*, 197, 40–44.
20 Mills DS et al. (2010) *The Encyclopedia of Applied Animal Behaviour and Welfare*, CABI, Wallingford, OX.
21 Barrows EM (2011) *Animal Behavior Desk Reference: A Dictionary of Animal Behavior, Ecology, and Evolution*, 3rd ed., CRC Press, London. Barrows makes explicit reference to the problems of definition and urges researchers, "thoroughly research your concept and related concepts and their names." And indeed, one might add, the other meanings they bring with them to the definition.
22 Chaucher, *Legendary Good Women*: "And yit they were hethene, al the pak."
23 The *Complete Oxford English Dictionary* similarly includes this hunting purpose in the definition for a pack of hounds or wolves and indeed of birds, "which naturally associate for purposes of attack or defence," tracing the first use back to the 17th century in relation to fox hunting: "All joyn (like so many dogs in a pack) in pursuing these Foxes" (*Hunting the Fox*, 1648).
24 Property and intellectual property are also types of group nouns, which create objects or artefacts out of the sociality inhering in these relationships. This is discussed in more detail in 'Part 4, Altruism, the social age.'
25 As considered again in later chapters, the relationship between pack and herd also reflects a predatory property model, where herd is usually applied to groups of agricultural domestic animals, while pack is more often applied to wild predators.
26 Although perhaps without the same embedded literary and cultural metaphor, note also the similar problems relating to the term "dominance": Westgarth C (2016) Why Nobody Will Ever Agree about Dominance in Dogs, *Journal of Veterinary Behavior*, 11, 99–101.
27 Deleuze G & Guattari F (1980/[1987]) *A Thousand Plateaus: Capitalism and Schizophrenia*, B Massumi (trans.), U of Minnesota P, Minneapolis, 33.
28 Deleuze G & Guattari F (1980/[1987]) *A Thousand Plateaus: Capitalism and Schizophrenia*, B Massumi (trans.), U of Minnesota P, Minneapolis, 239.
29 Fernandes JG et al. (2017) Do Aversive-Based Training Methods Actually Compromise Dog Welfare? A Literature Review, *Applied Animal Behaviour Science*, 196, 1–12; Power ER (2012) Domestication and the Dog: Embodying Home, *Area*, 44(3), 371–378.
30 The carefully crafted mythic status of the National Geographic "Dog Whisperer" franchise, centred around Cesar Millan, is an outstanding example of this penetration of pack discourse in the popular psyche. Cesar Millan has been extensively criticised (both in the technical literature as well as more widely) for his slavish promotion of pack leadership and his use of aversive training methods. For example, see Ha JC & Campion TL (2019) *Dog Behavior: Modern Science and Our Canine Companions*, Academic Press, London: [I]t's dominance theory in its purest form, and it's purely misused" (167). See further Derr M (2006) Pack of Lies, *New York Times*, 31 August. Nevertheless, in a peer-reviewed article on access to expertise published in *Cognition*, albeit not authored by canine researchers (although perhaps this is precisely the point as it indicates the ubiquity of the myth), the authors use Cesar Millan as an example of perception of and access to expertise as an example of their thesis on recognition of expert knowledge. Millan is presented as the ultimate aim in access to dog training expertise: "For example, if someone has a question about how to train their dog, the best person to ask, arguably, would be the famous dog-whisperer Cesar Millan." See further Landrum AR & Mills CM (2015) Developing Expectations Regarding the Boundaries of Expertise, *Cognition*, 134, 215–231: p. 230. Two further examples come perhaps more surprisingly from critical animal studies. The first, notwithstanding

a brief paragraph acknowledging that Millan has faced criticism, proceeds with a somewhat uncritical celebration of Millan and his "exceptional gift" and replays the mythology of his own television biography: Smith JA (2012) The Meaning of "Energy" in Cesar Millan's Discourse on Dogs, in Smith JA & Mitchell RW (eds.) *Experiencing Animal Minds: An Anthology of Animal-Human Encounters*, Columbia UP, New York, 142–153. While the chapter is engaging in its discussion of kinaesthetics and dance, its choice of subject is unfortunate. It does not take account at all of the position of the dog, physically or mentally (or indeed the troubling and alarming stress postures and behaviours often offered by the dogs in the programme), within what are highly edited and contrived television excerpts. The second also undertakes a rather unexacting approach to Millan and the "excellent, transparent examples" in his television programme, in Pryor AE (2012) Heidegger and the Dog Whisperer: Imagining Interspecies Kindness, in Gross A & Vallely A (eds.) *Animals and the Human Imagination: A Companion to Animal Studies*, Columbia UP, New York, 289–306: p. 303. Both chapters have in common a somewhat trustful reading of the television programme and its highly edited and produced content, almost a blind faith, with a seemingly complete unawareness or lack of understanding of the actual behaviour presented in those programmes or the technical discourse surrounding them alone. In many cases the "remarkable transformation", as described by Pryor, is more often a case of tonic immobility or learned helplessness, with all the very serious welfare implications that indicates. Indeed, this is the potential problem when behaviour is analysed without engaging that dog as well, where that dog is taken for granted, as it were.

31 As Mech notes, "In the 448-page, 2003 book *Wolves: Behavior, Ecology, and Conservation*, edited by Luigi Boitani and myself and written by 23 authors, *alpha* is mentioned in only six places and then only to explain why the term is outdated. What gives? . . . science has come to understand that most wolf packs are merely family groups formed exactly the same way as human families are formed." See Mech LD (2008) Whatever Happened to the Term Alpha Wolf?, *International Wolf*, Winter, 4–8: p. 5.

32 Mech LD (1999) Alpha Status, Dominance, and Division of Labor in Wolf Packs, *Canadian Journal of Zoology*, 77, 1196–1203: p. 1196.

33 See Schenkel R (1947) Ausdrucks-Studien an Wölfen: Gefangenschafts-Beobachtungen, *Behaviour*, 1(2), 81–129, where it was hypothesised that packs formed in response to the onset of winter in order to facilitate greater hunting efficiency ahead of the more difficult season.

34 Mech LD (1999) Alpha Status, Dominance, and Division of Labor in Wolf Packs, *Canadian Journal of Zoology*, 77, 1196–1203: p. 1196. See further Mech LD and Boitani L (eds.) (2003) *Wolves: Behaviour, Ecology, and Conservation*, U of Chicago P, Chicago.

35 Schenkel R (1947) Ausdrucks-Studien an Wölfen: Gefangenschafts-Beobachtungen, *Behaviour*, 1(2), 81–129.

36 Schenkel R (1967) Submission: Its Features and Function in the Wolf and Dog, *American Zoologist*, 7(2), 319–329.

37 Compare the later research in free-ranging dogs: Bonanni R et al. (2010) Effect of Affiliative and Agonistic Relationships on Leadership Behaviour in Free-Ranging Dogs, *Animal Behaviour*, 79, 981–991. In this study, the authors conclude not only that leadership is not concentrated within a particular individual but also that "in free-ranging dogs leadership does not appear to be a simple function of dominance rank, and affiliation may play a role in mediating follower behaviour" (990). Free-ranging dogs are also recognised as "facultatively social" in Marshall-Pescini

S et al. (2017) Integrating Social Ecology in Explanations of Wolf-Dog Behavioural Differences, *Current Opinion in Behavioral Sciences*, 16, 80–86: p. 82. This is relevant not only to a confounding of the conventional notions of alpha and "pack leader" in popular training discourse but also to the discussion of training method and learning later in the Social Age. "Leadership" or better still, "prestige" (to borrow Tarde's term) benefits from an affiliative approach to learning these relationships, rather than an adversarial one, which is very relevant to the debate on positive reinforcement as compared to aversive or balanced training and the significance for incentive and enforcement paradigms in property (see the discussion in Chapter 10, "Shared interests").

38 For instance, see the comments in Sax B (2000/[2013]) *Animals in the Third Reich*, Yogh & Thorn Books, Pittsburgh, PA, 68. In its translation to dog training discourse, Schenkel's study was indeed flawed in terms of the artificial composition of the group, but at the same time, the interpretations of leadership battles and "dominant" personalities is a further misunderstanding of his observations, extrapolating them to the character of an individual from what are the stressors of a dynamic situation. Therefore, going into battle with pet dogs for the moniker of "pack leader" is a somewhat ludicrous misapplication of an already problematic study.

39 Schenkel R (1947) Ausdrucks-Studien an Wölfen: Gefangenschafts-Beobachtungen, *Behaviour*, 1(2), 81–129: p. 84.

40 Mech LD (1970/[1981]) *The Wolf: The Ecology and Behavior of an Endangered Species*, U of Minnesota P, Minneapolis.

41 Mech LD (1966) *The Wolves of Isle Royale*, United States Department of the Interior, Washington.

42 Mech LD (1966) *The Wolves of Isle Royale*, United States Department of the Interior, Washington, 61.

43 Schenkel R (1947) Ausdrucks-Studien an Wölfen: Gefangenschafts-Beobachtungen, *Behaviour*, 1(2), 81–129: pp. 87/11.

44 Anthony A (1955) Behavior Patterns in a Laboratory Colony of Prairie Dogs, *Cynomys Ludovicianus*, *Journal of Mammalogy*, 36(1), 69–78.

45 Gray GW (1955) The Yerkes Laboratories, *Scientific American*, 192(2), 67–77. Gray describes Alpha as "friendly, even-tempered, level-headed but not brilliant" (68).

46 Society for Science & the Public (1937) Apes Taught to Use Gestures to Enlist Aid in Joint Task, *The Science News-Letter*, 32(848), 23+30. Alpha, the chimpanzee, also appears in Robert Yerkes's studies of the same period. See further: Yerkes RM (1939) Social Dominance and Sexual Status in the Chimpanzee, *The Quarterly Review of Biology*, 14(2), 115–136; Yerkes RM & Nissen HW (1939) Pre-Linguistic Sign Behavior in Chimpanzee, *Science*, 89(2321), 585–587; Yerkes RM (1940) Laboratory Chimpanzees, *Science*, 91(2362), 336–337.

47 Society for Science & the Public (1940) Ape Babies to Be Trained in New Experimental Nursery, *The Science News-Letter*, 37(24), 374–375. There are indeed numerous studies in this period to which Alpha, the chimpanzee, contributes.

48 Simonds PE (1962) The Japan Monkey Center, *Current Anthropology*, 3(3), 303–305.

49 Ginsburg B & Allee WC (1942) Some Effects of Conditioning on Social Dominance and Subordination in Inbred Strains of Mice, *Physiological Zoology*, 15(4), 485–506. See also the use in chickens in Allee WC (1942) Group Organization among Vertebrates, *Science*, 95(2464), 289–293. And soon after in other species: Greenberg B & Noble GK (1944) Social Behavior of the American Chameleon (*Anolis carolinensis Voigt*), *Physiological Zoology*, 17(4), 392–439.

50 Mech LD (1999) Alpha Status, Dominance, and Division of Labor in Wolf Packs, *Canadian Journal of Zoology*, 77, 1196–1203: p. 1198.
51 Scott JP (1964) Leadership in Macaque Societies, *Science*, 144(3623), 1179.
52 Mech LD (1991) *The Way of the Wolf*, Voyageur Press, Stillwater, MN, 35. Indeed, this idea of dominance over animals is not unique to the human-dog relationship and is a somewhat pervasive manifestation of the nature/culture divide that fuels the narrative of human exceptionalism. I can recall from childhood many parents in pony club (although I hasten to add, not mine) yelling out to their children, "Show him who's boss!", "Don't let him get away with it," etc.
53 Mech LD (1991) *The Way of the Wolf*, Voyageur Press, Stillwater, MN, 14. See further the discussion of social bonding and pack structure, where the bonds between wolves are approximated to "a dog's bond to its master," which is described as "this very trait of the wolf that has remained in the dog and made that animal 'man's best friend'," in Mech LD (1970/[1981]) *The Wolf: The Ecology and Behavior of an Endangered Species*, U of Minnesota P, Minneapolis, 45–46.
54 Mech LD (1970/[1981]) *The Wolf: The Ecology and Behavior of an Endangered Species*, U of Minnesota P, Minneapolis: "To preserve its status, a wolf must constantly assert its position" (77).
55 Mech LD (1970/[1981]) *The Wolf: The Ecology and Behavior of an Endangered Species*, U of Minnesota P, Minneapolis, 73.
56 For example, owners are variously advised to eat first, to go through doors first, never to let the dog walk ahead, never to allow the dog to sit higher than the owner, never to let the dog sit on the sofa or sleep on the bed, all in the context of a discourse of boundaries and "knowing their place." When it comes to relationships with their dogs, trainers advising this kind of "balanced" training want to "build boundaries." See, for example, 5 Tips for Building Boundaries, www.cesarsway.com/5-tips-for-building-boundaries/ See further the discussion of training in Chapter 3 "Socialisation" and Chapter 10, "Shared interests."
57 Zimen E (1976) On the Regulation of Pack Size in Wolves, *Ethology*, 40(3), 300–341. See also Zimen E (1978/[1981]) *The Wolf: A Species in Danger*, E Mosbacher (trans.), Delacorte P, New York, in particular the discussion in Chapter 9.
58 Zimen E (1978/[1981]) *The Wolf: A Species in Danger*, E Mosbacher (trans.), Delacorte P, New York, 173 (emphasis added). See further, in particular, the discussion in Chapter 4. See also the discussion in Packard JM (2003) Wolf Behavior: Reproductive, Social, and Intelligent, in Mech LD & Boitani L (eds.) *Wolves: Behavior, Ecology, and Conservation*, U of Chicago P, Chicago, 35–65: pp. 53–54.
59 Mech LD (1999) Alpha Status, Dominance, and Division of Labor in Wolf Packs, *Canadian Journal of Zoology*, 77, 1196–1203.
60 Zimen E (1978/[1981]) *The Wolf: A Species in Danger*, E Mosbacher (trans.), Delacorte P, New York.
61 Mech LD (1999) Alpha Status, Dominance, and Division of Labor in Wolf Packs, *Canadian Journal of Zoology*, 77, 1196–1203: p. 1197.
62 Mech LD (1999) Alpha Status, Dominance, and Division of Labor in Wolf Packs, *Canadian Journal of Zoology*, 77, 1196–1203: p. 1198. As Mech notes, alpha status is not stable even in captive packs, and there is no inherent permanent social status (1197). In many respects this has much in common with the creative immanence of Deleuze and Guattari's pack. In other words, there is no inherent identity as "dominant." See further Deleuze G & Guattari F (1980/[1987]) *A Thousand Plateaus: Capitalism and Schizophrenia*, B Massumi (trans.), U of Minnesota P, Minneapolis, 239–243. The problems with the dominance concept are discussed later in this chapter.
63 Mech LD et al. (2015) *Wolves on the Hunt: The Behavior of Wolves Hunting Wild Prey*, U of Chicago P, Chicago, xii. See further the discussion in Mech LD (2008)

Whatever Happened to the Term Alpha Wolf?, *International Wolf*, Winter, 4–8: "Given this natural history of wolf packs, there is no more reason to refer to the parent wolves as alphas than there would be to refer to the parents of a human family as the 'alpha' pair. Thus, we now refer to these animals as the male breeder and female breeder and as the breeding pair or simply the parents" (6).
64 Mech LD & Boitani L (2003) Wolf Social Ecology, in Mech LD and Boitani L (eds.) *Wolves: Behaviour, Ecology, and Conservation*, U of Chicago P, Chicago, 1–34: p. 7.
65 For extensive material related to his revised position on alpha terminology, including videos and popularised outreach, see David Mech's own website: https://davemech.org
66 See the discussion in Bradshaw JWS et al. (2009) Dominance in Domestic Dogs: Useful Construct or Bad Habit?, *Journal of Veterinary Behavior*, 4, 135–144. Much of the (misplaced) advice on "becoming pack leader" follows a property-like model for evidence of prestige (as seen in Veblen's account of predatory capitalism). This includes references to a kind of esteem or prestige (for example, walking ahead) as well as to space (for example, setting boundaries on attention and place) and indeed resources (for example, eating first, controlling access to food, and so on). See further www.cesarsway.com for more examples of this approach.
67 For instance, see www.cesarsway.com
68 Bain M (2019) Overview of Animal Training: A Welfare Perspective, in Chun Choe J (ed.) (2019) *Encyclopedia of Animal Behavior*, Vol. 1, 2nd ed., Academic Press, Amsterdam, 203–213: pp. 203–204. The persistence of this misinformation is repeated in the popular training literature. See further the discussion of sources of information (including popular media) and education status in Todd Z (2018) Barriers to the Adoption of Humane Dog Training Methods, *Journal of Veterinary Behavior*, 25, 28–34. A study published in 2017 revealed a significant repetition of misleading or even dangerous misinformation in popular training texts: Brown CM et al. (2017) Examination of the Accuracy and Applicability of Information in Popular Books on Dog Training, *Society and Animals*, 25, 411–435. In this study, the authors selected a sample of five best-selling training books published in English and reviewed them for accuracy with respect to learning theory and human-directed cues. The five subject titles were chosen for their persistent popularity and thus likely influence (the first search was conducted in 2009 where the titles were in the top five, and repeated in 2012, where the titles remained in the top 11, and in 2014, where they were in the top 20, despite numerous publications of new training titles in the interim). See further Bradshaw JWS et al. (2009) Dominance in Domestic Dogs: Useful Construct or Bad Habit?, *Journal of Veterinary Behavior*, 4, 135–144.
69 Kerkhove W van (2004) A Fresh Look at the Wolf-Pack Theory of Companion-Animal Dog Social Behavior, *Journal of Applied Animal Welfare Science*, 7(4), 279–285.
70 As Mech explains, abandoning the old "loaded terminology" would do much to reform terminology and further "both science's and the public's more accurate perception of the wolf." See Mech D (2008) Whatever Happened to the Term Alpha Wolf?, *International Wolf*, Winter, 4–8: p. 8.
71 Mills DS et al. (2010) *The Encyclopedia of Applied Animal Behaviour and Welfare*, CAB International, Wallingford, OX, 182–183.
72 Mech LD (2008) Whatever Happened to the Term Alpha Wolf?, *International Wolf*, Winter, 4–8: p. 7. Mech's reference to political correctness is striking in the context of the often highly polarised positions in training. Intriguingly, the change in terminology has been vilified in aversive-based dog training circles as "political

correctness": "David Mech's wild wolf observations . . . simply decided to veer away from accurate terminology in the field of ethology and replace it with more 'politically correct terms.'" See Michael D'Abruzzo's post on the Schenkel studies at https://dogtraining.world/knowledge-base/expression-studies-on-wolves-rudolph-schenkel (note Schenkel's name is misspelled in the original). Many of the advocates of "balanced" training, which relies upon a lot of the outdated theory of pack behaviour, dispute the insistence on science-based training and criticise non-aversive methods as "political correctness" and the proponents of reinforcement training as "liberals," among other similarly contextual pejorative language. The relationship between political positions, populism, education, and dog training methods is a complex area that is well beyond the scope of the present text.

73 Tarde G (1890/[1903]) *The Laws of Imitation*, EC Parsons (trans.), Henry Holt & Co, New York, 382.
74 Schenkel R (1947) Ausdrucks-Studien an Wölfen: Gefangenschafts-Beobachtungen, *Behaviour*, 1(2), 81–129: pp. 84/6.
75 Mech LD (2008) Whatever Happened to the Term Alpha Wolf?, *International Wolf*, Winter, 4–8: p. 6.
76 Simmel G (1950) *The Sociology of Georg Simmel*, KH Wolff (trans.), The Free Press, Glencoe, IL, 181.
77 Simmel G (1950) *The Sociology of Georg Simmel*, KH Wolff (trans.), The Free Press, Glencoe, IL, 181–182.
78 See for example the response by Barbara Smuts to Bernstein IS (1981) Dominance: The Baby and the Bathwater, *The Behavioral and Brain Sciences*, 4, 419–457. Smuts notes the emphasis in research on the presumed reliability, generality, and stability of these relationships and suggests that "Developing a general and universally agreed upon concept of dominance should not be a primary goal of primatologists." See Smuts B (1981) Dominance: An Alternative View, *The Behavioral and Brain Sciences*, 4, 448–449. See further the response of Vessey SH (1981) Dominance as Control, *The Behavioral and Brain Sciences*, 4, 449, in which the author emphasises instead the "communicative aspects" of dominance.
79 Bradshaw JWS et al. (2009) Dominance in Domestic Dogs: Useful Construct or Bad Habit?, *Journal of Veterinary Behavior*, 4, 135–144: p. 135. The authors note that in training and behaviour literature, dominance "tends to be misapplied as a motivation for social interactions, rather than simply a quality of that relationship. Hence, it is commonly suggested that a desire 'to be dominant' actually drives behavior, especially aggression, in the domestic dog" (135).
80 Simmel G (1950) *The Sociology of Georg Simmel*, KH Wolff (trans.), The Free Press, Glencoe, IL, 185.
81 Zimen E (1978/[1981]) *The Wolf: A Species in Danger*, E Mosbacher (trans.), Delacorte P, New York, 173. See also the observations in Bonanni R et al. (2010) Effect of Affiliative and Agonistic Relationships on Leadership Behaviour in Free-Ranging Dogs, *Animal Behaviour*, 79, 981–999.
82 Devereux G (1967) *From Anxiety to Method in the Behavioral Sciences*, Mouton & Co, The Hague, 31.
83 Simmel G (1950) *The Sociology of Georg Simmel*, KH Wolff (trans.), The Free Press, Glencoe, IL, 186.
84 Bhabha HK (1985) Signs Taken for Wonders: Questions of Ambivalence and Authority under a Tree Outside Delhi, May 1817, *Critical Inquiry*, 12(1), 144–165: p. 153.
85 Hobson JA (1902) The Scientific Basis of Imperialism, *Political Science Quarterly*, 17(3), 460–489.

86 Lehrman DS (1953) A Critique of Konrad Lorenz's Theory of Instinctive Behavior, *Quarterly Review of Biology*, 28(4), 337–363; Kalikow TJ (1983) Konrad Lorenz's Ethological Theory: Explanation and Ideology, 1938–1943, *Journal of the History of Biology*, 16(1), 39–73; Sax B (1997) What Is a "Jewish Dog"? Konrad Lorenz and the Cult of Wildness, *Society and Animals*, 5(1), 3–21.

87 See the contemporaneous discussion and literature review in Bartlett D & Bartlett F (1971) Social Implications of Biological Determinism, *Science and Society*, 35(2), 209–219. The authors note, "In recent years, there has been an astonishing spate of publications hailing the 'new biology' as the means for understanding the crises and dilemmas of our century" (209).

88 Sax B (2000/[2013]) *Animals in the Third Reich*, Yogh & Thorn Books, Pittsburgh, PA, 67. Sax goes on to note Schenkel's gendered dominance hierarchies, with a different hierarchy for males and females, and compares this to the hierarchy imposed on women in Nazi Germany: "This corresponded exactly to the hierarchal structure that the Nazis endeavored to create in their society. The hierarchy of women in Nazi Germany was somewhat distinct from that of men" (68).

89 Schenkel R (1967) Submission: Its Features and Function in the Wolf and Dog, *American Zoologist*, 7(2), 319–329.

90 Sax B (2000/[2013]) *Animals in the Third Reich*, Yogh & Thorn Books, Pittsburgh, PA, 81.

91 Medawar PB & Medawar JS (1983) *Aristotle to Zoos*, Harvard UP, Cambridge, MA, 4.

92 This can be seen through a range of examples and legislative responses, including racial profiling in humans and "breed profiling" in dogs, with dangerous dogs' legislation around the world and an almost consistent approach to regulating breeds and prohibiting ownership of certain breeds (and thus the dog as property) rather than responding to the welfare aspects of training methods, owner responsibility, and so on: *you cannot change nature*.

93 For example, see Essler JL et al. (2017) Domestication Does Not Explain the Presence of Inequity Aversion in Dogs, *Current Biology*, 27(12), 1861–1865.e3. See further Ha JC & Campion TL (2019) *Dog Behavior: Modern Science and Our Canine Companions*, Academic Press, London, 139–154.

94 Canedo JC et al. (2019) Let's Make Performance Management Work for New Hires: They Are the Future, *Organizational Dynamics*, 47, 229–233: p. 231.

95 Gilbert DH et al. (2015) Osmotic Strategy: Innovating at the Core to Inspire at the Edges, *Organizational Dynamics*, 44, 217–225: p. 222.

96 Eccles DW & Groth PT (2007) Wolves, Bees, and Football: Enhancing Coordination in Sociotechnological Problem Solving Systems through the Study of Human and Animal Groups, *Computers in Human Behavior*, 23, 2778–2790.

97 Karen Pryor suggests that punishment can be reinforcing for the punisher, "because it demonstrates and helps to maintain dominance," and that "the punisher may be primarily interested not in behaviour but in being proved to be of higher status." As she argues: "Do you want the dog, the child, the spouse, the employee to alter a given behaviour? In that case, it's a training problem, and you need to be aware of the weaknesses of punishment as a training device. Or do you really want revenge? In that case you should seek more wholesome reinforcers for yourself." See Pryor K (2002) *Don't Shoot the Dog! The New Art of Teaching and Training*, Rev ed., Ringpress, Dorking, 108.

98 Kafka F (1913/[1992]) Excursion into the Mountains, W Muir & E Muir (trans.), *The Complete Stories of Franz Kafka*, Minerva, London, 383.

99 Simmel G (1950) *The Sociology of Georg Simmel*, KH Wolff (trans.), The Free Press, Glencoe, IL, 181.

Chapter 9
Wild abandon

Qu'ils retournent à leur niche soyeuse et capitonnée ! Je chante le chien crotté, le chien pauvre, le chien sans domicile, le chien flâneur, le chien saltimbanque, le chien dont l'instinct, comme celui du pauvre, du bohémien et de l'histrion, est merveilleusement aiguillonné par la nécessité, cette si bonne mère, cette vraie patronne des intelligences!
                        Baudelaire C, Petits poëmes en prose (le spleen de Paris),
                                          Louis Conard, Paris, 1926: p. 174

For I sing the mangy dog, the pitiful, the homeless dog, the roving dog, the circus dog, the dog whose instinct, like that of the gypsy and the strolling player, has been so wonderfully sharpened by necessity, marvelous mother and true patroness of native wit.
    Baudelaire C (1869) The Faithful Dog, L Varèse (trans), in Baudelaire C (1869/[1970]) *Paris Spleen*, New Directions, New York, 104–107: p. 105.[1]

The pathway to property, traced by domestication, introduced a whole new identity for the dog – that of the stray. The once self-possessing dog became the "resident alien."[2]

Stray dogs, abandoned dogs, lost dogs, feral dogs, street dogs, homeless dogs, rescue dogs, shelter dogs, stolen dogs – there are many descriptors of dogs related to the property narrative, facilitated by the predatory drift towards the bounded animal. There is even an explicit slogan of rescue campaigns that incorporates this positioning: "Rescue is my favourite breed." Although this is a strategic move,[3] addressing the fashions of various breeds and the stigma against mixed breeds (and even the language of mixed breed is problematic), it does nevertheless perpetuate the attachment to "brand" as fashioned through the commodified dog.[4] And then we have purebred dogs, pedigreed dogs, working dogs, dangerous dogs,[5] designer dogs, and pet dogs. And even "foreign dogs" with cross-border rescue initiatives provoking an undercurrent of xenophobia.[6]

An artefact of human exceptionalism that persists in the domestication story is that of the supposed human intentionality in domestication, at the same time establishing a boundary between the "noble savage," as it were, and the diminished domesticate. This manifests in the celebration of naturalness[7] and the "cult of the wild,"[8] denigrating the domesticate as a kind in decline.[9] This is yet another form of human exceptionalism (tinted with a disconcerting wash of social Darwinism) in protecting the distinction and erecting the boundaries between the natural world and the human.[10] As John Baird Callicott notes: "wilderness is an ethnocentric concept."[11]

Le chien flâneur

Baudelaire sings "le chien flâneur," the roving dog, the good dog. But from where does the good dog rove? And to where? What is the stray if not a wanderer and a composition produced entirely through the external construction of boundaries, through property and urbanity?

> I sing the luckless dog who wanders alone through the winding ravines of huge cities, or the one who blinks up at some poor outcast of society with his spiritual eyes, as much as to say: "take me with you, and out of our joint misery we will make a kind of happiness."[12]

The flâneur holds the regard of many literary perspectives, including that of Baudelaire himself. Walter Benjamin's famous expositions upon the urban wanderer, the flâneur, offer genuine insight into the wandering, straying, outlaw dog. In particular, the flâneur remarks upon space and sees through, so to speak, the exudative skin of property, recalling the sociable animal territories of the Space Age, and yet outlining the joints and divisions of the city's propertied anatomies, at once both sidetracked and heading off: "The flâneur plays the role of scout in the marketplace. As such, he is also the explorer of the crowd."[13]

Benjamin speaks of the "porosity" of the twentieth century and the simultaneity of being at once both inside and outside, in the development of the arcades and through the figure of the flaneur, released into the crowd:[14] "Landscape – that, in fact, is what Paris becomes for the flâneur. Or, more precisely: the city splits for him into its dialectical poles. It opens up to him as a landscape, even as it closes around him as a room."[15] The flâneur is at once undomesticated and yet at home, confounding the separation of private and public so instrumental to the predatory model of property.

The flâneur is similarly inside and outside, insight and outsight, both within the property framework and yet abandoned to the crowd: "Dialectic of flâneurie: on one side, the man who feels himself viewed by all and sundry as a true suspect and, on the other side, the man who is utterly undiscoverable, the hidden man."[16] The flâneur's straying is always already *in personam*, as it were. Thus, the flâneur, the stray, the spectator is the constant; it is the landscape that changes as a work in progress, constituted and reconstituted as it is by its changing perspectives.

Thus, the predatory drift towards boundary-making produces the stray, a legal fiction, as it were, one that is necessary in order to maintain the rules of property. It presumes a lack of territory, a lack of intentionality, a lack of kin, in order to sustain the legitimacy of exceptionalism and to conceal the construction of that distinction: "Legal fictions, of their nature, conceal what is going on. They are a pretence."[17] However, the stray is not without territory but realises it through use and through footwork. The flâneur's wandering, paradoxically, is not purposeless and getting lost is not valueless, unlike the usual reckoning of the stray. Rather, the flâneur's perambulations are creative and innovative in their perspective-taking:[18] "To the flâneur, his city is – even if, like Baudelaire, he happened to be born there – no longer native ground. It represents for him a theatrical display, an arena."[19] Thus, the landscape is always unfolding into the distance, always anew: *finally unfinished*. This resonates with Uexküll's *Umwelt*, the surrounding world of the world of action and the world-as-sensed.[20] The flâneur does not focus on one single aspect of the landscape, enucleating objects and cutting off conversations. The flâneur does not simply trace a map; the flâneur makes the map, and that takes some work, "quite a different schooling":

> Not to find one's way in a city may well be uninteresting and banal. It requires ignorance – nothing more. But to lose oneself in a city – as one loses oneself in a forest – that calls for quite a different schooling. Then, signboards and street names, passers-by, roofs, kiosks, or bars must speak to the wanderer like a cracking twig under his feet in the forest, like the startling call of a bittern in the distance, like the sudden stillness of a clearing with a lily standing erect at its center. Paris taught me this art of straying; it fulfilled a dream that had shown its first traces in the labyrinths on the blotting pages of my school exercise books.[21]

This is not a world of objects, but a field of desires. And we are looking for the tracks, not the lion.

The scavage beast

Similarly, the emphasis on the dog as scavenger (which is nevertheless still an intentional activity) propels a story of domestication as accident, the kind of wandering purposelessness that attends the stray, which is consistent with the reaffirmation of that dog's more marginal position in relation to the emerging tale of property.[22] Further, in obscuring the link between that dog's first action and the subsequent development of agriculture through the imitation of domestication, that dog is remembered as without impact, without history, simply an accident within an otherwise human narrative.

In the domestication story, then, the theory of that dog as scavenger, or even thief, raises an interesting presupposition. While the scavenger theory does dispute purposive actions, if any, on the part of the humans, these nevertheless persist in versions of the taming narrative. The ongoing popular acceptance of the taming theory (and thus a premise of control[23]) diminishes the actions of that dog almost entirely, creating a narrative through which the "stray" and "feral" dog become accepted stories, socially engineered legal fictions in the lore of human exceptionalism, as it were.[24] The scavenger theory (particularly as accompanied by theories of subsequent and purposive taming and selection) also moves away some distance from the intentionality of the dog as pastoralist, as inventor, and teacher. In fact, it is almost as though domestication happened by chance, strayed into completely by accident, and refined through human opportunity.

As in earlier discussion, the meaning of scavenger shares an etymological history with scavage.[25] Scavage was a type of taxation imposed by the City of London and other municipalities until the sixteenth century in the form of a toll or custom collected from stranger merchants for their foreign wares. This extended to their children as well (known as "strangers' sons"[26]): "such sons had always paid the duties of package, bailage, and scavage, as other strangers do, and ought to do."[27] Scavage, along with other taxes and duties, served as a boundary-making device, delimiting, policing the inside and outside of English society: "the duties of package, scavage, and bailage served as a point of friction for the boundaries of Englishness throughout the seventeenth century."[28] As distinct from the relatedness of pastoral territory-making, integral to the debtor of the scavage are the notions of exclusion, trespass, and rivalry. Indeed, the stranger. The scavenger is an artefact of society's "predatory drift."

And as scavenger that dog is constructed as a stranger, an interloper, an intruder, a trespasser. That dog is a nuisance! But of course, how can one trespass on property that does not exist? It was in fact that dog who introduced the possibility of settlement and territory and the potential for later civilisation. Perhaps some scraps were available along the way, but it was that dog who practised a form of property and territory. It was the humans who intruded upon the dogs.

This rendering of the scavenger domestication narrative is thus flawed for the fictions it presumes in order to float. Whether scavenger or otherwise, that dog offers and changes the relations with humans. The dog is thus the *scavage* beast, one who both inspects and shows, both guards and regards, both defends and displays.[29] Unlike the flâneur, who is in a relation with their territory, the *scavage*, the stranger merchant, like a tourist, a visitor, must depart. Notions of scavengers frame the dog as outsider, to be banished.[30] A question for contemporary property jurisprudence is thus the regard for the stray, the flâneur, and the potential for the other strays within the property paradigm – the trespassers, the users, the consumers.

The paradoxical nature of the stranger in the context of this revisiting of the domestication story is instructive – the stranger is both distant and yet close, unknown and yet desirable. The stranger bridges the distance between scouts and followers, inventors and imitators, householder and lodger, producers and consumers. And then in some ways, those bridges are burned in contemporary property frameworks. What is the nature of having? What is the nature of the wanderer?

What then of the dog as stranger, the stranger who came to stay? At this stage of the story, it is important to turn to the explicit construction of the animal and, in particular, the dog, within property frameworks. The notion of the stray as outcast, outlaw, and moral outsider[31] provides insight into the various and different beings involved in property relations more widely, including the status of consumers, users, trespassers, and other strays in contemporary property frameworks.

Stray thoughts

This carving up of animal territories from the natural, through the domesticated, to the pet and so on, organises the landscape along property boundaries and conceals the kind of "joint action," or *concurrence*, to use Tarde's terminology.[32] This includes the demarcation of pets as those without productive value, as distinct from other domestic animals which have a functional value, rather than recognising a complex interaction of roles within the one being. In other words, the social spheres of human-animal relationships become delineated following the lead of conventional property narratives, as distinct from embracing animal territories through a sociable property. When it comes to the pet dog, there is even a narrative of rewilding, *becoming feral*.[33] Once again, the discourse of naturalness as applied to the domesticated dog denies the intentionality of that dog in their own domestication (and the domestication of the human), instead rendering that dog unstable and enslaved by atavistic traits to which they will inevitably revert if not for their ongoing management and discipline by human beings.

The history of pet-keeping is an example of this presumed causality in the domestication narrative. Pet-keeping is often presumed to have been a development that emerged with the ruling classes and subsequently made popular by the establishment of the middle classes in the eighteenth century with the rise of mercantilism and consumer culture.[34] This narrative is obviously always already situating the pet as property, and indeed the "pet" is propagated by the changes in fortunes and fashions that attend the rise of the consumer in the eighteenth and nineteenth centuries. However, this dominant narrative completely obscures the much longer history of pet-keeping,[35] one that is far more social than it is proprietary[36] – the Stone Age of property, commencing with that dog.

This forgetting of earlier pet-keeping, or distinguishing it as something other than the "excess" and "familiarity" of middle-class sentimentality, is resonant of classical anthropology and the same kind of distinction drawn between the "property-less" primitive human and the private property of modern society. Nomads are mobile but not without territory. Nomads are not consumers but they are not without property. Indeed, the "pet" in primitive cultures and nomadic societies embodies the idea of a sociable, mobile property, not in the form of the "thing" with which we obsess today, but rather in the form of the familial, the familiar, the relation that might be revived through a more sociable approach to property. You can choose your family.

Inside out

> We must distinguish three kinds of animals. First, individuated animals, family pets, sentimental, Oedipal animals each with its own petty history, "my" cat, "my" dog. These animals invite us to regress, draw us into a narcissistic contemplation, and they are the only kind of animal psychoanalysis understands, the better to discover a daddy, a mommy, a little brother behind them (when psychoanalysis talks about animals, animals learn to laugh): *anyone who likes cats or dogs is a fool.*[37]

> What if we did learn to laugh about the obligatory narratives leading to the casting of an opposition between social and human values, and an asocial technico-scientific logic? What if we felt free to describe the innovation starting from the social and political question of the force relations which produced the difference between those who have got the means to intervene in this history and those whose right to do so has not been recognized?[38]

What if?

Deleuze and Guattari appear to presume the narrative of pet-keeping as a sentimental enterprise of the modern age, marking cats and dogs as Oedipal animals, thus setting themselves on an uncertain path. Haraway admonishes Deleuze and Guattari "in their disdain for the daily, the ordinary, the affectional rather than the sublime."[39] Haraway notes: "I am not sure I can find in philosophy a clearer display of misogyny, fear of aging, incuriosity about animals, and horror at the ordinariness of flesh, here covered by the alibi of an anti-Oedipal and anticapitalist project."[40] And perhaps this is all because Deleuze and Guattari have their history wrong and indeed their science. The history of the pet dog is much older than Victorian sentimentality, much more wide open than the emergence of nineteenth-century breed books. Indeed, in deriding the pet as a recent and sentimental invention, Deleuze and Guattari are astonishingly complicit with the doctrine of human exceptionalism that revises the history as such, with all the deafness to science and smugness of the bourgeois cult of the wild that goes with that.

In an eight-hour series of interviews with Claire Parnet, Deleuze explains:

> But the cats, the dogs . . . the problem is that they are familial and familiar animals. And it is true that familial and familiar animals, if domesticated or tamed, I do not like. Nevertheless, the domesticated animals that are not familial, not familiar, I like them much as I am sensitive in something in them. . . . What do I find unpleasant? I do not like things that *rub*. A cat spends its time rubbing itself against you. I do not like that. A dog is another matter, what I fundamentally reproach the dogs for, is to bark. Barking

seems to me the most stupid cry ever . . . the barking is the shame of the animal kingdom.[41]

And yet humans never stop.

But in this distinction between unfamiliar domesticated animals and familiar, once again Deleuze has been fooled by the myth and diminishes the social competence of farmed animals, again to the detriment of their welfare.[42] In many respects, adhering to these artificial distinctions imposed upon animal populations provides for the ongoing position of human dominance and power over the natural world. A reaction against sentimentality is thus also a reinforcement of that exceptionalism. It reinforces the view that domestication was and is simply a story of mastery, often obscuring the agency and affiliative competence of the domesticates themselves.[43] And while in many examples of the human imitation of that capital invention this has proven to be true, mastery was by no means the mechanism for that first domestication. In summarising the history of domestication as domination, the very capabilities of domesticated animals are forgotten.[44] Deleuze and Guattari may be right about the aspect of narcissistic contemplation, but it is in the vanity project of the human authorship for the dog's domestication.

What if we did learn to laugh?

> Learning to laugh again is not to be against speculation as such. Why should we abstain from speculating? It breaks up the closed field in which the interest and fate of these speculations is decided. This field is defined by the difference between those whose right to debate, to bear weight on history, to be interested, and to demand accountability is recognized . . . and the 'public' to whom an image of science as 'authoritative' is presented. The fact that science is no longer debated in salons, that it no longer makes us laugh, is in no way because the closed field is defined by relations of competence.[45]

At once we must learn to laugh. Like the fools that we are. Like animals.

Outside in

Tarde explains, in what has become a refrain, there is no such thing as the social contract: "We ceased long ago to believe in Rousseau's 'social contract.' We know that far from having been the first tie between human wills, contract was a bond of slow formation, that it took centuries of subjection to the empire of the coercive decree, of the passively obeyed command, to suggest the idea of the reciprocal decree, as it were, of the complex bond by which two wills are linked together in alternate command and obedience. Nevertheless, many people still believe, although the error is quite similar, that exchange was the first step taken by mankind. This was not so at all. Before the idea of exchanging came that of present making or that of thieving, much simpler relations."[46]

Giorgio Agamben similarly rejects this exchange as "the first tie," identifying instead the ban as the original juridico-political relation: "what the ban holds together is precisely bare life and sovereign power. All representations of the originary political act as a contract or convention marking the passage from nature to the State in a discrete and definite way must be left wholly behind."[47] The State of Nature, the "cult of the wild," is thus not the first or original tie, but rather, it is "the State tie,"[48] a mechanism of sovereign exceptionalism. Rather this state of nature is instrumental in the protection of a predatory social architecture: "This is why in Hobbes, the foundation of sovereign power is to be sought not in the subjects' free renunciation of their natural right but in the sovereign's preservation of his natural right to do anything to anyone, which now appears as the right to punish."[49]

At once the predatory drift of that "bond of slow formation" can be deciphered:

> Far from being a prejuridical condition that is indifferent to the law of the city, the Hobbesian state of nature is the exception and the threshold that constitutes and dwells within it. It is not so much a war of all against all as, more precisely, a condition in which everyone is bare life and a *homo sacer* for everyone else, and in which everyone is thus *wargus, gerit caput lupinum*.[50]

To the stranger everyone is a wolf: *homo homini lupus*.[51]

The ban is thus both the abandonment of the animal and the organisation of animal sociable territories into regulated and territorialised property: "The understanding of the Hobbesian mythologeme in terms of *contract* instead of *ban* condemned democracy to impotence every time it had to confront the problem of sovereign power and has also rendered modern democracy constitutionally incapable of truly thinking a politics freed from the form of the State."[52] As such, the cincture of exceptionalism is both gasping but unbreachable: "Here there is, instead, a much more complicated zone of indiscernibility between *nomos* and *physis*, in which the State tie, having the form of a ban, is always already also non-State and pseudo-nature, and in which nature always already appears as *nomos* and the state of exception."[53] Thus, the *homo sacer, wargus*, the bandit, the outcast, the outlier, the animal is both inside and outside the law, a legal fiction, inside out and outside in. A place of confinement and at once always already abandoned:

> He who has been banned is not, in fact, simply set outside the law and made indifferent to it but rather *abandoned* by it, that is, exposed and threatened on the threshold in which life and law, outside and inside, become indistinguishable. It is literally not possible to say whether the one who has been banned is outside or inside the juridical order. . . . It is in this sense that the paradox of sovereignty can take the form "There is nothing outside the law." *The originary relation of law to life is not application but Abandonment*.[54]

That dog is thus *impounded*.

That dog looked back

Thus, the ban is inescapably reciprocal.

> Let ourselves be abandoned to what, if not to what abandonment abandons to? The origin of "abandonment" is a putting at, *bandon*. *Bandon* (*bandum, band, bannen*) is an order, a prescription, a decree, a permission, and the power that holds these freely at its disposal. To *abandon* is to remit, entrust, or turn over to such a sovereign power, and to remit, entrust, or turn over to its *ban*, that is, to its proclaiming, to its convening, and to its sentencing.[55]

The ban at once involves a functional dialectic, an algebra of political and juridical relations. It is both an order and a permission, a submission and a claim, a desertion and a freedom:

> Abandonment respects the law; it cannot do otherwise. That does not mean that there is any question of a forced respect, one consequently deprived of the characteristic value of respect. That "it cannot do otherwise" means it cannot be otherwise, it is not otherwise. Abandonment is abandonment to respect of the law, to respect the wholeness of the law's other side. Prior to all other determinations, and as the origin of all other determinations (fear and trembling, submission, veneration, imitation, compliance), respect is a gaze, a regard (*respectus*). It is not an optical regard, and still less a speculative regard, which would stare at the law. It is a regard that does not raise its eyes, and perhaps does not open them. It is also, and in the first place, a look back (*re-spicere*): turned toward the *before* of abandonment, where there is nothing to see, which is not to be seen. It is not a regard for the invisible, it is not an ideal or ideational regard. It is the *consideration* of abandonment. By respecting the law, abandonment respects itself, so to speak (and the law respects it). It turns back – not to perceive itself, but to receive itself.[56]

The dog looked back.

In this respect, as it were, in this regard, this "fear and trembling, submission, veneration, imitation, compliance,", the fundamental social value of prestige tells the story.[57] In that respect, in that gaze, there is attention, and in that attention, intention. This resonates with Tarde's approach to being and having – the animal, the outcast, is not resolved through "to be" but through a dynamic and relational "having." Agamben's ontology of relations as distinct from the identity of being; Nancy's "being-with" in an always already circumstance of relations ("Being is in common. What could be simpler to establish?"[58]); Tarde's reciprocity in having is sounding, and is listening, inventing and imitating, showing and answering. This is an ontology of relations; a system of property through contact, not of alienation.

Donna Haraway, in her approach to *respecere*, sees respect as a looking back and a looking back again, a reconsideration and a reiteration of multispecies relationships. Respect is a performance, a relation, an offer: "Looking back in this way takes us to seeing again, to *respecere*, to the act of respect. To hold in regard, to respond, to look back reciprocally, to notice, to pay attention, to have courteous regard for, to esteem: all of that is tied to polite greeting, to constituting the polis, where and when species meet."[59] The polite greeting is important, with the emphasis on relation as distinct from boundaries in administering the circumstances of society. It is sympathetic, friendly, animated. Haraway speaks of *response-ability*, "which is always experienced in the company of significant others," including animals.[60] Response-ability is thus a fundamental expression of *becoming-with*, of the performance of respect. Some decades earlier, the gestalt theorist, Friedrick (Fritz) Perls, also referred to *response-ability* in the context of gestalt therapy, a form of psychotherapy focusing on the moment, the here and now; that is, the present situation and environment.[61] This environmental model of therapy suggests some useful interactions with the sensation of sociability and embodied communication that this book has been exploring. Rather than a representational model of development, this is a therapy of pure sensation. Perls's understanding of response-ability thus engages with a similar reciprocity through relations. He defines it as, "the ability to respond: The ability to be alive, to feel, to be sensitive," which he distinguishes from obligation as something which is compelled, rather than offered, as well as implying a certain taking over (responsibility for) the other person.[62] In this way, Perls's notion of response-ability is a similar kind of ethical encounter between two autonomous beings, as distinct from simply being responsible for the other. This has interesting historical germs of Haraway's enriched concept of *respecere*.

This reciprocity, this looking back, is also insistent in Tarde's perspective on manners and imitation: "Politeness is merely reciprocity of flattery . . . the general need of being flattered, waited on, and saluted like a nobleman, was the secret factor which little by little, in France and elsewhere, made every man polite."[63] In other words, the regulation of society, the Hobbesian divestment of the citizen of the right "to do whatsoever he thought necessary for his own preservation," indeed is established not through punishing, as such, but through the imitation of courtesy.[64]

As we have seen, the predatory drift that turns aside sociability has produced a distorted property in no need of courtesy. In attending to this attention, this encounter between beings, a jural relation that is always already between two beings,[65] there is the "understanding that meeting the look of the other is a condition of having face oneself."[66] Haraway speaks of this communality as "shared suffering,"[67] and in many respects it re-sounds with the concept of shared interests presented here in that both are concerned with attention that is produced in concert, as it were.

Émile Durkheim interprets Tarde's interpsychology[68] as a replacement of his earlier work in the collective and sociability and describes it as arbitrary and confusing.[69] However, Tarde illuminates that vital aspect of sociability that it is necessarily embodied between two beings, an embodied communication to attention, as it were. And that attention is dialectical. In both desire and repulsion, the desire of and for attention remains.[70]

Lost in abandon

Curiously, there is no clear law on abandonment in the United Kingdom,[71] and it may not even be possible to abandon property, at once in the useless, empty, unowned space between lost and found. Abandonment is dutifully exceptional: "The relation of exception is a relation of ban. He who has been banned is not, in fact, simply set outside the law and made indifferent to it but rather *abandoned* by it, that is, exposed and threatened on the threshold in which life and law, outside and inside, become indistinguishable. It is literally not possible to say whether the one who has been banned is outside or inside the juridical order."[72] What, therefore, is the legal fiction underpinning the possible impossibility of abandonment other than the sanctioned stray? "What has been banned is delivered over to its own separateness and, at the same time, consigned to the mercy of the one who abandons it – at once excluded and included, removed and at the same time captured."[73] That dog is abandoned and yet still owned, lost and always already found.

However, in the dialectic of abandonment, the stray interrupts the property narrative, wanders around and intrudes upon the conviction of inside and outside. In this respect, the clean lines of property are straining at the boundaries and that dog is recognised as "the form of a survival of the state of nature at the very heart of the state."[74] Attempts at regulating further that public space and transforming it into the private are identifiable in provisions such as the United Kingdom's Public Spaces Protection Orders,[75] which, in effect, give power to local authorities to render public spaces private, including (especially) public parks.[76] Through such orders, not only the stray but also the owned may be banned from social life, cast out and outlawed. The flâneur's wanderings are increasingly circumscribed and curtailed through the drift of a predatory property framework.

How indeed might these property relations be cast open, as it were? As the discussion moves from the Machine Age into the Social Age, an emphasis on relations as distinct from the biological essentialism of beings leads to more "fruitful interferences."[77] Recalling the domestication event, when that first dog went "inside" and enlarged the social world of humans, brought them out into the open, as it were, the potential of sociable property relations becomes enticing: "With all its eyes the creature world beholds the open."[78]

And what of incorporeal space? In terms of incorporeal property, in other words, intellectual property, attempts at this kind of prescribed use of space continue to attract debate and controversy. What the social dog teaches us is to consider the importance of the co-constitution of legal space – through the commons, through social media, through shared interests. How might we rethink the dialectic of the ban?

Les chiens fraudeurs

>As vain as ever; it had its memories, . . .
>It wasn't anything but a nest of black sheep,
>Lovers from the bush, a rat down on his luck,
>Stray dogs, benighted hobos – smugglers and customs-inspectors.[79]

An intriguing example of this abandonment to the law, existing both inside and outside the law, transgressing both legal and physical boundaries, is that of the smuggling dogs on the Franco-Belgian border in the late nineteenth and early twentieth centuries – *les chiens fraudeurs*. These dogs would have parts of their coat shaved and replaced by goatskin pouches, which were attached to their backs hairy-side up, filled with tobacco and matches – hiding their transgression in the wide open.

Smuggling dogs were countered by customs dogs in their patrolling of borders. Chris Pearson notes that both dogs were "agents in the construction and contestation of borders."[80] Smuggling dogs were thus transgressive, breaching borders as agents of immorality, straying from the centre, outlaws. At the same time, the border, the ban, produces that outlaw – a legal fiction. The border relies on representative thinking, whereas *les chiens fraudeurs* expose the border's porosity and arbitrary nature.

The customs dogs, on the contrary, appear to police and affirm the boundary, while at the same time penetrating the boundary – inspecting, showing they are the scavengers at the border, the *scavage* beasts: "Customs dogs served as emotive counter-images to those that romanticized smuggling or promoted free trade, combating the narratives of writers who brought the legendary exploits of the eighteenth-century smuggler Louis Mandrin to a mass audience in *fin-de-siècle* France, as well as liberal thinkers who attached the state's protectionist customs laws."[81]

The relationship between the smuggling dog and the customs dog is a wondrous example of the relationship between animal territories, inside and outside, across arbitrary borders and predatory boundaries, co-constituting not only their borders but also their very identities, always already in relation to each other – dominant and servient, producer and consumer, owner and trespasser. In a *stranger* way, this outlaw scenario plays out a new social world of property.[82]

Stranger things

The modern understanding of stranger is always already implicated in a sense of place. The stranger is "not from around here," a foreigner. As well as place, the stranger is also invoking time, its identity itself being a definition in time, a newcomer. And of course, the stranger is unknown, novel, unfamiliar – in every sense of the word. A stranger simply is not of that society.

Without territory, the stranger belongs and does not belong. The stranger is owned and yet does not own. In his 1908 essay, "The Stranger," Georg Simmel explains this elsewhere through ownership:

> The stranger is by nature no 'owner of soil' – soil not only in the physical, but also in the figurative sense of a life-substance which is fixed, if not in a point in space; at least in an ideal point of the social environment Although in more intimate relations, he may develop all kinds of charm and significance, as long as he is considered a stranger in the eyes of the other, he is not an 'owner of soil.'[83]

That dog in the first domestication did not remain a stranger for long, provoking as it did not only the establishment of territory where there was none but also the first social ties and with that the emergence of society. This was no stranger to sociability. It is all in the perspective.

The strangers, it would seem, were the human intruders. So, where does this take things? How is it possible to recuperate the stranger and the question of distance in contemporary property relations, particularly in terms of production – familiar production.[84] In particular, social production through social media platforms and other forms of distributed and interactive creativity in a sense both depend upon the stranger and recuperate the familiar.[85] Both keeping and going the distance. Throughout the pretension at groups of dogs – the pet dogs, the feral dogs, the rescue dogs, the smuggling dogs, the customs dogs, the stray dogs – the category is both provoked and undone by the construction of boundaries:

> As a group member, rather, he is near and far *at the same time*. . . . But between nearness and distance, there arises a specific tension when the consciousness that only the quite general is common, stresses that which is not common . . . this non-common element is once more nothing individual, but merely the strangeness of origin, which is or could be common to many strangers. For this reason, strangers are not really conceived as individuals, but as strangers of a particular type: the element of distance is no less general in regard to them than the element of nearness.[86]

An older meaning of "stranger" is one who belongs to others. That is, the stranger is not of one's own kin or family,[87] but nevertheless belongs, elsewhere. In that encounter between strangers, the hospitality and regard for the other enlarges that belonging. In other words, the stranger is not presumed to be known but is available to become known. This is a question of perception and the awareness of an always already situated perspective, the *Umwelt*. As Vinciane Despret explains, "[I]t requires us to learn to encounter animals as if they were strangers, so as to unlearn all of the idiotic assumptions that have been made about them."[88] In other words, we must unlearn our assumptions, our stereotypes, including the fictions of the pack, and dominance, and alphas, and all the other myths of predatory drift, in order to encounter the world of property anew. This is the dialectic of the stranger.

But how did that dog, making kin through that extraordinary invention of domestication, making home and opening worlds, become a stranger to its own family, ultimately belonging to others, as it were, through the predatory drift of property? When did everything get so inhospitable for some of the earliest beings to settle and "make home"? How did dogs become cast out as wanderers?

Friends close, strangers closer

> If wandering is the liberation from every given point in space, and thus the conceptional opposition to fixation at such a point, the sociological form of the "stranger" presents the unity, as it were, of these two characteristics.[89]

Simmel speaks of the "unity of nearness and remoteness involved in every human relation" as being organised in the stranger such that "distance means that he, who is close by, is far, and strangeness means that he, who also is far, is actually near."[90] This nearness is arguably manifest in the prestige of the stranger, as it were, whereby distance motivates attention, imitation, and innovation. Tarde makes a similar observation:

> In fact, the influence of the model's example is efficacious inversely to its *distance* as well as directly to its superiority. *Distance* is understood here in its sociological meaning. However distant in space a stranger may be, he is close by, from this point of view, if we have numerous and daily relations with him and if we have every facility to satisfy our desire to imitate him.[91]

At the same time, the stranger is "liberated," an emancipated spectator,[92] as it were, "freer practically and theoretically; he surveys conditions with less prejudice; his criteria for them are more general and more objective ideals; he is not tied down in his action by habit, piety, and precedent."[93] Jacques Rancière's concept of the emancipated spectator appears immediately relevant here, especially in the interrogation of the spectator and place: "Everywhere there are starting points, intersections and junctions that enable us to learn something new if we refuse, firstly, radical distance, secondly the distribution of roles, and thirdly the boundaries between territories. . . . Every spectator is already an actor in her story; every actor, every man of action, is the spectator of the same story."[94] The emancipated spectator engages not with fixed representations but rather with the relations of sensations of the world around them, the *Umwelt*. While the production is familiar, the landscape will always look unfamiliar, always already receding into the distance with every step of the flâneur's untethered gaze: "The artwork is the people to come and it is a monument to its expectation, a monument to its absence."[95]

In terms of sociability and community formation, the wandering stranger provides much needed insight into digital communities and social forms of production, as well as the nature of creativity itself. Indeed, the very definition of parody relies on proximity and a relationship to the original, but at the same time transformation and opposition to the original: the very difference in repetition. What might this say about innovation and the formation of property in that innovation? Simmel notes that "Throughout the history of economics the stranger everywhere appears as the trader, or the trader as stranger." Arguably there is a remarkable and innovative moment in the process of trade as a kind of "fruitful interference" in and of itself. Simmel explains further, "As long as economy is essentially self-sufficient, or products are exchanged within a spatially narrow group, it needs no middleman: a trader is only required for products that originate outside the group." This might suggest that the enlargement of the social group is propelled by the trade imitation of stranger inventive products, as it were. For this reason, "the trader *must* be a stranger."

There is an enticing resonance with the scavenger concept and the scavage as discussed earlier. The stranger merchant, the scavenger, facilitates ongoing assumptions about a disempowered outsider, a fringe-dweller, presumptions which then continue to permeate modern conceptions of property pastoralism. Such pastoral properties include the kind of multispecies pastoralism considered throughout this work, as well as consumer-producer communities, fan communities, and yet the displacement of the consumer occurs, even in acts of creativity, through the use of the term "user-generated works" to describe what are, indeed, simply works. The highly differentiated creative landscape continues to prioritise certain beings over others:

> Once an economy is somehow closed the land is divided up, and handicrafts are established that satisfy the demand for them, the trader, too, can find his existence. For in trade, which alone makes possible unlimited combinations, intelligence always finds expansions and new territories, an achievement which is very difficult to attain for the original producer with his lesser mobility and his dependence upon a circle of customers that can be increased only slowly. Trade can always absorb more people than primary production; it is, therefore, the sphere indicated for the stranger, who intrudes as a supernumerary, so to speak into a group in which the economic positions are actually occupied.[96]

It is here that the predatory drift of the property paradigm, from play to predation, can be quite clearly deciphered. And as we have seen, this is caught up in popular domestication discourse itself in the scavenger narrative and the popular discourse on taming, on the journey from sociable play to predatory property: "Science has made considerable use and, unfortunately, abuse of the relation of *proprietor* to *property*. The abuse has consisted primarily in having misunderstood this relation by failing to see that the real property of any proprietor is a set of other proprietors.⁹⁷

Arguably, within property law, including intellectual property law, this predatory drift is clear. Considering for a moment the intellectual property framework, the user or consumer is this stranger, wandering and yet firmly settled. Through use and imitation, the consumer becomes an abundant source of innovation and novelty, "expansions and new territories," but is not kin. The stranger is "no owner of soil." What is forgotten, as it were, is the play of sociability: "Here possession is reciprocal, as in every *intra-social* relation; but it can be unilateral, as in the *extra-social* relation of master to slave, or of the farmer to his cattle."⁹⁸ *Can the owned own?*

In this way, the consumer is constructed after the fact as intruder, trespasser, and is contained within boundaries. But is it indeed the producer that intrudes and must introduce its qualities to the group?

> In support of these speculations, I will add another which completes them and which seems to me to be equally probable. The idea of reducing men to slavery, instead of killing and eating them, must have arisen after the idea of training animals instead of feeding on them, for the same reason that war against wild beasts must have preceded that against alien tribes. When man enslaved and domesticated his kind, he substituted the idea of human beasts of burden for that of human prey.⁹⁹

But how to recuperate the scavenger? As noted earlier, what continues to haunt this playbook, as it were, is the relationship between the word scavage and the implication of scrutiny and inspection¹⁰⁰ in the responsibility of surveying the imported goods.¹⁰¹ The scavenger emerges as a kind of attentive actor, an inspector, a witness, an expert. Arguably, Simmel's concept of the stranger rewrites the relationship of the visitor to the owner, the consumer to the producer, the user to the law: "In spite of being inorganically appended to it, the stranger is yet an organic member of the group."¹⁰² Thus, the diminished concept of the scavenger, as both artefact and watcher of the domestication narrative, is untied. That dog, the marginal being at the edge of property, may be recuperated through the stranger, and the scavenger is thus a visitor today who stays tomorrow.

The importance of Simmel's stranger concept for contemporary property jurisprudence is the consequence for the group; that is, the stranger and the relational dynamic of the social structure.¹⁰³ Recalling the definition of domestication and the discussion of socialisation, it is thus not about folding the dog into human society; rather it is about the burgeoning of society itself. The feverish boundary-making is at odds with the landscape of animal territory: "As soon as we begin to find our bearings, the landscape vanishes at a stroke, like the façade of a house as we enter it."¹⁰⁴ That first domestication was not a one-way street, to borrow the obtuse humour of Benjamin's title of the same name. Similarly, the predatory drift of the property paradigm is not a one-way street, it is a sociable field of unfinished business. The taxonomic imperative of property's predatory drift simply cannot hold,[105] and the obsessive causality of incentives and risk is fallacious.

But what is that dog looking at?

Stranger, then fiction

> Look here: you've got to be a model thief if I'm to be a model judge. If you're a fake thief, I become a fake judge. Is that clear? . . . My executioner has hit hard . . . for he too has his function. We are bound together, you, he and I. For example, if he didn't hit, how could I stop him from hitting? Therefore, he must strike so that I can intervene and demonstrate my authority. And you must deny your guilt so that he can beat you.[106]

The legal fictions are starting to be told. Legal fictions establish models, create measures, sustain patterns, are deemed *to be*. However, a legal fiction is outside the law and yet is created to provide access to the law and its operation. In other words, certain presumptions are accepted in order to proceed. In many respects, survival of the fittest, "the struggle for life," persists as a legal fiction in property discourse, sustaining the momentum of predatory drift through the presumed value of competition at all costs. Fabrications such as pack fiction and human exceptionalism have narrated the course of property. However, the deeds are forged, the romance is dead, there is no basis for the inevitability of a property framework, *red in tooth and claw*.

The mythology of the pack and the alpha, explored in detail in the previous chapter, not only circulates through the popular discourse and literature but also infiltrates the construction of the research questions themselves. This was seen in the early wolf research and the apparent "forgetting" of the constructed nature of the captive pack.[107] In this respect, theories of seasonality and other reasons for pack formation render the pack a seasonal event, authored by external factors, rather than an intentional, purposive family unit managed by the wolves themselves.[108] In these studies of captive packs, every individual was a stranger and no "owner of soil," no keeper of territory. In this contrived pack fiction, this dishonest family, everyone belonged to someone else. Everybody was a stranger. In this way, not only the conservation programmes applied to wolves but also much of the subsequent research, as well as a lingering fallacy in some areas of dog training, have all been based upon temporary visitors, strangers corralled together where they are not supposed to be, ultimately expected to leave again.[109]

Similarly, as seen in earlier discussions, presumptions of property displaced primitive law in classical anthropology, where nomadic systems were disregarded as simply purposeless wandering, not unlike the rendering of that dog's territory.

Ferae culturae

> The life of the bandit, like that of the sacred man, is not a piece of animal nature without any relation to law and the city. It is, rather, a threshold of indistinction and of passage between animal and man, *physis* and *nomos*, exclusion and inclusion: the life of the bandit is the life of the *loup garou*, the werewolf, who is precisely *neither man nor beast*, and who dwells paradoxically within both while belonging to neither.[110]

Ferae naturae is a term in common law, meaning of a wild nature or wild disposition. When used in relation to animals (*ferae naturae animalia*) it is specifically to distinguish those animals from domesticated or tamed animals (*mansuetae naturae* or *domitae naturae animalia*). If a wild animal is kept, then there is strict liability imposed upon the keeper for any damage. *Ferae naturae* remains unowned unless and until it is tamed, kept, or killed, at which time the animal is rendered as property and may be stolen. A wild animal otherwise, and for all intents and purposes, cannot be stolen unless this keeping can be shown and the animal has been "reduced to possession."[111] However, the nature of this ownership is qualified in relation to protection of identified species and so on, restrictions on identified "pest" species, and so on.[112] At the same time, a wild animal has the capacity to change legal relations simply by wandering onto land, by shifting its territory. In this respect, and by virtue of that act, the animal has the power to change a person's legal relations to that animal.[113] In this way, the feral animal, *ferae naturae*, is both inside and outside the law. Indeed, the "feral dog" is in fact a constructed identity, manipulated through property discourse and the wilderness narrative and modified by legislation.

This point of view of that dog resonates with Hoebel's critique of the "parochial point of view" of property in primitive law and its explanation and relegation as mere "customary" systems.[114] In other words, "the cult of the wild," in many respects, has been so impressed in some corners of ethological and behaviour research, at least as a framing discourse, that any discussion of law or culture or even society has been resisted as anthropomorphism. However, to abandon the question is to preserve and observe human exceptionalism through the "natural dog" and a systematic and limiting anthropocentrism. Just as Hoebel suggested an "anthropological definition of law," this investigation continues towards an ethological definition of law – an interspecies form of justice.

In the following chapters of the Social Age, kinds of significant legal behaviour and maintenance of canid property systems, through embodied cognition, altruism, and even ownership begin to emerge. Sociability invokes duties and obligations to play fair. While at first the feral dog may appear to be the incarnation of "no right" in Hohfeld's scheme, the feral is nevertheless implicated; that is, the feral animal is a being within that legal scheme and the legal fictions underpinning domesticates and ferals in canine societies are unsustainable. In all fairness, "no right" begins to look like we are taking liberties.

Let's go for a walk

We enter the Social Age as emancipated wanderers, looking at smells, listening to landmarks, tasting the noise. There is a certain purpose in straying, an important business in play, and a remembered familiar in the stranger. Indeed, we find ourselves in strange and familiar territory.

Into the depths of the Unknown![115] Now we are getting somewhere.

Notes

1 A more recent translation from Martin Sorrell is, "I sing the poor, dirt-caked mutt, the homeless drifter, the circus dog, the dog whose instinct, like a down-and-out's, a gypsy's, an actor's, is wonderfully sharpened by necessity, real mother, true patron of intelligence!" in Baudelaire C (1869) Good Dogs, M Sorrell (trans), in Baudelaire C (1869/[2010]) *Paris Spleen and Wine and Hashish*, Alma, Richmond, 98–101: p. 99.
2 This is a term applied in US taxation law to identify a foreign person who is resident for the purposes of incurring taxation obligations but is not a US citizen. Rosalyn Deutsche describes this position as today's "stranger," drawing upon Georg Simmel's work on "the stranger," discussed in more detail later in this chapter. In many respects, the dog has become "resident alien" in the predatory drift of property discourse. See further Deutsche R (2002) Sharing Strangeness: Krzysztof Wodiczko's Ægis and the Question of Hospitality, *Grey Room*, 6, 26–43: p. 32–33.
3 For instance, Barbara Creed describes the stray as "a being without kin" where "a creature seems not to belong to a clearly definable species." See Creed B (2017) *Stray: Human-Animal Ethics in the Anthropocene*, Power Publications, Sydney, 79. This "strangeness" and "namelessness" is arguably replicated through the notion of breeds and the adherence to breeds, whereby a "mutt" is without family, without legacy, with all the attending undertones of class, race and ethnicity (particularly as arises in cross-border rescue, as discussed later in this chapter). These presumptions also underlie the human intentionality in the so-called "designer dog" product (selected mixed breeds), where the branded appeal to class status and prestige is explicit.
4 Indeed, rescue has also co-opted the same discourse attached to so-called designer breeds or the pedigree dog market in headlines such as Cavendish L (2017) "Rise of the Middle-Class Rescue Dog," *The Times*, 11 November.
5 Although a more detailed discussion of "dangerous dogs" is somewhat outside the scope of the present discussion, the intersection of breed determinism, social status, race, and animal commodities is especially critical in the interpretation and international contagion of breed-specific legislation in relation to "dangerous dogs."
6 For instance, headlines in the UK have couched foreign rescue in the discourse of uncontrolled migration: Warren J (2017) "Britain's Canine Migrant Problem," *Express*, 6 June; "Britain Faces a Migration Issue: European Rescue Dogs," Carter A (2016) *The Conversation*, 28 April. Headlines in the US have also emphasised nationalistic or demonised the dogs as a priori "bad dogs": Morris J (2019) "Are We Really Importing Countries' Stray Pets for Adoption?," *Mercury News*, 28 March; Shaw B (2019) "There Is Such a Thing as a Bad Dog," *Twin Cities*, 23 July. Romanian rescue dogs, often free-roaming and street dogs before capture, are frequently described as "feral" within rescuer communities,

when in fact in most cases the fear or otherwise is due to mistreatment from humans (i.e., the kind of contact and "management" that is actually at odds with the concept of feral, as discussed later in this chapter).

7 For an interesting account on the concept of "naturalness" in animal welfare, see Gygax L & Hillmann E (2018) "Naturalness" and Its Relation to Animal Welfare from an Ethological Perspective, *Agriculture*, 8, 136. The authors raise a concern with the concept which is somewhat consistent with the "predatory drift" towards a kind of essentialism that is identified in the present work, whereby the assumption of circumstances consistent with naturalness "is inconsistent with the existing flexibility of behaviour ("phenotypic plasticity"). For example, if, in human care, there is a behaviour to which an animal subject is no longer motivated, such as predator avoidance, the subject is not directly affected by the absence of such behaviour" (4). However, the absence of such "natural behaviour" could in fact indicate positive welfare, given the research on the chronic stress states of prey animals, despite such stress being the possible "norm in nature." See further Zanette LY et al. (2019) Predator-Induced Fear Causes PTSD-Like Changes in the Brains and Behaviour of Wild Animals, *Nature*, 9, 11474.

8 The "cult of the wild" has some disturbing resonances with eugenics, co-opted as it was by Konrad Lorenz in his writings during the Nazi period (see the earlier discussion in Chapter 8, "Pack fiction") in order to celebrate an innate superiority that is otherwise compromised by human domestication. See the posthumous publication, Lorenz K (1992/[1996]) *The Natural Science of the Human Species: An Introduction to Comparative Behavioral Research, the Russian Manuscript (1944–1948)*, A von Cranach (ed.), RD Martin (trans.), MIT Press, Cambridge, MA. See further the discussion in Sax B (2000/[2013]) *Animals in the Third Reich*, Yogh & Thorn Books, Pittsburgh, PA, Chapter 12; Sax B (1997) What Is a "Jewish Dog"? Konrad Lorenz and the Cult of Wildness, *Society and Animals*, 5(1), 3–21. As well as the discussion in Chapter 8, "Pack fiction." See further the critique of modern assumptions about animal behaviour, including Lorenz's own observations in relation to aggression, in Rensberger B (1977) *The Cult of the Wild*, Anchor Press, New York. This cultural distinction between "natural" and "domesticate" is also relevant to breed discussions and the very significant welfare and legislative area of breed determinism. It is not possible to address this in appropriate detail within the scope of the present work, but there are significant interactions between the property framework, liability, and commodification of type in breed clubs and in breed-specific legislation pertaining to "dangerous dogs."

9 Hemmer H (1990) *Domestication: The Decline of Environmental Appreciation*, Cambridge UP, Cambridge.

10 This resonates with colonialist discourse and the notion of the "empty" or "useless" or "unowned" space, legal fictions such as *terra nullius*, as previously imported in Australia prior to the recognition of native title, and to ideas of pristine wilderness in order to qualify for wilderness protection, and so on. As John Baird Callicott states (referring to US legislation): "we must re-examine the *received* wilderness idea, that is, the idea that wilderness is, as the Wilderness Act states, 'an area where the earth and its community of life are untrammelled by man, where man is a visitor who does not remain.'" See Baird Callicott J (2002) A Critique of and an Alternative to the Wilderness Idea, in Butler T (ed.) *Wild Earth: Wild Ideas for a World Out of Balance*, Milkweed, Minneapolis, 172–186: p. 173. What Callicott identifies is arguably a kind of predatory drift seeking to preserve the perfect "state of nature" in wilderness conservation, at times at odds with the dynamic nature of

ecosystems and the sociability, as it were, of strategies such as biosphere reserves: "wilderness *preservation* has often meant free-framing the status quo ante, maintaining things as they were when the 'white man' first came on the scene . . . the wilderness idea perpetuates the pre-Darwinian myth that "man" exists apart from nature" (176). These same presumptions underpin the kind of qualifications to primitive law seen in classical anthropology, as discussed earlier, where primitive legal systems and property are rendered a kind of "wilderness": "Students of law, enchanted with the intricate mazes of their stately formal garden, have generally looked on the field of primitive law as an undomesticated and infertile wilderness" (Hoebel EA (1942) Fundamental Legal Concepts as Applied in the Study of Primitive Law, *Yale Law Journal*, 51, 951–966: p. 951). See also Gibson J (2005) *Community Resources*, Ashgate, Aldershot, 36–37.

11 Baird Callicott J (2002) A Critique of and an Alternative to the Wilderness Idea, in Butler T (ed.) *Wild Earth: Wild Ideas for a World Out of Balance*, Milkweed, Minneapolis, 172–186: p. 175. See further Sprankling JG (1996) The Antiwilderness Bias in American Property Law, *The University of Chicago Law Review*, 63(2), 519–590: "a nineteenth-century antiwilderness bias still influences modern property law" (520) and "It is axiomatic that geography influences law; this precept applies particularly to property law, which regulates rights and duties concerning land" (523).

12 Baudelaire C (1869) The Faithful Dog, L Varèse (trans.), in Baudelaire C (1869/[1970]) *Paris Spleen*, New Directions, New York, 104–107: p. 105. See also the alternative translation by Martin Sorrell: "I sing of calamitous dogs, those that wander among the winding ravines of great cities, or those whose sparkling, winning eyes have asked some misfit: "Take me with you, and our combined wretchedness might make some sort of happiness!" See Baudelaire C (1869) Good Dogs, M Sorrell (trans.), in Baudelaire C (1869/[2010]) *Paris Spleen and Wine and Hashish*, Alma, Richmond, 98–101: p. 99.

13 Benjamin W (1982/[2002]) *The Arcades Project*, H Eiland & K McLaughlin (trans.), Harvard UP, Cambridge, MA, 21. Benjamin states: "He is a spy for the capitalists, on assignment in the realm of consumers: [M5,6].

14 Benjamin W (1982/[2002]) *The Arcades Project*, H Eiland & K McLaughlin (trans.), Harvard UP, Cambridge, MA, [I4,4]. See further I[The Interior, The Trace], and M[The Flâneur].

15 Benjamin W (1982/[2002]) *The Arcades Project*, H Eiland & K McLaughlin (trans.), Harvard UP, Cambridge, MA, [M1,4].

16 Benjamin W (1982/[2002]) *The Arcades Project*, H Eiland & K McLaughlin (trans.), Harvard UP, Cambridge, MA, M2,8.

17 *OBG Limited v Allan* [2007] UKHL 21, [2008] 1 AC 1, at [228] per Lord Nicholls. This recalls the discussion in the previous chapter of "pack fiction" and the rhetoric of alpha and pack leadership, together with the socio-political context in which this perspective and, ultimately, belief system would be generated.

18 "We do not know and actually it is not of importance WHAT he is looking at but how that looking-at-whatever-it-is constitutes his specific experience and makes him important enough to become a *sujet* for the painter . . . flâneurs are artists even if they do not write, because they are witnessing that what is going on in the city": Schiper I (2017) From Flâneur to Co-Producer: The Performative Spectator, in Leeker M et al. (eds.) *Performing the Digital*, Transcript Verlag, Bielefeld, 191–209: p. 192.

19 Benjamin W (1982/[2002]) *The Arcades Project*, H Eiland & K McLaughlin (trans.), Harvard UP, Cambridge, MA, J66a, 6.

20 Uexküll J von (1920/[1926]) *Theoretical Biology*, Harcourt, Brace & Co, New York, Chapter V.

21 Benjamin W (1978/[2007]) *Reflections*, E Jephcott (trans.), Schocken Books, New York, 8–9.
22 Indeed, the stray challenges the very margins of property, as discussed later in this chapter.
23 Indeed the populist language of control is ubiquitous in some areas of dog training discourse, particularly aversive-based methods (and reliance on rhetoric of "consequences"), such as "balanced" or dominance training both of which frequently rely upon the fictions of pack leadership and alpha, as discussed in the previous chapter. This notion of control and "civilised" behaviour is seen in other products as well, such as the UK Kennel Club's Good Citizen Award programme, the implementation of a canine code, and other campaigns, all of which suggest a relationship between control and civility. Similarly, government campaigns in intellectual property usually emphasise a type of "good citizen" in the straying consumer, rather than addressing production or access. Recall also the earlier discussion of socialisation in relation to the controlling of boundaries in Chapter 3, "Socialisation," as well as in training in Chapter 8, "Pack fiction." This concept of control (and also the rhetoric of purpose) is also related to incentive-based causalities in economic models (see Chapter 10, "Shared interests") and is explored further in relation to creativity narratives and "other" authors in Gibson J (forthcoming) *More Than Human Intellectual Property*, Routledge, London.
24 It is notable that in the scientific literature, the term "feral" is rare, the more accurate "free-roaming" being much more commonly applied to describe dogs that are living free.
25 The etymology of scavenger, including a discussion of the scavage (toll), is also explored in The Invention of Domestication.
26 Sons of strangers were also treated as strangers for the purposes of the tax, despite being English born. See the discussion in Selwood J (2005) "English-Born Reputed Strangers": Birth and Descent in Seventeenth-Century London, *Journal of British Studies*, 44(4), 728–753.
27 Register of the Privy Council, 1632–3 (PRO, PC 2/42, f. 375).
28 Selwood J (2005) "English-Born Reputed Strangers": Birth and Descent in Seventeenth-Century London, *Journal of British Studies*, 44(4), 728–753: p. 738.
29 The word "scavenger" comes from scavage from *escauwage*, to inspect, and *scauwen* (Flemish), to show. See further the discussion of defence and resources in "Part 2, Territory, the space age," as well as a perspective upon the mutually constitutive relationship of guarding and display in Chapter 5, "Resource guarding."
30 Indeed, this culture of banishment is manifest in both actual and literary accounts. In 1910, the Governor of Istanbul ordered the exile of all stray dogs to the small island of Sivriada (also known as Hayirsizada, and the events are sometimes known as the Hayirsizada Dog Massacre). The dogs died through the capture, hunger, heat exhaustion, and lack of shade, as well as drowning in trying to escape. Deaths have been estimated in the several tens of thousands and up to 80,000. See the reports in *Today's Zaman*: Activists apologize to stray dogs killed by Unionist government (2012) *Today's Zaman*, 4 June; Animal Party to commemorate four-legged massacre victims (2012) *Today's Zaman*, 1 June. *Today's Zaman* was an English language version of the daily *Zaman*, both of which were shut down by Erdogan in an executive decree in 2016 in the days immediately following the coup attempt: Johnston C (2016) Turkey Coup Attempt: Arrest Warrants Issued for Former Newspaper Staff, *Guardian*, 27 July. Turkish activists claim that such practices of exile of stray dogs still exist: "some municipalities collect dogs and dump them in forested areas, far away from the city, where

they will not be able to find food" (See Animal Party). See further Creed B (2017) *Stray: Human-Animal Ethics in the Anthropocene*, Power Publications, Sydney, 65. See also the depiction of the event in the animated, short film, *Chienne d'histoire/Barking Island* (2010) Serge Avedikian (dir.), winner of the 2010 Palme d'Or for best short film. See also Wes Anderson's 2018 dystopian film, *Isle of Dogs*, in which dogs are banished to an island, separated from humans, as they are feared to be "contagious" (canine flu): *Isle of Dogs* (2018) Wes Anderson (dir.).
31 Creed B (2017) *Stray: Human-Animal Ethics in the Anthropocene*, Power Publications, Sydney, 7.
32 Tarde G (1898) *Les lois Sociales: esquisses d'une sociologie*, Félix Alcan, Paris.
33 This is somewhat inconsistent with the science of domestication and plays out curiously in the literature. For instance, in her introduction to the excellent collection, *Pets and People*, Christine Overall makes a brief distinction between the kind of affection from dogs and cats that "have been created and modified through millennia of breeding practices to facilitate their lives with human beings," and "those who are feral," the former seeking to live with humans, the latter not. However, arguably this is somewhat inconsistent with the research on domestication, socialisation, and affiliative learning in dogs, including the particular insights from comparative work with wolves and dogs, and indicates the pervasiveness of these distinctions on domestication in other disciplines: Overall C (2017) Introduction, in Overall C (ed.) *Pets and People: The Ethics of Our Relationships with Companion Animals*, Oxford UP, Oxford, xvii–xxv: p. xix.
34 For instance, in Howell P (2015) *At Home and Astray: The Domestic Dog in Victorian Britain*, U of Virginia P, Charlottesville, Philip Howell sets aside the earlier interspecies relationship during domestication and suggests that the "pet" is to be understood in "the rise and acceptance of pet keeping in the last couple of hundred years. . . . And the case can be made that it is in the Victorian period specifically that the practice of keeping dogs as pets – with all its repercussions – developed most meaningfully" (11). Keith Thomas and James Serpell identify trace pet relations back to the seventeenth century in, respectively: Thomas K (1983) *Man and the Natural World: A History of the Modern Sensibility*, Pantheon, New York; Serpell J (1986/[1996]) *In the Company of Animals: A Study of Human-Animal Relationships*, Cambridge UP, Cambridge. See further, Kete K (1994) *The Beast in the Boudoir: Petkeeping in Nineteenth-Century Paris*, U of California P, Berkeley. However, recent archaeological evidence of burial rituals, specific care and attention unrelated to any purposeful value, and so on, suggests that an understanding of pet-keeping as an invention of Victorian middle-class sensibilities is problematic and must be revised. An adherence to the notion of pet-keeping as a relatively modern and consumer-led enterprise is problematic at best and ethnocentric at worst, in view of the most recent research. While Howell goes on to argue that domestication is itself a contested term, certainly within the scientific community the account of pet-keeping is broadly accepted as having very ancient beginnings and very clear similarities to modern pet relationships. See further the discussion in Chapter 3, "Socialisation," including the example of the Australian dingo in Balme J & O'Connor S (2016) Dingoes and Aboriginal Social Organization in Holocene Australia, *Journal of Archaeological Science, Reports*, 7, 775–781. The authors in this research identify the particular treatment of the dingoes as pets and describe the "lavish care" and affection bestowed upon them (777). See also Albizuri S et al. (2019) Dogs in Funerary Contexts during the Middle Neolithic in the Northeastern Iberian Peninsula (5th-Early 4th Millennium BCE), *Journal of Archaeological Science*, 24, 198–207.

35 Pet-keeping has been established as existing back more than 10,000 years. See Janssens L et al. (2018) A New Look at an Old Dog: Bonn-Oberkassel Reconsidered, *Journal of Archaeological Science*, 92, 126–138. See further the more detailed discussion in Chapter 3, "Socialisation."
36 Erica Fudge notably calls for a more social interaction in the pet relationship through her discussion of a "cross-species conversation," and a recognition of "animal capacity and human limitation." She writes: "By implication we must abandon our belief in our status as separate and superior to them if we are to live successfully with our pets; a conversation must take place." See Fudge E (2008) *Pets*, Acumen, Stocksfield, 54–55.
37 Deleuze G & Guattari F (1980/[1987]) *A Thousand Plateaus: Capitalism and Schizophrenia*, B Massumi (trans.), U of Minnesota P, Minneapolis, 240.
38 Stengers I (2000) Another Look: Relearning to Laugh, P Deutscher (trans.), *Hypatia*, 15(4), 41–54: p. 45.
39 Haraway D (2008) *When Species Meet*, U of Minnesota P, Minneapolis, 29.
40 Haraway D (2008) *When Species Meet*, U of Minnesota P, Minneapolis, 20. Brian Massumi argues Haraway takes the quote out of context: "Deleuze and Guattari are specifically speaking about the Oedipal familialization of companion animals (cats and dogs sentimentally treated as human children). The critique is against this *human* gesture of projective identification. It is in no way directed against dogs or cats, or pets in general – or even against humans who keep companion animals in general. Any animal, the passage continues, even dogs and cats, even zoo animals, can participate in becomings with the human." (Massumi B (2014) *What Animals Teach Us about Politics*, Durham UP, Durham, 116 note 11). Although Deleuze does indeed express a certain disdain for dogs in interview, as discussed later in this chapter.
41 Deleuze G (1994–1995) A comme animal/A as in Animal. Dominique Hurth (trans.). Transcription of the first part (first letter of the ABC) of the eight-hour series of interviews between Gilles Deleuze and Claire Parnet, filmed by Pierre-André Boutang in 1988–1989. Broadcast on Arte between November 1994 and Spring 1995.
42 Compare the findings of high levels of social competence in goats, including in interspecies communications with humans, in the extensive research programme led by Alan McElligott and colleagues: Nawroth C et al. (2018) Goats Prefer Positive Human Emotional Facial Expressions, *Royal Society Open Science*, 5, 180491; Baciadonna L & McElligott AG (2018) Cognitive and Social Skills in Goats: State of Art and Future Directions, in Bueno-Guerra N & Amici F (eds.) *Field and Laboratory Methods in Animal Cognition: A Comparative Guide*, Cambridge UP, Cambridge, Box 5.1, 107–118; and Baciadonna L et al. (2019) Goats Distinguish between Positive and Negative Emotion-Linked Vocalisations, *Frontiers of Zoology*, 16, 25.
43 For instance, in Tuan, Y-F (1984) *Dominance and Affection: The Making of Pets*, Yale UP, New Haven, Yi-Fu Tuan declares that "Domestication means domination: the two words have the same root sense of mastery over another being – of bringing it into one's house or domain." (99) The author goes on to relate the history of domestication as one of taming, presuming selection (and human intentionality in the process) of dogs with "juvenile traits." Of course, taming as a theory for the domestication of dogs has been refuted, the most common pet and the subject of much of the discussion in Yi-Fu Tuan's book. See further page 101–103 where much of the discussion is compromised by a misunderstanding of the basic science.
44 For instance, see the discussion on cross-species conversation in Fudge E (2008) *Pets*, Acumen, Stocksfield, 53–65.

45 Stengers I (2000) Another Look: Relearning to Laugh, P Deutscher (trans.), *Hypatia*, 15(4), 41–54: p. 50.
46 Tarde G (1890/[1903]) *The Laws of Imitation*, EC Parsons (trans.), Henry Holt & Co, New York, 371.
47 Agamben G (1995/[1998]) *Homo Sacer: Sovereign Power and Bare Life*, D Heller-Roazen (trans.), Stanford UP, Stanford, 109.
48 Agamben G (1995/[1998]) *Homo Sacer: Sovereign Power and Bare Life*, D Heller-Roazen (trans.), Stanford UP, Stanford, 109.
49 Agamben G (1995/[1998]) *Homo Sacer: Sovereign Power and Bare Life*, D Heller-Roazen (trans.), Stanford UP, Stanford, 106. In Chapter 28 of *Leviathan*, "Of Punishments, and Rewards," Hobbes identifies the right to punish as vested in the public authority through the making of the Commonwealth: "before the Institution of Common-wealth, every man had a right to every thing, and to do whatsoever he thought necessary for his own preservation; subduing, hurting, or killing any man in order thereunto. And this is the foundation of that right of Punishing, which is exercised in every Common-wealth."
50 Agamben G (1995/[1998]) *Homo Sacer: Sovereign Power and Bare Life*, D Heller-Roazen (trans.), Stanford UP, Stanford, 106.
51 Hobbes offers a version of the same Latin proverb in *De Cive, or The Citizen*, when he writes in his epistle dedicatory, "that man to man is a kind of God; and that man to man is an arrant wolf. The first is true, if we compare citizens amongst themselves; and the second, if we compare cities." See Hobbes T (1642/[1949]) *De Cive or the Citizen*, Appleton-Century-Crofts, New York, 1.
52 Agamben G (1995/[1998]) *Homo Sacer: Sovereign Power and Bare Life*, D Heller-Roazen (trans.), Stanford UP, Stanford, 109.
53 Agamben G (1995/[1998]) *Homo Sacer: Sovereign Power and Bare Life*, D Heller-Roazen (trans.), Stanford UP, Stanford, 109.
54 Agamben G (1995/[1998]) *Homo Sacer: Sovereign Power and Bare Life*, D Heller-Roazen (trans.), Stanford UP, Stanford, 28–29.
55 Nancy J-L (1993) *The Birth to Presence*, B Holmes et al. (trans.), Stanford UP, Stanford, 43–44.
56 Nancy J-L (1993) *The Birth to Presence*, B Holmes et al. (trans.), Stanford UP, Stanford, 44–45.
57 Tarde G (1890/[1903]) *The Laws of Imitation*, EC Parsons (trans.), Henry Holt & Co, New York, 78.
58 Nancy J-L (1991) Of Being-in-Common, in Miami Theory Collective (ed.) *Community at Loose Ends*, U of Minnesota P, Minneapolis, 1.
59 Haraway D (2008) *When Species Meet*, U of Minnesota P, Minneapolis, 19. Vinciane Despret describes Haraway's approach in connection with embodied communication: "It is an exemplary choreography, Haraway comments, of a relation of 'respect,' in the etymological sense of the term, namely, of 'looking back,' of learning to respond and to be respondent, to be responsible." See Despret V (2012/[2016]) *What Would Animals Say If We Asked the Right Questions?*, B Buchanan (trans.), U of Minnesota P, Minneapolis, 17.
60 Haraway D (2008) *When Species Meet*, U of Minnesota P, Minneapolis, 89.
61 This environmental model of therapy suggests some useful interactions with the sensation of sociability and embodied communication discussed throughout this book. Rather than a representational model of development, this is a therapy of pure sensation. The therapy also has interesting resonances with the notion of so-called "living in the moment," an idea often celebrated in relation to dogs despite having little scientific basis and rendering them historically ineffectual, suggesting a kind of romanticism of the animal, complicit with an overarching discourse of human exceptionalism. In the context of gestalt therapy, however, it

suggests an interest appeal to animality in the context of the therapeutic setting. Recall the earlier discussion in the introductory chapter, "Owned: a dogged tale of property."
62 Perls F (1969/[1992]) *Gestalt Therapy Verbatim*, Gestalt Journal Press, Gouldsboro, ME, 121.
63 Tarde G (1890/[1903]) *The Laws of Imitation*, EC Parsons (trans.), Henry Holt & Co, New York, 378.
64 This is significant in the context of dog training and learning as well, and the emphasis on "teaching manners" and the discourse in "balanced" training on aversives and consequences. Similarly, in intellectual property frameworks, the "legitimacy" of those frameworks and the use of intellectual property is likely more effectively addressed through manners and courtesy, mutual attention and regard, such as through workable exceptions, mechanisms for facilitating meaningful access, mutual respect for producers and consumers. This is discussed in much more detail "Part 4, Altruism, the social age."
65 See the further discussion of Hohfeld's legal conceptions of jural relations in Chapter 11, "Resocialisation."
66 Haraway D (2008) *When Species Meet*, U of Minnesota P, Minneapolis, 88.
67 Haraway D (2008) *When Species Meet*, U of Minnesota P, Minneapolis, Chapter 3 in particular.
68 Tarde G (1903) L'inter-psychologie, *Bulletin de l'institut general psychologique*, 2, 91–118.
69 Durkheim E (1904–1905) Review: L'interpsychologie by G Tarde, *L'Année sociologique (1896/1897–1924/1925)*, T9, 133–135: p. 133. Durkheim also resists the idea that all relations between beings are social, suggesting that negative relations are indeed obstacles to the social and that the distinctly social is only the positive values of sympathy, trust, and obedience (133). It is beyond the scope of the present discussion to explore the detail of the long-standing feud between Durkheim and Tarde, but it is notable (possibly even ironic) how indeed his opinion of Tarde (despite Durkheim's assertion that such opinions can never be social) have generated such a rich legacy of innovation in sociological thought. Perhaps indeed the suggestion of hatred is, despite Durkheim's critique, social after all.
70 Tarde G (1903) L'inter-Psychologie, *Bulletin de l'institut general psychologique*, 2, 91–118: pp. 105–106.
71 Indeed, a dog delivered to a rescue or pound is described as an "owner surrender," indicating a clear provenance for that dog.
72 Agamben G (1995/[1998]) *Homo Sacer: Sovereign Power and Bare Life*, D Heller-Roazen (trans.), Stanford UP, Stanford, 28–29.
73 Agamben G (1995/[1998]) *Homo Sacer: Sovereign Power and Bare Life*, D Heller-Roazen (trans.), Stanford UP, Stanford, 109–110.
74 Agamben G (1995/[1998]) *Homo Sacer: Sovereign Power and Bare Life*, D Heller-Roazen (trans.), Stanford UP, Stanford, 106.
75 Anti-social Behaviour, Crime and Policing Act 2014, ss 59–61. These were previously known as Dog Control Orders.
76 See also Anti-social Behaviour, Crime and Policing Act 2014, s 106 (Keeping dogs under proper control) and s 107 (Whether a dog is a danger to public safety); Section 106 amends section 3(1) of the Dangerous Dogs Act 1991 so that control extends into "any place in England or Wales (whether or not a public place)". Control again persists as a constant value, where the legislative response focuses instead on the dog as thing, as property, thus creating a fictive causality presented as contained entirely within a narrative of stimulus and reaction rather than on a relation and reciprocal responsibilities (and thus owner behaviour) between human and dog.

77 Tarde G (1890/[1903]) *The Laws of Imitation*, EC Parsons (trans.), Henry Holt & Co, New York, 382.
78 Rainer Maria Rilke, The Eighth Elegy, The Duino Elegies.
79 Tristan Corbière (1873/[1959], The Contrary Poet/*Le poète contumace*, Randall Jarrell (trans.), *Poetry*, 76(5), 249–256: p. 250.
80 Pearson C (2016) Canines and Contraband: Dogs, Nonhuman Agency and the Making of the Franco-Belgian Border during the French Third Republic, *Journal of Historical Geography*, 54, 50–62: p. 50.
81 Pearson C (2016) Canines and Contraband: Dogs, Nonhuman Agency and the Making of the Franco-Belgian Border during the French Third Republic, *Journal of Historical Geography*, 54, 50–62: pp. 50–51.
82 Pearson notes that these events were important also to the cultural and social representations of dogs more generally and "fed into a wider reconfiguration of human-canine relationships" and "a broader nineteenth-century reimagining of the role of dogs in Western countries and their colonies" (51).
83 Simmel G (1908/[1950]) The Stranger, in *The Sociology of Georg Simmel*, KH Wolff (trans.), The Free Press, New York, 402–408: p. 403.
84 Gibson J (2014) *The Logic of Innovation*, Ashgate, Aldershot, 38–44. See further the full discussion in *Res familiaris*.
85 This is discussed in more detail in "Part 4 Altruism, the social age."
86 Simmel G (1908/[1950]) *The Stranger, in The Sociology of Georg Simmel*, KH Wolff (trans.), The Free Press, New York, 402–408: p. 407.
87 *The Complete Oxford English Dictionary*.
88 Despret V (2012/[2016]) *What Would Animals Say If We Asked the Right Questions?*, B Buchanan (trans.), U of Minnesota P, Minneapolis, 161
89 Simmel G (1908/[1950]) The Stranger, in *The Sociology of Georg Simmel*, KH Wolff (trans.), The Free Press, New York, 402–408: p. 402.
90 Simmel G (1908/[1950]) The Stranger, in *The Sociology of Georg Simmel*, KH Wolff (trans.), The Free Press, New York, 402–408: p. 402.
91 Tarde G (1890/[1903]) *The Laws of Imitation*, EC Parsons (trans.), Henry Holt & Co, New York, 224.
92 Rancière J (2008/[2011]) *The Emancipated Spectator*, G Elliott (trans.), Verso, London.
93 Simmel G (1908/[1950]) The Stranger, in *The Sociology of Georg Simmel*, KH Wolff (trans.), The Free Press, New York, 402–408: p. 405.
94 Rancière J (2008/[2011]) *The Emancipated Spectator*, G Elliott (trans.), Verso, London, 17.
95 Rancière J (2008/[2011]) *The Emancipated Spectator*, G Elliott (trans.), Verso, London, 59.
96 Simmel G (1908/[1950]) The Stranger, in *The Sociology of Georg Simmel*, KH Wolff (trans.), The Free Press, New York, 402–408: p. 403.
97 Tarde G (1893/[2012]) *Monadology and Sociology*, T Lorenc (trans.), Re-Press, Melbourne, 53.
98 Tarde G (1893/[2012]) *Monadology and Sociology*, T Lorenc (trans.), Re-Press, Melbourne, 54.
99 Tarde G (1890/[1903]) *The Laws of Imitation*, EC Parsons (trans.), Henry Holt & Co, New York, 278–279.
100 Leo Spitzer notes in the etymology of the word "The basic of *scavage* is evidently 'inspection,' as appears also from its etymology. . . . The idea of 'inspection of roads etc.' leads easily to that of 'scavenging'." See Spiter L (1947) Scalawag, *American Speech*, 22(3), 188–191: p. 188.
101 Statt D (1990) The City of London and the Controversy Over Immigration, 1660–1722, *The Historic Journal*, 33(1), 45–61: p. 53.

102 Simmel G (1908/[1950]) *The Stranger*, in *The Sociology of Georg Simmel*, KH Wolff (trans.), The Free Press, New York, 402–408: p. 408.
103 In a review of the literature on the concept, undertaken by sociologist S Dale McLemore at what may be considered the peak of Simmel's influence and the development of his reputation in the mid-twentieth century, McLemore explains: "Thus far we have seen that Simmel's view of the 'stranger' has given impetus and visibility to the sociological study of the newcomer but that Simmel's principal interest clearly is not in the newcomer as such. His main interest is in a particular configuration of social attributes which may characterize a group member who has come from somewhere else. For Simmel the word "stranger" refers not just to the newcomer but to one who having come from some other place assumes, or is assigned, a particular position in the social structure." See further McLemore S Dale (1970) Simmel's "Stranger": A Critique of the Concept, *The Pacific Sociological Review*, 13(2), 86–94: pp. 88–89.
104 Benjamin W (1928/[2016]) *One-Way Street*, E Jephcott (trans.), Belknap-Harvard, Cambridge, MA, 63.
105 In his introduction to *One Way Street*, Michael W Jennings writes: "Avoiding all semblance of linear narrative, the book seems on first reading to offer a jumble of sixty apparently autonomous short prose pieces.... The book's title indicates the organizing conceit of this apparent textual miscellany." See Jennings MW (2016) Introduction, in Benjamin W (1928/[2016]) *One-Way Street*, E Jephcott (trans.), Belknap-Harvard, Cambridge, MA, 2016, 1–20: p. 1.
106 Jean Genet, *The Balcony*, Act I Scene II.
107 Schenkel R (1947) Expression Studies of Wolves, *Behaviour*, 1, 81–129. See further the discussion in Mech LD (1999) Alpha Status, Dominance, and Division of Labor in Wolf Packs, *Canadian Journal of Zoology*, 77, 1196–1203: p. 1196.
108 See Schenkel R (1947) Expression Studies on Wolves: Captivity Observations, *Behaviour*, 1, 81–129. See further the critique of this interpretation in Mech LD (1999) Alpha Status, Dominance, and Division of Labor in Wolf Packs, *Canadian Journal of Zoology*, 77, 1196–1203: p. 1196. See further Mech LD and Boitani L (eds.) (2003) *Wolves: Behaviour, Ecology, and Conservation*, U of Chicago P, Chicago.
109 Indeed, even the early wolf research interpreted the packs as temporary and described the way in which wolves would leave, before returning for certain seasonal advantages. See further the discussion in Chapter 8, "Pack fiction."
110 Agamben G (1995/[1998]) *Homo Sacer: Sovereign Power and Bare Life*, D Heller-Roazen (trans.), Stanford UP, Stanford, 105.
111 Theft Act 1968.
112 For example, in the UK, native UK wildlife is protected under the Wildlife and Countryside Act 1981 as well as a raft of legislation pertaining to specific species, subject to other policy actions (such as culling). In general, however, the wild is simply not just there for the taking.
113 This has interesting intersections with the wandering of users or consumers into different creative spaces in the context of intellectual property. Similarly, through offering a work (making it available, communicating to the public, and so on) the author is also in a position to change a user's legal relations. This is addressed in the chapters in Part 4 "Altruism, the social age," particularly Chapter 11, "Resocialisation" and Chapter 12, "*Res famliaris*."
114 Hoebel EA (1942) Fundamental Legal Concepts as Applied in the Study of Primitive Law, *Yale Law Journal*, 51, 951–966: p. 952.
115 Benjamin W (1982/[2002]) *The Arcades Project*, H Eiland & K McLaughlin (trans.), Harvard UP, Cambridge, MA, [J83,5].

Part 4

Altruism, the social age

> If property has social origins, then property law is about shaping the contours of social relationships. That is where we should properly focus our attention.
>
> Joseph William Singer & Jack M Beermann,
> The Social Origins of Property, 1993.

> The difficulties in the transition from the power politics of the international peck order to a system based on international cooperation are impressive. The change is possible.
>
> Warder C Allee, Where Angels Fear to Tread, 1943

Chapter 10

Shared interests

> The etymology of "interest" is "to be situated between." The question, "Is this scientific?" could be understood as "Is this interesting?" This means, "Does it have the power to create a new link between us which nobody could reduce to a matter of belief or of interpretation?" In other words, does it have the power to situate itself between us?
>
> Stengers I (2000) Another Look: Relearning to Laugh,
> P Deutscher (trans), *Hypatia*, 15(4), 41–54: p. 48

> Being-*in*-common means that being is nothing that we would have as common property, even though we *are*, or even though being is not common to us except in the mode of *being shared*.
>
> Nancy J-L (1988/[1993]) *The Experience of Freedom*,
> B McDonald (trans), Stanford UP, Stanford, 69

> Nothing will cool passionate interests. Imagining an economy that is wise at last, reigning coolly over individuals who are rational and reasonable at last, ruled by good governance, is like imagining an ecological system with no animals, plants, viruses, or earthworms.
>
> Latour B & Lepinjay VA (2009) *The Science of Passionate Interests*, Prickly Paradigm P, Chicago, 42

We have been travelling from the familiar engagement of domestication through the sociable territory of animal spaces to the rivalry of property's predatory drift and the erasure of the individual. This erasure of the individual is not only in terms of a perceived or actual determinism and reductionism in biology, where the individual is merely indexical of the population, the species, and so on, but also persists in the positivism and scientism of the law. As seen throughout this canid history, the conscientiously collective professionalisation of a range of disciplines in the late nineteenth and early twentieth centuries not only provided a kind of functionalism with respect to science, sociology, and law but also negated the requirement for kinship in order to attain a sense of collective accomplishment. It negated the need for manners, as it were: *Property has no need of manners*.

Emerging from the combative property environment of the Machine Age, the discussion now embarks upon the present Social Age of property, as it were. To do this, attention will be focused on intellectual property in particular as a kind of culmination of the predatory drift of property, the narrative of things, and the imperative for resocialisation of property discourse and protection frameworks, before a campaign of coercion and punishment in the law leads to "sullen inaction, a numbness, a complete waste of potential."[1]

Thinking outside the puzzle box

The investigation of learning and cognition in laboratory-based animal behaviour research has almost invariably relied upon the capture and containment of that individual's capacities – whether that containment or direction is through a maze, or a cage, or a chamber, and so on. Of course, one of the most famous incarnations of this apparatus is the Skinner box, named after Burrhus Frederic Skinner (more commonly known as BF Skinner) and his work in a series of experiments on operant behaviour in rats, published in 1938.[2] Skinner's method grew out of work on reflexes and drives,[3] and he describes his project as simply "convenient representations of things already known."[4] The Skinner box is a small box fitted with some sort of manipulandum (this may be a lever, or a button, or a bell, and so on) and a mechanism for dispensing rewards (usually food or water as reinforcement) and possibly punishment. In his own experiments, Skinner explains: "Confinement is used as a means of excluding extraneous stimuli, and it is well to choose an organism for which this exclusion is as simply arranged as possible."[5]

In an interesting example of the kinds of "fictions" discussed in the previous Machine Age, the concept of "learning quadrants," which is ubiquitous in dog training discourse, is frequently attributed to Skinner. Although the explanation of reinforcement and punishment is never presented as quadrants anywhere in Skinner's work, this appears to be the basis for the model: that is, Skinner identified two kinds of reinforcing stimuli (those which presented or added something desirable, referred to as positive reinforcers, and those which removed something undesirable, referred to as negative reinforcers)[6] as well as two kinds of punishment (those which withdrew a positive reinforcer, and those which presented a negative reinforcer).[7][8] Thus, the quadrants may be understood as follows: write a book and obtain copyright protection (positive reinforcement); or fail to register a trade mark and risk having someone else register it instead (negative punishment when the mark is taken away[9]); or risk prosecution for selling counterfeit trade mark handbags (positive punishment); or stop everyone from casually copying a sign you intend to use as a mark[10] by registering it as a trade mark (negative reinforcement).[11] The original source of this representation of the quadrant scheme appears to be lost, but an unfortunate legacy of this interpretation of Skinner's work is the implication that the quadrants are somehow equal and opposite or even all recommended.[12] In particular, this quadrant representation implies a simplicity with respect to punishment as though it is the opposite of reward, quite contrary to Skinner's own analysis.[13]

Skinner, on the other hand, viewed punishment as "a questionable technique"[14] and recognised much of what has now been demonstrated in the more recent scientific literature,[15] namely, that punishment does not lead to lasting conditioned behaviours or lasting extinction of unwanted behaviours: "Even under severe and prolonged punishment, the rate of responding will rise when punishment has been discontinued, and although under these circumstances it is not easy to show that all the responses originally available will eventually appear, it has been found that after a given time the rate of responding is no lower than if no punishment had taken place."[16] As Skinner goes on to explain: "Behaviour which is conspicuously due to *emotional* circumstances, for example, is often likely to be punished, but it may often be more effectively controlled by modifying the circumstances."[17]

From the perspective of incentives in research, Skinner's methodology is a curious analogy of the research question itself: "It is often objected that a positivistic system offers no incentive to experimentation. The hypothesis, even the bad hypothesis, is said to be justified by its effect in producing research (presumably even bad research), and it is held or implied that some such device is usually needed. This is an historical question about the motivation of human behavior."[18]

With this work Skinner continues to be identified with radical behaviourism, a branch of animal psychology and learning that had been introduced as a research approach some two decades earlier by psychologist John Broadus Watson. In a lecture to Columbia University in 1913, Watson puts forth the foundations for a purely physiological approach to animal psychology: "The time seems to have come when psychology must discard all reference to consciousness; when it need no longer delude itself into thinking that it is making mental states the object of observation."[19] Radical behaviourism is consistent with the compulsion to scientific discipline identified in sociology and in law during the same period. In that same address, Watson states that psychology "has failed signally, I believe, during the fifty-odd years of its existence as an experimental discipline to make its place in the world as an undisputed natural science. Psychology, as it is generally thought of, has something esoteric in its methods."[20] According to radical behaviourism, all behaviour is construed to be consequential and contrived upon stimulus and response mechanisms: "Why don't we make what we can observe the real field of psychology? Let us limit ourselves to things that can be observed and formulate laws concerning only the observed things. Now what can we observe? Well, we can observe *behavior – what the organism does or says*. And let me make this fundamental point at once: that *saying* is doing – that is, *behaving*. Speaking overtly or silently is just as objective a type of behavior as baseball."[21]

This somewhat mechanical approach to behaviour betrays a Cartesian conceptualisation of animals: "In the latter part of the nineteenth century the concept of the reflex arc was applied to the adaptive behavior of animals. It had been thought to explain the strictly mechanical actions of the body ever since Descartes. Reflexes had stimuli . . . the outcome was a general stimulus-response psychology."[22] Thus, behaviour would be reduced to thingness, disregarding all notions of mental life. Since these early days, cognitive ethology has moved on from this radical behaviourism.[23] As Gordon Burghardt states: "Viewing learning as always and ultimately a product of primary drive reduction (hunger, thirst, sex, pain), so basic to studies of learning during the era in which most classic behaviorist approaches were developed . . is no longer viable."[24] Nevertheless, this *fin-de-siècle* pessimism, as it were, continues, with considerable faith in this stimulus-response approach to learning persisting in the training world as indeed it does in simple economic policy narratives. This betrays a presumption that the animal (or indeed, the consumer, the crowd) is simply expressing a predictable physiological reaction rather than an autonomous, receptive perception; or as Conwy Lloyd Morgan said of Julian Huxley's approach, "Huxley thus far invites us to believe that animals at their perceptive best are no more than conscious automata."[25]

Just a few years after Watson's lecture, Margaret Floy Washburn published *Movement and Mental Imagery*,[26] which introduced a relationship between mental life and the body, by all accounts an early investigation into embodied communication. In *The Animal Mind*, Washburn cautions: "The danger besetting the attempt at a purely physical explanation of animal behavior is that the facts shall be unduly simplified to fit the theory."[27] However, Watson's radical behaviourism took hold and "ousted the study of mental life from scientific psychology."[28] Since the dominance of behaviourism there has been a "cognitive revolution":[29] "We are witnessing the emergence of a new interdisciplinary field, namely the field of affective science."[30] Washburn's legacy, however, is important to remember and recall to the foreground today: "Behaviorism was vanquished, but in the ensuing enthusiasm for studying the mind, the relation that Washburn had seen as so worthy of study – that human consciousness is grounded in the human body and movements – was nearly forgotten. . . . Today, though, the view of disembodied cognition is being challenged by approaches that emphasize the importance of embodiment."[31]

Rather than accepting the representation of behaviour (and forgetting the unrepresentability of representation) as a purely physiological event, embodied cognition is an insight into the observation relation: "This perspective contrasts with approaches in psychology that conceptualize psychological functioning in terms of a closed loop of symbols or an internal model of the world, with the meaning of each symbol defined only by other symbols. . . . If psychological functioning is treated as internal models of the world, and thus a closed loop of symbols, then there is no place for adaptive action."[32]

The very question of incentives in this stimulus-response scenario, and the supposed causality that is implied, is similarly an inscrutable preoccupation of intellectual property discourse and indeed economics policy discourse more generally. Intellectual property is the ultimate nothingness of property rewritten as things. It is time to think outside the puzzle box of intellectual property frameworks, and of property causalities, more widely speaking. Towards achieving this, the concept of shared interests is concerned with getting to a point of genuine convergence through autonomy and choice rather than through coercion and discipline alone. But first of all, this will need a condition report.

A condition report

The concept of interest is arguably central to a resocialisation of property discourse, ushering in the relationality that has been somewhat obscured in a predatory model. This relationality is what animates the concept of shared interests being developed here in that the focus of attention is the bond rather than the behaviour offered in that relationship, rather than the object, as it were. In this way, shared interests suggest a similar set of relations as those to be explored in the next chapter in the context of Hohfeld's legal conceptions. In order to rethink the dominance paradigm of incentives and effectives – one that is almost obsessively tied to the cause and effect of radical behaviourism and the intentionality of the owner, the producer, the human – shared interests are more prosocial, a behavioural dyad, generating creativity and production rather than compliance and learned helplessness.

For example, in dog learning and training, there is a common advice that if a dog is doing something that is undesirable, something in which you have no interest, then you ignore it.[33] The rationale is that by ignoring it you are removing the reinforcement of the behaviour and thereby removing the incentive to continue the behaviour. In other words, the advice is to remove a positive reinforcer (attention), which is a kind of punishment.[34] Therefore, following this advice, if the dog is jumping up and this is an unwanted behaviour, the advice then is to turn away (sometimes also with crossed arms, thus removing the hands as well as the gaze and other possible sources of communication from the interaction). Or if the dog barks, ignore it. The overwhelming problem with this approach is that it presumes that the dog is indifferent to indifference.[35]

Then of course there is another kind of advice which emphasises more overt consequences for the "choices" the dog makes, such as "corrections," more commonly known as punishment (the language matters). The presumption is that punishment in this context also acts as an incentive because of the ongoing expectation of it.[36] Thus consequences can also be interpreted as incentives in this way. This training ethos is often branded "balanced," an intriguing development out of the increasingly polarised environment in dog training between positive reinforcement and punishment. Dog training is indeed full of semantics. In this approach, the advice is to create a consequence for the unwanted behaviour so that it is extinguished by negative reinforcement (removing something undesirable) or positive punishment (the use of aversives, such as a loud noise, shouting, hitting, jerking the lead, application of shock, and so on). Both negative reinforcement and positive punishment can occur in the one interaction.

Both of these approaches – one broadly positive and one broadly aversive – nevertheless presume the same kind of peculiarly oversimplified narrative with respect to the situation. Provide an incentive and reward the desired behaviour, and this behaviour will increase. Ignore or even punish the undesired behaviour, and these behaviours will diminish. Both reactions represent consequences for the dog. And both scenarios are based upon incentives (positive and negative); that is, the construction of a motive to act in a particular way through the application of external factors (such as external governance and so on),[37] as well as an implied counterpoint between rewards and punishments as somehow opposite and equal. The language of incentives is ambiguous in that the concept is inseparable from both reward and punishment. What is perhaps common to the mechanism of all types of incentive is a logic of expectation. In this respect, the language of incentives is thus the language of conditioning,[38] and when applied in the context of economic and property policy, the presumption is the possibility to condition certain behaviours across a population.

The advice to ignore an unwanted behaviour is a form of negative punishment (removing the desired attention) and of course positive punishment delivers a clearly negative consequence for the behaviour (physical and mental). In other words, both focus upon the stimulus (the incentive, the expectation of the consequence, correction, or punishment, the expectation of the reward, and so on) and a kind of physiological response to that stimulus. Contrary to Skinner's advice, both presume an expected and predictable effect of punishment and place confidence in that causal narrative; however, as seen in earlier discussion, this is unlikely to change the behaviour permanently. Although there are far more welfare concerns associated with directly aversive training methods (positive punishment), both methods presume a somewhat diminished mental life of the canine subject.

Arguably, the emphasis in training discourse on basic conditioning causalities is a damaging oversimplification of the cognitive abilities of dogs, as well as the kind of affiliative and empathetic competences considered later in this chapter. Indeed, it is a persistent oversimplification of economic models of property and of what is at stake in intellectual property as well. The drive model in the laboratory and in training is the same simplified causality that is applied to property (as seen throughout the development of the "predatory drift" concept in property discourse) as well as in incentives (and intellectual property) more broadly. This rationale is based upon a popular rendition of the puzzle box, as it were. Provide an incentive and reward the desired behaviours and these behaviours will increase. Ignore or even punish the undesired behaviours and they will diminish. However, interaction is the first law of attribution, so to speak, and attribution is the first law of intellectual property. What is really at stake in the training relationship, in the property relationship, in the consumer-producer dyad, is not a question of incentive and reward; rather it is the need for the understanding, recognition and acknowledgment of shared interests. Where then is the kinship in this characterisation of the creative property relationship? In the persistent and ubiquitous language of incentives to research, incentives to create, incentives to innovate, this is radical behaviourism applied to economic models of intellectual property and, to recall Morgenstern's words, "Economists simply don't know what science means."[39] Or as Latour and Lepinjay remark, "we must make do otherwise than by trusting in the economics of economists."[40] And we must make do otherwise than by trusting in the science of economists as well. Economists and lawyers need to update their science and start to think outside the puzzle box.

Let us return to the dog who is jumping up. The dog jumps up, but in both scenarios above, the treatment is of the action. But why does the dog jump up?

Perhaps it is because humans are usually taller, standing awkwardly upright. There is thus a physical obstacle to communication.[41] Perhaps the dog is merely frustrated.[42] Therefore, in thwarting that opportunity to communicate is there not also a basic welfare issue?[43] Perhaps instead of treating an effect there should be more dynamic engagement with interest.[44] When a dog in my family jumps up what do I do? I kneel down, I greet them, and they are satisfied. I am also satisfied through my own interaction. I am offered reciprocated affection and attention. My dogs and I share similar interests in communicating, and we have acknowledged those in each other in this simple interaction. I have become "a trusted subject."[45] Training and learning become a creative collaboration of shared interests, shared perspectives, shared attention. As Skinner himself declares, "Direct positive reinforcement is to be preferred because it appears to have fewer objectionable by-products."[46]

Returning to the training protocols, in non-aversive training methods[47] those shared interests are usually acknowledged by what is largely described as a reward. This is often food, but may include a marker (such as a clicker or whistle) which becomes primed as a reinforcer through the pairing with food rewards.[48] The notable common factor is the language of rewards, and a lot of this training is described and understood as "rewards-based," usually through food. While the criticism of this training (for example, the criticism that dogs will become overweight and food has to be withheld in order for treats to work in motivating the dog to learn,[49] and other mythologies) actually follows a lack of understanding of the methods, the preoccupation of that criticism with the rhetoric of reward is important. One of the most common criticisms of all is that the food treat is a bribe. On that point, in speaking of positive reinforcement in the context of children's education, Skinner has the ultimate retort to the critics: "A bribe is something paid to induce someone to do something illegal or wrong. Those who call positive reinforcement bribery are confessing to a very low opinion of school work."[50]

And in fact, perhaps even describing them as rewards is inaccurate. Karen Pryor states: "Reinforcement training is not a system of reward and punishment. . . . The concept of reward and punishment carries a great freight of emotional associations and interpretations,"[51] noting further, "Reinforcement is information – it's information about what you are doing that is *working*."[52] This is startling in its resonance with social learning and the concept of information that is socially transmitted through behaviour. And notably, this quality of the reinforcer as informative has been advocated for some time in psychology, somewhat before the "cognitive revolution" of the 1980s. James J Gibson explains:

> [I]t is reasonable to assume that stimuli *carry information* about the terrestrial environment. That is, they specify things about objects, places, events, animals, people, and the actions of people. The rules by which they do so are to be determined, but there is at least enough evidence to warrant discarding the opposite assumption under which we have been operating for centuries – that stimuli are necessarily and intrinsically meaningless.[53]

In many respects, what Pryor describes in her system of positive reinforcement training is the identification of something similar to the concept of shared interests proposed here. In the emphasis on timing (rather than consequence, "the reinforcer has to occur in the very instant the behavior is taking place. Bingo!"[54]) and mutual affection and attachment,[55] rather than a stimulus-response repertoire, the training relationship is articulated through a genuine convergence of those interests ultimately through the action or behaviour. And that affection is manifestly adjudicated, as it were, through that encounter, the justness of the training relationship: "A curious but important corollary to training by reinforcement is that it breeds affection in both subject and trainer. . . . The animals behave as if they love the trainer."[56] Pryor identifies this reinforcement of interests in the trainer as well, not merely in terms of achieving desired outcomes, but through the communicative process of the training relationship:

> The trainer rapidly develops an attachment, too. . . . What happens, I believe, is that the success of the training interchange tends to turn the participants into generalized conditioned reinforcers for each other. The trainer is the source of interesting, exciting, rewarding, life-enhancing events for the subject, and the subject's responses are interesting and rewarding for the trainer, so that they really become attached. Not dependent just attached. Comrades in the battle of life.[57]

The triadic nature of this relationship is clear – a relation between two beings communicated through an object, a property, a behaviour. This provides much-needed insight into the property model. Indeed, the dyad of property has become abrogated to that between the individual and the object in a narrative of absolute control as propelled through predatory drift: "It seems likely that the oversimplified conceptualization of the property relation in dyadic rather than triadic terms, is at the root of the essential ambiguity which has characterized the term property in common speech and sometimes in law. For property is a term commonly applied to both *objects* that are said to be owned as well as the *rights* exercised over such objects."[58] A fuller relationship of the triadic nature and the fundamental relations between two beings is crucial. The central principle is the relationship; the behaviour is, quite literally, incidental and spontaneous.

The one problem of property

> In a sense, there is only one problem of psychophysics, namely the definition of the stimulus. In this same sense there is only one problem in all of psychology – and that is the same problem. The definition of the stimulus is thus a bigger problem than it appears at first sight. The reason for equating psychology to the problem of defining stimuli can be stated thus: the complete definition of the stimulus to a given response involves the specification of all the transformations of the environment, both internal and external, that leave the response invariant.[59]

In this statement, the psychologist and founder of Harvard's Psycho-Acoustic Laboratory, Stanley Smith Stevens, identifies the "object" problem of psychology – the stimulus: *"does a stimulus motivate the individual or does it merely trigger a response?"*[60] This is arguably the one problem of intellectual property – the stimulus, that is, the incentive.[61] Do incentives genuinely motivate innovation and creativity? And indeed, are the ones devised even presenting the right stimuli? In the manner in which it is applied in intellectual property policy discourse, within the concept of incentive inheres the crucial preoccupation with predictability and measurement of the property relation and the creative or innovative narrative in the production of intellectual property.[62] Since Watson and the advent of radical behaviorism, the stimulus has dominated: "[W]e may say that the goal of psychological study is the *ascertaining of such data and laws that, given the stimulus, psychology can predict what the response will be; or, on the other hand, given the response, it can specify the nature of the stimulus.*"[63]

And for psychology and property alike, the problem of the stimulus is also one of definition.[64] And the difficulty with the translation of conditioning into the economic and property context is the over-simplification of the system as an unproblematic stimulus-response mechanism: "Labelling all our motivations as incentives suits some economists, because it is a sly way of reducing the rich complexity of human psychology to the one-dimensional motivation of *homo economicus.*"[65] In this context, any interest in the processes of innovation and creativity is displaced by an emphasis on incentives to participate in the economic model, and so any attention to the circumstances of innovative behaviour is somewhat deferred: "So long as we cling to the view that a person is an initiating doer, actor, or causer of behavior, we shall probably continue to neglect the conditions which must be changed if we are to solve our problems."[66] Indeed, the almost despotic influence of the incentives narrative risks an artificial causality: *the facts shall be unduly simplified to fit the theory.*[67]

What is necessary is a rethinking of the relational nature of reinforcement towards a sociability in the otherwise predominantly economic models of innovative and creative behaviour. That is, the nature of the emphasis on incentives betrays a (flawed) biological narrative in the economic model of innovation and creativity, explaining policy in terms of simple drives to dominance.[68] In reviewing approaches to motivation and incentives in psychological research, the ethologist Gordon Burghardt argues that what is missing is attention to emotions and affect. That is, the relationship is not wholly revealed by the box. Indeed, it is necessary to start thinking outside the puzzle box:

> Today we are also seeing that researchers wedded to a behavioral psychology based on reinforcers and contingencies of reinforcement are beginning to revamp some of their distinctive views about core concepts such as reinforcers and 'reinforcement' (rewards). Since the value of a specific reinforcer can vary with the individual, reinforcers are not intrinsic aspects of things. Rather, reinforcement is a relationship among affordances, the observer, and

his/her current state and prior history. Indeed, what is reinforcing is not only dependent on the individual, his/her prior experience and heredity, but also may involve hedonistic and affective properties underlying learning.[69]

Burghardt also distinguishes between the kind of drives underpinning conditioning paradigms and the nature of emotions and moods that may indeed constitute the "conditions" of which Skinner was speaking in his research. In advocating a behaviour systems approach, Burghardt is in many ways rethinking incentive as a question of perception, use, and meaning making. Indeed, it is arguably a question of *Umwelt*: "incorporating affective and cognitive processes into behavior systems approaches in new, rigorous and imaginative ways, may help bring about a true integrative psychological science that can address the rich diversity and mechanisms of behavior in all species."[70]

Thus, the relational nature of an incentive paradigm emerges, whereby the observer's always partial and situated account is affirmed:

> Coal and snow and food have mass and location and motion. Without observers, they have neither taste nor color nor brightness nor smell. To different observers, they have different tastes and colors and brightness and smells. . . . It is the same with reinforcers. . . . Reinforcers, like the secondary qualities of physics, are not intrinsic – they are not aspects of the thing, but rather of the relation between what the thing affords, its context, the observer, and his or her history. They are about what the observer is motivated to and is able to do with the thing, given his or her state of mind at that time. In turn, the state is determined by the immediate and historic context.[71]

In other words, once again, it is necessary to acknowledge the nuisance, to "reinsert the observer – the sometimes reinforceable organism – back into the *operant* and amend its 'three-term contingency' notation."[72] In this way, in that the relevant "stimulus," as it were, is in respect of the relationship itself, then the fundamental value in which such shared interest must invariably converge is that of attribution: that is, reciprocal possession and mutual respect, *respecere*.

Thus, in this reconfiguration of the conventional incentives model, the *Umwelt* of creators is more relevant than the application of "enforcement" (reinforcement or punishment) after the event. The relevant "incentive," as it were, is the environment for innovation and the opportunity for recognition and reciprocation within that environment, of which attribution is a fundamental basis. In the Social Age, enforcement cannot be about the object alone but rather should be principally about attribution, that is, the establishment and maintenance of sociality. This requires transformation beyond the adversarial, predatory drift of combative, objective demands, manifest only ever after the object. This is the fundamental failing of consequence-based approaches to property as distinct from attending to the social life, the conditions of property – that is, at the very least, "fewer objectionable by-products."[73]

Incentive relations

Considering this relational approach to incentives, the nature of altruism in property, and indeed in animal behaviour, is immediately relevant. Indeed, altruism is, to a great extent, concerned with a sociable property paradigm, whether that property is in terms of an object or in terms of personal, bodily integrity, and so on, the fundamental nature of altruism is a form of reciprocal possession and a kind of abundance generated through cooperation.

As seen in earlier discussions, conventional predatory property is structured around scarcity as a mechanism of desire.[74] Indeed, scarcity, not the intellectual property as such, is the incentive in the intellectual property system in that the award of intellectual property in return for labour, investment, skill, and so on, is scarcity itself. *The motive for the motive*.[75] This emphasis on scarcity is over and above the attention to attribution. Scarcity is the fundamental characteristic of predatory drift in terms of the narrative of survival of the fittest, where competition is valued and the preeminence of egoism over altruism is celebrated. In fact, while scarcity is presented as a solution to market failure, it is likely a failure as an incentive for sociability.

In relation to common pool natural resources, Sylvia Roch and Charles Samuelson have demonstrated the way in which scarcity of resources may lead to less cooperative behaviour, but regular replenishment may lead to more cooperative behaviour. Indeed, as conditions become more uncertain, more precarious, indeed more predatory, noncooperative individuals will simply take more: "Noncooperators are motivated to obtain more resources than other group members because they regard this resource allocation situation as a competition for power or dominance. Cooperators evaluate the same situation in terms of morality and fairness. When there is little uncertainty about the replenishment rate, noncooperators may see less opportunity for exploiting the uncertainty of the situation."[76] Further, scarcity may actually facilitate the conditions for further noncooperative behaviour simply by offering an external excuse: "Further, if the resource pool is depleted quickly, a noncooperator can easily blame the negative outcome on an unpredictable and unforgiving environment (e.g., "it was unavoidable or beyond my control")."[77] In other words, noncooperators may simply refer a critic to the biological narrative of survival of the fittest, and cut their social ties.

Thus, while scarcity drives predatory drift, certainty of resources (however that may be defined) becomes an incentive to altruism. Arguably, in terms of the resources of sociable property relations, attribution becomes a key value in this dynamic and a vital resource.

Imitating life

> We learn nothing from those who say: 'Do as I do'. Our only teachers are those who tell us to 'do with me', and are able to emit signs to be developed in heterogeneity rather than propose gestures for us to reproduce.[78]

A fundamental aspect of this incentive relation is a kind of affiliative or social learning. In other words, reinforcement learning is not a pure example of operant conditioning but rather a relationship of social learning and, thus, shared interests. Social learning is learning by observation (curiously resonant with Watson's emphatic departure from discussions of consciousness and mental life) of a demonstration through a relationship between two beings (observer and demonstrator).[79] Importantly, it is not merely an intraspecific relationship (between conspecifics) but rather can occur between beings from two different species (heterospecifics) – between human and dog, for example. To put it (perhaps too) simply – it is learning by imitation. Social learning by imitation is also significant in this context because it is learning that is usually understood outside of a narrative of instinctive reaction. It is creative. And it is innovative. Indeed, in this social relationship of reciprocation, imitation is the basis for interpretations of culture within animal societies.[80] As Tarde affirms: *imitation is a social tie*.[81]

Nevertheless, despite the potential cultural life of imitation, there continues in some areas of biological research an adherence to the reduction to thingness, to the box, that is also characteristic of the dominant ownership model in property. Property has no manners. Property is not cultural. And animals, according to this object-led perspective, have no culture. The British ethologist, William Homan Thorpe, in his consideration of local enhancement, takes an object-led approach, where there is "apparent imitation resulting from directing the animal's attention to a particular object or to a particular part of the environment."[82] However, the interpretation of imitation may describe something more expressive, but nevertheless still directed away from the relationship and towards goals, such as in goal or social emulation, where the imitation is directed towards a particular goal and thus is functional and adapted to that particular goal. In such imitation, "the observer copies the goals or outcomes of another animal's behavior but without necessarily copying the form of the action."[83] The difference or innovation in imitation is thus reconciled by the adherence to the goal.

However, particularly interesting in the context of animal cultures is the phenomenon of over-imitation;[84] in other words, "Imitation of actions that offer no discernable evidence of serving a function in achieving a given goal."[85] Much of the work on over-imitation has been in relation to human groups; however, it has now been identified in not only humans but also other animals, including dogs.[86] In that over-imitation is strongly linked to cultural transmission and ritualistic learning, it would seem that over-imitation potentially broaches the exceptionalism divide.[87]

The research on imitation, and the definition of imitation itself, is moving beyond motor imitation alone. Indeed, the emphasis on only the observable, as advocated by radical behaviourism, forgets the situated perspectives of the observers themselves. As Herbert Terrace explains: "[I]n virtually every experiment performed on imitation, imitation was defined with respect to motor tasks. That has lead [sic] to a lot of confusion because measures of what a naïve student sees while observing an expert perform a task are poorly defined, as are the criteria for determining which actions count as imitative."[88] Through the emerging field of embodied cognition and experiments specifically on cognitive imitation, "a form of social learning that does not require motor imitation,"[89] in many respects the experimental environment has similarly transformed beyond the supposedly observable (and all that is fraught about that) to the relational. Where cognitive imitation "involves nothing more or less than the ability to copy one or more abstract rules,"[90] it reinserts both observers – the researcher and the reinforceable organism – back into the equation, as it were.

As Terrace himself explains, attention to the stimulus "has taken us from orthodox behaviorism to animal cognition, and from exteroceptive stimuli that can be fully described by their physical characteristics to representations that, at present, can only be described by their functional properties."[91] Animal cognition has thus dragged the Platonic ideals of early radical behaviourism into a meaningful, relational, modal logic attuned to the fallibility and impossibility of representing representation. That dog is a welcome nuisance who will not stop barking.

There is considerable evidence of the proficiency of dogs in behavioural synchrony and social referencing,[92] a social competence not explained by human-centred reasons for domestication (i.e., human intentionality in selection and taming), as explored in earlier chapters.[93] Further, this kind of mutual imitation is associated with greater rapport[94] and potentially greater cooperation,[95] whether between dog and human, or between human and human. Notably, the link between imitation and imputations of prestige (as in the concept of charisma[96]) reaffirm not only the affiliative and social aspect of this learning but also the fundamental quality of attribution as both the locus of value and the steward of this sociality. In terms of the incentives to sociality, cooperation, and thus innovation, and returning to the pack mythology discussed earlier, rather than a hierarchy based on adversarial and agonistic combat, individuals are more likely to follow the leader with whom they have an affiliative relationship, rather than one based upon fear.[97] Apart from the obvious implications for training and learning, this is extremely relevant to the legitimacy of other social relations, including contagion and productive imitation. Indeed the social quality of prestige in a relationality of reciprocal possession is thus integral not only to Tarde's sociology but also to the sociality of dogs as well.[98] In other words, this affiliative behaviour is emerging as a basis for innovation, rather than a weakness in a competitive world, and is the fundamental foundation for empathy and compassion in a commercial environment. That is, this affiliative sociality is the basis for the ethical character of a truly modern property system.

Reciprocal altruism

> We have erred in thinking that societies in becoming civilized have favoured economic at the expense of juristic relations. In doing this, we forget that all labour and service and exchange is based upon a true system of contract, a system which is guaranteed by more and more formal and complex

> legislation; and we forget that to this accumulation of legal rules are added commercial and other kinds of usages which have the force of law, besides a host of all kinds of procedures, from the simple but general formalities of polite manners to electoral and parliamentary practices. Society is far more a system of mutually determined engagements and agreements, of rights and duties, than a system of mutual services.[99]

In the late nineteenth century, the Russian zoologist Karl Federovic Kessler delivered a presidential address to the St Petersburg Society of Naturalists entitled "On the Law of Mutual Aid"[100] or "Law of Mutual Help,"[101] in which he put forth the theory that sociability, rather than the struggle for life, was a fundamental value in animal life and evolution, and "far more important than the law of mutual contest."[102] Kessler died just a few months after his address and so his theories went undeveloped until another Russian scientist, Peter Kropotkin, perhaps better known as an anarchist philosopher and activist, seized upon these ideas and developed them in his 1902 book, *Mutual Aid: A Factor of Evolution*.[103] As Kropotkin explains, "Sociability thus puts a limit to physical struggle, and leaves room for the development of better moral feelings,"[104] and he identifies in several species (wild, captive, and domestic) the central importance of sympathy in their associations.

Several decades later, the sociobiologist Robert Trivers coined the term reciprocal altruism to capture the kind of empathetic cooperation between reciprocating partners which "benefits another organism, not closely related, while being apparently detrimental to the organism performing the behavior."[105] In other words, altruism can be a costly exercise. It is thus characterised not only by the relationship of reciprocity but also by the nature of the relationship between two partners. That is, it is a behavior of social relations. In a sense, it is also the basis for moral or ethical relations in that the scientific interpretation of reciprocal altruism identifies a deferred and yet expected reciprocation. There are correlative responsibilities, therefore, created by the altruistic relationship.[106] In this way, the fundamental ethical character of property is necessarily in this reciprocity: *respecere*.

What is also notable about reciprocal altruism is that it is not necessarily driven by reproduction success or kin selection, the usual parameters imposed upon animal creativity or empathy in the most extreme biological determinism. Rather, this type of altruistic behaviour can be offered "even when the recipient is so distantly related to the organism performing the altruistic act that kin selection can be ruled out."[107] Indeed, it may be offered even between two different species, as in the human-dog relationship. Reciprocal altruism is thus a possible incarnation of sociality, but at the same time it is the likely prerequisite of sociality in that it extends the social circle.[108] Not only is the dog invited in, but also the human circle is opened out to the world.

Further, rather than necessarily benefiting the group, reciprocal altruism describes a relationship of perspectives: "No concept of group advantage is necessary to explain the function of human altruistic behavior."[109] This is a kind of microsociological biology, a Tardean system: "Models that attempt to explain altruistic behavior in terms of natural selection are models designed to take the altruism out of altruism."[110] Rather than the being of populations to be discovered, the dynamic of reciprocal altruism ignites the *having* of Tarde's creative relationships. In this relationship of having as distinct from the categorical imperative of being, Tarde's "almost always unknown inventor"[111] starts to attract attention and to merit recognition.

In the kind of perspective-taking necessarily implied, reciprocal altruism is thus inextricably bound up with sympathy: "the greater the sympathy and the more likely the altruistic gesture, even to strange or dislike individuals."[112] In other words, empathetic relations are somewhat self-reinforcing in that sympathy itself provides an incentive to altruism: "sympathy motivates altruistic behavior as a function of the plight of the individual arousing the sympathy."[113] Thus, in affiliative behaviours, synchrony and social learning are to be found the bases for greater convergence of interests and indeed empathy and compassion in the law. Further, the communicative nature of positive reinforcement is conducive to productive strategies in an innovative population, as distinct from aversive strategies which are ultimately counter-productive to the functioning of the system.

Reciprocal altruism is also not directly motivated or facilitated by immediate reward. Thus, cooperating towards an immediate benefit would not necessarily fulfil a relationship of reciprocal altruism.[114] In this respect, reciprocal altruism is similar to the principles of the gift economy, where the reciprocation of the gift may not be immediately enjoyed or may even be significantly deferred. However, although both relationships are based upon a similar expectation, where reciprocal altruism differs is that the relationship is not premised upon an exchange, as such. That is, it is a relationship *in personam*, rather than a relationship that is manifest in a thing, *in res*, and thus against the world, *in rem*. Therefore, in many respects, reciprocal altruism performs the kind of sociability of property that might be imagined through animal territories, as distinct from the thingness in predatory drift, even in a gift economy.

In this way, reciprocal altruism is arguably also the potential for an ethical relationship, not only in property but also through a kind of reciprocal possession more generally; a moralistic exchange, engendering positive emotions which in turn are said to motivate repeated altruistic behaviour. At the same time, the system of reciprocal altruism is fiercely community based, as it were, in that the possibility of cheaters is policed through recognition and knowledge of individuals, allowing for identification of and moralistic aggression against cheaters.[115] As such, reciprocal altruism coheres the group through the imitation of the behaviour, through a form of social learning and, therefore, altruistic culture. Frans de Waal notes this cultural and ultimately bonding or community effect of reciprocal altruism, together with the attending risk: "Reciprocal altruism differs from other patterns of cooperation in that it is fraught with risk, depends on trust, and requires that individuals whose contributions fall short be shunned or punished, lest the whole system collapse."[116] There must be recognition and sociality.

Reciprocal altruism is thus both facilitative of community and at the same time arguably motivated by community, that is, by sympathy: *sympathy is the primary source of sociability.*[117]

Indeed, in his psychology, Tarde describes this kind of reciprocity in terms of the use that different species may make of each other, towards a kind of "interphysiology."[118] *Do with me*: "there is no ideo-motivity, only sensory-motivity."[119] Altruism is not based upon command – the authoritarian dominance of *do as I do*. Rather, altruism both animates the reciprocity and risk-taking of a genuine sociality and is the manifestation of the always already relational functioning social system. As distinct from the predatory taking at will, altruism is benefit without compulsion, and altruism is indeed the anathema of the predatory drift in property: "Strong dominance hierarchies reduce the extent to which altruistic situations occur in which the less dominant individual is capable of performing a benefit for the more dominant which the more dominant individual could not simply take at will."[120] Property has no need of courtesy.

The one problem is the stimulus. That is, the one problem is the incentive. What is the incentive in this scenario? Indeed, it is empathy. The one problem for property, for the erroneous abbreviation as "the law of things," is the frustration of empathy. Indeed, lack of empathy is the one problem for law.

Reciprocal altruism is thus a complex relationship of shared interests, communicated and imitated through empathetic behaviour and attunement to the other. This is a genuine ethical basis for the reciprocity inhering in Hohfeld's system, to which the next chapter will turn. The law as communicative and reciprocal.

This relationship of reciprocity is integral to the concept of shared interests in that it articulates the kind of relational approach to sociable property shown in animal territories. Reciprocity is not merely cooperation towards a goal, it is a relationship of trust. It is a relationship of belief.

It takes a village

> In human society we are accustomed to the idea of community organization. A village is composed of a number of people who are more or less grouped into families. These individuals and families are woven into a unit not only because they live in the same locality and so are forced to meet the same sort of problems as to food supply, protection from storms and from cold; they are also connected by numerous other bonds including those of kinship, of occupation and perhaps of tradition. All such forces knit the community into a working unit which at times may be remarkably effective.... In such a community as a village, men are associated not only with each other but also with other animals.... Unexpected interlocking of interests occurs between different animals in such a community.[121]

> Among our Teutonic forefathers the village community was apparently the chief sphere of sympathy and mutual aid for the commons all through the "dark" and Middle Ages, and for many purposes it remains so in rural districts at the present day.[122]

Interest is attention and, importantly, it is a selective attention, a particular perspective; that is, the concept of shared interests not only implies but also invites and indeed depends upon a kind of perspective-taking. In this way, shared interests comprise fundamentally affiliative and empathetic relations and, as such, generate a genuinely ethical encounter. Trust is thus immanent to shared interests.

Trust is similarly the basis of the relations in Wesley Newcomb Hohfeld's conscientious assemblage of judicial conceptions. His expressions of correlatives and opposites are engaged in more detail in the follow chapter, but for now it is almost exhilarating to note the interplay between Hohfeld's relations, Tarde's biological sociology, and the emergence of affective science – synchrony, as it were, both historically and cognitively, producing a genuinely affiliative jurisprudence. An ethological jurisprudence, if you will.

> Suppose, by contrast, that the basic task were to communicate to a child that much of her environment is such that several people (and other creatures) have need of it and claims on it – that is, it is "shared." Here her selfhood would not be hammered out in possession, but developed in the context of the rules of reciprocal connection. We would end up with a different picture of sharing and of the self that shares.[123]

In law, an interest is a kind of relationship or connection. How that may and does include interspecies relationships is an area of rigorous current scholarship.[124] It may arise through rights or through duties or any kind of meaningful relation in respect of the thing or being and is ordinarily positive or beneficial, as has been the case in the many and varied ways in which the term has been used over many years. Most importantly, particularly in the context of the model proposed here, an interest is usually accompanied by expectations. Whether that is because the interest is in relation to something which is deferred (such as in a sum payable on a loan, where money literally buys nothing) or entirely contrary to the concept of possession (such as a vested interest in land, where the interest is apposite to possession). The nature of interest thus suggests a kind of productive potential on the meeting of interests, on the encounter between interests – in other words, shared interests. Thus, shared interests are an inspirited communication, a motivated and social encounter of "fruitful interference of repetitions."[125] Recalling the positive reinforcement model of training, participation is elicited and motivated through an acknowledgement of shared interests towards a collective assemblage of enunciation in the training context. In contrast to this, aversive methods and punishment are illegitimate and indeed ineffective in the context of the kind of reciprocity at the heart of a resocialised system of property. There is, as it were, no interest in this model of aversive and punitive delimitation of resources.

Returning to the problem of "thingness," and the impact of predatory drift, it is perhaps no accident that the language of rights is almost always used in a narrative of property and indeed used loosely in a general sense. Whether it is in terms of actual property or in terms of the possession of certain privileges, the discourse of rights is frequently possessory and rivalrous and expresses a dominion in terms of privileges, powers, and prerogatives. In this respect, rights discourse betrays some of the more limiting effects of predatory drift, as explored through property.

This possessory discourse thus extends beyond the "things" associated with property and starts to imbue all relations with a sense of a predatory property imperative. As Jennifer Nedelsky points out, liberty and freedom are encircled by boundaries of possession and property,[126] and this reinforces the predatory drift in the property system itself. These are the same kinds of dividers affixed to the traditional view of domestication as a tale of human exceptionalism and intentionality, of taming and selection. The same immuration of that dog in the same way has resulted in the appearance of stray dogs, feral dogs, rescue dogs, and so on. Thus, following the slippage of property in this way, the dyad returns as one of individual and object: for example, dogs are often compared to chairs,[127] in a reflection of the predatory drift not only within property but also in socio-economic discourse more widely. However, in the actual functioning of the property system these are not comparable and certainly not interchangeable. The chair is an object within the system, available to be destroyed or abandoned at will. The dog is a relation within the system, a social interest, an interested socialiser. Indeed, the term of free-roaming and free-ranging, more favoured in the scientific discourse, is a definition of dog with respect to animal territories, not an objectification of dog within the predatory drift of property discourse. The difficulty is the unhelpful ambiguity in the system that has been accelerated by the predatory drift of a rivalrous property narrative of control. What is imperative is an animation of the fundamental relations within the property system and a displacement of the misapprehension of the system as object-led. And that one problem, as it were, is the effectuation of empathy as a fundamental incentive within that system.

An equitable interest, however, is always already a relationship between two beings.[128] It is never a right *in rem*, and in this respect the concept of shared interests reaffirms the fundamental jural relation *in personam* that qualifies Hohfeld's approach. Further, as Hohfeld affirms, an interest is not about things, but about relations: "[A]ll legal interests are "incorporeal" – consisting, as they do, of more or less limited aggregates of *abstract* legal relations. . . . Much of the difficulty, as regards legal terminology, arises from the fact that many of our words were originally applicable only to physical things; so that their use in connection with legal relations is, strictly speaking, figurative or fictional."[129] Hohfeld's scheme is indeed a scheme of interests – rights, privileges, power, immunities are all legal interests in this approach. Further, through the relations between jural correlatives and jural opposites, there is always a relation of two, an encounter, beyond a simple grid of binaries. It takes a village, as it were – a multiplicity.

In emphasising the *in personam* nature of shared interests, and in following Hohfeld's scheme as to the fundamental legal relation between two beings, this is not a perspective that is infused by rights-based discourse. Indeed, the concept of shared interests is also concerned with reasserting attention within the sociality of the jural relation and away from the ambiguous rhetoric of rights. As Hohfeld declares: "One of the greatest hindrances to the clear understanding, the incisive statement, and the true solution of legal problems frequently arises from the express or tacit assumption that all legal relations may be reduced to "rights" and "duties," and that these latter categories are therefore adequate for the purpose of analyzing even the most complex legal interests."[130] Further, the prosociality of this approach to property relations is necessarily forthcoming, as it were, whereby participation is active rather than compelled, autonomous rather than authoritarian.

Through reciprocal possession, in this respect, identity is contingent upon this relationship of having-in-common, rather than a static prefiguring of an inert property model: "If being is sharing, *our* sharing, then "to be" (to exist) is to share."[131] Thus, shared interests encompass *being-with*, that is, the communicative nature of "having." In this way, identity is not the one-sided identity of *to be*, but the reciprocal possession of sharing through these relations of *being-in-common*:

> This is relation: not a tendential relation, need, or drive of portions of being that are oriented toward their own re-union (this would not be relation, but a self-presence mediated by desire or will), but existence delivered to the incommensurability of being-in-common. What measures itself against the incommensurable is freedom. We could even say that to be in relation is to measure oneself with being as sharing, that is, with the birth or de-liverance of existence as such (as what through essence de-livers itself), and it is here that we have already recognized freedom.[132]

At the risk of being interested

> *It may be that denouncing the ideals of objectivity or neutrality associated with the sciences leads us into a trap: that of accepting, in order to criticize it, that there would be a common identity for the many ways to produce science. Learning to laugh, we choose to laugh with and laugh at. But we accept the risk of being interested, that is, of giving up the position of a judge.*[133]

Rats trust a human more if that human can make them laugh.[134] And (an as yet untested hypothesis) humans trust more when they learn that rats can laugh.

To be is to share, to accept the risk of being interested. Accept the risk. Learn to laugh.

Notes

1 Skinner BF (1979) The Non-Punitive Society, Commemorative Lecture, Keio University, Japan, 25 September. Available from the BF Skinner Foundation.
2 Skinner BF (1938) *The Behavior of Organisms: An Experimental Analysis*, Appleton-Century-Crofts, New York. Although named for Skinner, the confinement

device had in fact been introduced some time earlier by Edward L Thorndike in his experiments in the early twentieth century. See Thorndike EL (1911) *Animal Intelligence: Experimental Studies*, Macmillan, New York, 29–34.

3 Skinner BF (1938) *The Behavior of Organisms: An Experimental Analysis*, Appleton-Century-Crofts, New York, Chapter 2, where Skinner also attributes Pavlov's work on reflexes as foundational (45).
4 Skinner BF (1938) *The Behavior of Organisms: An Experimental Analysis*, Appleton-Century-Crofts, New York, 44.
5 Skinner BF (1938) *The Behavior of Organisms: An Experimental Analysis*, Appleton-Century-Crofts, New York, 48.
6 Skinner BF (1953) *Science and Human Behavior*, The Free Press, New York, 73.
7 Skinner BF (1953) *Science and Human Behavior*, The Free Press, New York, 185.
8 For a full discussion of his theories of reinforcers and punishers, see in particular Skinner BF (1953) *Science and Human Behavior*, The Free Press, New York.
9 Although this could be affected by unregistered accrued, if applicable.
10 Again, assuming no unregistered rights yet accrued.
11 This is somewhat similar to the celebrity baby name model, such as Blue Ivy Carter, daughter of Beyoncé and Jay-Z, who applied to register her name as a trade mark shortly after her birth (USTM 86883293, filing date 22 January 2016).
12 The imposition of a kind of categorial imperative upon the scheme is similar to the interpretation of Hohfeld's jural relations, as will be discussed in Chapter 11, "Resocialisation."
13 Skinner BF (1953) *Science and Human Behavior*, The Free Press, New York, 184.
14 Skinner BF (1953) *Science and Human Behavior*, The Free Press, New York, 182.
15 Sankey C et al. (2010) Positive Interactions Lead to Lasting Positive Memories in Horses, *Equus Caballus, Animal Behaviour*, 79, 869–875. In this study the researchers found that "The association of a reward with a learning task in an interactional context, which in this case was the training of young horses by humans, induced positive reactions towards humans during training. It also increased contact and interest, not only just after training, but also several months later, despite no further interaction with humans. In addition, this 'positive memory' of humans extended to novel persons. . . . Overall, positive reinforcement enhanced learning and memorization of the task itself" (873–874). This is described in the literature as "fading affect bias" which maintains that emotions linked to pleasant events fade more slowly than those linked to unpleasant events (Walker R et al. (2003) Life Is Pleasant: And Memory Helps to Keep It That Way!, *Review of General Psychology*, 7, 203–210. See further the discussion of inappropriate training methods in a rescue context in Preshaw L et al. (2017) Application of Learning Theory in Horse Rescues in England and Wales, *Applied Animal Behaviour Science*, 190, 82–89, where the authors note the importance of an ethological approach to welfare: "Inappropriate training practices can affect learning and have a negative impact on a horse's welfare, potentially leading to confusion and the development of flight responses and behaviours indicative of conflict" (83). See further McLean AN (2008) Overshadowing: A Silver Lining to a Dark Cloud in Horse Training, *Journal of Applied Animal Welfare Science*, 11, 236–248; Doherty O et al. (2017) The Importance of Learning Theory and Equitation Science to the Veterinarian, *Applied Animal Behaviour Science*, 190, 111–122. See further the effect of oxytocin in overall positive expectancy bias in

dogs, suggesting the importance of the human-dog bond in well-being in different situations: Kis A et al. (2015) Oxytocin Induces Positive Expectations about Ambivalent Stimuli (Cognitive bias) in Dogs, *Hormones and Behavior*, 69, 1–7. For a general review of the literature on oxytocin and social competence in dogs, see Kis et al. (2017) The Effect of Oxytocin on Human-Directed Social Behavior in Dogs (*Canis Familiaris*), *Hormones and Behavior*, 94, 40–52.

16 Skinner BF (1953) *Science and Human Behavior*, The Free Press, New York, 184. Skinner notes: "More recently, the suspicion has also arisen that punishment does not in fact do what it is supposed to do. An immediate effect in reducing a tendency to behave is clear enough, but this may be misleading. The reduction in strength may not be permanent" (183). See further the full discussion, Skinner BF (1953) *Science and Human Behavior*, The Free Press, New York, 182–184.

17 Skinner BF (1953) *Science and Human Behavior*, The Free Press, New York, 191. See further Overall KL (2011) That Dog Is Smarter Than You Know: Advances in Understanding Canine Learning, Memory, and Cognition, *Topics in Companion Animal Medicine*, 26(1), 2–9. Overall provides a clear explanation of learning at the cellular level and the relationship between rewards and acquired behaviours. Overall explains that continuous reward is most effective in acquiring a behaviour after which intermittent reward maintains that behaviour. However, "a really horrible experience can stimulate the amygdala to encode learned panic or phobia at the molecular level" (3). Karen Pryor describes this kind of intermittent reward as a kind of gambling: "The power of the variable schedule is at the root of all gambling . . . it's the variable schedule of reinforcement that does the hooking" (Pryor K (2002) *Don't Shoot the Dog! The New Art of Teaching and Training*, Revised ed., Ringpress, Dorking, 22).

18 Skinner BF (1938) *The Behavior of Organisms: An Experimental Analysis*, Appleton-Century-Crofts, New York, 44.

19 Watson JB (1913) Psychology as the Behaviorist Views It, *Psychological Review*, 20, 158–177: p. 163. See further Edward Titchener's critique of Watson's position in Titchener EB (1914) On "Psychology as the Behaviorist Views It", *Proceedings of the American Philosophical Society*, 53(213), 1–17.

20 Watson JB (1913) Psychology as the Behaviorist Views It, *Psychological Review*, 20, 158–177: p. 163. Indeed, one possible perspective offered is that "Historically, the origins of behaviourism may be seen as a flight from the subject-matter (the contents of conscious experience) and methodology (introspection) of 19th century structuralist psychology." See Fennell MJV (1977) Radical Behaviourist v Cognitive Psychology: A Pseudo-Quarrel?, *BABP Bulletin*, 5(5), 97–102: p. 97.

21 Watson JB and Mc Dougall W (1929) Behaviorism: The Modern Note in Psychology, in Watson JB & McDougall W (eds.) *The Battle of Behaviorism: An Exposition and An Exposure*, WW Norton & Co, London, 19. See further Watson JB (1919) *Psychology from the Standpoint of a Behaviorist*, JB Lippincott Co, Philadelphia.

22 Gibson JJ (1960) The Concept of the Stimulus in Psychology, *American Psychologist*, 15(11), 694–703: p. 694.

23 See further the useful review of differing learning theories, including behaviourist learning theory, in Guney A & Al S (2012) Effective Learning Environments in Relation to Different Learning Theories, *Procedia: Social and Behavioral Sciences*, 46, 2334–2338.

24 Burghardt GM (2019) A Place for Emotions in Behaviour Systems Research, *Behavioural Processes*, 166, 103881: pp. 2–3.

25 Morgan CL (1930) *The Animal Mind*, Edward Arnold & Co, London, 265.
26 Washburn MF (1916) *Movement and Mental Imagery: Outlines of a Motor Theory of the Complexer Mental Processes*, Houghton Mifflin, Boston. Washburn was the first woman to achieve a PhD in psychology, which was awarded in 1894 by Cornell University, under the supervision of Edward B Titchener, who had studied under Wilhelm Wundt, recognised today as one of the founders of modern experimental psychology. Washburn's PhD was also the first foreign study to be published in Wundt's *Philosophische Studien*. See further Dallenbach KM (1940) Margaret Floy Washburn 1871–1939, *The American Journal of Psychology*, 53(1), 1–5.
27 Washburn MF (1908) *The Animal Mind*, Macmillan, New York, 18.
28 Glenberg AM et al. (2010) From the Revolution to Embodiment: 25 Years of Cognitive Psychology, *Perspectives on Psychological Science*, 8(5), 573–585: p. 573.
29 Glenberg AM et al. (2010) From the Revolution to Embodiment: 25 Years of Cognitive Psychology, *Perspectives on Psychological Science*, 8(5), 573–585: p. 573.
30 Gross JJ & Barrett LF (2013) The Emerging Field of Affective Science, *Emotion*, 13(6), 997–998: p. 997.
31 Glenberg AM et al. (2010) From the Revolution to Embodiment: 25 Years of Cognitive Psychology, *Perspectives on Psychological Science*, 8(5), 573–585: p. 573. See further Glenberg AM (2010) Embodiment as a Unifying Perspective for Psychology, *WIREs Cognitive Science*, 1, 586–596. See also the edited collection Semin GR & Smith ER (eds.) (2008) *Embodied Grounding: Social, Cognitive, Affective, and Neuroscientific Approaches*, Cambridge UP, Cambridge.
32 Schubert TW & Semin GR (2009) Special Issue Introduction: Embodiment as a Unifying Perspective for Psychology, *European Journal of Social Psychology*, 39, 1135–1141: p. 1135.
33 For example, see the advice of The Dogs Trust UK, www.dogstrustdogschool.org.uk
34 Skinner BF (1953) *Science and Human Behavior*, The Free Press, New York, 184–185.
35 Despret V (2012/[2016]) *What Would Animals Say If We Asked the Right Questions?*, B Buchanan (trans.), U of Minnesota P, Minneapolis. Despret describes the attempts by researchers to be "invisible" when observing primates: "Practicing habituation by becoming invisible, however, is an extremely slow and arduous process and one that all primatologists agree is often doomed to fail. And if it is doomed to fail, it is so for one simple reason: because it is based on the idea that baboons will be indifferent to indifference" (16).
36 But, of course, this in and of itself can cause problems of fear and apprehension. See further the discussion of punishment in Chapter 8, "Pack fiction."
37 On the nature of these external factors in relation to the maintenance of the commons, see further the discussion in Chapter 12, "*Res familiaris.*"
38 In its simplest sense, conditioning is the behaviour that arises or is learned through the correlation of two events. Pavlovian conditioning is usually referred to as classical conditioning (where two external events are correlated); in these original experiments this was the correlation of a bell with the appearance of food (at which the dog salivated). In instrumental or operant conditioning, a specific response is elicited through the association with a positive or negative stimulus (such as pushing a bar for food). Some have argued that the two forms of conditioning are basically the same; however, others argue that the simplest stimulus-response model is less accurate in explaining operant conditioning. See Mills et al. (2010). See further Pavlov IP (1927) *Conditioned Reflexes:*

An Investigation of the Physiological Activity of the Cerebral Cortex, GV Anrep (trans.), OUP, Oxford; Skinner BF (1976) *About Behaviorism*, Vintage, New York, Chapter 4.

39 April-May 1942. Cited in Leonard RJ (1995) From Parlor Games to Social Science: Von Neumann, Morgenstern, and the Creation of Game Theory 1928–1944, *Journal of Economic Literature*, 33(2), 730–761: p. 730.
40 Latour B & Lepinjay VA (2009) *The Science of Passionate Interests*, Prickly Paradigm Press, Chicago, 68.
41 In fact, this social intuition, as it were, has also been established in the experimental context. Rezac et al. have suggested that jumping up is not a behaviour of value in and of itself, but rather is linked to the imperative to communicate and match a human's gaze: "dogs are probably not interested in jumping on people, but they only need to get close to their face". Further, the advice to turn one's back to the dog will clearly lead to further frustration in attempts to communicate: "when owners stood upright with their back to their dog immediately after entering the house, nearly two fifth of the dogs ran around their owner and jumped on the front side of his/her body." See Rezac P et al. (2017) Factors Affecting Dog Jumping on People, *Applied Animal Behaviour Science*, 197, 40–44.
42 Dzik V et al. (2019) Do Dogs Experience Frustration? New Contributions on Successive Negative Contrast in Domestic Dogs (*Canis Familiaris*), *Behavioural Processes*, 162, 14–19.
43 Recent research has identified various behaviours that dogs use to communicate with humans, translating these gestures into an interspecific "gestural repertoire." See Worsley HK & O'Hara SJ (2018) Cross-Species Referential Signalling Events in Domestic Dogs (*Canis Familiaris*), *Animal Cognition*, 21, 457–465. See further Skinner BF (1953) *Science and Human Behavior*, The Free Press, New York, where Skinner observes that punishment in one context can interfere with the same behaviour in an otherwise socially acceptable setting elsewhere: "In general, then, as a second effect of punishment, behaviour which has consistently been punished becomes the source of conditioned stimuli which evoke incompatible behaviour" (187).
44 This is also an important consideration in modern laboratory testing environments and in approving research protocols. Vinciane Despret has noted: "In place of routine and repetitive protocols, scientists could instead substitute inventive test through which the animals could *show what they are capable of* when we take the trouble of giving them propositions that are likely to interest them." Despret V (2012/[2016]) *What Would Animals Say If We Asked the Right Questions?*, B Buchanan (trans.), U of Minnesota P, Minneapolis, 35. This is a similar problem in many training regimes.
45 Despret V (2012/[2016]) *What Would Animals Say If We Asked the Right Questions?*, B Buchanan (trans.), U of Minnesota P, Minneapolis, 17.
46 Skinner BF (1953) *Science and Human Behavior*, The Free Press, New York, 192.
47 Non-aversive training is variously referred to as positive training, force-free training (as in avoiding coercive force), R+, or reinforcement-based training. Generally, it is training that avoids punishment (and negative reinforcement) or other aversive methods such as noises, shouting (positive punishment) or withdrawing affection (negative punishment) and so on in the learning context and as learning tools. As Karen Pryor explains: "I am not saying that clicker trainers never say no. Of course, you might reprimand a dog for eyeing the hors d'oeuvres on the coffee table, or restrain it with a leash on a crowded sidewalk. But we avoid using punishment, or its euphemism "correction," as a learning tool. During a training session the animal is free to take a chance, to make a guess, to try to come up on its own with reinforceable behavior. If it guesses wrong, fine. The

worst that can happen is no click. In this safe arena learners quickly discover ways to show you the very best they are capable of, and that leads to wonderful results." See Pryor K (2002) *Don't Shoot the Dog! The New Art of Teaching and Training*, Rev ed., Ringpress, Dorking, 174.

48 For further detail on these methods and "clicker training," see Pryor K (2002) *Clicker Training for Dogs*, Ringpress Books, Dorking.

49 In fact, research shows that hunger will diminish performance. For example, search dogs will search more accurately if they are not hungry (see Miller HC & Bender C (2012) The Breakfast Effect: Dogs (*Canis Familiaris*) Search More Accurately When They Are Less Hungry, *Behavioural Processes*, 91, 313–317). Considerable work on hunger, cognitive bias, and learning has been undertaken in relation to chickens (Buckley LA et al. (2015) Feed-Restricted Broiler Breeders: State-Dependent Learning as a Novel Welfare Assessment Tool to Evaluate Their Hunger State?, *Applied Animal Behaviour Science*, 165, 124–132; Buckley LA et al. (2011) Quantifying Hungry Broiler Breeder Dietary Preferences Using a Closed Economy T-Maze Task, *Applied Animal Behaviour Science*, 133, 216–227) as well as in sheep (Verbeek E et al. (2014) Are Hungry Sheep More Pessimistic? The Effects of Food Restriction on Cognitive Bias and the Involvement of Ghrelin in Its Regulation, *Physiology and Behavior*, 123, 67–75).

50 Skinner BF (1990) The Non-Punitive Society, *Japanese Journal of Behavior Analysis*, reprint of Commemorative lecture on the occasion of the award of honorary doctorate, Keio University, Japan, 25 September 1979.

51 Pryor K (2002) *Don't Shoot the Dog! The New Art of Teaching and Training*, Rev ed., Ringpress, Dorking, x.

52 Pryor K (2002) *Don't Shoot the Dog! The New Art of Teaching and Training*, Rev ed., Ringpress, Dorking, 159.

53 Gibson JJ (1960) The Concept of the Stimulus in Psychology, *American Psychologist*, 15(11), 694–703: p. 702.

54 Pryor K (2002) *Don't Shoot the Dog! The New Art of Teaching and Training*, Rev ed., Ringpress, Dorking, xi.

55 Pryor K (2002) *Don't Shoot the Dog! The New Art of Teaching and Training*, Rev ed., Ringpress, Dorking, 160. See earlier further the discussion of attachment and socialisation in Chapter 3, "Socialisation."

56 Pryor K (2002) *Don't Shoot the Dog! The New Art of Teaching and Training*, Rev ed., Ringpress, Dorking, 160.

57 Pryor K (2002) *Don't Shoot the Dog! The New Art of Teaching and Training*, Rev ed., Ringpress, Dorking, 160.

58 Hallowell AI (1942) The Nature and Function of Property as a Social Institution, *Journal of Legal and Political Sociology*, 1, 115–138: p. 120.

59 Stevens SS (1951) *Handbook of Experimental Psychology*, 1st ed., John Wiley & Sons, New York, 31–32. The psychologist, Stanley Smith Stevens, is the founder of Harvard's Psycho-Acoustic Laboratory.

60 Gibson JJ (1960) The Concept of the Stimulus in Psychology, *American Psychologist*, 15(11), 694–703: p. 695.

61 Notably, Freud uses the term stimulus in conjunction with the pleasure principle: Freud S (1916–1917/[1973]) *Introductory Lectures on Psychoanalysis*, J Strachey (trans.), Penguin, London, 401–403: p. 422. James J Gibson interprets Freud's meaning of stimulus in the language of an incentive, that is, "a motivating force . . . something that arouses or impels to action". See Gibson JJ (1960) The Concept of the Stimulus in Psychology, *American Psychologist*, 15(11), 694–703: p. 695.

62 Marks LE (1986) Introduction, in Stevens SS (1975/[1986]) *Psychophysics: Introduction to Its Perceptual, Neural, and Social Prospects*, Transaction Publishers, New Brunswick, vi. Notably, since the first edition of Stevens's foundational work, *Handbook of Experimental Psychology*, the single volume has grown to five in its present fourth edition, primarily reflecting the growth in qualitative research, beyond the "mainly quantitative in nature" focus of the first three editions, and is now re-titled *Stevens' Handbook of Experimental Psychology and Cognitive Neuroscience*, reflecting the development of the field, beyond the one problem, as it were. See wiley.com product page.

63 Watson JB (1919) *Psychology from the Standpoint of a Behaviorist*, JB Lippincott Co, Philadelphia, 10.

64 Gibson JJ (1960) The Concept of the Stimulus in Psychology, *American Psychologist*, 15(11), 694–703.

65 Aldred J (2019) *Licence to be Bad*, Allen Lane, London, 156. Elinor Ostrom also emphasised incentives, although arguably in the more relational sense being developed in the present discussion: "[W]e do not wish to ascribe altruistic behavior to appropriators of a common resource. Altruism solves too much, since altruistic individuals would cooperate even if others defected. Rather, we are interested in the change of incentives that could encourage rational and self-interested appropriators to cooperate when others do the same." See further Elinor Ostrom's work in relation to the commons in *Res familiaris*.

66 Skinner BF (1981) Selection by Consequences, *Science*, 213(4507), 501–504: p. 504.

67 Washburn MF (1908) *The Animal Mind*, Macmillan, New York, 18.

68 This reductive approach to motivation has been criticised recently by Jonathan Aldred, who argues that incentives may be potentially damaging to autonomy: "Many economists still assume that incentives don't normally conflict with a worker's sense of autonomy, because ordinary people don't work to express their autonomy. They just do it for the money." See Aldred J (2019) *Licence to be Bad*, Allen Lane, London, 164. See further Samuel Bowles's critique of incentives as obscuring the altruistic inclinations, or tendencies towards sociability, in Bowles S (2016) *The Moral Economy*, Yale UP, New Haven.

69 Burghardt GM (2019) A Place for Emotions in Behaviour Systems Research, *Behavioural Processes*, 166, 103881: p. 3.

70 Burghardt GM (2019) A Place for Emotions in Behaviour Systems Research, *Behavioural Processes*, 166, 103881: p. 5.

71 Killeen PR & Jacobs KW (2017) Coal Is Not Black, Snow Is Not White, Food Is Not a Reinforcer: The Roles of Affordances and Dispositions in the Analysis of Behavior, *The Behavior Analyst*, 40, 17–38: p. 18. This question of the relation between the reinforcer and the subject is under investigation in recent research into reinforcement training and dogs. This includes research into the relationship between performance and quality and preference of the reinforcer which shows quality improves performance where quantity does not (Riemer S et al. (2018) Reinforcer Effectiveness in Dogs: The Influence of Quantity and Quality, *Applied Animal Behaviour Science*, 206, 87–93) and notably, the interaction between social learning and influence and reinforcement, where social influence may override the incentive power of a particular reward quality (Pongrácz P et al. (2013) "We Will Work for You": Social Influence May Suppress Individual Food Preferences in a Communicative Situation in Dogs, *Learning and Motivation*, 44, 270–281).

72 Killeen PR & Jacobs KW (2017) Coal Is Not Black, Snow Is Not White, Food Is Not a Reinforcer: The Roles of Affordances and Dispositions in the Analysis of Behavior, *The Behavior Analyst*, 40, 17–38: p. 18.

73 Skinner BF (1953) *Science and Human Behavior*, The Free Press, New York, 192.
74 See further the discussion of scarcity in Chapter 2, "The imitation of domestication."
75 Saleilles R (1898/[1911]) *The Individualization of Punishment*, R Szold Jastrow (trans.), Little, Brown, & Co, Boston, 242.
76 Roch SG & Samuelson CD (1997) Effects of Environmental Uncertainty and Social Value Orientation in Resource Dilemmas, *Organizational Behavior and Human Decision Processes*, 70(3), 221–235: p. 230.
77 Roch SG & Samuelson CD (1997) Effects of Environmental Uncertainty and Social Value Orientation in Resource Dilemmas, *Organizational Behavior and Human Decision Processes*, 70(3), 221–235: p. 230.
78 Deleuze G (1968/[1994]) *Difference and Repetition*, P Patton (trans.), Columbia UP, New York, 23.
79 Mills DS et al. (2010) *The Encyclopedia of Applied Animal Behaviour and Welfare*, CAB International, Wallingford, OX, 563.
80 Galef B (1992) The Question of Animal Culture, *Human Nature*, 3(2), 157–178: pp. 161–162; Legare CH & Nielsen M (2015) Imitation and Innovation: The Dual Engines of Cultural Learning, *Trends in Cognitive Sciences*, 19(11), 688–699. Social learning and culture are being studied across a diverse range of species, from insects to nonhuman primates. For example, see Bridges AD & Chittka L (2019) Animal Behaviour: Conformity and the Beginnings of Culture in an Insect, *Current Biology*, 29, R150–R172; Aplin LM (2019) Culture and Cultural Evolution in Birds: A Review of the Evidence, *Animal Behaviour*, 147, 179–187; Whiten A & Waal E van de (2017) Social Learning, Culture and the "Socio-Cultural" Brain of Human and Non-Human Primates, *Neuroscience and Biobehavioral Reviews*, 82, 58–75. See further the collection of papers in Laland KN & Galef BG (eds.) (2009) *The Question of Animal Culture*, Harvard UP, Cambridge, MA. See further the two volumes edited by Susan Hurley and Nick Chater on imitation: Hurley S & Chater N (eds.) (2005) *Perspectives on Imitation: From Neuroscience to Social Science, Volume 1: Mechanisms of Imitation and Imitation in Animals*, MIT Press, Cambridge, MA; Hurley S & Chater N (eds.) (2005) *Perspectives on Imitation: From Neuroscience to Social Science, Volume 2: Imitation, Human Development, and Culture*, MIT Press, Cambridge, MA. See further the discussion in Laland KN & Janik VM (2006) The Animal Cultures Debate, *TRENDS in Ecology and Evolution*, 21(10), 542–547, where the authors note: "an anthropocentric perspective acts as a barrier to understanding the evolutionary roots of culture, and jeopardises our ability to see relationships among culture-like phenomena in diverse taxa" (542).
81 Tarde G (1890/[1903]) *The Laws of Imitation*, EC Parsons (trans.), Henry Holt & Co, New York, xvi.
82 Thorpe WH (1963) *Learning and Instinct in Animals*, 2nd ed., Methuen, London, 134.
83 Kubinyi E et al. (2009) Dog as a Model for Studying Conspecific and Heterospecific Social Learning, *Journal of Veterinary Behavior*, 4, 31–41: p. 32.
84 The term was introduced in Lyon DE et al. (2007) The Hidden Structure of Overimitation, *PNAS*, 104(50), 19751–19756.
85 Hoehl S et al. (2019) "Over-Imitation": A Review and Appraisal of a Decade of Research, *Developmental Review*, 51, 90–108: p. 90.
86 Huber L et al. (2018) Would Dogs Copy Irrelevant Actions from Their Human Caregiver?, *Learning & Behavior*, 46, 387–397.
87 Legare CH & Nielsen M (2015) Imitation and Innovation: The Dual Engines of Cultural Learning, *Trends in Cognitive Sciences*, 19(11), 688–699: "Whereas learning an instrumental skill allows for variability and innovation in methods

of execution, learning cultural conventions requires close conformity to the way other group members perform the actions through high fidelity imitation" (695–696). Over-imitation and overproduction are also powerful sources of creativity in animal communities. This question of creative and innovative behaviour is considered in more detail in Gibson J (forthcoming) *More Than Human Intellectual Property*, Routledge, London.
88 Terrace H (2010) Defining the Stimulus: A Memoir, *Behavioral Processes*, 83(2), 139–153: p. 150.
89 Terrace H (2010) Defining the Stimulus: A Memoir, *Behavioral Processes*, 83(2), 139–153: p. 150.
90 Terrace H (2010) Defining the Stimulus: A Memoir, *Behavioral Processes*, 83(2), 139–153: p. 150.
91 Terrace H (2010) Defining the Stimulus: A Memoir, *Behavioral Processes*, 83(2), 139–153: p. 152.
92 Duranton C & Gaunet F (2015) *Canis Sensitivus*: Affiliation and Dogs' Sensitivity to Others' Behaviour as the Basis for Synchronization with Humans?, *Journal of Veterinary Behavior*, 10, 513–524. See further Duranton C et al. (2016) When Facing an Unfamiliar Person, Pet Dogs Present Social Referencing Based on Their Owners' Direction of Movement Alone, *Animal Behaviour*, 113, 147–156. See further, in the context of animal-assisted interventions, in Pirrone F et al. (2017) Measuring Social Synchrony and Stress in the Handler-Dog Dyad during Animal-Assisted Activities: A Pilot Study, *Journal of Veterinary Behavior*, 21, 45–52.
93 See in particular the chapters in Part 1, "Domestication, the stone age." See also Udell MAR et al. (2008) Wolves Outperform Dogs in Following Human Social Cues, *Animal Behaviour*, 76, 1767–1773.
94 Chartrand TL & Baaren R van (2009) Human Mimicry, *Advances in Experimental Social Psychology*, 41, 219–274.
95 Lang M et al. (2017) Sync to Link: Endorphin-Mediated Synchrony Effects on Cooperation, *Biological Psychology*, 127, 191–197.
96 Castelnovo O et al. (2017) The Innate Code of Charisma, *The Leadership Quarterly*, 28, 543–554. See further the relevance of charisma in social referencing between dogs and humans, as discussed later in this chapter.
97 Duranton C & Gaunet F (2015) *Canis Sensitivus*: Affiliation and Dogs' Sensitivity to Others' Behaviour as the Basis for Synchronization with Humans?, *Journal of Veterinary Behavior*, 10, 513–524: "At group level, dogs more readily follow a leader toward whom they show affiliative behaviour than other individuals" (520). See further the study of the social organisation of free-ranging dogs in Bonanni R et al. (2010) Effect of Affiliative and Agonistic Relationships on Leadership Behaviour in Free-Ranging Dogs, *Animal Behaviour*, 79, 981–991: "high-ranking dogs that received affiliative submissions in greeting ceremonies were more likely to lead than dominant dogs receiving submissions only in agonistic contexts" (981).
98 Duranton C & Gaunet F (2015) *Canis Sensitivus*: Affiliation and Dogs' Sensitivity to Others' Behaviour as the Basis for Synchronization with Humans?, *Journal of Veterinary Behavior*, 10, 513–524; Yong MH & Ruffman T (2014) Emotional Contagion: Dogs and Humans Show a Similar Physiological Response to Human Infant Crying, *Behavioural Processes*, 108, 155–165.
99 Tarde G (1890/[1903]) *The Laws of Imitation*, EC Parsons (trans.), Henry Holt & Co, New York, 761.
100 The title as translated in Kropotkin P (1902) *Mutual Aid: A Factor in Evolution*, McClure Phillips & Co, New York, x.
101 The title as translated in the short English summary in Scientific Serials, Memoirs of the St Petersburg Society of Naturalists, *Nature*, 17 March 1881, 474.

102 Kropotkin P (1902) *Mutual Aid: A Factor in Evolution*, McClure Phillips & Co, New York, x.
103 Kropotkin P (1902) *Mutual Aid: A Factor in Evolution*, McClure Phillips & Co, New York.
104 Kropotkin P (1902) *Mutual Aid: A Factor in Evolution*, McClure Phillips & Co, New York, 59.
105 Trivers RL (1971) The Evolution of Reciprocal Altruism, *Quarterly Review of Biology*, 46(1), 35–57: p. 35. See further Axelrod R & Hamilton WD (1981) The Evolution of Cooperation, *Science*, 211(4489), 1390–1396; Axelrod R (1984) *The Evolution of Cooperation*, Penguin, London; and Axelrod R & Dion D (1988) The Further Evolution of Cooperation, *Science*, 242(4884), 1385–1390. Note also the discussion of the significant investments in the early human-canid partnerships in Lupo KD (2019) Hounds Follow Those Who Feed Them: What Can the Ethnographic Record of Hunter-Gatherers Reveal about Early Human-Canid Partnerships?, *Journal of Anthropological Archaeology*, 55, 101081.
106 How this might operate in a more formal legal context is examined in Chapter 11, "Resocialisation," drawing upon the jural conceptions of Wesley Newcomb Hohfeld, writing in the early twentieth century.
107 Trivers RL (1971) The Evolution of Reciprocal Altruism, *Quarterly Review of Biology*, 46(1), 35–57: p. 35.
108 Trivers RL (1971) The Evolution of Reciprocal Altruism, *Quarterly Review of Biology*, 46(1), 35–57: p. 52.
109 Trivers RL (1971) The Evolution of Reciprocal Altruism, *Quarterly Review of Biology*, 46(1), 35–57: p. 48.
110 Trivers RL (1971) The Evolution of Reciprocal Altruism, *Quarterly Review of Biology*, 46(1), 35–57: p. 35.
111 Tarde G (1890/[1903]) *The Laws of Imitation*, EC Parsons (trans.), Henry Holt & Co, New York, 90. To provide a fuller account of Tarde's criticism of the conventional approach: "The anthropologist utterly ignores the biography of the Cro-Magnon or Neanderthal man whom he is examining. He cares nothing at all for this. . . . The archaeologist likewise ignores, three-quarters of the time, the names of the dead whose ashes remain to be deciphered like an enigma and looks for and sees in them only the artistic or industrial process, or the characteristic desires or beliefs, or the rites, dogmas, words, and grammatical forms that are revealed by the contents of their tombs. And yet all these things were transmitted and propagated by imitation from some single and almost always unknown inventor for whose radiant invention every one of the anonymous unearthed objects was but an ephemeral vehicle, a mere place for growth" (89–90).
112 Trivers RL (1971) The Evolution of Reciprocal Altruism, *Quarterly Review of Biology*, 46(1), 35–57: p. 49.
113 Trivers RL (1971) The Evolution of Reciprocal Altruism, *Quarterly Review of Biology*, 46(1), 35-57: pp. 49–50.
114 Waal F de (1996) *Good Natured: The Origins of Right and Wrong in Humans and Other Animals*, Harvard UP, Cambridge, MA, 24.
115 Trivers RL (1971) The Evolution of Reciprocal Altruism, *Quarterly Review of Biology*, 46(1), 35–57: p. 49. Frans de Waal states: "Robert Trivers' theory of reciprocal altruism, published in 1971, is and will remain the centrepiece of any viable theory of moral evolution." See Waal F de (1996) *Good Natured: The Origins of Right and Wrong in Humans and Other Animals*, Harvard UP, Cambridge, MA, 25. See further de Waal's discussion of the links with morality at pages 136–144.
116 Waal F de (1996) *Good Natured: The Origins of Right and Wrong in Humans and Other Animals*, Harvard UP, Cambridge, MA, 24.

117 Tarde G (1890/[1903]) *The Laws of Imitation*, EC Parsons (trans.), Henry Holt & Co, New York, 79.
118 Tarde G (1903) L'inter-Psychologie, *Bulletin de l'institut general psychologique*, 2, 91–118: p. 93. Vinciane Despret notes the host-parasite relation in this inter-physiology as an important way in which to expand the relation beyond the harmonious (as Durkheim seems to presume): Despret V (2012/[2016]) *What Would Animals Say If We Asked the Right Questions?*, B Buchanan (trans.), U of Minnesota P, Minneapolis, 215–216 n 5. See further the discussion of interpsychology in Chapter 9, "Wild abandon."
119 Deleuze G (1968/[1994]) *Difference and Repetition*, P Patton (trans.), Columbia UP, New York, 23.
120 Trivers RL (1971) The Evolution of Reciprocal Altruism, *The Quarterly Review of Biology*, 46(1), 35–57: p. 38.
121 Allee WC (1932) *Animal Life and Social Growth*, The Williams & Wilkins Company, Baltimore, MD, 4–5.
122 Cooley CH (1961) Primary Groups, in Parsons T et al. (eds.) *Theories of Society: Foundations of Modern Sociological Theory*, Vol. 1, The Free Press of Glencoe, New York, 315–318: p. 316.
123 Nedelsky J (1990) Law, Boundaries, and the Bounded Self, *Representations*, 30, 162–189: p. 172.
124 Including my own forthcoming work, which investigates creativity and authorship, as well as the relational aspects of rights and protection frameworks. See Gibson J (forthcoming) *More Than Human Intellectual Property*, Routledge, London.
125 Tarde G (1890/[1903]) *The Laws of Imitation*, EC Parsons (trans.), Henry Holt & Co, New York, 382.
126 Nedelsky J (1990) Law, Boundaries, and the Bounded Self, *Representations*, 30, 162–189: p. 167.
127 For example, see Horowitz A (2019) When It Comes to Dogs, We Shouldn't Call Ourselves "Owners", *The Globe and Mail*, 8 September. It is interesting that the chair is the frequent comparator that is chosen, given its central role in the explanation of Platonic ideals, which resonates with the object-led approach to property.
128 Maitland (1909) *Equity: A Course of Lectures*, Cambridge UP, Cambridge: "[T]he thesis that I have to maintain is this, that equitable estates and interest are not *jura in rem*. For reasons that we shall perceive by and by, they have come to look very like *jura in rem*; but just for this very reason it is the more necessary for us to observe that they are essentially *jura in personam*, not rights against the world at large, but rights against certain persons" (Lect IX, 107).
129 Hohfeld WH (1913) Some Fundamental Legal Conceptions as Applied in Judicial Reasoning, *Yale Law Journal*, 23(1), 16–59: p. 24.
130 Hohfeld WH (1913) Some Fundamental Legal Conceptions as Applied in Judicial Reasoning, *Yale Law Journal*, 23(1), 16–59: p. 28.
131 Nancy J-L (1988/[1993]) *The Experience of Freedom*, B McDonald (trans.), Stanford UP, Stanford, 72.
132 Nancy J-L (1988/[1993]) *The Experience of Freedom*, B McDonald (trans.), Stanford UP, Stanford, 72–73.
133 Stengers I (2000) Another Look: Relearning to Laugh, P Deutscher (trans.), *Hypatia*, 15(4), 41–54: p. 41.
134 Cloutier S et al. (2012) Playful Handling by Caretakers Reduces Fear of Humans in the Laboratory Rat, *Applied Animal Behaviour Science*, 140, 161–171. See further Panksepp J & Burgdorf J (2003) "Laughing" Rats and the Evolutionary Antecedents of Human Joy?, *Physiology & Behavior*, 79, 533–547.

Chapter 11

Resocialisation

> Geese and swans also migrate on a similar principle, but the flight of these is seen. They travel in a pointed formation like fast galleys, so cleaving the air more easily than if they drove at it with a straight front; while in the rear the flight stretches out in a gradually widening wedge, and presents a broad surface to the drive of a following breeze. They place their necks on the birds in front of them, and when the leaders are tired they receive them to the rear.
>
> Pliny the Elder, *Natural History*, Book X, XXXII

One of the more astonishing and recognisable feats of collective animal behaviour[1] is the flight formation of some migratory bird species, a source of fascination for observers for at least two thousand years.[2] By organising into a V formation (and other organised clusters) the now accepted view is that the birds not only conserve energy while travelling over long distances but also are able to respond as a group with rapid changes in direction. As a bird flies it must battle against the detrimental drag force as it tries to produce lift against the forces of its weight and the air itself, at the same time producing upward- and downward-moving air. Research has established that individuals in a V formation flap their wings in such a way so as to capture the benefits of the upwash and minimise the drag of the downwash. In so doing the birds literally lift each other, all the while tracing the path of upwash of the bird in front.[3] Indeed, the researchers found that the birds synchronised their movements in order to make the most of the cooperative structure, such that they "timed their wing beats perfectly to match the good air off the bird in front."[4] One of the researchers, Steven Portugal, explains it thus: "It's like walking through the snow with your parents when you're a kid. . . . If you follow their footprints, they make your job easier because they've crunched the snow down."[5] The efficiency of the formation is not only in terms of the group but also the individual, who can conserve energy by flapping less frequently. However, the lead bird obviously has to work the hardest, and so birds will take turns at the front of the formation in displaying a kind of reciprocal altruism in what is socially agreed, as it were, collective behaviour.[6] The V formation is thus a compelling demonstration of cooperation. An individual will always "step up," so to speak, to assume this position despite the adverse effects it will have on it as an individual, and leaders will take turns, arguably because of that. In the V formation there is "no clear leader."[7] Free-riding, in every sense, is not only permitted, it is encouraged.

What is particularly significant about the insight provided by the V formation is that the actions and benefits to each bird come not from the complete formation as such, not from the spectacle, but from the fundamental relation between two birds; that is, between two individual beings. This is a group formation and a will of the collective but one for which the individual social relations are key. Indeed, the spectacle of the V formation is visible only to those outside the formation, not to the birds within, for whom each individual social unit of cooperation is the vitally important world. Somewhat tellingly, the reality of the relations within the formation is quite different from what is presumed by an anthropocentric perspective upon this spectacle, imposing the language of rank and order upon the V formation through military terms such as "echelon" formation. Once again, the predatory drift moves far from the actual relations.

The ethology of the V formation is strikingly resonant with Tarde's sociology, and with Hohfeld's perspective upon jural relations, with its correlative motivations of upwash and downwash, as it were. In the V formation it is possible to see how the interests of the collective may nevertheless be exacted to the relationships between two beings as the fundamental social unit, not as rivalry but as cooperation. That is, the V-formation demonstrates how *in rem* is always already a question of *in personam*. In the V formation these clever birds resolve any perceived anti-individualism of the assemblage, clarifying that the "lowest common denominator" is the relation between two birds, the fundamental unit of the collective will. Collective responsibility is exercised through the importance of the relations between two beings, through shared interests, giving effect ultimately to the shared interests of the group.

The science of resocialising property

> The deep and accelerating divergence between the course of science strictly speaking and that of philosophy comes from the fact that the former, happily, has chosen for its guide the verb Have. For science, everything is explained by *properties*, not by entities. . . . But science has made considerable use and, unfortunately, abuse of the relation of *proprietor* to *property*. The abuse has consisted primarily in having misunderstood this relation by failing to see that the real property of any proprietor is a set of other proprietors.[8]

Throughout, the reciprocity of Tarde's sociological approach to innovation and development has countered the artifice and alienation of predatory drift in property. Indeed, Tarde's interpsychology becomes an instrumental lens through which to resolve the *one problem* of incentive, that is, of empathy, in the law. Tarde notes: "Stuart Mill, most determinist of logicians and most logical of determinists saw concisely that everything could marvelously well be explained by means of laws, excepting the material the laws were made of and the point at which their operation began, that is to say an assemblage of data of facts essentially irrational."[9] In other words, how does one speak of the law when we are always already within the law itself?

Tarde's monadology offers reassurance: "However this question is resolved, these tiny beings which we call infinitesimal will be the real *agents*, and these tiny variations which we call infinitesimal will be the real *actions*."[10] Jorge Luis Borges approaches this question of accountability and representation in the story, *The Aleph*:[11] "I saw the Aleph from all points; I saw the earth in the Aleph and in the earth the Aleph once more and the earth in the Aleph . . . the inconceivable universe."[12] The Aleph is "One of the points in space containing all points."[13] Thus, the logic of the Aleph is that of the Leibnizian monad: "As a complement to the closure of his monads, Leibniz made each one a *camera obscura* where the whole universe of other monads is represented in a reduced form and from a particular angle."[14]

Tarde's observation of "*the tendency of monads to assemble*"[15] is part of the anti-Cartesianism of an ethological approach to property and the fundamental sociability and multiplicity of reciprocal possession: "It is reciprocal possession which explains the formation of those beautiful celestial mechanisms in which, by the power of mutual attraction, every point is a centre. Reciprocal possession explains the creation of these admirable living organisms whose parts are all united and solidary, and where everything is both an end and a means at once."[16] This is arguably the source of an ethological philosophy within Tarde's own thinking:

> In truth, one might justifiably wonder . . . whether it is really certain that our own intelligence and will, those great *egos* disposing of the vast resources of a gigantic cerebral state, are superior to those of the tiny egos confined in the miniscule city of an animal or even plant cell. Surely, if we were not blinded by the prejudice of always considering ourselves superior to everything, such comparisons would not be to our advantage. At root, it is this prejudice which prevents us from believing in the monads.[17]

Gilles Deleuze recognises in the anti-Cartesianism of monadological thought the potential for a kind of "animal monadology," that is, "With the union of the soul and the body, the other who now springs forth amid my effects – in order to throw them topsy-turvy – is the animal."[18] Further, this animal monadology is part of what Deleuze recognises as "putting the element of Having in place of that of Being. Clearly, there is nothing new about the formula of 'having a body,' but what is new is that this analysis bears upon species, degrees, relations, and variables of possession in order to use it to fashion the content or the development of the notion of Being."[19] Indeed, this monadological thought also characterises the system of jural relations developed by Hohfeld with a somewhat ethological character – that is, rather than external relations, Hohfeld's legal conceptions offer a kind of reciprocal possession through the analysis of the fundamental relations between two beings, mutually constituted through the relationship, as distinct from imposed through the application of external principles. As Hohfeld's analysis shows, any interest on its own (whether right, or privilege, or power and so on) is meaningless without what it fulfils in the assemblage of correlatives and opposites. Indeed, Tarde expresses a similar interpretation: "Thus, left to its own devices, a monad can achieve nothing. This is the crucial fact, and it immediately explains another, *the tendency of monads to assemble.*"[20] This is the monadological perspective of shared interests. And this is a fundamental starting point for an ethological jurisprudence: "We must, however, look to the social world to see monads laid bare, grasping each other in the intimacy of their transitory characters, each fully unfolded before the other, in the other, by the other. This is the relation *par excellence*, the paradigm of possession of which all others are only sketches or reflections."[21]

Indeed, only traces.

Reciprocal legacies

> The shift from substance to relation as a basic concept was one of the most significant changes in the growth of modern philosophy. One can illustrate this change by the similar shift that occurred about two decades ago in legal analysis. A legal right, formerly regarded as a thing-in-itself (a creation of "substantive law"), was reduced by Hohfeld and others to a relation between a person, a right-holder, and a determinate person or determinate persons (*right in personam*), or a class of indeterminate persons (*right in rem*). . . . To say these events were causally related because relativity or relationalism was "in the air" during the early decades of the present century, may be to conjure a Platonic ghost out of a metaphysical coincidence.[22]

The nature of predatory drift in the language of property and more widely has quite a legacy. Indeed, Hobbes prefigures the language of predatory drift, whereby the individual renders themselves prey in a relationship of predation and warfare: "For as long as every man holdeth this Right, of doing any thing he liketh; so long are all men in the condition of Warre."[23] However, there is also an important legacy to this reciprocity and empathy in the law. After the First and Fundamental Law of Nature that every individual should strive for peace, Hobbes incorporates a fundamental principle of reciprocity in his Second Law, and the attainment of peace through the relinquishment of natural rights: "*That a man be willing, when others are so too, as farre-forth, as for Peace, and defence of himself he shall think it necessary, to lay down this right to all things; and be contented with so much liberty against other men, as he would allow other men against himself*. . . . *Whatsoever you require that others should do to you, that do ye to them.* And that Law of all men, *Quod tibi fieri non vis, alteri ne feceris.*"[24] Further, the reciprocity of legal relations to be found in Hobbes's own elaboration of the Second Law suggests the correlativity in Hohfeld's scheme centuries later:

> And when a man hath in either manner abandoned, or granted away his Right; then is he said to be OBLIGED, or BOUND, not to hinder those, to whom such Right is granted, or abandoned, from the benefit of it: and that he *Ought*, and it is his DUTY not to make voyd that voluntary act of his own: and that such hindrance is INJUSTICE, and INJURY, as being *Sine Jure*; the Right being before renounced, or transferred. So that *Injury*, or

> *Injustice*, in the controversies of the world, is somewhat like to that, which in the disputations of Scholers is called *Absurdity*.[25]

However, this does not mean that such rights become purely Hohfeldian privileges (and thus unenforceable political rights). Indeed, this has been the traditional analysis of Hobbes's treatment of rights,[26] and this interpretation has been described as resulting in a distortion of Hobbes's work on rights.[27] Rather, this renunciation should be interpreted through what is generated by that renunciation. That is, not new privileges, as is the common interpretation, but new rights: "Only if we limit ourselves to an understanding of Hobbesian rights as Hohfeldian privileges do we fail to recognize the introduction of claims as a new *kind* of right."[28] Further, in the context of incorporeal property, or intellectual property, relevant to this discussion is the emphasis in some areas of policy and scholarship in the last couple of decades on a shift from a language of rights to a language of privileges.[29] Arguably, however, this linguistic compulsion is misled by the persistent ambiguity and expansion of the language of rights and maintains an adherence to the agonistic paradigm: "The use of a rights rhetoric by academics and activists concedes the rhetorical landscape to anti-regulatory advocates before a discussion of the appropriate allocation of interests can even begin."[30] The present discussion instead seeks to clarify the nature of the right through Hohfeld's monadology:

> One of the greatest hindrances to the clear understanding, the incisive statement, and the true solution of legal problems frequently arises from the express or tacit assumption that all legal relations may be reduced to "rights" and "duties," and that these latter categories are therefore adequate for the purpose of analyzing even the most complex legal interests, such as trusts, options, escrows, "future" interests, corporate interests, etc. Even if the difficulty related merely to inadequacy and ambiguity of terminology, its seriousness would nevertheless be worthy of definite recognition and persistent effort toward improvement; for in any closely reasoned problem, whether legal or non-legal, chameleon-hued words are a peril both to clear thought and to lucid expression.[31]

Recalling the mobility of animal territories, as distinct from the boundary-making of property, it is interesting at this point to consider Warder Clyde Allee's discussion of pecking orders as a kind of set of jural relations, albeit in a combative framework: "In other animal groups leadership may be expressed by the arrogation of certain rights and privileges. This is very well illustrated in the organization of a flock of domestic hens. Such groups, again, are an open, not a closed society but the newly admitted members must fight for any privileged standing which is accorded them by the community."[32]

Thus, Hohfeld's property monadology, as it were, also reinvigorates the creative assemblages in intellectual property through the co-presence of the user or consumer not only through the work in its consumption, but through the work in its conception and recognition. This contest in property is perhaps at odds with contemporary developments in "properties," including intellectual property, where a certain tolerance and negotiation is crucial. This is suggested as a kind of co-presence, as it were, which emerges as a fundamental character of intellectual property within this property model. The user is always already present in the work; indeed the user or consumer is fundamental to the creation of rights in the work. The user defines the work, not only in terms of its scope but also very much with respect to the work itself. Arguably this co-presence is even enshrined within conventional intellectual property frameworks through a range of user identities that define intellectual property,[33] but to what extent is this displaced by the predatory drift in intellectual property discourse?

For that we need a kind of "ethology" of property.

A conceptual approach

The reciprocity that is in a respect the substance or quality of an ethological jurisprudence is also intrinsically constitutive of Hohfeld's system of correlatives and opposites.[34] In this respect in particular, Hohfeld's scheme suggests a kind of perspective-taking and empathetic behaviour through the recognition of the very jural relations themselves. In many respects, Hohfeld's work suggests a revelatory moment in the history of property jurisprudence. In a brief career, cut short by his premature death, Hohfeld's scheme presents a revolutionary philosophical turn in the law that has perhaps since been reterritorialized, as it were, through its reconsideration in jurisprudential scholarship. Nevertheless, Hohfeld's task was arguably a philosophical one. Hohfeld set about to create concepts – always in combination, always in assemblage, monadological, as it were.

> [I]t cannot be doubted that Professor Hohfeld and his learned colleagues inaugurated a new era in legal science. Prior to the year 1917, when the Hohfeld system of juristic terminology was first vigorously advanced as a technical program, it had been supposed that it is possible to resolve all legal problems by reasoning directly from legal rules to juridical results without the aid of an intermediate technical principle best described as legal relation.... [H]is name deserves to be canonized in jurisprudence for initiating one of the most significant movements since the time of Austin for the scientific improvement of the technical method of legal reasoning.[35]

It is not unnoticed that Hohfeld and Tarde were writing at a very similar time in history, and to an extent perhaps it might be said that their work reflects the *fin de siècle* preoccupation with science – making sociology a science, making law a science, making ethology a science. In their analysis of Tarde's economic psychology, Latour and Lepinjay observe that Tarde's sociology was:

> Written amidst the first great era of globalization, grappling with all of the technological innovations of the times, taken with the moral and political problem of class struggles, profounding involved in bio-sociology, founded

on quantitative methods which at the time could only be dreamed of but which have today become available thanks to the extension of digitization techniques, it is because it seems freshly minted that we are presenting the work, a century later, in the middle of another period of globalization, at a time of moral, social, financial, political and ecological crisis.[36]

Indeed, in this present time of crisis, in an impassioned plea for a resolution to the one problem of empathy, what is striking about both Hohfeld and Tarde is the deterritorialization of concepts as productive, complex, and collective. The critical nature of Hohfeld's conceptual thinking is something which, at times, is underestimated in the process of its interpretation.

Hohfeld very artfully and conscientiously resocialised the law, as it were, through his refinement of all legal relations to the most intimate relation, that between individuals: "he tried to break down the notion of in rem relations to collections of smaller relations holding individually between pairs of people."[37] This facilitates a perspective upon property that incorporates the user, the consumer, rather than an adherence to a relationship to things and a unilateral discourse of exclusion.[38]

One of the persistent hesitations in the literature on Hohfeld's system is the supposed simplicity of its rendition of purportedly universal legal concepts and their consequences. But is this simplicity being oversimplified? Published around two decades after Hohfeld's Legal Conceptions, the "restatement" from Max Radin takes great issue with Hohfeld's enterprise: "Unambiguously! To say so much is to recognize the character of the task. It simply cannot be done. It cannot be done because of the very nature of human speech which did not grow out of a need of stating things precisely. There rarely was such a need."[39] Nevertheless, Hohfeld himself declared his own metaphor for his legal conceptions, at once reflecting *fin de siècle* thinking, calling them "the lowest common denominators of the law."[40] Commentators have focused upon this concept-based analysis in Hohfeld,[41] and throughout the consideration of Hohfeld's work is the characterisation of his correlatives as a kind of set of building blocks for more complex legal definitions.[42] While in many respects the basis for this approach is found in Hohfeld's articles, it is a contraction of the scheme. Hohfeld's table does indeed draw upon terms already in use in legal scholarship, and perhaps this is where some of the difficulties begin: "Obviously, every concept has a history."[43] And as Hohfeld insightfully recognises, this legacy of terms betrays an ongoing emphasis on things: "Much of the difficulty, as regards legal terminology, arises from the fact that many of our words were originally applicable only to physical things; so that their use in connection with legal relations is, strictly speaking, figurative or fictional."[44] This emphasis on thingness continues to monopolise, as it were, property discourse today, such that the ongoing debate on property and rights becomes a largely combative account between the holding of rights and the property in things. Hohfeld's correlatives, however, offer considerable connections of creativity through his explication of the aggregate nature of jural relations,[45] with each concept necessarily and fundamentally identified through relation and not through external account: "Possible worlds have a long history."[46] But what followed the "invention" that Hohfeld performs upon these terms is a certain unrest and a persistent point of conflict over the definition of Hohfeld's concepts, with considerable work devoted to revising and rethinking his terms,[47] renaming the concepts,[48] adding more,[49] or doing away with some of them altogether.[50] This reasoning on the nature and naming of the concepts in many respects shows the way in which the legal community has focused upon the concept as a kind of universal and categorising term, rather than as the more creative way in which arguably Hohfeld's work was emerging before his premature death: "His effort was less an attempt to elucidate the conceptions of others than to expose their confusions and to establish his own taxonomy."[51] In other words, the precise meaning of Hohfeld's concepts is also in relation, in combination, and through use. Indeed, Hohfeld's scheme is a territory, as it were, rather than the traditional boundary-making of much rights-based discourse.

In this respect, Jack Balkin calls Hohfeld "the first legal semiotician" and identifies his work as "the first to systematically and self-consciously discuss legal concepts such as rights, duties, and privileges rhetorically and as a system of mutually self-defining relations."[52] However, the subsequent enterprise within scholarship to refine or replace Hohfeld's terms betrays an adherence to the arbitral function of the concept, as it were, and so ultimately becomes a resistance to the potential of the concepts themselves. As such, the potential of Hohfeld's ethology, so to speak, is contained and tamed: *And they never looked back.*

One of the most important distinctions of Hohfeld's scheme is that the concepts are not discrete things, as such, but come about only as and through relations: "give up on seeing rights, duties, powers, and so forth as discrete identities. Instead, start viewing them as relations."[53] Further, the nature of the legal relations is that they are themselves contingencies.[54] Indeed, the error, so to speak, of much of the commentary on Hohfeld's approach is a logical one: "it wants to turn the concept into a function."[55] However, as Deleuze and Guattari have pointed out, "A relation of dependence or correspondence (necessary reason) defines the function. But this means first of all not only that the function must be defined in a mathematical or scientific proposition but that it characterizes a more general order of the proposition as what is expressed by the sentences of a natural language. Thus a new, specifically logical type of function must be invented."[56] In other words, where Hohfeld traces relations, much of the application restores the consequentialism of rights-based discourse: "In short, *in becoming propositional, the concept loses all the characteristics it possessed as philosophical concept:* its self-reference, its endoconsistency and its exoconsistency. This is because a regime of independence (of variables, axioms, and undecidable propositions) has replaced that of inseparability."[57] Thus, the very sociability of law that is animated by Hohfeld's system is obscured. It is to give Hohfeld's concepts, the footprints of justice, feet of clay.

Hohfeld's ethology

Arguably, rather than attempting to define a set of norms through his system, Hohfeld achieves something much more remarkable and enriching. In many respects, his deceptively simple table presents the resources not only to understand the judicial experiences of his day but also the means by which to think through these relations from scratch, as it were. In other words, Hohfeld's table is not simply representative of the judicial relations; rather it is a tool through which to continue to interrogate and transform. In this way, Hohfeld provides genuine philosophical concepts for property jurisprudence, but not in the form of Platonic Ideals or universals; rather, as a creative grid traversing the terrain. Unlike traditional universals, what is perhaps possible through Hohfeld's system is a genuinely discursive philosophical jurisprudence of property. What his table suggests is the means for a resocialisation of property. As his contemporary and colleague, Walter Wheeler Cook, explains:[58]

> It is also true that nearly all the concepts which these terms represent in Hohfeld's system have been recognized and discussed by more than one writer upon jurisprudence. A brief consideration serves to show, however, that the concepts and terms which are new are needed to logically complete the scheme and make of it a useful tool in the analysis of problems. When so completed, these legal concepts become the 'lowest common denominators' in terms of which all legal problems can be stated, and stated so as to bring out with greater distinctness than would otherwise be possible the real questions involved.

Indeed, all legal problems, all legal disputes, are always already relations. Thus, Hohfeld's concepts do not determine legal consequences, as such;[59] rather, they offer ways in which to identify new connections in property jurisprudence: "There are no simple concepts. Every concept has components and is defined by them. It therefore has a combination. It is a multiplicity."[60] The very nature of Hohfeld's scheme, of concepts presented as correlatives, always already doubled and in communication with each other, shows at once the potential within this creative jurisprudence. Deleuze and Guattari have identified the importance of not only the question "What to put in a concept?" but also "What to put with it?" This latter doubling and redoubling of the jurisprudential model offered by Hohfeld is deceptively simple and yet full of movement and creativity: "Hohfeld asserts that his conceptual framework is comprehensive, that is, capable of encompassing any and all jural relations among person, regardless of their normative content."[61] To embrace Hohfeld's model is indeed to explore the kind of productive thought advocated by Deleuze and Guattari in relation to the creation of concepts: "Immanence is redoubled. This is where one thinks no longer with figures but with concepts."[62] Indeed, this is the splendour of

Hohfeld's philosophy, as it were, and it has been an emancipation to rediscover his work.

In attempts to capture Hohfeld's system in a more substantive way, the mathematical and visual characterisation of Hohfeld's system has captured many commentators, and there has been considerable effort in depicting Hohfeld's relations mathematically,[63] an effort that has not been without criticism.[64] Disconcertingly, however, the overwhelming preoccupation has been with the nature of the relations as opposites; that is, jural relations as confronting and ultimately in contention. Indeed, this dominant mishandling of Hohfeld's system leads to its characterisation as primarily a binary system of opposites, reducing it methodically to a "Square of Opposition."[65] This immediately recalls the refiguring of Skinner's reinforcers and punishers through a misleading set of quadrants, considered in the previous chapter. The scheme is conceptualised as sets of equals and opposites, as distinct from dynamic relations, and thus the system is immediately adversarial in what amounts to an action of distortive predatory drift upon Hohfeld's otherwise extensive model. Hohfeld's table sets out not only what he calls jural opposites, but also jural correlatives, in a potential of extensive combination: "Concepts, therefore, extend to infinite and, being created, are never created from nothing. . . . Components, or what defines the *consistency* of the concept, its endoconsistency, are distinct, heterogeneous, and yet not separable. The point is that each partially overlaps, has a zone of neighbourhood, or a threshold of indiscernibility, with another."[66] Further, and very importantly, it is argued that, in contrast to a predominant view of Hohfeld's system, the "opposites" are not actually contrasting relationships as such but rather are different relationships. And those relationships are meaningful through the aggregate with correlatives. That is, the "opposite" is applied with respect to the two relationships, not in understanding the relationship between the two terms and it is in the aggregate relationships that the concepts become meaningful:[67] "Whereas a jural correlative is what others *must* have if one has a legally protected interest, a jural opposite is what one *cannot* have if one has a legally protected interest with respect to a certain type of act."[68] Importantly, "Correlatives express a single legal relation from the point of view of the two parties."[69] Thus, the terms simply do not operate in isolation but must be viewed in a series of interrelationships.[70] They are always already double, and both beings are always already complicit in the constitution of the right. In this respect, the meaning of the right is generated by the relationship, as it were.[71] Hohfeld explains, "At the very outset it seems necessary to emphasize the importance of differentiating purely legal relations from the physical and mental facts that call such relations into being . . . a considerable number of judicial opinions afford ample evidence of the inveterate and unfortunate tendency to confuse and blend the legal and the nonlegal quantities in a given problem."[72] Fundamentally, through Hohfeld is a genuine mechanism for meaningful reciprocity and a kind of reciprocal altruism within the law, and within property law in particular, the significance of which is not only for law but also towards a wider understanding of responsibility, accountability and empathy. These concepts are not discrete identities, not objective things; they come about only as and through relations.[73]

As such, and this recalls the problem with interpretive models based upon opposition, the opposites themselves are not necessarily negatives or mere negations of each other. Rather, "They are also *affirmations* that society will not penalize the holder of the privilege when he acts in the privileged way. So also are duty and right negations, for they negative the existence of privilege and no-right. They are also *affirmations* that society will penalize the holder of the duty when he acts in the un-privileged way. Each concept can be put in either a positive or negative *form* . . . but the concept expressed remains identical."[74] In this respect also, there is not a privileged "half" to the relation; this is a relation of genuine mutalism with no rank or hierarchy implied between rights and any so-called "lesser entitlement."[75] Balkin explains this arbitrary and contingent nature of Hohfeld's jural relations through his semiotic analysis of the scheme: "If Saussure offers a theory of the arbitrary nature of the sign, Hohfeld offers us a theory of the arbitrary nature of a right, or more generally, of any legally protected interest. The nature and extent of a person's rights are dependent upon the correlative duties of others. Just as a signifier does not take its meaning from the connection between itself and its signified, a right does not owe its existence to its connection to an individual, or a piece of property."[76]

Recalling Tarde's sociological monadology, Hohfeld's system is thus one of jural monadology, anatomising the fundamental legal relations, as it were, without constructing a substantive teleological approach to resolving those relations: "Hohfeld does not offer a *substantive theory* of law or entitlements or property or contracts or anything of the sort. All he offers is an *analytical method*."[77] This is the problem of the Aleph, Anti-Platonism in law, so to speak, and the politics of representation.[78] In other words, and crucially, this system achieves a transformative approach to perspectives upon legal relations, including how we may view those relations within their orientation through property: "[A]ll legal interest are 'incorporeal' – consisting, as they do, of more or less limited aggregates of *abstract* legal relations."[79] Hohfeld's scheme does indeed describe actual things, but importantly does not offer a definitive, substantive account. It is thus both engaging and engaged, dynamising and dynamic, and never descriptive and ossified.[80] In other words, an ethological approach is not about throwing property away, not abandoning property, not discarding it, but about realising it is not a definite thing. It is always already a relation, and the crucial issue is how we conduct those relations. In many respects, it is a resocialisation of property that Joseph Singer prefigures when he notes: "Whether we speak in the language of justice or utility, we will do a better job of understanding our own values and the consequences of alternative property regimes if we direct our attention to the kinds of relationships we want the legal rules to foster or discourage."[81] It is a way of looking, not the way things look.[82] Things begin to look different. And we must start to look back.

Sticky things

> The rules laid down in statutes and decision have often been constructed with the idea that property is a physical *res* – an object of sensation. As such property would always have a "*situs*" – a relation in space to other objects of sense. But a chose in action is also property, although it is not a thing or *res* – an object of sense. Our concept of property has shifted; incorporeal rights have become property. And finally, "property" has ceased to describe any *res*, or object of sense, at all, and has become merely a bundle of legal relations – rights, powers, privileges, immunities. Such is the case whether these relations affect the consumption and enjoyment of some particular object of sense or not.[83]

Hohfeld's scheme does much to disturb the obsessive thinking about things in property through his "complex aggregate of jural relations,"[84] used as the basis for the" bundle of sticks" ("bundle of rights)" theory in property ownership. Understanding property as a bundle of rights thus returns to the fore the dynamic experience of property through relations (within the bundle) as distinct from any particular thing. Arguably, more than any other concept in property, bundle of sticks creates a field of sociability rather than a one-sided dominion over a thing: "it gives a weak sense of the 'thingness' of private property."[85] Bundle of sticks is thus a bundle of relations, a busy, noisy sociability of contingent territories: "[B]y conceiving of ownership of property as a bundle of sticks, with each stick representing a distinct incident of ownership, it is possible to portray deprivation of a distinct interest rather than a mere restriction on an otherwise intact property interest."[86]

Hohfeld's relations systematically discredit the abridgment of property within the predatory drift of "the struggle for life," the will of the individual, and yet this is the dominant understanding of property rights – as rights of will, absolute and immutable – perverse in the context of an intra-social relationality. Huntington Cairns explains that "the fundamental idea of the common law is, as Pound has shown, relation, not will."[87] Huntington Cairns subsequently develops this into a theory of the triadic relations in property where that intra-sociality, that dialogue, in a manner of speaking, is always already three: "A owns B against C."[88] In this triadic relationality, C is *in rem*, all other individuals, the universal. However, Hohfeld's system is more exacting, more personal, and studies the relation between two beings, always already *in personam* in the very first instance, both encountering each other responsibly. In contrast to this, the apparent totality of *in rem* is a potential relation, but is not a dialogue, a communication. The "all other individuals," the *in rem*, is an inauthentic flourish, a Platonic ideal of the image of property. And it is the nature of defence, not the relation of display. In generalising the other being, the interpretation is from one perspective only: that of the owner. And that object, B, is subject to just one perspective: that of the owner. That dog is left in the shadows. But in Hohfeld's system, the "fruitful interference" of that dog is once again accountable.

From the public domain to the public interest, the ongoing attachment to thingness maintains an acceptance of the notion of boundaries and their transgression as a measure of potential harm, as distinct from the notion of boundaries as a negotiation, a point of contact. Joseph Singer argues that the law of nuisance provides a needed disruption to the boundary metaphor of property discourse: "[B]oundaries are not simply a mark of separation but of relationship. The ownership model uses the boundary metaphor to separate the space where an owner rules from the space where the owner's rights cease and nonowners take over. Ownership in this conception confers absolute powers within boundaries. The nuisance model recognizes that the boundary is a place of relationship among owners."[89] In this way, Singer's analysis of nuisance returns the sociable animal territories of overlapping tracks and negotiated space.

An ethology of owners

Paradoxically, in the predatory drift away from the sociable property relations of the earliest domestication, there is to be found nevertheless a resilience of the dogged sociability of canid property. The very conflict within property necessarily operates in its very use, for it is in use that the relational and sociable quality of property arguably persists. The sociability of property is translated into what we understand and recognise as "property" precisely through the kinds of relationships it creates, or roles it generates, and this occurs through its use. Without use, the integrity of property begins to disintegrate. Private land is such because there is someone to trespass upon it. In many ways, it comes into being through that encounter, as seen in the very earliest incarnations of property when human settlement behaviour first started to emerge. Similarly, in intellectual property, the concept of use is integral to the definition and operation of such property.[90] For example, if there is no intention to use, there may be no trade mark at all.[91] It is from this perspective that the potential of property, not as mere objectification or commodification of individuals, but in this relational aspect of use, becomes clear with respect to the welfare of the "propertyless":[92] "[A]lthough the idea of property as 'things' commands great cultural and rhetorical power, it fails to reflect the rich meanings of property in social discourse and law."[93]

This returns the discussion to the question of the other potential owners and, in particular, the question of that dog.[94] Disturbing the concept of predatory drift is important in revealing the importance of reciprocity, the ability to reciprocate, and the correlative duties that implies. Recalling Hallowell's dismissal of the notion of animal property on the basis that there are "no sanctions" in animal societies, advances in cognitive ethology and affective science confound this conclusion. Research on perspective-taking and affiliative and social learning, synchrony, altruism, cooperation, and other empathetic behaviours across a range of species are necessarily unravelling the conventional arguments against a fuller understanding of autonomous actions and claims for animals.

The anxiety that follows such considerations is, if animals, why not machines? There is considerable uncertainty at present over the potential status of artificial intelligence as authors. Arguably, the problem for most of the academic inquiry into the question of ownership in this context is a problem of predatory drift and a compulsive concern with the objects, the things. However, property is anything but the law of things. This is simply a convenient legal fiction that sustains predatory drift. And the discussions of authorship continue to focus on the nature of authorship as a right, without necessarily exploring the nature of authorship as a relation. In looking at this fundamental basis for property, that is, the recognition of a capacity for rights through the existence of correlative duties, the generalisation of animals and artificial intelligence all in the one "nonhuman" box is untenable. Animals do indeed have systems of property. But does all artificial intelligence? Or even any? It is in these relations and the capacity for reciprocity that the real insight into nonhuman property can be found.

At the moment when authorship is largely defined by the object, the rights are understood through the object in a monopolistic, as it were, relationship with that object. This is the issue for artifical intelligence art. Something has been created; therefore, there is a question of authorship *and* a question of property. But authorship is a relation, and this argument misunderstands the nature of authorship as a property right. In order for a robot to hold a property right, there must be some evidence of a correlative obligation for which the object is a vehicle. Property is an organisation of kin, *res familiaris*.

That dog is indeed a nuisance! Thank goodness for that dog.

Things are beginning to look different.

Notes

1 For a concise discussion of collective animal behaviour, see Biro D et al. (2016) Bringing a Time-Depth Perspective to Collective Animal Behaviour, *Trends in Ecology and Evolution*, 31(7), 550–562.
2 Bajec IL & Heppner FH (2009) Organized Flight in Birds, *Animal Behaviour*, 78, 777–789. While the formation has been a source of interest since the earliest documentation of natural history, systematic experimental investigation into the why and how of the V formation did not really get underway until the 1970s (777).
3 Portugal SJ et al. (2014) Upwash Exploitation and Downwash Avoidance Buy Flap Phasing in Ibis Formation Flight, *Nature*, 505, 399–404. The following bird will exactly trace the flap movement of the bird in front. Similarly, if confronted by a downwash, the individual will counter the downwash by doing exactly the opposite.
4 Steven Portugal quoted in Gill V (2014) Fly Like a Bird: The V Formation Finally Explained, *BBC News*, 16 January.
5 Steven Portugal, quoted in Yong E (2014) Birds That Fly in a V Formation Use an Amazing Trick, *National Geographic*, 15 January.
6 Voelki B et al. (2015) Matching Times of Leading and Following Suggest Cooperation through Direct Reciprocity during V-Formation Flight in Ibis, *PNAS*, 112(7), 2115–2120.

7 Portugal SJ et al. (2014) Upwash Exploitation and Downwash Avoidance Buy Flap Phasing in Ibis Formation Flight, *Nature*, 505, 399–404: p. 400.
8 Tarde G (1893/[2012]) *Monadology and Sociology*, T Lorenc (trans.), Re-Press, Melbourne, 53.
9 Tarde G (1890/[1912]) *Penal Philosophy*, R Howell (trans.), Little, Brown, and Co, Boston, 21–22.
10 Tarde G (1893/[2012]) *Monadology and Sociology*, T Lorenc (trans.), Re-Press, Melbourne, 11.
11 Borges JL (1945/[1967]) The Aleph, in *Jorges Luis Borges: A Personal Anthology*, A Kerrigan (trans.), Grove, New York, 138–154.
12 Borges JL (1945/[1967]) The Aleph, in *Jorges Luis Borges: A Personal Anthology*, A Kerrigan (trans.), Grove, New York, 138–154: p. 151.
13 Borges JL (1945/[1967]) The Aleph, in *Jorges Luis Borges: A Personal Anthology*, A Kerrigan (trans.), Grove, New York, 138–154: p. 146.
14 Tarde G (1893/[2012]) *Monadology and Sociology*, T Lorenc (trans.), Re-Press, Melbourne, 26.
15 Tarde G (1893/[2012]) *Monadology and Sociology*, T Lorenc (trans.), Re-Press, Melbourne, 34.
16 Tarde G (1893/[2012]) *Monadology and Sociology*, T Lorenc (trans.), Re-Press, Melbourne, 56–57.
17 Tarde G (1893/[2012]) *Monadology and Sociology*, T Lorenc (trans.), Re-Press, Melbourne, 22.
18 Deleuze G (1988/[1993]) *The Fold: Leibniz and the Baroque*, T Conley (trans.), U of Minnesota P, Minneapolis, 109.
19 Deleuze G (1988/[1993]) *The Fold: Leibniz and the Baroque*, T Conley (trans.), U of Minnesota P, Minneapolis, 109.
20 Tarde G (1893/[2012]) *Monadology and Sociology*, T Lorenc (trans.), Re-Press, Melbourne, 34.
21 Tarde G (1893/[2012]) *Monadology and Sociology*, T Lorenc (trans.), Re-Press, Melbourne, 56.
22 Patterson EW (1942) Logic in the Law, *University of Pennsylvania Law Review and American Law Register*, 90(8), 875–909: pp. 877–878.
23 Hobbes T (1651/[1968]) *Leviathan*, CB Macpherson (ed. and introd.), Penguin, London, Chapter 14, The second Law of Nature. See further the discussion of the concept of predatory drift in the Domination Age chapters.
24 Hobbes T (1651/[1968 *Leviathan*, CB Macpherson (ed. and introd.), Penguin, London, Chapter 14, The second Law of Nature.
25 Hobbes T (1651/[1968]) *Leviathan*, CB Macpherson (ed. and introd.), Penguin, London, Chapter 14, What it is to lay down a Right. Arthur Yates notes, "Contrary to those scholars who limit Hobbes's treatment of rights to Hohfeldian privileges, we must recognize that the privileges or liberties retained in civil society (the right to movement, to defend one's body, etc.) are combined with claims (with correlated duties of others)." See Yates A (2013) A Hohfeldian Analysis of Hobbesian Rights, *Law and Philosophy*, 32(4), 405–434: p. 410.
26 For instance, see Dalgarno MT (1975–1976) Analysing Hobbes's Contract, *Proceedings of the Aristotelian Society*, 76, 209–226; see the extensive treatment by Eleonor Curran in a series of articles: Curran E (2013) An Immodest Proposal: Hobbes Rather than Locke Provides a Forerunner for Modern Rights Theory, *Law and Philosophy*, 32(4), 515–538; Curran E (2010) Blinded by the Light of Hohfeld: Hobbes's Notion of Liberty, *Jurisprudence: An International Journal of Legal and Political Thought*, 1, 85–104; Curran E (2006) Can Rights Curb the Hobbesian Sovereign? The Full Right to Self-Preservation, Duties of Sovereignty and the Limitations of Hohfeld, *Law and Philosophy*, 25(2), 243–265; Curran

E (2006) Lost in Translation: Some Problems with a Hohfeldian Analysis of Hobbesian Rights, *Hobbes Studies*, 19(1), 58–76; and Curran E (2002) Hobbes's Theory of Rights: A Modern Interest Theory, *The Journal of Ethics*, 6(1), 63–86.

27 This is recognised both by those criticising the Hohfeldian analysis of Hobbesian rights (see Curran E (2006) Lost in Translation: Some Problems with a Hohfeldian Analysis of Hobbesian Rights, *Hobbes Studies*, 19(1), 58–76) and those advocating a Hohfeldian analysis in order to right, as it were, a fundamental misunderstanding of both the Hohfeldian analysis and Hobbes's theory of rights (see Yates A (2013) A Hohfeldian Analysis of Hobbesian Rights, *Law and Philosophy*, 32(4), 405–434). What these approaches have in common is that they both challenge the rendering of Hobbesian rights purely as Hohfeldian privileges.

28 Yates A (2013) A Hohfeldian Analysis of Hobbesian Rights, *Law and Philosophy*, 32(4), 405–434: pp. 409–410. See further the discussion of the right to resist punishment and the interpretation of this as a liberty through an application of Hohfeld's jural relations, in Schrock TS (1991) The Rights to Punish and Resist Punishment in Hobbes's *Leviathan*, *The Western Political Quarterly*, 44(4), 853–890. There the author explains the nature of Hobbesian rights as Hohfeldian privileges in the context of a confusion between the privilege/no-right pair and the right/duty pair: "Their confusion is understandable because, though it is true that privilege/no-right is different from right/duty, it is also true that both pairs are frequently created in the same moment by the same utterance" (879).

29 Economic and Social Council (2001) Economic Social and Cultural Rights: Intellectual Property Rights and Human Rights, Report of the Secretary-General, Addendum, 3 July, E/CN.4/Sub.2/2001/12/Add.1: "Indeed, it might be helpful to re-think the language used to describe IPRs and call them instead intellectual property privileges, which is what they are, and thus remove the possible confusion with human rights" (17). See further, Commission on Intellectual Property Rights (2002) *Integrating Intellectual Property and Development Policy*, Department for International Development, London: "Regardless of the term used for them, we prefer to regard IPRs as instruments of public policy which confer economic *privileges* on individuals or institutions solely for the purposes of contributing to the greater public good. The *privilege* is therefore a means to an end, not an end in itself" (6).

30 Long JA (2012) Waiting for Hohfeld: Property Rights, Property Privileges, and the Physical Consequences of Word Choice, *Gonzaga Law Review*, 48(2), 306–364: p. 353.

31 Hohfeld WN (1913) Some Fundamental Legal Conceptions as Applied in Judicial Reasoning, *Yale Law Journal*, 23(1), 16–59: pp. 28–29.

32 Allee WC (1932) *Animal Life and Social Growth*, The Williams & Wilkins Company, Baltimore, MD, 154.

33 Gibson J (2014) *The Logic of Innovation*, Ashgate, Aldershot, 48–49.

34 Hohfeld's correlatives are right/duty; privilege/no-right; power/liability' and immunity/disability. The jural opposites are right/no-right; privilege/duty; power/disability/ and immunity/liability. See further Hohfeld WN (1913) Some Fundamental Legal Conceptions as Applied in Judicial Reasoning, *Yale Law Journal*, 23(1), 16–59.

35 Kocourek A (1923) The Alphabet of Legal Relations, *American Bar Association Journal*, 9(4), 237–239: p. 237.

36 Latour B & Lepinjay VA (2009) *The Science of Passionate Interests*, Prickly Paradigm Press, Chicago, 3.

37 Smith HE (2012) On the Economy of Concepts in Property, *University of Pennsylvania Law Review*, 160(7), 2097–2128: p. 2102. See further the discussion in Campbell AH (1940) Some Footnotes to Salmond's Jurisprudence, *Cambridge Law Journal*, 7, 706–223.

38 Compare the work of James Penner, who argues, "It is my contention that the law of property is driven by an analysis which takes the perspective of exclusion, rather than one which elaborates a right to use. In other words, in order to understand property, we must look to the way that the law contours the duties it imposes on people to exclude themselves from the property of others, rather than regarding the law as instituting a series of positive liberties or powers to use particular things." See Penner J (1997) *The Idea of Property in Law*, Clarendon Press, Oxford, 71. Elsewhere in the same work, Penner rejects Hohfeld's jural relation between two beings as the fundamental legal relation, denouncing the subsequent controversy in the distinction between rights *in personam* and rights *in rem*: "Much of this controversy can be traced to Hohfeld, whose work is responsible for enthralling a generation of legal scholars with a bad, though appealing, characterization of the distinction," when he "famously argued that we should understand each right *in rem* as a multitude of more or less identical individual rights, each of which is held by the right *in rem*-holder against one of a very large and indefinite group of persons, essentially all subjects of the legal system. In other words, rights *in rem* are to be conceived of as a myriad of rights *in personam*" (23). Penner describes Hohfeld as "mad for the symmetry between rights and duties" and maintains, "To understand rights *in rem* we must not only discard Hohfeld's dogma that rights are always relations between two persons, but also the idea that a right *in rem* is a simple relation between one person and a set of indefinitely many others" (25).
39 Radin M (1938) A Restatement of Hohfeld, *Harvard Law Review*, 51(7), 1141–1164: p. 1142.
40 Hohfeld WH (1913) Some Fundamental Legal Conceptions as Applied in Judicial Reasoning, *Yale Law Journal*, 23(1), 16–59: p. 58.
41 For instance, see the discussion in Vatiero M (2010) From WN Hohfeld to JR Commons, and Beyond? A "Law and Economics" Enquiry on Jural Relations, *The American Journal of Economics and Sociology*, 69(2), 840–866; Smith HE (2012) On the Economy of Concepts in Property, *University of Pennsylvania Law Review*, 160(7), 2097–2128.
42 Arthur L Corbin, a contemporary of Hohfeld's was largely in support of a perceived quantitative analysis of legal behaviour. In Hohfeld's table of eight terms, Corbin saw the basic elements upon which to build "other important complexities": "They are fundamental because they are the conceptions out of which in various combinations we construct our conceptions of property, ownership, trust, easement, license, right of entry, patent, franchise, chose in action, contract, debt, quasi-contract, and other important complexities. They are fundamental because they are *constant* elements, into which all of our variable combinations can be analyzed, common denominators to which the superficially dissimilar, like law and equity, property and contract, can be reduced." See Corbin AL (1924) Jural Relations and Their Classification, *The Yale Law Journal*, 30(3), 226–238: p. 229.
43 Deleuze G & Guattari F (1991/[1994]) *What Is Philosophy?*, H Tomlinson & G Burchill (trans.), Verso, London, 17. In identifying his terminology, Hohfeld himself recognises the many and varied uses of terms throughout scholarship and everyday use: Hohfeld WN (1913) Some Fundamental Legal Conceptions as Applied in Judicial Reasoning, *Yale Law Journal*, 23(1), 16–59. See further the discussion of privilege in Robinson RE et al. (1983) The Logic of Rights, *The University of Toronto Law Journal*, 33(3), 267–278.
44 Hohfeld WN (1913) Some Fundamental Legal Conceptions as Applied in Judicial Reasoning, *Yale Law Journal*, 23(1), 16–59: p. 24. Indeed, this conceptual difficulty, as it were, influences what is arguably a frequent misreading of Hohfeld's

conceptual enterprise as an account of property, that is, as an account that implies things into relations.
45 As Pierre Schlag notes, "[L]egal concepts can be seen as jural composites – aggregates of different jural relations running to different parties concerning different acts." See Schlag P (2015) How to Do Things with Hohfeld, *Law and Contemporary Problems*, 78, 185–234: p. 217. Schlag goes on to explain: "the Hohfeldian insight into the decomposition of legal concepts has considerable virtues. For one thing, it helps restrain us from false inferences. It forces us to specify the legal relations between types of persons, kinds of acts, and identifiable jural relations. For another thing, once one views legal concepts (e.g., the fee simple) as composites of jural relations running to different parties regarding different actions, it becomes possible to question which jural relations should (or should not) be included in these jural composites. Decomposition, reshuffling, and recomposition of jural composites thus becomes analytically possible" (218).
46 Deleuze G & Guattari F (1991/[1994]) *What Is Philosophy?*, H Tomlinson & G Burchill (trans.), Verso, London, 18.
47 For a critique contemporary with Hohfeld's work see, for example: Randall HJ (1925) Hohfeld on Jurisprudence, *Law Quarterly Review*, 41, 86–94; Husik I (1923–1924) Hohfeld's Jurisprudence, *University of Pennsylvania Law Review*, 72, 263–277. The use of the term "liability" has historically raised the greatest unrest. Max Radin states: "Obviously the terms are defective since 'liability' is commonly used as the equivalent of 'obligation'. . . . In the case of 'liability,' it is unfortunate that some better term cannot be discovered. A literary equivalent may perhaps be found in the word 'subjection,' but the associations are quite wrong and the word has practically no legal history, that is, it has scarcely been used by lawyers at all." See Radin M (1938) A Restatement of Hohfeld, *Harvard Law Review*, 51(7), 1141–1164, p. 1158. See further the discussion in Singer JW (1982) The Legal Rights Debate in Analytical Jurisprudence from Bentham to Hohfeld, *Wisconsin Law Review*, 976–1060: pp. 992–993.
48 For example, see Lyons D (1970) The Correlativity of Rights and Duties, *Noûs*, 4(1), 45–55 (demands).
49 Kocourek A (1920) The Hohfeld System of Fundamental Legal Concepts, *Illinois Law Review*, 15(1), 24–39; Kocourek A (1923) The Alphabet of Legal Relations, *American Bar Association Journal*, 9(4), 237–239.
50 Halpin AKW (1985) Hohfeld's Conceptions: From Eight to Two, *Cambridge Law Journal*, 44(3), 435–457. See further Roy L Stone's somewhat unambiguously drafted critique: "Hohfeld's fundamental legal conceptions are not fundamental, or are fundamental only in the curious way in which Hohfeld makes them fundamental, that they are artificial, that they are probably infertile, that they are possibly impractical and that they are founded upon an American realism which itself misconceives the nature of law." See Stone RL (1963) An Analysis of Hohfeld, *Minnesota Law Review*, 48, 313–337: p. 337.
51 Schlag P (2015) How to Do Things with Hohfeld, *Law and Contemporary Problems*, 78, 185–234: p. 188.
52 Balkin JM (1990) The Hohfeldian Approach to Law and Semiotics, *University of Miami Law Review*, 44(5), 1119–1142: p. 1120. Although Balkin does not suggest that Hohfeld was directly influenced by Saussure, it is notable that both emerged from the same historical period of attention to the sciences and, in Saussure's case, move away from the notion of language as some sort of pre-existing essentialism towards a "scientific" study of language, "as naturalists, that is, in its natural ecological and social environment" (Seuren PAM (2016) Saussure and His Intellectual Environment, *History of European Ideas*, 42(6), 819–847:

p. 824). Similarly, Hohfeld's approach to legal concepts as relations also shows the constructedness of rights and other interests through use in a particular social and political context. Balkin notes: "A property right, then, is not an attribute or thing that inheres in the property itself, or in its owner. . . . It follows from Hohfeld's work that what constitutes a legally protected interest is arbitrary, and is not defined by the nature of things. Rather, the 'nature of things' in a legal sense is defined by the mutually self-defined relations of legal ideas. Just as reality is shaped and created by language, so too legal and political reality is shaped and created by mutually defined legal and political rights, powers, and duties. . . . Put another way, concepts like private property, consent, and liberty do not simply re-present previously existing things in the world. Rather, they result from the system of differences between legal and moral concepts, and in so doing constitute the political world that we live in" (1122–1123).

53 Schlag P (2015) How to Do Things with Hohfeld, *Law and Contemporary Problems*, 78, 185–234: p. 200. Schlag explains further: "Hohfeldian conceptions (right, duty, privilege, etc.) belong to a small self-referential world of legal form in which each legal conception acquires meaning through its relations to the others" (203).

54 As Balkin argues, "And indeed, emboldened by Hohfeld's critique, one could go further and argue that the concept of property itself had no essential content, but was merely defined in opposition to other rights of contract, criminal law, and so on. Thus, the ultimate point of the Hohfeldian analytic was that contract and property rights did not refer to real entities, but to particular contingent allocations of power created and enforced by state actors, that divided up the permissible forms of private power." See Balkin JM (1990) The Hohfeldian Approach to Law and Semiotics, *University of Miami Law Review*, 44(5), 1119–1142: pp. 1124–1125.

55 Deleuze G & Guattari F (1991/[1994]) *What Is Philosophy?*, H Tomlinson & G Burchill (trans.), Verso, London, 135.

56 Deleuze G & Guattari F (1991/[1994]) *What Is Philosophy?*, H Tomlinson & G Burchill (trans.), Verso, London, 135.

57 Deleuze G & Guattari F (1991/[1994]) *What Is Philosophy?*, H Tomlinson & G Burchill (trans.), Verso, London, 137–138.

58 Cook WW (1919) Hohfeld's Contributions to the Science of Law, *The Yale Law Journal*, 28(8), 721–738: p. 724.

59 Indeed, Joseph Singer considers Hohfeld an anticonceptualist in the response of his schema to classical analytical jurisprudence and describes his analytical scheme in terms resonant with semiotics and the arbitrary relationship of signified and signifier in the sign: "Hohfeld is property understood as a participant in the anticonceptualist revolt, even though some participants in the Hohfeldian debate thought he was a neoconceptualist. Hohfeld demonstrated that any supposed connection between liberties and duties did not result from logical necessity." See Singer JW (1982) The Legal Rights Debate in Analytical Jurisprudence from Bentham to Hohfeld, *Wisconsin Law Review*, 976–1060: p. 1053.

60 Deleuze G & Guattari F (1991/[1994]) *What Is Philosophy?*, H Tomlinson & G Burchill (trans.), Verso, London, 15.

61 Westen P (2018) Poor Wesley Hohfeld, *San Diego Law Review*, 55, 449–467: p. 459. Indeed, the frequent charge of minimalism and incompleteness that is often rendered against Hohfeld is arguably down to a misapplication of the analytic framework found in Hohfeld's concepts and an attenuation of the productive connections that are not only possible but integral to his conceptual framework of jural relations.

62 Deleuze G & Guattari F (1991/[1994]) *What Is Philosophy?*, H Tomlinson & G Burchill (trans.), Verso, London, 90.
63 This has included the proposal of "Hohfeld's Cube" as well as the use of Venn diagrams: Andrews M (1983) Hohfeld's Cube, *Akron Law Review*, 16(3), 471–485. In his proposal for a cube, Andrews identifies the aggregate as distinct from a purely adversarial structure: "The eight jural relations defined by Wesley N Hohfeld thus divide and unite the legal world" (485). The cube is also useful in that it prefigures the productive connections that are possible through Hohfeld's legal conceptions. Note also the discussion of the cube and the prefiguring of reciprocity and reciprocal altruism in Radin M (1929) Correlation, *Columbia Law Review*, 29(7), 901–905: "If we look at 'correlative' here, we find a number of closely similar usages. . . . In Biology, reciprocal relations in structure are correlatives. In Geometry, a point in plane may be the correlative of a line in a cube" (902).
64 For instance, note the critique of the attempts to deploy Hohfeld's table in a logical analysis of the law in Robinson RE et al. (1983) The Logic of Rights, *The University of Toronto Law Journal*, 33(3), 267–278. The authors note: "In fairness to Hohfeld, however, he did not set out to create a logical structure. If that had been his aim, he would have had to use propositions about legal relationships rather than the bare names of the relations themselves" (278).
65 O'Reilly DT (1995) Using the Square of Opposition to Illustrate the Deontic and Alethic Relations Constituting Rights, *The University of Toronto Law Journal*, 45(3), 279–310. See further the discussion in Robinson RE et al. (1983) The Logic of Rights, *The University of Toronto Law Journal*, 33(3), 267–278. The "square of opposition" is said to be derived from the work of Albert Kocourek: see Halpin A (2003) Fundamental Legal Concepts Reconsidered, *Canadian Journal of Law and Jurisprudence*, 16, 41–54: p. 41. However, Kocourek explicitly addressed the limiting nature of an analysis based upon this dynamic of binary opposition. Kocourek A (1921) Tabulae Minores Jurisprudentiae, *The Yale Law Journal*, 30(3), 215–225: "[W]hat Professor Hohfeld probably intended to outline was not a table of opposites in the sense of logic, but a table of negatives (contradictories)" (220, n 7). See further Kocourek A (1920) The Hohfeld System of Fundamental Legal Concepts, *Illinois Law Review*, 15(1), 24–39.
66 Deleuze G & Guattari F (1991/[1994]) *What Is Philosophy?*, H Tomlinson & G Burchill (trans.), Verso, London, 19.
67 Robinson et al. describe them as complements. See Robinson RE et al. (1983) The Logic of Rights, *The University of Toronto Law Journal*, 33(3), 267–278.
68 Balkin JM (1990) The Hohfeldian Approach to Law and Semiotics, *University of Miami Law Review*, 44(5), 1119–1142: p. 1122.
69 Singer JW (1982) The Legal Rights Debate in Analytical Jurisprudence from Bentham to Hohfeld, *Wisconsin Law Review*, 976–1060: p. 987.
70 As Balkin notes, "The nature and extent of a person's rights are dependent upon the correlative duties of others." See Balkin JM (1990) The Hohfeldian Approach to Law and Semiotics, *University of Miami Law Review*, 44(5), 1119–1142: p. 1122.
71 An early influence on Hohfeld, Oliver Wendell Holmes notes in *The Common Law*, "Every right is a consequence attached by the law to one or more facts which the law defines," and further, that "Legal duties are logically antecedent to legal rights" (214, 219). See Holmes OW (1882) *The Common Law*, Macmillan, London. See further Daniel Bromley's comment, "A property right is not the cause of protection but rather its effect," IN Bromley D (2002) This Land Is Whose Land?, *Wisconsin Academy Review*, 48(3), 60–63. In other words, "property

is fundamentally social" – see Long JA (2012) Waiting for Hohfeld: Property Rights, Property Privileges, and the Physical Consequences of Word Choice, *Gonzaga Law Review*, 48(2), 306–364: p. 355. See Singer & Beermann – "property rights can and should be defined through consideration of policies or values, and . . . property rights are instituted through the social and political construction of human relationships." Singer JW & Beermann JM (1993) The Social Origins of Property, *Canadian Journal of Law and Jurisprudence*, 6(2), 217–248: p. 218. The authors note, "the Court should shift its attention from natural law and formalistic conceptualizing and turn instead to consider the role that property plays in shaping the contours of social relationships." (220). See also Engle E (2010) Taking the Right Seriously: Hohfeldian Semiotics and Rights Discourse, *The Crit: A Critical Studies Journal*, 3(1), 84–107: p. 93. Peter Westen puts it clearly when he states, "Hohfeld emphasizes that his framework applies to legal relations that otherwise arise from antecedent mental and physical events, *not* to the antecedent mental and physical events themselves." See Westen P (2018) Poor Wesley Hohfeld, *San Diego Law Review*, 55, 449–467: p. 457.
72 Hohfeld WN (1913) Some Fundamental Legal Conceptions as Applied in Judicial Reasoning, *Yale Law Journal*, 23(1), 16–59: p. 20.
73 Schlag P (2015) How to Do Things with Hohfeld, *Law and Contemporary Problems*, 78, 185–234: p. 200.
74 Corbin AL (1921) Jural Relations and Their Classification, *Yale Law Journal*, 30(3), 226–238: p. 234, n6.
75 Compare the analysis of Cole DH & Grossman PZ (2002) The Meaning of Property Rights: Law versus Economics?, *Land Economics*, 78(3), 3178–330: p. 318. Compare also the use of the term "platform" to describe Hohfeld's scheme, offered in Schlag P (2015) How to Do Things with Hohfeld, *Law and Contemporary Problems*, 78, 185–234.
76 Balkin JM (1990) The Hohfeldian Approach to Law and Semiotics, *University of Miami Law Review*, 44(5), 1119–1142: p. 1122.
77 Schlag P (2015) How to Do Things with Hohfeld, *Law and Contemporary Problems*, 78, 185–234: p. 190.
78 Balkin situates Hohfeld's work within a more critical legal realism, "concerned with showing that seemingly neutral, natural, and apolitical concepts like the market, private property, or consent depended upon a set of political choices that were not necessary – choices that could be altered in the public interest once their contingent nature was made clear. It is this aspect of legal realism that depended so heavily on Hohfeld's theories." See Balkin JM (1990) The Hohfeldian Approach to Law and Semiotics, *University of Miami Law Review*, 44(5), 1119–1142: p. 1124. This anti-Platonism is identified by Balkin as "radically anti-essentialist," that is, it is not concerned with universals but rather with the analytical framework: "it stands to reason that a Saussurian or Hohfeldian theory of legal concepts would also be sceptical about essences" (1135).
79 Hohfeld WN (1913) Some Fundamental Legal Conceptions as Applied in Judicial Reasoning, *Yale Law Journal*, 23(1), 16–59: p. 24.
80 On the criticism of Hohfeld's approach as failing to distinguish between property and other relations, Pierre Schlag responds: "there is virtue in Hohfeld's approach to jural composites – namely, that it calls for us to think about why and how certain jural relations are condensed into what we call a property regime as opposed to a tort or contract or some other regime. It is precisely the incompleteness or, more charitably, the austere formal minimalism of Hohfeld's approach, that creates the motivation and the intellectual space necessary to inquire into the how and the why of our extant legal concepts – the principles of their organization

and assembly." See Schlag P (2015) How to Do Things with Hohfeld, *Law and Contemporary Problems*, 78, 185–234: p. 227. Jack Balkin sees this as a strength of Hohfeld's analysis: "his theories about judicial language were not specific to any type of rights. Thus, although the legal realists were mainly concerned with contract and property rights, and the general subject of economic regulation, the Hohfeldian analytic applies equally well to rights of free expression, sexual autonomy, equal treatment, or any other particular interest that the law might seek to protect." See Balkin JM (1990) The Hohfeldian Approach to Law and Semiotics, *University of Miami Law Review*, 44(5), 1119–1142: p. 1125. Balkin goes on to explain the fundamental semiotics of Hohfeld's schema: "First, legal concepts, no less than other linguistic concepts, result from a system of differences. Second, because of the semiotic characteristics of legal thought, the basic structure of legal arguments about rules and about the application of rules does not change, but repeats across various areas of doctrine" (1135).
81 Singer JW (2000) *Entitlement: The Paradoxes of Property*, Yale UP, New Haven, 134.
82 Pierre Schlag notes that Hohfeld's writings "can fundamentally alter the way one things about law." See Schlag P (2015) How to Do Things with Hohfeld, *Law and Contemporary Problems*, 78, 185–234: p. 186.
83 Corbin AL (1922) Taxation of Seats on the Stock Exchange, *Yale Law Journal*, 31(4), 429–431: p. 429.
84 Hohfeld WN (1917) Fundamental Legal Conceptions as Applied in Judicial Reasoning, *Yale Law Journal*, 26(8), 710–770: p. 746.
85 Heller MA (1999) The Boundaries of Private Property, *Yale Law Journal*, 108(6), 1163–1223: p. 1993.
86 Singer JW & Beermann JM (1993) The Social Origins of Property, *Canadian Journal of Law and Jurisprudence*, 6(2), 217–248: p. 222.
87 Cairns H (1935) *Law and the Social Sciences*, Kegan Paul, Trench, Trubner & Co, London, 59.
88 Cairns H (1935) *Law and the Social Sciences*, Kegan Paul, Trench, Trubner & Co, London, 59.
89 Singer JW (2000) *Entitlement: The Paradoxes of Property*, Yale UP, New Haven, 90.
90 Gibson J (2014) *The Logic of Innovation*, Ashgate, Aldershot.
91 Trade Marks Act 1994, 32(3). See further Johnson P (2018) "So Precisely What Will You Use Your Trade Mark For?" Bad Faith and Clarity in Trade Mark Specifications, *IIC*, 49, 940–970: pp. 954–969.
92 Gibson J (2006) *Creating Selves*, Ashgate, Aldershot, 15–16.
93 Underkuffler LS (2003) *The Idea of Property: Its Meaning and Power*, Oxford UP, Oxford, 12.
94 For a more comprehensive examination of the question of ownership in animals and machines, see Gibson J (forthcoming) *More Than Human Intellectual Property*, Routledge, London.

Chapter 12

Res familiaris

> And in the realm of the infinitely small, which, much more than the infinitely large, has remained inaccessible to our observations, does one not still dream of the philosopher's stone in a thousand forms, the identical atoms of the chemist, or the so-called homogenous protoplasm of the naturalists?
> Tarde G (1893/[2012]) *Monadology and Sociology*,
> T Lorenc (trans), re-press, Melbourne, 39

> To be a good sociologist one should refuse to go up, to take a larger view, to compile huge vistas! Look down, you sociologists. Be even more blind, even more narrow, even more down to earth, even more myopic.
> Latour B (2002) Gabriel Tarde and the end of the social,
> in Joyce P (ed) (2002) *The Social in Question: New bearings in history and the social sciences*, Routledge,
> London, 117–132: p. 124

Be familiar.

From the first domestication, through the sociable and sensory animal territories, to the "legal fictions" of property's predatory drift, and now opening out onto the shared interests of familiar ground, this has been a considerable journey. From making home to making kin, the relearning of sociability and resocialisation of property.

This chapter brings together the concept of shared interests, introduced earlier, with familiar production[1] in the context of a resocialised perspective on property, away from the legal fictions of the struggle for life, of the pack and the alpha, and fulfilled through the mutual regard of shared interests, and introduces a new term for an old understanding of property – *res familiaris*.

The trouble with things

The term *res* is of course familiar, in a manner of speaking, to legal discourse. In the legal context, *res* ordinarily refers to a thing in which a person may claim a right.[2] That is, the *res* is the thing from which a cause of action may arise; that is, property.[3]

In this understanding of *res*, the use is decidedly individual and obviously focused upon the object of proprietary interest. In other words, property rights *in rem* and *in personam* are understood as inextricably bound to the source, the thing. Thus, the use of the term in *res communes* or *res communis* does not necessarily imply a collective sociability of property;[4] rather, it is simply that these are things (and still things), like light and air, that are outside appropriation frameworks, at least to an extent. Although this apparent incapacity for appropriation is seemingly mitigated by claims such as right to light, the counter to this is that the party or neighbour seeking to obstruct the light is unable to appropriate it in this way.[5] This complexity in terms of the always already relational aspect of appropriation, as seen in the previous chapter, is the crack through which the light starts to stream.

This thingness of property, this possessive materiality, the triumph of the object, is almost inextricably bound up with notions of ownership. Indeed, the concept of *res nullius*, taken to mean a thing with no owner in a legal context, actually translates roughly as "no matter." Deemed ownership, it is thus appropriable. Without an owner, where is the body of evidence?[6] *Terra nullius*.

All the more, the presumptions regarding ownership and the object-based interpretation of property have also underpinned studies of behaviour, from early interpretations of territory and prior residence, through to assumptions of pack hierarchies, dominance identities and the mythic alpha, and the predatory drift of property as a combative, perilous, survival of the fittest. That dog's repertoire of behaviour becomes summarised through the resources linked to survival, where even territory becomes a "thing," regardless of any particular resources that may or may not be available within it.[7] Even that dog, the inventor of domestication, is presumed *res nullius* until ownership constitutes an identity within the property framework. That once sociable dog, purveyor of territory, artist of scent, curious flâneur, is immured within the scaffolding of property. George Romanes accepts this, writing in 1883: "Akin to this inborn idea of protecting the property of his master, is the idea which the dog has of himself as constituting a part of that property – *i.e.*, the idea of ownership as extended to himself."[8] The social contract is presumed as innate, "inborn," the very thing Tarde cautioned against. That dog, after introducing humans to sociable animal territories through domestication, is thus rendered *res nullius*, no matter, through the predatory drift of the property framework.

Ernest Beaglehole, writing in 1931, describes this construction of ownership by Romanes as identifying a kind of instinct of ownership in the owned:

> The domestic dog defends not only his food or his kennel but also other objects to which he has been conditioned by his master. So impressed was Romanes with his observations on domestic dogs that he urged that "the idea of defending his master's property has become in this animal truly instinctive" and is not due to individual instruction. "Akin to this inborn idea of protecting the property of his master," Romanes continues, "is the idea the dog has of himself constituting a part of that property – the idea of ownership as extended to himself."[9]

In this way, *res*, that thing, including that incorporeal thing of intellectual property, is presumed to have an inborn sense of completeness, of its own property and even of ownership, but not in the sense of the owner. Rather, this is achieved through the rendering of the owned. Even the internet has been colonised as "of things." Throughout property discourse, including intellectual property in particular, this notion of the "work" of the owned is a compelling mechanism in the service of a contrived predatory drift:

> The notion of accumulation does not do justice to this process of differentiation. It describes a phase – but only a phase – of the industry during which only the author of the repetition is active. It only marks a moment, albeit one necessary to development, which allows markets to grow, but never to change paths. It is also the product of an economic science – starting with economic sociology – which treats entities – humans and assets, services and technologies – as interchangeable, since they are seen from a distance, without capturing the small differences that would explain that change is not an exogenous shock suddenly befalling monomaniacal capitalists.[10]

An intriguing reinterpretation of this animal property, and indeed the case of Romanes's dog, is offered by Walter Heape. Instead of identifying the dog's sense of ownership as a displaced obligation of the owned, Heape offers a theory of an instinctive right to territory, and of the dog acting in self-interest, not through obligation:

> Everyone knows how keenly the domestic dog will defend the territory, however small, on which it is established by its master. . . . This attitude of the dog is generally regarded as an exhibition of its loyalty to its master as a duty to be preformed for the conservation of his master's property. A dog may be trained to perform this office of guardian with regard to human trespassers or strange visitors; but its attitude towards other dogs who seek to trespass is not the result of training, is not excited by loyalty to its master, it is assumed purely on account of its own interests; it is based on an instinctive *right* to preserve its own territory, and the *obligation*, which all other dogs recognise and very generally respect, to defend that territory.[11]

In many ways, although still viewed through the predatory drift of property discourse, Heape's interpretation of the dog's relationship to territory is arguably more sociable and certainly more autonomous than the one imagined by Romanes. In this account there is the opportunity for overlapping interests and territories and, most importantly, the operation of recognition and respect in the realisation of those territories.

What then of a property of sociability, a property through affiliation and sympathy, rather than defence and combat? This is the developing concept of *res familiaris*. The value of Hohfeld's conception of the law as fundamentally of relations, a law of sociability and mutual glances, is not as simple as it looks, perhaps all puns intended. Like the sociability of the senses, it will take work.

In the context of the predatory drift model of property development, Romanes's further observations of property along "classes" of predator and prey are striking yet not surprising. Property belongs to the "captor."[12] The human becomes the captor and the original sociability and wondrous reciprocity of that first domestication is rewritten as a discourse of unilateral acquisitive instinct, taming, and containment: "From the germ thus supplied by nature the art of man has operated in the case of the dog, till now the idea of defending his master's property has become in this animal truly instinctive. Without any training, and even sometimes against training, many dogs will bark and fly at strangers passing the gates or doors which bound their master's premises."[13]

Of course, with subsequent developments in the understanding of altruism, cooperation and mutual aid, of a kind of social reciprocity not only within species but between species, these "natural" examples defending the predatory drift of property are starting to seem like fictions: "*Fighting against* would be a curious form of *adapting to*!"[14] Building on the discussions in Chapter 10, "Shared interests," and Chapter 11, "Resocialisation," the biological and legal framework for a change in perspective is robust. It is thus possible to revise this early parable of property and rewrite the story as one of attachment and affiliative learning. And so, this perspective-taking might cause us to revisit conventional property frameworks, to question the value of the struggle, and the drive for better and better competition.

The original ownership model is based on a flawed premise, a legal fiction. As an example of what we knew then compared to what we know now, what Romanes observes as a kind of sense of ownership, drawn along the lines of a combative model, can be interpreted more meaningfully today through affiliative learning. Romanes describes the dog's sense of ownership thus:

> This abstract idea of ownership is well developed in many, if not in most dogs; so that, for instance, it is not at all an unusual thing to find that if a master consigns his dog to the care of a friend previously unknown to the animal, the latter will feel quite safe under the charge of one whom he has seen to be his master's friend. For the time being the allegiance of the animal is transferred, and he feels to his master's friend, not as to a stranger, but as to a deputed owner. It is not, I think, improbable that what appears to be the acquired instinct of barking is, as it were, an offshoot from this acquired instinct of property, and of protecting self as property, by drawing the attention of a master to the approach of strangers or enemies.[15]

What Romanes identifies as property, in the predatory sense of the term, is actually more reasonably a relationship of "being-with," in the sociable sense of that dog. A dog will in fact gauge from its human the acceptability of a stranger. In research on social referencing and synchrony in dogs, it has been found that dogs will look towards their humans for information and guidance, including the acceptance of strangers.¹⁶ Further, if a person behaves negatively towards a dog's owner, the dog will avoid them.¹⁷ Thus, while both examples provide evidence of social competence and even a kind of moral judgment, Romanes (and the traditions that followed) interprets this kind of behaviour as proprietary instinct, rather than sociability and creativity.

A personal anecdote illustrates this kind of social referencing. Recently the front garden wall of my mother's house suffered some considerable damage when a driver failed to set the handbrake on his car, leaving the car to roll down the hill and into my mother's wall. A few weeks later, after the insurance company had finally ordered the work, several workers arrived at my mother's house to fix the wall. The workers (three men) arrived early in the morning and started walking into my mother's garden for instructions. Her three dogs (Simba the Great Dane, YumYum the Miniature Poodle, and Benny the Maltese-Shih Tzu cross), all rescues and all with varying states of distrust regarding strangers, raced out of the house, ran down, confronted the workers, and started barking at them. My mother quickly followed them and said, "It's all right everyone, they are John's friends [my brother]," at which point all three dogs stopped barking and started greeting them instead: *Rex familiaris*.

What these dogs can teach humans, in terms of these "proprietary" or territory interactions, is the much more fundamental value of trust together with embodied communication. These are examples of synchrony in shared interests, rather than combat over a thing. As Brian Massumi has noted, in his advocacy for an animal politics, "*Animal politics actively affirms a logic of mutual inclusion. It greets the included middle with enthusiasm, in the form of performed effective paradoxes.*"¹⁸

What have been explored in the previous chapters in this, the Social Age, are the various ways in which an affiliative model of learning holds much potential, especially in digital territories, where attempts at the model of dominion become not only inefficient but also very regularly ineffective. Thus, by interpreting ownership, property, and its management through the concepts of shared interests and familiar production within the framework of sociability, *res familiaris* is mobilised. A more than human property.¹⁹

Every thing is a society.²⁰ For Tarde, society is not a fixed artefact to be defined from outside in an isolated and fixed observation, *to be*; but rather, it is embodied through having, through possession, "the universal fact."²¹ Indeed, society is always unfinished through the relations and sociality of *being-with*. Tarde's emphasis on the sociality of "having" over the fixation of (and upon) being, this is the character of reciprocal possession visited throughout this discussion, a property of relations: "What is society? It could be defined, from our point of view, as each individual's reciprocal possession, in many highly varied forms, of every other."²² The "thing" is sociability, a field of relations rather than static objects. Boundaries imposed within and around sociable territories, around things, can be only contingent, an artificial limitation on otherwise unfinished business: *finally unfinished*.

Reciprocal possession explains the creation of these admirable living organisms whose parts are all united and solidary, and where everything is both an end and a means at once. By reciprocal possession, finally, in the free cities of antiquity and in modern states, mutuality of service and equality of right bring about the prodigious achievements of our sciences, industries, and arts.[23]

The Cartesian thinking that underlines radical behaviourism, alienable objects, and human exceptionalism is thus confounded by this microsociology:

But, it will be objected, even if we cannot thus attain the limits of the psychic, nonetheless common sense affirms that, by and large, beings much smaller than ourselves are much less intelligent; and, following this progression, we are sure to arrive, on the path of increasing smallness, at the absolute absence of intelligence. Common sense indeed! Common sense also tells us that intelligence is incompatible with excessive size and in this, it must be admitted, experience proves it right. But if we juxtapose these two commonsensical affirmations, the one unmotivated, the other likely, it is clear that they emerge from the prejudice of anthropocentrism. In reality, we judge beings to be less intelligent the less we understand them, and the error of thinking the unknown to be unintelligent goes hand in hand with the error . . . of thinking the unknown to be indistinct, undifferentiated, and homogenous.[24]

These are thus functional boundaries, functional limits, but necessarily contingent and inadequate: "However infinite one may suppose thought or divine will to be, if it has to be *one* thing, it will *ipso facto* become inadequate as an explanation of reality."[25]

The common markers of a presumed human exceptionalism are usually language, symbolic thought, culture and justice, notwithstanding the challenges to these conclusions.[26] However, as well as the privileged viewpoints on these distinctions, it has been shown throughout this discussion that the predatory drift in property and its conventional rendering as a combative, competitive, mannerless object, contributes to the architecture of human exceptionalism. Even the notion of cooperation has been somewhat reconfigured as unique to humans, through theories of shared or collective intentionality as distinctively human capacities.[27] In this dominant and resilient model, society is about being through things, that materialism makes us uniquely human,[28] and that without ownership an animal is no matter, *res nullius*. That dog's being is wholly constructed and exhausted through property: "If having seems to indicate being, being surely implies having. Being, that hollow abstraction, is never conceived except as the *property* of something, of some other being, which is itself composed of *properties*, and so on to infinite. At root the whole concept of being is exhausted by the concept of having. But the converse is not true: being is not the whole content of the idea of property."[29] That dog, world's first inventor, becomes a thing incapable of achieving the "being" that is characterised by property.[30]

BL: When you criticize a-cosmicism, you don't come back to the object. For you the object is active socialized, something to which a lot of bizarre things happen. On the other hand, for you society does not have the characteristics attributed to it by the social sciences. It is once again filled with things.
MS: Humanity begins with things; animals don't have things.
BL: *The misunderstanding is complete.*[31]

Familiar territory

But we are looking for the tracks, not the lion.

It is in the social model of property that familiar production becomes most invigorated.[32] Familiar production anticipates, and responds to, Tarde's critique of the social contract, embodying the sociality that characterises animal territories, transforming the social of 'contract.'[33] Familiar production is always already *being-with*, where the things ("production") are in some way incidental, the appurtenance of social life – happenstance. Rather than the institutionalised, conventional narrative of progress, incentives, and ends, here is the world of pure expression of chance, shared interests, and the infinite sociability of the finally unfinished.

Familiar production is thus meaningful within Tarde's microsociology and at the same time resonates with domestication, that first "capital invention" and the making of home and kin. To be "familiar" ushers in not only meanings of community and neighbourhood but also the intimacy, openness, and mutuality that is at the heart of this sociality, the 'abode' of ethics;[34] that is, an ethics through use and mutual responsibility.[35] This is the world of manners and relations, rather than combat and competition. Familiar production is thus also de-institutionalised, disorganised, playful production, generated through relations and sociability, through living. In many respects this is consistent with Haraway's concept of *becoming-with*, in that familiar production is perhaps more concerned with the production of affiliative assemblages than with the particular products that may be produced through, and indexical of, those relations.[36]

The "boundaries" or "limits" of the "finished" products of familiar production, as it were, are indicated not from outside (*to be*), but rather through use, through "having." That is, any "marking" of territory among products is as a point of contact, an introduction, and information, rather than a defence or exclusion, relying on manners in communication.[37] In this way, familiar production is always *finally unfinished*, transforming the teleology of conventional property paradigms in the process.

The objects of familiar production may even be worthless in and of themselves, but the value to be found instead in the relations, the experiences, the repetitions generated through the "useless" object can be breathtaking: *money buys literally nothing*.[38]

The thing about the commons

> Mr Donaldson himself must be undone by this Victory. . . . Now the Door is open to every body, and his exclusive Title to share in this Right is at an End. The Field wherein he claimed an equal Right to graze his Cattle with the supposed Proprietor is laid open to be trampled on and rendered useless by all the Cattle in the Neighbourhood.[39]

The above is an extract from a letter on literary property, published in 1774, which includes what is possibly the very first reference to the so-called "tragedy of the commons,"[40] almost fifty years before the lectures of 1832 by the Rev Professor William Forster Lloyd, ordinarily credited with the revision of the commons.[41] Renewed attention to Lloyd's arguments came in 1968 with Garret Hardin's now famous essay, "The Tragedy of the Commons."[42] Hardin cites Lloyd's "little-known pamphlet" in his analysis of the depletion of the commons through unfettered access and overpopulation:

> The tragedy of the commons develops in this way. Picture a pasture open to all. It is to be expected that each herdsman will try to keep as many cattle as possible on the commons. Such an arrangement may work reasonably satisfactorily for centuries because tribal wars, poaching, and disease keep the numbers of both man and beast well below the carrying capacity of the land. Finally, however, comes the day of reckoning, that is, the day when the long-desired goal of social stability becomes a reality. At this point, the inherent logic of the commons remorselessly generates tragedy.[43]

Indeed, one might say it is "laid open to be trampled on and rendered useless by all the Cattle in the Neighbourhood."[44]

Hardin goes on to advocate for, in his words, a mutually agreed mutual coercion in order to address the anticipated crisis before the commons is used to uselessness: "The social arrangements that produce responsibility are arrangements that create coercion, of some sort."[45] This assertion resonates with the conventional model of predatory drift that has dominated not only the development of property but also the law more generally.

In contrast to Hardin's argument for external coercive regulatory control of the commons, Elinor Ostrom's influential work[46] maintains that the commons may be solved through internal cooperation and voluntary organisations; that is, a sociable solution delivered by the very people using it.[47] She illustrates this by developing a game based on a pastoral model of the herders (rather than focusing on the resources), "in which the herders themselves can make a binding contract to commit themselves to a cooperative strategy that they themselves will work out."[48] Fundamental to Ostrom's model is the contact and familiar production between herders: "They are not dependent on the accuracy of the information obtained by a distant government official regarding their strategies."[49] Reciprocity and trust, and face-to-face communication are thus key to the sustainability of the commons.[50] Responding to Ostrom's work, Arun Agrawal notes: "Without trust and reciprocity, sustained collective action is not possible – whether on the commons or in other settings."[51] In addition, Ostrom emphasises the importance of "shared interests and understandings," which she identifies as vulnerable to the forces of globalisation and reculturation:[52] "Ostrom's insight that social capital must be present before the construction of an institution designed to resolve a community dilemma is important."[53]

In contrast to Ostrom's herder game, characterised as it is by its sociability and familiar production, an adherence to a predatory property approach carves up and erects boundaries resulting in less for all: "Those recommending the imposition of privatization on the herders would divide the meadow in half and assign half of the meadow to one herder and the other half to the second herder. Now each herder will be playing a *game against nature* in a smaller terrain, rather than a game against another player in a larger terrain. The herders now will need to invest in fences and their maintenance, as well as in monitoring and sanctioning activities to enforce their division of the grazing area."[54] This is the game of the Looking-glass cake, the cake of familiar production, shared and consumed before it is quantified: *hand it round first, and cut it afterwards.*[55] As Hoebel declares, "The proof of the pudding is in the eating."[56] That is, the sociality of use and familiar production is what sustains the commons; through intra-social relations, rather than external governance.

As discussed earlier in relation to traditional knowledge,[57] the language of communalism and apportionment sustains the conceptualisation of the commons as something real in which individuals have a share. This perspective is nevertheless framed by the predatory drift of property towards an acceptance of rivalry, combat, and competition. In this way, the commons inheres as something preexistent, finite, and separate from those who visit upon the commons. Within the dominant economic models, the commons emerges as a thing in which to prevent overuse (thus justifying enclosure), not a relation to nurture and flourish (in which the emphasis would be on not only cooperation but also altruism and reciprocity). In the dominant perspectives, the commons reemerges as a thing, not a relation: "a remorseless tragedy."[58]

One thing that is seemingly at no risk of depletion is the enormous literature on the commons, some of which has been critical of Hardin's approach, and others which have deployed a mirror, as it were, of Hardin's analysis in order to consider other commons, such as in the commons concept of the public domain[59] as well as the "mirror" of the anticommons.[60] Arguably, the commons in intellectual property does not really work in the same way as a grazing commons, although the analogy has been reworked in often artful ways. Nevertheless, an adherence to the traditional narrative of the commons continues to situate it within conventional property rights or at least as a product of those rights.: "thinking about the commons itself has been enclosed all too often in a far too narrow set of presumptions. . . . As a result, thinking has often been polarized between private-property solutions or authoritarian state intervention. From a political perspective, the whole issue has been clouded over by a gut reaction either for or against enclosure."⁶¹ Indeed, even the discourse of the commons appears to succumb to the binarising logic of predatory drift.

The commons, so to speak, in intellectual property actually proliferates through use, through commutualism – through shared interests. In other words, overuse of the commons, as it were, can lead to its flourishing – the difference in repetition, the innovation in imitation: "The supreme law of imitation seems to be its tendency towards indefinite progression. . . . It seems to impel every discovery or innovation, however futile, to scatter itself through the whole of the indefinitely broadened social field."⁶² As Latour and Lepinjay explain, "Tarde does not set up an opposition between the mysterious origin of the individual genius and the slavish imitation of past models. He shifts levels: a genius is an individual in whom the multitudes of repetitions and imitations (those lively firings of the brain) lead, dare we say, a life of their own."⁶³ This tendency towards imitation nevertheless must be supported by the "coming together of inventions" and the legitimacy of "the prestige which belongs to alleged superiorities," then that propulsion of innovation "is checked by the different obstacles which it has successively to overcome or to turn aside."⁶⁴

This coming together, this innovative friendship, is what is proposed here as the *amity of the commons*.

The amity of the commons

> *Progress*, then, is a kind of collective thinking, which lacks a brain of its own, but which is made possible, thanks to imitation, by the solidarity of the brains of numerous scholars and inventors who interchange their successive discoveries.⁶⁵

The commons in intellectual property is thus a curious paradox for the conventional narrative of incentives, of cause and effect in innovation. Tarde's economics is not concerned with trade, but rather with the building of relations towards a market: "Trade does indeed exist, but it is brought back to its proper role in the genealogy of markets. What launches a market, what builds an economy, is not trade, which is but a zero-sum game; it is rather the pooling and the coordinating of previously scattered energies. Tarde places faith and trust at the center of this pooling effort."⁶⁶ The market is thus transformed as fundamentally sociable.

The pooling of energies is an integral part of the laws of imitation, this coming together. The products themselves thus circulate as part of those relations across and between each other, defeating notions of cause and effect, model and copy, tool and product: "There is no product that is not or cannot become the auxiliary of another, the *tool* of another. The distinction between tool and product possesses a merely superficial or relative truth."⁶⁷ The notion of "commoning" in environmental and ecological literature is very relevant in this respect. Building upon Ostrom's fundamental work, the concept of the commons in environmental literature is increasingly facilitated by an understanding of the commons as social practice, countering the traditional good-based interpretation: "The social form is what gives the matter its specific way of being (and becoming)."[68]

Attribution and credit, however, remain resilient and arguably essential to the sociability and manners of Tarde's economics. A product not only communicates with others in terms of its provenance, but also "allies itself to all the previous products that it utilises":[69]

> One consumes riches, that is, in order to employ them one must destroy them with greater or lesser speed; and perhaps one could also say that one consumes a power by exercising it, or abusing it; but does one consume one's glory, or even one's credit? Does one consume one's beliefs by thinking about them or the masterpieces that one admires by looking at them. On the contrary, there are two ideas that economists use in a far too restricted manner, those of alliances and struggles, of *adaptation* and *opposition*, ideas which are eminently capable of being generalized. Economists only deal with opposition in terms of the competition between productions or consumptions, and they neglect the hidden and continuous opposition of products which plays a crucial economic role, and they pay no mind either to the invisible alliances of products, to their fecund adaptations.[70]

This resonates with the altruism of shared interests, not merely a collaboration or cooperation, but a genuine offering and exchange, a vital reciprocity – a relationship of use.[71] Tarde's market is genuinely *response-able* and trade thus arises as part of this genealogy of relations through which markets are established. The intellectual property system has an abundance of examples where owners have managed to achieve such a pool of energies, as it were. A fundamental feature for participants in such energetic pooling is not the value realised in the object, the thing, as such, but rather the quality of attribution; that is, acknowledging the maker, however that may be adequately achieved, and the *response-ability* and trust within the pool that this sustains. The "value" to the system, and to the "owners," is thus the preservation of that attribution, which may indeed comprise also the opportunity for remunerative developments based upon this model.

Through these shared interests, the producer and consumer necessarily coincide on the desire for identification of the maker through the work. On the one hand, the producer has an interest in its dissemination and acknowledgement, as the maker, as offering the sensation. On the other hand, the consumer desires to acknowledge and disseminate it, to impart their alliance and affiliation with the work and maker, to show their attachment through recognition.[72] As an economic model, remuneration is possible not in spite of a work being shared for free, but precisely because that work is shared. The model does not depend upon the consumer to pay for its attention, as it were, but rather thrives upon the proliferative and free play of relations that are generated – the passionate interests. In this way, other "strangers" are invited into the conversation – brands, affiliates, and so on – and the value itself is thus to be found in that conversation and the quality of that conversation. It is upon this foundation, this launching of markets, as it were, into which trade can then be introduced, that the economic relationship may be subsequently established.[73] Monetary value is thus located elsewhere, but the value is generated precisely because of the sharing.

This is the olfactory mirror for intellectual property models. In sharing the smell the object is always elsewhere, the "having" is the sensation. *But for* the sharing, that value would not necessarily be realized: *hand it round first, and cut it afterwards.*[74] These amicable results, so to speak, are not structural impossibilities for intellectual property. Indeed, they are radically achievable. But they present certain socio-political challenges. They defy the expectations of predatory drift.

The reckoning of this is consistent with Tarde's metaphor of the cotyledon, as applied to capital, which distinguishes between what he terms "ruling inventions" and "auxiliary capital": "These two elements are different in more or less the same way as, in a plant seed, the germ is different from those little supplies of nutrients which envelope it and which we call cotyledons. Cotyledons are not indispensable; there are plants that reproduce without them. They are just very useful. The difficult is not in noticing them, when the seed is opened, for they are relatively large. The tiny germ is hidden by them. The economists who saw capital as consisting solely in the saving and accumulation of earlier products are like botanists who would view a seed as being entirely made up of cotyledons."[75] We are looking for the tracks, not the lion. We are looking for the germ, not the cotyledon.

The artificial scarcity[76] contrived by intellectual property frameworks is premised upon a conventional interpretation of the commons and the predatory drift underpinning the assumptions of relevant incentives.[77] Such confusion of the productive collision of intellectual works with the notion of the stimulation of trade is objectionable to Tarde: "We must distinguish, for commodities as well as books, between two forms of combat: *competition* and *contradiction*. Their competition, that is to say, their emulation in pursuit of the best solution to the same problem, the satisfaction of the same need, is excellent and praiseworthy, even when it is accompanied by an indirect and implicit contradiction, that of their contrary claims; but their direct collision, their violent contradiction, in the guise of literary polemics of trade wars, is odious."[78] Tarde revives a notion of "combat" and "competition" as a kind of mutual interest, but when this is reconfigured in terms of the violence of the predatory drift in trade it is "odious." In this scenario, trade is about defiance of each other, rather than converging through trust in each other:

> Only half of the truth is being told in seeing the trade contract as the essential and seminal economic event. Trade, in truth, favors and develops directly only consumption. The direct agent of production is another contract, which is no less seminal and no less fundamental: the loan contract. Through trade, we do each other favors, but all while defying one another: give and take; through loans, we place trust in one another.[79]

Tarde's laws of imitation thrive through amity, through contact, through looking back. In the Amity of the Commons it is possible to recognise what Tarde describes as "the passing of unilateral into reciprocal imitation," a fundamental life force of familiar production: "The mere play of imitation has resulted, then, not only in extending it, but in making it two-sided as well. Now, this effect which imitation produces upon itself, it also produces upon many other connections between people. Ultimately it transforms all unilateral into mutual relations."[80]

Shared interests and common ground

> But how to avoid the tragedy of the commons? Through co-operation. . . . I came to the conclusion that cattle were not the real cult object of the western ranchers' religion. Private property is . . . John Locke is the theologian of cattlepersons. As I envision a Paradise Valley Ungulate Commons – a key part of the Greater Yellowstone Biosphere Reserve Buffer Zone – private 'real' property would remain in private hands. Privately owned 'animal units' are what would go, along with fences, one purpose of which is to mark real estate boundaries and segregate one rancher's privately owned herd from another's.
>
> Would this be so un-American? Not if we think more expansively, in historical terms. That's more or less the way the Indians – bona fide Americans if anyone is – did it. Each group had a territory to which they claimed and enforced the property rights. But the animals were their own bosses.[81]

The ways in which animals manage overlapping territories through communication and points of contact contrast with the increasingly bifurcated character of western societies, not least in terms of current politics. Through this bifurcation, engagement on areas of convergence diminishes, and positions become entrenched belief systems. As seen in the previous chapters, this is arguably the nature of predatory drift and the structure of conventional property paradigms as well.

The predatory drift creates (and contrives to justify) a strict division between propertied predator and prey, between owner and trespasser, producer and consumer, and human and all other animals, through a series of (legal) fictions perpetuated as organising assumptions. The result of this predatory paradigm is an increasingly adversarial, combative model, where the middle of shared interests is what is arguably necessarily forgotten in order to represent the assumed natural totality of this property model. There is even further differentiation, such as the example of the term "user-generated creativity." This is a curious differentiation of creativity, presenting a specious distinction between creators on the one hand and users who might create on the other, resulting in an ongoing fictional hierarchy of genuine creators; the alphas, as it were, and the followers, the rest of the pack. Absorbing the somewhat class-based fiction of the pack, property drifts from the sociable territories to the predatory, rivalrous and uncooperative property paradigm, a narrative replicated in the first interpretations of the wolf pack, and perpetuated through the continuing spread of misinformation today, thus obscuring the family and the "familiar" of production. The mythical wolf pack is rallied to justify interactions as at once intensely competitive and aggressive, territorial and unequal, the predatory drift of social discourse.

This imperative of differentiation is also recognised in the nature of scientific evidence. Vinciane Despret laments the denigration of anecdotal evidence in science, such as the evidence of owners or guardians of dogs. Referring to the example of Harry Harlow and his research on attachment bonds using social isolation experiments in rhesus monkeys (or as Latour suggests, "The Sadistic Harlow and His Monkeys"[82]), Despret notes that "it is almost impossible to speak about attachment, even among humans, without evoking his name, as though it is due to him that we know that when an infant is separated from any meaningful contact, psychological and/or physical death follows."[83] As Despret explains, in order to represent the knowledge in this way, as a fact caused by Harlow, as it were, it is necessary "to implicitly endorse the manner by which he proposed to 'know' it: through a system of evidence, which, in this context, means a system of destruction."[84] Despret is describing a predatory drift within research, where the evidence destroyed is that of shared interests, that *becoming-with*, as Haraway describes. Despret argues that when a researcher "accepts to learn *with* them, and not *about* them, which is to say *against* them," this then produces the best knowledge of "those one is questioning."[85] The olfactory mirror, as it were.

In other words, in the dominant model of predatory property frameworks, there is no "commons." In this model, the concept of shared interests could not even be entertained as a logical possibility, but rather, becomes a conceptual improbability. This is some way from the sociability of animal territories and property as it was inaugurated by dogs in that first domestication, property that circulates on cooperation. Conventional notions of property are characterised by desire as lack, an always already unsatisfied instinct for consumption. In contrast to this, in the sociability of that dog's territories, production is motivated through the social and productive assemblage of sharing, of familiar production. This is property as flows, *fluxus*, if you will – *finally unfinished*.

What is needed is a different perspective, a different question, a different test. What is needed is a different mirror. Through advocating an ethological jurisprudence of property, that smelly mirror, that mutual glance, that commons of shared interests, is opened up to the world.

The commons is thus a co-constituted space, a kind of embodied communication, like the kind of pastoralism suggested in that first domestication. And just like the pastoralism in that first domestication, it is a legal space co-constituted by humans and animals. There is a kind of mutual dependence that is necessary in territory building. Even the Iguana cannot build her burrow alone. In some respect, some evolutionary remnants of animal territories continue to inhere in property models – the relationship between law and equity within real property, and the importance of the user in refining the scope of intellectual property. But what of the use itself? What of overlapping territories and coexisting access? What of shared interests? Departing from the "property" model that has been traversing the commons, a renewed perspective on the commons is possible – that of animal territories, *res familiaris*.

Res familiaris, in action

> In conceiving of the *homo œconomicus* economists have engaged in a double abstraction. First, the unwarranted one of having conceived of a man with nothing human in his heart; second, of having represented this individual as detached from any group, corporation, sect, party, homeland, or association of any sort.[86]

Endowed with Wesley Newcomb Hohfeld's scheme, the previous chapters marked out the footing for a relational interpretation of property. Hohfeld's legal conceptions have much in common with Tarde's monadological thinking: *Every thing is society.*

While *res familiaris* may be taken to mean simply "familiar thing," especially in the context of the usual legal reckoning of *res*, it can also be translated as friend. This is especially apt and felicitous for the sociable territories of *res familiaris*. Things become friends, as it were, not through a fixated possessory intentionality, but rather through the instrumentality of relations and contact: "Tarde describes the book-as-asset as that which becomes capable of creating friends and enemies, attractions and repulsions, through a game of quotations and reference."[87]

Thus, instead of focusing on the product alone, the intellectual property, it is possible to return producers and consumers meaningfully to the system, not as simply work, but through giving effect to genuine reciprocity and shared interests: "[T]he error of the first architects of political economy and of their successors has been that of persuading themselves that, in order to unify their speculations into a scientific corpus, the only means, but the certain means, was to attend to the material and external aspect of things."[88] What *res familiaris* means is to give life, to hold up an olfactory mirror to producers, consumers, to all users, and to their passionate interests, "sensations, emotions, ideas or volitions."[89] Tarde admonishes economic theory for its unfriendliness, as it were: "Never, in any period of history, have a producer and a consumer, a seller and a buyer been in each other's presence without having first been united to one another by some entirely sentimental relation – being neighbours, sharing citizenship or religious communion, enjoying a community of civilisation."[90] As Tarde explains, invention is not work, it is joy, and "it is for his joy, not his toil, that humanity remunerates him."[91]

Through these relations, through Hohfeld's "normative modalities,"[92] the nature of property in other contexts and systems becomes not only recognisable but also acknowledged. Instead of the presumed objectivity and inevitability of property's predatory drift, Hohfeld's system draws attention to the appearance of property, to the constructed and arbitrary nature of dominant rights-based discourse. It is as though he has devised a jurisprudence of the *Umwelt*, exposing the affectation and predatory pretext for all its presumptions and imperfections. This has enabled a repositioning on the predatory drift in property, bringing into focus the defensive territoriality and emphatic characterisation of property as an all or nothing battle for survival of the fittest, the struggle for life. This interpretation of territoriality has instead emerged as a social construction and a categorical imperative, rather than an inevitability, biological or otherwise. This journey has thus been one of unlearning those presumptions and recalling the animality that has been obscured and forgotten.

In this way, Hohfeld's model lends itself to different cultures, different species, different ethologies. Hoebel wrote of the potential of Hohfeld's scholarship for establishing an "ethnological jurisprudence," stating, "this is possible because Hohfeld's fundamental concepts are more universal than even their inventor himself realized. They fit not only the fundamental legal relations, but also the fundamentals of any complex of imperative social reciprocity."[93] Hohfeld's fundamental legal conceptions are the tools of a sociable property jurisprudence.

The operation of the assumptions and legal fictions of the predatory drift in law has, at best, produced confusion when dealing with anything other than a western legal paradigm. As seen in earlier discussions, much of the conflict and uncertainty regarding the protection of traditional knowledge has continued unresolved in terms of international cooperation, not least because predatory drift takes on a kind of biological imperative in the dominant property paradigm that frames these intergovernmental discussions. The transposition of the predatory model into other systems is quite often simply not relevant, meaningful, or applicable. In contrast to this persistent understanding of property in terms of a defensive territoriality, the sociality of use, the friendship of social reciprocity, is both a practical as well as a productive social convention in relation to territory and property. As the anthropologist, Alfred Irving Hallowell, said in 1942 in relation to classical anthropology's blindness to other systems of property in so-called primitive societies, "A naive view of property combined with a cultural bias has produced confusion."[94] So very little has changed.

Rehoming the stray

> So let us stop saying that work is the only source of value. The first source is invention, which is not a work; for work is a steady stream of imitation, a periodic series of concatenated acts, each of which has had to be taught by another's example and fortified by the repetition of oneself, by habit.[95]

A sociable *res familiaris* returns the producer and consumer to the economy of intellectual property, multiplying social connections through innovation rather than a quantification of products alone. In this way, the sensational exuberance of familiar production circulates freely, "the free play of passionate interests"; indeed, of shared interests.[96]

[T]he error of the first architects of political economy and of their successors has been that of persuading themselves that, in order to unify their speculations into a scientific corpus, the only means, but the certain means, was to attend to the material and external aspect of things, or, when this proved impossible, to attend to the abstract, rather than the concrete, aspect of things. For example, it was a question of concerning oneself with products rather than producers or consumers; and, when it came to the producer or the consumer – for in the end one could not avoid speaking about them – it was necessary to consider an expenditure of motor force (work) or a replenishment of force, and not sensations, emotions, ideas or volitions.[97]

We are looking for the tracks, not the lion. The property system pretends at completeness, authenticity in its representations. But the paradox of this model is that there is a necessary forgetting or erasure in order to assume that completeness. For property to appear as a coherent and complete, perfectly silent system, a self-judging, self-identical, and self-defining system, it necessarily "forgets" the third – the space in territory, the play in the system, the consumer in intellectual property, that dog in the cave . . . barking. All arrive after the event, in the footprints.[98] Predatory drift outruns the barking. But in invoking an ethological jurisprudence of property, that dog reinvigorates that use, that relationality, that play, that forgotten space of familiar production.[99]

As we have seen from that first domestication, through to the sociable pastoral territories, property is a productive sociality based upon the tracking of space not only between human and dog but also with the ungulate herds that cooperate, as it were, in the making of territory. This is the triadic nature of those earliest property relations and resonates loudly with Tarde's microsociology of imitations and repetitions, oppositions and adaptations, as well as the landscapes of familiar production.

This is not to suggest the position of that dog as object, as property *over which* A might have responsibility. It is instead an ethical encounter between responsible beings. Does this work? It is a bit like the Looking-glass cake. *The proof of the pudding is in the eating.*

When rats laugh

There is much we can learn from watching dogs playing. New dogs come and join the game, the game grows, the play configures the game itself, remaking territories, and finding new connections.

After all, the commons were originally about animals – creating and changing and making legal spaces with humans. An ethological jurisprudence is about addressing that reciprocity, finding that space, and making rats laugh.

Notes

1 Gibson J (2014) *The Logic of Innovation*, Ashgate, Aldershot, 38–44, and *passim*.
2 Greenberg D et al. (eds.), *Jowitt's Dictionary of English Law*, 5th edition, Sweet & Maxwell, London, 2019.
3 The *res* may also be a ship or cargo, as well as other property, in an Admiralty action *in rem*: Greenberg D et al. (eds.), *Jowitt's Dictionary of English Law*, 5th edition, Sweet & Maxwell, London, 2019.
4 See the discussion of the concept in relation to traditional knowledge and traditional cultural expressions in Gibson J (2005) *Community Resources*, Ashgate, Aldershot, 189–190.
5 The right to light was considered extensively by the Law Commission (2014) in *Rights to Light*, Law Commission No 356.
6 The relationship between owner and property object thus becomes a kind of conundrum. In relation to intellectual property this becomes even more critical. For example, in relation to the difficult interaction between traditional knowledge and intellectual property, see Gibson J (2005) *Community Resources*, Ashgate, Aldershot, 46: "The possessive relationship between individual and information that justifies and sustains intellectual property exists in a reciprocal legitimation with the individualistic sense of self that dominates western legal paradigms. This conundrum within conventional legal frameworks operates between the normative individual's possessive relationship to property and the generation (through the very exercise of that individual production and possession) of the individual legal subjectivity that is necessary to access such rights."
7 See further the discussion in Chapter 4, "Marking territory."
8 Romanes GR (1885) *Mental Evolution in Animals*, Kegan Paul Trench & Co, London, 234.
9 Beaglehole E (1931) *Property: A Study in Social Psychology*, George Allen & Unwin, London, 110.
10 Latour B & Lepinjay VA (2009) *The Science of Passionate Interests*, Prickly Paradigm Press, Chicago, 36.
11 Heape W (1931) *Emigration, Migration and Nomadism*, W Heffer & Sons, Cambridge, 31.
12 Romanes GR (1885) *Mental Evolution in Animals*, Kegan Paul Trench & Co, London, 234. This has interesting interactions with the prior residence effect, discussed in Chapter 4 "Marking territory."
13 Romanes GR (1885) *Mental Evolution in Animals*, Kegan Paul Trench & Co, London, 234.
14 Tarde G (1893/[2012]) *Monadology and Sociology*, T Lorenc (trans.), Re-Press, Melbourne, 55.
15 Romanes GR (1885) *Mental Evolution in Animals*, Kegan Paul Trench & Co, London, 235.
16 Duranton C et al. (2016) When Facing an Unfamiliar Person, Pet Dogs Present Social Referencing Based on Their Owners' Direction of Movement Alone, *Animal Behaviour*, 113, 147–156.
17 Chijiiwa H et al. (2015) Dogs Avoid People Who Behave Negatively to Their Owner: Third-Party Affective Evaluation, *Animal Behaviour*, 106, 123–127.
18 Massumi B (2014) *What Animals Teach Us about Politics*, Duke UP, Durham, 45.
19 A comprehensive examination of the application of these concepts in the understanding of authorship and ownership of intellectual property in artificial intelligence and animal creativity is the subject of my forthcoming book, Gibson J *More Than Human Intellectual Property*, Routledge, London.

20 Tarde G (1893/[2012]) *Monadology and Sociology*, T Lorenc (trans.), Re-Press, Melbourne, 28.
21 Tarde G (1893/[2012]) *Monadology and Sociology*, T Lorenc (trans.), Re-Press, Melbourne, 55.
22 Tarde G (1893/[2012]) *Monadology and Sociology*, T Lorenc (trans.), Re-Press, Melbourne, 51.
23 Tarde G (1893/[2012]) *Monadology and Sociology*, T Lorenc (trans.), Re-Press, Melbourne, 57.
24 Tarde G (1893/[2012]) *Monadology and Sociology*, T Lorenc (trans.), Re-Press, Melbourne, 24.
25 Tarde G (1893/[2012]) *Monadology and Sociology*, T Lorenc (trans.), Re-Press, Melbourne, 25.
26 It is beyond the scope of the present work to address these arguments in any detail here, however for a more comprehensive development of this discussion in the context of intellectual property, see Gibson J (forthcoming) *More Than Human Intellectual Property*, Routledge, London.
27 Tomasello M (2014) *A Natural History of Human Thinking*, Harvard UP, Cambridge, MA.
28 Lawton G (2014) The First Things Humans Owned, *New Scientist*, 25 March.
29 Tarde G (1893/[2012]) *Monadology and Sociology*, T Lorenc (trans.), Re-Press, Melbourne, 52.
30 For a more comprehensive examination of the position of animals within intellectual property frameworks, see Gibson J (forthcoming) *More Than Human Intellectual Property*, Routledge, London.
31 Serres M & Latour B (1990/[1995]) *Conversations on Science, Culture, and Time*, R Lapidus (trans.), U of Michigan P, Ann Arbor, 165–166.
32 For a detailed account of the concept of familiar production when first proposed, pleased see *The Logic of Innovation*.
33 Gibson J (2014) *The Logic of Innovation*, Ashgate, Aldershot, 38.
34 Gibson J (2014) *The Logic of Innovation*, Ashgate, Aldershot, 38.
35 In terms of intellectual property, the ethical character of the system arguably inheres in the relationships of contact and use (such as the scope of the intellectual property in relation to the defined user, or the application of limitations and exceptions). See further Gibson J (2014) *The Logic of Innovation*, Ashgate, Aldershot, 193.
36 Gibson J (2014) *The Logic of Innovation*, Ashgate, Aldershot, 39.
37 This is in contrast to the predatory model of property, combative and rivalrous, with no provision for information and thus no need for manners.
38 Gibson J (2014) *The Logic of Innovation*, Ashgate, Aldershot, 194–195.
39 Letter to a Celebrated Author on the Subject of Literary Property, *Public Advertiser*, 7 March, 1774. I am indebted to the keen historical research of Phillip Johnson for discovering this.
40 Although Elinor Ostrom contends that it was in fact Aristotle who was the first to make this observation in *Politics*, Book II, chapter 3. Aristotle wrote: "that which is common to the greatest number has the least care bestowed upon it." See *The Complete Works of Aristotle*, Vol. 2, Princeton UP, Princeton. See further Ostrom E (1990) *Governing the Commons: The Evolution of Institutions for Collective Action*, Cambridge UP, Cambridge, 2.
41 Lloyd WF (1832/[1980]) WF Lloyd on the Checks to Population, *Population and Development Review*, 6(3), 473–496.
42 Hardin G (1968) The Tragedy of the Commons, *Science*, 162, 1243–1248.
43 Hardin G (1968) The Tragedy of the Commons, *Science*, 162, 1243–1248: p. 1244.

44 Letter to a Celebrated Author on the Subject of Literary Property, *Public Advertiser*, 7 March, 1774.
45 Hardin G (1968) The Tragedy of the Commons, *Science*, 162, 1243–1248: p. 1247.
46 Ostrom became the first woman to be awarded the Nobel memorial Prize in Economic Sciences in 2009.
47 Ostrom E (1990) *Governing the Commons: The Evolution of Institutions for Collective Action*, Cambridge UP, Cambridge. In their introduction to a special issue of *Environmental Science and Policy*, dedicated to Ostrom's work, the editors note: "There is something in her work that enchants us. 'Community!' we intone with conviction. 'Social capital!', and we murmur approvingly. I believe the communitarian ethic moved her." See Lejano RP et al. (2014) Interrogating the Commons: Introduction to a Special Issue, *Environmental Science and Policy*, 36, 1–7: p. 1.
48 Ostrom E (1990) *Governing the Commons: The Evolution of Institutions for Collective Action*, Cambridge UP, Cambridge, 15.
49 Ostrom E (1990) *Governing the Commons: The Evolution of Institutions for Collective Action*, Cambridge UP, Cambridge, 16.
50 Ostrom E (2012) *The Future of the Commons*, The Institute of Economic Affairs, London, 80. See further the analysis of altruism in Ostrom's work in collaboration with her husband, Vincent Ostrom in Dietz T (2005) The Darwinian Trope in the Drama of the Commons: Variations on Some Themes by the Ostroms, *Journal of Economic Behavior & Organization*, 57, 205–225. The discussion also acknowledges the difficulty for evolutionary biologists in reconciling altruism (see further the more detailed discussion of this area in Chapter 10, "Shared interests").
51 Agrawal A (2014) Studying the Commons, Governing Common-Pool Resource Outcomes, *Environmental Science and Policy*, 36, 86–91: p. 87.
52 Ostrom E et al. (1999) Revisiting the Commons: Local Lessons, Global Challenges, *Science*, 284(5412), 278–282. See further Ostrom's related critique in relation to socio-ecological systems and the research context, in Young OR et al. (2006) The Globalization of Socio-Ecological Systems: An Agenda for Scientific Research, *Global Environmental Change*, 16, 304–316.
53 Willis P (2012) Engaging Communities: Ostrom's Economic Commons, Social Capital and Public Relations, *Public Relations Review*, 38, 116–122: p. 121.
54 Ostrom E (1990) *Governing the Commons: The Evolution of Institutions for Collective Action*, Cambridge UP, Cambridge, 12.
55 Gibson J (2014) *The Logic of Innovation*, Ashgate, Aldershot, 314. See further 313–316.
56 Hoebel EA (1946) Law and Anthropology, *Virginia Law Review*, 32(4), 835–854: p. 849.
57 See in particular the Chapter 7, "Predatory drift."
58 Ostrom E (1990) *Governing the Commons: The Evolution of Institutions for Collective Action*, Cambridge UP, Cambridge, 7.
59 Possibly one of the earliest examples is a 1990 essay by Jessica Litman, which refers to Hardin's article only briefly in a footnote for support of the assertion of the public domain as a "true commons": Litman J (1990) The Public Domain, *Emory Law Journal*, 39(4), 965–1023: p. 975, note 61. Interestingly, the areas that seem currently most active in exploring the concept of the "tragedy of the commons" are the laws of space, air and sea.
60 The tragedy of the anticommons was first proposed in 1998 by Michael Heller and Rebecca Eisenberg as the problem where too many owners can lead to under-grazing, as it were, of the commons and research and products deteriorating through lack of use: Heller MA (1998) The Tragedy of the

Anticommons: Property in the Transition from Marx to Markets, *Harvard Law Review*, 111(3), 621–688. See further: Heller MA & Eisenberg RS (1998) Can Patents Deter Innovation? The Anticommons in Biomedical Research, *Science*, 280, 698–701.
61 Harvey D (2011) The Future of the Commons, *Radical History Review*, 109, 101–106: p. 101.
62 Tarde G (1890/[1903]) *The Laws of Imitation*, EC Parsons (trans.), Henry Holt & Co, New York, 366.
63 Latour B & Lepinjay VA (2009) *The Science of Passionate Interests*, Prickly Paradigm Press, Chicago, 38.
64 Tarde G (1890/[1903]) *The Laws of Imitation*, EC Parsons (trans.), Henry Holt & Co, New York, 366–367.
65 Tarde G (1890/[1903]) *The Laws of Imitation*, EC Parsons (trans.), Henry Holt & Co, New York, 148–149.
66 Latour B & Lepinjay VA (2009) *The Science of Passionate Interests*, Prickly Paradigm Press, Chicago, 14.
67 Tarde G (1890/[1903]) *The Laws of Imitation*, EC Parsons (trans.), Henry Holt & Co, New York, particularly 366–367.
68 Euler J (2018) Conceptualizing the Commons: Moving Beyond the Goods-Based Definition by Introducing the Social Practices of Commoning as Vital Determinant, *Ecological Economics*, 143, 10–16: p. 12.
69 Tarde G (1902/[2007]) Economic Psychology, A Toscano (trans.), *Economy and Society*, 36(4), 614–643: p. 621.
70 Tarde G (1902/[2007]) Economic psychology, A Toscano (trans), *Economy and Society*, 36(4), 614–643: p. 620.
71 Hoebel EA (1942) Fundamental Legal Concepts as Applied in the Study of Primitive Law, *Yale Law Journal*, 51, 951–966: p. 963: "With such conceptions in mind it is not difficult to deal with the question of the existence of incorporeal property in primitive society, as well as tangible chattels. The subject first received anthropological attention in the writings of Professor Lowie, who contends that the notion of legal historians that incorporeal property is the result of advanced legal sophistication is a rationalistic prejudice belied by the data from primitive societies." For instance, in debates over the protection of traditional knowledge, one kind of creativity is verified, as it were, by the intellectual property system, and the other traditional models are unimaginable within the system. See further the discussion in Gibson J (2005) *Community Resources*, Aldershot, Ashgate, as well as in Gibson J (2006) *Creating Selves*, on the intellectual property system creating classes of creators (20, 22, 64–66).
72 See further the discussion of attachment and sociability in Chapter 3, "Socialisation."
73 Latour B & Lepinjay VA (2009) *The Science of Passionate Interests*, Prickly Paradigm Press, Chicago, 14.
74 See the discussion of the Looking-glass cake in LOGIC page 313–316.
75 Gabriel Tarde cited in Latour B & Lepinjay VA (2009) *The Science of Passionate Interests*, Prickly Paradigm Press, Chicago, 50. Latour and Lepinjay explain cotyledon capital thus: "[W]hile germ capital always meets invention (or adaptation), cotyledon capital draws opposition to itself. The germ survives only by its versatility and its ability not to be frozen in a static formula but rather to explore new connections – and to avoid opposition by constantly adapting. Fixed capital, material capital, is never so lucky; it attracts opposition like a lightning rod" (56).
76 See in particularly the earlier discussion of scarcity in Chapter 2 "The imitation of domestication" and Chapter 7, "Predatory drift."

77 See the discussion in Chapter 10, "Shared interests."
78 Tarde G (1902/[2007]) Economic Psychology, A Toscano (trans.), *Economy and Society*, 36(4), 614–643: p. 621.
79 Gabriel Tarde cited in Latour B & Lepinjay VA (2009) *The Science of Passionate Interests*, Prickly Paradigm Press, Chicago, 38.
80 Tarde G (1890/[1903]) *The Laws of Imitation*, EC Parsons (trans.), Henry Holt & Co, New York, 371.
81 Baird Callicott J (2002) A Critique of and an Alternative to the Wilderness Idea, in Butler T (ed.) *Wild Earth: Wild Ideas for a World Out of Balance*, Milkweed, Minneapolis, 172–186: pp. 184–185.
82 Latour B (2016) The Scientific Fables of an Empirical La Fontaine, Foreword to Despret V (2012/[2016]) *What Would Animals Say If We Asked the Right Questions?*, B Buchanan (trans.), U of Minnesota P, Minneapolis, vii–xiv: p. x.
83 Despret V (2012/[2016]) *What Would Animals Say If We Asked the Right Questions?*, B Buchanan (trans.), U of Minnesota P, Minneapolis, 145.
84 Despret V (2012/[2016]) *What Would Animals Say If We Asked the Right Questions?*, B Buchanan (trans.), U of Minnesota P, Minneapolis, 145.
85 Despret V (2012/[2016]) *What Would Animals Say If We Asked the Right Questions?*, B Buchanan (trans.), U of Minnesota P, Minneapolis, 146.
86 Tarde G (1902/[2007]) Economic Psychology, A Toscano (trans.), *Economy and Society*, 36(4), 614–643: p. 631.
87 Latour B & Lepinjay VA (2009) *The Science of Passionate Interests*, Prickly Paradigm Press, Chicago, 57.
88 Tarde G (1902/[2007]) Economic Psychology, A Toscano (trans.), *Economy and Society*, 36(4), 614–643: p. 629.
89 Tarde G (1902/[2007]) Economic Psychology, A Toscano (trans.), *Economy and Society*, 36(4), 614–643: p. 630.
90 Tarde G (1902/[2007]) Economic psychology, A Toscano (trans.), *Economy and Society*, 36(4), 614–643: p. 631.
91 Tarde G (1902/[2007]) Economic Psychology, A Toscano (trans.), *Economy and Society*, 36(4), 614–643: p. 640.
92 See further Clarke A & Kohler P (2005) Ownership, in *Property Law: Commentary and Materials*, Cambridge UP, Cambridge, 180–258: p. 206.
93 Hoebel EA (1942) Fundamental Legal Concepts as Applied in the Study of Primitive Law, *Yale Law Journal*, 51, 951–966: p. 966.
94 Hallowell AI (1942) The Nature and Function of Property as a Social Institution, *Journal of Legal and Political Sociology*, 1, 115–138: p. 129.
95 Tarde G (1902/[2007]) Economic Psychology, A Toscano (trans.), *Economy and Society*, 36(4), 614–643: p. 640.
96 Latour B & Lepinjay VA (2009) *The Science of Passionate Interests*, Prickly Paradigm Press, Chicago, 87.
97 Tarde G (1902/[2007]) Economic Psychology, A Toscano (trans.), *Economy and Society*, 36(4), 614–643: pp. 629–630.
98 In relation to intellectual property, the proper names (trade mark, copyright, patent, design) are taken as standing in for the object and are by definition accepting as possessing all the qualities of originality, distinctiveness and so on. The forgotten "third party," as it were, is the user. In intellectual property, *nobody*, the user, gets in the way: Gibson J (2014) *The Logic of Innovation*, Ashgate, Aldershot, 31.
99 Michel Serres explains the problem of the third man in terms of interference and noise through the example of all mathematicians, at once agreeing on the representation and recognition of a particular form, accepting the various "assumptions"

or "legal fictions" in order to give effect to that form as a universalist representation: "[T]he act of eliminating cacography, the attempt to eliminate noise, is at the same time the condition of the apprehension of the abstract form and the condition of the success of communication. If the mathematician becomes impatient, it is because he thinks inside a society that has triumphed over noise so well and for such a long time that he is amazed when the problem is raised anew." Serres M (1982) *Hermes: Literature, Science, Philosophy*, Johns Hopkins UP, Baltimore, MD, 68.

Not the end of it

> Clearly there are in the mind no objects or events – no pigs, no coconut palms, and no mothers. The mind contains only transforms, percepts, images, etc., and rules for making these transforms, percepts, etc. In what form these rules exist we do not know, but presumably they are embodied in the very machinery which creates the transforms. . . . In any case, it is nonsense to say that a man was frightened by a lion, because a lion is not an idea. The man makes an *idea* of the lion.[1]

I have been looking for the tracks, not the lion. Not through fear of the ferocious battle, the predatory drift of an ancient conflict, but through attention to the relations instead.

I'm off to the park now with some friends, some best friends. Let's make tracks together, for this story is resolutely unfinished.

Not the end of it, not by a long shot.

Note

1 Bateson G (1972/[2000]) *Steps to an Ecology of Mind*, U of Chicago P, Chicago, 271.

Finally unfinished.

Bibliography

Agamben G (1995/[1998]) *Homo Sacer: Sovereign Power and Bare Life*, D Heller-Roazen (trans.), Stanford UP, Stanford.
Agassi J (1989) The Role of the Philosopher among the Scientists: Nuisance or Necessity?, *Social Epistemology*, 3(4), 297–309.
Agnvall B et al. (2018) Is Evolution of Domestication Driven by Tameness? A Selective Review with Focus on Chickens, *Applied Animal Behaviour Science*, 205, 227–233.
Agrawal A (2014) Studying the Commons, Governing Common-Pool Resource Outcomes, *Environmental Science and Policy*, 36, 86–91.
Alberts AC (1992) Constraints on the Design of Chemical Communication Systems in Terrestrial Vertebrates, *American Naturalist*, 139, S62–S89.
Albizuri S et al. (2019) Dogs in Funerary Contexts during the Middle Neolithic in the Northeastern Iberian Peninsula (5th-Early 4th Millennium BCE), *Journal of Archaeological Science*, 24, 198–207.
Aldred J (2019) *Licence to Be Bad*, Allen Lane, London.
Allee WC (1932) *Animal Life and Social Growth*, The Williams & Wilkins Company, Baltimore, MD, 4–5.
Allee WC (1942) Group Organization among Vertebrates, *Science*, 95(2464), 289–293.
Allee WC (1943) Where Angels Fear to Tread: A Contribution from General Sociology to Human Ethics, *Science*, 97(2528), 517–525.
Allee WC (1945) Social Biology of Subhuman Groups, *Sociometry*, 8(1), 21–29: p. 23.
Allen G & Denslow J (1975) *Tracks and Signs (Clue Books)*, N Tinbergen & EAR Ennion (illus.), Oxford UP, Oxford.
Allini A et al. (2018) Pecking Order and Market Timing Theory in Emerging Markets: The Case of Egyptian Firms, *Research in International Business and Finance*, 44, 297–308.
Amat M et al. (2009) Aggressive Behaviour in the English Cocker Spaniel, *Journal of Veterinary Behavior*, 4, 111–117.
Andrews M (1983) Hohfeld's Cube, *Akron Law Review*, 16(3), 471–485.
Anthony A (1955) Behavior Patterns in a Laboratory Colony of Prairie Dogs, *Cynomys Ludovicianus, Journal of Mammalogy*, 36(1), 69–78.
Aplin LM (2019) Culture and Cultural Evolution in Birds: A Review of the Evidence, *Animal Behaviour*, 147, 179–187.

Ardrey R (1967) *The Territorial Imperative*, Collins, London.
Aristotle (1912/[1984]) *The Complete Works of Aristotle*, J Barnes (ed.), Revised Oxford Translation, Princeton UP, Princeton.
Armstrong Oma K (2010) Between Trust and Domination: Social Contracts between Humans and Animals, *World Archaeology*, 42(2), 175–187.
Asfahl KL & Dandekar AA (2018) Social Evolution: Selection on Multiple Cooperative Traits Optimizes Cost-Benefit Relationships, *Current Biology*, 28, R737–R759.
Avedikian S (dir.) (2010) *Chienne d'histoire/Barking Island*.
Axelrod R (1984) *The Evolution of Cooperation*, Penguin, London.
Axelrod R & Dion D (1988) The Further Evolution of Cooperation, *Science*, 242(4884), 1385–1390.
Axelrod R & Hamilton WD (1981) The Evolution of Cooperation, *Science*, 211(4489), 1390–1396.
Baciadonna L & McElligott AG (2018) Cognitive and Social Skills in Goats: State of Art and Future Directions, in Bueno-Guerra N & Amici F (eds.) *Field and Laboratory Methods in Animal Cognition: A Comparative Guide*, Cambridge UP, Cambridge, Box 5.1, 107–118.
Baciadonna L et al. (2019) Goats Distinguish between Positive and Negative Emotion-Linked Vocalisations, *Frontiers of Zoology*, 16, 25.
Baddeley B et al. (2012) A Model of Ant Route Navigation Driven by Scene Familiarity, *PLoS Computational Biology*, 8, e1002336.
Bain M (2019) Overview of Animal Training: A Welfare Perspective, in Chun Choe J (ed.) *Encyclopedia of Animal Behavior*, Vol. 1, 2nd ed., Academic Press, Amsterdam, 203–213.
Baird Callicott J (2002) A Critique of and an Alternative to the Wilderness Idea, in Butler T (ed.) *Wild Earth: Wild Ideas for a World Out of Balance*, Milkweed, Minneapolis, 172–186.
Bajec IL & Heppner FH (2009) Organized Flight in Birds, *Animal Behaviour*, 78, 777–789.
Balkin JM (1990) The Hohfeldian Approach to Law and Semiotics, *University of Miami Law Review*, 44(5), 1119–1142.
Balme J & O'Connor S (2016) Dingoes and Aboriginal Social Organization in Holocene Australia, *Journal of Archaeological Science: Reports*, 7, 775–781.
Bao X et al. (2019) Grid-Like Neural Representations Support Olfactory Navigation of a Two-Dimensional Odor Space, *Neuron*, 102(5), 1066–1075e.
Baratay É (2015) Building an Animal History, S Posthumus (trans.), in Mackenzie L & Posthuman S (eds.) *French Thinking about Animals*, Michigan State UP, East Lansing, MI, 3–14.
Barras C (2013) Wolves Turned Into Dogs by European Hunter-Gatherers, *New Scientist*, November.
Barrows EM (2011) *Animal Behavior Desk Reference: A Dictionary of Animal Behavior, Ecology, and Evolution*, 3rd ed., CRC Press, London.
Barsalou LW (2008) Grounded Cognition, *Annual Review of Psychology*, 59, 617–645.
Barsalou LW (2016) Situated Conceptualization: Theory and Applications, in Coello Y & Fischer MH (eds.) *Foundations of Embodied Cognition, Volume 1: Perceptual and Emotional Embodiment*, Psychology Press, East Sussex, 11–37.
Bartlett D & Bartlett F (1971) Social Implications of Biological Determinism, *Science and Society*, 35(2), 209–219.

Bassin M (2003) Between Realism and the 'New Right': Geopolitics in Germany in the 1990s, *Transactions of the Institute of British Geographers*, 28(3), 350–366.
Bates M (1990/[1950]) *The Nature of Natural History*, Princeton UP, Princeton.
Bateson G (1972/[2000]) *Steps to an Ecology of Mind*, U of Chicago P, Chicago.
Bateson P (2015) Playfulness and Creativity, *Current Biology*, 25(1), R12–R16.
Batty C (2009) What's That Smell?, *The Southern Journal of Philosophy*, 47(4), 321–348.
Batty C (2010) What the Nose Doesn't Know: Non-Veridicality and Olfactory Experience, *Journal of Consciousness Studies*, 17(3–4), 10–17.
Batty C (2011) Smelling Lessons, *Philosophical Studies*, 153(1), 161–174.
Baudelaire C (1869a) Good Dogs, M Sorrell (trans.), in Baudelaire C (1869/[2010]) *Paris Spleen and Wine and Hashish*, Alma, Richmond, 98–101.
Baudelaire C (1869b) The Faithful Dog, L Varèse (trans.), in Baudelaire C (1869/[1970]) *Paris Spleen*, New Directions, New York, 104–107.
Baudelaire C (1926) *Petits poëmes en prose (le spleen de Paris)*, Louis Conard, Paris.
Baudelaire C (1989) *Le spleen de Paris, ou les cinquante petits poèmes du prose de Charles Baudelaire*, Émil-Paul, Paris.
Beaglehole E (1931) *Property: A Study in Social Psychology*, Allen & Unwin, London.
Bekoff M (1979) Ground Scratching by Male Composite Dogs: A Composite Signal, *Journal of Mammalogy*, 60(4), 847–848.
Bekoff M (1995) Play Signals as Punctuation: The Structure of Social Play in Canids, *Behaviour*, 132(5/6), 419–429.
Bekoff M (ed.) (1998) *Encyclopedia of Animal Rights and Animal Welfare*, Fitzroy Dearborn Publishers, London.
Bekoff M (2000) Animal Emotions: Exploring Passionate Natures, *BioScience*, 50(10), 861–870.
Bekoff M (2001a) Observations of Scent-Marking and Discriminating Self from Others by a Domestic Dog (*Canis familiaris*): Tales of Displaced Yellow Snow, *Behavioural Processes*, 55, 75–79.
Bekoff M (2001b) Social Play Behaviour: Cooperation, Fairness, Trust, and the Evolution of Morality, *Journal of Consciousness Studies*, 8(2), 81–90.
Bekoff M (2002) Animal Reflections, *Nature*, 419, 255.
Bekoff M (2007) *The Emotional Lives of Animals*, New World Library, Novato, CA.
Bekoff M (2015) Playful Fun in Dogs, *Current Biology*, 25(1), R4–R7.
Bekoff M (2017) It's OK for Dogs to Engage in Zoomies and Enjoy FRAPs, *Psychology Today*, 26 September.
Bekoff M & Pierce J (2009) *Wild Justice: The Moral Lives of Animals*, Chicago UP, Chicago.
Benjamin W (1928/[2016]) *One-Way Street*, E Jephcott (trans.), Belknap-Harvard, Cambridge, MA.
Benjamin W (1978/[2007]) *Reflections*, E Jephcott (trans.), Schocken Books, New York.
Benjamin W (1982/[2002]) *The Arcades Project*, H Eiland & K McLaughlin (trans.), Harvard UP, Cambridge, MA.
Bennett ATD (1996) Do Animals Have Cognitive Maps?, *The Journal of Experimental Biology*, 199, 219–224.
Benson E (2014) The Biopolitics of the Border, *RCC Perspectives: The Edges of Environmental History*, 81–86.

Berger AE (2014) Reigning Cats or Dogs? Baudelaire's Cynicism, *Yale French Studies*, 125/126, 149–164.

Bergson H (1907/[1944]) *Creative Evolution*, A Mitchell (trans.), Random House, New York.

Berns GS et al. (2015) Scent of the Familiar: An fMRI Study of Canine Brain Responses to Familiar and Unfamiliar Human and Dog Odors, *Behavioural Processes*, 110, 37–46.

Bernstein IS (1981) Dominance: The Baby and the Bathwater, *The Behavioral and Brain Sciences*, 4, 419–457.

Bhabha HK (1985) Signs Taken for Wonders: Questions of Ambivalence and Authority under a Tree Outside Delhi, May 1817, *Critical Inquiry*, 12(1), 144–165.

Biro D et al. (2016) Bringing a Time-Depth Perspective to Collective Animal Behaviour, *Trends in Ecology and Evolution*, 31(7), 550–562.

Blacker CP and DVG (1966) Obituary: Sir Alexander Carr-Saunders, *Population Studies*, 20(3), 365–369.

Bleus G (1978) *The Thrill of Working with Odours: Smell Manifesto*. Available at www.mailart.be/thrill.html

Blomley N (2016) The Territory of Property, *Progress in Human Geography*, 593–609.

Bonanni R et al. (2010) Effect of Affiliative and Agonistic Relationships on Leadership Behaviour in Free-Ranging Dogs, *Animal Behaviour*, 79, 981–991.

Borges JL (1942/[1962]) Funes, the Memorious, in *Ficciones*, A Kerrigan (trans.), Grove Press, New York, 107–115.

Borges JL (1945/[1967]) The Aleph, in *Jorges Luis Borges: A Personal Anthology*, A Kerrigan (trans.), Grove Press, New York, 138–154.

Borges JL (1983/[1992]) Paracelsus and the Rose, *The Antioch Review*, NT Di Giovanni (trans.) 50(1/2), 395–398.

Botigué LR et al. (2017) Ancient European Dog Genomes Reveal Continuity since the Early Neolithic, *Nature*, 18 July.

Bowlby J (1969) *Attachment and Loss*, Vol. 1 Attachment, Pimlico-Random House, London.

Bowles S (2016) *The Moral Economy*, Yale UP, New Haven.

Bowles S & Choi J-K (2013) Coevolution of Farming and Private Property during the Early Holocene, *PNAS*, 110(22), 8830–8835.

Boyce AA (1954) The Foundation and Birthday of Rome: In Legend and History, *Archaeology*, 7(1), 9–14.

Bradshaw JWS et al. (2009) Dominance in Domestic Dogs: Useful Construct or Bad Habit?, *Journal of Veterinary Behavior*, 4, 135–144.

Breland K & Breland M (1961) The Misbehavior of Organisms, *American Psychologist*, 16(11), 681–684.

Breton A & Duchamp M (1942) *First Papers of Surrealism: Hanging by André Breton, His Twine Marcel Duchamp*, Coordinating Council of French Relief Societies, New York.

Bridges AD & Chittka L (2019) Animal Behaviour: Conformity and the Beginnings of Culture in an Insect, *Current Biology*, 29, R150–R172.

Briffault R (1931) *The Mothers: The Matriarchal Theory of Social Origins*, Macmillan, New York.

Brighenti AM (2006) On Territory as Relationship and Law as Territory, *Canadian Journal of Law and Society/Revue Canadienne Droit et Société*, 21(2), 65–86.

Brighenti AM (2010a) Lines, Barred Lines: Movement, Territory and the Law, *International Journal of Law in Context*, 6(3), 217–227.

Brighenti AM (2010b) On Territorology: Towards a General Science of Territory, *Theory, Culture & Society*, 27(1), 52–72.
British Medical Journal (1942) The Shape of a Smell, *British Medical Journal*, 2(4262), 315.
Bromley D (2002) This Land Is Whose Land?, *Wisconsin Academy Review*, 48(3), 60–63.
Brown CM et al. (2017) Examination of the Accuracy and Applicability of Information in Popular Books on Dog Training, *Society and Animals*, 25, 411–435.
Buckley LA et al. (2011) Quantifying hungry Broiler Breeder Dietary Preferences Using a Closed Economy T-Maze Task, *Applied Animal Behaviour Science*, 133, 216–227.
Buckley LA et al. (2015) Feed-Restricted Broiler Breeders: State-Dependent Learning as a Novel Welfare Assessment Tool to Evaluate Their Hunger State?, *Applied Animal Behaviour Science*, 165, 124–132.
Buehlmann C et al. (2015) Desert Ants Use Olfactory Scenes for Navigation, *Animal Behaviour*, 106, 99–105.
Bulliet RW (2005) *Hunters, Herders, and Hamburgers: The Past and Future of Human-Animal Relationships*, Columbia UP, New York, 89.
Bunford N et al. (2017) *Canis familiaris* as a Model for Non-Invasive Comparative Neuroscience, *Trends in Neurosciences*, 40(7), 438–452.
Bunzel R (1938) The Economic Organization of Primitive Peoples, in Boas F (ed.) *General Anthropology*, Heath, Boston, 327–408.
Burgen S (2019) Town Near Barcelona Uses Wolf Urine to Keep Wild Boar away, *Guardian*, 22 August.
Burghardt GM (1985) Animal Awareness: Current Perceptions and Historical Perspective, *American Psychologist*, 40(8), 905–919.
Burghardt GM (2007) Critical Anthropomorphism, Uncritical Anthropocentrism, and Naïve Nominalism, *Comparative Cognition and Behavior Reviews*, 2, 136–138.
Burghardt GM (2019) A Place for Emotions in Behaviour Systems Research, *Behavioural Processes*, 166, 103881.
Burghardt GM & Herzog Jr HA (1980) Beyond Conspecifics: Is Brer Rabbit Our Brother?, *BioScience*, 30(11), 763–768.
Burkhardt Jr RW (2005) *Patterns of Behavior: Konrad Lorenz, Niko Tinbergen, and the Founding of Ethology*, U of Chicago P, Chicago.
Burkhardt Jr RW (2008) The Nature of Evidence: How Well Do 'Facts' Travel?, London School of Economics, London, Working Paper 32/08.
Burt WH (1949) Territoriality, *Journal of Mammalogy*, 30(1), 25–27.
Buttner AP (2016) Neurobiological Underpinnings of Dogs' Human-Like Social Competence: How Interactions between Stress Response Systems and Oxytocin Mediate Dogs' Social Skills, *Neuroscience and Biobehavioral Reviews*, 71, 198–214.
Cairns H (1931) Law and Anthropology, *Columbia Law Review*, 31(1), 32–55.
Cairns H (1935) *Law and the Social Sciences*, Kegan Paul, Trench, Trubner & Co, London.
Cairns H (1941) *The Theory of Legal Science*, U of North Carolina P, Chapel Hill.
Callaway E (2008) Wolves Make Dog's Dinner Out of Domestication Theory, *New Scientist*, September.
Calvino I (1986/[1993]) The Name, the Nose, in *Under the Jaguar Sun*, W Weaver (trans.), Vintage, London.

Campbell AH (1940) Some Footnotes to Salmond's Jurisprudence, *Cambridge Law Journal*, 7, 706–223.
Campbell WE (1972) A Behaviour Test for Puppy Selection, *Modern Veterinary Practice*, 12, 29–33.
Campbell-Palmer R & Rosell F (2011) The Importance of Chemical Communication Studies to Mammalian Conservation Biology, *Biological Conservation*, 144, 1919–1930.
Candea M (2016) Revisiting Tarde's House, in Candea M (ed.) *The Social after Gabriel Tarde: Debates and Assessments*, 2nd ed., Routledge, London, 1–27.
Canedo JC et al. (2019) Let's Make Performance Management Work for New Hires: They Are the Future, *Organizational Dynamics*, 47, 229–233.
Carpenter CR (1958) Territoriality: A Review of Concepts and Problems, in Roe A & Simpson GG (eds.) *Behavior and Evolution*, Yale UP, New Haven, 224–250.
Carr-Saunders AM & Wilson PA (1933) *The Professions*, Clarendon Press, Oxford.
Carter A (2016) Britain Faces a Migration Issue: European Rescue Dogs, *The Conversation*, 28 April.
Cassidy R & Mullin M (eds.) (2007) *Where the Wild Things Are Now: Domestication Reconsidered*, Berg, Oxford, 71–99.
Castelnovo O et al. (2017) The Innate Code of Charisma, *The Leadership Quarterly*, 28, 543–554.
Chan E et al. (2012) From Objects to Landmarks: The Function of Visual Location Information in Spatial Navigation, *Frontiers in Psychology*, 3(304), 1–11.
Chartrand TL & Baaren R van (2009) Human Mimicry, *Advances in Experimental Social Psychology*, 41, 219–274.
Chijiiwa H et al. (2015) Dogs Avoid People Who Behave Negatively to Their Owner: Third-Party Affective Evaluation, *Animal Behaviour*, 106, 123–127.
Chittka L & Jensen K (2011) Animal Cognition: Concepts from Apes to Bees, *Current Biology*, 21(3), R116–R119.
Clancy K (2017) Survival of the Friendliest, *Nautilus*, 23 March.
Clapham M et al. (2013) The Function of Strategic Tree Selectivity in the Chemical Signaling of Brown Bears, *Animal Behaviour*, 85, 1351–1357.
Clark N (2007) Animal Interface: The Generosity of Domestication, in Cassidy R & Mullin M (eds.) *Where the Wild Things Are Now: Domestication Reconsidered*, Berg, Oxford, 49–70.
Clarke A & Kohler P (2005) Ownership, in *Property Law: Commentary and Materials*, Cambridge UP, Cambridge.
Classen C (1993) *Worlds of Sense: Exploring the Senses in History and Across Cultures*, Routledge, London.
Classen C et al. (1994) *Aroma: A Cultural History of Smell*, Routledge, London.
Cloutier S et al. (2012) Playful Handling by Caretakers Reduces Fear of Humans in the Laboratory Rat, *Applied Animal Behaviour Science*, 140, 161–171.
Clutton-Brock J (1989a/[2015]) Introduction, in Clutton-Brock J (ed.) *The Walking Larder: Patterns of Domestication, Pastoralism, and Predation*, Routledge, London, 1–3.
Clutton-Brock J (ed.) (1989b/[2015]) *The Walking Larder: Patterns of Domestication, Pastoralism, and Predation*, Routledge, London.
Clutton-Brock J (2017) Origins of the Dog: The Archaeological Evidence, in Serpell J (ed.) *The Domestic Dog: Its Evolution, Behavior and Interactions with People*, 2nd ed., Cambridge UP, Cambridge, 7–21.

Coello Y & Fischer MH (eds.) (2016) *Foundations of Embodied Cognition, Volume 1: Perceptual and Emotional Embodiment*, Psychology Press, East Sussex.

Cole DH & Grossman PZ (2002) The Meaning of Property Rights: Law versus Economics?, *Land Economics*, 78(3), 317–330.

Cook WW (1917) The Alienability of Choses in Action: A Reply to Professor Williston, *Harvard Law Review*, 30(5), 449–485.

Cook WW (1919) Hohfeld's Contributions to the Science of Law, *The Yale Law Journal*, 28(8), 721–738.

Cooke F (2017) Canine Aggression and the Law: An International Perspective, in Mills DS & Westgarth C (eds.) *Dog Bites: A Muiltidisciplinary Perspective*, 5m Publishing, Sheffield, 191–204.

Cooley CH (1961) Primary Groups, in Parsons T et al. (eds.) *Theories of Society: Foundations of Modern Sociological Theory*, Vol. 1, The Free Press of Glencoe, New York, 315–318.

Cooper JJ et al. (2003) Clever Hounds: Social Cognition in the Domestic Dog (*Canis familiaris*), *Applied Animal Behaviour Science*, 81, 229–244.

Coppinger R & Coppinger L (2016) *What Is a Dog?*, U of Chicago P, Chicago.

Corbin AL (1982/[1994]) *The Foul and the Fragrant: Odour and the Social Imagination*, Picador, London.

Corbin AL (1921) Jural Relations and Their Classification, *Yale Law Journal*, 30(3), 226–238.

Corbin AL (1922) Taxation of Seats on the Stock Exchange, *Yale Law Journal*, 31(4), 429–431.

Costa JT (2019) Social Evolution in 'Other' Insects and Arachnids, in Choe JC (ed.) *Encyclopedia of Animal Behavior*, Vol. 4, 2nd ed., Academic Press, Amsterdam, 617–631.

Courchamp F et al. (2008) *Allee Effects: In Ecology and Conservation*, Oxford UP, Oxford.

Creed B (2017) *Stray: Human-Animal Ethics in the Anthropocene*, Power Publications, Sydney.

Cupere, Peter de (2016) *Scent in Context: Olfactory Art*, Stockmans Publishers, Brussels.

Curr EM (1886) *The Australian Race: Its Origin, Languages, Customs, Place of Landing in Australia and the Routes by Which It Spread Itself over the Continent*, John Ferres Government Printer, Melbourne.

Curran E (2002) Hobbes's Theory of Rights: A Modern Interest Theory, *The Journal of Ethics*, 6(1), 63–86.

Curran E (2006a) Can Rights Curb the Hobbesian Sovereign? The Full Right to Self-Preservation, Duties of Sovereignty and the Limitations of Hohfeld, *Law and Philosophy*, 25(2), 243–265.

Curran E (2006b) Lost in Translation: Some Problems with a Hohfeldian Analysis of Hobbesian Rights, *Hobbes Studies*, 19(1), 58–76.

Curran E (2010) Blinded by the Light of Hohfeld: Hobbes's Notion of Liberty, *Jurisprudence: An International Journal of Legal and Political Thought*, 1, 85–104.

Curran E (2013) An Immodest Proposal: Hobbes Rather Than Locke Provides a Forerunner for Modern Rights Theory, *Law and Philosophy*, 32(4), 515–538.

Daley J (2017) New Study Has a Bone to Pick with Dog Domestication Findings, *Smithsonian*, 19 July.

Dalgarno MT (1975–1976) Analysing Hobbes's Contract, *Proceedings of the Aristotelian Society*, 76, 209–226.
Dalibard GH (2009) Parameters Influencing Service Dogs' Quality of Response to Commands: Retrospective Study of 71 Dogs, *Journal of Veterinary Behavior*, 4, 19–24.
Dallenbach KM (1940) Margaret Floy Washburn 1871–1939, *The American Journal of Psychology*, 53(1), 1–5.
Da Rold F (2018) Defining Embodied Cognition: The Problem of Situatedness, *New Ideas in Psychology*, 51, 9–14.
Darwin C (1859/[2008]) *On the Origin of Species*, Oxford UP, Oxford.
Darwin C (1871/[2004]) *The Descent of Man, and Selection in Relation to Sex*, Penguin, London.
Davidson DS (1928a) Family Hunting Territories of the Tribes of Tierra del Fuego, *Indian Notes*, 5(1), 395–410.
Davidson DS (1928b) The Family Hunting Territory in Australia, *American Anthropologist*, 30(4), 614–631.
Davis H & Balfour D (eds.) (1992) *The Inevitable Bond: Examining Scientist-Animal Interactions*, Cambridge UP, Cambridge.
Davis MM (1906) *Gabriel Tarde: An Essay in Sociological Theory*, Columbia University Dissertation, New York.
Deleuze G (1968/[1994]) *Difference and Repetition*, P Patton (trans.), Columbia UP, New York.
Deleuze G (1988/[1986]) *Foucault*, S Hand (trans.), U of Minnesota P, Minneapolis.
Deleuze G (1988/[1993]) *The Fold: Leibniz and the Baroque*, T Conley (trans.), U of Minnesota P, Minneapolis.
Deleuze G (1994–1995) A Comme Animal/A as in Animal, Dominique Hurth (trans.). Transcription of the First Part (First Letter of the ABC) of the Eight-Hour Series of Interviews between Gilles Deleuze and Claire Parnet, Filmed by Pierre-André Boutang in 1988–1989. Broadcast on Arte between November 1994 and Spring 1995.
Deleuze G (1996) In Interview with Claire Parnét, in Pierre-André Boutang & Michel Pamart (dirs.), Transcript D Hurth (trans.) *L'abécédaire de Gilles Deleuze*.
Deleuze G & Guattari F (1980/[1987]) *A Thousand Plateaus: Capitalism and Schizophrenia*, B Massumi (trans.), U of Minnesota P, Minneapolis.
Deleuze G & Guattari F (1991/[1994]) *What Is Philosophy?*, H Tomlinson & G Burchill (trans.), Verso, London.
Demsetz H (1967) Toward a Theory of Property Rights, *The American Economic Review*, 57(2), 347–359.
Demsetz H (2002) Toward a Theory of Property Rights II: The Competition between Private and Collective Ownership, *The Journal of Legal Studies*, 31(S2), S653–S672.
Derrida J (1982/[1988]) *The Ear of the Other*, P Kamuf (trans.), U of Nebraska P, Lincoln.
Despret V (2004) The Body We Care For: Figures of Anthropo-zoo-genesis, *Body & Society*, 10(2–3), 111–134.
Despret V (2012/[2016]) *What Would Animals Say If We Asked the Right Questions?*, B Buchanan (trans.), U of Minnesota P, Minneapolis.

Deutsche R (2002) Sharing Strangeness: Krzysztof Wodiczko's Ægis and the Question of Hospitality, *Grey Room*, 6, 26–43.

Devereux G (1967) *From Anxiety to Method in the Behavioral Sciences*, Mouton & Co, The Hague.

Diaconu M (2006) Reflections on an Aesthetics of Touch, Smell and Taste, *Contemporary Aesthetics*, 4, 1–10.

Dietz T (2005) The Darwinian Trope in the Drama of the Commons: Variations on Some Themes by the Ostroms, *Journal of Economic Behavior & Organization*, 57, 205–225.

Doherty O et al. (2017) The Importance of Learning Theory and Equitation Science to the Veterinarian, *Applied Animal Behaviour Science*, 190, 111–122.

Donaldson J (1996/[2013]) *The Culture Clash*, Dogwise Publishing, Wenatchee, WA.

Donaldson J (2004) *Fight! A Guide to Dog-Dog Aggression*, Dogwise Publishing, Wenatchee, WA.

Donaldson J (2008) *Oh Behave! Dogs from Pavlov to Premack to Pinker*, Dogwise Publishing, Wenatchee, WA.

Donati K (2019) 'Herding Is His Favourite Thing in the World': Convivial World-Making on a Multispecies Farm, *Journal of Rural Studies*, 66, 119–129.

Drake AG et al. (2015) 3D Morphometric Analysis of Fossil Canid Skulls Contradicts the Suggested Domestication of Dogs during the Late Paleolithic, *Scientific Reports: Nature*, 5, 1–8.

Duchamp M (1973) *The Writings of Marcel Duchamp*, M Sanouillet & E Peterson (eds.), Da Capo, New York.

Ducos P (1978) Domestication Defined and Methodological Approaches to Its Recognition in Faunal Assemblages, in Meadow RH & Zeder M (eds.) *Approaches to Faunal Analysis in the Middle East*, Peabody Museum, Cambridge, MA, 53–56.

Dugatkin LA & Bekoff M (2003) Play and the Evolution of Fairness: A Game Theory Model, *Behavioural Processes*, 60, 209–214.

Duranton C & Gaunet F (2015) Canis Sensitives: Affiliation and Dogs' Sensitivity to Others' Behaviour as the Basis for Synchronization with Humans?, *Journal of Veterinary Behavior*, 10, 513–524.

Duranton C & Horowitz A (2019) Let Me Sniff! Nosework Induces Positive Judgment Bias in Pet Dogs, *Applied Animal Behaviour Science*, 211, 61–66.

Duranton C et al. (2016) When Facing an Unfamiliar Person, Pet Dogs Present Social Referencing Based on Their Owners' Direction of Movement Alone, *Animal Behaviour*, 113, 147–156.

Durkheim É (1904–1905) Review: L'interpsychologie by G Tarde, *L'Année sociologique (1896/1897–1924/1925)*, T9, 133–135.

Dzik V et al. (2019) Do Dogs Experience Frustration? New Contributions on Successive Negative Contrast in Domestic Dogs (*Canis familiaris*), *Behavioural Processes*, 162, 14–19.

Earle T (2000) Archaeology, Property, and Prehistory, *Annual Review of Anthropology*, 29, 39–60.

Eccles DW & Groth PT (2007) Wolves, Bees, and Football: Enhancing Coordination in Sociotechnological Problem Solving Systems through the Study of Human and Animal Groups, *Computers in Human Behavior*, 23, 2778–2790.

Ehrlich E (1936) *Fundamental Principles of the Sociology of Law*, Harvard UP, Cambridge, MA.
Engle E (2010) Taking the Right Seriously: Hohfeldian Semiotics and Rights Discourse, *The Crit: A Critical Studies Journal*, 3(1), 84–107.
Ennion EAR & Tinbergen N (1967) *Tracks*, Oxford UP, London.
Essler JL et al. (2017) Domestication Does Not Explain the Presence of Inequity Aversion in Dogs, *Current Biology*, 27, 1861–1865.
Estalrrich A et al. (2017) Dietary Reconstruction of the El Sidrón Neandertal Familial Group (Spain) in the Context of Other Neandertal and Modern Hunter-Gatherer Groups: A Molar Microwear Texture Analysis, *Journal of Human Evolution*, 104, 13–22.
Euler J (2018) Conceptualizing the Commons: Moving Beyond the Goods-Based Definition by Introducing the Social Practices of Commoning as Vital Determinant, *Ecological Economics*, 143, 10–16.
Evans EP (1894) The Ethics of Tribal Society, *Popular Science Monthly*, 44, 289–207.
Faraci D (2014) Do Property Rights Presuppose Scarcity?, *Journal of Business Ethics*, 125(3), 531–537.
Fennell MJV (1977) Radical Behaviourist v Cognitive Psychology: A Pseudo-Quarrel?, *BABP Bulletin*, 5(5), 97–102.
Fentress JC (1992) The Covalent Animal: On Bonds and Their Boundaries in Behavioural Research, in Davis H & Balfour D (eds.) *The Inevitable Bond: Examining Scientist-Animal Interactions*, Cambridge UP, Cambridge, 44–71.
Fernandes JG et al. (2017) Do aversive-based training methods actually compromise dog welfare? A literature review, *Applied Animal Behaviour Science*, 196, 1–12.
Fiorenza L et al. (2015) To Meat or Not to Meat? New Perspectives on Neandertal Ecology, *American Journal of Physical Anthropology*, 156(S59), 43–71.
Fiset S (2009) Evidence for Averaging of Distance from Landmarks in the Domestic Dog, *Behavioural Processes*, 81, 429–438.
Fourier C (1808/[1996]) *The Theory of the Four Movements*, I Patterson (trans.), Cambridge UP, Cambridge.
Frank J (1949) *Law and the Modern Mind*, Stevens & Sons, London, 37.
Frank MZ & Goyal VK (2003) Testing the Pecking Order Theory of Capital Structure, *Journal of Financial Economics*, 67(2), 217–248.
Frantz LAF et al. (2016) Genomic and Archaeological Evidence Suggests a Dual Origin of Domestic Dogs, *Science*, 352, 1228–1231.
Freas CA et al. (2019) Experimental Ethology of Learning in Desert Ants: Becoming Expert Navigators, *Behavioural Processes*, 158, 181–191.
Freedman AH et al. (2014) Genome Sequencing Highlights the Dynamic Early History of Dogs, *PLoS Genetics*, 10(1), e1004631.
Freud S (1916–1917/[1973]) *Introductory Lectures on Psychoanalysis*, J Strachey (trans.), Penguin, London.
Frisby D & Featherstone M (eds.) *Simmel on Culture*, Sage, London.
Fudge E (2008) *Pets*, Acumen, Stocksfield, 54–55.
Fuxiu Jiang et al. (2017) A Pecking Order of Shareholder Structure, *Journal of Corporate Finance*, 44, 1–14.
Gácsi M et al. (2013) Wolves Do Not Join the Dance: Sophisticated Aggression Control by Adjusting to Human Social Signals in Dogs, *Applied Animal Behaviour Science*, 145, 109–122.

Galbraith JK (2007) Taming Predatory Capitalism, in Rogers J et al. (2006) Taming Global Capitalism Anew, *The Nation*, 17 April.
Galbraith JK (2008) *The Predator State*, Free Press, New York.
Galef BG (1992) The Question of Animal Culture, *Human Nature*, 3(2), 157–178.
Galef BG (2010) Animal Traditions: Experimental Evidence of Learning by Imitation in an Unlikely Animal, *Current Biology*, 20(13), R555–R556.
Galibert F et al. (2016) The Genetics of Canine Olfaction, *Journal of Veterinary Behavior*, 16, 86–93.
Gallup Jr GG (1970) Chimpanzees: Self-Recognition, *Science*, 167.
Gallup Jr GG (1975) Toward an Operational Definition of Self-Awareness, in Tuttle RH (ed.) *Socioecology and Psychology of Primates*, Mouton, The Hague, 309–341.
Galton, Sir Francis (1865) The First Steps towards the Domestication of Animals, *Transactions of the Ethnological Society*, 3, 122–138.
Gaudry Q et al. (2012) Smelling on the Fly: Sensory Cues and Strategies for Olfactory Navigation in Drosophila, *Current Opinion in Neurobiology*, 22(2), 216–222.
Gauthier D (1979) David Hume, Contractarian, *The Philosophical Review*, 88(1), 3–38.
Gazit I & Terkel J (2003) Domination of Olfaction over Vision in Explosives Detection by Dogs, *Applied Animal Behaviour Science*, 82, 65–73.
Gergely A et al. (2014) Dogs Are Able to Generalise Directional Acoustic Signals to Different Contexts and Tasks, *Applied Animal Behaviour Science*, 156, 54–61.
Germonpré M et al. (2012) Paleolithic Dog Skulls at the Gravettian Předmostí Site, the Czech Republic, *Journal of Archaeological Science*, 39, 184–202.
Germonpré M et al. (2013) Paleolithic Dogs and the Early Domestication of the Wolf: A Reply to the Comments of Crockford and Kuzmin (2012), *Journal of Archaeological Science*, 40, 786–792.
Germonpré M et al. (2014) Paleolithic Dogs and Pleistocene Wolves Revisited: A Reply to Morey, *Journal of Archaeological Science*, 54(2015), 210–236.
Germonpré M et al. (2015a) Fossil Dogs and Wolves from Palaeolithic Sites in Belgium, the Ukraine and Russia: Osteometry, Ancient DNA and Stable Isotopes, *Journal of Archaeological Science*, 36, 473–490.
Germonpré M et al. (2015b) Large Canids at the Gravettian Předmostí Site, the Czech Republic: The Mandible, *Quarternary International*, 359–360: pp. 261–279.
Germonpré M et al. (2017) Palaeolitihic and Prehistoric Dogs and Pleistocene Wolves from Yakutia: Identification of Isolated Skulls, *Journal of Archaeological Science*, 78, 1–19.
Gibson J (2005) *Community Resources*, Ashgate, Aldershot.
Gibson J (2006) *Creating Selves*, Ashgate, Aldershot.
Gibson J (2008) The Law of the Land, in Graber CB & Burri-Nenova M (eds.) *Intellectual Property and Traditional Cutlural Expressions in a Digital Environment*, Edward Elgar, Cheltenham, 182–201.
Gibson J (2014) *The Logic of Innovation*, Ashgate, Aldershot.
Gibson J (forthcoming) *More Than Human Intellectual Property: Animal Authors and Human Machines*, Routledge, London.
Gibson JJ (1950) *The Perception of the Visual World*, Houghton Mifflin Company, Boston.
Gibson JJ (1960) The Concept of the Stimulus in Psychology, *American Psychologist*, 15(11), 694–703.

Gibson JJ (1979/[2015]) *The Ecological Approach to Visual Perception*, Psychology Press, New York.
Giddings FH (1903) Introduction, in Tarde G (ed.) (1890/[1903]) *The Laws of Imitation*, EC Parsons (trans.), Henry Holt & Co, New York, iii–vii.
Gilbert DH et al. (2015) Osmotic Strategy: Innovating at the Core to Inspire at the Edges, *Organizational Dynamics*, 44, 217–225.
Gill F & Wolf LL (1975) Economics of Feeding Territoriality in the Golden-Winged Sunbird, *Ecology*, 56, 333–345.
Gilmore KM & Greer KA (2015) Why Is the Dog an Ideal Model for Aging Research?, *Experimental Gerontology*, 71, 14–20.
Ginsburg B & Allee WC (1942) Some Effects of Conditioning on Social Dominance and Subordination in Inbred Strains of Mice, *Physiological Zoology*, 15(4), 485–506.
Glenberg AM (2010) Embodiment as a Unifying Perspective for Psychology, *WIREs Cognitive Science*, 1, 586–596.
Glenberg AM & Kaschak MP (2002) Grounding Language in Action, *Psychonomic Bulletin & Review*, 9, 558–565.
Glenberg AM et al. (2010) From the Revolution to Embodiment: 25 Years of Cognitive Psychology, *Perspectives on Psychological Science*, 8(5), 573–585.
Goffman E (1961) *Asylums: Essays on the Social Situation of Mental Patients and Other Inmates*, Anchor Books-Doubleday, New York.
Goldsmith O (1824) *A History of the Earth, and Animated Nature, Volume II, Part Third, History of Animated Nature, Birds*, Henry Fisher, Caxton Press, London.
Goldsmith O (1854) *The Works of Oliver Goldsmith*, P Cunningham (ed.), John Murray, London.
González-Martínez Á et al. (2019) Association between Puppy Classes and Adulthood Behavior of the Dog, *Journal of Veterinary Behavior*, in press.
Gosling LM & Roberts SC (2001) Scent-Marking by Male Mammals: Cheat-Proof Signals to Competitors and Mates, *Advances in the Study of Behaviour*, 30, 169–217.
Goymann W (2019) On the Importance of Studying Animal Behaviour: Or Any Other Kind of 'Blue Sky' Research, *Ethology*, 125, 501–502.
Gray GW (1955) The Yerkes Laboratories, *Scientific American*, 192(2), 67–77.
Greenberg B & Noble GK (1944) Social Behavior of the American Chameleon (*Anolis carolinensis* Voigt), *Physiological Zoology*, 17(4), 392–439.
Griffin DR (1976) *The Question of Animal Awareness: Evolutionary Continuity of Mental Experience*, The Rockefeller UP, New York.
Griffin DR (1977) Anthropomorphism, *BioScience*, 27(7), 445–446.
Grøn O (2005) A Siberian Perspective on the North European Hamburgian Culture: A Study in Applied Hunter-Gatherer Ethnoarchaeology, *Before Farming*, 1, 1–29.
Gross JJ & Barrett LF (2013) The Emerging Field of Affective Science, *Emotion*, 13(6), 997–998.
Grubb TC (1974) Olfactory Navigation to the Nesting Burrow in Leach's Petrel (*Oceanodroma Leucorrhoa*), *Animal Behaviour*, 22(1), 192–202.
Guarino B (2017) Your Dog's Ancestor Came from a Group of Wolves 40,000 Years Ago, Study Says, *The Washington Post*, 18 July.
Guenther MG (1981) Bushman and Hunter-Gatherer Territoriality, *Zeitschrift für Ethnologie*, 106(1/2), 109–120.
Guney A & Al S (2012) Effective Learning Environments in Relation to Different Learning Theories, *Procedia: Social and Behavioral Sciences*, 46, 2334–2338.

Gygax L & Hillmann E (2018) 'Naturalness' and Its Relation to Animal Welfare from an Ethological Perspective, *Agriculture*, 8, 136.
Ha JC & Campion TL (2019) *Dog Behavior: Modern Science and Our Canine Companions*, Academic Press, London.
Hall AJ (2010) *Earth into Property: Colonization, Decolonization and Capital*, McGill-Queen's UP, Montreal-Kingston.
Hallowell AI (1942) The Nature and Function of Property as a Social Institution, *Journal of Legal and Political Sociology*, 1, 115–138.
Hallowell AI (1949) The Size of Algonkian Hunting Territories: A Function of Ecological Adjustment, *American Anthropologist*, 51(1), 35–45.
Halpin AKW (1985) Hohfeld's Conceptions: From Eight to Two, *Cambridge Law Journal*, 44(3), 435–457.
Halpin AKW (2003) Fundamental Legal Concepts Reconsidered, *Canadian Journal of Law and Jurisprudence*, 16, 41–54.
Haraway D (2008) *When Species Meet*, U of Minnesota P, Minneapolis.
Hardin G (1968) The Tragedy of the Commons, *Science*, 162, 1243–1248.
Hardy K et al. (2015) The Importance of Dietary Carbohydrate in Human Evolution, *The Quarterly Review of Biology*, 90(3), c251–c268.
Hare B (2008) The Dog: A Biologist's Best Friend, *Current Biology*, 18(13), R543–R544.
Hare B & Tomasello M (2005) Human-Like Social Skills in Dogs?, *TRENDS in Cognitive Sciences*, 9(9), 439–444.
Hare B & Woods V (2013) We Didn't Domesticate Dogs: They Domesticated Us, *National Geographic News*, 3 March.
Hare B et al. (2002) The Domestication of Social Cognition in Dogs, *Science*, 298, 1634–1636.
Harman O (2011) *The Price of Altruism*, Vintage, London.
Harris G (2019) What am I Actually Buying?, *The Art Newspaper*, 29 August.
Harvey D (2011) The Future of the Commons, *Radical History Review*, 109, 101–106.
Heap S et al. (2012) The Adoption of Landmarks for Territorial Boundaries, *Animal Behaviour*, 83, 871–878: pp. 871–872.
Heape W (1931) *Emigration, Migration and Nomadism*, W Heffer & Sons, Cambridge.
Hedhammar Å & Hultin-Jäderlund K (2007) Behaviour and Disease in Dogs, in Jensen P (ed.) *The Behavioural Biology of Dogs*, CABI, Wallingford, OX, 243–261.
Hediger H (1959) *Wild Animals in Captivity*, Butterworths, London.
Hediger H (1968) *The Psychology and Behaviour of Animals in Zoos and Circuses*, Dover Publications, New York.
Heinz HJ (1972) Territoriality among the Bushmen in General and the !Ko in Particular, *Anthropos*, 67, 404–416.
Heller MA (1998) The Tragedy of the Anticommons: Property in the Transition from Marx to Markets, *Harvard Law Review*, 111(3), 621–688.
Heller MA (1999) The Boundaries of Private Property, *Yale Law Journal*, 108(6), 1163–1223.
Heller MA & Eisenberg RS (1998) Can Patents Deter Innovation? The Anticommons in Biomedical Research, *Science*, 280, 698–701.

Hemmer H (1990) *Domestication: The Decline of Environmental Appreciation*, Cambridge UP, Cambridge.
Hemsworth PH & Coleman GJ (2010) *Human-Livestock Interactions: The Stockperson and the Productivity and Welfare of Intensively Farmed Animals*, 2nd ed., CAB International, Wallingford.
Higgins H (2002) *Fluxus Experience*, U of California P, Berkeley.
Hirschler B (2016) How Dogs Became Man's Best Friend: Twice Over, *Reuters*, 2 June.
Hobbes T (1642/[1949]) *De Cive or the Citizen*, Appleton-Century-Crofts, New York.
Hobbes T (1651/[1968]) *Leviathan*, CB Macpherson (ed. & introd.), Penguin, London.
Hobson JA (1902) The Scientific Basis of Imperialism, *Political Science Quarterly*, 17(3), 460–489.
Hoebel EA (1940) *The Political Organization and Law-Ways of the Comanche Indians*, American Anthropological Association, Menasha, WI, 45–48.
Hoebel EA (1942) Fundamental Legal Concepts as Applied in the Study of Primitive Law, *Yale Law Journal*, 51, 951–966.
Hoebel EA (1946) Law and Anthropology, *Virginia Law Review*, 32(4), 835–854.
Hoebel EA (1954) *The Law of Primitive Man: A Study in Comparative Legal Dynamics*, Harvard UP, Cambridge, MA.
Hoehl S et al. (2019) 'Over-Imitation': A Review and Appraisal of a Decade of Research, *Developmental Review*, 51, 90–108.
Hohfeld WN (1913a) The Relations between Equity and Law, *Michigan Law Review*, 537–571.
Hohfeld WN (1913b) Some Fundamental Legal Conceptions as Applied in Judicial Reasoning, *Yale Law Journal*, 23(1), 16–59.
Hohfeld WN (1917) Fundamental Legal Conceptions as Applied in Judicial Reasoning, *Yale Law Journal*, 26(8), 710–770.
Holland TE (1916) *Jurisprudence*, 12th ed., Clarendon Press, Oxford.
Holmberg T (2019) Walking, Eating, Sleeping: Rhythm Analysis of Human/Dog Intimacy, *Emotion, Space and Society*, 26–31.
Holmes OW (1882) *The Common Law*, Macmillan, London.
Hopkins D (2014) Duchamp, Childhood, Work and Play: The Vernissage for *First Papers of Surrealism*, New York 1942, *Tate Papers*, 22.
Horowitz A (2013a) *On Looking: About Everything There Is to See*, Simon & Schuster, London.
Horowitz A (2013b) Sensitivity to Unequal Rewards in the Domestic Dog: Quantity over Fairness, *Journal of Veterinary Behavior*, 8(4) e30–e31.
Horowitz A (2016) *Being a Dog: Following the Dog Into a World of Smell*, Simon & Schuster, London.
Horowitz A (2017) Smelling Themselves: Dogs Investigate Their Own Odours Longer When Modified in an 'Olfactory Mirror' Test, *Behavioural Processes*, 143, 17–24.
Horowitz A (2019) When It Comes to Dogs, We Shouldn't Call Ourselves 'Owners', *The Globe and Mail*, 8 September.
Horowitz A et al. (2013) Smelling More or Less: Investigating the Olfactory Experience of the Domestic Dog, *Learning and Motivation*, 44, 207–217.
Horwitz S (2012) How Capitalism and the Bourgeois Virtues Transformed and Humanized the Family, *The Journal of Socio-Economics*, 41, 792–795.

Howard HE (1920) *Territory in Bird Life*, EP Dutton & Co, New York.
Howard HE (1929) *An Introduction to the Study of Bird Behaviour*, Cambridge UP, Cambridge.
Howell P (2015) *At Home and Astray: The Domestic Dog in Victorian Britain*, U of Virginia P, Charlottesville.
Howell TJ & Bennett PC (2011) Can Dogs (*Canis familiaris*) Use a Mirror to Solve a Problem?, *Journal of Veterinary Behavior*, 6, 306–312.
Howell TJ et al. (2013) Do Dogs Use a Mirror to Find Hidden Food?, *Journal of Veterinary Behavior*, 8, 425–430.
Howes D (2003) *Sensual Relations: Engaging the Senses in Culture and Social Theory*, U of Michigan P, Ann Arbor.
Howes D (2013) The Social Life of the Senses, *Ars Vivendi Journal*, 3, 4–23.
Howes D & Classen C (2014) *Ways of Sensing: Understanding the Senses in Society*, Routledge, London.
Huber L et al. (2018) Would Dogs Copy Irrelevant Actions from Their Human Caregiver?, *Learning & Behavior*, 46, 387–397.
Hume D (1739–1740/[1969]) *A Treatise of Human Nature*, Penguin, London.
Hurley S & Chater N (eds.) (2005a) *Perspectives on Imitation: From Neuroscience to Social Science, Volume 1: Mechanisms of Imitation and Imitation in Animals*, MIT Press, Cambridge, MA.
Hurley S & Chater N (eds.) (2005b) *Perspectives on Imitation: From Neuroscience to Social Science, Volume 2: Imitation, Human Development, and Culture*, MIT Press, Cambridge, MA.
Hurst JL & Beynon RJ (2004) Scent Wars: The Chemobiology of Competitive Signaling in Mice, *BioEssays*, 26, 1288–1298.
Huxley A (1932) *Brave New World*, Chatto & Windus, London.
Huxley J (1952) Foreword, in Lorenz KZ *King Solomon's Ring: New Light on Animal Ways*, M Kerr Wilson (trans.), Methuen & Co, London, 9–13.
Ingold T (1994) From Trust to Domination: An Alternative History of Human-Animal Relations, in Manning A & Serpell J (eds.) *Animals and Human Society: Changing Perspectives*, Routledge, London, 1–22.
Ingold T (2000) *The Perception of the Environment: Essays in Livelihood, Dwelling and Skill*, Routledge, London.
Jacobs JA (1893) The Folk, *Folklore*, 4(2), 233–238.
Jacobs JA et al. (2017) Ability of Owners to Identify Resource Guarding Behaviour in the Domestic Dog, *Applied Animal Behaviour Science*, 188, 77–83.
Jacobs JA et al. (2018a) Factors Associated with Canine Resource Guarding Behaviour in the Presence of Dogs: A Cross-Sectional Survey of Dog Owners, *Preventive Veterinary Medicine*, 161, 134–142.
Jacobs JA et al. (2018b) Factors Associated with Canine Resource Guarding Behaviour in the Presence of People: A Cross-Sectional Survey of Dog Owners, *Preventive Veterinary Medicine*, 161, 143–153.
Janssens L et al. (2018) A New Look at an Old Dog: Bonn-Oberkassel Reconsidered, *Journal of Archaeological Science*, 92, 126–138.
Jennings MW (2016) Introduction, in Benjamin W (1928/[2016]) *One-Way Street*, E Jephcott (trans.), Belknap-Harvard, Cambridge, MA, 1–20.
Jhering R von (1913) *Law as a Means to an End*, Boston Book Company, Boston.

Johnston AM et al. (2017) Uncovering the Origins of Dog-Human Eye Contact: Dingoes Establish Eye Contact More Than Wolves, But Less Than Dogs, *Animal Behaviour*, 133, 123–129.
Kachur L (2001) *Displaying the Marvellous Marcel Duchamp, Salvador Dali, and Surrealist Exhibition Installations*, MIT Press, Cambridge, MA.
Kafka F (1913/[1992]) Excursion Into the Mountains, W Muir & E Muir (trans.), in *The Complete Stories of Franz Kafka*, Minerva, London, 383.
Kafka F (1931/[1992]) Investigations of a Dog, W Muir & E Muir (trans.), in Kafka F (1992) *Kafka: The Complete Short Stories*, Minerva, London, 278–316.
Kalikow TJ (1983) Konrad Lorenz's Ethological Theory: Explanation and Ideology, 1938–1943, *Journal of the History of Biology*, 16(1), 39–73.
Kaminski J & Marshall-Pescini S (eds.) (2014) *The Social Dog: Behaviour and Cognition*, Academic Press, London.
Kaplan G (2009) Animals and Music: Between Cultural Definitions and Sensory Evidence, *Sign System Studies*, 37(3/4), 75–101.
Kaplan G (2015) *Bird Minds: Cognition and Behaviour of Australian Native Birds*, CSIRO, Clayton South, VIC.
Kaplan G & Rogers LJ (2007) Elephants That Paint, Birds That Make Music: Do Animals Have an Aesthetic Sense? in Read CA (ed), *Cerebrum 2007: Emerging Ideas in Brain Science*, Dana Foundation Press, New York, 1–14.
Kaplan HS & Zimmer M (2018) Sensorimotor Integration for Decision Making: How the Worm Steers, *Neuron*, 97(2), 258–260.
Kaufman AB & Kaufman JC (eds.) (2015) *Animal Creativity and Innovation*, Academic Press, London.
Kellein T (2007) *The Dream of Fluxus: George Maciunas: An Artist's Biography*, Edition Hansjörg Mayer, London.
Kerkhove W van (2004) A Fresh Look at the Wolf-Pack Theory of Companion-Animal Dog Social Behavior, *Journal of Applied Animal Welfare Science*, 7(4), 279–285.
Kete K (1994) *The Beast in the Boudoir: Petkeeping in Nineteenth-Century Paris*, U of California P, Berkeley.
Killeen PR & Jacobs KW (2017) Coal Is Not Black, Snow Is Not White, Food Is Not a Reinforcer: The Roles of Affordances and Dispositions in the Analysis of Behavior, *The Behavior Analyst*, 40, 17–38.
Kis A et al. (2015) Oxytocin Induces Positive Expectations about Ambivalent Stimuli (Cognitive Bias) in Dogs, *Hormones and Behavior*, 69, 1–7.
Kis A et al. (2017) The Effect of Oxytocin on Human-Directed Social Behavior in Dogs (*Canis familiaris*), *Hormones and Behavior*, 94, 40–52.
Kocourek A (1915) Law and Other Fields of Knowledge, *International Journal of Ethics*, 25(2), 179–187: pp. 186–187.
Kocourek A (1917) The Nature of Interests and Their Classification, *American Journal of Sociology*, 23(3), 359–368.
Kocourek A (1920) The Hohfeld System of Fundamental Legal Concepts, *Illinois Law Review*, 15(1), 24–39.
Kocourek A (1921) Tabulae Minores Jurisprudentiae, *The Yale Law Journal*, 30(3), 215–225.
Kocourek A (1923) The Alphabet of Legal Relations, *American Bar Association Journal*, 9(4), 237–239.

Kokko H et al. (2006) From Hawks and Doves to Self-Consistent Games of Territorial Behavior, *The American Naturalist*, 167(6), 901–912.
Krier JE (2009) Evolutionary Theory and the Origin of Property Rights, *Cornell Law Review*, 95(1), 139–159.
Krofel M et al. (2017) Does Human Infrastructure Shape Scent Marking in a Solitary Felid?, *Mammalian Biology*, 87, 36–39.
Kropotkin P (1902) *Mutual Aid: A Factor in Evolution*, McClure Phillips & Co, New York.
Kubinyi E et al. (2009) Dog as a Model for Studying Conspecific and Heterospecific Social Learning, *Journal of Veterinary Behavior*, 4, 31–41: p. 32.
Kuhne F (2016) Behavioural Responses of Dogs to Dog-Human Social Conflict Situations, *Applied Animal Behaviour Science*, 182, 38–43.
LaFollette MR et al. (2018) Practical Rat Tickling: Determining an Efficient and Effective Dosage of Heterospecific Play, *Applied Animal Behaviour Science*, 208, 82–91.
Laland KN & Galef BG (2009a) Introduction, in Laland KN & Galef BG (eds.) *The Question of Animal Culture*, Harvard UP, Cambridge, MA.
Laland KN & Galef BG (eds.) (2009b) *The Question of Animal Culture*, Harvard UP, Cambridge, MA.
Laland KN & Janik VM (2006) The Animal Cultures Debate, *TRENDS in Ecology and Evolution*, 21(10), 542–547.
Landrum AR & Mills CM (2015) Developing Expectations Regarding the Boundaries of Expertise, *Cognition*, 134, 215–231.
Lang M et al. (2017) Sync to Link: Endorphin-Mediated Synchrony Effects on Cooperation, *Biological Psychology*, 127, 191–197.
Laplantine F (2015) *The Life of the Senses: Introduction to a Modal Anthropology*, J Furniss (trans.), Bloomsbury, London, 82.
Largey GP & Watson DR (1972) The Sociology of Odors, *American Journal of Sociology*, 77(6), 1021–1034.
Larson G & Burger J (2013) A Population Genetics View of Animal Domestication, *Trends in Genetics*, 29(4), 197–205.
Larson G & Fuller DQ (2014) The Evolution of Animal Domestication, *Annual Review of Ecology, Evolution, and Systematics*, 45, 115–136.
Larson G et al. (2012) Rethinking Dog Domestication by Integrating Genetics, Archeology, and Biogeography, *PNAS*, 109, 8878–8883.
Latour B (2001) Gabriel Tarde and the End of the Social, *Soziale Welt: Zeitschrift für Sozialwissenschaftliche Forschung und Praxis*, 52, 361–381.
Latour B (2002) Gabriel Tarde and the End of the Social, in Joyce P (ed.) *The Social in Question: New Bearings in History and the Social Sciences*, Routledge, London, 117–132.
Latour B (2008) *What Is the Style of Matters of Concern?*, Van Gorcum, Amsterdam.
Latour B (2016) The Scientific Fables of an Empirical La Fontaine, Foreword, in Despret V (ed.) (2012/[2016]) *What Would Animals Say If We Asked the Right Questions?*, B Buchanan (trans.), U of Minnesota P, Minneapolis, vii–xiv.
Latour B & Lepinjay VA (2009) *The Science of Passionate Interests*, Prickly Paradigm Press, Chicago.
Lawton G (2014) The First Things Humans Owned, *New Scientist*, 25 March.

Leach HM (2003) Human Domestication Reconsidered, *Current Anthropology*, 44(3), 349–360.
Leach HM (2007) Selection and the Unforeseen Consequences of Domestication, in Cassidy R & Mullin M (eds.) *Where the Wild Things Are Now: Domestication Reconsidered*, Berg, Oxford, 71–99.
Legare CH & Nielsen M (2015) Imitation and Innovation: The Dual Engines of Cultural Learning, *Trends in Cognitive Sciences*, 19(11), 688–699.
Lehrman DS (1953) A Critique of Konrad Lorenz's Theory of Instinctive Behavior, *Quarterly Review of Biology*, 28(4), 337–363.
Lejano RP et al. (2014) Interrogating the Commons: Introduction to a Special Issue, *Environmental Science and Policy*, 36, 1–7.
Leonard RJ (1995) From Parlor Games to Social Science: Von Neumann, Morgenstern, and the Creation of Game Theory 1928–1944, *Journal of Economic Literature*, 33(2), 730–761.
Leys R (1993) Mead's Voices: Imitation as Foundation, or, the Struggle against Mimesis, *Critical Inquiry*, 19(2), 277–307.
Litman J (1990) The Public Domain, *Emory Law Journal*, 39(4), 965–1023.
Lloyd WF (1832/[1980]) WF Lloyd on the Checks to Population, *Population and Development Review*, 6(3), 473–496.
Lombroso C (1876) *L'Uomo Delinquente*, Ulrico Hoepli, Milano.
Lombroso C (1911) *Criminal Man, According to the Classification of Cesare Lombroso*, G Lombroso-Ferrero (ed.), GP Putnam's Sons, New York.
Long AA (1997) Stoic Philosophers on Persons, Property-Ownership and Community, *Bulletin of the Institute of Classical Studies*, 68, Aristotle and After, 13–31.
Long JA (2012) Waiting for Hohfeld: Property Rights, Property Privileges, and the Physical Consequences of Word Choice, *Gonzaga Law Review*, 48(2), 306–364.
Lorenz KZ (1935) Der Kumpan in der Umwelt des Vogels. Der Artgenosse als auslösendes Moment sozialer Verhaltensweisen, *Journal für Ornithologie*, 83, 137–215, 289–413.
Lorenz KZ (1952) *King Solomon's Ring: New Light on Animal Ways*, M Kerr Wilson (trans.), Methuen & Co, London.
Lorenz KZ (1988/[1991]) *Here Am I: Where Are You? The Behavior of the Greylag Goose*, RD Martin (trans.), Harcourt Brace Jovanovich, New York.
Lorenz KZ (1992/[1996]) *The Natural Science of the Human Species: An Introduction to Comparative Behavioral Research, the 'Russian Manuscript' (1944–1948)*, A von Cranach (ed.), RD Martin (trans.), MIT Press, Cambridge, MA, 75.
Lorimer H (2006) Herding Memories of Humans and Animals, *Environment and Planning D: Society and Space*, 24, 497–518.
Losey RJ et al. (2011) Canids as Persons: Early Neolithic Dog and Wolf Burials, Cis-Baikal, Siberia, *Journal of Anthropological Archaeology*, 30, 174–189.
Lowie RH (1928) Incorporeal Property in Primitive Society, *Yale Law Journal*, 37(5), 551–563.
Lupo KD (2019) Hounds Follow Those Who Feed Them: What Can the Ethnographic Record of Hunter-Gatherers Reveal about Early Human-Canid Partnerships?, *Journal of Anthropological Archaeology*, 55, 101081.
Lushetich N (2014) *Fluxus: The Practice of Non-Duality*, Rodopi, Amsterdam.
Lyman SM & Scott MB (1967) Territoriality: A Neglected Sociological Dimension, *Social Problems*, 15(2), 236–249.

Lyon DE et al. (2007) The Hidden Structure of Overimitation, *Proceedings of the National Academy of Sciences of the United States of America*, 104(50), 19751–19756.
Lyons D (1970) The Correlativity of Rights and Duties, *Noûs*, 4(1), 45–55.
Maciunas G (1963) *Fluxus Manifesto I*. Available at georgemaciunas.com
Maciunas G (1971) *Fluxmanifesto*. Available at georgemaciunas.com
MacLean EL et al. (2017) Individual Differences in Cooperative Communication Skills Are More Similar between Dogs and Humans Than Chimpanzees, *Animal Behaviour*, 126, 41–51.
Maitland (1909) *Equity: A Course of Lectures*, Cambridge UP, Cambridge.
Malinowski B (1922) *Argonauts of the Western Pacific*, Routledge Kegan Paul, London.
Malinowski B (1926) *Crime and Custom in Savage Society*, Harcourt Brace & Co, New York.
Malinowski B (1942) A New Instrument for the Interpretation of Law: Especially Primitive, *The Yale Law Journal*, 51(8), 1237–1254.
Malinowski B (1944) *A Scientific Theory of Culture and Other Essays*, U of North Carolina P, Chapel Hill.
Maloney JP (1937) Restatement of the Law of Property, *St John's Law Review*, 12, 1–21.
Manning A & Serpell J (eds.) (1994) *Animals and Human Society: Changing Perspectives*, Routledge, London.
Marks LE (1986) Introduction, in Stevens SS (1975/[1986]) *Psychophysics: Introduction to Its Perceptual, Neural, and Social Prospects*, Transaction Publishers, New Brunswick.
Marshall A (1925) *Memorials of Alfred Marshall*, AC Pigou (ed.), Macmillan, London.
Marshall-Pescini S & Kaminski J (2014) The Social Dog: History and Evolution, in Kaminski J & Marshall-Pescini S (eds.) *The Social Dog: Behaviour and Cognition*, Academic Press, London, 3–33.
Marshall-Pescini S et al. (2017a) Integrating Social Ecology in Explanations of Wolf-Dog Behavioural Differences, *Current Opinion in Behavioral Sciences*, 16, 80–86.
Marshall-Pescini S et al. (2017b) The Role of Domestication and Experience in 'Looking Back' towards Humans in an Unsolvable Task, *Nature*, 7, 46636.
Massumi B (2014) *What Animals Teach Us about Politics*, Durham UP, Durham.
Maynard Smith J (1979) Game Theory and the Evolution of Behaviour, *Proceedings of the Royal Society of London*, 205(1161), 475–488.
Maynard Smith J (1982) *Evolution and the Theory of Games*, Cambridge UP, Cambridge.
Maynard Smith J & Price GR (1973) The Logic of Animal Conflict, *Nature*, 246, 15–18.
Mayr E (1935) Bernard Altum and the Territory Theory, *Proceedings of the Linnaean Society of New York*, 45–46: pp. 24–38.
Mazzatenta A et al. (2017) The Companion Dog as a Unique Translational Model for Aging, *Seminars in Cell & Developmental Biology*, 70, 141–153.
McClure SB (2015) The Pastoral Effect, *Current Anthropology*, 56(6), 901–910.
McGuire B & Bemis KE (2017) Scent Marking in Shelter Dogs: Effects of Body Size, *Applied Animal Behaviour Science*, 186, 49–55: p. 49.

McGuire B et al. (2018) Urine Marking in Male Domestic Dogs: Honest or Dishonest, *Journal of Zoology*, 306, 163–170.
McKenzie RD (1924) The Ecological Approach to the Study of the Human Community, *American Journal of Sociology*, 30(3), 287–301.
McLean AN (2008) Overshadowing: A Silver Lining to a Dark Cloud in Horse Training, *Journal of Applied Animal Welfare Science*, 11, 236–248.
McLemore S Dale (1970) Simmel's 'Stranger': A Critique of the Concept, *The Pacific Sociological Review*, 13(2), 86–94.
Mead M (1961) Some Anthropological Considerations Concerning Natural Law, *Natural Law Forum*, 6, 51–64.
Mech LD (1966) *The Wolves of Isle Royale*, United States Department of the Interior, Washington.
Mech LD (1970/[1981]) *The Wolf: The Ecology and Behavior of an Endangered Species*, U of Minnesota P, Minneapolis.
Mech LD (1991) *The Way of the Wolf*, Voyageur Press, Stillwater, MN.
Mech LD (1999) Alpha Status, Dominance, and Division of Labor in Wolf Packs, *Canadian Journal of Zoology*, 77(8), 1196–1203.
Mech LD (ed.) (2000) *The Wolves of Minnesota: Howl in the Heartland*, Voyageur Press, Stillwater, MN.
Mech LD (2008) Whatever Happened to the Term Alpha Wolf?, *International Wolf*, Winter, 4–8.
Mech LD & Boitani L (2003a) Wolf Social Ecology, in Mech LD and Boitani L (eds.) *Wolves: Behaviour, Ecology, and Conservation*, U of Chicago P, Chicago, 1–34: p. 7.
Mech LD and Boitani L (eds.) (2003b) *Wolves: Behaviour, Ecology, and Conservation*, U of Chicago P, Chicago.
Mech LD et al. (2015) *Wolves on the Hunt: The Behavior of Wolves Hunting Wild Prey*, U of Chicago P, Chicago.
Medawar PB & Medawar JS (1983) *Aristotle to Zoos*, Harvard UP, Cambridge, MA.
Menzel R (2009) Learning and Memory in Invertebrates: Honey Bee, in LS Squire (ed.) *Encyclopedia of Neuroscience*, Academic Press, Cambridge, MA, 435–439.
Mercier D et al. (2018) Olfactory Landmark-Based Communication in Interacting Drosophila, *Current Biology*, 28(16), 2624–2631.e5.
Merskovits MJ (1940/[1952]) *Economic Anthropology*, Alfred A Knopf, New York.
Mesterton-Gibbons M & Adams ES (2003) Landmarks in Territory Partitioning: A Strategically Stable Convention?, *The American Naturalist*, 161(5), 685–697.
Mesterton-Gibbons M & Sherratt TN (2014) Bourgeois versus Anti-Bourgeois: A Model of Infinite Regress, *Animal Behaviour*, 89, 171–183.
Miklósi Á (2015) *Dog Behaviour, Evolution, and Cognition*, 2nd ed., Oxford UP, Oxford.
Miklósi A & Soporoni K (2006) A Comparative Analysis of Animals' Understanding of the Human Pointing Gesture, *Animal Cognition*, 1, 113–121.
Miklósi A et al. (2003) A Simple Reason for a Big Difference: Wolves Do Not Look Back at Humans, But Dogs Do, *Current Biology*, 13, 763–766.
Miklósi Á et al. (2004) Comparative Social Cognition: What Can Dogs Teach Us?, *Animal Behaviour*, 67, 995–1004.
Milet J (1970) *Gabriel Tarde et la philosophie de l'histoire*, Vrin, Paris.

Milet J (1972) Gabriel Tarde et al psychologie sociale, *Revue française de sociologie*, 13(4), 472–484.
Miller HC & Bender C (2012) The Breakfast Effect: Dogs (*Canis familiaris*) Search More Accurately When They Are Less Hungry, *Behavioural Processes*, 91, 313–317.
Mills D et al. (2010) *The Encyclopedia of Applied Animal Behaviour and Welfare*, CABI, Wallingford, OX.
Milson SFC (2003) *A Natural History of the Common Law*, Columbia UP, New York.
Mitchell RW (2015) Creativity in the Interaction: The Case of Dog-Human Play, in Kaufman AB & Kaufman JC (eds.) *Animal Creativity and Innovation*, Academic Press, London, 31–42.
Möller R & Vardy A (2006) Local Visual Homing by Matched-Filter Descent in Image Distances, *Biological Cybernetics*, 95, 413–430.
Morey DF (2014) In Search of Paleolithic Dogs: A Quest with Mixed Results, *Journal of Archaeological Science*, 52, 300–307.
Morey DF & Jeger R (2015) Paleolithic Dogs: Why Sustained Domestication Then?, *Journal of Archaeological Science: Reports*, 3, 420–428.
Morgan CL (1930) *The Animal Mind*, Edward Arnold & Co, London.
Morgan LH (1877) *Ancient People, or Researches in the Line of Human Progress, from Savagery through Barbarism to Civilization*, Charles H Kerr & Co, Chicago.
Mosse GL (1966) The Genesis of Fascism, *Journal of Contemporary History*, 1(1), 14–26.
Mugford RA (1984) Aggressive Behaviour in the English Cocker Spaniel, *The Veterinary Annual*, 24, 310–314.
Müller CA & Cant MA (2010) Imitation and Traditions in Wild Banded Mongooses, *Current Biology*, 20(13), 1171–1175.
Nagasawa M et al. (2015) Oxytocin-Gaze Positive Loop and the Coevolution of Human-Dog Bonds, *Science*, 348, 333–336.
Nancy J-L (1991) Of Being-in-Common, in Miami Theory Collective (ed.) *Community at Loose Ends*, U of Minnesota P, Minneapolis, 1.
Nancy J-L (1993) *The Birth to Presence*, B Holmes et al. (trans.), Stanford UP, Stanford, 43–44.
Nancy J-L (2003) *A Finite Thinking*, Stanford UP, Stanford, 154.
Nawroth C et al. (2018) Goats Prefer Positive Human Emotional Facial Expressions, *Royal Society Open Science*, 5, 18049.
Nedelsky J (1990) Law, Boundaries and the Bounded Self, *Representations*, 30, 162–189.
Nedelsky J (2011) *Law's Relations: A Relational Theory of Self, Autonomy and Law*, Oxford UP, Oxford.
Nice MM (1933) The Theory of Territorialism and Its Development, in *Fifty Years' Progress of American Ornithology, 1883–1933*, American Ornithologists' Union, Lancaster, PA, 89–100.
Nice MM (1941a) The Role of Territory in Bird Life, *The American Midland Naturalist*, 26(3), 441–487.
Nice MM (1941b) The Role of Territory in Bird Life, *The American Midland Naturalist*, 46(3), 441–487.
Nietzsche F (1874/[2015]) *The Use and Abuse of History*, A Collins (trans.), Martino Press, Mansfield.

Nietzsche F (1882/[1974]) *The Gay Science*, W Kaufman (trans.), Vintage Books, New York.
Nietzsche F (1883/[1969]) *Thus Spoke Zarathustra*, Penguin, London.
Nietzsche F (1886/[1973]) *Beyond Good and Evil*, Penguin, London, 199.
Nietzsche F (1887/[1989]) *On the Genealogy of Morals and Ecce Homo*, W Kauffman (trans.), Vintage, New York.
Noble GK (1939) The Role of Dominance in the Social Life of Birds, *The Auk*, 56(3), 263–273.
O'Connor TP (1997) Working on Relationships: Another Look at Animal Domestication, *Antiquity*, 71, 149–156.
O'Reilly DT (1995) Using the Square of Opposition to Illustrate the Deontic and Alethic Relations Constituting Rights, *The University of Toronto Law Journal*, 45(3), 279–310.
Ojalammi S & Blomley N (2015) Dancing with Wolves: Making Legal Territory in a More-Than-Human World, *Geoforum*, 62, 51–60.
Orton D (2010) Both Subject and Object Herding, Inalienability and Sentient Property in Prehistory, *World Archaeology*, 42(2), 188–200.
Osborne H (1977) Odours and Appreciation, *British Journal of Aesthetics*, 17(1), 37–48.
Ostrom E (1990) *Governing the Commons: The Evolution of Institutions for Collective Action*, Cambridge UP, Cambridge.
Ostrom E (2012) *The Future of the Commons*, The Institute of Economic Affairs, London.
Ostrom E et al. (1999) Revisiting the Commons: Local Lessons, Global Challenges, *Science*, 284(5412), 278–282.
Overall C (2017a) Introduction, in Overall C (ed.) *Pets and People: The Ethics of Our Relationships with Companion Animals*, Oxford UP, Oxford, xvii–xxv.
Overall C (ed.) (2017b) *Pets and People: The Ethics of Our Relationships with Companion Animals*, Oxford UP, Oxford.
Overall KL (2011) That Dog Is Smarter Than You Know: Advances in Understanding Canine Learning, Memory, and Cognition, *Topics in Companion Animal Medicine*, 26(1), 2–9.
Packard JM (2003) Wolf Behavior: Reproductive, Social, and Intelligent, in Mech LD & Boitani L (eds.) *Wolves: Behavior, Ecology, and Conservation*, U of Chicago P, Chicago, 35–65.
Panksepp J (2000) The Riddle of Laughter: Neural and Psychoevolutionary Underpinnings of Joy, *Current Directions in Psychological Science*, 9, 183–186.
Panksepp J & Burgdorf J (2003) 'Laughing' Rats and the Evolutionary Antecedents of Human Joy?, *Physiology & Behavior*, 79, 533–547.
Park RE & Burgess EW (1921) *Introduction to the Science of Sociology*, U of Chicago P, Chicago.
Parker GA (1974) Assessment Strategy and the Evolution of Animal Conflicts, *Journal of Theoretical Biology*, 47, 223–243.
Patou-Mathis et al. (2018) The Evidence from Vindija Cave (Croatia) Reveals Diversity of Neandertal Behaviour in Europe, *Quarternary International*, 23(6), 314–326.
Patterson EW (1942) Logic in the Law, *University of Pennsylvania Law Review and American Law Register*, 90(8), 875–909.

Pavlov IP (1927) *Conditioned Reflexes: An Investigation of the Physiological Activity of the Cerebral Cortex*, GV Anrep (trans.), Oxford UP, Oxford.
Paz O (1968/[1990]) *Marcel Duchamp: Appearance Stripped Bare*, Arcade Publishing, New York.
Pearson C (2016) Canines and Contraband: Dogs, Nonhuman Agency and the Making of the Franco-Belgian Border during the French Third Republic, *Journal of Historical Geography*, 54, 50–62.
Penner J (1997) *The Idea of Property in Law*, Clarendon Press, Oxford.
Pérez-Guisado J et al. (2006) Heritability of Dominant-Aggressive Behaviour in English Cocker Spaniels, *Applied Animal Behaviour Science*, 100, 219–227.
Perls F (1969/[1992]) *Gestalt Therapy Verbatim*, Gestalt Journal Press, Gouldsboro, ME.
Perrin G (1955) 'Pecking Order' 1924–54, *American Speech*, 30(4), 265–268.
Pfaller-Sadovsky N et al. (2017) It Is Mine! Using Clicker Training as a Treatment of Object Guarding in 4 Companion Dogs (*Canis lupus familiaris*), *Journal of Veterinary Behavior*, 22, 57–65.
Pierotti R (2016) The Role of Myth in Understanding Nature, *Ethnobiology Letters*, 7(2), 6–13.
Pierotti R & Fogg BR (2017) *The First Domestication: How Wolves and Humans Coevolved*, Yale UP, New Haven.
Pionnier-Capitan M et al. (2011) New Evidence for Upper Paleolithic Small Domestic Dogs in South-Western Europe, *Journal of Archaeological Science*, 38, 2123–2140.
Pirrone F et al. (2017) Measuring Social Synchrony and Stress in the Handler-Dog Dyad during Animal-Assisted Activities: A Pilot Study, *Journal of Veterinary Behavior*, 21, 45–52.
Pittenger M (1987) Science, Culture and the New Socialist Intellectuals before World War I, *American Studies*, 28(1), 73–91.
Pitulko VV & Kasparov AK (2017) Archaeological Dogs from the Early Holocene Zhokhov Site in the Eastern Siberia Arctic, *Journal of Archaeological Science Reports*, 13, 491–515.
Plotnik JM et al. (2019) Elephants Have a Nose for Quantity, *PNAS*, 116(25), 12566–12571.
Podberscek AL & Serpell JA (1996) The English Cocker Spaniel: Preliminary Findings on Aggressive Behaviour, *Applied Animal Behaviour Science*, 47, 75–89.
Pongrácz P et al. (2013) 'We Will Work for You': Social Influence May Suppress Individual Food Preferences in a Communicative Situation in Dogs, *Learning and Motivation*, 44, 270–281.
Pongrácz P et al. (2017) Do You See What I See? The Difference between Dog and Human Visual Perception May Affect the Outcome of Experiments, *Behavioural Processes*, 140, 53–60.
Portugal SJ et al. (2014) Upwash Exploitation and Downwash Avoidance Buy Flap Phasing in Ibis Formation Flight, *Nature*, 505, 399–404.
Power ER (2012) Domestication and the Dog: Embodying Home, *Area*, 44(3), 371–378.
Preshaw L et al. (2017) Application of Learning Theory in Horse Rescues in England and Wales, *Applied Animal Behaviour Science*, 190, 82–89.
Previde EP & Valsecchi P (2014) The Immaterial Cord: The Dog-Human Attachment Bond, in Kaminski J & Marshall-Pescini S (eds.) *The Social Dog: Behaviour and Cognition*, Academic Press, San Diego, 165–189.

Pryor AE (2012) Heidegger and the Dog Whisperer: Imagining Interspecies Kindness, in Gross A & Vallely A (eds.) *Animals and the Human Imagination: A Companion to Animal Studies*, Columbia UP, New York, 289–306.
Pryor K (2002a) *Clicker Training for Dogs*, Ringpress Books, Dorking.
Pryor K (2002b) *Don't Shoot the Dog! The New Art of Teaching and Training*, Rev ed., Ringpress, Dorking.
Pulvermuller F (2005) Brain Mechanisms Linking Language and Action, *Nature Reviews Neuroscience*, 6, 576–582.
Pyyhtinen O (2009) Being-with: Georg Simmel's Sociology of Association, *Theory, Culture & Society*, 26(5), 108–128.
Radin M (1929) Correlation, *Columbia Law Review*, 29(7), 901–905.
Radin M (1938) A Restatement of Hohfeld, *Harvard Law Review*, 51(7), 1141–1164.
Ralls K (1971) Mammalian Scent Marking, *Science*, 171(3970), 443–449.
Rancière J (2008/[2011]) *The Emancipated Spectator*, G Elliott (trans.), Verso, London.
Randall HJ (1918) Law and Geography, in Kocourek A & Wigmore JH *Evolution of Law, Select Readings on the Origin and Development of Legal Institutions: Volume III, Formative Influences of Legal Development*, Little, Brown, & Co, Boston.
Randall HJ (1925) Hohfeld on Jurisprudence, *Law Quarterly Review*, 41, 86–94; Husik I (1923–1924) Hohfeld's Jurisprudence, *University of Pennsylvania Law Review*, 72, 263–277.
Range F et al. (2009) Effort and Reward: Inequity Aversion in Domestic Dogs?, *Journal of Veterinary Behavior*, 4(2) 45–46.
Raymer EJ (2013) A Man of His Time: Thorstein Veblen and the University of Chicago Darwinists, *Journal of the History of Biology*, 46(4), 669–698.
Reinhard J et al. (2004) Olfaction: Scent-Triggered Navigation in Honeybees, *Nature*, 427, 411.
Rensberger B (1977) *The Cult of the Wild*, Anchor Press, New York.
Rezáč P et al. (2011) Factors Affecting Dog-Dog Interactions on Walks with Their Owners, *Applied Animal Behaviour Science*, 134, 170–176.
Rezac P et al. (2017) Factors Affecting Dog Jumping on People, *Applied Animal Behaviour Science*, 197, 40–44.
Riach AC et al. (2017) Length of Time Domestic Dogs (*Canis familiaris*) Spend Smelling Urine of Gonadectomised and Intact Conspecifics, *Behavioural Processes*, 143, 138–140.
Riemer S et al. (2018) Reinforcer Effectiveness in Dogs: The Influence of Quantity and Quality, *Applied Animal Behaviour Science*, 206, 87–93.
Rindisbacher HJ (2015) What's This Smell? Shifting Worlds of Olfactory Perception, *KulturPoetik*, 15(1), 70–104.
Rindos D (1984) *The Origins of Agriculture: An Evolutionary Perspective*, Academic Press, San Diego.
Rivers WHR (1924) *Social Organization*, Routledge, London.
Robinson RE et al. (1983) The Logic of Rights, *The University of Toronto Law Journal*, 33(3), 267–278.
Roch SG & Samuelson CD (1997) Effects of Environmental Uncertainty and Social Value Orientation in Resource Dilemmas, *Organizational Behavior and Human Decision Processes*, 70(3), 221–235.

Roe A & Simpson GG (eds.) (1958) *Behavior and Evolution*, Yale UP, New Haven.
Rogers J et al. (2006) Taming Global Capitalism Anew, *The Nation*, 17 April.
Romanes GR (1885) *Mental Evolution in Animals*, Kegan Paul Trench & Co, London.
Rooney NJ & Bradshaw JWS (2002) An Experimental Study of the Effects of Play Upon the Dog-Human Relationship, *Applied Animal Behaviour Science*, 75, 161–176.
Rose DB (1992/[2000]) *Dingo Makes Us Human: Life and Land in an Australian Aboriginal Culture*, Cambridge UP, Cambridge.
Rudlin WA (1934) Review: The Professions by AM Carr-Saunders and PA Wilson, *The Economic Journal*, 44(174), 322–324.
Russell N (2002) The Wild Side of Animal Domestication, *Society & Animals*, 10(3), 285–302.
Russell N (2012) *Social Zooarchaeology*, Cambridge UP, Cambridge.
Ruvinsky A & Sampson J (2001) *The Genetics of the Dog*, CAB International, Wallingford, OX.
Sabido Ramos O (2017) The Senses as a Resource of Meaning in the Construction of the Stranger: An Approach from Georg Simmel's Relational Sociology, *Simmel Studies*, 21(1), 15–41.
Sack RD (1983) Human Territoriality: A Theory, *Annals of the Association of American Geographers*, 73(1), 55–74.
Sack RD (1986) *Human Territoriality: Its Theory and History*, Cambridge UP, Cambridge.
Sagan D (2010) Umwelt after Uexküll, in Uexküll J von (ed.) (1934/[2010]) *A Foray Into the Worlds of Animals and Humans*, U of Minnesota P, Minneapolis, 1–34.
Sahlins M (1995) *How 'Natives' Thinks: About Captain Cook, for Example*, U of Chicago P, Chicago.
Saint-Exupéry A de (1943/[1995]) *The Little Prince*, I Testot-Ferry (trans.), Wordsworth, London.
Saleilles R (1898/[1911]) *The Individualization of Punishment*, R Szold Jastrow (trans.), Little, Brown, & Co, Boston.
Sankey C et al. (2010) Positive Interactions Lead to Lasting Positive Memories in Horses, *Equus caballus, Animal Behaviour*, 79, 869–875.
Sassen S (2006) *Territory, Author, Rights: From Medieval to Global Assemblages*, Princeton UP, Princeton.
Sauvet G (2019) The Lifeworld of Hunter-Gatherers and the Concepts of Territory, *Quarternary International*, 503, 191–199.
Savolainen P et al. (2002) Genetic Evidence for an East Asian Origin of Domestic Dogs, *Science*, 298, 1610–1613.
Sax B (1997) What Is a 'Jewish Dog'? Konrad Lorenz and the Cult of Wildness, *Society and Animals*, 5(1), 3–21.
Sax B (2000/[2013]) *Animals in the Third Reich*, Yogh & Thorn Books, Pittsburgh.
Schenkel R (1947) Ausdrucks-Studien an Wölfen: Gefangenschafts-Beobachtungen, *Behaviour*, 1(2), 81–129. (Expression Studies of Wolves).
Schenkel R (1967) Submission: Its Features and Function in the Wolf and Dog, *American Zoologist*, 7(2), 319–329.

Schiper I (2017) From Flâneur to Co-Producer: The Performative Spectator, in Leeker M et al. (eds.) *Performing the Digital*, Transcript Verlag, Bielefeld, 191–209.

Schjelderup-Ebbe T (1922) Beiträge zur Sozialpsychologie des haushuhns/Contributions to the Social Psychology of the Domestic Chicken, *Zeitschrift für Psychologie*, 88, 225–252, M Schleidt & WM Schleidt (trans.), in Schein MW (ed.) (1975) *Social Hierarchy and Dominance*, Dowden, Hutchinson & Ross, Stroudsburg, PA, 7–49.

Schlag P (2015) How to Do Things with Hohfeld, *Law and Contemporary Problems*, 78, 185–234.

Schleidt WM (1998) Is Humaneness Canine?, *Human Ethology Bulletin*, 13(4), 14–20.

Schleidt WM & Shalter MD (2003) Co-Evolution of Humans and Canids: An Alternative View of Dog Domestication: *Homo Homini Lupus?*, *Evolution and Cognition*, 9(1), 57–71.

Schleidt WM & Shalter MD (2018) Dogs and Mankind: Coeevolution on the Move: An Update, *Human Ethology Bulletin*, 33(1), 15–38.

Schrock TS (1991) The Rights to Punish and Resist Punishment in Hobbes's *Leviathan*, *The Western Political Quarterly*, 44(4), 853–890.

Schubert TW & Semin GR (2009) Special Issue Introduction: Embodiment as a Unifying Perspective for Psychology, *European Journal of Social Psychology*, 39, 1135–1141.

Schwartz B (1993) Why Altruism Is Impossible . . . and Ubiquitous, *Social Service Review*, 67(3), 314–343.

Scott JP (1964) Leadership in Macaque Societies, *Science*, 144(3623), 1179.

Seifert B & Gonenc H (2008) The International Evidence on the Pecking Order Hypothesis, *Journal of Multinational Financial Management*, 18(3), 244–260.

Seltzer LF (2012) Are You a Victim of Predatory Capitalism?, *Psychology Today*, 21 September.

Selwood J (2005) 'English-Born Reputed Strangers': Birth and Descent in Seventeenth-Century London, *Journal of British Studies*, 44(4), 728–753.

Semin GR & Smith ER (eds.) (2008) *Embodied Grounding: Social, Cognitive, Affective, and Neuroscientific Approaches*, Cambridge UP, Cambridge.

Serpell J (1986/[1996]) *In the Company of Animals: A Study of Human-Animal Relationships*, Cambridge UP, Cambridge.

Serpell J (ed.) (2017) *The Domestic Dog: Its Evolution, Behavior and Interactions with People*, 2nd ed., Cambridge UP, Cambridge.

Serres M (1982) *Hermes: Literature, Science, Philosophy*, Johns Hopkins UP, Baltimore, MD.

Serres M (1985[2008]) *The Five Senses: A Philosophy of Mingled Bodies*, Continuum, London.

Serres M & Latour B (1990/[1995]) *Conversations on Science, Culture, and Time*, R Lapidus (trans.), U of Michigan P, Ann Arbor.

Seton ET (1909) *Life-Histories of Northern Mammals: Volume 1, Grass-Eaters*, Charles Scribner's Sons, New York City.

Seuren PAM (2016) Saussure and His Intellectual Environment, *History of European Ideas*, 42(6), 819–847.

Sharpe LL (2015) Handstand Scent Marking: Height Matters to Dwarf Mongooses, *Animal Behaviour*, 105, 173–179.
Sharpe LL et al. (2012) Handstand Scent Marking in the Dwarf Mongoose (*Helogale parvula*), *Ethology*, 118, 575–583.
Shaw WH (1984) Marx and Morgan, *History and Theory*, 23(2), 215–228.
Simmel G (1907/[2000]) Sociology of the Senses, M Riter & D Frisby (trans.), in Frisby D & Featherstone M (eds.) *Simmel on Culture*, Sage, London, 109–120.
Simmel G (1908/[1950]) The Stranger, in *The Sociology of Georg Simmel*, KH Wolff (trans.), The Free Press, New York, 402–408.
Simmel G (1910/[1949]) The Sociology of Sociability, EC Hughes (trans.), *American Journal of Sociology*, 55(3), 254–261.
Simmel G (1921) Sociology of the Senses: Visual Interaction, in Park RE & Burgess EW (eds.) *Introduction to the Science of Sociology*, U of Chicago P, Chicago, 356–361.
Simmel G (1950) *The Sociology of Georg Simmel*, KH Wolff (trans.), The Free Press, Glencoe, IL.
Simonds PE (1962) The Japan Monkey Center, *Current Anthropology*, 3(3), 303–305.
Singer JW (1982) The Legal Rights Debate in Analytical Jurisprudence from Bentham to Hohfeld, *Wisconsin Law Review*, 976–1060.
Singer JW (2000) *Entitlement*, Yale UP, New Haven.
Singer JW & Beermann JM (1993) The Social Origins of Property, *Canadian Journal of Law and Jurisprudence*, 6(2), 217–248.
Skinner BF (1938) *The Behavior of Organisms: An Experimental Analysis*, Appleton-Century-Crofts, New York.
Skinner BF (1953) *Science and Human Behavior*, The Free Press, New York.
Skinner BF (1976) *About Behaviorism*, Vintage, New York.
Skinner BF (1979) The Non-Punitive Society, Commemorative Lecture, Keio University, Japan, 25 September. Available from the BF Skinner Foundation.
Skinner BF (1981) Selection by Consequences, *Science*, 213(4507), 501–504.
Skloglund P et al. (2015) Ancient Wolf Genome Reveals an Early Divergence of Domestic Dog Ancestors and Admixture Into High Latitude Breeds, *Current Biology*, 25, 1515–1519.
Slezak M (2015) Ancient DNA Suggests Dogs Split from Wolves 40,000 Years Ago, *New Scientist*, 21 May.
Smith BD (2006) Niche Construction and the Behavioral Context of Plant and Animal Domestication, *Evolutionary Anthropology*, 16, 118–199.
Smith HE (2012) On the Economy of Concepts in Property, *University of Pennsylvania Law Review*, 160(7), 2097–2128.
Smith JA (2012) The Meaning of 'Energy' in Cesar Millan's Discourse on Dogs, in Smith JA & Mitchell RW (eds.) *Experiencing Animal Minds: An Anthology of Animal-Human Encounters*, Columbia UP, New York, 142–153.
Smuts B (1981) Dominance: An Alternative View, *The Behavioral and Brain Sciences*, 4, 448–449.
Smuts B (2007) Embodied Communication in Non-Human Animals, in Fogel A et al. (eds.) *Human Development in the Twenty-First Century*, Cambridge UP, Cambridge, 136–146.
Speck FG (1914–1915) The Basis of American Indian Ownership of the Land, University of Pennsylvania Faculty, Public Lectures, Philadelphia, 181–196.

Speck FG (1926) Land Ownership among Hunting Peoples in Primitive America and the World's Marginal Areas, Proceedings, Twenty-Second International Congress of Americanists, Rome 323–332.
Spencer H (1892) *The Principles of Ethics*, D Appleton & Co, New York.
Sperber D (1974/[1975]) *Rethinking Symbolism*, A Morton (trans.), Cambridge UP, Cambridge.
Spetch ML & Kelly DM (2006) Comparative Spatial Cognition: Processes in Landmark- and Surface-Based Place Finding, in Wasserman EA & Zentall TR (eds.) *Comparative Cognition: Experimental Explorations of Animal Intelligence*, Oxford UP, Oxford, 210–228.
Spiter L (1947) Scalawag, *American Speech*, 22(3), 188–191.
Sprankling JG (1996) The Antiwilderness Bias in American Property Law, *The University of Chicago Law Review*, 63(2), 519–590.
Stamp J (2013) The First Major Museum Show to Focus on Smell, *Smithsonian*, 16 January.
Statt D (1990) The City of London and the Controversy over Immigration, 1660–1722, *The Historic Journal*, 33(1), 45–61.
Steck K (2012) Just Follow Your Nose: Homing by Olfactory Cues in Ants, *Current Opinion in Neurobiology*, 22(2), 231–235.
Stengers I (2000) Another Look: Relearning to Laugh, P Deutscher (trans.), *Hypatia*, 15(4), 41–54.
Stetter MG et al. (2017) How to Make a Domesticate, *Current Biology*, 27, R896–R900.
Stevens SS (1951) *Handbook of Experimental Psychology*, 1st ed., John Wiley & Sons, New York.
Stevens SS (1975/[1986]) *Psychophysics: Introduction to Its Perceptual, Neural, and Social Prospects*, Transaction Publishers, New Brunswick.
Stone RL (1963) An Analysis of Hohfeld, *Minnesota Law Review*, 48, 313–337.
Studzinski CM et al. (2005) The Canine Model of Human Cognitive Aging and Dementia: Pharmacological Validity of the Model for Assessment of Human Cognitive-Enhancing Drugs, *Progress in Neuro-Psychopharmacology & Biological Psychiatry*, 29, 489–498.
Studzinski CM et al. (2006) Visuospatial Function in the Beagle Dog: An Early Marker of Cognitive Decline in a Model of Human Aging and Dementia, *Neurobiology of Learning and Memory*, 86, 197–204.
Szeemann H (2018) *Selected Writings*, D Chon et al. (ed.), J Blower & E Tucker (trans.), Getty Research Institute, Los Angeles.
Tanimoto Y & Kiimura KD (2019) Neuronal, Mathematical, and Molecular Bases of Perceptual Decision-Making in *C. elegans*, *Neuroscience Research*, 140, 3–13.
Tarde G (1884) Darwinisme Naturel et Darwinisme Social, *Revue Philosophique de la France et de l'Étranger*, 17, 607–637.
Tarde G (1890/[1903]) *The Laws of Imitation*, EC Parsons (trans.), Henry Holt & Co, New York.
Tarde G (1890/[1912]) *Penal Philosophy*, R Howell (trans.), Little, Brown, & Co, Boston.
Tarde G (1893/[2012]) *Monadology and Sociology*, T Lorenc (trans.), Re-Press, Melbourne, 22–23.
Tarde G (1898) *Les lois Sociales: esquisses d'une sociologie*, Félix Alcan, Paris.

Tarde G (1899) *Social Laws: An Outline of Sociology*, HC Warren (trans.), Macmillan, New York.
Tarde G (1902/[2007]) Economic Psychology, A Toscano (trans.), *Economy and Society*, 36(4), 614–643.
Tarde G (1903) L'interpsychologie, *Bulletin de l'institut general psychologique*, 2, 91–118.
Tarde G (1910) Les Possibles: Fragment d'un ouvrage de jeunesse inédit, *Archives d'anthropologie criminelle*, 25, 8–41.
Tarde G (1969) *On Communication and Social Influence*, TN Clark (ed.), U of Chicago P, Chicago.
Tarde G & Durkheim É (2008) The Debate between Tarde and Durkheim, EV Vargas et al. (script), A Damle & M Candea (trans.), *Environment and Planning D: Society and Space*, 26, 761–777.
Tawney RH (1921) *The Acquisitive Society*, Harcourt Brace & Co, New York, 56–57.
Terrace H (2010) Defining the Stimulus: A Memoir, *Behavioral Processes*, 83(2), 139–153.
Thalmann O et al. (2013) Complete Mitochondrial Genomes of Ancient Canids Suggest a Curopean Origin of Domestic Dogs, *Science*, 342, 871–874.
Thomas K (1983) *Man and the Natural World: A History of the Modern Sensibility*, Pantheon, New York.
Thompson EP (1851) *The Passions of Animals*, Chapman & Hall, London.
Thorndike EL (1911) *Animal Intelligence: Experimental Studies*, Macmillan, New York, 29–34.
Thorpe WH (1963) *Learning and Instinct in Animals*, 2nd ed., Methuen, London.
Tiger L & Fox R (1966) The Zoological Perspective in Social Science, *Man*, 1, 75–81.
Tinbergen N (1954) *Bird Life*, Oxford UP, London.
Tinbergen N (1958) *Curious Naturalists*, Doubleday, New York.
Tinbergen N (1960/[1971]) *The Herring Gull's World: A Study of the Social Behaviour of Birds*, Harper Torchbook, New York.
Tinbergen N (1972) *The Animal in Its World: Volume I, Field Studies*, Harvard UP, Cambridge.
Tinbergen N & Falkus H (1970) *Signals for Survival*, E Ennion (illus.), Clarendon Press, Oxford.
Titchener EB (1914) On 'Psychology as the Behaviorist Views It', *Proceedings of the American Philosophical Society*, 53(213), 1–17.
Todd Z (2018) Barriers to the Adoption of Humane Dog Training Methods, *Journal of Veterinary Behavior*, 25, 28–34.
Tomasello M (2014) *A Natural History of Human Thinking*, Harvard UP, Cambridge, MA.
Tomasello M and Call J (1997) *Primate Cognition*, Oxford UP, Oxford.
Tonkonoff S (2017) *From Tarde to Deleuze and Foucault: The Infinitesimal Revolution*, Palgrave Macmillan, Cham, Switzerland.
Topál J (2009) Understanding the Dog: What Is It Like to Be a Human Creation?, *Journal of Veterinary Behavior*, 4(2), 45.
Topál J et al. (2005) Attachment to Humans: A Comparative Study on Hand-Reared Wolves and Differently Socialized Dog Puppies, *Animal Behaviour*, 70, 1367–1375.

Tristan Corbière (1873/[1959]) The Contrary Poet/*Le poète contumace*, Randall Jarrell (trans.), *Poetry*, 76(5), 249–256.
Trivers RL (1971) The Evolution of Reciprocal Altruism, *Quarterly Review of Biology*, 46(1), 35–57.
Tuan, Yi-Fu (1984) *Dominance and Affection: The Making of Pets*, Yale UP, New Haven.
Turda M (2014) Biology and Eugenics, in Saler M (ed.) *The Fin-de-Siècle World*, Routledge, London, Chapter 29.
Udell MAR et al. (2008) Wolves Outperform Dogs in Following Human Social Cues, *Animal Behaviour*, 76, 1767–1773.
Uexküll J von (1920/[1926]) *Theoretical Biology*, Harcourt, Brace & Co, New York.
Underkuffler L (2003) *The Idea of Property: Its Meaning and Power*, Oxford UP, Oxford.
Våge J et al. (2008) Behavioral Characteristics of English Cocker Spaniels with Owner-Defined Aggressive Behaviour, *Journal of Veterinary Behavior*, 3, 248–254.
Vance WR (1937–1938) Restatement of the Law of Property, *U of Pennsylvania Law Review*, 86, 173–188.
Vatiero M (2010) From WN Hohfeld to JR Commons, and Beyond? A 'Law and Economics' Enquiry on Jural Relations, *The American Journal of Economics and Sociology*, 69(2), 840–866.
Vauclair J (1996) *Animal Cognition*, Harvard UP, Cambridge, MA.
Veblen T (1898) The Instinct of Workmanship and the Irksomeness of Labor, *American Journal of Sociology*, 4(2), 187–201: p. 196.
Veblen T (1899/[2007]) *The Theory of the Leisure Class*, Oxford UP, Oxford.
Ventós E (2011) The World of Smell, in ACTAR/Arts Santa Mònica (ed.) *Smell Colour: Chemistry, Art and Pedagogy*, ACTAR, Barcelona, 17–27.
Verbeek E et al. (2014) Are Hungry Sheep More Pessimistic? The Effects of Food Restriction on Cognitive Bias and the Involvement of Ghrelin in Its Regulation, *Physiology and Behavior*, 123, 67–75.
Vessey SH (1981) Dominance as Control, *The Behavioral and Brain Sciences*, 4, 449.
Vilà C et al. (1997) Multiple and Ancient Origins of the Domestic Dog, *Science*, 276, 1687–1689.
Viveiros de Castro E (2015) *The Relative Native: Essays on Indigenous Conceptual Worlds*, Hau Books, Chicago.
Voelki B et al. (2015) Matching Times of Leading and Following Suggest Cooperation through Direct Reciprocity during V-Formation Flight in Ibis, *PNAS*, 112(7), 2115–2120.
Waal F de (1996) *Good Natured: The Origins of Right and Wrong in Humans and Other Animals*, Harvard UP, Cambridge, MA.
Waal F de (1999) Anthropomorphism and Anthropodenial: Consistency in Our Thinking about Humans and Other Animals, *Philosophical Topics*, 27, 255–280.
Waal F de (2016) *Are We Smart Enough to Know How Smart Animals Are?*, Granta, London.
Waddington CH (1961) *The Ethical Animal*, Atheneum, New York.
Walker R et al. (2003) Life Is Pleasant: And Memory Helps to Keep It That Way!, *Review of General Psychology*, 7, 203–210.

Wallraff HG (2004) Avian Olfactory Navigation: Its Empirical Foundation and Conceptual State, *Animal Behaviour*, 67(2), 189–204.

Wallraff HG (2014) Do Olfactory Stimuli Provide Positional Information for Home-Oriented Avian Navigation?, *Animal Behaviour*, 90, 31–36.

Waskul DD & Vannini P (2008) Smell, Odor, and Somatic Work: Sense-Making and Sensory Management, *Social Psychology Quarterly*, 71(1), 53–71.

Wasserman EA & Zentall TR (eds.) (2006) *Comparative Cognition: Experimental Explorations of Animal Intelligence*, Oxford UP, Oxford.

Watson JB (1913) Psychology as the Behaviorist Views It, *Psychological Review*, 20, 158–177.

Watson JB (1919) *Psychology from the Standpoint of a Behaviorist*, JB Lippincott Co, Philadelphia.

Watson JB (1924/[1929]) Behaviorism: The Modern Note in Psychology, in Watson JB & McDougall W (1929) *The Battle of Behaviorism: An Exposition and an Exposure*, WW Norton & Co, London.

Watson JB & McDougall W (1929) *The Battle of Behaviorism: An Exposition and an Exposure*, WW Norton & Co, London.

Weil K (2012) *Thinking Animals: Why Animal Studies Now?*, Columbia UP, New York.

Westen P (2018) Poor Wesley Hohfeld, *San Diego Law Review*, 55, 449–467.

Westgarth C (2016) Why Nobody Will Ever Agree about Dominance in Dogs, *Journal of Veterinary Behavior*, 11, 99–101.

Whiten A & Waal E van de (2017) Social Learning, Culture and the 'Socio-Cultural' Brain of Human and Non-Human Primates, *Neuroscience and Biobehavioral Reviews*, 82, 58–75.

Wiegmann DD (2019) Nocturnal Navigation by Whip Spiders: Antenniform Legs Mediate Near-Distance Olfactory Localization of a Shelter, *Animal Behaviour*, 149, 45–54.

Willis P (2012) Engaging Communities: Ostrom's Economic Commons, Social Capital and Public Relations, *Public Relations Review*, 38, 116–122.

Willughby F et al. (1678) *The Ornithology of Francis Willughby of Middleton in the County of Warwick, esq*, John Martyn, London.

Wilson PJ (2009) *The Domestication of the Human Species*, Yale UP, New Haven.

Winthrop-Young G (2010) Bubbles and Webs: A Backdoor Stroll through the Readings of Uexküll, Afterword to Uexküll J von (1934/[2010]) *A Foray into the Worlds of Animals and Humans*, J D O'Neil (trans), U of Minnesota P, Minneapolis, 209–243: p. 220.

Worsley HK & O'Hara SJ (2018) Cross-Species Referential Signalling Events in Domestic Dogs (*Canis familiaris*), *Animal Cognition*, 21, 457–465.

Wyatt TD (2014) *Pheromones and Animal Behaviour: Chemical Signals and Signatures*, 2nd ed., Cambridge UP, Cambridge, 263–273.

Wystrach A & Graham P (2012) What Can We Learn from Studies of Insect Navigation?, *Animal Behaviour*, 84, 13–20.

Xenos N (1987) Liberalism and the Postulate of Scarcity, *Political Theory*, 15(2), 225–243.

Yates A (2013) A Hohfeldian Analysis of Hobbesian Rights, *Law and Philosophy*, 32(4), 405–434.

Yerkes RM (1939) Social Dominance and Sexual Status in the Chimpanzee, *The Quarterly Review of Biology*, 14(2), 115–136.

Yerkes RM (1940) Laboratory Chimpanzees, *Science*, 91(2362), 336–337.

Yerkes RM & Nissen HW (1939) Pre-Linguistic Sign Behavior in Chimpanzee, *Science*, 89(2321), 585–587.

Yong MH & Ruffman T (2014) Emotional Contagion: Dogs and Humans Show a Similar Physiological Response to Human Infant Crying, *Behavioural Processes*, 108, 155–165.

Young OR et al. (2006) The Globalization of Socio-Ecological Systems: An Agenda for Scientific Research, *Global Environmental Change*, 16, 304–316.

Zanette LY et al. (2019) Predator-Induced Fear Causes PTSD-Like Changes in the Brains and Behaviour of Wild Animals, *Nature*, 9, 11474.

Zeder MA (2012) The Domestication of Animals, *Journal of Anthropological Research*, 68(2), 161–190.

Zeder MA (2015) Core Questions in Domestication Research, *PNAS*, 112(11), 3191–3198.

Zeiden R et al. (2018) Do Ultimate Owners Follow the Pecking Order Theory?, *The Quarterly Review of Economics and Finance*, 67, 45–50.

Zeil J et al. (2003) Catchment Areas of Panoramic Snapshots in Outdoor Scenes, *Journal of the Optical Society of America A: Optics Image Science and Vision*, 20, 450–469.

Zeuner FE (1963) *A History of Domesticated Animals*, Harper & Row, New York.

Zimen E (1976) On the Regulation of Pack Size in Wolves, *Ethology*, 40(3), 300–341.

Zimen E (1978/[1981]) *The Wolf: A Species in Danger*, E Mosbacher (trans.), Delacorte Press, New York.

Ziv G (2017) The Effects of Using Aversive Training Methods in Dogs, *Journal of Veterinary Behavior*, 19, 50–60.

Zub K et al. (2003) Wolf Pack Territory Marking in the Białowieża Primeval Forest (Poland), *Behaviour*, 140(5), 635–648.

Index

abandonment 227–230
accountability 61, 62, 84, 85, 87, 88, 94, 114, 187, 226, 281, 290
acquisitive instinct 16, 107–108, 122n9, 181–182, 185–188, 193n20, 305
adaptation 41, 57–58, 71, 115, 179, 312, 318
affective science 2, 254, 267, 292
affirmations 222, 290, 307
Agamben, Giorgio 227
Agassi, Joseph 19
aggressiveness 118, 143, 192–193n14, 210
Agrawal, Arun 310
agriculturalism 14–15, 26n98, 38, 41, 44–45n5, 58–60, 64, 105, 119, 135, 137, 211n1, 222
alienation 184, 228, 281
Allee, Warder Clyde 17, 24n75, 147n42, 184
Allee effect 147n42
"alpha" concept 86, 97n45, 178–179, 184, 201, 203–207, 209, 214n31, 214–215n37, 216n62, 216–217n63, 232, 236, 240n16, 241n22, 302, 303, 314
altruism 17, 73n17, 115, 147n42, 261, 275n65, 305, 312; reciprocal 145n7, 263–266, 278n110, 289; see also sympathy
Altum, Johann Bernard Theodor 110, 111
Animal Behavior Enterprises 178
animal modelling 7–8
animal societies 73n12
animal training 2; humane 178; see also dog training

animal welfare 19n3, 89, 98n59, 211n2, 238n6
animals: cats 52n70; dingoes 96n23, 242n33; as "exotic other" 188, 197n79; goats 243n41; horses 270n15; human 2; iguana 8, 108, 190, 315; individuated 225; mouse 205; nonhuman 1–2; Oedipal 225, 243n39; predator/prey 97n38; primates 272n35; property relations of 2; psychology of 253; rats 269, 318; sharing of territory by 167; social competence in 243n41; souls of 85; tame/domesticated 237; territorial behaviours of 109–114; territoriality among 123n30; tracks of 134–135; wild 237; see also birds; consciousness; dogs; intelligence; wolves
animism 46n9, 85
anthropocentrism 6, 20n20, 36, 90, 130–131n120, 136, 138, 139, 149n62, 156, 181, 189, 212n17, 237, 276n79, 281, 307
anthropodenial 6
anthropomorphism 5, 6, 7, 9, 22n52, 237; critical 5, 6, 7
anthropology 118, 188, 189, 278n107, 317; archaeological 59–60
anti-Cartesianism 83, 282
anticonceptualism 298n59
archaeology 278n107
Aristotle 65
art: and artificial intelligence 293; and dogs 162–163; Fluxus 164–165, 173n87, 174n96; olfactory 153–157, 163–167; Surrealism 164
Art for Dogs 162–163

artificial intelligence (AI) 2, 159, 293, 319n19
assemblages 62, 75–76n49, 207, 267
attachment bonds 315; and the training relationship 258
attachment theories 83–84, 95n13
attribution 7, 32, 38, 83, 90, 106, 109–110, 134, 153, 156, 159, 166–167, 256, 260–261, 263, 312
attunement 70–71, 129n96, 266; somatic 159
authorship 32, 33, 39, 109, 112, 153, 164, 210, 226, 293, 319n19
autonomy 4, 23n61, 42, 116, 127n79, 129n96, 189, 254, 275n68
aversive training methods 9, 89, 129n96, 203, 213n30, 214–215n37, 217–218n72, 241n22, 244n83, 255–257, 265, 267, 273n47

Bain, Melissa 207
Balkin, Jack 287, 290
banishment 241n29
Barth, John 164
Bates, Marston 110, 111
Baudelaire, Charles 164, 220–221
Beaglehole, Ernest 107, 117, 122n9, 303
becoming-with 7, 98n60
behaviourism 5, 16, 271–272n26; origins of 271n20; radical 2, 161, 253–255, 256, 259, 263, 307
being-in-common 202, 269
being-with 7, 98n60, 269, 305
Bekoff, Marc 88–89
Benjamin, Walter 221, 235
Benson, Etienne 114
Bergson, Henri 12, 62, 63, 83
Beuys, Joseph 164
biological determinism 56, 121, 128–129n94, 179, 189, 209, 251, 264
biological essentialism 230
biology, micro-sociological 265
birds, flight formations of 280–281, 293n2, 293n3
Bleus, Guy 165
Bonn-Oberkassel dog 84–85
Borges, Jorge Luis 4, 29, 282
boundaries 135–136, 139, 146n29, 149–150nn65–67, 306; and the stranger 232

boundary-making 16, 110, 129n96, 140, 142, 150n67, 155, 157, 222, 235, 284, 287; and scavage 223
Bowles, Samuel 15
Brecht, George 164
Breland, Keller 178–179
Breland, Marian 178–179
Breton, André 163
Burghardt, Gordon 254, 259–260

Cage, John 164
Cairns, Huntington 290
Callicott, John Baird 221, 239n9
camera obscura 282
cannibalism 77n74
capital, cotyledon 313, 322n74
capitalism: predatory 182, 183, 207, 217n66; predatory drift of 183
Carpenter, Clarence Ray 113
Carr-Saunders, Alexander Morris 12
Cartesianism 11
cats, domestication of 52n70
Choi, Jung-Kyoo 15
civilization: agriculturalist 14–15, 26n98, 38, 41, 44–45n5, 58–60, 64, 105, 119, 135, 137, 211n1, 222; communistic stage 185–186, 188; consumer-producer communities 234; herder societies 309–310; hunter-gatherers 14, 120, 135, 211n1; pastoral societies 41–43, 48n35, 56, 58–59, 60, 65, 66–67, 76n52, 105, 112, 135, 137, 211n1, 234, 309, 318; stages of 187
Clutton-Brook, Juliet 33
co-evolution 37, 65, 66; see also evolution
cognition, embodied 2, 75n38, 237, 254, 262
cognitive ethology 5, 20n18, 86, 121, 253, 292
cognitive revolution 257
collaboration 140, 257, 312
collective behavior 147n42, 280
colonialism 185–188, 239n9
colonisation 209
commensalism 126n71
common law 196n72, 237
commons 15, 120, 138, 141, 191, 230, 266, 309–311, 315, 316, 318; amity of 311–314; tragedy of 309–311, 321n59

communication: with dogs 257; embodied 62–63, 74–75n37, 75n42, 92, 159, 229, 244n58, 315; by looking 93–94; by scent-marking 154–155, 158–159; use of gesture by dogs 90, 273n43
communism 185–186, 187, 188; primitive 195–196n60
competition 15, 17, 46n17, 58, 65, 71, 79n110, 86, 90, 116, 136–137, 155, 161, 180–184, 187, 190, 194n22, 204, 207, 208, 236, 261, 305, 308, 310, 312, 313
conditioning 45–46n9, 255–256, 259, 272n38
consciousness 5, 9, 16, 56, 67, 161, 190, 232, 253, 254
constitutionalism, American 116
contractarianism 79–80n112
contradiction 184, 313
conversation 69, 83, 92, 312; cross-species 243n35, 243n42
Cook, Walter Wheeler 119, 288
cooperation 261, 265, 312; among birds 280–281; natural 27n122; *see also* altruism, reciprocal
Corbin, Alain 139
correlatives 96n21, 267, 268, 282, 285, 286, 288, 289, 295n34, 299n63
Coverly, Dave 81
creativity 67, 72, 109, 234, 259, 276n86, 286; user-generated 314
cult of the wild 221, 225, 227, 237, 239n7
culture: altruistic 265; animal 262; determinism of 197n85; predatory phase of 183
culture contact 73n11, 114
custom(s) 81, 118–119, 188, 191, 223

Dadaism 164
Darwin, Charles 11, 17, 31, 44–45n5, 91; on social instincts 86–87; Tarde's interest in 57
Darwinism 11, 114, 137, 184; evolutionary theory 36; social 137, 179, 184, 221
Davidson, Daniel Sutherland 119
Deleuze, Gilles 7–8, 10, 75–76n49, 142, 203, 225, 243n39, 243n40, 282, 286, 288
Derrida, Jacques 92

Descartes, René 253
Despret, Vinciane 7, 70, 232, 273n44, 315
determinism 55, 197n85; bio-colonial 188–191; biological 55, 121, 128–129n94, 179, 189, 209, 251, 264; ethological 128–129n94
Diaconu, Malinda 158
differentiation 33, 56, 70, 72, 90, 157, 304, 314, 315
dog training 89–90, 95n7, 99n72, 129n96, 146n31, 178, 207, 211n2, 213–214n30, 216n56, 217n68, 217–218n72, 255–258, 273n41; aversive 9, 89, 129n96, 203, 213n30, 214–215n37, 217–218n72, 241n22, 244n83, 255–257, 265, 267, 273n47; and learning quadrants 252; non-aversive 89, 217–218n72, 257, 273n47; and the notion of control 241n22; reinforcement 257; "teaching manners" 245n63; using clickers 273n47
dogs: aggressive 192–193n14; as artists 64–65, 153–157; Bonn-Oberkassel dog 84–85; and breed determinism 238–239n7; breed profiling of 219n92; burials of 84–85, 96n31, 97n35, 241–242n33; cognitive abilities of 7, 256; customs of 231; dangerous 219n92, 220, 238n3, 238n4, 245n75; designer 220, 238n2, 238n3; divergence from wolves 36, 50n45, 58; domestic 1; domestication of 15–16, 22n52, 31–40, 52n70, 56, 59–61, 93–94, 211–212n3, 235; eye contact with humans 211–212n3; feral 8, 13, 16, 190, 220, 223, 224, 232, 237, 238n5, 241n23, 242n32, 268; free-ranging 214–215n37, 277n95; greeting ceremonies of 277n95; impounded 227; and the instinctive right to territory 304–305; as inventors 42–44, 60–61, 307; "le chien flâneur" 220–222, 223, 240n17; "les chiens fraudeurs" 231; nuisance behaviours of 18–19, 38–39, 201–202, 263, 291, 293; and ownership 303; Paleolithic 36, 48–49n41; as pets 84–85, 223–224, 241–242n33; and predatory drift

9–10, 16, 61; and the property system 268; relationship to history 8–9; relationships with humans 2; rescue 238n5; resource guarding by 132–134, 144n2, 145n13; as scavengers 8, 38–39, 42–43, 51nn65–66, 66–67, 70, 84, 91, 200, 222–224, 231, 234–235, 241n24, 241n25; smuggling 231; social competence of 7, 67; social morality of 67; socialisation of 81–82, 92, 100n95, 211–212n3; sociality of 263; as strangers 223, 231–232; stray 2, 8, 10, 16, 18, 220–223, 230, 231, 232, 238n2; use of gesture to communicate 90; welfare of 1; *see also* animals; dog training; "pack" concept; scent marking

domestication 8–9, 15; accidental 43; and attachment theories 83–84; defined 31–33, 44n4; of the dog 15–16, 22n52, 31–40, 52n70, 56, 59–61, 93–94, 211–212n3, 235; as dominance over nature 44n2; as domination 243n42; history of 36–38; human authorship of 226; of humans 59–60; invention of 34–35, 40–41; and the "pack" concept 200–211; paradox of 33–34; self- 37, 39–40, 52n70, 56, 60, 87; science of 32, 59, 83, 242n32; and territory 142–143; through imitation 70–71; *see also* domestication theories

domestication theories 45n6; pastoral apprenticeship model 66; scavenger theories 38–39, 43, 66, 222, 223, 224; taming theory 223

dominance hierarchies 86, 89, 97n47, 117, 203, 205, 206, 208, 266; gendered 219n88

dominance theory 178, 201, 204, 206–209, 218n78, 218n79

Donati, Kelly 137–138

downwash 280–281, 293n3

dualism 5, 61, 96n32; sociological 118, 119

Duchamp, Marcel 163

Durkheim, Emile, on social relations 244–245n68

ecology, behavioural 145n11
economics 182, 256, 316; evolutionary 108, 194n27

economy: of incentives 138; of passionate interests 138

embodied cognition 2, 75n38, 237, 254, 262

empathy 1, 3, 85, 92, 116, 133, 145n7, 263–266, 268, 281, 283, 286, 290

enculturation 84, 92

Engels, Friedrich 14, 45n6

Ennion, Eric 134

equality 4, 6, 307

equity 59, 187, 196n72, 315; *see also* inequity aversion

essentialism, biological 230

ethnocentrism 189, 221, 241–242n33

ethnological jurisprudence 317

ethological jurisprudence 4, 6, 18–19, 121, 267; and property 1–2

ethology: beginnings of 12; cognitive 5, 20n18, 86, 121, 253, 292; comparative 112, 114–115; of Hohfeld 286, 287–290; and observation 5–7; of owners 292–293; philosophical 7; and property 2

eugenics 137, 179, 239n7

Evans, Edward Payson 110

evolution 11, 79n110; co-evolution 37, 65, 66; moral 278n110; role of sociability in 264; social 57, 137

evolutionarily stable strategy (ESS) 108–109

evolutionary theory 17, 45n6, 184, 187; Darwinian 36, 137; game theory and 167–168n10; of production 14; of property 13; social theory of 13–14

expectancy bias 270n15

eye contact 211–212n3; *see also* gaze

familiar production 6, 10, 11, 17, 47n29, 66, 107, 109, 112, 138, 147n42, 156, 166, 302, 306, 308–310, 314, 315, 317, 318

ferae naturae 237

ferals 8, 13, 16, 190, 220, 223, 224, 232, 237, 238n5, 241n23, 242n32, 268

Fluxus 164–165, 173n87, 174n96, 315

Fourier, Charles 138

Freud, Sigmund 274n61

Fudge, Erica 243n35

Galbraith, James K. 182

Gallup, Gordon 156

Galton, Francis 39, 87

gaze 93, 149n62, 162, 164, 228, 255, 273n41; olfactory 159
geography 114, 118; influence on law 240n10
geopolitics 17–18
gestalt therapy 229, 244n60
Gibson, James J. 159, 257
globalisation 16, 285–286, 310
goats 243n41
Goffman, Erving 114
Goldsmith, Oliver 109
Griffin, Donald 5, 6, 20n18
Guattari, Félix 7–8, 10, 75–76n49, 142, 151–152n90, 203, 225, 243n39, 243n40, 286, 288
Guenther, Mathias Georg 120–121

habituation 33, 37, 55, 82, 272n35
Hallowell, Alfred Irving 107–108, 118, 132–133, 292, 317
Hamilton, William Donald 147n42
Haraway, Donna 7, 35, 43, 61, 228–289, 243n39, 244n58
Hardin, Garrett 309–310
Harlow, Harry 315
Hayirsizada Dog Massacre 241n29
Heape, Walter 105–106, 304
herd instinct 85, 87, 93
herd morality 85–86
heredity 13, 59, 65, 260
Herskovits, Melville J. 186
Herzog, Harold 20n20
Hobbes, Thomas 107, 227, 229, 244n48, 244n50; on rights 283–284; theory of rights 295nn27–28
Hoebel, Edward Adamson 6, 118, 188, 190–191, 237, 310, 322n70
Hohfeld, Wesley Newcomb 4, 11, 17, 88, 117–118, 119, 183, 187, 255, 267, 268, 286; as anticonceptualist 298n59; ethology of 287–290; normative modaliities of 316–317; on privileges 295nn27–28; on property 316; property monadology 284–285; on rights 282–284; Square of Opposition 289; system of correlatives and opposites 285–287; system of jural relations 281, 290, 297n45, 297n47, 297n50, 297–298n52, 299n64, 299–300n71, 300–301n80, 316; Westen's defense of 298n61
Holocene revolution 26n99
Horowitz, Alexandra 156

host-parasite relations 278n113
Howard, Henry Eliot 110–111
Howell, Philip 241–242n33
Howes, David 157
human exceptionalism 2, 6, 9, 22n53, 32, 55, 60, 63, 71, 89, 115, 118, 189, 203, 307; and domestication 220; as fabrication 236; and pets 225
human rights 6, 295n29
human-animal relationships 33, 44n1, 44n4, 224, 243n35, 246n81; *see also* dogs
humaneness 56, 92–94, 137, 210
Hume, David 71–72
hunter-gatherers 14, 120, 135, 211n1
Huxley, Aldous 179
Huxley, Julian 179, 187, 254
Huxley, Thomas 179

iguana 8, 108, 190, 315
imitation 65–66, 69, 73n12, 78n81, 91–92, 119, 197n85, 276n86; cognitive 262; laws of 311; mutual 263; as social tie 262; society as 66–67
immanence 216n62, 288
impartiality 5
imperialism 209
imprinting 83
incentive relations 261
incentives 2, 236, 259–260, 275n65, 275n68, 281; for behaviors 253–254; in the consumer-producer dyad 256; in dog training 255–256; economy of 138; empathy as 266
individualism 186
industrial attraction 138
industrialisation 4, 12, 16
inequity aversion 94, 108, 189
Ingold, Tim 14, 33
innovation 184, 259, 262, 281, 311
insect navigation 148n53
instinct 2, 63, 107; acquisitive 181–182, 185–188, 193n20; aggressive 210; social 86
instinctive drift (instinctual drift) 178–182
intellectual property 2, 89, 98n59, 109, 125n57, 162, 182, 213n24, 319n19, 320n35, 323n97; and the commons 311; and the concept of incentives 258–259; and creative space 247n111; IP rights 80n109,

295n29; models of 313; and property law 235; role of domestication in 107; and smell 166; sociability of 166–167
intelligence 41, 48n35, 63, 83, 149n62, 159, 204, 234, 282, 307; artificial 1, 159, 293; social 92
intentionality 106, 200, 220–221; human 9, 31–33, 39, 40, 44n2, 44–45n5, 47n30, 60, 67, 220–221, 238n2, 243n42, 255, 263, 268, 307; individual 4; non–human 37, 40, 47n25, 55, 187, 189, 211–212n3, 222, 224; possessory 316; and smelling 157, 160
interest 267, 269; equitable 268
interpsychology 229, 281
intuition 63, 67, 83; social 273n41
invention 69–70, 73n7, 136–137; by dogs 42–44, 60–61; of society 66–68

Jennings, Michael W. 247n103
Jhering, Rudolf von 82, 184
justice, inter-species 237

Kessler, Karl Federovich 17, 264
knowledge, traditional 14, 185, 188, 191, 310, 317, 319n6, 322n70
!Ko people 120–121
Kropotkin, Peter 17, 264

landmarks 8, 16, 39, 64, 135–136, 138–140, 142–144, 148nn53–54, 149n57, 149–150nn64–67, 150n69, 152n93, 153–154, 157, 160–161, 167–168n10, 183, 187, 237
Laplantine, François 162
Larson, Gerger 37
Latour, Bruno 256, 285–286, 311, 315
laughter 225, 269, 318
law: anthropological definition of 187, 237; ethological definition of 237; primitive 107, 186, 187, 189, 190, 236–237, 239n9
Law of Mutual Aid (Mutual Help) 264
Law of Nature 184, 283
laws of imitation 311
Leach, Helen 32
learned helplessness 255
learning: affiliative/social 262–263; by imitation 262–263
learning quadrants 252
Lebensraum 16
legal fictions 201, 212n15, 236, 239n9, 293, 305, 323–324n98

Leibniz, Gottfried Wilhelm 282
Lepinjay, V.A. 256, 285–286, 311
liberty 4, 6, 34, 116, 125n50, 268, 283
Little Prince vignette 68–70, 141
Lloyd, William Forster 309
Locke, John 107, 314
Lombroso, Cesare 179
Lorenz, Konrad 42, 83, 84, 93, 210, 238–239n7
Lowie, R. H. 190, 322n70
Lushetich, Natasha 163

Machine Age 16, 40, 82, 160, 230, 252
Maciunas, George 164–165
Malinowski, Bronislaw 12, 58, 118, 119, 186–187, 188, 190, 191
Mandrin, Louis 231
Marx, Karl 11, 14, 45n6
Massumi, Brian 243n39, 306
Mayr, Ernst 110
McLemore, S. Dale 247n101
Mead, Margaret 186
Mech, David 204, 205–206, 207, 208
microsociology 11, 307
milieu 142, 151–152n90
Mill, John Stuart 71, 281
Millan, Cesar 99n75, 211n2, 213–214n30
mirror self-recognition (MSR) test 149n62, 156, 169–170n32, 170n36
monadology 281–282; jural 290; property 284–285; sociological 290
monumentalisation 148n53
monumentalism 139
moral judgment 306
moral justice 90, 93–94
morality 85–87; and play 88–91; social 88, 118; and territory 115
Morgan, Conwy Lloyd 254
Morgan, Lewis Henry 13, 45n6, 119
Morgenstern, Oskar 17–18, 256
motivations 253, 275n68
mutual aid 305; Law of Mutual Aid (Mutual Help) 264
mutuality 118, 119, 120, 209, 307, 308

Nancy, Jean-Luc 201
Natural law 187
natural rights 107–108, 227
natural selection 58, 65, 79n110, 182
Nazi ideology 16, 219n88
Nedelsky, Jennifer 116, 268
negative reinforcement 252

Nice, Margaret Morse 110–111, 124n39
Nietzsche, Friedrich 85–86, 91
Noble, Gladwyn Kingsley 115, 117
nomadic peoples 119–120
nonhuman: animals 185; terminology 1–2; *see also* animals

objectivity 4, 5, 6, 63, 159, 201, 269, 316
observation 5–7
olfactory mirror 156
Ono, Yoko 164
opposites 267, 268, 282, 285, 289–290
Ostrom, Elinor 309–310, 311
Overall, Christine 242n32
ownership 19n8, 190–191; discourse 118; and the dog 303; ethology of 292–293; extrinsicality of 4; history of 8–9; of land 119–121, 130n109; vs. private property 15; of territory 120

"pack" concept 9, 16, 43, 47n30, 58–59, 83, 86, 89–92, 95n7, 97n38, 97n44, 97n45, 97n47, 99n80, 113, 121, 129n96, 136, 178, 179, 200–211, 213–214n30, 214n31, 214n33, 214–215n37, 215n38, 216n53, 216–217n63, 217–218n72, 232, 236, 240n16, 241n22, 247n107, 263, 302–303, 314–315; as myth 235–236
Paracelsus 4
Parnet, Claire 225, 243n40
pastoral societies 41–43, 48n35, 56, 58–59, 60, 65, 66–67, 76n52, 105, 112, 135, 137, 211n1, 234, 309, 318
patent law 73n7
Pavlov, Ivan 272n38
Paz, Octavio 163–164
Pearson, Chris 231
pecking order 116–117
Penner, James 296n38
Péret, Benjamin 163
Perls, Fredrick (Fritz) 229
personhood 84
pet-keeping 84, 224–225, 241–242n33, 242n34
Platonism and anti-Platonism 290, 300n78
play 87–88; morality 88–91; social 8, 88, 90–91, 94, 108, 132
pleasure principle 274n61
populism 12, 217–218n72

Portugal, Steven 280
positive reinforcement 252, 255, 257–258, 270n15
possession, reciprocal 118, 261, 269, 282, 306
Pound, Ezra 290
predatory drift: in animal behavior 178, 179; in art 165; as artificial narrative 180; of behavior 144n3, 146n31; of the "bond of slow formation" 226; toward boundary-making 222; towards the bounded animal 220, 221; of capitalism 183; in commercial relationships 204; and competition 86, 260–261; in dog training 181, 207, 208; and domestication 40, 202; driven by scarcity 261; in economic discourse 210; evolutionary narrative of 189; of knowledge systems 188; language of 283; in legal discourse 210, 226; and the predator/prey relationship 314; in primitive law 186; in property 61, 76n52, 82, 84, 97n38, 106–108, 116, 135, 136, 142, 144n3, 160, 180–185, 190–191, 194n27, 229, 232, 234–235, 238n1, 251, 256, 267–268, 302, 305; in property language 112, 198–199n98; and reciprocity 292–293; in relationships 106; and scarcity 261; social narrative of 189, 204; and territory 115, 118, 123n29, 135; violence of 313; of the visual 141
prior-residence effect 167–168n10
private property 15, 58, 181, 188; in primitive societies 186, 188
private space 230
professionalisation 12
property: "ages" of 15–18; in agricultural societies 14–15, 26n98; and animals 1–2, 292; communistic stage of ownership 185–186; defined 2–4; in developed societies 14; economic theories of 46n17; ethology of 8–9, 285–287; evolutionary language of 182; evolutionary theory of 13; in hunter-gatherer societies 14; and the idea of territory 105–107; jurisprudence of 288; language of 90; in the Machine Age 16; movable 119–121; and natural rights 107–108; in nomadic societies

13–14, 224; as organisation of kin 293; ownership of 127–128n84; as part of the personality or self 117; pets as 224; Platonic ideal of the image of 290; and predatory drift 61, 76n52, 82, 84, 97n38, 106–108, 116, 135, 136, 142, 144n3, 160, 180–185, 190–191, 194n27, 229, 232, 234–235, 238n1, 251, 256, 267–268, 302, 305; predatory model of 320n37; in primitive societies 25n87, 317; resocialisation of 6–7, 281–283; sociability of 292; in the Social Age 17; as social institution 14–15, 118; social model of 308; sociality of 190; in the Space Age 16; in the Stone Age 15–16; terminology associated with 128n89
property discourse 106
property law 201, 235, 289; antiwilderness bias in 240n10
property relationships 2–3, 180, 316; with owner 319n6; sociability of 8; sociable connection of 4
property rights 83, 198–199n98, 296n38; in hunting grounds 25n93; and scarcity 71–72
Pryor, Karen 257–258, 273n47
psychology 161, 259; animal 253; behavioral 259; comparative 20n18; experimental 271–272n26, 274–275n62; inter- 229, 281; psychophysics 258
psychophysics 258
psychotherapy, gestalt 229, 244n60
public space 230
punishment 219n97, 244n48, 255–256, 257, 271n16, 273n43, 289; aversive training methods 9, 89, 129n96, 203, 213n30, 214–215n37, 217–218n72, 241n22, 244n83, 255–257, 265, 267, 273n47

Radin, Max 183, 286
Rancière, Jacques 233
Randall, Henry James 113–114
realism, legal 300n78
reciprocal possession 118, 261, 269, 282, 306
reciprocity 94, 118, 261, 289, 312; and altruism 263–266; legacies of 283–285; and predatory drift 292–293; social 305

reductionism 5, 251
reinforcement 259, 271n17, 275n71, 289
res communes (*res communis*) 303
res familiaris 11, 17, 112, 140, 143, 147n42, 293, 302, 304, 306, 316, 317
res nullius 303, 307
resident aliens 238n1; *see also* strangers
resocialisation 88, 280–281; conceptual approach 285–287; and an ethology of owners 292–293; Hohfeld's ethology of 287–290; of property 281–283; and reciprocal legacies 283–285; and the science of resocialising property 281–283; sticky things 291–292
resource guarding 132–144, 185; by dogs 144n2, 145n13
respecere 7, 228, 260, 264
respect 4, 7, 34, 83, 84, 106, 132, 155, 169n29, 228–299, 245n63, 260, 304
response-ability 229
rhizomes 7–8
rights discourse 3, 282–284
Rivers, William Halse Rivers (WHR) 185, 187
Roch, Sylvia 261
Romanes, George 303–305
rookeries 124n46
Rousseau, Jean-Jacques 41, 226
rule of law 193n22
Russell, Nerissa 33, 184

Saint-Exupèry, Antoine de 69, 141
Saito, Takako 165
Samuelson, Charles 261
Sax, Boria 210
scarcity 79n110, 116, 261; artificial 80n113, 90, 313; and property rights 71–72
scavage 39, 51n66, 222–223, 231, 234, 235, 241n28
scavenger 8, 38–39, 42–43, 51nn65–66, 66–67, 70, 84, 91, 200, 222–223, 231, 234–235, 241n24, 241n25
scavenging 38–39, 43, 51n64, 61, 66, 91, 222–223, 234–235
scent 138–144, 149n57, 149n60, 172n66; as art 153–157; as communication 157–160; *see also* smell
scent marking 139, 153–156, 167n4, 167n6, 168n12, 168–169n20, 169n23

Schenkel, Rudolf 135, 204, 208, 208–210, 215n38, 217–218n72, 219n88
Schjelderup-Ebbe, Thorleif 116–117
Schlag, Pierre 300–301n80
Schleidt, Wolfgang 41, 58, 65
self-awareness 149n62, 156
self-recognition 156, 169–170n32
semiotics 287, 290
senses 171n55; olfactory 160–162, 171n45, 172n66; visual 161
sentientism 3
Serpell, James 241–242n33
Serres, Michel 159
Shalter, Michael 41, 58, 65
shared interests 17, 71, 84, 133, 138, 140, 147n42, 150n66, 180, 194n22, 254–258, 260, 262, 266–269, 281, 282, 302, 306, 308–310, 312; and common ground 314–317
Simmel, Georg 12, 87–88, 158, 161, 173n77, 208, 232, 233, 234, 235, 247n101
Singer, Joseph 193n22, 290, 291, 298n59
Skinner, Burrhus Frederic (BF) 252–253, 256, 257, 260, 289
Skinner box 252, 269n2
slavery 235
smell 18, 94, 135–144, 149n60, 160–162, 166–167, 170n44, 171n45, 237, 260, 313; and art 153–160, 162–165; as communication 154–156, 159, 161–162; human sense of 157–158; and intellectual property 18, 153, 160, 198n97; use to mark property 135, 138–139, 141–142, 153, 156–157; as self-recognition 156; *see also* scent
Smith, Adam 71
smuggling 231
Smuts, Barbara 61
sociability 48n35; creative 83 and embodied communication 229; and evolution 264; of intellectual property 166–167; interspecies 136; of law 286; origins of 110; and play 87–88; of property 292; and smell 158, 166; of space 147n44; of territory 315
Social Age 10, 17, 194n22, 214–215n37, 230, 238, 252, 260, 306

social bonding 216n53
social class, biological theory of 209
social contract 41, 79–80n112, 86, 92, 226, 303, 308
social Darwinism 137, 179, 184, 221
social ethics 17
social hierarchy 210
social instincts 86
social intelligence 92
social learning 73n12
social media 230, 232
social morality 118, 210
social referencing 263, 305–306
social theory 23n58
socialisation 81–94, 95n7, 100n91, 133; in animal behaviour 81–82; critical periods for 83; of the dog 92, 100n95, 211–212n3; and dog training 241n22
sociality: affiliative 263; among insects 133; collective 147n42; cooperative 147n42; of the dog 263; domestication as 66; dynamic 62; imitative 75–76n49; interactive 62; interspecies 44n1; of knowledge 72; morality of 85; through territory 133
society: as imitation 66–67; invention of 66–68
sociology 182, 201–202; associative 62; bio- 285; ecological school 115; of imitation 11; micro- 307; and territory 115; territory concept in 121; universal 10–11, 137; zoological turn in 121
Space Age 16, 153, 157, 181, 183, 221
Spencer, H. 58
stealing 58
Stevens, Stanley Smith 259, 274–275n62
stimulus 159, 180, 256, 258–259, 260, 263; and response 245n75, 253–254, 256, 257–258, 259, 272n38
stoic philosophy 122n11
Stone Age 15–16, 81, 189, 224
stranger 231–236, 238n1, 241n25, 247n101
strays, 2, 8, 10, 16, 18, 220–224, 230, 231, 232, 238n2
subjectivities 92; interspecies 85
surrealism 164
survival of the fittest 83, 136–137, 184, 261

sympathy 62–3, 76n52, 91–92, 115, 266; *see also* altruism
synchrony 263, 265, 267, 292, 305, 306

Tarde, Gabriel: on adaptation 57–58; associative sociology 62; on being 228; on capital 313; on concurrence 224; on conversation 69; on creative relationships 264; on culture contact 183; on domestication 34–35, 38, 42–43, 56, 64–65; economics of 80n113, 89, 311–312, 316; on evolution 17; on genius 311; on imitation 63, 262; on innovation 281; on logical dualism 119; on monads 24n70, 283, 290, 316; name of 19n12; on possession 117; on property 14–15; on reciprocity 265–266; on the social contract 226, 303, 308; on socialization 83; on social relations 244–245n68; on society 4–5, 59, 82, 306; sociology of 10–12, 137, 263, 281, 285–286; on somnambulism 201; on spontaneous appearance 67; on the stranger 233; on trade relations 188, 311; on trust 71
technologisation 12
Terrace, Herbert 262–263
territoriality 110, 115, 120–121, 317; among animals 123n30; economic theory of 132; and power 123n29; as social phenomenon 113
territory 105–107; among animals 314; among the !Ko people 120–121; and birds 109–111, 113, 124n39, 124n46, 126–127n75; boundaries between 135–136, 139; comparative ethology of 112, 114–115; covering 114–116; defending 116–119, 132–144, 150n69; defined 123n25; and hunter-gatherer societies 120; instinctive right to 304; making of 109–114; marking of 106, 107–109, 138–144, 146n29, 153–157, 167n4, 167n6, 168n12, 168–169n20, 169n23; and morality 115; organisation of 227; ownership of 120; sociability of 315; as strategy 130–131n120
theory of relations 88
thingness 3, 10, 159, 267

Thomas, Keith 241–242n33
Thorpe, William Homan 262
three-term contingency 260
Tinbergen, Nikolaas 113, 134
Titchener, Edward B 271–272n26
Topál, József 22n52
tracks, of animals 134–135
tragedy of the anticommons 321–322n60
Tragedy of the Commons 309–311, 321n59
Trivers, Robert 264
trust 33, 71, 115, 211n1, 265, 266–267, 269, 306, 309, 310, 311, 312, 313

Uexküll, Jakob von 6, 161, 222
Umwelt 6–7, 34, 148n53, 159, 222, 232–233, 260, 316
Unconscious Selection 31, 44–45n5
universals 288, 300n78
upwash 280–281

variability 65, 276n86
Veblen, Thorstein 108, 182, 183, 194n27, 207, 217n66
visual perception 16, 61, 138, 140, 141, 154, 156, 158, 159, 160, 161, 163

Waddington, Conrad 187
Washburn, Margaret Floy 11, 254, 271–272n26
Watson, John Broadus 161, 253–254, 259, 262
Wilcox, Dominic 162
wilderness conservation 239n9
wilderness narrative 190, 221, 237, 239n9
Willughby, Francis 109
Wilson, Paul Alexander 12
wolves 36–37, 41, 43, 49n43, 58–59, 83, 203–205, 216–217n63; families of 86; Lorenz's work with 210; research on 125n60, 135–136, 209; social bonding among 216n53; social hierarchy of 86, 97nn45–46; and territory 113; *see also* "alpha" concept; "pack" concept
Wundt, Wilhelm 271–272n26
Wynne, Clive 45–46n9

Zeder, Melinda 32
Zimen, Erik 206

For Product Safety Concerns and Information please contact our EU representative GPSR@taylorandfrancis.com
Taylor & Francis Verlag GmbH, Kaufingerstraße 24, 80331 München, Germany

www.ingramcontent.com/pod-product-compliance
Ingram Content Group UK Ltd.
Pitfield, Milton Keynes, MK11 3LW, UK
UKHW021811170325
456245UK00030B/242